ECONOMIC AND SOCIAL

SECURITY

Public and Private Measures Against

Economic Insecurity

JOHN G. TURNBULL
PROFESSOR OF ECONOMICS AND INDUSTRIAL RELATIONS
UNIVERSITY OF MINNESOTA

C. ARTHUR WILLIAMS, JR.
ASSOCIATE PROFESSOR OF ECONOMICS AND INSURANCE
UNIVERSITY OF MINNESOTA

EARL F. CHEIT
ASSOCIATE PROFESSOR OF ECONOMICS
SAINT LOUIS UNIVERSITY

THE RONALD PRESS COMPANY · NEW YORK

Copyright, ©, 1957, by

THE RONALD PRESS COMPANY

All Rights Reserved

4

Library of Congress Catalog Card Number: 57–7480
PRINTED IN THE UNITED STATES OF AMERICA

To

OUR FAMILIES

who would prefer more attention
and less *Economic and Social Security*

Preface

This book is an introduction to economic security, to the problems arising from the pressures of economic insecurity, and to the ways in which society has sought to accommodate itself to these problems. The text was developed to meet the needs of the increasing number of courses in the field.

We should like to note here a number of facts about the book. First, this text treats not only the customary fields of social insurances and assistances, but also includes the private insurances as well as substandard conditions. We conceive the economic security problem as arising essentially out of the operation of the labor market, and on that basis these basic categories are logical inclusions. We have found this approach particularly useful in our own courses in the several institutions in which we teach.

Second, our approach makes it necessary that we deal with a broader framework of subject matter than if we treated only the social—or the private—assistances and insurances. We have not, however, tried to be less exacting in our treatment of the social or private insurances than are several excellent volumes in this field. Conversely, we have included a number of chapters on the problems of substandard conditions.

Third, we have limited our discussion of economic insecurity essentially to the operation of the labor market in its relation to job-oriented insecurity. It is perfectly true, for example, that substandard conditions in housing can be viewed as giving rise to economic insecurity and, in fact, have been so treated by some analysts. But we view this type of problem as somewhat outside the scope of our treatment. We have had to limit our boundaries in order to secure a manageable volume, and our decisions are reflected in the following pages.

Fourth, our approach is essentially economic in nature. We cannot claim competence as legal practitioners, political scientists, or social workers. Hence we do not treat in detail these phases of the subject matter involved. We do claim, however, some training and interest beyond the narrow confines of economics as such.

Fifth, we do not feel that we have pioneered in our analytical techniques, in our evaluations, and in our proposals for improvements in the American economic security system, although we have introduced some differing and possibly original ideas on the nature of economic security.

But, sixth, we do feel that we have developed a new and original approach in the treatment of the subject matter. With each of the subareas in the field of economic security we have attempted to synthesize and integrate public and private approaches to the problem, and to show how society in the larger sense has sought to adjust itself to the issues involved. It is with respect to this synthesis and integration that we do claim more originality.

Seventh, with respect to a mechanical item, we have deliberately used different years in a number of the tabular presentations so as to permit comparisons of various types.

Finally, we feel this volume is an excellent example, if not of interdisciplinary research, at least of interdisciplinary cooperation. We do not feel one man could have written this text. Our joint undertaking has been a happy one with none of the traumatic experiences that occasionally come in collaborative ventures.

It is not possible to list the many researchers and administrators who have contributed to an understanding of economic security programs. In footnotes throughout the book we have sought to indicate the sources of materials and ideas upon which we have relied and which have been so valuable in the preparation of the book. We must express here, however, our debt to our colleagues at the University of Minnesota, Saint Louis University, and The Massachusetts Institute of Technology, who, during the preparation of the text, read portions of the manuscript and provided valuable suggestions and encouragement; to John M. Briggs, C.L.U., C.P.C.U., and William Brandow, C.P.C.U., for very helpful commentary; to Robert J. Myers, Chief Actuary, Social Security Administration, for patiently helping us correct a number of our slips; to Beatrice A. Rogers and Mary M. Pepple for editorial help; and to our wives, who aided in the editing and typing of the manuscript or who suffered through its completion.

John G. Turnbull
C. Arthur Williams, Jr.
Earl F. Cheit

Minneapolis, Minnesota
St. Louis, Missouri
   February, 1957

Contents

ECONOMIC AND SOCIAL SECURITY

1

Economic Security in Our Society

"The best way to security is to marry the boss's daughter."
—Anon.
"The best security for old age is a large family."—Anon.

Introduction

Whether marrying the boss's daughter is the best way to achieve personal security may be a debatable matter. And whether a large family is the best security for old age also may be debatable. But those sayings point up two problems with which society has long concerned itself: the existence of insecurity and the desire to overcome this insecurity.

This book concerns itself with these two problems. More specifically, this book concerns itself with the nature and causes of *economic* insecurity essentially arising out of the operations of labor markets, and the ways in which society has sought to adjust or accommodate itself to *economic* insecurity.[1] Within this context the focus is upon the individual as his economic destiny is influenced by the ebb and flow of job-oriented insecurity.

In the preceding paragraph the term insecurity is qualified by the adjective *economic*. This qualification is deliberate. While security has many dimensions—anthropological, legal, political, psychological, sociological—the economic component is critically important. Protracted unemployment, for example, may have serious psychological implications for the individual, as well as important political and sociological consequences for society.[2] But the special-

[1] For an interesting historical résumé see I. M. Rubinow, *The Quest For Security* (New York: Henry Holt & Co., Inc., 1934).
[2] See, for example, E. Wight Bakke, *The Unemployed Worker* (New Haven: Yale University Press, 1940).

3

ized analysis of these psychological, political, and social matters and the prescription of remedies are best left to the specialist in those fields. This book will, therefore, focus primarily upon economic issues and will comment upon these other problems only where such comment is relevant to the main stream of thought.

Finally, we shall not concern ourselves with certain other forms of "insecurity" which are not labor market oriented and which have only an indirect economic relation to the more general problem, as, for example, the "insecurity" asociated with entrepreneurial risk-taking (such as starting a new business) or insecurity involved in the failure to get a job promotion or in the worry about losing one's position. Nor shall we deal with national or international security insofar as these matters involve relations among states and nations. The focus of this book is instead upon the basic categories of individual economic insecurities existent in our system, upon their causes, and upon the ways in which society has sought to accomodate itself to these insecurities, that is, what it has tried to do about them.

Plan of the Book

Following this introductory section, each of the major categories of economic insecurity is discussed in some detail. In turn, for each of these areas a systematic exposition is used. This includes, first, a discussion of the nature of the problem; second, the action society has taken in trying to solve the problem, including *both* public and private approaches; and third, an analysis of the consequences of the actions taken.

Throughout the volume, emphasis is placed upon the broader features of problems and programs and upon basic principles, rather than upon detailed facts and statistics. This volume is designed to provide a basis for understanding the nature and causes of economic insecurity in our society and the social adjustments to it. It is not a handbook designed to answer such questions as, for example, whether an individual can collect unemployment compensation in a given state under a given set of complex job separation circumstances. Such questions can best be answered by the administrative agencies set up for such purposes.

Nor is this volume a statistical compendium of facts and figures on economic security; this information can be obtained readily via statistical and other summaries published by various agencies. Such materials tend to be short-lived, and therefore of limited usefulness in a book of this type. This should not be taken to imply that we will have no concern with facts and figures. Patently, this could not be the case. But our emphasis will be upon understanding, rather than upon memorization, upon the more basic economic and social forces involved, rather than upon administrative complexities, legal niceties, or statistical detail.

Nature and Causes of Economic Insecurity

While it is not easy to define economic insecurity in one sentence, it is easy to suggest in more detail the basic factors involved.

Economic insecurity for the individual can be viewed first of all as involving a loss (or threat of loss) of income—whether a relative or absolute loss—and/or additional expenses. The primary proximate cause is the loss of his job by the individual concerned, whether this be a temporary or permanent loss. But a job loss may not always be involved. The individual may, for example, be injured and yet able to continue work, but incurring various medical costs. Or, members of his family may become victims of various accidents or illnesses. As the term is commonly employed today, economic insecurity would embrace all such cases involving income loss or additional expenses.

Where job separation is the factor in question, any one of several additional causal factors may be involved. It is important to note these, as listed below, since separate programs to combat insecurity have been built up around each of them.

Job separation arising from old age. We are not concerned here as to whether the older worker should or should not retire, or if he should, at what age. Suffice it to say that a retirement custom has developed in this country, that "compulsory retirement" (and hence job separation) is the rule, and that the age for such retirement is most commonly sixty-five. Unless, however, the retiring employee has accumulated a fund upon which to live, this very fact of job separation creates for him an economic insecurity (excepting, of course, cases where he is able to live with his offspring or relatives for the balance of his days).

It is interesting to note that programs designed to overcome this type of insecurity do not necessarily have as their goal the continuance of the individual in his job (nor, incidentally, a cultural pattern in which the children or relatives take the retired person in to live with them). Rather, such programs aim at permitting the individual to accumulate a fund so that when job separation *does* occur at retirement, economic insecurities are not created.

Job separation arising from accidents and sickness, with death as the extreme case. In these cases it is also apparent that the very fact of job separation creates an income (salary or wage) loss. But such accidents and sickness may involve additional economic hazards. These are the additional expenses arising out of medical and allied therapeutic treatment, or burial expenses in the case of death; and possible future losses in earning power if the accident involves a loss of bodily members such as a hand or leg, or death in the extreme case. If permanent and total disability results from the accident or sickness, the degree of economic insecurity created becomes particularly critical. But even if only temporary and partial disability are involved, a serious problem may present itself to the individual. Until recently, programs designed to meet these types of insecurities protected the employee only, and then only against the hazards of job-connected accidents and later certain job-connected diseases. Increasingly, however, there is a tendency to protect the employee *and* his family also against this hazard, regardless of the source. This type of development is designed to get at economic insecurities of the form earlier noted where job separation is not necessarily involved.

Job separation arising from "economic" causes. Old age and accidents and sickness all contain an element of "economic" causality in that the individual's productivity diminishes, becoming zero in the extreme case of total incapacitation. But there are cases where individual productivity does not change at all and yet where separation occurs for economic reasons beyond the individual's control. This is the familiar case of "unemployment"—where business conditions require employers to curtail their work forces, whether for secular, cyclical, seasonal, technological, or other reasons.

The above three cases typify the major causal forces giving rise to economic insecurity. In general, the analysis in this book will stop at these causality levels. If one goes much beyond these stages, one finds himself in specialized areas beyond the boundaries of the field of economic security as it is viewed here. For example, the prevention of industrial accidents, as a phase of programs designed to reduce one type of economic insecurity, involves individual physiological and psychological causal forces requiring the attention of psychologists and others. Or, the further analysis of unemployment leads one into the field of fiscal and monetary theory, and here also the role of the specialist becomes evident.

Conventional treatment of the topics of security and insecurity tends to stop with the types of subject matter discussed above. When this is the case, the term "social security" frequently has been used to denote public approaches particularly, although in this text we include private approaches also. And, if the emphasis has been upon public insurance programs designed to combat the insecurities involved, "social insurance" customarily has been the applicable term. (These matters of terminology will be more fully discussed in a later section in this chapter.)

Increasingly, however, there has been a tendency to include another subject area within the general framework of economic security.[3] This newer inclusion is that of "substandard conditions," the term "conditions" here referring commonly to wages, hours, and other conditions of employment.

Substandard conditions. It is contended that economic insecurity is inherent in substandard working conditions, hours, or wages. Here it is not the inability of an individual to secure a job that is at issue, but rather his inability to get an employment contract that meets the minimum standards under which society will permit its members to be employed. When this subject matter is included in the discussion along with "social security," there has been some usage of the term "economic security." Since this book addresses itself to both of these subject-matter categories as being inherent in labor market operation, we have adopted the term "economic security" as best describing the scope of our treatment.

Social Adjustment to Economic Insecurity

GENERAL APPROACHES EMPLOYED

If society does not passively accept the consequences of economic insecurity, a number of alternative courses are open to it. These courses may be followed individually or collectively. Historically, society has attacked the insecurity problem simultaneously in a number of ways. The following are the most common alternatives.

Alleviation of the undesirable economic consequences of the specific act or factor giving rise to the economic insecurity. An industrial accident takes place; a wage loss is incurred for the individual involved; and medical expenses are created. One social approach to such problems is to compensate the individual for the medical expenses and for a portion of the wage loss. This is "curative" rather than "preventive" medicine. That is, in and of itself

[3] Professor Stefan A. Riesenfeld was a pioneer in this approach. See Stefan A. Riesenfeld and Richard C. Maxwell, *Modern Social Legislation* (Brooklyn: The Foundation Press, 1950). But see also, for an earlier view, Barbara N. Armstrong, *Insuring the Essentials* (New York: The Macmillan Co., 1932).

such a method of indemnifying the individual seeks to alleviate consequences rather than prevent occurrences. Note also that this indemnification approach is essentially economic in nature; there is no payment for physical pain, psychological suffering, and so on.

Prevention (or reduction in incidence) of the occurrence of the event giving rise to the economic insecurity. Consider again the case of industrial accidents. One obvious way to prevent economic insecurity from this source is to prevent the accident: no occurrence, no insecurity. Prevention may be "true" prevention which seeks to eliminate or reduce the chance of loss, or, that which seeks to minimize the severity of the loss. The use of safety guards on plant equipment is an example of a preventive method which seeks to reduce accident risks; prompt medical care in case of accidents illustrates minimization of the severity of loss. Preventive programs of the above types have followed a number of different courses. In some cases the programs have been independent of any particular system of indemnification. Thus, a business enterprise seeks to reduce accidents, irrespective of the indemnification method used. Why should the business enterprise do this? Quite apart from the humanitarian factor involved, such an approach is simply good industrial relations practice. In many cases, however, economic incentives may be stronger than sheer humanitarianism. Hence, one may find indemnification and prevention systems linked in one way or another. For example, an employer may seek to protect his employees against the undesirable consequences of industrial accidents through the use of an insurance system. The insurance system may in turn provide for a reduction in premiums (costs) if there is a reduction in accidents. Hence, the employer has a very real economic motivation to reduce the incidence of accidents. In most contemporary alleviative programs there is a link between the indemnification and preventive aspects, although there are various preventive approaches not directly tied to alleviative programs.

Government regulation. In one respect, regulation is inherent in any program of alleviation or prevention where the government is concerned. But regulation may also apply in other cases, primarily those of substandard conditions. Regulation may be preventive or punitive in nature. Thus, in certain jurisdictions, children below a certain age may be prohibited from seeking gainful employment. Or, women may be prohibited from working in certain types of establishments between the hours of midnight and 7:00 A.M. Or, women and children may not be allowed to work over a certain number of hours in given types of operations.

In other cases the regulation may be punitive. Thus, a forty-hour ceiling may be placed upon the work week. If this were an absolute prohibition, forty hours would be the outside limit. But the regulation may be punitive: an employer may work his employees over forty hours per week, but only upon paying them a penalty rate, such as time-and-one-half for the excess hours.

METHODS OF COMBATING ECONOMIC INSECURITY: PRIVATE APPROACHES

Alleviation, prevention, and regulation constitute the principal approaches to the problems of economic insecurity. Given these approaches, there are a number of specific methods through which these approaches can be applied. These methods can be divided into two basic categories: private and public. Let us first consider, private methods.

Private approaches to insecurity, without the use of insurance. In this method the individual assumes the risks of insecurity and seeks to combat them through the mechanism of saving or by other means. In some cases, group activity of a noninsurance nature may be used.

One alternative involves the individual only. By accumulating a fund of savings—a reserve—the individual may be able to protect himself from the undesirable economic consequences of industrial accidents and sickness and unemployment. Likewise, the accumulation of such a fund may permit retirement at "old age." (We do not at this point evaluate these methods. Thus we do not analyze here the question of how effectively, in fact, an individual can protect himself by this method, or for how many individuals in society it is likely to prove effective. We merely note that it is one possible system.)

A second alternative involves the individual and his family and/or friends. Should job separation place the individual in impoverished circumstances, his family or friends may tide him over for the short run or may take care of him from then on. A worker suffers an accident, is temporarily displaced from his job, and is supported by his family. Or, an older employee retires and lives with his children until his death. Or, the retired employee and/or his spouse retire to a denominationally or fraternally supported old-folks' home. This alternative typified the American economy during the nineteenth as well as a good part of the twentieth century and is still to be found.

While the above examples illustrate essentially alleviative methods, a third alternative involves the individual, his employer, and in a significant proportion of cases, also a labor organization, and is basically preventive in nature. Thus, conventional employment guarantees may be viewed as a private noninsurance approach which seeks to get at one type of insecurity problem, and does it through the preventive route. Health and safety measures provide another preventive example. Such methods are likely to increase considerably in importance in the future.

Private approaches to insecurity utilizing a system of insurance. This method is an extension of that discussed above. Instead, however, of "saving" in the individual sense, the person pools his risks with others and employs a practice commonly called insurance. When an individual buys an annuity for old age from a commercial insurance company, he is using this method. The same is true when an accident insurance policy is purchased. For actuarial reasons, this type of insurance has not been privately written by commercial insurers in the field of unemployment; hence there is a gap in the risks which this approach can cover. (It is true, however, that we have historical record of some private unemployment "insurance" programs, and the newer wage guarantees are a form of "insurance.")

Formal groups as well as individuals as such may utilize this method. Thus, fraternal associations, labor organizations, and others, either by themselves or through collective negotiations with others, use insurance programs. And again, while the insurance approach is basically alleviative, preventions may accompany it, as in the case of health and safety programming and workmen's compensation.

The private insurance approach, including individuals and groups, has come to play a very important part in present-day attempts to combat economic insecurity in the United States. Whereas the noninsurance method was important in an earlier day, it has become less so today in the cases of old age and accidents and illness.

Private approaches, mixed, where various combinations of the above methods are used. Realistically this mixed system typifies present practice in the United States. For some individuals and/or groups and for some risks, insurance systems are used; for other individuals or risks, they are not. Detailed discussion of these programs will constitute a major portion of this book.

Methods of Combating Economic Insecurity: Public Approaches

In addition to private approaches, there are different ways in which governments may seek to attack the problems of economic insecurity. Here also there are specific variations in governmental methods, and in real life one finds political bodies utilizing a number of these variations. These different approaches are not mutually exclusive; in the American economy there is a tendency to use varied programs.

Government regulation, service not provided either by public or private agencies. In specific situations, particularly those relating to substandard conditions, the government spells out the framework of rules, but beyond that, except for administration of the rules and compliance with them, neither government nor private agencies provide any continuing service in combating economic insecurity. The Fair Labor Standards Act of 1938 (the Wage and Hour Law) provides the best illustration of this type of governmental regulation. Here the federal government has set down a framework of regulations including a floor on wages and a "ceiling" on hours. A federal agency administers the Act in its various phases. But beyond this the government is not in "business," and the only obligation business enterprises have is to comply with the statute. Other federal and state laws regulating wages, hours, and working conditions illustrate this type of public approach. These regulatory methods are all essentially preventive in nature.

Government regulation, with service provided by private agencies. In this case, there is also a state-administered statute. But compliance in this case involves the provision of continuing service, either by the complying business enterprise or, through it, by other outside private agencies.

The approach to industrial accidents illustrates this case. A state enacts a law placing certain responsibilities upon the employer as to indemnification of wage losses suffered and medical costs incurred by an employee injured in an accident upon the employer's premises. The law may permit the employer himself, under certain circumstances, to assume directly the financial responsibilities involved, that is, to become "self-insured." The average employer will, however, comply with the law by taking out an insurance policy with a commercial company writing this type of coverage. Thus, while the state legislates the framework of regulation, it is the private agency—the employer himself or an insurance company —which undertakes the economic activity required for statutory compliance. This approach is applied today to industrial accidents and sickness in a number of states in this country under statutory requirements of workmen's compensation laws.

Government regulation, with service also provided by the government. In addition to writing a framework of economic security regulation, governments may also provide the services required by the regulation. This may be done in two ways: (1) by providing the service directly or (2) by making income payments to individuals permitting them to purchase the service.

1. Direct provision of economic security service is found in a variety of situations. A given county in a state sets up a poorhouse, or poor farm, or an old people's home. In such cases the service— food, lodging, clothing, medical care—is provided directly on a service basis to the needy person; and there is customarily no intermediate transfer of money. Other illustrations are easily found on local, state, and national levels: the visiting nurse, schools for the blind, medical assistance to the veteran.

2. Income payment systems have become increasingly important since the middle of the 1930's. Such systems may be of two basic types. In one case the government makes the income payments to the individual in need, who then, within certain limitations, is free to spend the income to meet his needs. Here the government acts as a sort of middleman: it raises monies from various sources, and then passes them on to individuals for use in combating insecurities they face. The "dole," "poor relief," and "old-age assistance" are examples of this approach.

In the other case the government also uses the income approach, but it engages in continuing economic activity in the process. The government is in business, so to speak. This method exists, first, on the federal level in the Old Age and Survivors Insurance (OASI) program, wherein the government is in the insurance business, particularly the annuity branch of it. On the combined federal-state level, the Unemployment Compensation (UC) program provides an illustration; here the several states, operating within a federal framework, are in the unemployment insurance business. Finally, in some states, the state is in the casualty insurance business, underwriting workmen's compensation risks. Public works afford a different type of illustration for all levels of government, particularly in recent decades.

INDIRECT PUBLIC AND PRIVATE APPROACHES TO
ECONOMIC INSECURITY

In addition to the types of programs noted above, there are other and somewhat more indirect approaches to economic insecurity. These include both public and private methods, in which preventive aspects are perhaps more strongly stressed. Two illustrations can be given. As a public measure on the federal level, the use of appropriate fiscal and monetary policies may permit the maintenance of high levels of employment. This in turn reduces the possibility of economic insecurity due to job separation for economic reasons. The Employment Act of 1946 provides an example of a statute oriented to problems of this type.

In the private sector of the economy, the complex series of procedures included in employment stabilization typify this more indirect approach. Various provisions in state unemployment insurance laws do provide a stimulus for stabilization efforts by giving reduced "insurance" rates to the employer who succeeds in his employment stabilization attempts. But additionally there are numerous cases of informal stabilization programs that are preventive in nature.

In both of the above public and private examples, the preventive program is not necessarily linked to any specific alleviative program. Thus, the use of various policies to maintain high levels of employment is not in and of itself linked to unemployment compensation systems; such policies are undertaken for broader and more basic economic and social purposes.

In the United States today we utilize all the foregoing direct and indirect public and private systems. The proportions vary, depending upon the specific causal factor in economic insecurity for which the program is set up. The body of this book will concern itself with discussing and analyzing the variety of programs existing in the framework sketched above[4]

Basic Problems in Economic Security Programs

The application of any concrete economic security program requires that a number of operational questions be answered. Since each of these questions is relevant to the programs subsequently discussed in this book, we shall outline them at this point. The

[4] Although the subject matter is beyond the scope of this book, it is clear that collective bargaining and its related public policy are designed to make employees more secure through their own efforts.

questions involved are operational; we do not raise at this point
the more basic problems that need to be solved in order to evaluate
a given program and decide if it should or should not be introduced
or should or should not be eliminated. For the moment we accept
the system as it is. This is not an unrealistic point of view, since
it is hard to conceive, for example, of the Old-Age and Survivors
Insurance system being wiped off the books. This neither suggests
that such programs cannot be amended or improved, nor does it
mean that they cannot be criticized. But for purposes of exposition
in this text, it is perhaps better to present first the system as it
exists and then later evaluate it on the basis of specific criteria set
up for the purpose.

The operational questions involved in any given economic security program are as follows.[5]

Who shall be covered by the program? In the case of public
programs, administrative, constitutional, economic, political, and
other pressures are intertwined, along with "need," in determining
coverage. The Old-Age and Survivors Insurance program will serve
as an example. In the early years following the passage of this act,
certain classes of employees such as agricultural laborers and domestic servants were excluded, partly because of administrative
difficulties involved in handling their records. As record-keeping
experience was gained by the OASI administration, this became
less of a problem, and such employees have since been brought
under the act. Or, there is little doubt that economic considerations
were important in originally excluding farm groups, for example,
from coverage. Again, the political representation of medical practitioners has probably been instrumental in enabling them to remain
out of the OASI program even though most other categories of
self-employed are now covered.

In the case of unemployment insurance, differences in coverage
have been in part based upon the number of employees the employer had and, additionally, in some states, upon the size of the
community in which the company was located. Thus, in a case in
point, otherwise eligible employers of *one* or more employees in
towns of 10,000 and over would come under the act, but in towns of
less than 10,000 only employers of *eight* or more (after December
31, 1955, four or more) employees would be covered. The logic of
the community size factor was based in part, at least, upon the
belief that in small towns employment was "inherently" more stable,

[5] For a useful reference, see Eveline M. Burns, *Social Security and Public Policy*
(New York: McGraw-Hill Book Co., Inc., 1956).

and also that where unemployment did occur, the individual frequently had other resources, such as a quarter-acre of land to help tide him over. Thus, it was argued that the same degree of need did not exist.

Similar considerations enter into private programs, such as employer-sponsored or collectively bargained pension programs or "guaranteed wage" programs. A wage guarantee may be extended only to employees with two years' service with the company, this restriction arising in part out of the belief that the company does not have such an obligation to employees who do not intend to remain with it, that is, to "floaters." Or, if such a plan is collectively bargained, it may extend only to "seniority" workers. In part, this may be based upon cost factors, in part upon ethical considerations noted above. Other reasons may also be involved, varying to some extent with the specific program involved.

In general, there is a tendency for the coverage of economic security programs to become more extensive. This is true for public as well as private programs. The increase in coverage under the OASI amendments, particularly of 1950 and 1954, illustrates this for public programs, and the extension of company and union health and welfare programs to the family of the employee provides an example for private programs. There are some exceptions; unemployment insurance is a case where coverage has been extended relatively little. And there are some cases where the program contracts because of the well-being of the economy or because of the substitution of other programs. Thus, the county poor farm is gradually becoming a thing of the past as newer programs of economic security take its place.

What are qualifications for collection of benefits? Where economic security programs involve the payment of benefits, as to an injured, retired, or unemployed individual, it is customary to require that the "covered" individual also meet certain other requirements. These are usually of three types.

First are requirements relating to coverage itself. Thus the individual frequently must have been in the program for a certain period of time and in some cases also must have had certain minimum wages or earnings. The specific requirements vary with program types, and again are a result of a combination of administrative, economic, political, and other considerations. The reasoning behind such requirements is that benefits should only be payable to one who has a bona fide attachment to the labor force or to a given company and that there should be some sort of "ethical" minimum to this attachment. Thus, for example, it is not held to be economically or ethically desirable to pay unemployment benefits to a housewife who works as a retail clerk during the Christmas season but who retires from the labor force after the season is over.

A second requirement relates to the specific factor "causing" the economic insecurity. Thus, where discharge is for cause, or where an individual quits for certain reasons, unemployment insurance may be denied or there may be a longer waiting period required. Parallel illustrations can be given for accident and for old age security programs. Private economic security systems probably are currently less restrictive in these respects than are public. Subsequent to job separation, other qualifications are also found. In unemployment compensation, for example, a person must be able to work and willing to work before he can become an eligible claimant; the previously mentioned housewife who worked at Christmas would not be eligible for benefits (assuming that she had sufficient coverage) if she dropped out of the labor force on January 1 and did not make herself available for employment.

Third, some public programs involve continuing requirements, once benefits have started. Thus, under unemployment compensation, a beneficiary may lose part or all of his benefits if he earns above a certain maximum amount in part-time, casual, or other employment while he is technically unemployed. The same is true of a beneficiary under OASI, who, if he is in a certain age group and earns more than a certain sum, has his benefits reduced.

The net effect of all these restrictions is to set up a series of rules under which benefits can and under which they cannot be claimed. Ethical and economic reasons underlie such requirements, with political pressures evident in a variety of instances. Public assistance programs strikingly illustrate, in a different way, all of the above characteristics.

What benefits should be paid the recipients of economic security programs in varying situations? Here public and private programs differ markedly. In the private insurance program there is usually a close correspondence with actuarial principles. A person collects what is related actuarially to the specific cost outlays made under the program; under a given annuity plan a higher in-payment will result in an actuarially related higher benefit. Hence the major determinant is impersonal and mathematical. In the noninsurance type of private economic security program, such as the dismissal wage or the wage guarantee, actuarial relations do not hold, and the benefit levels are usually a matter of individual or pooled judgment, as well as of collective bargaining.

In the public insurance programs, such as OASI or UC, actuarial relations are less important. This is true not only for the relation between over-all total benefits and over-all total costs of the program, but also for individual benefits and costs. These social insurance systems emphasize the social aspect more than they do the actuarial. (Indeed, some critics have held that social "assurance" would be a more logical term.) Thus, under OASI, per given dollar of in-payment, a low-wage worker receives a proportionately greater benefit than does the high-wage earner. This is true because the benefit computation formula is structured so as to pay a higher percentage benefit for the lower wage increments. Under public assistance programs "need" is critical in determining benefits. The influence of political pressures is apparent with respect to the above.

What are the costs? A complicated set of factors lies behind cost considerations, of which the following are among the more basic.

Costs are, of course, closely related on one side to need and on the other to the ability and willingness of the individual, company, or governmental unit to bear the cost. Thus, a given county's ability to take care of its aged poor or needy (assuming no grants are available from other political units) depends not only upon the degree of need, but upon how much revenue can be directed to this purpose.

If there is leeway in how much can be expended, the actual expenditures will be determined by a number of factors. First are the economic factors involved in the benefit levels desired. For example, there is a considerable difference in the benefits collectible under the Railroad Retirement Act as compared with OASI. But there is also a considerable difference in the level of in-payments. Political pressures may influence benefit levels; thus under UC, experience rating has probably contributed to keeping benefits down in order to keep costs down. Second, for private plans, where the actuarial relationship is much tighter, it is more obvious that the benefit structure desired will have a direct bearing upon costs. Here, also, political pressures are evident, though they are the pressures of management, unionism, and collective bargaining, rather than of government. If a wage increase is forthcoming, the union membership may prefer it in "here-and-now pay raises" rather than as part of an increase in security benefits.

Who shall pay the costs? Here again diverse pressures are evident. In public programs, political and constitutional considerations are relevant. Thus, in the OASI program, both employer and employee contribute. In the UC program, only the employer contributes. Why this difference? One reason is that it was felt the UC program would have a greater chance of meeting the test of constitutionality if the given approach were used. In private programs, both ethics and economics are involved. Some persons hold that the employee as well as the employer should contribute to security programs as a matter of "right." Against this is set the fact that, dollar for dollar, contributions made only by the employer are the more economical, since they are tax deductible, while the employee's are not. Also, it has been held that it is much more economical to administer a program where only the employer contributes. Compromise, not necessarily in the worst sense of the term, usually produces the final result.

What method of financing should be used? Should the program be put completely upon a pay-as-you-go basis or should the system be set up so as to provide also for an accumulation of funds for past service (as in the case of retirement) as well as for possible future increases in costs?

In general, the type of insecurity involved, and hence the program utilized, has an important bearing upon the answer to this last question. For example, most accident and health programs tend, by their inherent nature, to be operated upon a pay-as-you-go basis; there is little logic in any other approach. Public unemployment insurance programs stand in an intermediate position; in part the employer (given varying state laws) pays in yearly on a pay-as-you-go basis. But, if he builds up the account for his own enterprise, and his firm has little unemployment, his rates in subsequent years may be lowered. At the other extreme are situations, primarily involving retirement, where a choice can be made between pay-as-you-go and other systems. Thus, a university may provide for its retired employees by meeting retirement payments through a year-by-year budgetary allowance. This is, in fact, the way many such institutions operated until 1930–1935. But this approach entails heavy financial burdens if the retirement rolls grow and if no reserve has been built up. Hence, in most private retirement programs the pay-as-you-go approach has been abandoned in favor of other more financially sound means. In the OASI program the approach has veered from one extreme to the other, with political and other pressures as important as economic ones. In passing, it ought to be noted that the same type of financial logic need not necessarily hold for both public and private programs. Thus, "pay-

administration involves, first, execution of the program in terms of its intent and, second, that such execution be honest. Recent experiences with some private health and welfare programs provide examples of poor administration. Structural soundness implies not only an economical plan, but one whose features do not produce on balance undesirable operational, economic, and social consequences.

3. Does the program produce undesirable economic consequences? Does it artificially distort resource allocation? Pricing? What is its impact upon the functioning of the economy? For example, do different state unemployment insurance laws artificially influence the location of industry? Does experience rating in unemployment compensation add to cyclical movement rather than act as a counter-cyclical force? Do private pension programs unduly restrict labor mobility?

The criteria problem not only involves the choice of yardsticks, but also requires the collection of information so as to apply the yardsticks.[7] Information is becoming increasingly available in many areas of economic security, and this is perhaps a less difficult problem than the specification of standards. We shall use the above-noted three criteria throughout the book as we discuss economic security programs.

Three Introductory Problems

We have found students very much interested in a number of economic security problems at the outset of their study. Hence we are introducing three of these problems at this point.[8]

HAS ECONOMIC INSECURITY INCREASED OR DECREASED WITH TIME?

One issue about which students frequently raise questions is whether economic insecurity has increased or decreased over the years. While quantitative answers are difficult to secure for this problem it can be approached in a number of ways.

1. Certainly the "forms" of insecurity—or the "ultimate" causal factors—have changed over the past several hundred years. Nature, as in the case of crop failures, has become less significant in the American scene; institutional forces in an urbanized society have become more important, as in the case of periods of cyclical unem-

[7] For an interesting example of an economic framework in evaluating an economic security program, see Jerome Rothenberg, "Welfare Implications of Alternative Methods of Financing Medical Care," *American Economic Review*, XLI, No. 2 (May, 1951), pp. 676–87.

[8] The student should consult, not only here, but as a generally informative source, *Economic Security For Americans* (New York: The American Assembly, Graduate School of Business, Columbia University, 1954).

ployment. Which of these is the more severe is hard to say; probably the former is less so, for a community of primarily agricultural peoples can keep body and soul together by eking out an existence on the land. (We by no means deny the crushing impact of dustbowls, hurricanes, floods, and so on.) Beyond this, it is difficult to judge.[9]

2. Given an urban and industrial system, preventive actions taken by society have tended increasingly to lessen the actual risks of certain types of insecurity. This is most notable in the case of industrial accidents. A person's chances of being killed or injured in industry are less than they were twenty-five or fifty years ago. For example, industrial deaths in 1913 (the earliest year for which the figures appear to have any reliability) were 25,000; in 1955, preliminary estimates set them at 14,200.[10] If one uses relative figures, relating deaths to the size of the labor force, the reduction in risks becomes even more striking. These results have been brought about by the combined action of employers, employees, unions, insurance companies, public agencies, and others through the operation of safety programs. Hence, in this area at least, the causes of aggregate insecurity appear to have lessened.

Unemployment and old age present a different picture. While aggregate insecurity due to unemployment has lessened in the past fifteen years, the picture in the prior decade was as black as it has ever been in American economic history. It is probably safe to say, however, that governmental policy is likely to be such in the future as to prevent any repetition of the post-1929 experience. Thus it may be expected that insecurity arising from this source will not be of the magnitude of previous periods. Old age is probably the least changed of the three factors under discussion; in major part this results, of course, from the inexorable march of age itself. And while individual incomes have increased through the years—and, hence, also the ability to set up a fund for old age—so also have expenditures. The result is a race, with normal marginal propensities to save not necessarily guaranteeing the accumulation of a fund sufficient to provide financial independence upon retirement.

On balance, taking all three causal types into account, it is reasonable to conclude that aggregate economic insecurity has quan-

[9] Fiction frequently may be better than fact in portraying such pictures. For a very useful bibliography in this connection, see Virginia Prestridge (compiler), *The Worker in American Fiction, An Annotated Bibliography, Bibliographic Contributions No. 4* (Champaign: Institute of Labor and Industrial Relations, University of Illinois, 1954).

[10] See "Preliminary Estimates of Work Injuries in 1955," *Monthly Labor Review,* LXXIX, No. 4 (April, 1956), pp. 438–39.

titatively lessened through the years. While it is not possible to say how much, the direction seems clear. Preventive actions of one type or another have been introduced, and effectively, on balance.

3. If one now considers not the form, not the causal factors, not the preventive programs in economic insecurity, but rather the programs of alleviation, then it is clear that the consequences of insecurity are less critical than they were in the past. This does not mean that an ideal system has been achieved. But through public and/or private programs relating to old age, to unemployment, and to accidents and illness, it is clear that the covered individual is afforded a degree of protection nonexistent in earlier times.

Summarizing, we may say, therefore: (1) that the forms of economic insecurity and causal factors have altered, and it is difficult to say whether the risks of economic insecurity are "inherently" greater or less than they used to be; (2) that via preventive programs, actual risks have been lessened for industrial accidents and sickness and probably for unemployment; and (3) that alleviation programs have significantly lessened the undesirable consequences of incidents that do take place.

SECURITY AND INCENTIVE

What are the effects of economic security programs upon incentive? Does unemployment insurance, for example, tend to create a class of persons who prefer to collect benefits rather than work? Does workmen's compensation create a class of medical malingerers? Do wage guarantees and other forms of security programs reduce productivity and increase complacency? We may try to find the answer to these questions in a number of ways.

1. We have little fundamental empirical knowledge on the relation of security to incentives, and still less of it translatable to security and incentives in the work environment. There is much more speculation than information surrounding this subject. Partisan groups on both sides of the question tend to discuss the problem in terms of stereotyped and unproven beliefs. Hence, there is not much that can be said on this basic level. It is our belief that a Scottish verdict—not proven—must be rendered with respect to those who say that security dulls incentive (or for that matter, that insecurity increases incentive).[11]

[11] We do not attempt to get into the larger question of the impact of security upon the ability of a society to survive. See for example, Arnold J. Toynbee, A Study of History (one volume abridgment by D. C. Somervell) (New York: Oxford University Press, 1947), chap. vi-viii.

2. On the level of operating experience we have a better basis upon which to make a judgment, although not by any means as complete a basis as we should like. First, it is the relatively rare case where a person deliberately severs himself from employment so as to collect benefits. True, there are safeguards written into most systems which seek to prevent this. Certainly it would be the very rare case where a person would deliberately injure himself to collect workmen's compensation (although he may feign injury). Probably if there were no safeguards in the law, more people would quit jobs to collect unemployment compensation. While this may indicate that security would dull incentive, it also might mean that more people would try to locate themselves in more suitable jobs. The fact that safeguards exist prevents any full empirical test. The problem does not, of course, exist with respect to old age.

Second, for the group eligible to collect unemployment or workmen's compensation, there is little doubt that some abuses exist. There is no doubt that some malingering exists in accident cases. And there is little doubt that some undesirable practices occur in unemployment compensation.[12] But the level of benefit payments under the unemployment insurance system during high levels of employment leaves little doubt that people prefer to work rather than to collect benefits.

3. The conclusions seem warranted that: (a) the present economic security system in the United States has not damaged the well-being of the economy by destroying incentive; (b) abuses probably exist in all the economic security programs, but they are neither important relative to the whole program nor in general outside of administrative control; and (c) although economic security programs as presently constituted appear not to have impaired incentives, they would tend to do so if benefits restored all or nearly all wage losses.

The Government and Economic Security Programs

Government has come to play an increasingly important role in economic security. Is this a justifiable role? The answer to this question largely depends upon how one defines "justifiable." Prior to seeking such an answer, it may be interesting to note how governments came to assume their roles.

Following industrialization in the United States, government action first involved intervention in substandard conditions, par-

---

[12] See the interesting study by Joseph M. Becker, *The Problem of Abuse in Unemployment Benefits* (New York: Columbia University Press, 1953), particularly Part IV.

ticularly working conditions and hours of work for women and children. Such regulation began as early as the period 1840–1850, and developed from two parallel beliefs: (1) that, because of their position in society, women and children merited special consideration and protection in the economy, and (2) that the labor-marketing mechanism, as an economic institution, did not necessarily guarantee such consideration and protection. Hence, governmental regulation was viewed as necessary. Subsequently, though slowly, came intervention in other substandard areas, as in regulating the maximum working hours of males in transportation where the public safety was involved.

Over a half-century later, state governments crystallized employee protection against industrial accidents and illness through the enactment of workmen's compensation legislation. In some cases the state became an entrepreneur by going into the insurance business; in others it merely passed conformity legislation, requiring private businesses to provide protection, but permitting private insurance carriers to underwrite the risks.

A generation later saw the passage, on the federal or federal-state level, of old age and unemployment insurance. In both these cases, government became the underwriter, going into the social insurance business. Still later the Employment Act of 1946 was passed.

All these programs arose from needs which culminated in social legislation at given points in time. Moreover, all through this period, government units at the local level were affording protection (even if only minimal) to the needy, the aged, and the impoverished. Therefore, to ask whether the state has a justifiable role in economic security is to talk about a *fait accompli* which has existed for over a century.

But the mere fact of existence does not necessarily provide justification. We feel, however, that justification can be found on a number of grounds.

First, the state has a basis for specifying minimum standards of performance for its economic institutions. There is no inherently necessary reason for assuming the institutions will perform optimally. Thus, just as rules of the game are logical in athletic contests, so are they also applicable to economic contests to prevent the latter from being played in socially undesirable ways. Minimum governmental standards for child labor, for hours of work for women and children, and for working conditions have a place in society.

Second, the government may be the only agency which effectively can act in certain economic security fields. Thus, the maintenance of high levels of employment involves the use of fiscal and monetary policy essentially or only within the province of government. While we would prefer to see a maximization of self-regulation by economic institutions, there is no necessary guarantee that this will be forthcoming. The adage about that government governing best which governs least is not necessarily applicable here.

Third, government programs may be the only ones which will permit coverage to be extended to those who most need protection. Moreover, such programs create greater uniformity and standardization, thus lessening the chance of patchwork systems.

But two additional remarks might be made. First, it is our present feeling that the government serves its most useful function in providing a "basic layer" of protection upon which private supplements can be built. Second, we would feel that a preferable approach is for private enterprise to operate within a governmental framework, where feasible.

In conclusion, we would make two comments. First, we feel that government plays a necessary and useful role in economic security and that its activity here is not leading the nation down the road to the "socialist" or "welfare" state. To the contrary, government action may help us to preserve and strengthen the type of system we cherish so much. Second, we would prefer to see, within the governmental framework, a maximizing of the area in which private enterprise can operate.

A Note on Terminology

We have noted in this chapter a number of the terms used in the field of economic security. Here we should like to present a more detailed picture and, in so doing, provide an over-all view of the pattern of terminology. Then, in future sections of this book, it should be clear what is meant by a term and what its relationship is to other terms.

Our presentation is in diagrammatic form, with appended explanation where needed. (See Fig. 1.1) It should be noted that preventive, alleviative, and regulatory methods are intertwined throughout.

Summary

This introductory section has been designed to trace the principal features of the subject of economic insecurity. Such insecurity

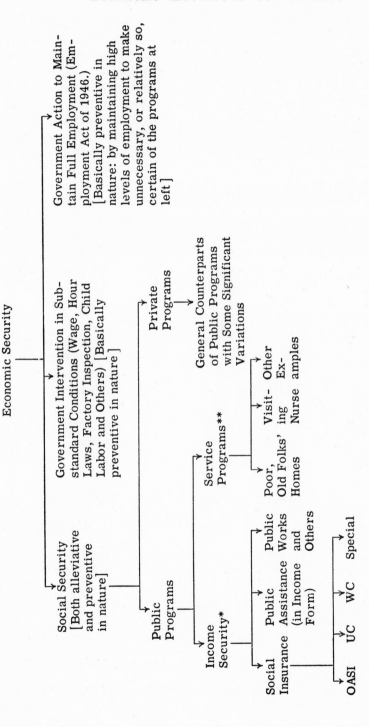

Fig. 1.1 Principal Economic Security Terms and Their Relationships

*Where recipient receives cash and in expending it secures needed services.
**Where recipient receives service directly.

arises out of the loss of income and/or the creation of additional expenses for the individual. In turn, the most important cause giving rise to the loss of income is the loss of gainful employment: the insecurity is job-oriented. Additional expenses may be incurred through accidents or sickness; here there may or may not be an accompanying job loss. Society may try to adjust to these forms of economic insecurity in a variety of ways: alleviation of the undesirable consequences, reduction or prevention of the incidence, and government regulation. Both public and private methods to combat insecurity may be utilized, and in the United States a combined system, in fact, exists.

The conventional treatment of the problem of economic security tends to limit itself to the topics of public and private assistance and insurance as they seek to combat insecurity of the types noted above. Substandard conditions in wages, hours, and other conditions of employment are important causal factors in economic insecurity. Hence this section has also noted the relevance of such factors and how society has sought, through government regulation, to adjust itself to the particular problems created.

The presentation here has been deliberately abstract, the purpose being to provide the reader with a series of concepts and problems. We have not felt it desirable to introduce institutional facts until the student has the equipment with which he can make the facts intelligible, analyze them, and evaluate them.

With this background, we now clothe our analytical skeleton and turn to a concrete examination of the American economic security system.

Suggestions for Additional Reading

ARMSTRONG, BARBARA NACHTRIEB. *Insuring the Essentials.* New York: The Macmillan Co., 1932.
A quarter-century old, but a very comprehensive analysis of economic insecurity and how to attack it. The analysis covers more than "insurance"; it also deals, as do we, with substandard conditions.

HABER, WILLIAM and WILBUR J. COHEN, (eds.). *Readings in Social Security.* Englewood Cliffs, N. J.: Prentice-Hall, Inc., 1948.
A very interesting and well-selected series of readings covering many phases of economic security. The historical and analytical material is particularly useful.

HOGAN, JOHN D. and FRANCIS A. J. IANNI. *American Social Legislation.* New York: Harper & Bros., 1956.
An informative account of American social legislation, which usefully supplements the material in this text.

LAUTERBACH, ALBERT. *Economic Security and Individual Freedom, Can We Have Both?* Ithaca: Cornell University Press, 1948.
A discussion along broad lines of the basic issues involved in freedom and security. Worth perusing along with F. A. Hayek, *The Road to Serfdom,* and J. M. Clark, *Alternative to Serfdom.*

THE AMERICAN ASSEMBLY, GRADUATE SCHOOL OF BUSINESS, COLUMBIA UNIVERSITY. *Economic Security For Americans.* New York: Columbia University, 1954.
Background papers and findings of a conference on economic security for Americans. Excellent factual material as well as thought-provoking discussion.

WITTE, EDWIN E. *Five Lectures on Social Security.* Rio Piedras, Puerto Rico: University of Puerto Rico, 1951.
An extremely useful description and anaylsis of economic security programs by one of the outstanding authorities on the subject.

2

The American Economic
Security System

Introduction

The American economic security system attacks financial uncertainties associated with old age, premature death, unemployment, and accidental injury and sickness; and substandard conditions. The system includes the preventive, alleviative, and regulatory approaches discussed in Chapter 1.

Preventive approaches include public and private attempts to reduce the frequency and severity of financial losses associated with death and old age, accidents and sickness, and unemployment; and government regulations designed to eliminate substandard working conditions.

The alleviative approaches, which seek to offset the undesirable effects of economic insecurity, are, first, the public regulatory-alleviative programs and, second, the private alleviative programs. The public regulatory-alleviative programs include government regulation with alleviating service or income payments being provided by the government on a social insurance or public assistance basis, and government regulation with the alleviating service or income payments being provided by private agencies. The private alleviative approaches include assistance from relatives, payments from friends, private charities, employers, and others, and private insurance.[1] Private insurance, as the term is used in this text, includes all types

[1] Assumption of the loss by the individual himself is one way of handling the problem, but this is not an alleviative approach in a technical sense.

of definite benefit plans. Examples are: individual insurance issued by a commercial insurer; a pension plan self-insured by an employer; a hospital service plan underwritten by a hospital; and the recently negotiated supplementary unemployment benefit plans.

The purpose of this chapter is to enumerate the specific programs comprising the American economic security system and to classify these programs according to the insecurities covered, the sponsorship: public (federal, state, or local) or private, and the basic approach. This summary view of the system clothes with reality the somewhat abstract concepts developed in the last chapter, and will help us keep in mind the interrelationships among the programs as we study their specific details in later sections of this book.

Some Important Distinctions

This enumeration and classification of the American economic security system will be more meaningful if we distinguish first between alleviative service and income payments; second between public assistance and social insurance; and third between private insurance and social insurance.

Service Versus Income Payments

Under a service program, the recipient receives payments in kind instead of in cash, while under an income program the recipient receives cash which he may use to purchase the services he needs and desires. Both service and income programs exist in the United States today, although as will be seen, the latter predominates.

The recipient of service benefits must accept the program benefits, but the recipient of income benefits can purchase those services which he deems most important. The recipient loses freedom of economic choice when a loss of income is replaced with specific services. For example, there is a loss of freedom if an individual is provided with free room and board instead of, say, a cash payment of $100 a month when he reaches age sixty-five. The loss of freedom is less, however, when the program provides specific services instead of reimbursing the individual for expenses incurred in purchasing the specific types of services. In fact, the loss of freedom may be very slight if the services under the service program may be obtained from all or most of the available providers of that service. For example, a medical expense program may provide service benefits or cash reimbursements for expenses incurred. In either case, the program is limited to medical services. The loss of freedom under the service program depends upon the ability of the insured to choose his own doctors, hospitals, nurses, and other suppliers of medical service. If the service program makes available all or most of the medical facilities of the nation on equal terms, the relative loss of freedom of choice is slight.

A variety of other considerations, some administrative, some economic, are relevant to the issue of service versus income payments. Among them are the following:

1. Service benefits make it possible for the sponsoring body to exercise more control over the quality and cost of the services.
2. An insured person may use cash payments for purposes which are not socially or economically desirable; hence service programs provide more rigorous controls, not only in quality and cost, but also in use.
3. Service benefits may, however, be more costly to administer, for there may be many more administrative and other details to be considered.
4. Public service benefits may make it necessary for the government to enter an area which, in the past, has been reserved for private enterprise.
5. Service benefits may not be affected directly or immediately by price changes; income benefits are. For example, a promise to provide hospital care in a semi-private room for thirty days is not reduced by an increase in the costs of providing this service. A $10 per day allowance may be sufficient to pay all the cost when the promise is made but only part of the cost later when the insured is hospitalized.
6. Service benefits replacing lost income are less "popular" than income benefits because of the loss of freedom of economic choice. Therefore, some who are eligible do not apply for the benefits. This tends to reduce the cost of the program. Freedom of choice is frequently a critical factor.

Granted these considerations, it is nevertheless true that, essentially because of the importance attached to the freedom of economic choice by our population, most of the alleviative payments under the American economic security system are payments in cash.[2] The services provided by some nonprofit medical expense associations are the most notable exception, and under these programs the loss of economic freedom is not great.

[2] Eveline M. Burns, *Social Security and Public Policy* (New York: McGraw-Hill Book Co., Inc., 1956), pp. 5-9. This excellent book discusses in detail the major questions arising in connection with public social security programs.

Public Assistance Versus Social Insurance[3]

Public assistance programs tend to be "charity" programs. Public assistance benefits customarily are paid only to those individuals who can demonstrate need, and the amount of the benefit is based upon the extent of the demonstrated need. Final decisions on both eligibility and benefit amounts are made on a discretionary basis by the officials administering the public assistance programs.

Social insurance programs include all of the public regulatory-alleviative programs which provide benefits as a matter of right instead of on the basis of demonstrated need. Social insurance benefits are paid to all persons who satisfy certain eligibility requirements, regardless of their need. The benefit amounts are also determined on some basis other than actual need, although under many social insurance programs one factor affecting general benefit schedules is the presumed average need of the beneficiaries. The actual need may be more or less than the social insurance benefits. The officials administering the social insurance programs exercise little or no discretion in the determination of eligibility or benefit amounts in the general case.

Other differences between public assistance and social insurance programs may be summarized as follows:

1. The only direct participants under a public assistance program are the recipients. The direct participants under a social insurance plan are the insureds, only a small fraction of whom are beneficiaries at any given time. Thus, many more persons are directly concerned with social insurance programs.

2. Many persons who otherwise would be eligible for public assistance benefits do not apply because of the test of need. Participation in most social insurance programs is compulsory, but the participants need not claim their benefits. Of course, very few persons who are eligible for social insurance benefits refuse to make a claim, for there is no stigma attached to the receipt of the benefits.

3. Because of the character of public assistance programs, they are usually financed out of general revenues which usually are derived from a more progressive tax system than earmarked revenues. Social insurance programs, on the other hand, are generally financed out of earmarked taxes, and there is usually some relationship between an individual's benefit and the contributions made by the individual or on his behalf. It is held generally desirable to maintain some relationship between contributions and benefits because of the favorable effect on economic incentives.

[3] For an extensive discussion, see Eveline M. Burns, *The American Social Security System* (Boston: Houghton Mifflin Co., 1951), pp. 28–39.

4. Federal, state, and local funds are used to finance public assistance programs, but the programs are administered only by state or local government units. The amount of discretion involved in the programs is the principal reason advanced for the lack of federal administration. Federal and state funds plus private insurance premiums are used to finance social insurance programs. Because the amount of discretion involved is slight and because uniformity among the states is highly desirable, many of the programs are administered solely by the federal government.

5. Public assistance benefits are difficult to forecast because of the discretionary means test for both eligibility and benefit amounts. Therefore, most American families do not consider public assistance benefits in their economic security plans (except as emergency measures) because they do not expect or want to be needy. Social insurance benefits, on the other hand, can be reasonably forecast and participants are eligible for the benefits as a matter of right. Therefore, social insurance benefits are and should be included in the economic security plans of the American family.

Social insurance programs are much more "popular" than public assistance programs because definite benefits payable as a matter of right are preferred to indefinite benefits payable on the basis of need. Therefore, as interest in more adequate public economic security schemes has increased, social insurance programs have gradually replaced public assistance programs as the basic approach to these financial problems. Public assistance programs today protect only those persons who are both needy and ineligible for adequate social insurance benefits. Such programs are relatively least important in economic insecurities involving premature death and old age, for which social insurance programs are highly developed, and most important in cases such as disability where economic security programs are inadequate.

Social Insurance Versus Private Insurance

Insurance may be defined as a social device by means of which the risks or uncertainties of many persons are combined through actual or promised contributions to a fund out of which claimants are paid.[4] Because the proportion of losses becomes more predictable as the number of persons or objects independently exposed to the loss increases, the risk or uncertainty of the insurer is slight if the insured group is large. Thus insurance is beneficial because it (1) reduces risk and its undesirable consequences and (2) sub-

---

[4] On page 30 we stated that private insurance includes all types of definite benefit plans. This is true because all the definite benefit plans of which the authors are aware can and usually do involve some pooling of the risks of many persons.

stitutes many small losses in the form of premiums for a few large losses, thus reducing the *real* economic burden on society. The economic burden is less because, according to the law of diminishing utility, the loss in utility is much less if $100 is taken from each of 1000 families than if $10,000 is taken from each of ten families.[5]

A sound insurance system should possess the following characteristics: First, the number of insureds should be large and they should be independently exposed to the potential loss. Otherwise the risk is not reduced sufficiently to permit safe operation. Second, the losses covered should be definite in time and place to facilitate loss adjustments. Third, the chance of loss should be measurable. Otherwise the cost of the program is indefinite. Fourth, the loss should be accidental from the viewpoint of the insured. It is unwise to insure against losses which the insured can bring about or against losses which are bound to happen. (Death, for example, is "bound to happen"; but the date of death is uncertain.)

Private insurance plans generally possess the following characteristics, although there are some important exceptions primarily associated with group insurance.

1. The protection is voluntary. Insureds must be "sold" on the need for protection. As a result, some persons buy either no protection or inadequate protection. On the other hand, they do retain their freedom of economic choice.

2. The insurance contract is a legal instrument which cannot be changed and which can be enforced in the courts.

3. The cost of each individual's protection is determined on an actuarial basis. His benefit amounts and his loss and expense-producing potentialities are considered in determining the price, for the price of the protection should equal the expected cost. It is true that most insureds are not rated individually, for there is a desire to base rates on past experience and the experience of a single insured is not usually credible. (This is obvious in the case of death.) Moreover, rating each person individually is a complicated procedure. Therefore, usually all insureds with *approximately* the same loss and expense characteristics are grouped together in a class and charged the same rate. For example, life insurance premiums vary with the amount and type of life insurance purchased, but for a given benefit the rates depend upon only one factor—age. There are undoubtedly differences among standard lives in the

[5] See Paul A. Samuelson, *Economics* (3rd ed.; New York: McGraw-Hill Book Co., Inc., 1955), pp. 419–20; also Allan H. Willett, *The Economic Theory of Risk and Insurance* (New York: Columbia University Press, 1901. Reprinted, Philadelphia: University of Pennsylvania Press, 1951).

same age groups, but these differences are assumed to be slight.[6] Insofar as practical considerations will permit, price equals expected cost.

Private insurers may become bankrupt if their premiums plus assessments, if any, are consistently not sufficient to pay their actual expenses and losses, which may differ considerably from their expected losses and expenses. Private insurer experience in this respect has, however, been excellent.

4. The protection is provided by many insurers of various types who compete with one another for insureds. There are stock insurers, mutual insurers, self-insurers, medical service associations, and many others. Competition forces these insurers to reassess their contracts and prices periodically.

Social insurance includes a variety of insurance arrangements. At one extreme we have the type of private insurance required by law, such as workmen's compensation insurance, and public insurance, such as government life insurance for World War II veterans, which operate on essentially the same basis as private insurance. At the other extreme we have programs which differ from private insurance in many respects and which some persons believe should not be considered insurance. However, these programs do satisfy the definition of insurance used in this text.

The most important social insurance program—Old-Age and Survivors Insurance—is the best example of this latter "extreme." This program carries out a social and economic public policy decision: it provides a floor of protection for all participants against financial losses caused by premature death, disability, or old age.[7] It differs from the most common forms of private insurance in four important respects:

1. Participation is compulsory for all eligible persons. Otherwise some individuals would elect not to be covered and the policy objective of a floor of protection for all members of a defined group would be thwarted.

2. The benefits are prescribed by law. There are no contracts, and it is possible (but highly improbable) that Congress will rescind the benefits in the future. Periodic changes in the benefit structure are very likely through changes in the law.

3. The system redistributes income in addition to providing protection through a pooling arrangement. The lower-income groups, the insureds with many dependents, and the participants who were elderly

[6] Substandard lives may pay a higher premium, but there are relatively few substandard lives.

[7] For a concise description of the principles underlying this program, see J. Douglas Brown, "Concepts in Old Age and Survivors Insurance," *Proceedings* of the First Annual Meeting of the Industrial Relations Research Association, 1948, pp. 100–06.

when the system was inaugurated receive more benefits for their contributions than most other participants. If this were not true, it would be impossible to achieve the public policy objective of a floor of protection for all participants, since some insureds would be unable to afford adequate protection. The benefits are not equitable in the private insurance sense, but they are not meant to be. Other standards of performance have been deemed more important.

The contribution rates are scheduled, but Congress may and has revised the schedule periodically. Consequently, bankruptcy is impossible as long as the government has an effective taxing power, although it is conceivable that the taxes may become unbearable. An individual's contribution may vary yearly even though the tax rate remains fixed, for the base (annual income) upon which the tax is levied may fluctuate from year to year. These fluctuations may have little or no effect on the benefits.

4. The government system is a monopolistic system. However, public pressure forces a continual reassessment of benefits and contribution rates.

Because the benefits and the contribution rates may be made noncontractual and flexible, and because the government has the taxing power, some risks which are noninsurable by sound private insurance standards are insurable under social insurance programs. For example, Old-Age and Survivors Insurance, as it presently exists, could not be underwritten by a private insurer, as there are too many unpredictable variables in the program. Another case in point is unemployment insurance, which is not underwritten by private commercial insurers because they consider the chance of loss to be unpredictable and the exposure units to be interdependent. However, some employers have developed self-insured unemployment "insurance" plans.

Other social insurance programs may not be as different from private insurance as OASI. We shall not consider here any of these other programs, but as each is discussed in detail in later chapters the student should compare and contrast that program with private insurance in order to increase his appreciation and understanding of the important differences between private and social insurance. Since the purposes of the two devices differ, we should expect to find differences in their nature and application.

The American Economic Security System

Classifying the various programs included in the American economic security system is a difficult task, if for no other reason than that the system is complex.[8] Numerous program classes and sub-classes must be considered. In this text, for each insured economic insecurity we shall classify the program utilized according to sponsorship, public or private, and according to the basic approach. In order to simplify the discussion, we shall discuss the preventive and alleviative programs separately.

PREVENTIVE PROGRAMS

Most people do not think of preventive programs when economic security measures are being discussed, but the preventive approaches decrease the cost of nonpreventive programs and produce greater social and economic benefits when they are successful. Preventive efforts include programs aimed at one or both of the following objectives: (1) reduction or elimination of the chance of loss (*true prevention*); (2) minimization of the severity of the losses.[9] The preventive efforts may be general programs aimed at problems affecting all or most of our population or they may be selective programs designed to aid one person, firm, area, or other subdivision of the population.

Death, old age, and illness.[10] Since the preventive programs dealing with the problems of death, old age, accidental injuries and sickness overlap to a large extent, they will be treated in this discussion as one unit. All levels of government participate in the extensive public preventive programs. It is impossible to enumerate all of these activities, but an example of each approach will indicate their nature. General programs illustrating the true prevention and minimization objectives are inspections under the Pure Food and Drug Act and quarantine programs. Illustrative selective programs are physical examinations of school children and rehabilitation programs for veterans. Private efforts may be divided into the same categories. Illustrative general programs are medical research into the causes of certain diseases and first-aid classes. Illustrative selective programs are physical examinations for employees and the assignment of a lighter work load to an employee following a heart attack. It is interesting to note that while all the above measures

[8] For a useful classification of the public social security programs, see *Systems of Social Security: United States* (Geneva: International Labour Office, 1953). See also, Edwin E. Witte, *Five Lectures on Social Security* (Rio Piedras, Puerto Rico: University of Puerto Rico, 1951).

[9] A. H. Mowbray and R. H. Blanchard, *Insurance* (4th ed.; New York: McGraw-Hill Book Co., Inc., 1955), pp. 30–36. The salvage operations described by these authors have been included under the efforts to minimize the loss.

[10] We use "illness" here and later in the text as a generalized term which includes accidental injuries and sickness.

have an important job-oriented relationship, it is indirect in many cases. In general, in this text, we shall be concerned with the more direct relationships.

Unemployment. Public preventive measures against unemployment may be categorized in the same way. Most of the programs are sponsored by the federal government. True prevention includes monetary and fiscal policies aimed at maintaining full employment. The same policies when aimed at re-achieving full employment following a decline in economic activity illustrates the minimizing approach. Other examples are public works programs and "automatic stabilizers," such as the income tax whose burden decreases in periods of unemployment, thus tending to increase purchasing power. Public employment services for veterans illustrates a selective preventive approach, while the allocation of government contracts to critical unemployment areas is a selective minimizing approach. Private industry also has introduced stabilization programs which attempt to reduce unemployment through various techniques.

Substandard conditions. Government intervention in substandard conditions is essentially truly preventive in nature. There are no alleviative aspects to these programs. Before we investigate the scope of this intervention, we should note two facts. First, any improvement in substandard conditions indirectly improves the condition of the population with respect to the economic insecurities associated with death, old age, illness, and unemployment. Second, any public actions designed to increase the average real wage of employees indirectly attack substandard conditions.

Government intervention in substandard conditions essentially consists of a set of rules with which employers are expected to comply. The federal Fair Labor Standards Act contains the most important set of rules, for it establishes a minimum wage and a maximum work week at standard rates for most employments in interstate commerce. The act also regulates the use of child labor. The Davis-Bacon Act and the Walsh-Healey Act provide for the payment of prevailing minimum wage rates by private firms serving the government. The Walsh-Healey Act, which applies to suppliers, also establishes a maximum work week at standard rates, prohibits child labor, and specifies certain health and safety standards.

All states have child labor laws and laws which regulate in some way the maximum work week for women. A few have laws which regulate the maximum work week for men. Eight have minimum wage laws applying to all workers, while twenty-one have similar laws applying to women and children only. Other working conditions such as minimum work space are also prescribed under some state laws.

Private attempts to improve the working conditions of the wage earner include the voluntary actions of employers, the efforts of labor unions, collective actions through collective bargaining, and measures of one type or another inspired by the public conscience.

ALLEVIATIVE PROGRAMS

Preventive programs are only a partial solution to the problem of economic security. There may be limitations as to what can be accomplished; for example, premature death can probably never be eliminated. In other cases, the results do not justify the commitment of more economic resources to the preventive program.

Alleviative programs not only supplement but are the alternative solution when preventive efforts fail. They reimburse the insured for the financial loss that he or his family suffers when he becomes ill, dies prematurely, terminates his earning career because of old age, or is unemployed. In this section we shall list the alleviative programs dealing with each of these problems and classify them as social insurance programs, public assistance programs, or private approaches. Whether the programs provide service or cash benefits will be indicated in the text.

Death and old age. 1. *Social insurance.* The most important program providing death and retirement benefits is the Federal Old-Age and Survivors Insurance System established under the Social Security Act of 1935. This social insurance program pays benefits in cash, and its coverage is becoming almost universal.

Other social insurance programs, all of which are underwritten by the federal government and all of which pay income benefits, are the Railroad Retirement System, the Civil Service Retirement System, government life insurance for servicemen and veterans, veterans' benefits, and retirement programs of the armed services. State and local governments also have retirement systems for certain of their employees. That these programs are designed for special groups is evident from their titles.

Death due to occupational causes is covered under both federal and state workmen's compensation laws. The state acts are the most important. These acts require employers to pay cash benefits to the beneficiaries of deceased employees whose deaths were job-connected. Employers may self-insure this obligation with the state's permission, but usually the employer is insured by a private insurer or a state insurer. Seven states have monopolistic state funds, while eleven have funds which compete with commercial insurers.

2. *Public assistance.* The public program dealing specifically with old age is Old-Age Assistance. The federal government makes grants-in-aid to approved state programs which are in turn administered by state and local governmental authorities. A similar program—Aid to Dependent Children—provides benefits for children who are deprived of parental support because of death, incapacity, or absence of a parent. Both programs pay income benefits.

3. *Private approaches.* The most important private measure is private insurance, which consists primarily of individual insurance contracts issued by commercial insurers and group insurance plans underwritten by commercial insurers or self-insured by employers and/or unions. Reliance on relatives and charity, while still extensive, is less important than in the past.

Unemployment. 1. *Social insurance.* Each of the forty-eight states has an unemployment insurance system covering most of the employees in the state. The federal government participates indirectly, for it levies a tax on employers to pay the administrative costs of the state funds. The tax is reduced if the employer contributes to a state unemployment insurance scheme. Thus the states have a strong incentive for maintaining an unemployment compensation fund. Moreover, all taxes paid to the states are deposited in a federal unemployment insurance fund from which the states withdraw needed benefit amounts. The state plans provide cash payments to the *temporarily* unemployed.

The only other active unemployment insurance system is the federally written Railroad Unemployment Insurance System which provides similar benefits for a special class of workers.

2. *Private approaches.* No commercial insurer underwrites unemployment insurance, but we do have private unemployment "insurance" and, more commonly, supplementary unemployment insurance self-insured by an employer or union. The benefits are cash payments. Work and wage guarantees, including supplementary unemployment insurance, are of major interest currently.

Reliance on relatives and charity is necessary in some cases; here benefits may be in cash or in kind.

Accidental injury and sickness. 1. *Social insurance.* The Federal Old-Age and Survivors Insurance System provides two limited benefits in case of disability caused by accidental injury or sickness. The first benefit is a monthly income for certain totally and permanently disabled persons. The second benefit enables a totally and permanently disabled person to retain the death and retirement benefits to which he was entitled at the date the disability began.

The other social insurance programs provide benefits for only (1) job-connected injury or disease or (2) special groups.

The federal and state workmen's compensation laws protect most employees against loss of income and medical expenses caused by job-connected injuries and disease. Income benefits are paid in cash; medical bills are paid by the insurer. These laws have already been discussed as an alleviative approach to the financial problems caused by death.

Federal social insurance programs dealing with special groups include (1) the Railroad Retirement System which pays a lifetime income in case of total and permanent disability, (2) the Railroad Temporary Disability Insurance System which pays income benefits to participants who are totally disabled for a short period, (3) the Public Health Service which, in addition to its other functions, provides free medical services in its hospitals for qualified seamen, (4) a federal law which requires that shipowners continue the wages and provide full medical care for a seaman during the voyage and, in the event of continued illness, for a reasonable time thereafter, (5) the disability pensions and medical care services provided by the Veterans Administration, and (6) the continued salary and medical benefits for members of the armed services.

Four states—Rhode Island, California, New Jersey, and New York—have enacted temporary nonoccupational disability insurance legislation which affects most of the industrial workers in those states. The purpose is to provide income to workers who are disabled for short periods because of nonoccupational injuries and sickness. The California act also provides cash allowances toward hospital bills. The insurance is provided by a monopolistic state fund in Rhode Island; the other three states have competitive state funds.

2. *Public assistance.* Special public assistance programs providing income benefits in case of disability include Aid to Dependent Children (already mentioned in connection with death), Aid to the Blind, and Aid to the Totally and Permanently Disabled. Under all four special public assistance programs—these three and Old-Age Assistance—medical care allowances are included in the assistance payments made to recipients. Direct payments are also made to suppliers of medical service.

3. *Private approaches.* Private approaches are especially important in this area because the public programs are so limited. The

insurance approach is, by far, the most important. Many types of insurers are active, the two leading types being the commercial insurers and the Blue Cross and Blue Shield associations. Commercial insurers under individual or group contracts promise income benefits in case of long-term or short-term disability and pay cash allowances toward medical expenses. They also protect an individual against the loss of his death, retirement, or accidental injury and sickness insurance, through his inability to pay premiums while totally and permanently disabled. Blue Cross and Blue Shield associations provide medical expense protection, usually on a service basis. Other plans, called independent plans, include a variety of approaches to the medical expense problem.

As in the case of other risks, it may be necessary to rely on assistance from relatives or gifts from nonrelatives. The benefits may be in cash or in kind.

General. 1. *Public assistance.* Needy persons who do not qualify for benefits under any of the social insurance or special public assistance programs may receive aid from the general assistance programs financed and administered by the states, local governments, or both. Payments are made in cash or in services to persons who can demonstrate need, regardless of the cause, if they satisfy the eligibility requirements. These are residual programs whose importance depends upon the coverage and benefit levels of other programs as well as upon general economic conditions.

2. *Private approaches.* Assistance from relatives and gifts from friends, charities, and help from employers, unions, and others are the basic private approaches available. The benefits may be in cash or in kind.

Recent Growth

The American insurance system, as a component of the American economic security system, has expanded tremendously in the past twenty-five years. Table 2.1 shows how the financial protection of a typical United States employee's family against death, old age, unemployment, and illness improved from 1929 to 1954. The table "does not present an average and is not symbolic of all workers, but it shows the situation of some millions of workers."[11] The most striking feature of the table is the increase in the number of kinds of public and private protection against economic insecurity.

---

[11] Chester C. Nash, "The Contribution of Life Insurance to Social Security in the United States," *International Labour Review*, LXXII, No. 1 (July, 1955), 39. The comparison presented in the text is based on a table in this article.

TABLE 2.1

FINANCIAL PROTECTION OF A TYPICAL UNITED STATES WORKER'S FAMILY
AGAINST DEATH, OLD AGE, UNEMPLOYMENT AND ACCIDENTAL INJURY
AND SICKNESS, 1929 and 1954

Type of protection	1929	1954
Death:		
Old-Age and Survivors Insurance	None	Up to $200 monthly while child is dependent
Private life insurance	$3,000	$8,000
Old age:		
Old-Age and Survivors Insurance	None	Up to $162.80 monthly
Private annuities and pensions . .	None	$100 monthly
Unemployment:		
State unemployment compensation .	None	Up to $200 monthly
Illness:		
Occupational:		
Workmen's compensation . . .	Yes	Yes
Nonoccupational:		
Private medical expense insurance	None	Protection against most medical expenses associated with short-term illnesses.

Source: Derived and adapted from Table VII in Chester C. Nash, "The Contribution of Life Insurance to Social Security in the United States," *International Labour Review*, LXXII, No. 1 (July, 1955), 39.

Most of the public programs were initiated under the Social Security Act which was not passed until 1935. Workmen's compensation was the only important public program in existence prior to that time. Other countries had adopted extensive public social insurance programs at a much earlier date. Germany had a fairly complete national insurance system in operation by the close of the nineteenth century. Great Britain introduced a series of public programs during the first two decades of the present century. Other foreign countries were also active about the same time. Why did the United States lag behind?

This lag has been explained by the superior economic status and individualistic nature of our population, our federal form of government, and the retention by the states of powers not expressly delegated to the federal government, social and economic variations among the states, and competition among the states for business interests.[12] The Great Depression and changes in our social mores lessened the retarding effect of these factors and an extensive social insurance program was born. However, the program characteristics reflect the continuing importance of these factors.

[12] Mowbray and Blanchard, *op. cit.*, pp. 492–94.

Private insurance, on the other hand, was important twenty-five years ago, but it was much less developed and much less popular than it is today. In fact, private insurance in the United States dates back to the colonial period, but the industry was a very small one until the middle of the ninetenth century when it began a period of steady growth. The Depression marked the beginning of a period of extremely rapid growth. The factors favoring the tremendous increase in the benefits and the proportion of the insured population are the Depression experiences, the excellent record of the private commercial insurers during this period, increased public interest in economic security, the introduction of public programs, the increasing importance of industry programs for employees, the government insurance program for servicemen and veterans, the changes in income distribution, an improved insurance industry sales force, the introduction of new coverages, and a higher average level of education among our population.

Forecasting is a hazardous occupation, but we can be almost certain that the typical employee will be much better protected in 1979 than he was in 1954. The existing types of benefits should more adequately cover his losses, and some new disability income benefits—private or public—will probably be included in the list. By 1956 an OASI total and permanent disability income benefit up to $108.50 had already been added.

A Final Comment

The American economic security system seems unnecessarily complicated when judged on a strictly logical basis. We may wonder how such a complex system came into being. The major reason is that the system was developed piecemeal in response to what seemed to be the most important need at the time. This statement applies to both public and private programs.

Political factors were important in public programs as well as were social and economic needs, and, conversely, a private insurance program had to promise to be a safe operation before it could be initiated. Thus the system is a compromise between the desire to provide the optimum economic security at the minimum cost, make the system self-supporting, maintain individual responsibility, respect states' rights, and please the voting public. Few, if any, persons are completely satisfied with the present system, but the critics, with feelings ranging from mild to intense, are not united in their objections. Some argue for a completely logical system, however that may be defined. Others believe that some, but not all, of the other considerations should be ignored, while still others believe that it is possible to establish a superior compromise system. Each of these three groups may be divided into many subgroups on other bases, such as the method of implementing their proposals.

We shall not attempt to evaluate the system at this point because we need to know more about the provisions and operations of these programs. We will, however, present a series of evaluations in the final chapter of this text.

We shall now explore in some detail the nature of the financial problems caused by death, old age, unemployment, accidental injury and sickness, and substandard conditions and the public and private programs providing some degree of economic security against these risks.

Summary

The American Economic Security System includes preventive and alleviative programs, public and private. The preventive programs include general and selective efforts to reduce or eliminate the chance of loss due to death, superannuation, illness, and unemployment, or to minimize the extent of such losses, and government regulations such as the Fair Labor Standards Act which establish sets of operating rules affecting such working conditions as the wage rate and maximum work week.

The alleviative programs include social insurance, public assistance, and private approaches, the most important of which is private insurance. Social insurance differs from public assistance primarily in that the benefits are established by formula and are available as a matter of right, while public assistance payments are determined on a discretionary basis and are payable only to the needy. It is difficult to compare social insurance with private insurance because each term includes many different types of programs, but the most important social insurance program, Old-Age and Survivors Insurance, can be contrasted with the most important private insurance protection, individual insurance contracts issued by commercial insurers. OASI is compulsory, the benefits are prescribed by law and subject to change, the system redistributes income in addition to pooling the risks, and the government is a monopoly insurer. Individual life insurance written by commercial insurers is voluntary, the benefits are prescribed in a contract, the price is determined by the cost of the benefits insofar as practical considerations will permit, and there is intense competition.

Some programs provide service benefits, but most pay cash benefits. The loss of freedom of economic choice under a service program is greatest when lost income is replaced by limited specific services.

Social insurance programs providing death and retirement benefits include OASI and the programs for special groups such as railroad workers, civil service employees, servicemen and veterans. Workmen's compensation laws provide protection against death due to occupational causes. Public assistance programs attacking these perils specifically are Old-Age Assistance and Aid to Dependent Children. Private protection consists primarily of individual insurance and group insurance underwritten by commercial insurers or self-insured by employers and/or unions.

Social insurance programs providing unemployment insurance benefits include the state unemployment insurance funds and the special federal program for railroad workers. Private protection is afforded through self-insured industry plans.

Social insurance attacking accidental injury and sickness consists of the OASI provisions providing an income for certain totally and permanently disabled persons and preventing a loss of retirement and death benefits due to total and permanent disability, workmen's compensation insurance, and programs for special groups such as railroad workers, seamen, veterans, servicemen, and the industrial workers in four states. Public assistance programs include cash payments under Aid to the Blind and Aid to the Totally and Permanently Disabled programs and medical expense allowances or payments under all four federally supported state programs. Private protection includes individual and group insurance underwritten primarily by commercial insurers and nonprofit medical expense associations.

Residual protection for the needy is provided through state and local general public assistance programs. Private residual protection includes reliance on relatives and charity.

Suggestions for Additional Reading

BURNS, EVELINE M. *The American Social Security System*. Boston: Houghton Mifflin Co., 1951. Chapters 2 and 3.
These chapters contain a detailed discussion of the various public alleviative approaches and the structure of the American Social Security System.
—— *Social Security and Public Policy*. New York: McGraw-Hill Book Co., Inc., 1956. Introduction.
A highly respected student of social security presents a brief and stimulating discussion of the historical development of social security measures and the important decisions to be made before establishing a program.
EPSTEIN, ABRAHAM. *Insecurity, A Challenge to America*, 2d rev. ed. New York: Random House, Inc., 1938. Chapters 1 through 5. In these chapters,

an ardent advocate of social insurance discusses its fundamentals and problems.

GAGLIARDO, DOMENICO. *American Social Insurance,* rev. ed. New York: Harper & Bros., 1955. Pp. 14-21.
These pages present a detailed analysis of the differences between private insurance and social insurance.

Systems of Social Security: United States. Geneva: International Labour Office, 1953.
A concise and detailed analysis of the public programs in the American Social Security System.

WILLETT, ALLAN H. *The Economic Theory of Risk and Insurance.* Philadelphia: University of Pennsylvania Press, 1951. Chapters 1, 6, and 7.
This reprint of a 1901 doctoral dissertation discusses the adverse economic effects of risk, the various methods of handling risk, and the theory of insurance.

3

Problems of Death and Old Age

Introduction

Each person faces the possibility that premature death will cut short his earning power period or that he will live to such an advanced age that his earning power will have stopped and he will have consumed all of his accumulated assets. Both situations pose serious financial problems which most persons are anxious to solve through private or public means. We start our discussion in this text with the topics of death and old age, since these tend to be the most "final" as forms of job severance and hence as causes of economic insecurity. Unemployment, except in the rare case is of finite duration; occupational injuries and sickness, the same except for permanent disabilities.

In this chapter we shall explore the nature and importance of the financial problems associated with premature death and old age. We shall also consider the probability that a person will die prematurely and the probability that a person will survive to retirement age and beyond, and how these probabilities are related to economic insecurity.

The general preventive and alleviative approaches to these problems will then be discussed so as to emphasize the important roles played by social insurance, public assistance, and private insurance. Each of these approaches is discussed in detail in the next two chapters.

Finally, note will be made of the current economic resources of the aged, from all private and public sources, in order to indicate the need for improvements in the present approaches to the problems of old age.

The Economic Problems of Premature Death

NATURE AND IMPORTANCE

Premature death causes two types of financial loss to dependents. First, the deceased's earning power stops. Second, extra expenses are incurred in the form of burial expenses, estate taxes, forced liquidation losses, and others.

The earning power loss is the most important for most families, but few persons appreciate its possible magnitude. An example will illustrate this point. Assume that an individual, aged thirty-five, is earning $6,000 a year after income taxes. In order to simplify the explanation, further assume that his salary is not expected to change until age sixty-five, at which time he expects to retire. Under these assumptions, his future income will total 30 × $6,000 = $180,000. If he should die at age thirty-five, this income will never be earned. However, it is not fair to state that his dependents will suffer a loss of $180,000 because, first, he would have consumed some of this income if he had lived and, second, this income would have been spread over a thirty-year period.

If it is assumed that $1,500 would have been required each year to maintain the deceased and prepare for his retirement, the annual income loss to the dependents is $4,500, making a total income loss of $135,000. The fact that this income would have been spread over a thirty-year period means that some allowance must be made for the interest earnings on a lump sum available at the present time. In more technical terms it is necessary to discount the future incomes in order to determine their present values. If it is assumed that this lump sum can earn 2 per cent interest compounded annually and that the incomes would have been available at the end of the year in which they were earned, the lump sum (or the present value of the future incomes) is computed as follows:

$$\$4500 \ (1+.02)^{-1} \ = 4500 \ (.9804)$$
$$4500 \ (1+.02)^{-2} \ = 4500 \ (.9612)$$
$$4500 \ (1+.02)^{-3} \ = 4500 \ (.9423)$$
$$\cdots \qquad \cdots$$
$$4500 \ (1+.02)^{-28} = 4500 \ (.5744)$$
$$4500 \ (1+.02)^{-29} = 4500 \ (.5631)$$
$$4500 \ (1+.02)^{-30} = 4500 \ (.5521)$$

$100,000, approximately

$101,000, approximately

In other words, if $101,000 is invested at 2 per cent interest compounded annually, periodic withdrawals of $4,500 at the end of each year for thirty years would exhaust the fund. Therefore,

$101,000 is a good *estimate* of the earning power loss to the dependents in this case. Even if it were in error by as much as $20,000 or $30,000, it is still a useful figure because it reveals the magnitude of the loss.

The earning power loss varies directly with the level of future earnings, inversely with age. When the individual whose situation was discussed in the last paragraph reaches age fifty, the possible earning power loss will have dropped to approximately $60,000. At retirement age, it will be zero. Annual income typically increases in the early years of employment and the drop in earning power loss is usually not as rapid as in the case discussed.[1] However, it is still generally true that, other things being equal, the family suffers the greatest earning power loss when the breadwinner dies at an early age.

PROBABILITY OF PREMATURE DEATH

Because of medical advances and improved social and economic conditions, premature death is much less likely to occur today than it was in the earlier part of the twentieth century. However, a large number of people still die early in life and the probability that this will happen is greater than most people choose to believe. Table 3.1 shows the mortality rates at various ages over the first half of this century. Notice that most of the improvement has occurred at the younger ages. This improvement is expected to continue, but at a less rapid pace, in the future.

Table 3.2 presents the most recent data in a different setting. It indicates the probability that a person aged twenty, thirty, forty, fifty, and sixty will die before reaching age sixty-five, which is a typical retirement age. Note that on the basis of 1949–51 mortality rates, about one out of every four persons, aged twenty, will have his earning power period shortened by a premature death.

The Economic Problems of Old Age

NATURE AND IMPORTANCE

Old age also presents serious economic security problems. Earnings may stop or be considerably reduced, but expenses continue. The economic security problem involved is how to meet expenses not covered by current earnings. Again it is fair to say that the

---

[1] If the difference between the starting and final incomes is great, it is possible that the large interest discounts may result in an increasing earning power loss during the first few years.

TABLE 3.1

DEATHS PER 1000 TOTAL POPULATION LIVING AT
SPECIFIED AGES AT TEN-YEAR INTERVALS, 1910–1950

Age	1909–11*	1919–21*†	1929–31*†	1939–41	1949–51
0	114.62	80.25	62.32	47.10	29.76
10	2.27	2.11	1.47	.90	.53
20	4.68	4.27	3.18	2.17	1.35
30	6.51	5.73	4.13	3.07	1.79
40	9.39	7.50	6.79	5.24	3.68
50	14.37	11.74	12.78	10.76	8.76
60	28.58	24.62	26.44	22.51	19.77
70	59.52	54.63	57.96	48.73	42.49
80	130.28	119.73	129.97	114.91	98.41
90	249.62	238.19	245.50	230.81	212.49
100	401.91	442.44	470.37	360.05	389.04

* Death registrations were not available for all states until 1933.
† Data for 1919–21 and 1929–31 apply to white males only.

Source: U. S. Department of Commerce, Bureau of the Census. *United States Life Tables, 1910, 1930, 1940, and 1950.* Washington: U. S. Government Printing Office, 1916, 1936, 1946, and 1954.

average person does not appreciate the magnitude of this problem. For example, assume that a retired person, aged sixty-five, has expenses totaling $1,200 a year. If these expenses are to be paid at the end of each year solely out of interest payments on accumulated investments, the principal would have to be $40,000 if the interest rate after taxes is 3 per cent, $60,000 if the interest rate after taxes is 2 per cent.

If it is assumed that expenses are to be paid out of periodic withdrawals of the principal plus interest on the unpaid balance, it is necessary to know how many years the person will live in order to determine the amount he must have accumulated by the date of retirement. If he will live ten more years, the required principal is

TABLE 3.2

PROBABILITY OF DYING PRIOR TO AGE 65, 1949–51

Present Age	Probability
20	.29
30	.28
40	.26
50	.22
60	.11

Source: *United States Life Tables, 1950.*

about $10,200 at 3 per cent interest, $10,800 at 2 per cent. If he will live twenty more years, the required principal is $17,900 at 3 per cent interest, $19,600 at 2 per cent. If he will live to age one hundred, the amount required is $25,800 at 3 per cent interest, $30,000 at 2 per cent interest. The amount varies directly with the number of years and inversely with the interest rate.

Thus there are two problems created by old age. First, a large sum of money must be accumulated to provide for even a short period of retirement. Second, the period of retirement is unknown and may be lengthy. Therefore the necessary individual accumulation is unknown.

PROBABILITY OF SURVIVAL TO RETIREMENT AGE AND BEYOND

A person either dies or lives. Consequently the chance that a person will live to reach a certain age is equal to unity minus the probability that he will die before reaching that age. Therefore, Table 3.3, which shows the probability that a person aged twenty, thirty, forty, fifty, or sixty will reach age sixty-five, is based upon the data presented in Table 3.2.

TABLE 3.3

PROBABILITY OF SURVIVAL TO AGE 65 AND AVERAGE
LIFE EXPECTANCY AT SPECIFIED AGES, 1949–51

Present Age	Probability	Average Life Expectancy	Average Life Expectancy Beyond Age 65
20	.71	51.20	6.20
30	.72	41.91	6.91
40	.74	32.81	7.81
50	.78	24.40	9.40
60	.89	17.04	12.04

Source: *United States Life Tables, 1950.*

Table 3.3 also indicates the average life expectancy for each age or the average number of years that persons in that age group will live beyond their present age. For ages twenty and forty, the median number of remaining life years is slightly higher than the average; for ages sixty and eighty, the median is less. The third column in the table shows the number of years by which the average life expectancy will carry the person beyond sixty-five. Notice that these figures increase as the person grows older because he has moved closer to age sixty-five and his chances of surviving to that age have improved.

As mortality rates decrease over time, the probability of surviving to retirement age and beyond increases. Table 3.4 shows how the average life expectancies at ages twenty, forty, sixty, and eighty have increased over time. Note that the improvements at the older ages are slight, but those at the younger ages are great.

TABLE 3.4

AVERAGE LIFE EXPECTANCIES AT SPECIFIED AGES
AT TEN YEAR INTERVALS, 1910–50*

Age	1909–11	1919–21†	1929–31†	1939–41	1949–51
0	51.49	56.34	59.12	63.62	68.07
20	43.53	45.60	46.02	48.54	51.20
40	28.20	29.86	29.22	31.03	32.81
60	14.42	15.25	14.72	15.91	17.04
80	5.25	5.47	5.26	5.73	6.34

* Death registrations not available for all states until 1933.
† Data for 1919–21 and 1929–31 apply to white males only.
Source: *United States Life Tables, 1910, 1930, 1940, and 1950.*

Table 3.5 classifies 1949–51 average life expectancies by age, sex, and race. Females have a higher average life expectancy than males, while the average white person will reach a more advanced age than the average non-white person. Other mortality data indicate that the average life span of a country dweller is slightly longer than that of a city dweller. At older ages, the sex of the individual is the most important factor.

TABLE 3.5

AVERAGE LIFE EXPECTANCY CLASSIFIED BY
AGE, SEX, AND RACE, 1949–51

Age	White		Non-Whites		All Races	
	Male	Female	Male	Female	Male	Female
0	66.31	72.03	58.91	62.70	65.47	70.96
20	49.52	54.56	43.73	46.77	48.92	53.73
40	31.17	35.64	27.29	29.82	30.79	35.06
60	15.76	18.64	14.91	16.95	15.68	18.50
80	5.88	6.59	7.07	8.15	5.94	6.67

Source: *United States Life Tables, 1950.*

AGE COMPOSITION OF THE TOTAL POPULATION

Decreasing mortality rates, especially at the younger ages, tend to increase the proportion of the population who are sixty-five years of age or over. This is one reason why problems created by old age are becoming more important from society's point of view. Decreasing birth rates (until recent years) and reduced immigration have intensified the effect of the decreasing mortality rates. The changes in the age composition of the United States population that have already occurred and are expected to occur in the future are presented in Table 3.6. Note that the proportion of persons aged sixty-five and over has increased from 4 per cent in 1900 to about 8 per cent in 1950. By 1980 it is expected to be 11 per cent. Since the total population has and is expected to grow steadily over this period, the change in the number of aged persons is even more dramatic.

TABLE 3.6

AGE COMPOSITION OF THE UNITED STATES TOTAL POPULATION
AT TWENTY-YEAR INTERVALS, 1900–2000

| Year | Per Cent of Population in Each Age Group | | |
	Under 20	20–64	65 and over
1900	44	52	4
1920	41	54	5
1940	34	59	7
1960	37	54	9
1980	34	55	11
2000	33	56	11

Source: Based on Robert J. Myers and Eugene A. Rasor, "Illustrative United States Population Projections, 1952," *Actuarial Study No. 33* (Federal Security Agency, Social Security Administration), November, 1952.

General Approaches to the Economic Problems of Premature Death

Society has attacked the problem of premature death in many ways. Private preventive and alleviative methods have been used as well as public preventive and alleviative methods.

PREVENTIVE METHODS

Preventive methods have reduced mortality rates, as evidenced by the data presented in Tables 3.1 and 3.4. Advancements in medical knowledge and the more extensive application of that knowledge have been the most important factors, but higher average standards of living have also contributed to the increasing life span.

A variety of specific private preventive methods have been developed: medical research which seeks to reduce the possibilities of premature death; the distribution of health information; individual physical examinations; safety programs. Individuals, employers, unions, and private institutions such as hospitals, charitable foundations, and commercial insurers participate in these activities. Public preventive methods include, among others, public health programs and safety regulations. Many public methods, while job-oriented, are only indirectly so, and in keeping with the focus of this book, we shall not analyze them in detail. As noted in the preface, substandard housing is an example of such an indirectly related item.

Preventive methods can never be completely successful, however, and there is tremendous variation in the extent to which they are used by each person. Furthermore, our society is continually creating new possible causes of premature death, such as the automobile and the airplane. For these reasons, alleviative measures are also necessary.

PRIVATE ALLEVIATIVE METHODS

Private methods of alleviating the financial loss caused by premature death have changed materially since the beginning of the Industrial Revolution. As long as families were largely self-sufficient —a common occurrence in a predominantly agricultural economy— the dependents of a deceased person were welcome in some relative's home because they were able to make valuable contributions to the household's consumption needs. Today these dependents can usually make a positive contribution only if they have some source of money income, such as wages or savings.

Furthemore, even if the dependents have sufficient money income, it has become less "convenient" for relatives to care for them because of smaller living quarters, longer and more expensive dependency periods for children, varied interests, and increased mobility. Moreover, the size of the average family has decreased and hence there are fewer relatives to turn to for support.

Dependents still move in with relatives (for example, a daughter and her children still may live with her parents), but in general, social and economic forces have reduced the frequency and effectiveness of this approach to the problem.

Private charities help in alleviation, but this aid is necessarily very limited. Community Chest or United Fund agencies exemplify this approach. Churches, labor unions, fraternal societies, and charitable institutions of various types have been active in providing assistance. But, if private charity is the only support available, a drastic reduction in the family's standard of living is almost certain to result. Furthermore, most families do not consider charity to be an acceptable solution to their problems.

The employer of the deceased may continue part of the deceased's salary for a period following death or make a lump sum payment, but these payments are in most cases only a temporary aid. Given present practices, most dependents receive relatively little permanent aid from this source.

Hence, if dependents are to maintain an independent household, they must have sufficient money income of their own. A young widow without any children may be able to work, although her income will probably be much less than that of her husband. A young mother may also be able to work, but her home life may suffer as a result. In many cases it is impossible for the mother to work.

Young couples seldom have much accumulated capital in the form of real estate, savings accounts and securities; older couples may. The reasons why it may be difficult to accumulate sufficient capital over a lifetime are discussed on page 62. The problem is more acute when the family is young. Unfortunately, this is the group for whom the economic losses caused by premature death are greatest.

Fortunately, life insurance makes it possible for a deceased to leave his dependents a large sum of money even if he should die at an early age. Because mortality rates are relatively low, small premium payments by many people make it possible to pay the beneficiaries of the deceased substantial sums of money. For example, for about $50 a year, a man, aged thirty, can purchase a contract which will pay his family $8,000 if he dies between thirty and thirty-five.[2] However, some persons may not be able to qualify for individual life insurance for physical or other reasons, while others consider the cost too high. Also, many persons with dependents may mistakenly feel that they do not need any insurance; relatively few have an adequate amount of insurance.

Group life insurance has extended the coverage because every member of an eligible group is eligible for insurance and the wholesale merchandising of the coverage cuts the cost.[3] However, many persons are not members of an eligible group, and the amount of protection available under a group plan is limited.

Private life insurance has expanded tremendously during the past decade. The amount of life insurance owned by all families at

[2] This contract is a five-year term policy. The major types of life insurance contracts are discussed in Chapter 5.

[3] See Chapter 5 for a discussion of the nature of group life insurance.

the end of 1955 was $372 billion. This is an impressive total, but the average amount of insurance per family was only $6,900, or one and one-third of the average disposable income. Four out of five families had some life insurance protection, but the range in protection was great.[4] Hence society has utilized additional methods.

PUBLIC ALLEVIATIVE METHODS

Because the financial loss caused by premature death is so great, and because most families have not voluntarily protected themselves adequately against this loss, the government has often been forced to aid the deceased's dependents. Poorhouses and orphanages represent the major approach used prior to the twentieth century. Limited state cash assistance programs made their appearance at the beginning of this century, but these programs varied greatly among states and, in general, were very inadequate.

The Social Security Act of 1935 was responsible for the first large scale use of public alleviative methods. This Act provided, among other things, for federal grants-in-aid to state public assistance programs dealing with the problems caused by premature death. In 1939 the social insurance provisions of the Act were amended to include what Congress considered to be basic minimum death benefits. Because the provisions of the Social Security Act are discussed in detail in Chapter 4, the Act will not be described here, but it should be mentioned that the benefits under these programs are sizable and affect most of the population.

Death benefits are also available under the federal government's Railroad Retirement System, Civil Service Retirement System, veterans' programs, and Armed Services' programs, a selective discussion of which is found in Chapter 13.

LAYERS OF PROTECTION

The average American family has two layers of protection against the financial loss caused by premature death. Social insurance provides the basic layer, while private insurance supplements the coverage. In most cases this private insurance consists of individual insurance, but for a strong and increasing number of families, group insurance is the second layer and individual insurance the third. All three layers are desirable if the dependents are to be adequately protected. These three layers of protection plus public assistance programs are discussed in the two chapters which follow.

[4] Institute of Life Insurance. *Life Insurance Fact Book, 1956,* New York, New York, 1956.

General Approaches to the Economic Problems of Old Age

Methods of attacking the economic problems of old age are largely alleviative, but the preventive programs discussed in connection with premature death do diminish the old-age problems if a larger proportion of the persons attaining advanced ages are capable of earning a limited income and if a place can be found to employ their talents. Otherwise, increasing average life expectancies intensify the problems of old age.

PREVENTIVE METHODS

Preventive efforts, then, take the form of continued employment. Table 3.7 indicates that although an increasing proportion of the labor force is sixty-five years of age and over, the percentage of the population over sixty-five in the labor force is decreasing. The first result can be explained by the increased value of technical knowledge and experience in the modern industrial world. The second finding may be due to the fact that the demand is not adequate to absorb all the qualified aged persons, or it may be due to the fact that the majority of the aged do not possess the talents that are in demand, or it may result from institutional pressures toward forced retirement.

TABLE 3.7

AGED PERSONS IN THE LABOR FORCE, 1900–1955

Year	Proportion of Labor Force* 65 years and over		Proportion of persons 65 years and over in the labor force*	
	Men	Women	Men	Women
1900	4.5	2.6	68.4	8.5
1910	4.2	2.5	63.7	8.6
1920	4.4	2.4	60.2	7.9
1930	5.1	2.6	58.3	7.9
1940	4.6	2.2	41.5	5.8
1950	5.4	3.1	41.0	7.3
Week ending December 10, 1955	5.6	3.9	39.2	11.2

* 1900–1930 data are for the gainfully occupied. 1940–55 data relate to the labor force.

Source: Data for 1900–1940 based on Tables 1 and 4 in S. J. Mushkin and Alan Berman, "Factors Influencing Trends in Employment of the Aged," *Social Security Bulletin*, X, No. 8 (August, 1947), 18–23. Data for 1950 from U. S. Department of Commerce, Bureau of the Census, *Seventeenth Census of the United States, 1950*, II, Part I, 97, 247. Data for December, 1955 based on U. S. Department of Commerce, Bureau of the Census, "The Monthly Report on the Labor Force: December, 1955," *Current Population Reports, Labor Force*, Series P–57, No. 163 (January, 1956), 8, 10.

A recently completed study on the economic implications of an aging population by the Institute of Industrial Relations at the University of California revealed some important and disturbing facts concerning the earning status of the aged. First, 80 per cent of the aged who are not in the labor force left their jobs because of their health or because their employer asked them or institutional pressures required them to leave. Second, 77 per cent of the aged not in the labor force do not feel well enough to work. Third, the skills of aged persons have obsolesced. Many of them spent most of their lives in nonskilled occupations, while about two-thirds of the aged who had spent most of their lives working in professional, technical, and skilled trades were working in other occupations at the time they retired.[5]

Compulsory retirement ages and maximum hiring ages reduce the probability of employment for aged workers who have retained their health and technical abilities. The most common retirement age is sixty-five, which is the age at which the worker becomes eligible for retirement benefits under Old-Age and Survivors Insurance.

Companies which use a specific age limit instead of a discretionary one feel that an objective standard is the only workable one. According to them, most aged workers are held to be poor employees, especially since their minimum wages are set by law or collective bargaining. Their health may be poor; they are inflexible; they may be more likely to cause personnel problems; they raise insurance and pension costs; and they block the promotion lanes for younger people.

Some persons do not believe that the employment possibilities for the aged are this poor. It has been argued that many of the aged who do not consider themselves well enough to work might change their attitudes if they had something challenging to which they could look forward.[6] Furthermore, many of the aged might have retained their health if they had continued their normal work.[7]

Those who feel optimistic about the prospects for employing the aged also remind us that increasing emphasis on training and decreasing emphasis on physical strength have already increased the proportion of the labor force that is sixty-five and over. They

[5] Robert Dorfman, "The Labor Force Status of Persons Aged Sixty-five and Over," *American Economic Review*, XLIV, No. 2 (May, 1954), 635–36. See also the papers by Peter O. Steiner on "The Size, Nature, and Adequacy of the Resources of the Aged," pp. 645–60, and Melvin W. Reder, "Age and Income," pp. 661–70, both in the same issue.

[6] Floyd Bond, discussion of Robert Dorfman article, *op. cit.*, p. 673.

[7] Elizabeth Wallace, discussion of Robert Dorfman article, *op. cit.*, p. 675.

believe that this trend will continue. They point to the fact that the educational levels of the aged and non-aged will be more alike in the future. They believe that modern industry should take another look at compulsory retirement ages and maximum hiring ages because many able persons have been forced to retire too early in life, thus wasting human resources. Many business enterprises have already taken steps in this direction.

In short, it is argued that a retirement philosophy appropriate when the aged formed a relatively small segment of the population, or perhaps appropriate in periods of economic depression such as 1930–1940, is not and will not be appropriate in the future. This alternative viewpoint has attracted much interest and merits serious consideration.

PRIVATE METHODS OF ALLEVIATION

About 70 per cent of the aged population are not wage earners or spouses of wage earners. If present trends continue, this percentage will increase. If not, and the percentage decreases, the improvement will probably be slight and there will always be a sizable proportion of the aged who will have either no earnings or inadequate earnings. Sources of money receipts other than earnings include cash contributions from friends or relatives; interest, dividends, and rents; dissavings of liquid assets; individual annuities and life insurance proceeds; and private group pension plans. Private charities and private homes provide some aid, but their role in the aggregate is less important than formerly and they are not considered here. Given lowered earnings (or other income), expenses can be reduced, but this is not always an easy matter either culturally or procedurally. Thus, it is not easy to take up the home production of food, for example, after never having done it during one's lifetime, or to move in with relatives.

The following data provide some information on incomes of the aged. Table 3.8 shows the estimated annual money income from various private sources at the end of 1954. In addition to the money income of $13.5 billion noted in the table, about 20 per cent of the aged dissaved approximately $1.1 billion.[8] Since there were approximately 13.9 million aged persons at that time, the average amount of money income from private sources plus dissavings was about $1,050.

[8] Lenore A. Epstein, "Economic Resources of Persons Aged 65 and Over," *Social Security Bulletin*, XVIII, No. 6 (June, 1955), 3–19, 32–33. This excellent article summarizes and interprets the results of several studies in this area.

TABLE 3.8

PRIVATE SOURCES OF MONEY INCOME FOR THE AGED, 1954

Source	Per cent of aged receiving money from source	Total annual receipts from source (in billions)
Earnings	30%	$9.0
Cash contributions from funds or relatives . .	1–30*	—
Interest, dividends, and rents	20–33⅓	3.6
Individual annuities and insurance	5–10	.4
Group pension plans	7	.5

* Regular cash contributions are rare; occasional cash gifts are common. Total amount is negligible.

Source: Adapted from Lenore A. Epstein, "Economic Resources of Persons Aged 65 and Over," *Social Security Bulletin*, XVIII, No. 6 (June, 1955), 3–19, 32–33.

The most important source of money income was earnings, but only 30 per cent of the aged benefit from earnings. Even if it is assumed that the entire $5.6 billion from other private sources was received by the other ten million aged, each person in this group would have received, on the average, less than $600. However, interest, dividends, and rents—the next largest source—were available to no more than 33⅓ per cent of the aged. If it is assumed that 63⅓ per cent of the aged absorb the total income from earnings, interest, dividends, and rents, but no more, 36⅔ per cent of the aged would have received a little more than $2 billion from other private sources, or about $400 per person. Because these assumptions are so unrealistic and because it is known that some of the aged receive sizable annual money receipts, we may conclude that the status of a large part of the population is worse than the data indicate. Even if the assumptions were true, there would appear to be need for some public action.

Reasons given to explain the low money receipts from private sources include the relatively low income status of a large part of the population, an upward trend in prices, high income taxes, the importance to Americans of "keeping up with the Joneses," the bank and business failures of the thirties, personal misfortunes, the weakening of family ties, and a human tendency to postpone preparation for retirement. Most of these forces are beyond the control of the individual, but the last is definitely not.

As noted earlier, another method of attacking the financial problems caused by old age is to reduce expenses. At the end of 1951, about 40 per cent of the aged were living with relatives. As pointed out earlier, people in need are less likely to live with relatives now than in earlier centuries. More than half of the aged living with their relatives had money receipts from private sources of less than $500; but in some cases they were supporting their relatives. About 25 per cent received free rent by living with relatives while slightly over 50 per cent owned their own homes, 80 per cent of the homes being free of mortgages. About 35 per cent lived outside urban areas and produced some of their own food. Income in kind from home ownership, free rent, and food production is liberally estimated to have amounted to about $2.5 billion in 1951. Because there were declines from 1951 to 1954 in the proportion of those aged over sixty-five living with relatives, in the proportion of the aged in rural areas, and in farm prices, the estimates for 1954 would probably be the same or less.[9] Adding this income in kind would increase the private money receipts by about 17 per cent in 1954. This income is important, but does not alter the conclusion that present private sources of support in old age are inadequate.

PUBLIC METHODS OF ALLEVIATION

Before the twentieth century, government assistance to the aged consisted almost entirely of poorhouses. A few states made cash grants to the needy aged during the first thirty years of this century, but, until the federal government through the Social Security Act made grants-in-aid to the states, the vast majority of the states made no cash grants and those that did paid very small amounts to very few people. At present, all forty-eight states have public assistance programs for the aged. About 20 per cent of the aged received $1.6 billion in benefits during 1954.

Social insurance plans for the aged originally took the form of retirement plans for persons rendering service to the government. State and local government employees, federal government civil service employees, and members of the armed services have been covered for the greater part of this century. Railroad workers became the first nongovernmental employees to be covered under a social insurance plan when the Railroad Retirement System began to operate in 1937 as a substitute for private employer plans. The most important social insurance program—Old-Age and Survivors Insurance—began to operate in the same year and has expanded in coverage and benefits since that time. About 50 per cent of the aged received $4.8 billion in payments under these Systems in 1954.

[9] *Ibid.*, p. 32.

LAYERS OF PROTECTION

The average American family has three or four layers of protection against the financial dilemma posed by old age: social insurance, savings and investments, and individual annuities and life insurance contracts; or, social insurance, group pensions, savings and investments, and individual annuities and life insurance contracts. The social insurance provides a floor of protection; the private investments and insurance make it possible for a person with initiative, foresight, and some luck to convert this minimum level of income into a more comfortable one. The provisions of social insurance and private insurance plans are discussed along with public assistance plans in the next two chapters. Prior to analyzing these matters it may be instructive to look a little more fully at the resources of the aged.

Economic Resources of the Aged

What are the current economic resources of the aged? On pages 61-63, some general information was provided on the economic status of the aged with respect to private sources of money income. Fortunately, more detailed information is available, providing no attempt is made to distinguish between private and public resources.

Table 3.9 shows that 7.3 per cent of the aged couples, 15.9 per cent of the aged nonmarried men, and 34.6 per cent of the nonmarried women had no form of money income in 1951. For each of the five sources of money income, the table lists the proportion receiving income from that source, the proportion for which it was the primary source, and the proportion for which it was the only source. Pensions include social insurance and related programs and group pensions; while asset income includes interest, dividends, rents, and individual annuities and income from supplementary contracts.[10] Earnings were the most important income source followed by pensions except for nonmarried women for whom the most important sources were public assistance, pensions, and asset income.

Married couples had a median income of $1,387 while nonmarried men and nonmarried women had median incomes of $662 and $403 respectively.[11] Among those with some money income, the median incomes were $1,460, $777, and $623 respectively. Median incomes for the 30 per cent of the aged population which had no

---

[10] If the proceeds of a life insurance policy are paid out in installments, the installments are considered to be income from a supplementary contract. See Chapter 5.

[11] Epstein, op. cit., p. 8.

TABLE 3.9

PROPORTION OF AGED WITH MONEY INCOME,* BY TYPE OF UNIT
AND SOURCE OF MONEY INCOME, 1951

(Noninstitutional Population, Continental United States)

Source of Money income	Married couples	Nonmarried men	Nonmarried women
Any source	92.7%	84.1%	65.4%
Earnings	56.6	33.7	12.6
Primary source	42.1	22.8	7.8
Only source	29.1	17.5	6.0
Pensions	35.6	33.6	21.4
Primary source	22.6	25.8	14.6
Only source	12.5	16.0	10.1
Asset income	25.5	17.0	21.6
Primary source	8.6	6.2	12.0
Only source	4.3	4.5	9.0
Public assistance	16.4	26.2	25.6
Primary source	12.0	19.3	23.4
Only source	8.8	16.7	20.7
Regular contributions of money from persons not in the household . .	.8	1.5	2.6

* Persons reporting earnings, pensions, etc., represents those with $1 or more from that source. Percentage reporting designated source as the only or primary source excludes those (generally few in number) receiving less than $200 from that source. Dissavings and the portion of lump-sum inheritances or insurance settlements used for current living were taken into account in this study in determining the only or primary source of income.

Source: Table 4. Lenore A. Epstein, "Economic Resources of Persons Aged 65 and Over," *Social Security Bulletin*, XVIII, No. 6 (June, 1955), 8.

earnings were less than $1,000 for married couples and less than $500 for nonmarried persons.

Thirteen per cent of the married couples, 34 per cent of the non-married men, and 26 per cent of the nonmarried women reported that they owned no assets in the form of bank accounts, cash, life insurance, stocks and bonds, and homes or other property.[12] On the other hand, 71 per cent, 41 per cent, and 42 per cent, respectively, owned $3,000 or more in assets. Almost all of this latter group owned their own homes and there is a strong positive correlation between asset ownership and size of money income. About 80 per cent of the aged with assets did not use them to supplement income, but about 10 per cent used $500 or more. There is a strong negative correlation between the use of savings and money income.

Table 3.10 shows that over half of the aged economic units had total money income and total money receipts less than $1,000.

[12] *Ibid.,* p. 17.

Money receipts are defined as money income plus dissavings and the portion of lump-sum insurance payments or inheritances used for current living. Less than 12 per cent had money receipts of $3,000 and over. The table also indicates the extent to which the economic status of those persons living alone is superior to that of those living with relatives.

TABLE 3.10

PROPORTIONS OF AGED WITH MONEY INCOME AND MONEY RECEIPTS LESS THAN $1,000, AND, $3,000 OR MORE, BY TYPE OF UNIT AND LIVING ARRANGEMENTS, 1951

(Noninstitutional Population, Continental United States)

Income and Receipt Levels	All Units	Married Couples	Nonmarried Men	Nonmarried Women
Total				
Less than $1,000				
Money income	65.1%	38.1%	70.2%	86.9%
Money receipts . . .	60.8	34.2	65.4	83.2
$3,000 and over				
Money income	10.9	22.0	7.9	2.5
Money receipts . . .	11.7	22.7	8.5	3.1
Living Alone				
Less than $1,000				
Money income	55.9	35.3	68.7	80.9
Money receipts . . .	50.6	30.8	63.7	75.8
$3,000 and over				
Money income	14.5	24.4	8.6	2.7
Money receipts . . .	15.9	25.4	10.0	3.3
Living with Relatives				
Less than $1,000				
Money income	75.4	44.5	71.6	90.9
Money receipts . . .	72.0	41.7	67.0	87.7
$3,000 and over				
Money income	6.9	16.3	7.2	2.4
Money receipts . . .	7.2	16.3	7.8	2.9

Source: Table 12. Lenore A. Epstein, "Economic Resources of Persons Aged 65 and Over," *Social Security Bulletin*, XVIII, No. 6 (June, 1955), 19.

On the basis of these data we may conclude that in 1951 the economic resources of most of the aged were inadequate. Since that time, social insurance benefits have been liberalized and the number of beneficiaries has about doubled. Private employer pensions (collectively bargained or provided unilaterally) have also become more important. However, the average money income per aged person still only approximates $1,500 and there is a wide variation among individuals. The situation should, however, continue to improve as the various social insurance programs approach maturity.

Public Versus Private Action

The need for some level of public action in this area is obvious. However, since increased public benefits may occur at the expense of increased private benefits, it is not clear at present whether the two types of action have been combined in the optimum proportions. An answer to this question would, of course, contain important policy implications for the future. However, in order to discuss the question, it is necessary to understand the major characteristics of the present public assistance, social insurance, and private insurance plans. We shall consider the public plans in Chapter 4 and the private plans in Chapter 5.

Summary

Premature death causes a loss of earning power and unexpected expenses such as funeral expenses and estate taxes. For most families, the most important loss is the loss of the present value of future incomes. About one out of four persons, aged twenty, will die prior to age sixty-five.

When a person reaches an advanced age, his earnings may stop or be reduced but his expenses continue, even if at a lower level. He must save during his earning career to prepare for retirement, but he does not know how much to save because the date of death is unknown. On the average, about three out of four persons, aged twenty, will reach age sixty-five. Decreasing mortality rates, low birth rates during the Depression, and reduced immigration have increased greatly the proportion of our population faced with the problems of old age.

Preventive methods such as medical research and safety programs have reduced the probability of premature death, but alleviative methods are still essential. Prior to the Industrial Revolution, the dependents of deceased persons moved in with relatives, but social and economic forces have reduced the importance of this solution. Private insurance is the most acceptable and effective alleviative approach, but relatively few persons are adequately protected through this medium for various reasons.

The Social Security Act initiated the first extensive public programs dealing with premature death. State public assistance programs became eligible for federal grants-in-aid in 1935 and the social insurance system was amended in 1939 to include death benefits.

The most important preventive approach to the problems of old age is continued employment of the aged. However, 70 per cent of the aged are not wage earners nor are their spouses. Private sources such as dissaving; interest, dividends, and rent; and insurance provide about $400 annually per aged person, and the distribution of this income is very uneven. The inadequacy of these private sources has been attributed to many factors including the low income status of part of the population, high taxes, and personal failures to prepare for retirement.

The Social Security Act also initiated the public programs dealing with old age. State public assistance programs were made eligible for federal grants-in-aid and a social insurance pension system was established.

Despite the public and private layers of protection and the continued employment of some aged persons, the current economic resources of the aged are inadequate. Currently the average money income per aged person is about $1,500 and the income is distributed very unevenly.

Suggestions for Additional Reading

CORSON, JOHN J. and JOHN W. MCCONNELL. *Economic Needs of Older People.* New York: The Twentieth Century Fund, 1956.
    The economic problems of the aged are discussed in some detail in this extensive study, particularly in Chapters 1 through 5.
DUBLIN, LOUIS I. and ALFRED J. LOTKA. *The Money Value of a Man,* rev. ed. New York: The Ronald Press Co., 1946.
    A detailed discussion of a method for measuring the value of a human life in terms of earning power.
EPSTEIN, ABRAHAM. *Insecurity, A Challenge to America,* 2d rev. ed. New York: Random House, Inc., 1938. Chapters 6–11.
    A strong advocate discusses the need for social insurance programs providing protection against premature death and old age.
EPSTEIN, LENORE A. "Economic Resources of Persons Aged 65 and Over," *Social Security Bulletin,* XVIII, No. 6 (June, 1955), 3–19, 32–33.
    This article summarizes and interprets the results of several studies on the economic problems of the aged.
HUEBNER, SOLOMON S. *The Economics of Life Insurance,* rev. ed. New York: Appleton-Century-Crofts, Inc., 1944.
    A pioneering discussion of human life values and their relationship to property values.
U. S. DEPARTMENT OF COMMERCE, BUREAU OF THE CENSUS. *United States Life Tables, 1950.* Washington, D. C.: U. S. Government Printing Office, 1954.
    Detailed mortality tables applicable to the total population.

4

The Social Security Act

Introduction

The need for some public protection against the financial problems of death and old age has been discussed in Chapter 3. In this chapter we shall consider the Social Security Act and its relationship to these problems.

First we shall describe the conditions that led to the passage of the Social Security Act. Then we shall analyze the public assistance and social insurance programs established under the Act.

Two of the four types of state public assistance programs made eligible for federal financial support under the Act deal with death and old age. The nature of the federal support, the characteristics of these state programs, and important trends are issues which will bear analysis. The bulk of the chapter deals with the social insurance program established under the Social Security Act. Eligibility requirements, death and old age benefits, reasons for terminating or suspending the benefits, method of financing the benefits, administration of the insurance system, and significant trends will be described in detail.

Finally we shall consider the extent to which the social insurance system has reduced the need for the special public assistance programs dealing with the economic problems of death and old age, and how the social insurance system fits into the over-all American economic security program.

Historical Development

Prior to the passage of the Social Security Act in 1935, only limited public financial assistance was provided for the aged and for the dependents of deceased workers. Energetic social reformers wrote and talked at length about the problem, but only seven states had passed old-age assistance laws prior to the Great Depression, and two of these laws had been declared unconstitutional. More than half of the states had passed mothers' pension laws which provided cash payments for widowed mothers, but the benefits were small. The federal government itself had taken no action, although bills had been introduced in the Congress at various times.

The Depression increased and dramatized the problem, and over half the states had an old-age assistance law by the middle thirties. However, these laws covered but a very small segment of the aged population because of severe age, citizenship, residence, income, and property requirements. In addition, during the depth of the Depression, only about one out of every ten eligibles was actually receiving a pension, primarily because of financial problems experienced by state and local governmental units. All but two states had mothers' aid laws, but these programs were also badly in need of financial assistance.

In June, 1934, President Franklin D. Roosevelt appointed a Committee on Economic Security to study the general problem of economic security. After extensive deliberations concerning the employments to be covered, the benefits to be included, and the method of financing, the Committee reported its findings in January, 1935. Congress did not accept all the recommendations of the Committee, but it did pass the Social Security Act.

Important amendments to the Act were passed in 1939, 1946, 1950, 1952, 1954, and 1956. The Act as it now stands provides for the following:

1. Grants to the states for assistance to the needy aged, blind, totally and permanently disabled, and dependent children
2. Grants to the states for services provided for maternal and child welfare
3. Grants to the states for the administration of state unemployment compensation funds
4. A Federal Old-Age and Survivors Insurance System

The grants made under the first group of provisions were designed to solve an immediate problem by strengthening the state special public assistance programs. The Federal Old-Age and Survivors Insurance System represents a long-range approach to the problems of death, old-age and disability. The grants under the second and third set of provisions deal with problems certain of which will be discussed later.

Special Public Assistance Programs

Under the Social Security Act, the federal government makes grants-in-aid to states having a public assistance program for the needy aged, blind, totally and permanently disabled, and dependent children. Unlike the social insurance program to be discussed later, the public assistance programs (1) distribute funds only in the case of need and (2) rely usually upon general revenues for their support. The social insurance program does not eliminate the need for public assistance because many persons are not covered under the social insurance program, while others, who are covered, are not eligible for adequate benefits and require supplementary assistance.

Since old age and death are the insecurities under consideration in this chapter, the discussion will be limited to the programs providing aid for the needy aged and needy dependent children. The other special public assistance programs are discussed in Chapter 11.

FEDERAL GRANTS FOR OLD-AGE ASSISTANCE PROGRAMS

All forty-eight states now have old-age assistance programs that are eligible for federal aid. The purpose of federal grants-in-aid is to provide financial support for state programs which meet certain minimum standards; however, the detailed provisions and administration of the programs are left to the state and local governmental units.

At the present time, the federal government pays, in addition to one-half the administrative expenses, the following portion of the *average* monthly pension provided under an approved state program:

> 80 per cent of the first $30, plus
> 50 per cent of the remainder.

In determining the average monthly pension, only the first $60 of each individual pension is counted. As a result of this formula, the federal government's share of the benefits paid is greatest when the average pension payment is low. Therefore, the formula is favorable to the poorer states and to those states whose programs include liberal eligibility requirements.

The basic minimum requirements for federal approval are as follows:[1] The logic underlying each requirement is appended in parentheses.

[1] U. S. Department of Health, Education and Welfare, Social Security Administration, "Characteristics of State Public Assistance Plans under the Social Security Act," *Public Assistance Report No. 27*, 1956.

1. The program must cover all counties in the state, but it may be administered by local governmental units. (Otherwise certain counties could be discriminated against.)

2. A single state agency must either administer the program itself or supervise the local governmental units administering the program. (This promotes uniformity of treatment among localities.)

3. The state must participate financially in the program. (The state government should aid the local governmental units in the same way that the federal government is aiding the state.)

4. Personnel in the administrative unit must be selected and retained through the merit system. (This provision is designed to improve the caliber of employed personnel.)

5. The Secretary of Health, Education, and Welfare is entitled to any information he may require concerning the operation of the program. (This information is used primarily to determine whether the minimum federal requirements are being met, and for informational and research purposes.)

6. Information divulged by applicants and recipients must be regarded as confidential, but interested persons may look at the rolls for other than political or commercial purposes. (The privacy of the individual is to be preserved.)

7. The age requirement must be sixty-five years or less. (Sixty-five is the retirement age under the OASI program.)

8. The residence requirement must not exceed five out of the preceding nine years and one year immediately preceding the date of application. (The durational residence requirement should be as short as possible.)

9. The citizenship requirement must not exclude any citizen of the United States.

10. Benefits must be granted only in case of need. An applicant's income and assets must be considered in determining his needs. (This requirement follows from the nature of the grants.)

11. A dissatisfied applicant must have the right to a fair hearing before the supervising state agency. (This right is regarded as essential in a democracy.)

12. A state authority must establish and maintain standards for public and private institutions housing recipients of the benefits. (Otherwise some institutions might profit at the expense of the public assistance program.)

STATE OLD-AGE ASSISTANCE PROGRAMS

The forty-eight state programs meet these federal standards; but given these minimal standards, there are considerable differences in the details of state programs, especially as regards the concept of need and the amount of the benefits. The most important features of the current state programs are summarized in the following paragraphs.[2]

All state programs require that the recipient be sixty-five years of age. In about two-thirds of the states, there is no citizenship requirement; and in about the same proportion of the states, the residence requirement is less than the federal requirement for approval. Some states have reciprocal agreements with other states which reduce the durational residence requirements for some applicants.

An applicant is generally considered to be "needy" if he has insufficient income or other resources to provide reasonable subsistence compatible with decency and health. Definite income limits are seldom used, but almost all the states set definite limits on the amount of property which an eligible person may own. These property limits tend to reduce the amount of discretion involved in individual cases. They vary by amount, the method of valuation, and the type of property included. An applicant who disposes of property in order to qualify for assistance is ineligible under almost all state laws.

If there are relatives who are legally responsible for and financially able to support the aged person, this may disqualify him, not affect him at all, or reduce the amount of his benefit. In a few states, the state may pay the benefit on the assumption that no relatives exist and then collect from said relatives.

The amount of assistance is determined by subtracting the applicant's resources from his personal requirements as determined by the administering agency. A few states have established statutory minimums for assistance plus other income.

A majority of the states have a specified maximum benefit. Most of them set the federal matching limit or a higher limit. About two-thirds of the limits are statutory, while the others are administrative.

A majority of states reserve the right to recover at least part of the assistance granted from the recipient or his estate. Usually this claim is not enforceable against any house or homestead if there is a surviving spouse or minor children.

Trends in old-age assistance programs. The old-age assistance programs have been liberalized in various ways over the years. Income and property limits as a condition of eligibility have been reduced; the circle of relatives considered legally responsible for

[2] *Ibid.* The student should consult this source, *Public Assistance Report No. 27,* for more detailed information.

the support of aged persons has been narrowed and, in some cases, ignored; pensions are now paid to persons in approved public and private institutions; and the monthly benefits have been considerably increased.

The formulas that have been used since 1935 to determine the contribution of the federal government are given in Table 4.1. Two important changes have occurred. First, the contribution has been considerably increased through increases in the maximum monthly benefits included in the average and the fraction of the average benefit paid. Second, instead of contributing the same percentage of all average benefits, the federal government now pays a larger share of the low average grants than of the high average grants.

TABLE 4.1

FORMULAS FOR DETERMINING FEDERAL CONTRIBUTIONS TO STATE OLD-AGE ASSISTANCE PROGRAMS, 1935–56

Year	Maximum monthly benefits included in average	Fraction of average benefit paid by federal government
1935	$30	½
1939	40	½
1946	45	⅔ of first $15, ½ of balance
1948	50	¾ of first $20, ½ of balance
1952	55	⅘ of first $25, ½ of balance
1956	60	⅘ of first $30, ½ of balance

Because it is more convenient to discuss the operations of old-age assistance plans at the same time that we discuss the operations of the plans providing aid to dependent children, we shall consider next the nature of the latter group of plans. An evaluation of both groups of plans will follow the discussion of their operations.

FEDERAL GRANTS FOR PROGRAMS PROVIDING AID TO DEPENDENT CHILDREN

All states in the Union have federally approved plans providing aid to dependent children. These benefits are payable in case of death, continued absence from the home, or physical or mental incapacity of a parent. A few states also make payments for other reasons, but the federal government does not contribute to these special benefits.

As in the case of old-age assistance, the federal government pays one-half the administrative expenses. It also pays the following portion of the *average* monthly benefit per recipient (not family):

$\frac{14}{17}$ of the first $17, plus
50 per cent of the excess.

Only family benefits up to and including $32 for the first child, plus $32 for one adult in each family, plus $23 for each additional child are counted in computing the *average* monthly benefit. The formula is similar to that used in determining the federal contribution to old-age assistance in that the contribution is relatively greatest when the average benefit is low.

The requirements for federal approval are essentially the same as those established for old-age assistance plans, but the residence requirement is considerably more liberal from the viewpoint of the recipient. No state may impose a resident requirement which denies aid to any child residing in the state who has resided in the state for one year immediately preceding the application or who was born within one year immediately preceding the application, if his parent or other relative with whom he is living has resided in the state for one year immediately preceding the birth. No age requirement is necessary for approval, but the federal government will contribute only to those cases involving dependents under eighteen.

STATE PROGRAMS PROVIDING AID TO DEPENDENT CHILDREN

The details of the state programs may be summarized briefly as follows. Under about four-fifths of the plans, a dependent child must be under sixteen or under eighteen if regularly attending school. Until the 1956 amendments the federal government would not share in assistance payments to children aged sixteen and seventeen unless they attended school regularly. The minimum age requirement is fourteen; the maximum, twenty-one. Only one plan has a citizenship requirement. Four-fifths of the plans have the residence requirement established for federal approval; the others have none. About one-sixth of the plans provide payments on behalf of unborn children.

In almost all states, the child recipient must be living with a close relative. The child is generally assumed to be needy if he or the person with whom he is living has insufficient income or other resources to provide the child with a reasonable subsistence compatible with decency and health. No specific income limits have been established in any state, but about three-fourths of the programs set limits on the property owned by the child and his family. As in the case of old-age assistance, these property limits vary by amount, the method of valuation, and the type of property involved.

The amount of the benefit is determined in the same way as the old-age assistance benefit. A majority of states have established a maximum benefit. Most of these are administrative, the others are statutory. About two-thirds of the maximum payments are at least as liberal as the federal matching limit.

Most states do not reserve the right to recover payments made to an infant. This policy differs from the one adopted in the case of old-age assistance. The aid does not represent a loan against future earning power.

Trends in aid-to-dependent-children programs. The aid-to-dependent-children programs have been continually liberalized since the thirties in the same ways as the old-age assistance programs. The changes in the federal contribution formula over the years are given in Table 4.2.

TABLE 4.2

FORMULAS FOR DETERMINING FEDERAL CONTRIBUTIONS TO STATE
AID-TO-DEPENDENT-CHILDREN PROGRAMS: 1935–56

Year	Maximum monthly benefits included in average		Fraction of average benefit per recipient paid by federal government
	First Child	*Each Additional Child*	
1935	$18	$12	⅓
1939	18	12	½
1946	24	15	⅔ of first $9, ½ of balance
1948	27	18	¾ of first $12, ½ of balance
1950	27 plus 27 per adult	18	¾ of first $12, ½ of balance
1952	30 plus 30 per adult	21	⅘ of first $15, ½ of balance
1956	32 plus 32 per adult	23	14⁄17 of first $32, ½ of balance

Until 1939 the federal government paid less than half the average benefits under the state programs. Until 1946 the federal contribution was a fixed percentage of all average benefits, but since that date the share paid by the federal government has increased as the average benefit has increased. Until 1950 the federal government contributed nothing toward payments made to the adults with whom the child is living. The total federal contribution has increased significantly over the years.

OPERATIONS

A study of the more important operations of these two special public assistance programs enables one to understand more clearly their nature and scope.

The changes over time in the number of recipients, total payments, and average monthly payments under the public assistance programs are given in Table 4.3. The number of old-age recipients increased up to 1950 except during the war years, but it has de-

TABLE 4.3

PUBLIC ASSISTANCE: RECIPIENTS, TOTAL PAYMENTS, AND AVERAGE MONTHLY PAYMENTS, BY PROGRAM, 1936–55

| | Recipients (in thousands)* | | | | Total Payments (in thousands)† | | Average Monthly Payment*† | | |
| | Old-Age Assistance | Aid to Dependent Children | | | Old-Age Assistance | Aid to Dependent Children | Old-Age Assistance | Aid to Dependent Children | |
Year		Families	Total Recipients	Children				Per Family	Per Recipient
1936	1,106	162	—	404	$ 155,241	$ 49,654	$18.79	$29.82	—
1937	1,577	228	—	565	310,442	70,451	19.46	31.46	—
1938	1,776	280	—	648	392,384	97,442	19.56	31.96	—
1939	1,909	315	—	760	430,480	114,949	19.30	31.77	—
1940	2,066	370	—	891	474,952	133,243	20.26	32.38	—
1941	2,234	390	—	941	541,519	153,153	21.27	33.62	—
1942	2,227	348	—	849	595,152	158,435	23.37	36.25	—
1943	2,149	272	—	676	653,171	140,942	26.66	41.57	—
1944	2,066	254	—	639	693,338	135,015	28.43	45.58	—
1945	2,056	274	—	701	726,550	149,667	30.88	52.05	—
1946	2,196	346	—	885	822,061	208,857	35.31	62.23	—
1947	2,332	416	—	1,060	989,716	294,961	37.42	63.01	—
1948	2,498	475	—	1,214	1,132,604	364,160	42.02	71.88	—
1949	2,736	599	—	1,521	1,380,398	475,361	44.76	74.19	—
1950	2,789	652	2,234	1,662	1,469,869	553,697	43.95	72.42	21.13
1951	2,708	593	2,044	1,524	1,474,513	561,691	46.00	77.08	22.36
1952	2,646	570	1,992	1,495	1,532,907	553,836	50.90	83.83	23.98
1953	2,591	548	1,942	1,464	1,596,696	562,257	51.50	84.22	23.77
1954	2,565	604	2,174	1,640	1,592,778	593,512	51.90	86.24	23.96
1955	2,553	603	2,193	1,661	1,608,137	639,072	53.93	88.61	24.35

* Data shown are for December of each year.
† Includes vendor payments for medical care from 1950 on.

Source: Social Security Bulletin, Annual Statistical Supplement, 1955, p. 49.

creased slightly since 1950 when OASI was extended to cover many new groups of employees. The number of recipients under the aid-to-dependent-children programs has increased very rapidly except for temporary setbacks during World War II and 1952–53. The average monthly payments have increased about 190 per cent for old-age assistance and almost 200 per cent for aid to dependent children. The future should be marked by a slight decline in old-age assistance recipients as more people become eligible for OASI, but the number of persons receiving support under the aid-to-dependent-children program will probably increase because OASI provides assistance only in case of death. The average monthly payments will increase if the trend of the price-level is upward.

Part of the increase in the number of recipients is due to the changing age composition of the population and the size of the population. Table 4.4 indicates that the number of old-age assistance recipients relative to the number of persons sixty-five or over has actually declined slightly, while the number of child recipients relative to the total population under eighteen has increased, but not as rapidly as the absolute number has increased.

TABLE 4.4

PROPORTION OF POPULATION RECEIVING ASSISTANCE, BY PROGRAM, 1943–56

Month and Year		Number of old-age-assistance recipients relative to 1000 population sixty-five and over	Number of child recipients relative to 1000 population under eighteen
July,	1943	223	18
December,	1944	208	15
	1945	204	17
	1946	213	21
	1947	219	24
	1948	228	26
	1949	241	33
	1950	224	34
June,	1952	201	32
	1953	191	30
	1954	184	28
	1955	179	29
	1956	173	29

Source: *Social Security Bulletins.*

The variations among states are very wide. In June, 1956, the number of old-age assistance recipients per 1,000 aged population ranged from forty-one in New Jersey to 604 in Louisiana. The number of children receiving aid to dependent children per 1,000 population under eighteen ranged from ten in New Jersey to sixty-eight in West Virginia (ninety-six in Puerto Rico). The average old-age assistance benefit varied between $28.45 in West Virginia ($7.93 in Puerto Rico and $18.54 in the Virgin Islands) and $90.18 in Connecticut. Mississippi paid the lowest average aid-to-dependent-children benefit per recipient, $7.48 ($2.94 in Puerto Rico), while Connecticut paid the highest, $42.29. These variations are caused by differences in the economic status of the state populations, the percentage of the populations covered under OASI, and the provisions of state plans.

Federal contributions have become more important over the years, as would be expected from the formula changes discussed earlier. In 1936, the federal government paid 42.8 per cent of the expenditures for assistance and administration under the old-age assistance programs. The state paid 45.0 per cent and the local units paid 12.2 per cent. In 1955, the three corresponding figures were 54.8 per cent, 38.2 per cent, and 7.0 per cent.

Federally approved aid-to-dependent-children programs were not enacted as rapidly as old-age assistance programs, and federal aid to these programs was more limited in the beginning. Therefore, the increasing importance of the federal contribution to these programs is even more marked. In 1936 the federal government paid 12.9 per cent of the expenditures, while the state paid 26.1 per cent and the local units 61.0 per cent. In 1955 the three corresponding figures were 56.3 per cent, 31.8 per cent, and 11.9 per cent. The state's share had increased to 46.2 per cent by 1939, decreased to 37.7 in 1940, increased again to 52.0 per cent in 1946, and has steadily decreased since that time.

The importance of federal aid varies among states depending upon the economic status of the state and the willingness of the state to appropriate funds for public assistance purposes. In 1955, the percentage of expenditures for old-age assistance and administration supplied by the federal government ranged from 36.8 per cent in Colorado (33.4 per cent in Puerto Rico) to 75.8 per cent in West Virginia. The federal share of the cost of the aid-to-dependent-children programs varied between 41.1 per cent in Connecticut (32.8 per cent in Puerto Rico) to 78.5 per cent in Arkansas.

EVALUATION

The purpose of the special programs providing aid to the aged and dependent children is to provide minimum subsistence to the needy persons in these two groups. The programs have been criticized in various ways, but few would argue that the programs have been self-defeating in the sense that recipients prefer assistance payments to private approaches to their problems. Furthermore, because there are social and economic reasons why dependent children and the aged (though the case is weaker here) should not be attached to the labor force, we are less concerned about whether the recipient prefers an assistance payment to earnings.

One advantage of these programs is that the individual is given a cash allowance which he may spend according to his individual needs and desires. Two important disadvantages are the adverse effects of a means test and the indefiniteness of the test and the benefits. Fortunately this indefiniteness is being reduced.

Perhaps the major objection to these programs is the heterogeneity among the states. This is the price which must be paid to preserve states' rights, but steps could be taken within the existing framework to make the programs less diverse. Thus, reciprocal arrangements should be made which prevent the loss of benefits when a person moves from one state to another.

While average benefits have increased over the years, the maximum benefits in many states are still far below the level required to provide minimum subsistence. As recently as 1956, the maximum old-age payment was as low as $30. The eligibility requirements in some states are as restrictive as the federal law will permit.

The variation among state laws is due primarily to the variations in wealth among the various states and their willingness to tax this wealth.[3] If it is agreed that more uniformity among states is desirable, it will be necessary for the federal government to contribute relatively more funds to the poorer states. The problem then is to determine how the willingness to tax can be equated among the states.[4] The present formula does charge the federal government with a larger share of the low grants, but this low grant may be due to poor economic status or unwillingness to tax.

From the evidence available, the administration of the special public assistance programs has been honest, but many claimants have complained about inequitable treatment. Such complaints are bound to arise when administrative discretion is involved, and, fortunately, the amount of arbitrary discretion is being reduced. The federal requirement that employees be hired and discharged

[3] See Eveline M. Burns, *The American Social Security System* (Boston: Houghton Mifflin Co., 1951). Chapter 12 contains an excellent discussion of the financing of special public assistance programs.

[4] *Ibid.*, pp. 374–75.

on a merit basis has raised the general level of competence, but low salaries are a source of continuing personnel problems.[5]

The present status of special public assistance plans may be summarized under two headings. First, efforts are being made to reduce the need for public assistance. Second, and at the same time, the eligibility requirements and benefit levels in the existing programs are being liberalized. These dual objectives are highly desirable.

Old-Age and Survivors Insurance

CONTENT OF THE ACT

The social insurance system created under the Social Security Act is known as the Federal Old-Age and Survivors Insurance System, or OASI in abbreviated form. This system provides certain protection against the problems created by death, old age, and disability. The provisions in the system which deal with disability are discussed in Chapter 11, but the provisions dealing with retirement and survivorship benefits are discussed below. These provisions are subject to change each time the Congress meets, but a study of the current provisions helps one to understand and appreciate the nature and magnitude of this operation.

COVERAGE

Classes of coverage. To receive benefits, a person must be what is called "fully insured" or "currently insured." In general, fully insured persons are eligible for the survivorship and retirement benefits provided by the system; currently insured persons are eligible only for the survivorship benefits.

Quarters of coverage and covered employment. In order to understand how one may become fully or currently insured it is necessary to define "a quarter of coverage." A quarter of coverage is a calendar quarter during which a wage earner received $50 or more in "covered" employment.

Most employments are covered employments on a compulsory or elective basis. The easiest way to define covered employment is to consider the employments which are excluded from coverage or included only under special conditions. The excluded occupations are:

    1. Family employment except when the service is performed by a child twenty-one years of age or over

[5] Jay L. Roney, "Twenty Years of Public Assistance," *Social Security Bulletin,* XVIII, No. 8 (August, 1955), 22–23.

2. Local newsboys under eighteen years of age
3. Student nurses and internes
4. Student workers in institutions of learning
5. Students performing domestic services for college clubs, fraternities and sororities
6. Railroad workers
7. Self-employed physicians
8. Policemen and firemen covered under an existing retirement system (except in five states)
9. Certain federal government employees covered by a public retirement system
10. Some special types of federal and state employees

The occupations included under special conditions are the following:

1. Agricultural labor is considered covered employment if the laborer earns $150 or more from any one employer in a calendar year or if he works for one employer on twenty or more days for cash pay figured on a time basis rather than a piece-rate basis.
2. Nonfarm domestic workers and casual laborers must earn $50 or more from one employer in a calendar quarter.
3. Clergymen earning at least $400 a year may, within a limited period, elect to be covered.
4. In order for employees of nonprofit organizations to be covered, the employer must consent and two-thirds of the employees must agree. Any employee who disagrees cannot be covered unless he elects coverage within twenty-four months after the end of the first month of the calendar quarter in which the coverage for the group becomes effective. All new employees are automatically covered.
5. State and local government employees not already under a retirement system may be covered if the state agrees. The employees under a retirement system may be covered if the state consents and at least half the employees under each system agree.

The exclusions have been justified on the following grounds. Railroad workers are covered under a separate public retirement system as are the federal employees excluded under the act. Nonprofit organizations have a tax-exempt status and a tax should not be levied without their consent, nor should the federal government intervene in their affairs. States cannot be taxed without their consent. Some state and local government employees fear that they will lose their benefits under their present public retirement systems if they are covered under OASI. The American Medical Association has held that doctors do not retire until a very advanced age and that they will not benefit from the act. Most of the other occupations are excluded for administrative reasons. Either the administrative problems seem insoluble at the present time or the efforts necessary to solve the problems are not justified by the benefits to be gained.

If a covered wage earner received $3,000 in covered employment in any year before 1951, the first quarter in that year during which he earned at least $50 and each succeeding quarter is considered a quarter of coverage. For earnings during the years 1951–1954, the wage earner receives credit for four quarters of coverage if his income in covered employment in the year was $3,600. For earnings during years after 1954, the same rule applies, but the annual income figure is $4,200.

Self-employed persons, who first became eligible for coverage in 1951, receive credit for four quarters of coverage for each year in which their annual self-employment income is $400 or more.[6]

Determination of insured status. To determine whether an individual is *fully insured,* the first step is to count the number of calendar quarters elapsing between December 31, 1950 (or the end of the quarter in which he became twenty-one, if later) and the beginning of the quarter in which he became sixty-five years of age (sixty-two for women) or died.[7] If the quarters of coverage credited to this person since January 1, 1937, are equal to at least half this number, he is fully insured. However, he must have at least six quarters of coverage and he is not required to have more than forty quarters of coverage.

A special rule will enable some persons who cannot qualify under the above definition to receive benefits. The rule states that a person is fully insured if all but four of the quarters between December 31, 1954, and July 1, 1957, or if later, the beginning of the quarter in which he reaches retirement age or dies are quarters of coverage. He must have at least six quarters of coverage. After 1960 this rule will have no effect, for anyone qualifying under the special rule will also qualify under the basic definition. The purpose of this rule is to help aged persons who were covered for the first time in 1955 and 1956.

---

[6] Self-employed farmers have an optional way of figuring self-employment earnings. If a farmer's gross farm income is $1,800 or less, he may report his actual net farm earnings or two-thirds of the gross income. If his gross farm income is more than $1,800, and his actual net farm earnings are less than $1,200, he may report his actual net earnings or $1,200. Otherwise, he must report his actual net farm earnings.

Farm laborers also receive special treatment. A farm laborer is credited with one quarter of coverage for each $100 of annual wages, the maximum annual credit being four quarters of coverage.

[7] If the total number of quarters elapsed is an odd number, one quarter is deducted.

Illustrations. The following illustrations should clarify the above definitions.

1. Assume that a person is sixty-five in March, 1962. Because he earned $5,000 a year in covered employment from 1951–1957, inclusive, he has been credited with twenty-eight quarters of coverage. He is fully insured because this is more than half the forty-four quarters which have elapsed between December 31, 1950 and January 1, 1962.

2. Another worker reaches age sixty-five in July, 1972. Because he earned at least $50 per quarter in covered employment from 1955–1964, inclusive, he has forty quarters of coverage, although eighty-six quarters have elapsed between December 31, 1950, and July 1, 1972. He is fully insured in this case because he has satisfied the maximum requirement.

3. A student will be twenty-one years of age in December, 1960. He expects to work in covered employment for five years beginning July 1, 1961, after which time he expects to go into the medical profession. He will not be fully insured when he reaches age sixty-five, for he will have only twenty quarters of coverage. This case is not typical. Most students will qualify by working ten years in covered employment. Some will be well on their way to a fully insured status by the time they graduate because of part-time work in college.

4. A worker, who was sixty-three years of age in January, 1956, first entered covered employment at that time. He earned $4,500 a year in his new job. He will be fully insured when he reaches age sixty-five in January, 1958, because of the special rule.

It is possible to achieve *currently insured* status at an early date, for the only requirement is that the person have six quarters of coverage out of the last thirteen quarters including the quarter in which he dies or reaches age sixty-five. A worker, aged twenty-two, could enter covered employment in June, 1960, at a salary of $200 a month and be currently insured by July, 1961. It is, of course, possible to be currently insured without being fully insured and vice versa.

BENEFITS

The benefits under the act may be divided into retirement and survivorship benefits. Unless otherwise specified, a person must be fully insured to qualify for retirement benefits, but survivorship benefits are provided for fully or currently insured individuals.

Retirement benefits. 1. *The primary insurance amount.* When the insured worker reaches age sixty-five, he is entitled to a monthly income for life called the primary insurance amount. All other benefits are expressed as a per cent of this amount.

A female worker may elect to receive her monthly retirement income as soon as she reaches age sixty-two, but her monthly income is reduced by ⁵⁄₉ of 1 per cent for each month prior to her sixty-fifth birthday that the benefits begin. For example, if her benefits begin on her sixty-third birthday, the amount of her monthly payments will be 86⅔ per cent of what she would receive if she were sixty-five. If there are three or more months before she reaches age sixty-five for which her benefit is suspended because she works, her benefit is automatically recomputed when she reaches age sixty-five.

The computation of the primary insurance amount is fairly complex because of the many amendments to the original act. The first step is to compute the average monthly wage on which the insured paid a social security tax between his starting date and his closing date. The starting date is usually December 31, 1950, or the last day of the calendar year in which the person was twenty-one years of age. However, the starting date is December 31, 1936, if the person does not have six quarters of coverage after 1950 or if moving the starting date back increases the benefit. Furthermore, if a person works in covered employment prior to the calendar year in which he reaches twenty-two years of age, those months of employment in any prior year in which less than two quarters were quarters of coverage will not be counted. The closing date is that one of the following dates which results in the highest benefit: (1) the first day of the year in which he was both fully insured and at least sixty-five (sixty-two years of age for females); (2) the first day of the year in which the person died or applied for retirement benefits; and (3) the first day of the following year. The total wages and/or self-employment income on which the individual has paid a social security tax over this period is divided by the number of months in the period to determine the average monthly wage. If the number of months in the denominator is less than eighteen, eighteen is used in the computation. Prior to 1951, the maximum average monthly wage was $250 because the annual income was taxed only up to $3,000. The annual income subject to tax was increased in 1951 to $3,600 and in 1955 to $4,200.

The "drop-out" provisions make it possible for a person who has six quarters of coverage after June 30, 1953, or who first became eligible for benefits after August, 1954, to drop the five calendar years of lowest earnings from the computation. For this reason, by April, 1956, some persons had an average monthly wage of $350. The purpose of these provisions is to enable persons covered for the first time in 1955 and 1956 to start off with a clean slate and to enable all workers to reach the new maximum.[8]

[8] The drop-out provisions are not applicable if the conversion table described on page 87 is used to compute the benefits.

In addition, special starting and closing dates may be used for persons who die or become entitled to benefits in 1956 or 1957. For a person dying or becoming entitled to benefits in 1956, December 31, 1954, may be used as the starting date and July 1, 1956, as the closing date, if the person acquired six quarters of coverage between December 31, 1954, and the end of the quarter in which he died or became eligible for benefits. A similar rule applies to a person dying or becoming eligible for benefits in 1957, with December 31, 1955, and July 1, 1957, being the respective starting and closing dates. Persons covered for the first time in 1955 or 1956 may find this special rule more useful than the drop-out provisions because complete calendar years must be dropped under those provisions and the number of months used in the computation must be at least eighteen. However, this special rule will affect a relatively small number of persons.

2. *Primary insurance amount calculation.* The next step is to apply the primary insurance amount formula to the average monthly wage. If the individual has at least six quarters of coverage after 1950, the following formula is used:

> 55 per cent of the first $110 of average monthly wage plus
> 20 per cent of the next $240 of average monthly wage.

However, if the average monthly income is less than $130, the following formula is used without the drop-out, if more favorable:

> 55 per cent of the first $100 of average monthly wage plus
> 15 per cent of the next $30 of average monthly wage plus $5.

Therefore, if the average monthly wage is $210, the primary insurance amount is

$$.55 \ (\$110) + .20 \ (\$100) = \$80.50$$

If the average monthly wage is $110 with or without the drop-out, the primary insurance amount is

$$.55 \ (\$100) + .15 \ (\$10) + \$5 = \$61.50$$

If the person is a female who has elected to retire at sixty-two years of age, the corresponding primary insurance amounts are

$$.80 \ (\$80.50) = \$64.50 \ \text{and}$$
$$.80 \ (\$61.50) = \$49.20$$

This formula represents a compromise between the desire to provide a floor of protection for all families and the desire to preserve some relationship between taxable earnings and benefits. The benefit is a larger percentage of lower earnings, but the benefit does vary directly with the income. The reason for the two formulas is that the 1954 amendments were designed to increase the 1952 benefit levels by at least $5 and the first formula does not accomplish this objective.

If the individual does not have six quarters of coverage after 1950, a primary insurance *benefit* is computed using the 1939 amendment formula and the benefit is converted to a primary insurance *amount* with the aid of a conversion table. The 1939 amendment formula is as follows:

> 40 per cent of the first $50 of average monthly wage plus
> 10 per cent of the next $200 of average monthly wage plus
> 1 per cent of the sum of the two preceding items times the number of years prior to 1951 in which the employee earned $200 or more in covered employment.

A portion of the conversion table is reproduced in Table 4.5. For example, assume that a worker was in covered employment from January, 1939, until December, 1948. He was sixty-five years of age in February, 1953. Because his average monthly wage was $150, his primary insurance *benefit* is:

.40 ($50) + .10 ($100) + .01 (10) (Sum of two preceding terms)
or $20   + $10   + .10 ($30) = $33

TABLE 4.5
CONVERSION TABLE

Primary insurance benefit (1939 formula)	Primary insurance amount (1954 amendment)
$10	$30.00
20	47.00
30	66.30
35	73.90
40	81.10
45	88.50

Source: *Questions and Answers on Your New Social Security Benefits* (Englewood Cliffs, N. J.: Prentice-Hall, Inc., 1954), p. 14.

The primary insurance *amount*, according to the *detailed* conversion table, is $71.10.[9]

The minimum primary insurance amount in either case is $30. Since the maximum average monthly wage is $350, the maximum primary insurance amount under the present law is (.55) $110 + (.20) $240, or $108.50.

[9] A few individuals with at least six quarters of coverage after 1950 would be entitled to larger benefits if this procedure were used to compute the primary insurance amount. If so, the more liberal procedure is used.

As already stated, the primary insurance amount increases as the average monthly wage increases, but the ratio of the primary insurance amount to the average monthly wage decreases as the wage increases. The number of years of service is included in the 1939 formula, but not in the 1954 formula, because it was felt that this feature of the 1939 formula placed too much emphasis on the relationship between taxable earnings and benefits. It penalized especially the dependents of wage earners who died at an early age. However, periods not spent in covered employment do tend to reduce the average monthly wage and consequently the primary insurance amount.

Persons who were in the Armed Forces between September 15, 1940, and January 1, 1957, receive a wage credit of $160 for each month of service during this period if they were honorably discharged. (Effective January 1, 1957, members of the armed services became eligible for full social security coverage on the same basis as those in other covered employments.) These wage credits may (1) enable a veteran to achieve fully or currently insured status at an earlier age and (2) increase the average monthly wage. These military wage credits are not counted if monthly benefits based at least in part on this military service period are paid under the Army, Navy, Civil Service, or other federal retirement systems except that for persons in service after 1956, 1951-56 wage credits are counted.

3. *Dependents' benefits.* The benefits for dependents of the retired worker are the following:

(a) Life income to wife of retired worker. The wife of a person receiving a primary insurance amount for life will receive 50 per cent of that amount if she is sixty-five years of age and has been married to the retired worker at least three years.

If she wishes, she may take reduced benefits beginning as soon as she reaches age sixty-two. The reduction in benefits is $\frac{25}{36}$ of 1 per cent times the number of months prior to age sixty-five that the benefits begin. Thus if she elects to receive benefits beginning on her sixty-third birthday, she will receive 83⅓ per cent of the amount she would receive if she waited until she was sixty-five.

If she elects to receive a reduced benefit and there are three or more months during which she does not receive this benefit because she has in her care a child entitled to a child's benefit or because she or her husband are employed, her benefit is automatically recomputed when she reaches age sixty-five to make allowance for those months.

(b) Income to a mother until her youngest child is eighteen years of age. The wife of a person receiving a primary insurance amount will receive 50 per cent of that amount as long as she has under her care a child of the worker under eighteen years of age.

(c) Income to age eighteen for children of retired worker. Each child of a person receiving a primary insurance amount will receive 50 per cent of that amount until he reaches eighteen or marries. At the time the benefit is applied for, the child must be dependent upon the worker.

(d) Life income to husband of retired worker. The husband of a person receiving a primary insurance amount will receive 50 per cent of that amount if he is sixty-five years of age and can prove that he depended upon his wife for at least one-half his support at the time she filed for benefits.[10] This benefit is available only if the wife is both *fully and currently insured.*

The minimum benefit for a retired worker and his dependents is $45. The maximum benefit is 80 per cent of the average monthly wage, but in no case more than $200. However, the application of this rule is not permitted to reduce the family benefit below $50 or one and one-half times the primary insurance amount, whichever is larger.

Illustrations. The following show the application of these rules.

(1) A worker, aged sixty-five, who retires in 1958 has an average monthly wage of $200. His primary insurance amount is $78.50. If his wife is also sixty-five years of age, the family benefit will be (1.00 + .50) $78.50, or $117.80.[11] The maximum benefit rule does not apply, since (.80) $200 = $160.

If his wife is sixty-two and elects to receive a reduced benefit, the family benefit will be (1.00 + (.75) .50) $78.50 = $108.

If the worker has a wife, aged forty-five, with a child, aged ten, in her care, the computed family benefit will be (1.00 + .50 + .50) $78.50, or $157.10.[12] The maximum benefit rule does not apply, and the family will receive $157.10 a month for eight years until the child reaches age eighteen. Unless the wife elects to receive a reduced wife's benefit between age sixty-two and age sixty-five, the worker will receive $78.50 a month for the next twelve years until the wife is sixty-five years of age. The benefit will then be increased to $117.80

(2) A worker, aged sixty-five, who retires in 1960 has an average monthly wage of $300. His primary insurance amount is $98.50. If he has a wife, aged fifty-five, and two children, aged seventeen and fifteen,

10 The payments to the dependents of a female worker are always based upon the unreduced old-age insurance benefit even if the worker elects to take benefits at a reduced rate.

11 Benefits are always increased to the next higher multiple of ten cents.

12 Because the Social Security Administration computes each individual benefit separately, the benefit is $157.10 instead of $157.

the computed family benefit is $(1.00 + .50 + .50 + .50)$ \$98.50, or \$246.40. However, the maximum benefit is $(.80)$ \$300 or \$200, whichever is less. Therefore, the family will receive \$200 a month until the first child is eighteen years of age. Unless the wife elects to receive a reduced wife's benefit between ages sixty-two and sixty-five, the benefit will be \$197.10 for two more years, \$98.50 for the next seven years, and \$147.80 after the wife is sixty-five years of age.

(3) A worker, aged sixty-five, who retires in 1962 has an average monthly wage of \$100. His primary insurance amount with a drop-out is \$55. If his wife is the same age, the computed family benefit is $(1.00 + .50)$ \$55, or \$82.50. The maximum benefit of $(.80)$ \$100, or \$80, is less than this, but this rule is not applied because it would reduce the benefit to less than one and one-half times the primary insurance amount.

Survivorship benefits. The survivorship benefits provided under OASI are the following:

1. Life income to widower. The widower of a *fully and currently* insured person will receive 75 per cent of the deceased's primary insurance amount if he is sixty-five years of age, has not remarried, and depended upon his wife for at least one-half his support when she died.

2. Life income to widow. The widow of a *fully insured* person will receive 75 per cent of the deceased's primary insurance amount if she is sixty-two years of age and has not remarried.

3. Income to a mother until her youngest child reaches eighteen years of age. The widow of a deceased person will receive 75 per cent of his primary insurance amount as long as she has a child of the deceased under eighteen years of age in her care and has not remarried. If she was divorced from the deceased at the time of his death, she must have depended upon him for at least one-half her support at the time of his death.

4. Income to age eighteen for children of deceased worker. Until he reaches eighteen or marries, each child of a deceased worker will receive 50 per cent of the deceased's primary insurance amount plus 25 per cent divided by the number of children. He must have been dependent upon the deceased at the date of death. One child would receive 75 per cent of the primary insurance amount; each of two children would receive 62.5 per cent; each of five children would receive 55 per cent; and so on.

5. Life income to parents. If there are no other survivors, each parent of a *fully insured* deceased will receive 75 per cent of the primary insurance amount if he is sixty-five years of age (sixty-two years of age for the mother) and depended upon the deceased for at least one-half his support.

6. Lump-sum death benefit. A lump-sum death benefit equal
to three times the primary insurance amount, but in no case more
than $255, is paid to the widow or widower, if eligible. Otherwise
the person(s) paying the burial expenses can be reimbursed.

The minimum benefit for a single survivor is $30. If a mother's
benefit is payable, the minimum family benefit is $45. The maxi-
mum family benefit payable to survivors is the same as the maximum family retirement benefit.

A few examples will illustrate the application of these benefits.

(1) A currently insured worker dies in 1960 leaving a wife, aged
thirty-five, and one child, aged eight. Since his average monthly wage
was $240, his primary insurance amount is $86.50. The lump-sum benefit
is $255, and the wife and child will receive $(.75 + .75)$ $86.50 = 129.80
for ten years. If the worker had been fully insured, the widow would
also begin to receive $64.90 after she reached age sixty-two.

(2) A fully insured person dies in 1960 leaving a wife, aged fifty-two.
Since his average monthly wage is $280, his primary insurance amount
is $94.50. The wife will receive a lump-sum benefit of $255, but she will
not receive any monthly income for ten years, at which time she will
begin to receive $(.75)$ $94.50 = 70.90. If her husband had been only
currently insured or if she remarried, she would not receive the income
benefit.

(3) A fully insured worker dies in 1964 leaving a wife, aged thirty-
five, and two children, aged eight and thirteen. His average monthly
wage was $350 and his primary insurance amount was $108.50. The
lump-sum benefit of $255 will be paid to the wife, and the family will
receive an income of $200 for five years. The computed benefit is
$(.75 + .625 + .625)$ $108.50 = 217.20, but the maximum benefit rule ap-
plies. For the second five years the benefit is $(.75 + .75)$ $108.50 = 162.80.
The income then stops until the widow becomes eligible for $81.40 a
month when she is sixty-two years of age.

LOSS OF BENEFITS

Benefits are *terminated* for several reasons, most of which have
been implied in the preceding discussion. A mother loses her benefit if for any reason she no longer has under her care a child en-
entitled to benefits. A child loses his benefit if he reaches eighteen,
marries, or is adopted by anyone other than his stepparent, grand-
parent, aunt, or uncle. A widow, surviving mother, or surviving
parent loses her benefit if she remarries. A wife's benefit continues
only so long as she remains married to the insured. Death, of course,
terminates the benefit of any deceased as of the preceding month.

There is one very important reason why the monthly payments
may be *suspended*. If a beneficiary under seventy-two years of age

earns more than $1,200 in any calendar year in covered or uncovered employment, he loses one month of benefit in that year for each $80 or fraction thereof in excess of $1,200. However, benefits are always paid for any month in which a person earns $80 or less in wages and does not render substantial services in self-employment, even if his annual earnings are in excess of $1,200. If a person is seventy-two years of age or older, there is no limit on the amount he can earn.

If a retired worker loses his benefit for this reason, his dependents lose theirs. If a dependent loses his benefit, the benefit of others is not affected.

The purpose of the earnings test is twofold. It encourages older persons to retire, thus providing job opportunities for younger persons, and, what is more important, it cuts the cost of the program. Chapter 14 discusses these issues in greater detail.

Other less important reasons for suspending payment are employment outside the United States in noncovered employment on seven or more calendar days; deportation because of illegal entry or conviction of crime; and conviction of treason, sedition, sabotage, or espionage.

Benefits are not duplicated, the largest being paid.

Financing

Taxes. OASI benefits are financed by a tax on the worker and his employer. The employee has been asked to contribute because (1) the problems created by death and old age are not entirely due to employment, (2) most employees want to contribute to the cost, (3) a direct contribution emphasizes the relationship between contributions and benefits, and (4) a direct contribution strengthens the employee's claim for a voice in the program. The employer's contribution is justified by the fact that the employer has a business interest in the welfare of his employees. The cost of adequate protection against the problems of death and old age is a proper charge against the business operations and, presumably, part of this charge can be shifted to consumers.[13]

At present the employer and the employee each pay 2¼ per cent on the first $4,200 of the employee's wage. A self-employed person pays 3⅜ per cent on his net earnings. The 3⅜ per cent figure represents a compromise between 2¼ per cent and 4½ per cent. The tax rates include a ¼ per cent tax on employees and employers and a

[13] Ida C. Merriam, "Social Security Financing," *Bureau Report No. 17* (Washington: Federal Security Agency, Social Security Administration, 1952), pp. 12–13.

⅜ per cent tax on the self-employed to finance the disability benefits discussed in Chapter 11.

Wages include all payment in cash or kind, with certain exceptions such as the employer's social security tax and unemployment insurance tax or payments in kind to domestic and farm workers. Net self-employment earnings do not include interest, dividends, and rent unless the self-employed person receives them in the course of his business as a real estate or securities dealer.

After 1959, the tax rates including the disability tax noted above are scheduled to increase as follows:

TAX RATE FOR

Year	Employer	Employee	Self-employed
1960–64	2¾%	2¾%	4⅛%
1964–69	3¼	3¼	4⅞
1970–74	3¾	3¾	5⅝
1975–on	4¼	4¼	6⅜

The purpose of the gradually increasing tax rates is to avoid the adverse effects, political and economic, of the sudden imposition of a large tax.

All persons in covered employment pay the tax even if they derive no benefit from the payment. For example, a fully insured person, who could retire with a maximum benefit, must pay a tax if he works in covered employment after age sixty-five.

Each employer withholds the social security tax from the pay of covered employees and sends twice this amount to the District Director of Internal Revenue with a detailed report on the employees covered. Self-employed persons pay their tax each year when they file their income tax return.

The trust fund. The funds collected less the disability taxes are appropriated to the Federal Old-Age and Survivors Insurance Fund. The Secretary of the Treasury is the Managing Trustee of the fund with broad powers over it. The other members of the Board of Trustees are the Secretary of Labor and the Secretary of Health, Education, and Welfare. That part of the fund which is not needed to pay the benefits and administrative costs is invested in interest-bearing United States government obligations.

The fund does not offset a legal reserve of the type required to be established by private life insurers. A private life insurer must carry as a liability item on its balance sheet the difference between the present value of future benefits promised under its contracts in force and the present value of future premium payments for these contracts. The private insurer could stop selling contracts at any time, and if its interest and mortality assumptions are correct, future premiums plus an amount equal to this liability item (known as the legal reserve) accumulated at interest would be sufficient to pay all contractual claims. The trust fund is not this large, but *if the system operates indefinitely,* the amount in the trust fund accumulated at interest plus future social security payroll taxes is expected to be enough to pay all benefits. Congress has stated that the system is to be self-supporting. The fund reduces the financial burden that must be borne by future social security taxes.

The Board of Trustees is required to report annually on the operation and status of the fund during the next ensuing five fiscal years. It must also report immediately to the Congress whenever it is of the opinion (1) that during the ensuing five years, the amount in the fund will exceed three times the highest annual expenditures during that period or (2) that the amount in the fund is unduly small. Congress is not required to take any action on this report, but this is the only reference to the size of the fund in the law. Apparently the fund is to act as a partial reserve fund. While not a full legal reserve fund, it is more than a contingency reserve fund.

ADMINISTRATION

Old-Age and Survivors Insurance is administered by the Bureau of Old-Age and Survivors Insurance. This bureau is a division of the Social Security Administration which is in turn a part of the Department of Health, Education, and Welfare. The Social Security Administration has district offices located throughout the country.[14]

Each worker covered under OASI has a social security account number which is used to keep a record of his earnings. The benefits are computed on the basis of this earnings record. This record is kept by the Social Security Administration at its central office in Baltimore, Maryland, and insureds are encouraged to check on their accounts every three years, since corrections must be made within approximately four years after the wages are paid.

Benefits must be applied for at a social security office. If the insured believes that there has been an error in his earnings record or in computing his benefit, he may ask the Bureau of Old-Age and Survivors Insurance to reconsider his case. Either after this recon-

---

[14] These offices are invaluable as information centers. If the student has any technical questions on social security, he will be able to get answers to them from such an office. The Social Security Administration publishes a series of useful informational booklets, copies of which can be secured from these offices.

sideration or without it, he may request a hearing before a referee. The referee's decision may be appealed to the Appeals Council of the Social Security Administration. Further appeal may be made to the federal courts, if necessary.

OPERATIONAL TRENDS

Since its original passage in 1935, the Social Security Act has been considerably liberalized by enlarging the scope of covered employment, reducing the requirements for insured status, adding new benefits, increasing their amount, and postponing scheduled tax increases. A consideration of the major amendments may indicate further the types of changes to be expected in the future.

Covered employment. Under the original Act, only six out of ten gainfully employed persons were in covered employment. Excluded were agricultural laborers, domestic employees, employees of federal, state, and local governments, casual laborers, employees of nonprofit charitable, religious, scientific, literary, or educational institutions, and self-employed persons. These exclusions were justified by the same arguments as current exclusions, but administrative difficulties seemed much more important in 1935 than now. For example, in 1935 the inclusion of any agricultural laborers, domestic workers, or self-employed seemed administratively impossible. The 1950, 1954, and 1956 amendments reduced the exclusions considerably, and at present more than nine out of ten gainfully employed persons are in covered employment. This fraction is expected to increase and may eventually become unity.

Insured status. Under the original Act, a worker aged sixty-five was entitled to retirement benefits if he (a) had worked in covered employment on at least one day in each of five years between December 31, 1936, and his sixty-fifth birthday and (b) had earned at least $2,000 in covered employment. No survivorship benefits were available. This eligibility requirement was restrictive, and meant that no benefits would be payable until 1942.

In 1939, survivorship benefits were added to the Act and the eligibility requirements liberalized because it was felt that the existing provisions were inadequate. The terms "fully insured" and "currently insured" were introduced and defined in the same way as at present, except that the starting point was January 1, 1937, instead of January 1, 1951.[15]

---

[15] Actually, until 1946 the requirement for currently insured status was six out of the last twelve quarters, not including the quarter in which the insured died or retired. The present provision is more liberal.

The number of covered employments was greatly increased by the 1950 amendments and the starting date was moved up to January 1, 1951, in order to make it easier for new entrants to qualify for fully insured status at an early date. When the list of covered employments was further extended in 1954 and 1956, the starting date was not changed because so few years had elapsed since 1950 and the new entrants were not nearly as numerous. However, special rules were adopted which enabled many new entrants to qualify with fewer quarters of coverage than the standard rule would require.

Benefits. Until 1939 the only benefit was a monthly income for a retired worker based on the total wages on which a social security tax should have been paid. The formula was as follows:

> ½ per cent of the first $3,000, plus
> $\frac{1}{12}$ per cent of the next $42,000, plus
> $\frac{1}{24}$ per cent of the excess.

The formula recognized both the level and duration of earnings.

The maximum benefit was $85; the minimum was $10. No benefit was payable for any month in which the worker was engaged in "regular" employment. If a worker died before he had received at least 3.5 per cent of his total taxed wages, the difference was returned to his estate. If he failed to qualify for monthly benefits at sixty-five, 3.5 per cent of his total taxed wages was returned to him in a lump sum. This return was considered to be a return of the worker's contributions plus interest.

The 1939 amendments made extensive changes in the benefits. The first important change was in the formula. An average monthly wage was to be computed in essentially the same way as at present, except that the starting date was always January 1, 1937. Because only the first $3,000 of income was taxed, the maximum average monthly wage was $250. The primary insurance benefit, as it was called at that time, was computed according to the 1939 formula discussed on page 87.

The effective maximum benefit was $40 plus ($.40 times years of coverage); the minimum was $10. No benefit was payable for any month in which the claimant earned at least $15 in covered employment.

These changes accomplished the following objectives. First, the benefit depended upon the average taxable earnings over the base period, instead of upon the total taxable earnings. This procedure increased the benefits available to those persons who were approaching retirement age at the time the formula was introduced. It also favored those who spread their total earnings over more years in the base period, the argument being that the person who pays taxes over a longer period of time should receive more benefits. Second, the formula favored low-income groups relatively more than did the old formula. The benefit was recognized more as a floor of protection than as a savings program. The reduction of the maximum benefit, and the introduction of dependents' allowances (as discussed in the next paragraph) were steps in the same direction. Finally, the introduction of a $15 earnings limit eliminated the discretionary determination of what regular employment was.

The second important 1939 change was the addition of new retirement benefits—the wife's, mother's, and children's benefits, and survivorship benefits—the widow's, mother's, children's, and parent's benefits; and the lump-sum benefit. The maximum family benefit was twice the monthly primary benefit, 80 per cent of the average monthly wage, or $85, whichever was the smallest.

No more extensive changes were made until 1950 when the formula was changed to reflect increases in the cost of living and in wage levels. The maximum taxable earnings, the maximum individual and family benefits, and the limit on earnings of beneficiaries were all increased. Under this revision, the percentage increases were greatest for the higher income groups, thus counteracting to some extent the effect of the previous revision. At the same time, the increment in the formula for years of coverage was dropped. The special dependents' allowances for widowers and divorced wives were added and some survivor benefits raised.

The cost of living continued to increase, and minor amendments in 1952 increased all the following: the benefits for average earnings amounts under $100, the earnings limitation of beneficiaries, and the maximum family benefit.

In 1954 the present formula, maximum taxable earnings, maximum individual and family benefits, and earnings limitation were adopted. Since the cost of living had increased only slightly, these changes increased the adequacy of the benefits.

The 1956 amendments lowered from sixty-five to sixty-two the age at which female workers, wives, widows, and mothers of insured persons could draw benefits.

If we are about to witness a period of continuing inflation as many economists appear to believe, we may expect another increase in the wage subject to tax and an increase in the benefits provided by the formula. The lower income groups will probably benefit most from the change, depending largely upon political fortunes.

The tax structure. In 1937 the employer and employee were each asked to pay a tax of 1 per cent on the first $3,000 of the worker's earnings. It was stipulated that this tax would increase by ½ per cent every three years until 1949 when it would have reached 3 per cent. As stated earlier, the purpose of the graduated increase was to lessen the impact of the tax.

Because a tax increase is unpopular and because many persons questioned the necessity for an increase for reasons to be discussed shortly, the original rates were not increased as scheduled. However, it was not until 1947 that this original tax schedule was abandoned in favor of one which called for a tax of 1 per cent in 1948–49, 1½ per cent in 1950–51, and 2 per cent thereafter.

The tax was increased in 1950 according to this revised schedule, but the important 1950 amendments in coverage and benefits also produced a new tax schedule. The tax was to remain at 1½ per cent until 1954 when it would be increased to 2 per cent. In 1960 the tax would jump to 2½ per cent, in 1965 to 3 per cent, and in 1970 to 3½ per cent, the maximum figure. Self-employed persons were to pay one and one-half times the employee tax.

In 1954 the tax was increased as scheduled, but a revised tax schedule was adopted which required employees and employers to pay a maximum tax rate of 4 per cent from 1975 on. In 1956, each of the tax rates in the 1954 schedule was increased to cover the cost of disability benefits.

Tax increases have been postponed in the past, but it is probable that there will be fewer postponements in the future as benefits are increased and the apparent cost of the program mounts. A higher tax schedule is not at all unlikely.

The reserve fund. Until 1940 the excess of the income over expenditures was kept in an Old-Age Reserve Account which was administered by the Secretary of the Treasury. The balance was invested in special 3 per cent government bonds. On January 1, 1940, the funds were transferred to the Federal Old-Age and Survivors Insurance Trust Fund which was to be administered by a Board of Trustees. The balance was invested in bonds bearing the average rate of interest on the public debt. The 1956 amendments increased the interest rate on these special bonds to the average rate of interest on all marketable obligations of the United States not due or callable until at least five years after the original date of issue.

The original tax schedule was expected to make the system self-supporting if it operated indefinitely. Because no pensions were to be paid for several years and because the taxes were to be increased to the maximum in twelve years, a sizable trust fund was to have been accumulated in the early years. However, it soon became apparent that the tax schedule might not be high enough. A further increase in tax rates would have created an even larger Trust Fund, and the opponents of higher taxes and a sizable Trust Fund became more outspoken in their protests. Their arguments included the following:

1. The tax schedule necessary to make the system self-supporting is almost impossible to estimate. The schedule gives an impression of accuracy which is not justified.
2. Because the funds are invested in government bonds, the national debt will increase and will never be eliminated.[16] Furthermore, the stated 3 per cent interest rate is too high.
3. The trust fund may provide the federal government with funds at a time when it cannot use them. Unwise expenditures may result.
4. The government debt must be paid out of taxes so that future benefits are to be paid out of taxes even if a trust fund is accumulated.
5. The tax is deflationary. In the late 1930's it was desirable to stimulate business activities.
6. The presence of a large trust fund may lead to a demand for more liberal benefits.

Those favoring a large reserve fund argued as follows:

1. The tax schedule necessary to make the system self-supporting may be crude, but it is much better than nothing and does reduce the financial burden that is passed on to future generations.
2. It will probably never be possible to retire completely the national debt. The 3 per cent interest rate can be reduced.
3. The needs of the government exceed the funds provided by the system. If the funds were not provided by the system, they would have to be borrowed elsewhere.
4. There is a difference between debt service costs and social insurance costs. Different segments of the population and different generations are involved.
5. Long-range social insurance policy should not be sacrificed to other short-run political and economic considerations.
6. If a small trust fund is accumulated, the cost is deceptively low. This is much more likely to lead to extravagant benefits than is a large fund.[17]

16 There were still hopes in 1938 that it could be eliminated.
17 James S. Parker, "Financial Policy in Old Age and Survivors Insurance, 1935–50," *Social Security Bulletin*, XIV, No. 6 (June, 1951), 3–10. This list of arguments and much of the discussion herein on the trust fund are based upon this article.

At the same time that the tax schedule was being debated, a much more liberal benefit schedule was being studied, and it was being recommended that the government contribute to the cost. It was argued that the government should bear at least part of the cost for those who would contribute for only a few years before retiring, since it was held to be unfair to tax the younger employees to pay for these benefits. It was also argued that the inclusion of these retirants would reduce the social assistance programs supported out of general revenues, thus lessening the financial burden of the federal government.

The intent of the actual changes in the financial provisions of the law are not clear. Political and immediate economic problems forced postponement of the scheduled tax increase in 1940, but no increase was recommended in later years to make up for this reduction. The trust fund's progress was slowed down significantly, particularly since the benefits were liberalized considerably. On the other hand, the federal government did not pledge itself to participate in the program. It was at this time that the Board of Trustees was asked to report immediately when the fund was unduly low or exceeded the maximum established by the "rule of three." This appeared to set a maximum limit on the fund, but the maximum was exceeded almost immediately and Congress did nothing except to continue postponing tax increases until 1947 when a stop-gap measure was enacted. The tax freezes were strongly opposed by the Commissioner of the Social Security Administration who argued that the immediate economic problems of the 1930's no longer existed.

The result of the freezes was that a larger share of the financial burden was passed on to future social security taxpayers. It also became apparent that the tax schedule was not sufficient to make the system self-supporting, and the Revenue Act of 1943 authorized Congress to make direct appropriations when necessary to finance the benefits provided.

In 1950 Congress reversed itself and declared that the system was to be self-supporting. It adopted a new higher tax schedule, and the tax increase scheduled for 1954 became a reality. The benefit increases in 1954 were accompanied by an even higher tax structure. The 1956 disability benefits are paid out of a separate fund. As a result the trust fund today is not as great as intended in 1935, but it is more than a contingency fund and, according to Congress, should be sufficient with future taxes to pay all benefits and expenses.

OPERATIONAL DATA

Old-Age and Survivors Insurance is, by far, the most important insurance operation in the country. In December, 1955, the civilian labor force was estimated at 66.6 million, of which only 2.4 million were unemployed. Out of the 64.2 million employed, it is estimated that 53.1 million were engaged in covered employment. Over 66 million persons worked in covered employment sometime during 1955. Seventy-one million people had already achieved fully insured or currently insured status, and millions of nonworkers are entitled to benefits as dependents of covered workers.

The increases in the number of insured living workers, the number of workers with taxable earnings, the number of new entrants, the amount of taxable earnings, the average taxable earnings per employee, and the number of employers reporting taxable wages are indicated in Table 4.6. All of the "sudden changes" appearing in the table can be attributed to amendments to the Social Security

TABLE 4.6

OLD-AGE AND SURVIVORS INSURANCE: INSURED LIVING WORKERS, NEW ENTRANTS, WORKERS WITH TAXABLE EARNINGS, TAXABLE EARNINGS, AND EMPLOYERS REPORTING TAXABLE EARNINGS, 1937–55

Year	Living workers at beginning of following year (in thousands) Insured	Uninsured	New entrants (in thousands)	Workers with taxable earnings during year (in thousands)	Taxable Earnings Total (in millions)	Average per worker	Employers reporting taxable wages (in thousands)
1937	——	——	32,904	32,904	$ 29,615	$ 900	2,421
1938	——	——	3,930	31,822	26,502	833	2,239
1939	22,900	17,800	4,450	33,751	29,745	881	2,366
1940	24,900	20,000	4,430	35,393	32,974	932	2,500
1941	27,500	23,500	6,436	40,976	41,848	1,021	2,646
1942	31,200	27,300	7,965	46,363	52,939	1,142	2,655
1943	34,900	30,500	7,337	47,656	62,423	1,310	2,394
1944	38,600	30,900	4,691	46,296	64,426	1,392	2,369
1945	40,300	32,100	3,477	46,392	62,945	1,357	2,614
1946	41,800	33,200	3,078	48,845	69,088	1,414	3,017
1947	43,400	33,700	2,685	48,908	78,372	1,602	3,246
1948	44,800	34,400	2,635	49,018	84,122	1,716	3,298
1949	45,700	34,900	1,958	46,796	81,808	1,748	3,316
1950	59,800	22,600	2,520	48,283	87,498	1,812	3,345
1951	62,800	25,100	6,170	58,100	121,060	2,084	4,440
1952*	68,200	22,700	3,800	59,600	128,700	2,160	4,450
1953*	71,000	22,500	3,400	61,000	136,000	2,230	4,350
1954*	70,900	24,300	2,500	60,000	134,000	2,230	4,350
1955*	71,300	28,600	6,000	66,000	159,000	2,400	5,000

* Preliminary estimates.

Source: Social Security Bulletin, Annual Statistical Supplement, 1955, p. 15.

Act and to the impacts of World War II. The effect of the 1950 amendments is the most noticeable. Steady increases in wage levels have also been partly responsible for an increase in the average taxable earnings per worker.

Information on changes in the status of the living insured workers is provided in Table 4.7. The number of fully insured persons relative to the total number of insured persons has always been at least 85 per cent, but the 100 per cent and near 100 per cent ratios of the past five years are temporary phenomena created by the 1950 "new start," and special eligibility rules in 1954 and 1956. The number of persons with only currently insured status will increase in the future. Furthermore, the percentage of fully insured persons who have a permanently insured status will increase as a larger number of persons accumulate at least forty quarters of coverage or quarters of coverage equal to one-half the number of quarters between December 31, 1950, and the quarter in which they either reached or expect to reach age sixty-five.

The number of persons receiving monthly benefits at the end of each year since 1940 and the total monthly benefits that they were receiving are shown in Table 4.8. The data are also classified

TABLE 4.7

LIVING WORKERS INSURED UNDER OASI, BY INSURANCE STATUS, 1940–56
(In Millions)

Beginning of year	Total insured	Fully Insured			Currently insured only
		Total	Permanently insured	Not permanently insured	
1940	22.9	22.9	0.6	22.3	( )
1941	24.9	24.2	1.1	23.1	0.7
1942	27.5	25.8	1.4	24.4	1.7
1943	31.2	28.1	1.8	26.3	3.1
1944	34.9	29.9	2.3	27.6	5.0
1945	38.6	31.9	2.8	29.1	6.7
1946	40.3	33.4	3.4	30.0	6.9
1947	41.8	35.4	8.6	26.8	6.4
1948	43.4	37.3	11.6	25.7	6.1
1949	44.8	38.9	13.2	25.7	5.9
1950	45.7	40.1	14.9	25.2	5.6
1951	59.8	59.8	21.0	38.8	( )
1952	62.8	62.8	22.9	39.9	( )
1953	68.2	68.2	25.4	42.8	( )
1954	71.0	71.0	27.4	43.6	( )
1955	70.9	70.3	29.6	40.7	0.6
1956	71.3	70.1	32.0	38.1	1.2

Source: *Social Security Bulletin, Annual Statistical Supplement,* 1955, p. 18.

TABLE 4.8

OLD-AGE AND SURVIVORS INSURANCE: NUMBER OF BENEFICIARIES AT END OF YEAR AND MONTHLY BENEFITS RECEIVED, BY TYPE OF BENEFITS, 1940–55

(Numbers and Amounts in Thousands)

Year	Total		Old-age		Wife's or Husband's		Child's		Widow's or Widower's		Mother's		Parent's	
	Number	Amount	Number	Amount	Number	Amount	Number	Amount	Number	Amount	Number	Amount	Number	Amount
1940	222	$ 4,070	112	$ 2,539	30	$ 361	55	$ 668	4	$ 90	20	$ 402	1	$ 11
1941	434	7,815	200	4,539	57	691	117	1,432	15	302	42	826	2	26
1942	598	10,782	260	5,989	77	941	173	2,112	29	577	57	1,124	3	39
1943	748	13,510	306	7,171	92	1,151	229	2,822	46	930	70	1,384	4	52
1944	955	17,344	378	8,980	116	1,460	298	3,691	68	1,367	90	1,781	5	65
1945	1,288	23,801	518	12,538	159	2,040	390	4,858	94	1,893	121	2,391	6	81
1946	1,642	31,081	702	17,230	216	2,805	462	5,804	127	2,568	128	2,577	7	97
1947	1,978	38,277	875	21,779	269	3,545	525	6,702	164	3,352	135	2,764	10	135
1948	2,315	45,872	1,048	26,564	321	4,307	581	7,549	210	4,331	142	2,959	12	162
1949	2,743	56,074	1,286	33,437	391	5,376	639	8,427	261	5,442	152	3,207	13	185
1950	3,477	126,857	1,771	77,678	508	11,995	700	19,366	314	11,481	169	5,801	15	535
1951	4,379	154,791	2,278	96,008	647	14,710	846	22,739	384	13,849	204	6,776	19	709
1952	5,026	205,179	2,644	130,217	738	19,178	939	28,141	455	18,482	299	8,273	21	887
1953	5,981	253,792	3,222	164,659	888	24,017	1,053	32,517	541	22,096	254	9,517	24	986
1954	6,886	339,342	3,775	223,272	1,016	32,271	1,161	40,996	638	29,526	272	12,089	25	1,189
1955	7,961	411,613	4,474	276,942	1,192	39,416	1,276	46,444	701	34,152	292	13,403	25	1,257

Source: *Social Security Bulletin, Annual Statistical Supplement,* 1955, p. 29.

by type of benefit. The increase in the number of beneficiaries and
monthly benefits for each type of benefit and for all benefits combined is the most important fact revealed by the table. The retirement beneficiaries and benefits have become a more important part
of the total beneficiaries and benefits as the number of persons
becoming eligible for these benefits has increased. The mother's
benefit and the child's benefit have become less important, partly
because of lower mortality rates at the younger ages and partly
because death benefit rolls reach maturity quickly.

Table 4.9 shows how improved benefits and rising wages have
increased the average monthly benefit of each type.

TABLE 4.9

AVERAGE OASI MONTHLY BENEFIT BEING RECEIVED AT END OF YEAR,
BY TYPE OF BENEFIT, 1940–55

Year	All Benefits	Old-age	Wife's or Husband's	Child's	Widow's or Widower's	Mother's	Parents
1940	$18.29	$22.60	$12.13	$12.22	$20.28	$19.61	$13*
1942	18.02	23.02	12.28	12.24	20.15	19.57	13*
1944	18.16	13.73	12.63	12.38	20.16	19.80	13*
1946	18.93	24.55	12.99	12.57	20.21	20.07	13*
1948	19.82	25.35	13.42	12.99	20.60	20.81	14*
1950	36.48	43.86	23.60	27.68	36.54	34.24	36.70
1952	40.83	49.25	25.99	29.98	40.66	36.13	41.33
1954	49.28	59.14	31.77	35.32	46.27	44.52	47.25
1955	51.70	61.90	33.07	36.40	48.72	45.90	50.24

* Rounded to two significant digits.

Source: Based on Table 4.8.

Although the number and amount of OASI benefits have continually increased, certain individuals have had their benefits withheld or terminated. About 300,000 benefits were being withheld
on December 31, 1955. The reason for withholding over 90 per
cent of these benefits was the employment or self-employment of
the beneficiary or an old-age beneficiary on whose earnings the
benefit was based. Over 550,000 benefits were terminated in 1954.
As would be expected, death was the most important cause of termination, except in the case of the children's and mother's benefit,
where attainment of age eighteen by the child was the most important reason. Another important reason for the loss of the
mother's benefit was remarriage.[18]

The growth of the OASI Trust Fund since 1937 is shown in Table
4.10. Social security taxes, transfers from the Railroad Retirement

[18] *Social Security Bulletin, Annual Statistical Supplement,* 1955, pp. 34–35.

Act, appropriations by Congress to cover benefits paid to veterans, and interest on investments have exceeded the benefits and administrative expenses every year. At the end of 1955, the fund consisted of $561 million in cash, $2.4 billion in regular government bonds, and $18.7 billion in special certificates of indebtedness.

TABLE 4.10

RECEIPTS, EXPENDITURES, AND ASSETS OF OASI TRUST FUND, 1937–56

(in thousands)

| Fiscal year | Receipts | | Expenditures | | Total assets |
	Net contribution income and transfers	Interest	Benefit payments	Administrative expenses	
1936–37	$ 265,000	$ 2,262	$ 27	$ ———	$ 267,235
1937–38	387,000	15,412	5,404	———	777,243
1938–39	503,000	26,951	13,892	———	1,180,302
1939–40	550,000	42,489	15,805	12,288	1,744,698
1940–41	688,141	55,958	64,342	26,840	2,397,615
1941–42	895,619	71,007	110,281	26,766	3,227,194
1942–43	1,130,495	87,403	149,304	27,492	4,268,296
1943–44	1,292,122	103,177	184,597	32,607	5,446,391
1944–45	1,309,919	123,584	239,834	26,950	6,613,381
1945–46	1,238,218	147,766	320,510	37,427	7,641,428
1946–47	1,459,867	163,466	425,582	40,788	8,798,390
1947–48	1,616,862	190,562	511,676	47,457	10,046,681
1948–49	1,693,575	230,194	607,036	53,465	11,309,949
1949–50	2,109,992	256,778	727,266	56,841	12,892,612
1950–51	3,124,098	287,392	1,498,088	70,447	14,735,567
1951–52	3,597,982	333,514	1,982,377	84,649	16,600,036
1952–53	4,096,602	386,640	2,627,492	89,429	18,366,356
1953–54	4,589,182	450,504	3,275,556	88,636	20,042,615
1954–55	5,086,154	447,580	4,333,147	103,202	21,140,643
1955–56*	6,442,326	494,889	5,360,813	124,339	22,593,064

* Preliminary data.

Source: *Social Security Bulletin,* XIX, No. 9 (September, 1956), p. 28.

Actuaries of the Social Security Administration periodically prepare actuarial estimates of the progress of the fund. The estimate prepared in 1954 on the assumption that the 1954 benefit schedule and tax schedule would remain in effect is summarized in Table 4.11.[19] While the schedule *has* changed, it will be instructive to examine the actuarial principles applied.

[19] See Robert J. Myers and Eugene A. Rasor, "Long Range Cost Estimates for Old-Age and Survivors Insurance," *Actuarial Study No. 39* (U. S. Department of Health, Education, and Welfare, 1954). For more recent data see Robert J. Myers, "Old-Age and Survivors Insurance: Financing Basis and Policy Under 1956 Amendments," *Social Security Bulletin,* XIX, No. 9 (September, 1956), pp. 16–20.

TABLE 4.11
Estimated Progress of OASI Trust Fund,
Assuming 2.4 Per Cent Interest
(in thousands)

Cal-endar year	Receipts		Expenditures		Assets at end of year
	Net contribution income and transfers	Interest	Benefit payments	Administrative expenses	
Low-cost Estimate					
1955	$ 5,939	$ 519	$ 4,495	$101	$ 22,798
1960	7,807	672	6,822	117	29,126
1970	12,526	1,061	10,654	145	46,115
1980	16,245	1,870	14,335	173	80,649
1990	17,734	2,607	17,398	199	111,309
2000	19,740	3,413	18,559	217	146,087
2025	24,175	6,801	25,272	280	289,476
2050	29,418	11,662	30,151	337	497,053
High-cost Estimate					
1955	$ 5,906	$ 512	$ 4,984	$127	$ 22,243
1960	7,736	568	7,736	153	24,139
1970	12,393	564	12,097	193	24,112
1980	13,819	722	16,235	232	30,497
1990	16,615	380	19,752	268	14,510
2000	17,753	——	21,470	289 (Fund exhausted in 1995)	
Intermediate-cost Estimate					
1955	$ 5,922	$ 516	$ 4,740	$114	$ 22,520
1960	7,772	620	7,279	135	26,623
1970	12,460	812	11,377	169	35,114
1980	16,032	1,296	15,285	202	55,573
1990	17,174	1,494	18,574	234	62,910
2000	18,747	1,436	20,014	253	60,494
2025	21,336	294	27,391	320	9,354
2050	24,293	——	29,918	352 (Fund exhausted in 2027)	

Source: Robert J. Myers and Eugene A. Rasor, "Long Range Cost Estimates for Old Age and Survivors Insurance," *Actuarial Study No. 39* (U. S. Department of Health, Education, and Welfare, 1954), p. 40.

Note that there are three estimates—a low-cost estimate, a high-cost estimate, and an intermediate-cost estimate. Under the low-cost estimate, the trust fund would continually increase, while under the high-cost estimate the fund would be exhausted in 1995. Under the intermediate-cost estimate, which is simply the mid-point between the high- and low-cost estimates, the fund would be exhausted in 2027. If the trust fund should be exhausted at some future date, Congress would have to raise the social security payroll tax or appropriate general revenue funds to help pay the benefits, but Congress has not committed itself to do the latter.

Under the low-cost estimate, the benefit payments were expected to increase to 7.89 per cent of payroll by 2050. Under the high-cost estimate, the figure was 11.92 per cent, and under the intermediate-cost estimate, 9.48 per cent.[20] These rates were assumed to be ultimate in the estimate. If OASI were operated on a pay-as-you-go basis, these rates approximate the tax that would be required to pay the benefits.

The actuaries also estimate periodically the level payroll tax (called the level premium rate) that would have to be paid annually if the system were to operate indefinitely and remain self-supporting. Table 4.12 shows the estimated level premium rates under the low-, high-, and intermediate-cost assumptions for interest rates of 2.25 per cent, 2.4 per cent—the present earnings rate (2.6 per cent after the 1956 amendments) of the trust fund—and 2.5 per cent.

The level premium expressed as a per cent of payroll is equal to the present value of future benefit payments and administrative expenses expressed as a per cent of the present value of future taxable payrolls less the balance in the trust fund expressed as a per cent of the present value of future taxable payrolls. Because self-employed persons pay only 75 per cent of the amount contributed by employers and employees, the level premium rate for the employer and employee combined is higher than the result of this computation.

Note that under the low-cost estimate, the present contribution rate exceeded the required rate, but the opposite was true under the high- and intermediate-cost estimates. According to the intermediate-cost, 2.4 per cent interest estimate, the required combined rate was 7.70 per cent, while the combined level premium rate under the current schedule was 7.23 per cent. This annual shortage of .47 per cent of payroll would exhaust the fund by 2027 if the assumptions turned out to be correct.

The assumptions made in these estimates involve many factors such as mortality rates, birth rates, immigration, total employment and the proportion acquiring quarters of coverage, marital and parental status, remarriage rates, and interest rates. Consequently the estimates are crude and new estimates must be made periodically. The operating question is whether the estimated required rate is reasonably close to the actual rate.

It should be re-emphasized that even if the assumptions were correct, the adoption of a 7.53 per cent level premium rate would

20 *Ibid.*, p. 38.

TABLE 4.12

ESTIMATED LEVEL PREMIUM RATES IN PERPETUITY UNDER THE
OASI SYSTEM, 1954

Present value of	Per cent of present value of future taxable payrolls		
	Low-cost estimate	High-cost estimate	Intermediate-cost estimate
Interest at 2.25%			
Benefit payments	6.73%	8.68%	7.63%
Administrative costs	.08	.12	.10
Trust Fund at end of 1954	.19	.22	.20
Level-premiums	6.62	8.58	7.53
Combined employer-employee level premiums	6.89	8.91	7.82
Present employer-employee level premiums	7.32	7.22	7.28
Interest at 2.4%			
Benefit payments	6.67	8.53	7.53
Administrative costs	.08	.12	.10
Trust Fund at end of 1954	.21	.24	.22
Level-premiums	6.54	8.41	7.41
Combined employer-employee level premiums	6.80	8.75	7.70
Present employer-employee level premiums	7.28	7.17	7.23
Interest at 2.5%			
Benefit payments	6.62	8.44	7.47
Administrative costs	.08	.12	.10
Trust Fund at end of 1954	.22	.25	.23
Level-premiums	6.48	8.31	7.34
Combined employer-employee level premiums	6.74	8.64	7.62
Present employer-employee level premiums	7.24	7.14	7.19

Source: Robert J. Myers and Eugene A. Rasor, "Long Range Cost Estimates for Old-Age and Survivors Insurance," *Actuarial Study No. 39* (U. S. Department of Health, Education, and Welfare, 1954), p. 41.

not have made it possible to terminate OASI, continue payments to current benefit recipients, and make proportional payments to other contributors. The assumption of an indefinite operation is crucial, for the level premium rate is computed on the assumption that there are only the following two objectives: first, all contributors should pay the normal rate which is the level premium rate sufficient to pay the costs for new entrants into the system; second, the deficiency in the trust fund due to the accrued liability not covered by the trust fund must not increase. This deficiency arises because present and former members of OASI have not and will not (at the normal rate) pay for the benefits they receive. If they had, the trust fund and the interest income from the investments in the fund would be larger, thus reducing the required level premium rate.

Payment of the interest on the deficiency in the fund is essential if the deficiency is not to increase. However, the deficiency will not and need not be eliminated as long as the system is expected to operate indefinitely. According to the intermediate-cost, 2.25 per cent interest assumption, the 7.53 per cent level premium rate consisted of a 5 per cent normal rate and a 2.53 per cent interest charge on the unfunded accrued liability. In other words, a 5 per cent tax would be sufficient to make the system self-supporting if there were no unfunded accrued liability and the underlying assumptions were correct.

It should also be emphasized that if OASI had been terminated at the end of 1954, the trust fund of $21 billion would not have been sufficient to pay the $34 billion present value of benefits to current recipients. However, since it is not expected that the system will stop operating, this is an academic issue.

Effect of OASI on Public Assistance Programs

The Social Security Act provided for a social insurance program at the federal level and for grants-in-aid for public assistance programs at the state level. It was felt that the importance of the public assistance programs would decline as the number of persons attaining insured status under OASI increased. Actually the number of persons receiving old-age assistance and aid to dependent children has increased since the early thirties, although the number of old-age recipients has decreased since 1950.

The increase in the number of persons receiving old-age assistance is due primarily to the rapidly increasing aged population and the many exclusions under OASI during the first fifteen years of its operations. The increasing number of persons receiving aid-to-dependent-children benefits is due primarily to a change in the principal cause of dependency from death of the father to absence of the father, usually because of marital difficulties.

In spite of their continued importance, the public assistance programs have been affected considerably by OASI. They would have been more important if there had been no OASI. Figure 4.1 shows a steady increase in the proportion of the aged population receiving

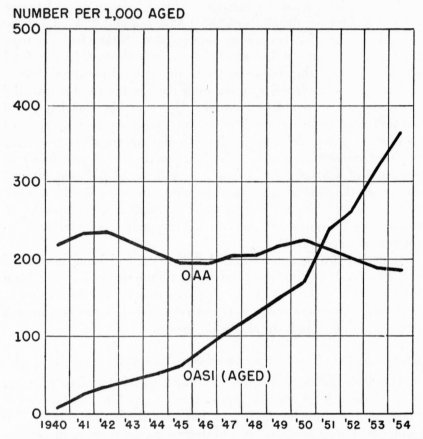

NUMBER PER 1,000 AGED

Average monthly number of beneficiaries and recipients, by years, per 1,000 persons aged 65 and over in the population.

Fig. 4.1. Growth in Social Insurance Protection for the Aged

Source: U. S. Department of Health, Education, and Welfare, *Annual Report* (Washington, D. C.: U. S. Government Printing Office, 1954), p. 45.

OASI retirement benefits, while the proportion of the aged population receiving old-age assistance benefits is less now than it was in 1940. The proportion currently receiving OASI benefits is almost twice the proportion receiving old-age assistance benefits.

Figure 4.2 shows that the OASI program is much more important than the aid-to-dependent-children programs when the cause of dependency is death. In fact, there is a decline in the *number* of children receiving public assistance payments because the father has died. In the future, OASI will have greater effects on both public assistance programs.

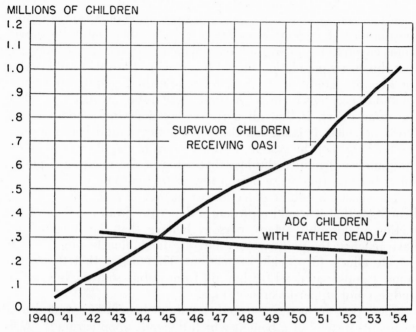

MILLIONS OF CHILDREN

¹ Data available only for October 1942, June 1948, and November 1953.

Fig. 4.2. Number of Children Receiving Aid to Dependent Children with Father Dead, and Number of Survivor Children Receiving Old-Age and Survivors Insurance, 1950–1954

Source: U. S. Department of Health, Education, and Welfare, *Annual Report* (Washington, D. C.: U. S. Government Printing Office, 1954), p. 47.

EVALUATION

The Federal Old-Age and Survivors Insurance System provides a floor of protection on a quasi-contractual basis. The system has apparently not reduced individual efforts to protect families against the problems created by death and old age. In fact, the commercial insurance industry has been stimulated, rather than hindered, by OASI.

The OASI program pays benefits which are related to the earnings record and presumptive need, while the taxes are collected on a relative ability-to-pay basis. The benefits are a larger proportion of low incomes and are directly related to the number of dependents, while the tax varies directly with the wage up to $4,200. The objective of a protective floor makes it impossible to relate the benefits entirely to the taxes paid because the lower income groups could not afford the actuarial cost of their benefits.

The current program covers most occupations and will probably eventually cover all occupations. This extension of coverage reduces the number of persons who lose their eligibility status by moving from covered to uncovered employment. It has been suggested that the *entire* population should be covered, but this would destroy the idea of a contributory system because the benefits could not be related to earnings records. A similar suggestion, which would have the same effect, is that all currently aged persons should receive OASI benefits. It is argued that such action would better indicate the final costs of the system, lower the cost of the old-age assistance programs, and reduce the loss that some of the uncovered persons suffer because they were born a few years too soon.

The most important objection to further liberalization of OASI benefits is that it would represent a departure from the floor of protection philosophy. Many persons believe that the benefit levels have reached the point where they are beginning to interfere with private efforts to provide protection. They argue that the low-income groups may need further aid from public sources, but not the middle- and upper-income groups.

Some persons have suggested that a flat benefit be granted to all recipients instead of a benefit which depends upon earnings. A flat benefit would reduce administrative costs and improve the relative position of low-income groups. However, a flat benefit would probably not appeal to most Americans, who prefer some relationship between contributions and benefits. In fact, some persons strongly believe that the present relationship is too weak.

The earnings limitation has been continually increased and there are many who favor its removal. For example, certain professional men, such as doctors, feel that this limitation will stop them from receiving any retirement benefits until they are seventy-two years of age. Others argue that the aged should not be discouraged from working, since their productive capacity will be needed as they become a larger proportion of the total population. On the other hand, a high earnings limitation (or conversely none at all) is not in keeping with the floor of protection philosophy. The removal of the earnings clause would also increase substantially the cost of the program. These issues are discussed more fully in Chapter 14.

Many persons favor the extension of OASI to presently uncovered occupations, an increase in the benefit levels for the low-income groups, and an increase in the earnings limit. These changes would reduce the problems created by "in and out" employment, improve the position of the low-income groups without destroying the floor of protection concept, and encourage the aged to continue working, but at a reduced pace.

Since OASI benefits the entire population directly or indirectly and the vast majority are affected directly, it has been argued that the government should pay the entire cost of the program out of general tax revenues. As a result, the high-income groups would bear a larger share of the cost of the program than they do at present. However, the direct benefits of the program are so much more important than the indirect benefits that it does not seem equitable to tax those persons who are not participants. Furthermore, an earmarked payroll is superior to a general revenue tax in that it emphasizes the cost of the benefits and supports the contributory principle. Chapter 14 further analyzes these matters, along with other economic issues.

A much stronger argument can be made for using a government contribution to pay the interest on the unfunded accrued liability, thus reducing the payroll tax to that which would be necessary if the system were to begin operations now. The cost of benefits for new entrants would still be emphasized and the contributory principle would remain intact. The sole question is whether it is more equitable to distribute the interest costs among the participants and their employers through payroll taxes or among the total population through progressive federal income taxes.

The advantages and disadvantages of a sizable trust fund have been discussed on pages 98-100. Many persons would be opposed to a strict pay-as-you-go plan because the tax burden of future generations would be too great. On the other hand, a large trust fund may lead to an unwarranted liberalization of benefits, essentially on political grounds. Therefore, the present arrangement appears to be a reasonable compromise position.

It should be pointed out, however, that reducing the tax burden of future generations through a trust fund is not the only objective of rational economic security programming. If the payroll tax is lower in 2010 than it would have been without a trust fund, but there are no more goods and services than they would have had under a pay-as-you-go plan, the sole effect of the trust fund would be to improve slightly the position of the taxpayer relative to that of OASI beneficiaries. A trust fund makes a real contribution to the economic welfare of future taxpayers only if it transfers funds from current consumption to investment, thus increasing production in the future. How effective the trust fund has been in this respect is a matter of conjecture.

The administration of the system is highly mechanized and efficiently conducted. Administrative expenses in 1955 were only 2.3 per cent of the benefits paid and the trend is downward. This excellent record may be due in part to the nondiscretionary aspects of the program, but the federal civil service program is also contributory.

Economic implications of the program will be analyzed in greater detail in Chapter 14. The discussion now turns to private approaches to the economic problems of old age and premature death as they provide supplements to the floor of protection afforded by the Social Security System.

Summary

The Social Security Act, which, among other contributions to economic security, created the first extensive public programs dealing with the economic problems of death and old age, was an outgrowth of the Depression.

Under the Act, the federal government makes grants-in-aid to states having public assistance programs for the needy aged and needy dependent children. To be eligible for federal support, the programs must meet certain minimum standards, but the state and local governments are responsible for the detailed provisions and the administration of the programs.

Old-Age and Survivors Insurance is the social insurance program established under the Social Security Act. Unlike the public assistance programs, OASI is entirely federally supported and federally administered.

To be eligible for OASI benefits, a person must be fully insured or currently insured. In general, a person must be fully insured to qualify for retirement benefits, but either a fully insured or currently insured person qualifies for death benefits.

The basic benefit is a retirement benefit for the insured person at age sixty-five. The benefit formula is a compromise between the desire to provide a floor of protection for all families and the desire to preserve some relationship between taxable earnings and benefits.

The benefits for the dependents of a retired worker are a life income to the wife after age sixty-two, income to a mother until her youngest child is age eighteen, income until age eighteen for children, and a life income to the husband of a retired female worker after age sixty-five.

The death benefits are a life income for a widower after age sixty-five, a life income to a widow after age sixty-two, income to a mother until her youngest child reaches age eighteen, a life income to parents after age sixty-five, and a lump-sum death benefit.

The most important reason for suspending the benefits is annual earnings by a beneficiary in excess of $1,200.

OASI benefits are financed entirely by a payroll tax paid by the worker and his employer. The present tax rate on each is 2¼ per cent. Self-employed persons pay 3⅜ per cent. Tax rates are scheduled to increase approximately every five years until 1975, although, of course, this schedule can change as in the past.

The most important liberalizations of OASI since its introduction in 1935 have been the addition of the survivorship benefits, the extension of coverage to more employments, the reduction of the eligibility requirements, and increases in all benefit amounts.

Arguments over the purpose and desirability of the trust fund have been frequent, extensive, and continuing.

OASI has not replaced the special public assistance programs, but it has reduced their relative importance.

Suggestions for Additional Reading

BROWN, J. DOUGLAS. "Concepts in Old Age and Survivors Insurance," *Proceedings* of the Industrial Relations Research Association, 1948. Pp. 100–06.
A concise description of the principles underlying the OASI program in 1948.

CHAMBER OF COMMERCE OF THE UNITED STATES. *Improving Social Security.* Washington, D. C., 1953.
One point of view on how our social security program could be improved. One of the suggestions is that OASI be financed on a pay-as-you-go basis.

COMMERCE CLEARING HOUSE, INC. *Explanation of Social Security Law as Amended in 1956.* Chicago: Commerce Clearing House, Inc., 1956.
A detailed explanation of the Social Security Act as amended in 1956.

CORSON, JOHN J. and JOHN W. McCONNELL. *Economic Needs of Older People.* New York: The Twentieth Century Fund, 1956.
Chapters 6 through 8 present an analysis of both old age assistance and social insurance for the aged. Chapters 9 through 11 present useful data on private pension plans.

MERIAM, IDA C. *Social Security Financing.* (Bureau Report No. 17.) Washington, D. C.: Federal Security Agency, Social Security Administration, 1952.
The various ways in which social security programs can be financed are discussed in this report.

Report to the President of the Committee on Economic Security. Washington, D. C.: U. S. Government Printing Office, 1935.
The committee report which led to the passage of the original Social Security Act.

U. S. Congress, 84th, Second Session, Senate, Hearings Before the Finance Committee. *Social Security Amendments of 1955.* Washington, D. C.: U. S. Government Printing Office, 1956.

Hearings on the 1956 amendments to the Social Security Act.

U. S. Department of Health, Education, and Welfare. *Annual Report.* Washington, D. C.: U. S. Government Printing Office, 1955.

The annual reports of the Department comment on the current operations of the special state public assistance programs and OASI.

5

Private Approaches:
Death and Old Age

Introduction

Social insurance provides a floor of protection against financial problems caused by premature death and old age. The coverage is extended on a compulsory basis and the benefits are paid for through taxes. Social insurance does not, and should not, provide complete protection against these problems, for it is generally agreed that the complete elimination of individual responsibility would affect adversely the moral and mental fiber of our population. Therefore, the individual who wants more than a floor of protection must supplement social insurance with private alleviative methods.

Private methods of alleviating the financial losses caused by premature death and old age were discussed in Chapter 3. Private insurance, which is the most important of these methods, is the subject of this chapter.

We shall first consider individual life insurance and annuity contracts issued by commercial insurers. The nature and uses of the basic types of contracts and some important special contracts will be discussed. The possible stumbling block of uninsurability will also be considered.

The second part of the chapter deals with group life insurance and group pension plans. Group life insurance is primarily underwritten by commercial insurers, but group pension plans are commonly underwritten by both commercial insurers and employers or unions. We shall trace the historical development of group insurance, note its distinctive features and contributions to economic security, and discuss the benefits provided under group pension plans.

Individual Insurance

Most of the private insurance in force today is purchased by persons acting as individuals. The responsibility for purchasing the insurance and paying the premiums is almost always the insured's. Ideally the protection is tailor-made to meet the insured's needs and desires.

TYPES OF LIFE INSURANCE CONTRACTS

The individual insurance contracts may protect the insured or his dependents against financial losses caused by premature death, old age, or both.

Term insurance is the simplest form of life insurance. If the insured dies during the term of the policy, the face amount of the policy is paid to his beneficiary. If he does not die, the insurer pays nothing. The period of a term insurance policy may be any number of years such as one year, five years, ten years, twenty years, or the years to age sixty-five.

Because there is no savings element in the term policy, the premium is relatively low. For this reason, term insurance is an excellent temporary form of protection against premature death. For example, term insurance may be purchased so as to complete the payments on a mortgage were the insured to die before the mortgage has been paid off. A person who will be currently insured under OASI in a few months may purchase term insurance to protect his family in the interim. A young man with excellent prospects but little current income may purchase term insurance to protect his family in the early years of marriage.

One of the major disadvantages of term insurance is that the protection terminates at the end of the period. This would not be important in the first and second examples cited above, but it would be extremely important in the third example because the need for protection continues and the insured may become uninsurable before the end of the term. However, term insurance policies are available which are renewable at least once without evidence of insurability. Each time the policy is renewed, the premium is increased because the probability of death increases. The premiums charged by one nonparticipating life insurer[1] for its five-year renewable term insurance contracts are presented in Table 5.1. At the advanced ages, the premiums are so high that the policy will probably be dropped or at least reduced. However, if the term insurance is also convertible, it may be converted within a specified period to a "permanent" contract as of the original date of issue or at the attained age.

TABLE 5.1

ANNUAL PREMIUMS CHARGED BY ONE NONPARTICIPATING LIFE INSURER
FOR FIVE-YEAR RENEWABLE TERM INSURANCE

Age	Premium per $1,000	Age	Premium per $1,000
20	$5.97	45	$12.11
25	6.10	50	17.20
30	6.55	55	24.89
35	7.44	60	35.11
40	9.16		

The basic permanent contracts are *the straight life contract, the limited payment life contract, and the endowment contract.* Under the first two contracts, the insurer promises to pay the face amount when the insured dies. The two contracts differ from one another in that under the straight life contract the insured pays premiums until death, while under the limited payment life contract the insured pays premiums until death or until the expiration of a stated period, if earlier. Examples of limited payment contracts are twenty-payment, thirty-payment, and paid-up at sixty-five contracts. Under an endowment contract the insurer promises to pay the face amount immediately if the insured dies within the endowment period *or* at the end of the period if the insured is still living. Examples of endowment contracts are twenty-year endowments, thirty-year endowments, and endowments at age sixty. Premiums charged for principal permanent contracts by the same nonparticipating insurer

[1] About two-thirds of the life insurance in force is written by mutual insurers, while about one-sixth of the insurance issued by stock insurers is written on a participating basis. This means that under about 70 per cent of the life insurance in force, dividends to policyholders must be subtracted from the premiums paid in order to determine the actual cost of continuing the insurance in force.

Participating insurers typically charge a higher initial premium than nonparticipating insurers, but the dividends will determine whether the actual cost of continuing the contract will be more, the same, or less.

Nonparticipating premiums as of 1956 are quoted in this text because they are actual cost figures. A fair illustration of the cost of continuing participating contracts would require dividend estimates as well as a table of the initial premiums.

whose term insurance rates have been quoted in Table 5.1 are presented in Table 5.2.

TABLE 5.2

ANNUAL PREMIUMS CHARGED BY ONE NONPARTICIPATING LIFE INSURER
FOR STRAIGHT LIFE, LIMITED PAYMENT, AND ENDOWMENT CONTRACTS

Age	Type of contract			
	Straight life	Twenty payment	Paid-up at sixty-five	Twenty-year endowment
20	$13.72	$24.63	$14.92	$46.69
25	15.64	27.12	17.53	46.74
30	18.00	29.84	20.96	46.79
35	21.08	33.01	25.45	47.21
40	25.10	36.78	31.86	48.64
50	37.50	47.19	57.14	54.75
60	59.08	66.05	——	70.39

If an insured continues the protection from age twenty-five to age sixty-five, it will cost him $592.80 to protect his family under a $1,000 five-year renewable term insurance policy. The premiums on a straight life policy will total $625.60. However, this comparison is unfair, for possible interest earnings are ignored. If the premiums could have been invested at 2½ per cent interest compounded annually, the true cost of continuing the term protection is $840.16, while the straight life policy will cost him $1,054.18.

On the other hand, there is one very important difference between permanent contracts and term insurance contracts. Under permanent contracts, the insurer accumulates at a guaranteed interest rate the difference between the level premium and the insured's share of the expected death benefits and administrative expenses. This accumulation process accomplishes two objectives. First, the cost of paying death benefits does not increase as rapidly as the mortality rate because the increasing accumulations are part of the face amount paid the beneficiary and the "net amount at risk" (the face amount less the accumulation) decreases. In fact the net premiums (the premiums charged, less the expense charges) plus the interest credited for the year is always more than enough to pay the benefits for that year, less the accumulations credited to the deceaseds. Consequently the accumulations continue to grow.

Second, the insured may claim these accumulations (called nonforfeiture values) at any time. For example, he may elect to retire at age sixty-five and use the accumulations to help finance his retirement. There are usually three nonforfeiture options. The insured may elect to take the accumulations in cash, use them as a single premium to purchase paid-up insurance, or use them as a single premium to purchase extended term insurance. The paid-up insurance is a policy of the same type as the original contract in a reduced amount. The extended term insurance provides the original amount of protection for a limited number of years.[2] For example, under a $1,000 straight life policy issued by one insurer to an insured, aged twenty-five, the insured may at age sixty-five stop paying premiums and obtain $614 in cash, have $807 of insurance protection continued for life, or have $1,000 of insurance protection continued for sixteen years and 321 days.

The amount of the cash value at the end of each policy year depends upon the type of contract, the age at issue, and the actuarial assumptions made by the insurer. Under all permanent contracts, the cash value continues to grow throughout the life of the contract, but the pattern of growth differs by policy type. Under a straight life contract, the cash value grows steadily until it equals the face value at age 100. The cash value must equal the face value at this age, for insurance actuaries have assumed in their premium calculations that no one will live beyond age 100.

Under a limited payment life contract, the cash value grows more rapidly during the premium-paying period because the premiums are higher. The cash value continues to grow at a less rapid pace after the premium-paying period because the interest on the cash value is more than is required to pay the insured's share of the benefits paid to the beneficiaries of the deceaseds. At age 100 the cash value equals the face value for the reason already cited.

Under an endowment contract, the cash value grows very rapidly and equals the face amount at the end of the endowment period. In a sense, the whole life and limited payment life contracts are endowments at age 100.

Thus, in addition to providing protection against financial losses caused by premature death, all permanent contracts help the insured to acquire a retirement fund through a systematic savings plan.

METHODS OF PAYING PROCEEDS

The death proceeds under life insurance contracts are payable in a lump sum or according to some settlement option selected by

[2] If the original contract is an endowment contract, the extended term insurance does not run beyond the maturity date of the original endowment contract. If the cash value is more than the premium required for term insurance to the maturity date, the excess is used to purchase a promise that some reduced amount will be paid to those who live to the maturity date.

the insured or his beneficiary. An increasing number of insurers also permit the insured to select some settlement option if he wishes to surrender the policy for cash before his death.

The four most common settlement options are the following:

1. Interest option. The proceeds are left with the insurer for some specified period and interest payments are made to the beneficiary. The beneficiary may or may not have the right to withdraw part or all of the principal.

2. Fixed amount option. The beneficiary receives a specified monthly income for as many months as the proceeds and the interest on the unpaid balance will afford.

3. Fixed period option. The beneficiary receives for a specified period a monthly income of whatever amount the proceeds and the interest on the unpaid balance will afford.

4. Annuity option. An annuity payable under this option may take one of several forms. It may be a straight life annuity under which the insurer promises to pay the beneficiary a monthly income for life. Usually, however, it is either an instalment refund annuity, a cash refund annuity, or an annuity with a period certain.

Under an instalment refund annuity, the payments are continued during the lifetime of the beneficiary, but if the annuitant should die before the annuity payments have equalled the proceeds, the payments are continued to another beneficiary until this equality is achieved. A cash refund annuity differs from the instalment refund annuity only in that upon death of the beneficiary the difference, if any, between the proceeds and the sum of the monthly payments is paid in cash to another beneficiary. Under an annuity with a period certain, the insurer promises to pay a monthly income for life, but the income is guaranteed for at least a specified period.

For proceeds of a given amount, the monthly income differs depending upon the option selected because of the differences in the guaranteed amounts and the loss of interest for varying periods. The annuities with some guaranteed amounts are a wise choice when dependents survive the beneficiary, but the price is a reduced monthly income for the beneficiary.

A table of settlement options appearing in one insurance contract is reproduced as Table 5.3. These options are useful because they enable the insured to have the proceeds paid in the manner he deems best. He may or may not give the beneficiary the right to change the program he sets up. If the insured does not elect any options, the beneficiary may usually elect them. The options provide a safe investment, with at least a guaranteed rate of interest and no management problems. The present tax code also favors their use.

TABLE 5.3

Settlement Option Values Used by One Insurer

Fixed instalment options		Monthly life income per $1,000 proceeds				
Number of years	Monthly income per $1,000 proceeds	Age		Five years certain	Ten years certain	Fifteen years certain
		Male	Female			
5	$17.70	15	20	$2.79	$2.79	$2.78
10	9.39	25	30	3.05	3.04	3.03
15	6.64	35	40	3.45	3.43	3.41
20	5.27	45	50	4.06	4.02	3.95
25	4.46	55	60	5.03	4.90	4.69
30	3.93	65	70	6.59	6.16	5.56

If the settlement option privilege also applies to cash values, the insured may usually elect a joint and survivorship annuity. This annuity provides a specified income per month during the lifetime of two beneficiaries plus a reduced income during the lifetime of the survivor. For example, a husband and wife may receive $100 a month, with $50 a month being paid to the surviving spouse.

When the settlement options may be applied to both death proceeds and living benefits such as cash values and matured endowments, permanent insurance contracts provide more complete protection against the financial problems associated with both premature death and old age. For example, an insured may purchase a straight life contract to protect his family and at retirement age have the cash value converted into an annuity. When the options may not be applied to living benefits, the only contribution to old-age protection is the accumulation of a retirement fund.

Settlement Options and Planning an Insurance Program

One of the important uses of a table of settlement options is the determination of the amount of insurance which is needed to carry out the desires of the insured. A highly simplified example follows. Assume that a young man, aged thirty, has a wife, aged thirty, and a son, aged three. If this young man were to die today, how much insurance would be required to provide the following benefits for his family?

$2,000 for last illness expenses, taxes, and funeral;
  $200 a month for the widow and child until the child reaches age
      eighteen; and
  $100 a month for life for the widow after the child reaches age
      eighteen.

One way of paying out the life insurance proceeds which would accomplish these objectives is the following:

$2,000 in a lump sum;

    $100 a month according to the settlement option which provides a life annuity with a fifteen-year certain period; and

    $100 a month according to the settlement option which provides a monthly income for fifteen years.

If the settlement option values in Table 5.3 are applicable, the following amounts of insurance will be needed in addition to the $2,000 lump sum:

$$\frac{\$100}{\$3.03} \times \$1,000 = \$33,000, \text{ approximately; and}$$

$$\frac{\$100}{\$6.64} \times \$1,000 = \$15,000, \text{ approximately.}$$

The total is approximately $50,000.

In actual practice the problem is far more complicated and the solution much more thorough. It is necessary to recognize changes through time, retirement needs, tax factors, existing insurance and noninsurance assets, and many other factors. Considerable skill is required in order to construct a satisfactory insurance program. The example, however, illustrates valid insurance planning principles.

Two additional remarks are appropriate here. First, the benefits provided under social insurance programs are usually deducted from the needs of the insured before the private insurance need is determined. This procedure emphasizes the supplementary nature of private insurance. Second, settlement option tables may be used to emphasize the importance of OASI benefits. The mother and son in the example cited could receive as much as $135.70 a month until the child reaches eighteen years of age and the widow $81.40 a month after she reaches age sixty-two. These benefits are equivalent to about $28,000 in private life insurance proceeds.

ANNUITY CONTRACTS

Life insurers issue annuities as separate contracts in addition to those issued under the settlement option provisions. These separate contracts may be classified into two major groups—immediate annuities and deferred annuities. The emphasis in these contracts is upon financial preparation for old age.

Under an immediate annuity, the annuitant pays the insurer a lump sum and receives a monthly income for life under one of the annuity forms discussed in connection with settlement options. The savings may be accumulated through some method other than insurance.

The more common type of annuity is the deferred annuity under which a person normally pays premiums from the issue date to the retirement date, at which time the insurer begins to pay him a monthly income according to the terms of one of the various annuity forms. Under a pure deferred annuity, no benefit is paid if the insured dies prior to reaching retirement age, but few contracts of this type are issued. Usually the premiums are refunded in case of death.

An important recent development is the variable annuity contract. A variable annuity differs from a conventional annuity in that (1) the premiums are usually invested entirely in equities and (2) at the retirement date the insured is promised a fixed number of units each month instead of a fixed number of dollars. The value of the unit fluctuates with the performance of the invested assets. Because the equities tend to rise and fall in value as consumers' prices rise and fall, the variable income tends to provide constant real purchasing power. However, because equities tend to fluctuate more in value than consumers' prices, it is recommended and sometimes required that an equal amount be invested in a conventional annuity. At this writing, only the District of Columbia and West Virginia have authorized the issuance of variable annuities by commercial insurers and only two or three insurers have issued such contracts. In addition, in 1952 New York granted permission to a special insurer which restricts its policies to staff members of colleges, private schools, foundations, and research organizations. This insurer issued the first variable annuity.[3]

Special Life Insurance and Annuity Contracts

Numerous modifications and combinations of term insurance contracts, basic permanent insurance contracts, and annuities are sold by insurers. The reader is referred to any standard text on life insurance for a detailed discussion of these contracts and life insurance in general.[4] However, a few special contracts are so im-

---

[3] For a discussion of the variable annuity concept, see William C. Greenough, "Pensions—Meeting Price Level Changes," *Pensions: Problems and Trends* (Homewood: Richard D. Irwin, Inc., 1955), pp. 138–60.

[4] For example, see S. S. Huebner, *Life Insurance* (4th ed.; New York: Appleton-Century-Crofts, 1950); J. B. Maclean, *Life Insurance* (7th ed.; New York: McGraw-

portant in the search for economic security that they merit a brief description here.

1. Under a *modified life contract*, the protection is for life, but the premium is less in the first three or five years and higher thereafter.

2. A *family income contract* is a straight life contract (or some other permanent contract) plus decreasing term insurance. If the insured dies within some specified family income period, such as ten or twenty years, the insurer will pay a monthly income of usually $10 or $20 per $1,000 of straight life protection until the expiration of the family income period. The face value of the straight life policy is payable at the end of the period. If the insured lives to the end of the family income period, the decreasing term insurance expires and the policy continues as a straight life policy. The family income policy is especially designed for a young man with a family whose need for protection is greatest when his children are young.

3. A *retirement income annuity* is a deferred annuity plus decreasing term insurance. For each $10 of monthly income provided at retirement age by the annuity, there is a promise that $1,000 will be paid to the beneficiary if this amount exceeds the cash value.

4. A *preferred risk policy* is issued in minimum amounts, such as $10,000, and is usually designed for insureds in above average health. The minimum size requirement makes it possible to reduce the premium.

BRANCHES OF INDIVIDUAL INSURANCE

The most important branch of individual insurance sold by commercial insurers is the ordinary insurance branch. These policies are written in amounts of $1,000 or more; premiums are designed to be paid annually but may be paid semi-annually, quarterly, or monthly; and all premiums other than the first are paid directly to the branch or home office of the insurer.

Another branch of commercial life insurance which is declining in relative importance, but which continues to grow, is industrial insurance. "Industrial" policies have provisions which differ slightly from those in ordinary policies and are sometimes written in amounts of $1,000 or less. In most cases, premiums are collected weekly or monthly at the home of the insured. The premiums are higher than the premiums for equivalent ordinary insurance, primarily because of the collection service. This insurance is designed to appeal to low-income groups.

Hill Book Co., Inc., 1951); J. H. Magee, *Life Insurance* (rev. ed.; Chicago: Richard D. Irwin, Inc., 1951); and R. I. Mehr and R. W. Osler, *Modern Life Insurance* (rev. ed.; New York: The Macmillan Co., 1956). For a detailed discussion in a general insurance text see R. Riegel and J. Miller, *Insurance Principles and Practices* (3rd. ed.; Englewood Cliffs, N. J.: Prentice-Hall, Inc., 1947), pp. 85–248.

Contracts similar to those sold by commercial insurers are issued by fraternal societies in all states and by mutual savings banks in Connecticut, Massachusetts, and New York.

INSURANCE IN FORCE, 1910–55

The spectacular growth in the total amount of private individual life insurance, especially during the past decade, and the increasingly important role played by commercial ordinary insurance are illustrated by the data in Table 5.4.

TABLE 5.4

INDIVIDUAL LIFE INSURANCE IN FORCE IN THE UNITED STATES, 1910–1955

(in millions)

Year	Commercial insurance		Fraternals	Mutual savings banks
	Ordinary	Industrial		
1910	$ 11,783	$ 3,125	$ 8,596	$ 1
1915	16,650	4,279	9,444	4
1920	32,022	6,948	10,500	15
1925	52,910	12,318	10,289	38
1930	78,622	17,963	9,539	77
1935	70,710	17,471	6,719.	110
1940	79,408	20,866	6,676	203
1945	101,651	27,675	7,422	331
1950	149,791	33,415	8,811	798
1955	216,000	39,682	10,507	860

Source: Institute of Life Insurance, *Life Insurance Fact Book, 1956*, pp. 8, 89; U. S. Department of Labor, Bureau of Labor Statistics, "Operation of Savings Bank Life Insurance in Massachusetts and New York," *Revision of Bulletin 615*, 1941; Alfred M. Best Co., *Best's Life Insurance Reports* (New York: 1941 and 1946).

Almost all the individual annuity contracts are sold by commercial insurers. The amount of annual income to be provided at maturity date under individual commercial annuity contracts has increased from $375 million in 1935 to about $610 million in 1955.[5] The slow rate of increase compared with the growth of life insurance in force is due in part to the tremendous increase in group annuities to be discussed later.

TYPES OF CONTRACTS IN FORCE

In Table 5.5 the ordinary life insurance contracts in force at the end of 1954 are analyzed according to the type of contract. The basic permanent insurance contracts account for almost 70 per cent

[5] Institute of Life Insurance, *Life Insurance Fact Book, 1956*, p. 30.

of the insurance in force. Clearly, most of the insurance in force is designed to protect the insureds against financial losses caused by both premature death and old age.

TABLE 5.5

ORDINARY LIFE INSURANCE CONTRACTS IN FORCE IN THE
UNITED STATES, BY TYPE OF CONTRACT, 1954
(in millions)

Type of contract	Amount
Term	
Regular	$ 10,000
Decreasing	3,100
Straight life	70,200
Limited payment life	43,200
Endowment	25,100
Family income and similar contracts	
Permanent	15,400
Term	16,100
Retirement income annuity	10,600
Others	6,900
Total	$200,700

Source: Institute of Life Insurance, *Life Insurance Fact Book, 1956*, p. 12.

However, more emphasis was placed on protection by persons buying policies during 1954. Decreasing term insurance and family income policies are becoming increasingly important.

UNINSURABILITY

An individual must be insurable from the viewpoint of the insurer before he can obtain a policy. The sources of information consulted by an insurance underwriter are the prospective insured's application, the agent's statement, an inspection bureau's report, and, commonly, the results of a medical examination by a doctor. If there is no medical examination, a detailed nonmedical form must be completed. Personal history, family history, physical condition, and personal habits are considered in making the underwriting decision.

No one knows how many persons fail to apply for insurance because they or their agents know that they are uninsurable, but data are available which indicate how many applicants are refused insurance because of the underwriting requirements. A 1954 survey revealed that only 2 per cent of the applications received were declined by the insurers.[6] This rate has decreased over the years. Nine per cent of the applicants did not take the insurance contract that they applied for or the alternative contract that the insurer was willing to issue.

Hence, individual insurance is a readily available form of protection against the economic insecurities of premature death and old age, and it has come to play an important role in the American economic security system. But another form of insurance, group insurance, has increased in importance recently, and we now turn to a discussion of it.

Group Insurance

DEVELOPMENT

Group insurance provided at the place of employment has played an increasingly important role in the average American's search for economic security. The characteristics of group insurance are discussed in detail subsequently in this chapter, but first we shall look at some of the historical background.[7]

At the turn of the century, the social and economic status of the average worker was far from Utopian, as will be noted in Chapter 15. Working conditions were poor and wages were low. Prominent reformers of the day emphasized the plight of the worker and the indifferent attitude of his employers. A spirit of reform was in the air. But labor-management strife persisted and it was not overnight that reforms were accomplished.

Most workers were expected to solve the problems caused by death, disability, and old age on their own, but few were financially able to do so. Some workers, however, belonged to mutual benefit associations which provided small benefits in case of death or disability. These associations included the employees of a given firm or the members of a trade union. Participation was almost always voluntary, and many workers did not join even though they were eligible. Employees usually managed the plans, with the employer contributing directly to the cost in about one-third of them. He contributed indirectly to the cost of other plans by performing some of the administrative duties or permitting employees to handle them on company time.[8]

Very few employees, other than railroad workers, received company pensions when they retired. Most of the pension plans that

[6] Ibid., p. 45.
[7] See Louise Wolters Ilse, Group Insurance and Employee Retirement Plans (Englewood Cliffs, N. J.: Prentice-Hall, Inc., 1953).
[8] Ibid., p. 24.

did exist were informal plans, with the amount and duration of each pension being determined by the employer at the date of retirement. Pensions were paid out of current income and varied with that income. There were a few formal pension plans that contained a formula for determining the benefit, but there was no guarantee that the given pension might not be discontinued. Since these pension funds also operated on a pay-as-you-go basis or, at best, with a partial reserve, the discontinuance or reduction of these benefits was a distinct possibility, which often happened.

Because each of the mutual benefit associations and pension funds covered a small number of persons, the benefit payments tended to vary greatly from year to year. This was especially noticeable in the case of death and disability, and many of the mutual benefit associations either failed or faced financial difficulties because of adverse loss experience in a single year.

In 1910 Montgomery Ward and Company decided to increase the death and disability benefits provided by its mutual benefit association. The company was concerned about possible unstable loss experience and thought that this risk could be eliminated by insuring the benefits with a commercial insurer. The negotiations with insurers were lengthy because the idea was novel, but an insurance contract ultimately was issued in 1912.[9] All employees at Chicago and Kansas City who had worked for the company for at least six months were covered, regardless of their individual insurability status. The company paid the entire premium. Because of the savings involved in wholesaling the benefits, the cost of the group protection was less than that of equivalent individual insurance contracts.

During this period, employers were becoming increasingly interested in providing death and disability protection for their employees, and the new group life insurance and group accidental injury and sickness insurance contracts appealed to them. Several reasons have been advanced to explain this employer interest in welfare benefits. Some argue that employers became more humanitarian and wanted to improve the lot of the workers for unselfish reasons. Others believe that selfish motives predominated. According to the latter, employers began to realize that a worker is more productive if he does not have to worry about possible or actual financial losses caused by death and disability; he develops loyalty to the firm; and he is less likely to leave the firm or to strike against the employer. Still others believe that employers were aware of the

[9] See *Ibid.*, chap. ii, for a more detailed discussion.

developing trends and attempted to wrest the initiative from labor leaders. Certainly, not all employers had the same motives, and many were probably motivated by all three factors. Part of the movement also can be credited to the salesmanship of the insurance industry.

Labor unions initially opposed the new group insurance idea as an example of paternalism which would destroy the labor union movement. Fraternals and a large segment of the commercial insurance industry also questioned the soundness of the idea, since there was no individual underwriting. They also argued that the contracts were discriminatory, threatened the continued existence of individual insurance, and emphasized term insurance, which they considered to be unsatisfactory except in special instances. The press and the general public, however, were generally sympathetic to the plan.

In order to assure sound underwriting and placate opposition in the insurance industry, many states passed legislation which limited the conditions under which group insurance could be written, and listed certain provisions the sense of which had to be included in every group insurance contract. Unions generally remained opposed to employer-sponsored benefits, but in the twenties many unions began to insure their own members under group insurance plans, in some cases forming their own insurance companies.

In 1926 the Amalgamated Association of Street and Electric Railway Employees became the first union to introduce life and disability insurance into a collective bargaining agreement.[10] In later years, collective bargaining agreements were to become a most important force in the growth of group insurance, but until the forties, most unions preferred to press directly for higher wages, shorter hours, and improved working conditions, and not for these "fringes."

The pension movement also grew, but much less rapidly. Pension costs were higher and the advantages of insuring the funds with a commercial insurer were less clear cut. The growth that did occur was due to the increased employer interest already discussed. However, in connection with pensions, two additional reasons should be added to the list. First, older employees could be retired when their usefulness declined. Second, the promotion lanes were continually being opened up for younger employees and their incentives increased as a result.

[10] *Ibid.*, p. 339.

Shortly after 1920, some employers, impressed by the success of the group life insurers, agreed to insure their pension plans on a group basis with commercial insurers. The major advantage to be gained through such an approach was the contractual guarantee of the insurer.[11] In the late twenties insured pension plans became popular, and during the thirties and early forties most of the new pension plans were insured plans.

During World War II, there was a tremendous increase in the importance of group life insurance, group accidental injury and sickness insurance, and pension plans. Wage increases were limited under the wartime government stabilization program, but welfare benefits customarily were not. Therefore, many employers, on their own or, more commonly through collective bargaining, substituted insurance benefits for wage increases. The high excess profits tax structure reduced the actual cost to employers.

The increase in growth continued after the war as many of the larger unions pressed for and obtained welfare benefits clauses in their collective bargaining agreements. Pensions were highlighted in these union demands. Some unions argued that the depreciation and obsolescence of manpower is a proper charge on industry. (This argument, incidentally, has been attacked on the grounds that a man ages even if he does not work.) A more common and more powerful argument advanced by the unions held that pensions are deferred wages. Current wages are reduced in order to provide pension benefits. However, unions were willing to accept plans under which the employees lost their deferred wages if they terminated their employment prior to retirement age. This concession was probably a wise tactic at the time because it reduced the cost of pensions to employers. Since (1) the investment climate had improved, (2) more persons were covered under each private pension plan, and (3) more flexible benefits were desired, especially under collective bargaining agreements, self-insured pension plans became increasingly more active competitors of insured plans.

An important benchmark in the pension movement was the establishment of the United Mine Workers Retirement Plan which became effective in 1947. The plan provided, in addition to certain death and accidental injury and sickness benefits, $100 a month to workers aged sixty who have completed twenty years of service. The fund is administered by three trustees representing both the union and the coal operators and is financed entirely by the operators through the payment of a "royalty" rate per ton of coal mined.

[11] The relative merits of insured and self-insured pension plans are discussed on pages 144–45.

In the development of pension programs, several important Supreme Court decisions were rendered two years later. In 1946 the Inland Steel Company of Chicago had refused to bargain with the United Steelworkers' Union on the issue of a compulsory retirement age in an existing retirement plan. The National Labor Relations Board ruled in 1948 that pensions were a form of wages and that the provisions of a pension plan were conditions of employment. Therefore, the company was required to bargain with the union on company pension plans. The NLRB issued a similar ruling concerning group life insurance benefits in the same year. Both rulings were sustained by the Supreme Court in 1949, and union interest in welfare benefits soared because of the clarified legal status. The United Steel Workers and the United Auto Workers negotiated important retirement plans in the same year.

Union and employer interest in group insurance continues. We may expect the introduction of new plans in the future and improvements in existing plans. We shall now consider in detail (1) group life insurance, which is written almost entirely by commercial insurers, and (2) pension plans, which may be insured or self-insured.

GROUP LIFE INSURANCE

Individual underwriting and the cost of individual insurance contracts plus the difficulties involved in selling life insurance to individuals tend to restrict the extension of ordinary and industrial insurance. Group life insurance, which is designed to get at these problems, is insurance of a group of persons bound together by some common interest. Examples of such groups include the employees of one employer (by far, the most common group), the members of a labor union, the debtors of a common creditor, and others. The contract is issued to the head of the group such as the employer, the labor union, the trustees of a welfare fund, or the creditor, while the participating members of the group receive individual certificates.

Group underwriting is substituted for individual underwriting. If the group is acceptable to the insurer, all members of the group are acceptable even if they would be unable to pass the individual underwriting standards. The cost is relatively low because of the reduction in administrative expenses due to the wholesaling principle and the fact that the head of the group usually performs some of the administrative duties. Moreover, the head of the group usually pays part or all of the cost.

Gregg illustrates how greatly group life insurance has extended life insurance coverage as follows: "At the end of 1955, about 30.5

million workers in the United States were covered by group life insurance. About 25 per cent of this group, over seven million persons, had no individual policies of life insurance. In addition it is estimated that about 50 per cent of the persons covered by group life insurance had less than $1,000 of life insurance under individual policies."[12]

If an insurer limits group life insurance protection to those groups which as a group have an expected mortality rate approximating that underlying the premium charged, group insurance is feasible. As a rule, the expected mortality rates are assumed to differ among groups only because of differences in the age composition of the groups.

In order to avoid adverse selection against the insurer and in order to maintain a low stable premium, only those types of groups which possess the following characteristics should be insured.[13]

1. Insurance should be an incidental purpose of the group.
2. Membership in the group should require a certain minimum degree of physical activity and health.
3. New entrants should be required to show a minimum grade of health.
4. There should be a continuous withdrawal of aged and impaired lives and a steady inflow of young and healthy lives.

The most insurable type of group, according to these criteria, is a group of employees under a common employer.

Of course, not all groups of an acceptable type are eligible for insurance. The group must be of a certain minimum size. The minimum size in about half the states is twenty-five. About one-quarter have established a minimum size of ten, while most of the other states require no minimum size. The major purpose of this requirement is to reduce the overhead expense per insured. Moreover, underwriters feel that the proportion of impaired lives in an eligible group decreases as the size of the group increases.

If the members of the group do not pay any of the cost (a noncontributing plan) all members of an eligible class must be covered. If the members pay part of the cost (a contributory plan), all members of a specified class must be eligible to participate, and at least 75 per cent of those eligible must participate. Otherwise the proportion of impaired lives among the insureds might be abnormally high.

---

[12] Reprinted by permission from Davis W. Gregg, *An Analysis of Group Life Insurance* (rev. ed.; Homewood: Richard D. Irwin, Inc., 1957), p. 17.

[13] Davis W. Gregg, *An Analysis of Group Life Insurance* (Philadelphia: University of Pennsylvania Press, 1950), pp. 27–30.

In addition to meeting these general requirements, each group must satisfy the insurer's underwriter that there are no special reasons why it should not qualify for group insurance.

The group insurance contract itself contains some additional underwriting safeguards. First, eligibility requirements are stated. What constitutes membership in the group is clearly defined; a probationary period of membership may be required in order to avoid the high cost of insuring "floaters"; and there may be a requirement that the member be actively at work or able to present some other evidence of reasonably good health. If the insurance is voluntary, eligible members usually must apply for the insurance within thirty days after the date of their eligibility if they wish to obtain the insurance without evidence of insurability.

Second, the amount of insurance is determined automatically by the member's earnings, position, years of membership, debt, or some other criterion. It may be a flat amount for all group members. The earnings basis has proved the most satisfactory for the employee group, and the amount of group life insurance is often some multiple of the annual earnings. If the amount of insurance were not determined automatically, the persons in poor health would tend to purchase the largest amounts of insurance.

Third, there is a minimum and maximum amount of insurance per person. A minimum of $500 of insurance is usually established in order to avoid unduly high expenses of administration. The maximum amount is a function of the total insurance in force and usually does not exceed $40,000. Setting a minimum and maximum amount in this way produces a safer distribution of insurance amounts from an underwriting point of view. Otherwise the insurer might have most of his eggs in a few baskets.

GROUP RENEWABLE TERM INSURANCE

Over 90 per cent of the group life insurance in force is one-year renewable term insurance. From the member's point of view, the insurer will pay the face amount to his beneficiary if he dies while insured as a member of the group, but there is no cash value if he leaves the group. The proceeds are payable in a lump sum or according to one of the optional modes of settlement, but the annuity and the interest options are often not available.

The major disadvantage of individual one-year renewable term insurance is that each year the premium increases and at the advanced ages the premium becomes prohibitive for most people. Fortunately, however, the total premium for a group does not change unless the age and benefit composition of the group changes.

If the group is carefully selected, these changes should be slight. If the head of the group pays the entire cost, it is possible for him to provide this low cost protection at an almost constant rate. If the plan is contributory, each member's share of the cost is usually kept constant during his period of participation and seldom exceeds 60¢ per month per $1,000 of insurance. The head of the group pays the almost constant additional cost. Under a contributory plan, the cost for the very young may exceed the premium for individual term insurance, but after a few years the cost will be much less. If the plan is voluntary, some of the younger members may wait until the group protection is cheaper than the individual contract, but they may become uninsurable in the meantime and be unable to participate.

A simplified example of the procedure used to compute the total annual premium for a group term life insurance contract will illustrate these principles. Assume that the group consists of 100 members grouped as follows:

Age	Benefit	Number
20	$1,000	10
	2,000	10
30	2,000	10
	3,000	10
40	3,000	10
	4,000	10
50	4,000	20
	4,000	20

The total premium is obtained by (1) multiplying the premium rate for each age by the amount of insurance in force at that age and (2) adding an additional loading charge to the total of the premiums obtained in the first step. The premium rates used are less than individual term insurance premium rates because they include only a 10 per cent loading charge.[14] The additional loading charge is usually $1.80 per $1,000 on the first $75,000 of insurance. Therefore, the total premium for this group is computed as follows:

Age	Total amount of insurance	Premium rate	Premium
20	$ 30,000	$ 2.60	$ 78.00
30	50,000	3.80	190.00
40	70,000	6.60	462.00
50	80,000	13.16	1052.80
60	80,000	28.40	2272.00
	$310,000		$4054.80

Total premium = $4,054.80 + 1.80 ($75) = $4,189.80

[14] In individual term insurance the loading is generally close to 50 per cent.

If no new members join the group and coverage is continued on all the old members, the total premium will increase over time, but if the older members are dropped from the group after a certain age and younger members take their place, the total cost will be fairly constant over time. Note that it is the age composition of the group which must remain fairly constant, not the average age. It costs more to insure two people, aged thirty and fifty, than two people, both aged forty, but the average age of the two groups is the same.

The actual cost of the group protection will probably be less than the computed premium, for participating insurers return dividends to policyholders and nonparticipating insurers make retroactive adjustments of the premium. The size of the dividends and the retroactive adjustments depend partly upon the total group experience of the insurer and partly upon the experience of the particular group.

An insured who terminates his connection with the group (other than a debtor group) has the right to purchase an individual life insurance contract up to the amount of the group coverage without evidence of insurability. Application for this coverage must be made within thirty-one days and the premium is that in effect for his attained age at the date of termination. Term insurance coverage is sometimes granted for one year, but usually the converted contract must be some form of permanent insurance. If the insurer or the employer terminates the group insurance, members who have been insured for five years (sometimes three) may convert their insurance under the same conditions, but the converted amount may not exceed $2,000. This conversion privilege is extremely important if a terminating member becomes uninsurable while a member of the insured group, but there is no premium advantage for *standard* lives.

OTHER FORMS OF GROUP LIFE INSURANCE

A major problem with group term insurance is that the conversion privilege is of little value to members retiring at an advanced age because the premiums on the individual contracts are very high. For this reason, insurers now underwrite two additional forms of group insurance: group paid-up insurance and level-premium group permanent insurance. In the description of these forms we shall assume a group of employees under a common employer.

A group paid-up plan combines term insurance with paid-up insurance. The total amount of insurance for each employee is determined in the same way as under a group term insurance plan, but the composition of the total differs. Usually small units of paid-up insurance are purchased annually during the insured's participation under the plan, while term insurance is written for the difference. If the total amount of protection is constant, paid-up insurance represents an increasing portion of the total, while the term insurance decreases. Two common plans are (1) the annual purchase of a specified number of units of paid-up insurance and (2) the annual purchase of a decreasing number of units of paid-up insurance with the employee's constant contributions. Under the second plan, the amount of paid-up insurance will depend upon the number of years of participation *and* the age at which the employee entered the group. If none of the paid-up insurance was purchased by employer contributions, the employee is entitled to the paid-up protection when he leaves the group. Paid-up insurance like individual insurance may be surrendered for its cash value if the insured wishes. In addition, the usual conversion rights apply to the term insurance portion of his protection. However, if the employer has contributed to the cost of the paid-up insurance, he may establish certain conditions which must be satisfied before the employee may claim that portion of the paid-up insurance purchased with his contributions. These conditions are called vesting conditions and plans may provide for no vesting at any time, full vesting immediately upon becoming a group member, or full or partial vesting after a specified age, years of membership, or both. (The problem of vesting is discussed more fully on pages 143–44 and in Chapter 14.)

Group permanent or level-premium life insurance plans emphasize the retirement aspects of insurance more than group paid-up plans. In fact they are often regarded as pension plans instead of life insurance plans because of the sizable cash values available at retirement age. Straight life, limited payment life, endowment, or retirement income contracts are issued to individuals on a group basis. They contain paid-up insurance and cash value options, and settlement options, except for the interest option. If an employee terminates his connection with the group, his claim to the nonforfeiture value will depend upon the vesting conditions mentioned in the preceding paragraph. If he wishes, he may convert in the usual way the difference between the total group coverage and the amount of the paid-up insurance.

The most common solution to the problem of retired employees, however, is to continue their insurance in a reduced amount under the regular group term contract.

Contributory Versus Noncontributory Plans

Most group insurance plans are contributory, but the trend is toward noncontributory plans. The major advantages of a contributory plan include the following:

1. A larger benefit can be purchased.
2. The member is possibly more likely to be interested in the plan and hence may derive more satisfaction from it as a result.
3. The plan is less likely to be discontinued.

The major advantages of a noncontributory plan are as follows:

1. The member does not have to pay an income tax on the premiums paid in his behalf.
2. All eligible members of the group are insured.
3. The administrative costs are less because there is less record-keeping.

Tax considerations and the inclusion of insurance benefits in collective bargaining agreements are the primary factors favoring noncontributory plans today.

Trends

The important trends in group insurance include the extension of group insurance to new types of groups and smaller groups; an increase in the maximum amount of group insurance written on a single life and in the average size of a group certificate; more frequent use of settlement options in paying out policy proceeds; liberalization in the conversion privilege by permitting the insured to convert his group protection to term insurance for at least one year; and an increase in the use of group permanent insurance or reduced group term insurance to solve the problem of the retiring member.

Group Life Insurance in Force, 1912–1955

Group life insurance is the fastest growing branch of insurance. The tremendous increase in the amount of group insurance in force since its introduction in 1912 is shown in Table 5.6. About thirty-two million persons are now insured under group life insurance contracts. Until 1947 the amount of industrial insurance in force exceeded the amount of group insurance in force, but there is now over $2,500 of group life insurance in force for each $1,000 of industrial insurance. Over the same period, the ratio of the amount of group insurance in force to the amount of ordinary insurance in force has increased from about 30 per cent to 50 per cent.

TABLE 5.6

GROUP LIFE INSURANCE IN FORCE IN THE UNITED STATES, 1912–1955

(in millions)

Year	Amount	Year	Amount
1912	$ 13	1935	$ 10,283
1915	100	1940	15,256
1920	1,570	1945	22,436
1925	4,247	1950	50,962
1930	9,828	1955	101,300

Source: Institute of Life Insurance, *Life Insurance Fact Book, 1956*, p. 25.

Group Pension Plans

Group life insurance in force is much less than individual life insurance in force, but group pensions are much more important than individual annuity contracts, with the impetus provided by collectively bargained plans significant. These pension plans may be formal or informal; they may be financed on a pay-as-you-go or on a funded basis. Since almost all the important pension plans today are formal funded plans, other types will not be discussed further in this text.

We shall limit our discussion to those plans which cover the employees of a single employer, but in recent years, as a result of collective bargaining, pooled welfare funds covering the employees of more than one employer have become more common. Examples are the plans of the United Brotherhood of Carpenters and Joiners of America, the Amalgamated Clothing Workers of America, and the United Mine Workers of America. These multi-employer plans are relatively few in number, but they cover many employees and have come to play an important role in our search for economic security.[15]

RETIREMENT BENEFITS

Benefits under these formal funded plans are determined in one of two ways:

Money purchase formula. Under this method, the benefit is that amount which can be provided on the basis of an annual con-

[15] For a discussion of pooled welfare plans, see Charles L. Dearing, *Industrial Pensions* (Washington: The Brookings Institution, 1954), pp. 89–106.

tribution to the plan equal to a percentage of the employee's earnings. This plan is seldom used because the benefits cannot easily be explained and they decrease rapidly as the age of the entrant increases. Furthermore the benefit depends more upon the earnings in the early years than in the later years because the early contributions are credited with compound interest over a longer period of time. The advantage to the employer is that the cost is known and it varies with his payroll.

Definite or unit benefit formula. Under this method, the benefit is a flat amount for all retirants or a specified function of earnings, service, or both. The contribution is the amount necessary to provide the benefit. Examples of definite benefit formulas include the following: $100 per month for all eligible retirants; 50 per cent of final earnings; 50 per cent of average earnings over the past five years; $5 per month for each year of service; 2 per cent of final earnings for each year of service; 2 per cent of average earnings during the past ten years for each year of service; and 2 per cent of average earnings for each year of service. The last example illustrates the type of plan which is by far the most common, but there is a trend toward the use of average earnings during the past five or ten years instead of the career average. Retirants, past and future, tend to judge plans on the relationship between their pension and their final earnings, not their average earnings; and over most earning careers, the final earnings are much greater than the average earnings. During periods of inflation they are markedly so.

Whenever length of service is a factor in determining the amount of the benefit, as it is in the case of money purchase plans and most definite purchase plans, a distinction is made between service rendered prior to and after the installation of the pension plan. Most plans count at least part of the past service in addition to the future service. Otherwise, employees approaching retirement age at the time the plan was introduced would receive a very small benefit. If the benefit depends upon career earnings, it is customary to assume for administrative reasons that the annual earnings prior to the installation of the plan were equal to the present earnings. Because this assumption almost always results in an overestimate of past earnings, a smaller percentage is applied to past earnings than to future earnings to determine the benefit.

Because most employees will receive OASI retirement benefits which the employer has paid for in part, the benefits under most private pension plans are affected in some way by OASI. It is customary to (1) deduct the social security benefits actually received from the private pension benefit, (2) exclude earnings under $4,200 from the private pension plan, or (3) apply a smaller percentage to the earnings under $4,200.[16] When the last two methods are used, the usual objective is to produce a maximum total benefit (OASI plus private pension benefit) expressed as a per cent of earnings which decreases as the earnings increase to $4,200 and remains the same for all higher incomes.

Retirement income is always paid during the lifetime of the pensioner, but there may be additional payments if the pensioner dies. The annuity form may be a straight life annuity, a cash refund annuity, an instalment refund annuity, a joint and last survivor annuity, or an annuity with a period certain. These annuity forms have been described on pages 122-23. The cash refund and instalment refund annuity forms are usually modified to the extent that the refund is limited to the employee's contributions to the plan.

Benefits under a pension plan are specified in terms of one annuity form, usually the straight life annuity or a cash refund annuity, but the employee almost always has the right to receive an actuarially equivalent income under another form. If the employee wishes to elect a form with larger death benefits, he must usually elect this form a stated number of years prior to retirement because of the possibility of adverse selection.

More than one-fifth of the university pension plans (underwritten by the special life insurer noted on page 125) and an increasing number of self-insured industrial pension plans provide a variable annuity.

QUALIFICATION FOR RETIREMENT BENEFITS

In order to qualify for retirement benefits, an employee must first have been eligible to participate under the plan. Participation may be limited to those employees who satisfy one or more of the following types of criteria: minimum age, maximum age, minimum length of service, minimum earnings, type of remuneration (hourly wage or salary), and type of work. For example, one plan may cover all employees over thirty years of age with at least five years of service. Another may cover all salaried employees earning over $4,200 a year. The minimum age and service requirements cut the cost of administration by excluding temporary employees; the maximum age limitation excludes those employees for whom it would be very expensive to provide pensions. The minimum earn-

[16] For a discussion of the relative merits of each method of integration, see Dan M. McGill, *Fundamentals of Private Pensions* (Homewood: Richard D. Irwin, Inc., 1955), pp. 42–48.

ings requirement is designed to integrate the plan with OASI. The other requirements may be used to cut the cost or may arise out of the special circumstances surrounding negotiated plans.

In order to receive the full retirement benefits, employees must almost always have attained a normal retirement age, usually sixty-five. Sometimes there is also a minimum service requirement. If an employee wishes to continue working beyond the normal retirement age, he may be able to do so under some circumstances, although institutional rules may make it increasingly difficult. However, there are seldom any further contributions to the plan in his behalf. The benefits may start at the normal retirement age even if he continues working, or the income may be postponed until the actual retirement date. The deferred benefit may be the same as that which he would have received at the normal retirement age or it may be the actuarial equivalent; that is, it may be adjusted upward to reflect additional interest earnings and the advanced age.

EARLY RETIREMENT, TERMINATION, AND DEATH BENEFITS

Some plans do not permit an employee to retire prior to the normal retirement date; others make an exception only in the case of total and permanent disability. However, most plans permit early retirement if the retirant meets a minimum age or minimum age and service requirement. The employer's consent may or may not be required. For example, the plan may permit an employee to retire with the employer's consent if he has attained the age of fifty-five. Another may require that a person reach fifty-five years of age and complete ten years of service before he can retire. If early retirement is permitted, the benefit is usually the actuarial equivalent of the normal retirement age benefit. This actuarial equivalent is much less than the benefit at the normal retirement age because fewer contributions are made to the plan, the period of compound interest earnings is much less, and the cost of providing an income beginning at an earlier age is much higher.

If an employee withdraws from employment prior to the normal or early retirement age, he is entitled to his own contributions to the plan, with or without interest. The vesting provisions of the plan determine his right to the employer's contributions in his behalf. There may be full, partial, or no vesting; the vesting may be immediate or, as is usually the case, there may be certain service or age and service requirements; and the vested amount may be returned in cash or as a paid-up annuity. For example, one plan may provide for immediate full vesting, but the employee must take his own and the employer's contributions in the form of a paid-up annuity. Another may entitle the employee to 25 per cent of the employer's contributions in cash after five years of service, 50 per cent after ten years, 75 per cent after fifteen years, and 100 per cent after twenty years. A third may provide full vesting of the employer's contributions in cash or as a paid-up annuity for all eligible employees with ten years of service.

Death benefits are usually limited to a return of the employee's contributions, but death benefits equal to one year's income or $1,000 per $10 of retirement income are sometimes included.

METHODS OF FINANCING AND FUNDING

The pension plan may be a self-insured trusteed plan or an insured plan. Under a self-insured trusteed plan, the contributions are paid to a trustee who invests the money and pays the benefits. There is no guarantee that the contributions will be sufficient to pay the benefits, but the plan is highly flexible. Unusual benefit formulas can be handled with relative ease under this arrangement. The earnings on investments tend to be high because the trust funds may be invested in equities.

Under an insured plan, the contributions are paid to an insurer who administers them in one of the following ways. Small firms usually have a *pension trust* under which a trustee purchases an individual level-premium retirement annuity or retirement income annuity contract for each eligible employee. However, the insured plans covering the most persons are *group annuity* plans under which the employer purchases each year from an insurer a number of paid-up deferred group annuities. Usually the benefit is expressed as a per cent of earnings for each year of service, and the annuity purchased in any year is sufficient to provide this benefit at the retirement date. Under either of these plans, the insurer guarantees performance under the contracts purchased. The yield on the invested funds is relatively low because the investments of life insurers are limited primarily to fixed obligations.

Insurers also operate two more flexible plans—*deposit administration plans* and the *immediate participation guarantee contracts*. Under a deposit administration plan, annuity contracts are not purchased until an employee retires. Annual contributions to the insurer are accumulated at a guaranteed rate of interest and may be used to purchase an annuity at a price fixed at the time the contribution is made. The contributions are made on the basis of an actuarial estimate, but there is no guarantee that they will be sufficient to provide the benefits specified under the plan. The insurer guarantees the benefits for retiring employees only. The deposit administration plan is becoming more popular because of the flexibility in financing that it affords the employer and because it may be used to fund the more popular final pay type of benefit.

Immediate participation guarantee contracts are even more flexible in that the insurer administers the retirement fund as if it were a self-insured trusteed fund, but the insurer reserves the right to convert the plan into a deferred group annuity plan if the fund drops to the level where it is just sufficient to provide the benefits for retired workers. In this way, the retired workers are guaranteed that their income will not be disturbed.

Most of the retirement plans are insured plans, but the self-administered trusteed plans cover more than twice as many employees. Combination plans are common. According to recent estimates, there are more than 20,000 pension plans covering at least thirteen million persons. The insured plans, which number 18,980, cover over four million persons. The breakdown by type of insured plan is given in Table 5.7.

TABLE 5.7

NUMBER OF INSURED PENSION PLANS AND NUMBER OF PERSONS COVERED, BY TYPE OF PLAN, 1955

Type of plan	Number of plans	Number of persons covered
Group annuities	3,760	2,410,000
Deposit administration	990	950,000
Individual policy		480,000
pension trusts	12,530	480,000
Other	1,700	310,000
Total	18,980	4,150,000

Source: Institute of Life Insurance, *Life Insurance Fact Book, 1956,* p. 33.

Since the 1920's the employee has usually paid at least part of the cost of the plan, but the trend is now in favor of noncontributory plans, for the reasons discussed on page 139.

Very few plans are fully funded; that is, the fund is seldom sufficient to pay all benefits earned up to the present date if the plan were to be terminated. However, most funds would be able to pay the future service benefits plus some of the past service benefits. Under some plans, terminal funding is used instead of advance funding. The benefits payable to retired employees are fully funded, but the benefits payable to others are not funded at all.

OPERATIONS AND TRENDS

The important trends in group pensions include an increase in the number of persons covered, a reduction in age and service eligibility requirements, increased benefits and a switch to a final pay formula, a movement from inflexible insured plans to more flexible insured plans and self-insured trusteed plans, more liberal vesting provisions, and the growth of industry-wide negotiated plans. Collective bargaining has played a significant role in these developments.

INSURED PENSION PLANS, 1940–1955

Table 5.8 shows the tremendous growth of insured pension plans since 1940. This table actually understates the development of group pensions, since self-insured pension plans have been becoming relatively more important since 1945. However, no reliable data are available on the growth of self-insured plans.

TABLE 5.8

INSURED PENSION PLANS IN THE UNITED STATES, 1940–1955

Year	Number of plans	Number of persons covered
1940	1,530	685,000
1945	6,700	1,500,000
1950	11,250	2,865,000
1955	18,980	4,150,000

Source: Institute of Life Insurance, *Life Insurance Fact Book, 1956,* p. 33.

Operations of Life Insurance

The life insurance industry is the largest private agency dealing with the financial problems of premature death and old age. Its operations indicate the scope of private activities in this area.

Over 60 per cent of the total population and over 80 per cent of United States families own some form of life insurance, and the percentages are increasing each year. The total amount of life insurance in force is about $370 billion, which is double the amount in force less than ten years ago. About 3 per cent of the total population owns annuities providing about $2 billion in annual income at maturity. Ten years ago both of these figures were less than one half their present value.

The significant growth in the income of the life insurance industry is shown in Table 5.9. Note that the annual income is now over $16 billion.

TABLE 5.9
INCOME OF UNITED STATES LIFE INSURERS, 1930–1955
(in millions)

Year	Premium income*	Investment and other income†	Total
1920	$ 1,381	$ 383	$ 1,764
1925	2,378	640	3,018
1930	3,517	1,077	4,594
1935	3,673	1,399	5,072
1940	3,887	1,771	5,658
1945	5,159	2,515	7,674
1950	8,189	3,148	11,337
1955	12,546	3,998	16,544

* Accidental injury and sickness premiums included in 1950 and 1955 figures.
† Other income includes proceeds left with the insurers under settlement options.
Source: Institute of Life Insurance, *Life Insurance Fact Book, 1956*, p. 51.

The benefits have also increased, but not as rapidly. Table 5.10 shows that annuity payments have shown the greatest increase since 1940, but death benefits are the most important type of benefit. Note, however, that the total living benefits listed approach the death benefits.

TABLE 5.10
BENEFIT PAYMENTS IN THE UNITED STATES, 1940–1955
(in thousands)

Year	Death benefits	Matured endowments	Annuity payments	Surrender values
1940	$ 994,950	$269,244	$176,492	$652,022
1945	1,279,667	406,669	216,422	210,874
1950	1,589,744	495,090	319,381	592,272
1955	2,240,731	613,919	462,240	895,970

Source: Institute of Life Insurance, *Life Insurance Fact Book, 1956*, p. 35.

Because income exceeds expenses and benefits, the assets of life insurers have grown rapidly and are approaching $100 billion. Table 5.11 records the growth of these assets and the legal reserves which are the most important liability item. Almost all the assets are invested in interest-bearing debt securities and mortgages.

EVALUATION

Private life insurers have made sizable contributions to the economic security of our population.[17] Most American families look

[17] See Chester C. Nash, "The Contribution of Life Insurance to Social Security in the United States," *International Labour Review*, LXXII, No. 1 (July, 1955), 1–19.

TABLE 5.11

ASSETS AND LEGAL RESERVES OF UNITED STATES LIFE INSURERS, 1920–1955
(in millions)

Year	Assets	Reserves
1920	$ 7,320	$ 6,338
1925	11,538	9,927
1930	18,880	16,231
1935	23,216	20,404
1940	30,802	27,238
1945	44,797	38,667
1950	64,020	54,946
1955	90,432	75,359

Source: Institute of Life Insurance, *Life Insurance Fact Book, 1956*, pp. 57, 60.

to private life insurance and annuities as their major supplement to the floor of protection provided by OASI.

The commercial insurer is, by far, the most important underwriter of private insurance. In this evaluation of private insurance, therefore, we shall discuss primarily the types of protection afforded, the underwriting practices, and the premium structures of commercial insurers.

Types of protection afforded. Commercial insurers issue a wide variety of life insurance and annuity contracts. Numerous combinations of pure protection against premature death and a systematic savings plan are obtainable from most of the leading insurers.

Very few persons question the advantages of life insurance as pure financial protection against premature death, but the following advantages of life insurance and annuity contracts as a systematic savings plan are less widely understood and appreciated. (1) Insureds are much less inclined to skip premium payments than savings bank deposits or security purchases. (2) The insurer guarantees a minimum interest rate on the savings fund. (3) The insured does not have to worry about managing the fund. (4) The present tax code favors saving through insurance. (5) The chance that the insurer will not be able to pay the savings fund on demand is almost nil. For these five reasons, life insurance and annuity contracts are an excellent way for most families to accumulate at least the minimum savings fund required for old age. In addition, annuity contracts and annuity settlement options on cash values or death proceeds make it possible to avoid exhausting the savings fund before the date of death.

The contracts tend to be liberal. For example, if the insured dies two or more years after the life insurance contract is issued, the insurer cannot refuse to pay the death claim because of misrepresentations by the insured at the time he applied for the contracts. The contracts are also flexible, as evidenced by the nonforfeiture options and the settlement options.

The promises of the life insurers are secure. The state regulatory bodies restrict the investments of commercial insurers to high-grade securities and require them to establish a legal reserve item on the liability side of their balance sheets. This legal reserve is equal to the difference between the present value of estimated future benefits and the present value of expected future premium payments under contracts already in force. The legal reserve differs from the OASI Trust Fund operation in that an indefinite operation is not and should not be assumed. If a commercial insurer sold no new contracts, the premium payments under the contracts in force plus assets corresponding to the legal reserve amount should be sufficient to discharge the obligations of the insurer.

However, it cannot be argued that all persons have received the optimum protection for their premium dollars. One of the most common failings is an overemphasis on contracts with savings fund aspects at a time when protection against premature death is the most important need. For example, many young workers with dependents have twenty-payment life contracts, but renewable and convertible term insurance would seem more appropriate. On the other hand, the authors do not agree with the fairly common suggestion that most persons would be better off (some might be) if they limited their life insurance programs solely to pure term insurance contracts.

This less-than-optimum protection in individual cases may be ascribed to many factors, the most important of which are (1) a lack of knowledge and appreciation of basic insurance principles by insureds and (2) the poor advice provided by a minority of insurance agents or other advisers. Fortunately, both situations are being rectified. Insureds have more opportunity than ever before to learn the basic principles of life insurance. Journals and magazines print more feature articles on insurance; competent authors have written helpful books on the subject;[18] and college insurance courses for the nonspecialist are becoming more common. As for the agents, the caliber of the average insurance agent has

[18] See the life insurance texts cited in fn. 4. For a different viewpoint, see consumer education books such as the one by Philip Gordis, *How to Buy Insurance* (New York: W. W. Norton & Co., Inc., 1947).

improved during the past two decades. Agents are required to know more about insurance contracts, law, rates, and reserves than in the past. Life insurance programming—a survey of the private insurance needs followed by the selection of the best insurance contracts and settlement options to meet those needs—has become a fairly common procedure. Some excellent training and educational programs have been established, one of which leads to a professional designation.

In the opinion of the authors, the insurance industry in the past has tended to de-emphasize term insurance to such an extent that it was not used in cases where it was the most appropriate form of protection. In recent years, many types of term insurance have become more readily available, and the insurance industry has enthusiastically supported the sale of family income contracts. However, the authors believe that term insurance is still being underemphasized by some insurers and agents.

The inadequacy of fixed-dollar obligations, such as life insurance and annuity contracts, during a long period of steady upward price movements is obvious. This inadequacy is primarily responsible for the interest in the variable annuity discussed on page 125. Opinion both within and outside the insurance industry is divided on the advisability of underwriting such an annuity,[19] but there are indications that variable annuity contracts will become more readily available. Many technical difficulties must be worked out before any insurer is likely to propose issuing a contract with death proceeds which fluctuate in amount.

The movement from relatively inflexible insured group plans to more flexible insured plans and self-insured plans is both encouraging and disturbing. The types of benefit formulas used under the more flexible plans are more satisfactory to the insureds, but the plans are more likely to run into financial difficulties because of this flexibility. Other important group insurance developments such as the continuance of life insurance protection on retired workers and improved vesting provisions are steps in the right direction.

Underwriting practices. A relatively few persons are unable to purchase private individual life insurance because they are uninsurable. Another relatively small group can purchase only substandard insurance which is either more expensive or more restricted than the contracts issued to standard lives. A very small number of persons will always be uninsurable, and contracts may

---

[19] It is not within the scope of this text to summarize the many arguments on both sides of this question. For an excellent summary of the issues involved, see *Insurance Law Journal,* June, 1956.

on occasion have war and aviation exclusions, but individual under-writing procedures are still being continually liberalized.

Group insurance provides relatively inexpensive protection for all participants and is especially valuable to persons who are uninsurable by individual insurance standards. On the other hand, the protection is not tailor-made for the individual. At present, group insurance plans cover about half the employed workers, and benefits are gradually being extended. The overall development of group insurance appears satisfactory, but a few insurers have underwritten groups and benefit amounts that appear unsound, or threaten the continued existence of individual insurance and tailor-made protection. On the other hand, the legislation of some states appears unnecessarily restrictive.

Premium structures. Private insurance premiums should not, on the average, exceed the expected losses and expected reasonable expenses plus a reasonable margin for contingencies and profit. In addition they should distribute the cost equitably among insureds. Life insurance premiums rate favorably on both counts. The manner in which premiums vary among insureds has been discussed at various points in this chapter. A few additional facts concerning the general level of rates should be noted here.

The initial cost of a life insurance or annuity contract is determined by the insurer's expected mortality rates, interest rates earned on invested assets, and expenses. If the actual experience is more favorable than the expected experience, the policyholders usually gain because, as indicated previously, most life insurance is issued on a participating basis. Moreover, competition forces the nonparticipating insurers to make their estimates as realistic as possible.

Mortality rates have been decreasing, thus decreasing actual life insurance costs and increasing annuity costs. Interest rates declined from about 5 per cent in 1930 to 2.88 per cent in 1947, but they have increased slowly to about 3.5 per cent in 1955. Most life insurance investments are limited by choice and by statute to debt obligations whose yield has been greatly affected by the monetary and fiscal policies of the federal government. Expenses average about 17 per cent of total income. Increasing mechanization, group coverages, and high-minimum policies tend to reduce the expenses, while increasing wages, rents, taxes, and other costs operate in the opposite direction. The expense ratio varies greatly among contracts and branches of insurance. All three factors vary among insurers.

SELF-INSURED PENSION PLANS

Self-insured pension plans are the other important type of private insurance protection. Their benefit formulas and financing provisions are usually more flexible than those of insured pension plans. Moreover, the pension funds may be invested in equities as well as in fixed-dollar securities. As a result, the funds accumulate more rapidly than insured funds in periods of rising stock prices, but they are probably less secure.

The lack of a third-party guarantee is not too important if the number of persons participating is large and the benefits are based upon competent actuarial advice, but the insured plans are superior in this respect.

ABUSES IN ADMINISTRATION

The Taft-Hartley Act of 1947 required that welfare and pension plans subject to collective bargaining be administered by a board of trustees representing management, labor, and the public. The purpose of this provision was to insure honest administration, but some cases of dishonest and irresponsible administration have occurred. For example, the trustees have in certain cases acted in collusion with insurance agents to embezzle premiums.[20] Fortunately, however, such cases are definitely in the minority. This is especially true of pension plans which are subject to some controls by the Bureau of Internal Revenue.

Other cases of improper administration in private insurance in recent years appear to be rare.

A COMMENT ON ECONOMIC ISSUES

The existence of private insurance has important economic consequences. The over-all effect of private insurance is that of increasing the fund of savings available for investments in the economy. Annuity premiums and the portions of life insurance premiums which are used to build up cash values represent a type of forced savings, which insurers must invest, thus increasing the production in the future when the insureds plan to retire. The term portions of the premiums probably also lead to an increase in available short-term investment funds, for the insurer can invest these amounts for the period elapsing between the payment of the premiums and the payment of the expenses and benefits. If investment opportunities

[20] For a further discussion, see Chapter 18.

are not available, private insurance may simply reduce current spending and hence national income.[21]

One important consequence of private programs is their effect upon labor mobility, as affected particularly by group insurance. The effect of group life insurance is slight because the employee's only loss in moving from one employer to another may be a period of no coverage during the waiting period. Group pensions are a more important factor, especially when the vesting provisions are a function of the length of service. Older workers are more likely to be affected by this consideration than younger workers. It should also be remembered that seniority carries with it other advantages which the worker must also consider.[22] Group insurance exerts its greatest influence when the proposed movement is from a firm with group insurance to one with no group insurance. Chapter 14 further analyzes these and other issues.

A CONCLUDING COMMENT

As long as we wish to preserve the freedom and responsibility of the individual, private insurance will continue to play an important role in our quest for economic security. Social insurance will provide the floor of protection; private insurance makes it possible to carpet this floor. It is hoped and expected that the thickness of the carpet will increase in the future.

Summary

Private life insurance and annuities include (1) individual life insurance and annuities, (2) group life insurance, and (3) group pension plans.

The basic types of individual life insurance contracts are the term insurance contracts and the permanent contracts including the straight life contract, the limited payment contract, and the endowment contract. Term insurance provides temporary protection against death losses only. The permanent contracts combine protection against death losses with a systematic savings plan.

The death proceeds are payable in a lump sum or according to some settlement option selected by the insured or his beneficiary.

The savings fund under the permanent contracts may be used to continue some life insurance protection if the insured wishes to

21 See Chapters 14 and 18 for further discussion of finance and investment issues.
22 Daniel H. Brill, "Economic Impact of Private Pension Plans," *Pensions: Problems and Trends* (Homewood: Richard D. Irwin, Inc., 1955), pp. 86–87.

stop paying premiums. If the insured prefers, he may receive the savings fund in a lump sum or according to some settlement option.

Annuity contracts are primarily designed to protect the insured against the problems of old age. The basic annuities may be classified as immediate or deferred annuities and as straight life, instalment refund, or cash refund annuities.

Applicants for individual insurance must be insurable, but less than 2 per cent of the applications for commercial insurance are declined.

Group life insurance was first written by a commercial insurer in 1912 for Montgomery Ward employees. Commercial insurers entered the group pension field in the twenties. Self-insured group pension plans were also becoming more important by that time. Almost all the early group plans were employer-initiated, but group insurance benefits are now an important issue for collective bargaining.

Each member of an eligible group is eligible for group life insurance even if he is not individually insurable. Another advantage to the insured is that the cost is lower than the cost of equivalent individual insurance.

Most group life insurance is yearly renewable term insurance. An insured who leaves the group may without proving insurability replace the group protection with an individual life insurance contract.

Group pension benefits are computed according to a unit benefit or money purchase formula. The benefits are specified in terms of one annuity form, but usually other forms may be elected.

Benefits available to employees terminating their employment at an early date depend upon the vesting provisions. Death benefits are usually limited to a return of the employee's contributions.

The pension plan may be a self-insured plan or an insured plan. The insured plans include a pension trust, a group annuity plan, a deposit administration plan, and an immediate participation guarantee plan. Most group pension plans are insured, but the self-insured plans cover more employees.

Most new group insurance plans are noncontributory, primarily because of the tax advantages and collective bargaining.

Suggestions for Additional Reading

DEARING, CHARLES L. *Industrial Pensions*. Washington: The Brookings Institution, 1954. Chapters 3 through 5.

A clear exposition of the nature and increasing importance of collective bargaining on industrial pensions and a concise description of the differences between single-firm and multi-firm plans.

GREGG, DAVIS W. *An Analysis of Group Life Insurance,* rev. ed. Homewood: Richard D. Irwin, Inc., 1957.
The theory and the practice of group life insurance are examined in this authoritative volume.

ILSE, LOUISE WOLTERS. *Group Insurance and Employee Retirement Plans.* Englewood Cliffs, N. J.: Prentice-Hall, Inc., 1953. Chapters 1 through 6; 12 and 13.
This text emphasizes the historical development of the group insurance movement.

McGILL, DAN MAYS. *Fundamentals of Private Pensions.* Homewood: Richard D. Irwin, Inc., 1955.
An excellent description and analysis of the fundamentals of group pension plans.

MEHR, ROBERT I., and ROBERT W. OSLER. *Modern Life Insurance,* rev. ed. New York: The Macmillan Co., 1956.
A recently published text on private life insurance and annuities.

STRONG, JAY. *Employee Benefit Plans in Operation.* Washington: The Bureau of National Affairs, Inc., 1951. Chapters 1 through 5, and 8.
An analysis of the group insurance plans of 923 firms. The last chapter discusses collective bargaining on welfare programs.

6

Problems of Unemployment

Introduction

In terms of the number of people directly or indirectly involved and the impacts upon them and upon society as a whole, unemployment has probably been the most important single factor in job connected economic insecurity in this country for the past half-century. If this statement is not wholly valid for the entire period, it is at least for several concentrated sub-periods, particularly in the decade after 1929. Unemployment in this sense is defined, as was noted in Chapter 1, as that type associated with changing economic circumstances, rather than with accidents, sickness, or old age. Unemployment associated with old age is discussed in the last section of this book; that associated with illness will be treated in the next. Major attention in the present section, therefore, will be devoted to "economic" unemployment, its causes, and to the ways in which society has tried to accommodate itself to the problems brought about by such unemployment.[1]

This chapter deals with the concepts of employment and unemployment, with their quantitative measurement, and with the ways in which society has sought to prevent or reduce unemployment through monetary and fiscal policy, public works, and selective measures; or has sought to improve the functioning of the labor market through employment exchanges.

[1] Two classics in the over-all field of unemployment with which the student should be familiar are: Paul H. Douglas and Aaron Director, *The Problem of Unemployment* (New York: The Macmillan Co., 1931); and W. H. Beveridge, *Unemployment: A Problem of Industry* (New York: Longmans, Green & Co., Inc., 1930).

The Problem of Unemployment

GENERAL NATURE

Involuntary unemployment may be defined quantitatively as the difference between the quantity of labor services offered at a given level of wages with a given set for working conditions, and the quantity of labor services taken at such levels. If this quantity is positive, then involuntary unemployment of a given magnitude exists. Translated from aggregate to individual terms, this means simply that a given person may not be able to find employment or may lose what he has.

But factors other than wage level relationships are causally important in unemployment. Because of inherent elements in a given economic situation, it may be possible that even an adjusted wage level would not reduce unemployment. Thus, in a secularly declining industry, say the production of carriages, a reduction in wages may not be a feasible means to increase, let alone maintain, employment. Or, in certain seasonal operations such as processing foodstuffs, if the raw materials are non-existent at the moment, wage rate changes may be able to accomplish little in providing work opportunities. Thus it is necessary in the first instance to distinguish between aggregate involuntary unemployment arising out of deficiencies in labor demand related to wage levels, and selective involuntary unemployment arising out of deficiencies in labor demand caused by, even if only temporarily, structural economic factors such as production conditions, changes in technology, and changes in consumer preferences.

The labor market does not, however, operate as impersonally as this type of discussion might indicate. The hiring process and the job-getting process are personalized, and hence some individuals might find it difficult to secure employment irrespective of the economic conditions noted above. Employer hiring selectivity tends to increase as economic conditions worsen, thus compounding the problem for certain individuals. Moreover, individual job-getting embodies many nonrational choices, which may have unemployment implications. Thus, this third factor is also important.

Hence, several factors are at work in creating unemployment: first, the impersonal operation of the labor market, reflecting aggregate demands for and supplies of labor at various wage levels (and with possibilities of involuntary unemployment at different wage levels); second, the more selective though still impersonal structural problems of industries or companies, reflecting demands for labor not necessarily wage oriented; and third, the personalized hiring *and* job-getting process, that is, the personalized operation of the labor market as seen by the individual. Notwithstanding this detailed breakdown, unemployment cannot be handled on the basis of statistical probability as was done for life expectancy in Chapter 3. The implications of this for policy are clear.

Unemployment is not an easy term to define precisely or to quantify, either conceptually or empirically, let alone in terms of the above threefold classification.[2] We have focused above on involuntary unemployment, on the basis that voluntary unemployment, by its very connotation, has no relevance for the problem of economic insecurity. But "voluntary" may be an elusive term in some respects: An individual may be "voluntarily" idle in the sense that his search for work has been discouraging and he has temporarily removed himself from participation in the labor force or in the sense that he is only interested if a certain type of job comes along. How much of this "involuntary voluntarism" exists is not definitely ascertainable; probably it is not large except for older age groups, where it may be significant. But there is little doubt that conceptually it creates a problem in the measurement of unemployment.

"Partial" employment poses another issue. For example, in the week of July 8–14, 1956, out of 59,175,000 persons at work, 13,627,000, or 22 per cent, worked less than forty hours. Table 6.1 illustrates this.

Not all this partial employment has an equivalent unemployment counterpart. For example, certain classes of employees, such as housewives, may prefer to work (and may be able to work) only a restricted number of hours per week. To the extent that this is true, productive capacity is expanded by any participation on their part in the labor force, and there is no involuntary unemployment. But there is no doubt that among these 13,627,000 persons there are many who are only "partially" employed and who would prefer a longer work week.

"Disguised" unemployment is a further problem that is both conceptually and realistically important, though quantifying it is an extremely difficult task. This type of unemployment occurs when persons are not placed in jobs where their capacities are utilized to

[2] The reader interested in pursuing this topic in greater detail is urged to look at the various papers presented at the Universities-National Bureau of Economic Research *Conference on the Measurement and Behavior of Unemployment* held at Princeton, New Jersey, September, 1954. See also L. J. Ducoff and M. J. Hagood, *Labor Force Definition and Measurement: Recent Experience in the United States* (New York: Social Science Research Council, Bulletin 56, 1947).

TABLE 6.1

HOURS WORKED, JULY 8–14, 1956

Total at work	59,175,000
1–14 hours	2,715,000
15–21 hours	2,727,000
22–29 hours	2,326,000
30–34 hours	2,327,000
35–39 hours	3,532,000
40 hours	22,910,000
✻	✻
✻	✻
90 or more hours	760,000

Average hours worked this week were 42.5. It should be noted that "over-" as well as "under-" employment exists (if, say, a mean work week of 40 hours is accepted).

Source: U. S. Department of Commerce, Bureau of the Census, *Current Population Reports, Labor Force,* Series P-57, No. 169 (August, 1956).

the fullest, either on an aggregate or individual basis. Such unemployment implies that a norm or standard of employment is not being met. Examples of such under-utilization are common: excess numbers of persons in given industries such as agriculture, or in given regions such as the South, who would make a greater contribution to national productivity if labor mobility operated so as to place them elsewhere. Or in a given company, industry, or area a similar case exists when an individual is not optimally producing because the placement process has not located him where his capacities would be best utilized.[3]

The Focus of This Chapter. In this chapter we shall be concerned essentially with involuntary and total unemployment. Partial and disguised unemployment will receive some attention, the former in the general discussion on unemployment, the latter in a more special way. However, any detailed analysis of and prescription for disguised unemployment not only raises broad areas of economic policy, but also leads us to a consideration of education, counseling, placement, and other topics far beyond the scope of this book. Partial unemployment, while involving some specialized characteristics, is of such a nature as to permit treatment under the analysis of general unemployment.

[3] For a useful discussion of both the above topics see the paper, "The Meaning and Measurement of Partial and Disguised Unemployment," by L. J. Ducoff and M. J. Hagood presented at the 1954 Universities-National Bureau of Economic Research *Conference on the Measurement and Behavior of Unemployment.* See also Fernando Sierra Berdecia and A. J. Jaffe, "The Concept and Measurement of Underemployment," *Monthly Labor Review,* LXXVIII, No. 3 (March, 1955), 283–87.

THE MEASUREMENT OF UNEMPLOYMENT:
AGGREGATE DATA

Not until 1940 was information available on a comprehensive and continuous basis on the extent of unemployment. Census data were available in earlier years in the form of gross figures on those totally unemployed during the census survey week. But these data are not entirely comparable from one census to another, and of course they did not constitute continuous annual series. Private estimates were prepared at least as far back as 1897, but they also are subject to limitations of various sorts.

Unemployment data, 1929 to date. Beginning with the application of the "labor force" concept in 1940, data have been available continuously since that year, and have been carried back to 1929. The data are published in the *Monthly Report on the Labor Force,* prepared by the Bureau of the Census. While one might question the concepts utilized in this labor force framework, the statistical techniques employed (though basic changes and improvements were made in 1954), and the possible sampling errors in the estimates, the data are nevertheless reliable indicators of changes in the volume of employment and unemployment. And they are far better than anything we have had in the past.

The relevant definitions in this labor force conceptual framework are as follows.[4]

1. *"Employed.*—Employed persons comprise those who, during the survey week, were either (a) "at work"—those who did any work for pay or profit, or worked without pay for 15 hours or more on a family farm or business; or (b) "with a job but not at work"— those who did not work and were not looking for work but had a job or business from which they were temporarily absent because of vacation, illness, industrial dispute, bad weather, or layoff with definite instructions to return to work within 30 days of layoff. Also included are persons who had new jobs to which they were scheduled to report within 30 days.
2. *"Unemployed.*—Unemployed persons include those who did not work at all during the survey week and were looking for work. Also included as unemployed are persons who would have been looking for work except that (a) they were temporarily ill, (b)

[4] See U. S. Department of Commerce, Bureau of the Census, "Concepts and Methods Used in the Current Labor Force Statistics . . . ," *Current Population Reports,* Series P–23, No. 2 (July 30, 1954), particularly p. 2. For a useful discussion see W. S. Woytinsky and Associates, *Employment and Wages in the United States* (New York: The Twentieth Century Fund, 1953), chaps. xxxii, xxxiii by Thomas C. Fichandler.

PROBLEMS OF UNEMPLOYMENT 161

they expected to return to a job from which they had been laid
off for an indefinite period, or (c) they believed no work was
available in their line of work or in the community.

3. *"Labor force.*—The civilian labor force comprises the total of all
civilians classified as employed or unemployed in accordance
with the criteria described above. The total labor force also includes members of the Armed Forces stationed either in the
United States or abroad."

Using these definitions, data on employment and unemployment
are available from 1929 on. Table 6.2 summarizes this information.

TABLE 6.2

EMPLOYMENT–UNEMPLOYMENT, 1929–1955

		In Labor Force			
	Total	Civilian Labor Force			
Annual	Including Armed			Unemployed	
Average	Forces	Civilian	Employed	Number	Per Cent
1929	49,440	49,180	47,630	1,550	3.2
1930	50,080	49,820	45,480	4,340	8.7
1931	50,680	50,420	42,400	8,020	15.9
1932	51,250	51,000	38,940	12,060	23.6
1933	51,840	51,590	38,760	12,830	24.9
1934	52,490	52,230	40,890	11,340	21.7
1935	53,140	52,870	42,260	10,610	20.1
1936	53,740	53,440	44,410	9,030	16.9
1937	54,320	54,000	46,300	7,700	14.3
1938	54,950	54,610	44,220	10,390	19.0
1939	55,600	55,230	45,750	9,480	17.2
1940	56,030	55,640	47,520	8,120	14.6
1941	57,380	55,910	50,350	5,560	9.9
1942	60,230	56,410	53,750	2,660	4.7
1943	64,410	55,540	54,470	1,070	1.9
1944	65,890	54,630	53,960	670	1.2
1945	65,140	53,860	52,820	1,040	1.9
1946	60,820	57,520	55,250	2,270	3.9
1947	61,608	60,168	58,027	2,142	3.6
1948	62,748	61,442	59,378	2,064	3.4
1949	63,571	62,105	58,710	3,395	5.5
1950	64,599	63,099	59,957	3,142	5.0
1951	65,832	62,884	61,005	1,879	3.0
1952	66,426	62,966	61,293	1,673	2.7
1953	66,965	63,418	61,894	1,523	2.5
1954*	67,819	64,468	61,238	3,230	5.0
1955	68,896	65,847	63,193	2,654	4.0

* Beginning in 1954 a new sample was used; data from this year on are therefore
not strictly comparable with those of previous periods.

Source: U. S. Department of Commerce, Bureau of the Census, *Statistical Abstract
of the United States, 1954,* Table 218, p. 195. Data for 1954 and 1955 from current
labor force reports. Figures in thousands.

Unemployment data, 1897–1929. Additional data, going back to 1897, are available to round out more fully the picture on employment and unemployment. These data, are, however, set in a conceptual framework different from that of the "labor force." Hence the pre- and post-1929 data are not comparable. Yet it may be useful to summarize this pre-1929 evidence. Douglas has analyzed the period 1897–1926 for manufacturing, transportation, building trades, and mining. His figures show full-time unemployment fluctuating between a low of 5.5 per cent in 1918 and a high of 23.1 per cent in 1921. The average approximates 10 per cent, rising above 15 per cent only in seven years.[5] Data prepared by the National Industrial Conference Board, using the "gainful worker" concept, indicate "full employment" for four years (1906, 1917–1919) between 1900 and 1928. In all other years, there was a net of full-time unemployment, ranging from .4 to 11 per cent, with both a median and mean of 3.6 per cent. Unemployment is defined in the Conference Board summaries as the difference between *estimates* of the total number of gainful workers and *estimates* of employment. New estimates made in 1951 by Herring parallel rather closely those of the Conference Board.[6]

Other sources of unemployment data. In conjunction with the operation of the Unemployment Insurance program, the Bureau of Employment Security prepares weekly figures on initial unemployment claims as well as on insured unemployment. For the week ending July 21, 1956, insured unemployment was 1,219,900, this comparing with a labor force unemployment total figure of 2,833,000.[7] Of necessity, insured unemployment figures are lower; for, quite apart from technical statistical differences, not all the unemployed are covered under the unemployment insurance system. The data are useful, however, for comparative purposes.

State agencies frequently provide monthly, annual, or other time-period estimates, useful on the local or regional level.[8]

[5] See Paul H. Douglas, *Real Wages in the United States, 1890–1926,* (Boston: Houghton Mifflin Co., 1930), Table 172, p. 460. See also the paper by Stanley Lebergott, "Annual Estimates of Unemployment in the United States, 1900–1950," presented at the Universities-National Bureau of Economic Research *Conference on the Measurement and Behavior of Unemployment.*

[6] See National Industrial Conference Board, *Economic Almanac,* New York, 1945–1946, pp. 38–39; and John P. Herring, *Labor Force, Employment and Unemployment* (Seattle: University of Washington Press, 1951), p. 47.

[7] See the handy "Combined Employment and Unemployment Release" appended to U. S. Department of Commerce, Bureau of the Census, *Current Population Reports, Labor Force,* Series P–57, No. 169, August, 1956.

[8] Such data can customarily be obtained, without cost, from the appropriate unemployment insurance administrative agency in the state.

THE MEASUREMENT OF UNEMPLOYMENT:
SPECIALIZED DATA

Unemployment has dimensions other than weekly, monthly or annual aggregates for the economy. Data—detailed in some cases, fragmentary in others—are available for various of these other dimensions and are discussed below. A knowledge of these other dimensions is important because attempts to deal with unemployment must take cognizance of them. The problem is far more complex than that of merely finding X number of additional jobs for the economy as a whole.

General employment and earnings. The Bureau of Labor Statistics, in its monthly publication *Employment and Earnings,* provides data on employment trends, employment, and labor turnover. Such data are technically of the same dimension as the averages noted above; these employment data are, however, useful supplements to labor force figures. The data are not directly comparable with those from the *Monthly Report on the Labor Force,* since the latter uses household reporting (receives its information from households) as compared with establishment reporting (receives its information from business firms) for the former. The approaches also are conceptually different. The BLS measures the number of jobs; the MRLF the number of individuals with jobs.

Unemployment by regions. Unemployment tends to vary by regions. In part this is a function of the types of industry located therein; and in part it arises out of broader regional economic forces; in part it may result from natural or other phenomena such as windstorms, floods, and so on. The Bureau of Employment Security presently classifies major labor markets ("regions") into six groups, ranging from labor shortage areas (with less than a 1.5 per cent ratio of unemployment to total labor force) to labor surplus areas (with an unemployment ratio of 12 per cent or more). At mid-year 1956 the following *major* continental U. S. labor market areas were classified as Group F with 12 per cent or more unemployment: Lawrence, Massachusetts; Scranton and Wilkes-Barre —Hazelton, Pennsylvania.[9] If one takes a figure of 3.0 to 5.9 per cent (and over) unemployment as a critical ratio, then 105 United States labor market areas were in such a position. The policy uses of such regional data are readily apparent; they afford a basis upon which assistance of one type or another can be given to the distressed area.

[9] *The Labor Market and Employment Security,* June, 1956, pp. 9–16.

Unemployment by occupation and industry. Unemployment also varies by occupation and industry. Thus, in 1954 the following occupational breakdown can be found.

TABLE 6.3

PERCENTAGE UNEMPLOYMENT, BY OCCUPATIONAL GROUP, 1954

Occupational Group	*October, 1954*
All experienced workers	4.2
Professional and semi-professional workers	1.7
Farmers and farm managers	0.2
Proprietors, managers, and officials, except farmers . . .	1.3
Clerical and kindred workers	3.3
Salesmen and saleswomen	3.4
Craftsmen, foremen and kindred workers	4.6
Operatives and kindred workers	6.6
Domestic service workers	5.4
Service workers, except domestic	4.5
Farm laborers and foremen	2.1
Laborers, except farm and mine	8.4

Source: U. S. Department of Commerce, Bureau of the Census, "Annual Report on the Labor Force, 1954," *Current Population Reports,* Series P–50, No. 59, Table IX, p. 9.

The reasons for these differences are explained in terms of the nature of the occupation, its seasonality, its skill levels, the "fixed cost" nature of certain occupational classes, and so on.

Industry variations likewise exist. Thus, construction tends to have a high percentage of unemployed; self-employed a low, with others in between. In part, the self-employment figures may be misleading, since many of the self-employed may continue in marginal businesses rather than look for employment elsewhere.[10]

Unemployment by age and sex. Hauser and Pearl found, except for the war years, no "striking differences over the past decade [1940–1950] between the unemployment rates of men and women."[11] In absolute numbers there have been changes, however, with unemployed men outnumbering unemployed women three to one in 1940, but only two and one-half to one or so at the end of the decade. By age there appears to be a higher rate for the teen-age group, tapering off to ages forty-five to fifty-four and then tending to rise again. This is the familiar "U-shaped" curve. The reasons for this are al-

[10] See T. C. Fichandler, cited in Woytinsky, *op. cit.,* pp. 412 ff., for an interesting discussion of these cases.

[11] See Philip M. Hauser and Robert B. Pearl, "Who Are the Unemployed?" *Journal of the American Statistical Association,* XLV, No. 252 (December, 1950), 486–89.

most self-evident in terms of employer and union policies, and of American cultural factors.[12]

Unemployment by duration of unemployment. The following table summarizes, in monthly averages, this information for 1955, for persons fourteen years and older. While short-term unemployment has its serious consequences, it is the individual who exhausts

TABLE 6.4

UNEMPLOYED PERSONS, BY DURATION OF UNEMPLOYMENT, 1955

	Duration of Unemployment				Average Duration of
Total Unemployed	4 Weeks and Under	5–14 Weeks	15–26 Weeks	Over 26 Weeks	Unemployment in Weeks
2,654,000	1,136,000	815,000	366,000	336,000	13.2

Source: See the tabular summary in *Economic Report of the President, January, 1956* (Washington, D. C.: U. S. Government Printing Office), p. 186.

his right to unemployment compensation who, with his family, faces the critical problem.[13] In periods of high-level employment, the number of such cases is not likely to be large, but even here there may be industry or regional cases where critical developments occur. In New England, for example, in the benefit years 1949–1950 (during the critical decline in employment) 38.5 per cent of the claimants exhausted their benefit rights.[14] Duration of unemployment appears to be higher for men than for women, and higher for older than for younger persons.

Other dimensions. The unemployment rate in the United States is consistently higher for nonwhite than for white workers, and this is true even during periods of "full" employment.[15] There is an inverse correlation between income group and unemployment. Here again the reasons are largely those of occupational association,

[12] For data on the older worker, see U. S. Department of Labor, Bureau of Labor Statistics, "Employment and Economic Status of Older Men and Women," *Bulletin 1092,* May, 1952.

[13] Professor George P. Shultz has suggested that it is not only aggregate unemployment figures that are important, but also who has been unemployed, how long, and other relevant characteristics. He suggests that the majority of unemployment in 1954–1956 was "transition" unemployment, and hence less serious than chronic unemployment.

[14] See Walter Galenson, *A Report on Unemployment Benefit Costs in Massachusetts* (Boston: Commonwealth of Massachusetts, 1950), p. 46.

[15] See Joseph W. Garbarino, *The Unemployed Worker during a Period of "Full" Employment,* Reprint No. 50 (Berkeley: University of California, Institute of Industrial Relations, 1954), pp. 16–23.

lower income tending to be associated with occupations having independently a higher unemployment rate.

"FULL EMPLOYMENT" AND THE HISTORICAL PATTERN OF UNEMPLOYMENT

If one accepts the maintenance of a high level of employment as a desirable goal of society, then it may be instructive to measure past performance of the economy with this yardstick. A "high level of employment" may, of course, be interpreted in different ways. In turn, the performance record will vary depending upon the standard selected.

At one extreme is the criterion of "full employment." Defined in its most rigorous sense the concept has been interpreted as

"Full employment . . . means having always more vacant jobs than unemployed men . . . it means that the normal lag between losing one job and finding another will be very short."[16]

A somewhat less rigorous definition, though not necessarily incompatible with Beveridge's, is found in a United Nations Report:

". . . We define full employment as a situation in which unemployment does not exceed the minimum allowances that must be made for the effects of seasonal and frictional forces."[17]

A yardstick which appears still less exacting is given in the 1953 *Economic Report of the President,* where it is noted:

"And it is assumed for purposes of this study that unemployment, which during the past 2 years has been below the 2-million mark, could rise to as much as 2½ million by 1955 without presenting a general unemployment problem. Such an unemployment figure in a considerably larger labor force would not depart so markedly from the Nation's legislated objective of "maximum employment" as to call for new counteracting public measures. . . ."[18]

Two and one-half million out of a labor force of 68.6 million (the 1955 projection) would amount to a percentage of 3.6. Various other views of "high-level" employment are to be found, ranging up to unemployment levels of 5 per cent or so.[19] (In some cases a

[16] See William H. Beveridge, *Full Employment in a Free Society* (New York: W. W. Norton & Co., 1945), p. 18.

[17] See *National and International Measures For Full Employment* (Lake Success: United Nations, 1949), p. 13.

[18] *The Economic Report of the President, January, 1953* (Washington, D. C.: U. S. Government Printing Office), p. 83.

[19] See Lloyd Reynolds, *Labor Economics and Labor Relations* (2d ed.; Englewood Cliffs, N. J.: Prentice-Hall, Inc., 1954), p. 460, where he notes: ". . . something like 5 per cent unemployment may be close to the point of price balance in our economy." The 5 per cent level is also the judgment of the Committee for Economic Development.

range of percentages is used, with variations allowed for seasonal and frictional factors.)

If one takes the least rigorous concept of "full employment" (or "high-level employment")—say 5 per cent unemployment—then in fourteen of the last twenty-seven years this standard has not been attained. Moreover, seven of the years in which it was reached were war years. If one looks at the years prior to 1929, using Douglas' figures, the record is also one of less than 50 per cent achievement. However, using Conference Board or Herring figures, the record is much better. Conversely, the record also has been much better since 1940, even in the nonwar years. And with both major political parties committed to some sort of "full-employment" plank, it is not likely that we shall see in our lifetime a duplication of the experience of the 1930's. It should be noted, however, that the reduction of unemployment is not necessarily a cost-free process; noneconomic as well as economic costs are involved. Moreover, "full employment" accompanied by rising prices is not a cost-free phenomenon.[20] The implications of these statements are patent.

THE IMPACTS OF UNEMPLOYMENT

Thus far we have talked about the dimensions of unemployment without specifying in any detail why it is an undesirable phenomenon. In one respect its undesirability may appear obvious; in others it may be well to go into more detail. These may be set down in a number of categories.

Impacts upon the economy. Unemployment has negative impacts upon the level of economic activity in the economy, the region, or the locality. (We make no distinction here as to "cause" and "result.") The experience of the United States in the 1930's, of various textile mill areas in the north for a longer period, or of the western "ghost town" illustrates this point. The impact upon industries and firms, and upon other businesses in various areas, is also clear, as is the influence upon future supplies of skilled labor.

Impacts upon the individual and his family. The direct economic impacts here are obvious. But there are indirect and noneconomic consequences. While it is hard to quantify these impacts, or even estimate their seriousness in some cases, there seems to be little doubt that they are undesirable rather than desirable in nature.

[20] Indeed, some labor economists view unemployment as a phenomenon which has a psychotic hold on the American consciousness and they suggest that overexpansion rather than deflation has been the tendency in the past fifty years. See, for example, Orme W. Phelps, *Introduction to Labor Economics* (New York: McGraw-Hill Book Co., Inc., 1950), pp. 155–59.

There appears to be some loss of skill in protracted unemployment, a worsening of the mental outlook, some increase in delinquency, physical debilitation, very frequently of children in the family, and some deterioration of the family as a unit.[21]

Impacts upon social institutions. Unemployment reaches beyond the individual, the family, and beyond economic forces to society as a whole. It affects social institutions of many types, changing the direction toward which political parties move, instituting new beliefs and new groups—Technocracy and the Technocrats, the Townsend plan and the Townsendites—and making for a realignment of the structure of society.[22]

Whether these societal changes can be held to be essentially undesirable (as were the impacts upon the individual and his family) is a matter of opinion. Certainly, however, unemployment has been an important instrumentality in making for change. Unemployment has been, to be sure, only a symptom of deeper-lying causes, yet there is little doubt that it was one of the symbols seized upon in the pressures of social change.

The Types of Unemployment

There are many ways of classifying the "types" of unemployment or, what is frequently construed as the same thing, the "causes" of unemployment. We shall adopt a classification that is useful in and of itself and which will also permit us to discuss, on the same basis, various approaches to the solution of unemployment. This classification is the same three-fold system developed earlier in this chapter and is as follows:[23]

1. "Aggregate" unemployment, reflecting "secular" or "cyclical" causal factors, including the idea of "permanent underemployment"

[21] Several useful, though older, sources which discuss this problem are Philip Klein, *The Burden of Unemployment* (New York: The Russell Sage Foundation, 1923); Stuart A. Rice, "The Effect of Unemployment upon the Worker and His Family," in *Business Cycles and Unemployment* (New York: McGraw-Hill Book Co., Inc., 1923); and *Men without Work, A Report Made to the Pilgrim Trust* (Cambridge: Cambridge University Press, 1938). Areas of interest change, and we have relatively little research of this type today as compared with a quarter-century ago. Perhaps the last big wave of data concerns the physical and mental condition of members of the armed forces in World War II and the relation of such condition to economic experiences of the post-1929 period.

[22] For an interesting analysis, see Robert S. and Helen M. Lynd, *Middletown in Transition* (New York: Harcourt, Brace and Co., Inc., 1937); and Frederick Lewis Allen's two books, *Only Yesterday* and *Since Yesterday* (New York: Harper & Brothers, 1931 and 1939 respectively).

[23] For a broader set of concepts, see *National and International Measures For Full Employment,* pp. 11 and ff.

2. "Selective" or "structural" unemployment, reflecting seasonal, technological, casual, and other causal factors
3. "Personal" unemployment, largely involving the personalized operation of the labor market: the ways in which jobs are gotten and the ways in which employers operate in the labor market.

We will take up each of these in turn.

AGGREGATE UNEMPLOYMENT

This type of unemployment is at first instance a reflection of the *aggregate* demand for labor. Given this statement, different analysts in the labor field approach the problem somewhat differently, although two main lines of thought can be found.

1. The first type of aggregate unemployment involves the idea that the customary state of the economy, particularly an industrialized economy, is characterized by an insufficiency and instability of effective demand. The key to understanding this effective demand problem lies in recognizing the fact that, under a private enterprise system, the decisions to save and to invest are to a considerable extent independent of each other. This approach reflects the course of developments culminating in Lord Keynes' *General Theory* in 1936. If permanent underemployment is not only a theoretical possibility but an empirical tendency, then appropriate counter-measures must be found, whether privately or publicly originated. Both major American political parties, whether they would grant the logical validity of such a type of underemployment (at least on a permanent basis), are seemingly committed to monetary and fiscal policies which would prevent the phenomenon from occurring.

2. A second type of aggregate or "mass" employment is that caused by cyclical forces.[24] The drop in production—and employment—may be triggered by a drop in spending occurring anywhere in the economy, but is most likely to develop in capital expenditures, government outlays, or consumer purchases of durables, with probably the first and second items the more important.[25] It is cyclical unemployment which has been the most serious and the most pro-

[24] See, for example, Lloyd Reynolds, *op. cit.*, pp. 455 and ff. It is interesting to note that, except for a footnote on p. 631, Reynolds does not mention Keynes—nor does he discuss permanent underemployment. Fashions change in this field as well as in others.

[25] Here is an example of where our analysis stops at the proximate stage; to get at the reasons for the change in expenditures would lead us into topics outside the province of this discussion. Obviously, however, any monetary and fiscal policy which tackles the unemployment problem cannot stop at the proximate level, but must go deeper.

longed type in the United States. Reference to Table 6.2 reveals this correspondence.

SELECTIVE OR STRUCTURAL UNEMPLOYMENT

In contrast to "mass" unemployment, with its impact upon the economy as a whole, there are numerous other types of unemployment affecting only particular individuals or groups in the economy. Such unemployment is sometimes called "normal," since some authorities hold it to be expected in a dynamically functioning economy. Given causal factors lie behind each of these types. These causal factors are all demand-deficiency oriented, but the deficiency is specialized rather than generalized as is the case in mass unemployment, and it arises out of structural features of the economy. Inasmuch as solutions to each type involve an understanding of causes, it is desirable to spell them out.

1. Seasonal unemployment is the single most important type of nonmass unemployment. Woytinsky notes that in the pre-World War II period, seasonal changes tended to make October (the high month) employment some 4.1 to 4.3 million higher than in the low month of January, although the latter month was not the seasonal trough for all industries.[26] Seasonality is essentially a function of two factors: first, weather conditions, influencing agriculture and outdoor construction, and second, "custom," affecting demand and production in industries such as automobiles, apparel, and retail trade. These two major factors exhibit some interdependence. Since there is likewise an interdependence among business enterprises in the economy, the economic impacts of seasonality may extend outward like the ripples made when a stone is cast into a millpond.

2. Casual unemployment can be viewed as a foreshortened form of the seasonal type. In this case the work is also intermittent in nature, but on a daily or weekly basis rather than by seasons. Longshoring provides a case in point. In such industries and occupations the problem may be heightened further by the attachment of an excessive labor force.

3. Technological unemployment results from the "displacement of men by machines." We do not argue here whether in the aggregate or in the long run such unemployment actually exists. In the short run and for certain individuals and groups, there is little doubt of the reality of job separations from this cause.[27] "Automation"

[26] See W. Woytinsky, op. cit., pp. 336–41.
[27] For two useful discussions, see the Work Projects Administration project reports, Survey of Economic Theory on Technological Change and Employment, and Unemployment and Technological Change (Philadelphia, 1940).

represents a contemporary illustration of this phenomenon.[28] The 1955 Congressional hearings on automation attest to the contemporary importance of—and fears about—the automation process.[29]

4. Secular declines in demand for specific types of goods and services—and hence declines in the derived demand for labor—are causes of unemployment. Again, while the long-run effects of such changes may be debatable, there is little doubt about the short-run displacement. Illustrations in this field are numerous: diesel for steam power, the synthetic revolution in fabrics, the change in styles of women's headgear, the decline in the use of men's hats. The first two of the above illustrations indicate demand changes linked with broadscale changes in technology; the latter two are indicative of changes in fashion.

5. Conversion-reconversion unemployment, noted in particular from 1940 on as the United States converted twice to war and back to peace again. While this form of displacement may be short-lived, and may not even result in a change of employers by the individuals involved, it may be sufficiently serious locally to warrant calling it an emergency.[30]

6. In all the above cases, regional unemployment may be a resultant. Thus, technological change may leave a community with heavy unemployment. Or, changes in demand for goods and services may do the same. But stranded areas may result from other causes: depletion of local natural resources, the migration of industry, or natural disasters.[31]

7. Finally, in the area of specific unemployment, there may be a miscellany of causes: industrial disputes, the failure of a specific business enterprise, temporary natural disasters (the floods of 1955 in New England are ample illustration of this), and other factors.

The above seven types are different from mass unemployment essentially in terms of the causes and of the numbers of people involved. On this basis the remedy to be applied may likewise be expected to be different. It is for this reason the story is spelled out in some detail.

[28] For a useful discussion, see George B. Baldwin and George P. Shultz, "Automation: A New Dimension to Old Problems," *Proceedings* of the Seventh Annual Meeting of the Industrial Relations Research Association, 1954.

[29] See *Monthly Labor Review*, LXXIX, No. 1 (January, 1956), 7–19; LXXVIII, No. 6 (June, 1955), 637–44; LXXVIII, No. 5 (May, 1955), 519–27.

[30] We have numerous examples of this type in the war and post-war periods. Reference to newspaper articles in states such as Michigan tell the story.

[31] For union commentary, see "The Distressed Area: A Growing National Problem," *The CIO Economic Outlook* XVI, No. 7–8 (July–August, 1955).

PERSONAL UNEMPLOYMENT

The above two major categories may be viewed as impersonal in form, in that the finger of unemployment beckons impartially. (We exempt here nonimpartial cases of "favoritism" in layoffs and discharges; the developing appliction of seniority and the use of grievance procedures have tended to lessen this.) But some individuals may find it difficult to obtain their first job; others, once displaced, may find re-employment difficult; and in the extreme case, the "unemployable" may result. In other instances, where workers are displaced for whatever cause, they may find other employment, but it may take an uneconomical amount of time. This problem is related to two factors: (1) the job-getting process: the way applicants look for jobs and the way in which employers look for employees (or, more broadly speaking, the process through which the labor market matches man and job), and (2) institutional restraints upon employment possibilities of various classes of people.[32]

The unemployment solution in such cases is quite different from that of aggregate or selective unemployment. In these latter two cases the approach is essentially through the "creation" of more jobs or through their regularization. In personal unemployment the approach is through the improvement of the job marketing process. "Frictional" unemployment of some magnitude is to be expected in any dynamic economy. But the duration of such unemployment can no doubt be lessened through the wide dissemination of information about job openings and through other techniques designed to bring applicant and job together. Moreover, a more rational labor marketing process would make for a better matching of applicant and job and thus tend to decrease disguised unemployment. Finally, a re-evaluation of employment standards may make possible a reduction in the hard core of the unemployables.

Approaches to the Problem of Unemployment

In this chapter we shall concern ourselves essentially with public preventive measures, reserving for the next chapter a discussion of the chief public alleviative measure (unemployment insurance) and for the following chapter a discussion of private approaches to unemployment.

[32] As a minimum assignment, the student should look at L. G. Reynolds and Joseph Shister, *Job Horizons* (New York: Harper and Brothers, 1949); L. G. Reynolds, *The Structure of Labor Markets* (New York: Harper and Brothers, 1951); and E. W. Noland and E. W. Bakke, *Workers Wanted* (New York: Harper and Brothers, 1949).

AGGREGATE UNEMPLOYMENT: GENERAL ISSUES

Any analysis of the prevention (or reduction) of aggregate or mass unemployment requires a prior consideration of five issues.

1. What is the line at which mass unemployment is construed as beginning? The answer is of paramount importance because public measures of one type or another may not be set into motion until this point is reached or approached. While there is no unanimous answer to the question, there is some agreement about a 3 to 5 per cent zone, with allowable variations for frictional and seasonal impacts. Interestingly enough, these figures result from two different types of beliefs. The first is that if unemployment goes over, for example, 5 per cent, a danger point has been reached, and mass unemployment, with detrimental effects upon the economy, is the next step. The second is that if *less* than 5 per cent unemployment is reached, inflationary pressures may throw the economy out of balance in the other direction. Trying to walk the 5 per cent tightrope is an obvious impossibility; in the thirties the United States economy was well over the figure, with deflationary consequences; in the forties the picture was the opposite. The best one can probably hope for is that excess pressures do not develop in either direction.

2. As a corollary of the above, if underemployment is construed as undesirable, so likewise is overemployment, with its inflationary pressures. Whereas the specter of the thirties was unemployment and deflation, the problem of the two decades since then has been (except for two short periods) in the opposite direction. And it may well be that the outlook for the near future is in a direction opposite from that of deflation. Hence public policy should be expected to deal with over- as well as with mass underemployment.

3. In this type of analysis it is not necessary to enter the equilibrium-at-less-than-full-employment controversy, nor to try to distinguish between those measures designed to counter cyclical mass unemployment and those to counter long-run equilibrium unemployment, if such is a possibility. There are two reasons for this. First, the anti-unemployment policies that have been suggested are in certain measure the same whether the phenomenon is cyclical or long-run. Second, at the present time, one has no way of knowing empirically whether any "downturn" is merely a cyclical indication or whether it has other implications.

4. In general, mass unemployment requires an attack on other than the labor front. That is, actions by employees, unions and/or employers are not, in themselves, likely to be enough to resolve

unemployment problems. Moreover, actions to reduce the labor supply to a given demand level are not as desirable as those of raising demand. Given these stipulations, mass unemployment requires action on broader monetary and fiscal fronts. This is noted in greater detail in Chapter 8, where it will be seen that the stabilizing activities of employers and unions, while of considerable value, are not in themselves sufficient to counteract mass unemployment movements.

5. If a broad attack is required, then governmental action is necessary. To some people and groups this intrusion by government may be undesirable. Such opposition is less formidable than it used to be, however, and there seems to be some general acceptance of the role of government in maintaining the well-being of the economy.

Aggregate Unemployment: Preventive Measures

Two basic preventive approaches exist in the United States today. The first involves the use of "automatic" devices, wherein unemployment (and a lowering of economic activity) call forth their own compensatory devices. The second includes using discretionary and consciously planned actions.[33]

The first category of devices includes what have come to be called "built-in stabilizers." There are a number of such stabilizers presently existent in the economy, some linked directly to employment, others not. Among the principal stabilizers are the following.

Unemployment insurance and other welfare payments. An increase in unemployment does not curtail purchasing power by an equivalent increment, because unemployment insurance shores up the purchasing power of the covered unemployed. This program is countercyclical in nature, collecting more in taxes than is paid out in benefits in prosperous times, and vice versa.[34] (The program may not be entirely countercyclical, insofar as "experience rating" modifies this characteristic.) Other transfer payments, such as public assistance, play an important role.[35]

The graduated income tax. This tax is of such a nature that a given increase in income occasions a greater than proportional in-

[33] For a useful discussion, see the articles in *Policies to Combat Depression,* A Report of the National Bureau of Economic Research (Princeton: Princeton University Press, 1956).

[34] We shall discuss in Chapter 14 the quantitative counterbalancing impact of unemployment insurance.

[35] For an excellent discussion of built-in economic security stabilizers see Ida C. Merriam, "Social Security Programs and Economic Stability," *Policies To Combat Depression, op. cit.*

crease in the tax, and vice versa. Thus, as economic activity lessens and incomes decrease, the income tax decreases proportionately. With given marginal propensities to consume, this stabilizer also is countercyclical.

Other measures. There are other types of built-in stabilizers. These include farm-aid programs, wherein compensatory payments tend to move in directions opposite from that of the cycle, and corporate and family savings which tend to exhibit the same tendency.

While these built-in stabilizers are of some countercyclical importance, they are not at present in and of themselves sufficient to create a balance in the economy. Therefore, other measures have been suggested and utilized in the past, of which public works and monetary and fiscal policy are the most important.

Public works. As countercyclical devices, public works have been exhaustively analyzed and discussed, particularly in the thirties.[36] It will be useful, however, to comment briefly on such measures.

The rationale of the public works approach is simple. Since various public projects—roads, airports, dams, office buildings, schools—must be undertaken from time to time, why not undertake such projects (or the majority of them) when the economy is operating at less than optimum capacity? Two purposes would be served by such an approach: first, "excessive" construction, adding fuel to the flames, would be avoided in prosperous times and, second, the economy would be shored up by the introduction of such construction in depressed times.

Various problems are raised by such an approach. One is planning. For a rational system to be used, there should be advance planning, so that construction undertaken returns the greatest possible yield per dollar of investment. On this basis we would hold that projects of this type are preferable to those which merely seek to get money into circulation. This in turn implies that the program should not seek to maximize direct employment at the expense of efficiency, and conversely that public works employees should be regarded as bona fide workers, not as relief clients, and should be paid going wages.

Another problem is timing, which raises a number of difficult issues. The public cannot postpone indefinitely all projects. This

---

[36] For useful summaries, see Arthur D. Gayer, *Public Works in Prosperity and Depression* (New York: National Bureau of Economic Research, 1935); and J. M. Clark, *Economics of Planning Public Works* (Washington, D. C.: U. S. Government Printing Office, 1935).

means that construction may have to be undertaken in prosperous times, defeating in part the countercyclical process. The school-building program since World War II illustrates this point. (There is little doubt, of course, that this building program has helped in part to create prosperity.) Again, while it is not likely that the public will "run out" of projects, some problems of this type might develop locally. Here again advance planning is useful. Still another difficulty is deciding when to turn on public works and when to turn them off. Turning them on may be easier than turning them off; thus, if a "danger point" of X per cent unemployed is reached, the program may be set in motion. But since projects require a definite construction period, it may not be so easy to curtail the program when unemployment falls below the danger point by a given amount.

Also, such projects may be of limited usefulness at the local level if they are financed and administered essentially at that level. A recent study concludes that even if state and local public works programs had been stabilized to the greatest degree practicable in the period 1920–1939 they would have changed gross national product in the average year by only a fraction of 1 per cent.[37] The study further raises serious doubts as to the potency of timed public works for alleviating the consequences of cyclical contractions. But, it is also noted that if federal money were made available on a sufficient scale, 25 per cent of the unemployment slack could be taken up by public works. Hence, there is a useful role to be played by such programs, though they may not be the primary measures they were once thought to be. Therefore other approaches must also be used.

Monetary and fiscal policy. The broadest public approach to the employment problem is through monetary and fiscal policy. Through changes in the structure of tax rates, through changes in the level of government expenditure, through debt increases or retirement, and via other means (including public works as noted above), public bodies may seek to maintain a high level employment economy. These control techniques appear to be powerful, and there is some empirical validation of their use. The test of such techniques is that they should accomplish the purposes for which they are introduced; they should neither be self-defeating nor have injurious side effects. Thus, public programs should not reduce the willingness of businessmen to make private capital expenditures nor

---

[37] See W. E. Upjohn Institute for Community Research, *Public Works and Employment From the Local Government Point of View* (Chicago: Public Administration Service, 1955).

should they unstabilize private investment. (As a passing comment, there is no empirical evidence that public programs in the United States have had these negative results; as an illustration one can look at the private expenditure figures during political administrations allegedly "unfriendly" to private enterprise.)

In general, it appears that monetary and fiscal techniques can play an important role in the maintaining of the well-being of the economy.[38] This is true not only in the "direct" sense, but also insofar as they may be used indirectly to promote the stability of private investment in a private enterprise economy. The indirect control approach may be the only feasible one for such an economy. Indirect monetary control methods tend to be more effective in placing upper limits to investment than in preventing downward movement. But special tax incentives may be instrumental in regularizing investment. And, where fluctuations in private investment still persist, countervailing public investment—a direct method—may be used. Obviously, such programs require careful planning and timing by the appropriate authorities.

SELECTIVE OR STRUCTURAL UNEMPLOYMENT

The incidence of selective unemployment upon individuals or groups is a normal function of a dynamic economy. To reduce this type of unemployment to zero would be equivalent to making the economy more rigid. But there is little doubt that a reduction is possible in given cases, that critical instances of such unemployment might be treated on some sort of emergency basis, and that the readjustments occasioned by this type of unemployment should be made as expeditiously as the situation allows.

There are a number of methods by which such selective unemployment can be attacked. First, employers and unions can seek to regularize employment, as, for example, in the case of seasonal variations; to assist in readjustment where job severance is involved, through the use of dismissal wages; to plan rationally the introduction of new equipment; to develop employment and wage guarantees. All these private methods are discussed in Chapter 8. Likewise, the government can seek to improve the operation of the labor market in providing information about jobs and job openings, and in trying to bring demands for and supplies of labor together. This method—the public employment service—is developed in the next section in this chapter.

[38] See *National and International Measures for Full Employment*, Part II, for a fuller discussion of this entire subject.

There are other ways, however, in which selective unemployment can be tackled, particularly by governmental agencies. Among such methods are the following.

Allocation of government defense or other contracts. Thus, if labor market area A is classed as a labor surplus area and if it has certain types of productive facilities, the government may specifically allocate contracts to it. This approach was used in the period 1950–1953. The usefulness of this method in reducing pockets of unemployment is obvious. The dangers are that it may become a political pressure problem with all the attendant dangers. This is pointedly illustrated in a converse problem: the closing of (or attempts to close) army and navy installations of various types.

Nonemergency "financial" relief afforded to industries or regions. The following mechanisms come to mind: stockpiling programs; accelerated depreciation allowances as for defense industries; changes in credit terms as for housing, automobiles, and home appliance producers; direct subsidies for various industries, such as shipbuilding; tariff changes, as for the watchmaking and bicycle industries; and so on. These selective measures may be disadvantageous to the consumer at large (as in the tariff illustration) and they may be unwise economically, but they may be of direct help in the local employment situation.

Direct emergency assistance. In the case of natural or other disasters—droughts, floods, hurricanes, tornadoes—government agencies may seek to assist in the restoration of business activity (and employment) by direct loans, emergency grants, and other measures. Thus, at the time of the western New England floods in the fall of 1955, federal and state emergency measures were taken to alleviate the situation.

"Minimum" federal program for relief of distressed areas. As an example, the CIO suggested coordinated administration, technical assistance, public works, loans to private investors, fast tax-writeoffs, procurement, training and transportation, unemployment compensation, and pensions.[39]

Reclamation of depressed industrial areas. The federal government has, as this book is written, a series of plans for the "reclamation of depressed industrial areas" through a variety of techniques including many of those specified above.[40]

[39] See *Economic Outlook*, XVI, No. 7–8 (July-August, 1955), p. 61.
[40] See the *Economic Report of the President, January, 1956* (Washington, D. C.: U. S. Government Printing Office), pp. 61–63.

The advantages of all the above mechanisms are obvious. The dangers are twofold. First, government assistance may be based primarily upon partisan political considerations. And, second, the assistance may perpetuate an already uneconomical situation. Thus, governmental measures to maintain farm employment opportunities would be open to serious debate, since one of the logical solutions of this problem appears to be increasing mobility *from* the farm. (Here is an exception to the rule of increasing demand rather than reducing supply; in this case a reduction in supply is called for.)[41] Yet if these measures are judiciously used, there is little doubt but that they can assist in mitigating the readjustment problems associated with selective unemployment.

PERSONAL UNEMPLOYMENT

The two categories of unemployment noted above tend to be impersonal in nature. But the labor market functions in a personal way: individuals try to get their first jobs, individuals become unemployed, given employers offer jobs, and so on. And in order for individuals to know of jobs and facts about them, and for employers to know of job applicants, it is necessary that the labor market maximize its flow of information. In so providing a two-way flow of information, the labor market will not only make it easier to secure the first job, but also facilitate the employment readjustments necessitated by mass or selective unemployment. This labor market procedure may be developed in two ways: first, by structuring an unstructured market, and second, by increasing the flow of information in a structured market.

An unstructured labor market may be viewed as one in which the only nexus is cash.[42] Structuring introduces other considerations into the market: occupational groupings, attachments of employers for given types of employees and vice versa, developing a flow of information about the job market, using rational techniques in job marketing. While certain of these structural characteristics impose restraints upon the market, others help to rationalize its operation. Interestingly enough, the entry of a union may assist in structuring a labor market, through the introduction of job structures, wage rationalization, information on job availability, and other procedures.

[41] For an interesting analysis of this problem, see H. L. Parsons, *The Impact of Fluctuations in National Income on Agricultural Wages and Employment*, Harvard Studies in Labor in Agriculture, No. 1–HL, 1952.

[42] For a more sophisticated treatment, see Clark Kerr, "The Balkanization of Labor Markets," *Labor Mobility and Economic Opportunity* (Cambridge: The Technology Press, 1954), particularly p. 95.

The employment exchange or service is the major mechanism by means of which the structured market increases the flow of information. In the United States two principal types of agencies, the private and the public employment services are found. While many private employment agencies had unsavory reputations in the past, public regulation has been imposed, and many such agencies perform a useful function today in bringing together job offerer and job seeker in clerical, secretarial, professional, and other fields. Many employers and unions have maintained employment services in one form or another: the hiring hall, preferential hiring, and maintenance of job opportunity lists illustrate these approaches. While these methods may be discriminatory in some instances—as in the case of the preferential treatment given union members—it is probable that the net result has been to increase the structured operation of the labor market.

Although the public employment service approach has a history dating back at least to the early 1900's, it was not until 1933, with the passage of the Wagner-Peyser Act, that the system was fully formalized. This act set up a federal-state system of public employment offices, the purposes of which were to structure the labor markets and to bring together those seeking and those offering jobs.[43] The system was federalized in 1942 as part of the war manpower program and was returned to the states shortly after the war.

The employment service performs a number of functions, including the following: (1) seeking to match workers and jobs through the local employment service office, (2) acting as a service arm of the unemployment insurance system in that those who have applied for unemployment insurance are required to register at such an office, and (3) performing broader service functions such as making labor market surveys.

The employment service is a meeting place for buyers and sellers. An unemployed individual may register for work. An employer may list job openings, specifying in some detail relevant job information. When a job request is received, the employment service provides a referral service by sending applicants to the job. There is no pressure upon the individual to accept the job (except in the case of an applicant drawing unemployment insurance).

The role of the employment service has become increasingly important in the United States.[44] Not only has the abstract objective of increasing the efficiency of labor markets been influenced, but the

---

[43] For a good short summary, see W. Woytinsky, op. cit., pp. 182–85.

[44] The student should become familiar with the monthly publication, The Labor Market and Employment Security.

concrete goal of job placements has annually increased. The employment service operates under a number of difficulties: the problem of securing all the relevant information about jobs and applicants, pressures from both job seekers and job offerers who each want "something better," the use of the service in many cases by "marginal" employers and employees, and the stigma of a political operation. While the quality and quantity of results vary from one state to another, it may be said in general that the service has been increasingly accepted by employers and applicants, that it has become increasingly effective in placement operations, particularly in the blue-collar job category, and that it has had a positive effect in increasing the economic operation of the labor market. It still has a good way to go, however, before its operation can be called optimal.[45]

The labor market should also channel information about job requirements and opportunities to institutions preparing the youth of the country for vocational pursuits. In turn, these institutions should provide means for evaluating the varying job aptitudes of these youths. Increasingly, vocational testing and counseling are being given in high schools, colleges and universities, and elsewhere. Such an approach not only increases the rational functioning of the labor market, but equally importantly, it helps minimize the amount of disguised unemployment.

An Evaluation

Tremendous strides have been made in the United States in the last twenty-five years in the identification and measurement of employment and unemployment. While one may not necessarily agree that the labor force concept, and particularly the Bureau of the Census definitions of employment and unemployment, are the most sophisticated possible, it is true that this approach is a great improvement over a quarter-century ago. And it is likely that continuing improvements will be made, increasing the accuracy of the measurements.

The approach to the unemployment problem requires as well an approach to the overemployment problem, or at least to the problem of a level of employment that invokes inflationary pressures. The American economy became so deflationary-conscious during the

---

[45] See, for example, J. J. Corson's statement: "After twenty years' development, the public employment service is far from an effective national placement institution to provide the service needed by society and the individual." ("The Placement Function in an Industrial Society," in National Manpower Council, *Improving the Work Skills of the Nation.* New York: Columbia University Press, 1955, p. 178).

thirties and forties, that it may well be that the opposite possibility is the greater future threat. There may be more truth than sophistry to the "Uneasy Triangle" argument that a society can have *no more* than any *two* of the following three objectives: free collective bargaining, full employment, and stable prices.[46] In the last decade we have chosen the first two, and the burden has fallen upon those whose incomes did not rise as fast as the average increase in prices. If the past presages the future, then over- as well as underemployment may be a critical problem.

All the techniques we have examined here—monetary and fiscal policies, public works, selective emergency measures, employment exchanges—seem capable of performing useful roles in the prevention or reduction of unemployment. In general, where various of these policies have been applied, the performance record has been good, including even the emergency "alphabet" agencies of the New Deal. But there seems to be little doubt that some measures may produce undesirable economic consequences. Thus, measures to prevent mass unemployment may lead to overemployment. Or, emergency measures designed to reduce unemployment in critical areas may do so, but may also perpetuate uneconomic situations instead of, say, encouraging the labor mobility necessary to rectify the situation.

In conclusion, the unemployment–overemployment problem is one of delicate balance. There is no necessary guarantee that the marketing mechanism will automatically achieve and maintain this balance for society. And if the government, broadly defined, seeks to assist in maintaining equilibrium, it has powerful tools at its command, but it also has several pressing problems. First, it may have to make a choice with respect to the alternatives that are open to society: free collective bargaining, full employment, and stable prices. Second, it must administer its policies so as to achieve the alternatives it selects. This requires establishing criteria of various "levels" of employment, securing a continuous flow of information thereon, choosing the correct policy, and timing the actions carefully.[47] The best we can probably hope for is achievement within a limited range. But there is little doubt that we can avoid the debacle of the thirties. And, with wisdom and a little courage, we

[46] See "The Uneasy Triangle" in *The Economist*, issues of August 9, 16, 23, 1952, pp. 322–23, 376–78, and 434–35, respectively. This trilogy was propounded earlier in this country by C. O. Hardy. For skepticism about its validity, see the paper by Milton Friedman in *The Impact of the Union*, edited by D. McC. Wright (New York: Harcourt, Brace and Co., 1951), particularly pp. 226 ff.

[47] See in this connection Charles D. Stewart, "Uses of Unemployment Statistics in Economic Policy," *Monthly Labor Review*, LXXVIII, No. 3 (March, 1955), 279–82.

should be able to avoid the opposite extreme. This is not wishful thinking.

Summary

"Economic unemployment" has been one of the most important causal factors giving rise to economic insecurity in the United States in this century. While unemployment is neither easy to define precisely nor to measure exactly, it is possible to conceive of three major types: aggregate, selective, and personal. Such a breakdown is useful, since programs to combat this type of insecurity have approached the problem on these three fronts. While unemployment data are not collected on the basis of the above threefold classification, the data we do have provide an increasingly reliable picture of employment and unemployment, particularly on a relative basis. Additionally, selective unemployment data of various types are becoming increasingly available: unemployment by regions, by occupation and industry, by age and sex, by duration of unemployment, and in other dimensions.

Aggregate unemployment requires for its minimization the maintenance of a high level of economic opportunity. While industry and labor can undertake useful positive action, governmental monetary and fiscal policies are likely to be the more important, particularly in critical periods. Selective unemployment may also require government assistance for its solution, although one should note that such solutions may tend to perpetuate an uneconomic situation, particularly where political pressures are strong. Personal unemployment can be attacked on a broad front through a series of measures which seek to improve the operation of the labor market by making more rational the ways in which jobs are offered and sought.

There is little doubt that we have at our command today powerful tools which, on the one hand, should make unlikely a repetition of the period 1930–1940, and, on the other, should make for a more rationally operating labor market. But vigilance needs to be exercised so that in our desire to avoid the insecurity of unemployment we do not fall heir to the dangers of overemployment.

Suggestions for Additional Reading

MILLIKAN, MAX F. *Income Stabilization for a Developing Democracy, A Study of the Politics and Economics of High Employment Without Inflation.* New Haven: Yale University Press, 1953.
A series of sixteen essays, presenting a stimulating discussion of the problems involved in full employment. See particularly the essay by Paul A. Samuelson.

UNITED NATIONS. *National and International Measures For Full Employment.* Lake Success: United Nations, 1949.
A compendium by a panel of economists on the nature, causes, and remedies for unemployment. Particularly useful for its inclusion of recent economic thinking.

U. S. CONGRESS, 84TH, FIRST SESSION, JOINT COMMITTEE ON THE ECONOMIC REPORT. Hearings on *Automation and Technological Change.* Washington, D. C.: U. S. Government Printing Office, 1955.
Discussion of the nature and impacts of automation and technological change. Particularly useful for its current material.

UNIVERSITIES-NATIONAL BUREAU COMMITTEE FOR ECONOMIC RESEARCH. Papers Presented at *Conference on the Measurement and Behavior of Unemployment* (held at Princeton, New Jersey, September, 1954). New York: National Bureau of Economic Research, 1954.
A collection of stimulating papers by various experts on the meaning and measurement of full employment, on unemployment statistics, and on other phases of the subject.

WOYTINSKY, W. S., and ASSOCIATES. *Employment and Wages in the United States.* New York: The Twentieth Century Fund, 1953.
A detailed institutional and theoretical examination of employment and wages. Part III, "Employment and Unemployment," is particularly relevant to the stream of thought in this text.

7

Unemployment Insurance

Introduction

The major public program in the United States for the alleviation of the undesirable consequences of unemployment is the unemployment insurance (or compensation) system which was developed in the Social Security Act of 1935. In addition to this basic system, there are a number of special programs to be found, as, for example, for railroad employees, which are discussed in Chapter 13.

The terms unemployment "compensation" and "insurance" as used above are commonly employed interchangeably. In the early days of the program "compensation" was used. After 1937, when the Social Security Act was declared constitutional, there was a tendency to use the term "insurance."[1] Technically, "compensation" might be a better term in light of the actuarial nature of the problem. Or, social "assurance" would be appropriate. But since "compensation" and "insurance" are both found in ordinary usage, we shall follow this custom here.

As was noted in Chapter 6, there are various ways in which society can approach the unemployment problem: prevention, or reduction, on a public or private basis; alleviation on the same grounds; or some combination of these two. The public preventive approach has been discussed in the last chapter; private systems will be covered in Chapter 8. This chapter, then, will focus upon the remaining major area—public alleviative programs of which unemployment compensation is the outstanding example.

[1] See Ruth Reticker, "Twenty Years of Unemployment Insurance," *Social Security Bulletin*, XVIII, No. 12 (December, 1955), 3–10.

Development of the Present System

If one accepts the premise that the unemployed are an overhead cost to society, though they may be a variable cost to the employer, then the question that must be answered is how society will provide for this overhead item. Various alternatives are to be found. At one extreme is the case where society lets the unemployed take care of themselves through private means: personal resources, relatives, friends, private charities. At the other extreme would be some complete public "cradle to the grave" system. The trend in the United States has changed from the almost completely private approach to one with a significant degree of public intervention. The chronological sequence of these alleviative program developments is interesting to note.

INDIVIDUAL INITIATIVE

There has always been a belief in the United States that, wherever possible, individuals themselves should make provision for economic emergencies such as might arise from unemployment. Although this doctrine has been tempered considerably through the years, for a long period it was the basis for social action. Applying this doctrine meant in turn that while society would not stand by and permit an individual to starve, it would provide assistance only in the critical case and not as the general rule. Private charities for many years carried the bulk of alleviative programs.

THE "RELIEF" DOCTRINE

Where public assistance was provided, it was commonly done under the "poor relief" or "work relief" doctrine.[2] Such relief might be "indoor," as in an almshouse, "outdoor," as through the receipt of cash, or "work relief," wherein the community sought some service in return for assistance. Such relief was customarily administered on the local or state level, was enmeshed in legal intricacies that frequently denied help to an individual, and tended to "disfranchise" the needy in a variety of ways, as, for example, in defining them as paupers.

DEVELOPMENT OF FEDERAL RELIEF

After a series of depressions in this country, beginning with the period of 1893–1894, there was an increasing tendency to formalize

[2] For a useful summary see Florence Peterson in D. D. Lescohier and E. Brandeis, *History of Labor in the United States, 1896–1932,* (New York: The Macmillan Co., 1935), III, chaps. xi and xii—Unemployment Relief.

public assistance and to apply it in a somewhat more rational social manner. (Prior to 1893–1894 there seems to have been little organized public response to the economic consequences of depression conditions.) And after 1929 there was increasing participation by the federal government in unemployment relief, culminating in the comprehensive programs developed in the New Deal era.

"UNEMPLOYMENT INSURANCE" PLANS

In addition to private and public *relief* approaches, a number of employers and/or unions sought to develop "unemployment insurance" plans of various types. These plans, to be discussed more fully in the next chapter, were insufficient to meet the general problem, though they were of some help in scattered instances. There was no attempt in this country to follow such European plans as those of Berne, Switzerland, or Ghent, Belgium, which, in the period 1893–1901 and later, provided for subsidization of private programs by municipal, provincial, and national governments.

UNEMPLOYMENT COMPENSATION LAWS

Hence, the nonrelief developments in the United States took the turn of governmental programming of unemployment insurance systems. Early attempts were made on a state basis, in Massachusetts in 1916, in Wisconsin, with the Huber bill in 1921; and, on a federal basis, with resolutions or bills introduced in the Congress in 1916, 1928, 1931, and 1934. Nothing developed from these sources, however, in no small measure because of the opposition of labor organizations. Such opposition arose because of a fear of government as such and a further fear that a system of this type could be turned against employees on strike. By 1932 the forces of economic necessity diminished labor opposition, and in that year Wisconsin passed the first unemployment compensation law in the United States. The law was a deferred statute, however, not to go into effect for two years. Four other states passed unemployment insurance laws prior to the Social Security Act of 1935, but only the New York law became effective.[3]

SOCIAL SECURITY ACT OF 1935

The insurance approach was crystallized in the Social Security Act of 1935, in which one of the several major components related

[3] See Harry Malisoff, "The Emergence of Unemployment Compensation," *Political Science Quarterly*, LIV, Nos. 2, 3, 4 (June, September, December, 1939), 237–58, 391–420, and 577–99, respectively.

to unemployment compensation. As noted in Chapter 4, in 1934 a national Committee on Economic Security had been created; out of its deliberations had come a series of recommendations, including a national system for old-age insurance, and a federal-state system in the unemployment field. Preference for a federal-state tax-offset plan rather than for a national system or a tax-rebate plan was based in part upon the belief that such an approach would be the most likely to survive the test of constitutionality, in part upon the fact that the committee included among its influential members persons who were responsible for the Wisconsin plan, in part upon disputes between adherents of different types of funds, which disputes could be resolved by letting each state go ahead, and in part upon a belief that a faster job could be done if each state were encouraged to act on its own. The 1935 Act, with subsequent modifications, is that which has come down to the present day and which we shall examine after commenting upon the compensation principle.

The Compensation Principle

If the labor market operated so that the principle of equal net advantage were fully applicable, then one would expect that wage rates for individual occupations would reflect their relative advantages and disadvantages, so that the final wage rate would equalize the advantages and disadvantages among all occupations.[4] And it would therefore follow that, other things being equal, occupations where the incidence of unemployment was high would pay correspondingly higher wage rates than similar occupations where the incidence was low. Demand and supply factors operating in such a labor market would work so as to bring about these optimal conditions.

Do wage rates, in fact, reflect such differences in the risks of unemployment? To some extent, yes. Various building trade rates for a long period tended to take account of the pressures of seasonal unemployment. But these cases are few; we have little correspondence, for example, of rates with the risks of cyclical, secular, or technological unemployment.

If this is the case, what alternatives are open to society if it wishes to take positive action? One approach would be for wages to be set legislatively or administratively so as to reflect differing unemployment risks. The serious ethical implications and enormous administrative difficulties in such an approach are readily apparent.

---

[4] See the parallel reasoning applied in Chapter 9 on Workmen's Compensation, in which field this type of argumentation has been used more extensively.

An alternative approach is to use the compensation principle, in which the cost of production includes a charge (tax) for the specific unemployment risk. If this cost is shared by the public (through higher prices), the employer (through reduced profits), and the employee (through lower wages), the burden is distributed. The utility of the compensation payment at the time of unemployment is greater than that of incremental increases in the wage rate which would occur under wage adjustment. Thus this method is more economically rational than that of administrative wage setting, to say nothing of being more feasible operationally.[5] Even if it be assumed that the employee bears the *full* burden of the cost, this method has merit. First, while it may be *forced insurance*, thus limiting freedom of choice, it is there, and the employee can draw upon it in time of need. (There is no assurance, for example, that "compensatory" wage rates would be used by the individual to provide for unemployment needs.) Second, the cost of the risk is spread beyond the particular risk, thus forcing a social sharing of the burden. (It should be noted, however, that experience rating —to be discussed in Chapter 14—may narrow this risk spreading to a point where "self insurance" is evident.) Hence there is both administrative feasibility and economic logic to the "compensation" or "insurance" principle.

This compensation approach is, in fact, the system embodied in the Social Security Act of 1935, to which the discussion now turns.

Unemployment Provisions of the 1935 Social Security Act

It should be noted initially that the federal Act had two distinguishing characteristics. First, it was an enabling Act designed to encourage the states to pass their own laws. And second, it provided a set of minimum standards for state laws, permitting the states to enact more liberal, but not more restrictive, laws. The basic elements in this federal statute are as follows.

COVERAGE

Coverage is a matter of numbers as well as of employment types. Taking numbers first, employers are covered who employ eight or more different individuals on any twenty or more days in the calendar year, each day being in a different week. This is a "minimum-

---

[5] See Chapter 9 for a more detailed analysis of the applicability of this approach in workmen's compensation.

minimum"; thus, an employer who meets the above stipulation is covered for the year, and pays taxes on his employees for the full year, even though he has, say, only seven or fewer employees for the balance of the year. In 1954, in one of the few amendments to the Act, the Congress lowered the limit from eight to four employees, effective January 1, 1956, and blanketed in civilian employees of the federal government as of January 1, 1955.

Employment types excluded are agriculture, domestic service, casual labor, certain public service, and nonprofit charitable, educational, literary, religious, and scientific pursuits. These criteria are applied to the employee in terms of the types of work he does, and not to the employee as employee. The 50 per cent rule is applied to determine coverage: if over 50 per cent of the work an employee does is within the meaning of the Act, he is covered for all his employment; if less than 50 per cent, he is excluded. This makes for administrative simplicity and does not work an injustice. While OASI has greatly broadened its coverage, the same has not been true in unemployment compensation. The Act originally covered employees in interstate transportation, but separate legislation is now provided for them.

Why these exclusions? The reasons are found in a complex of administrative, economic, and political circumstances. Thus, there was some belief that smaller employers could handle implicitly their unemployment problems; moreover, the administrative difficulties were felt to be of such a nature that it would not be feasible to include the employer of fewer than eight. Twenty weeks was used as a cut-off, since it would eliminate most seasonal employment related to agriculture. Certain employment classes—such as casual labor or domestic service—were excluded, partly because of administrative difficulties in blanketing in such groups, and additionally in the former case because of the belief that one should have some permanence of attachment to the labor force before one could rightly make a claim upon the system. Agricultural labor was excluded, in part for administrative and political reasons, and also because of the belief that the depressed farm economy could not bear the costs.

QUALIFICATIONS FOR BENEFITS

The Act leaves to the states the right to determine specific qualifications for benefits, such as allowable reasons for job separations, interpretations of the terms "able to work" and "available for work," and "allowable earnings" while unemployed. The federal Act does specify, however, a number of situations in which a state may not deny compensation to an otherwise eligible applicant. These include the stipulations that the applicant shall not be ineligible if he refuses to accept new work under any of the following conditions: (1) if the job opening is available because of a strike, lockout, or other labor dispute, (2) if the wages, hours, or working conditions are substantially less favorable than those prevailing for similar work in the locality, and (3) if, as a condition of employment the individual must join, resign from, or refrain from joining a bona fide labor organization. The rationale of these specifications is clear; they are designed to prevent an undercutting of desirable labor standards, and to preserve the neutrality of the state *vis-à-vis* employers and labor organizations, and, in labor disputes.

BENEFIT LEVELS

Benefit levels as such are not specified in the federal Act. There are, however, several indirect stipulations. First, such benefits as are paid must be paid through public employment offices or such other agencies as may be approved. Second, all money withdrawn from the unemployment fund of a state shall be used solely in the payment of unemployment compensation, with certain administrative and disability exceptions. The reasons for such requirements are clear.

COSTS AND FINANCING

It is here that the major feature of the federal Act is found. A federal tax of 3 per cent is levied upon the wages and salaries paid by covered employers, as previously defined. Up to 1939 the tax was levied on total wages; in that year an amendment set a limit of $3,000. The limitation was imposed because of the disparate relation between in-payments and possible benefits for higher income groups.[6]

The 3 per cent rate was selected for two basic reasons. First, it represented an "actuarial" figure that would have provided benefits at levels envisaged in a number of proposed bills for the period 1920–1932. Second, it was a compromise between "disaster relief" and "high benefit" plan proponents.

The important "enabling innovation" in the federal Act was as follows. The specified 3 per cent tax was to be paid to the federal

---

[6] It is interesting to note that, while the OASI tax base has gone to $4,200, the unemployment insurance base has held at the above-mentioned $3,000. The student should ask himself why this is so.

government. If, however, the state in question had an approved unemployment insurance law with its own tax structure, 90 per cent of the federal tax could be deducted, or "offset." (Numerically, if an employer's federal tax was, for example, $3,000, then $2,700 of it might be offset for the state.) The remaining 10 per cent was to be paid to the federal government for administrative costs. A state law would, of course, keep the "monies at home" for use within the state, instead of having them go to the federal government for commingled use in various states. There was thus considerable incentive for a state to pass its own law; and this, in fact, was what happened in all forty-eight states (and three territories).

Technically, *all* the monies collected by a state are sent to the Secretary of the Treasury and put into an Unemployment Trust Fund, thus centralizing and safeguarding the reserve. The "title" to a state's monies is, however, retained by it, and a separate book account maintained for it. The funds, other than those needed for current state withdrawals, are invested in United States bonds, either regular or special issues. Interest earned on these bonds is periodically added to the reserve. A state may draw on its account, but only to the limit of its balance, and only for the purpose of paying unemployment benefits. (A 1946 amendment permitted the states utilizing employee contributions to withdraw such contributions to pay disability benefits.) The federal Act does not require employee contributions, but does not prohibit them. Although nine states have at various times levied an employee tax, only two do so today.[7]

In order to assist in providing an economic incentive for the reduction of unemployment, an "additional credit" provision was incorporated in the Act. A state may write into its own program a provision whereby an employer with a favorable employment experience (low unemployment) pays a lower tax. But the 90 per cent federal offset applies only to such taxes as the employer pays to the state. Hence, unless a special provision were made, the employer with a reduced state tax would technically pay the balance to the federal government. Special provision, in fact, has been made in the law via the "additional credit" proviso. Hence, the employer with a reduced state tax is permitted to deduct not only what he *does* pay to the state, but what he *would have paid* had he paid the maximum tax, subject to the limitation of 90 per cent of the federal

---

[7] Under OASI, both employee and employer contribute. The student should ask himself why this is not also the case for unemployment compensation. See Chapter 4, page 92, for comments.

tax. In order to prevent abuse of this tax reduction procedure, the experience rating provisions (that is, the provisions which permit low unemployment employers to pay lower rates) of state acts must meet minimum federal standards. The federal standards require in general that an employer have a certain minimum time experience (formerly three years; as of January 1, 1955, one year) or have a certain maximum balance in his reserve account before he can become eligible for a reduced tax.

ADMINISTRATION

The federal law is now administered by the Secretary of Labor through the Bureau of Employment Security. The states retain considerable autonomy; their major responsibility is to comply with federal specifications, but, given that, they exercise operational initiative in the day-to-day administration of the state laws. The federal administrative specifications are five in number—the state must: (1) administer its law in such a way as will, within reason, permit full payment of unemployment compensation when due, (2) cooperate with state agencies administering public works or employment, (3) provide for a review system for denied claims, (4) make the necessary reports to the federal administration, and (5) after 1939, apply the merit system to its administrative staff. Hence, there is considerable variation in the details of state administration. Administrative costs are borne by the federal government through its retention of 10 per cent of the 3 per cent tax, and by subsequent reimbursement to the states.

State Unemployment Insurance Acts

In attempting to portray the present state unemployment insurance system in the United States, one faces a dilemma. On the one hand, a detailed presentation does not serve the purpose of this text, whose aim is analysis and evaluation. Moreover, a detailed presentation would become out of date as quickly as it was printed, so rapid are developments in this field.[8] Yet is is obvious that one cannot analyze and understand if one does not have some fund or stock of information with which to work. Hence, we shall adopt the compromise of sketching in the main informational threads with-

[8] This is even more the case in unemployment compensation, workmen's compensation and in public assistance than in old-age insurance, for in the latter instance there is only a single federal law; in the former the complex diversity of state laws is apparent.

out attempting in any way to suggest that this provides a definitive treatment of the full range of available data.[9]

COVERAGE

As was previously noted, the federal law sets a floor below which the states cannot go in restrictiveness. The states can, however, adopt more liberal provisions, and this is the trend that has developed. The following data illustrate the picture as of January 1, 1956.

First, as to the size of the firm, twenty-three states went beyond the federal Act and covered employees in firms with work forces ranging from one to four employees. Moreover, twenty states require the specified number of employees to be employed for a period shorter than the federal Act's twenty weeks. Additionally, all states which limit coverage by firm size provide that employing units with fewer than the required number of employees may elect to have them covered under the state law. The contractual relationship of employer and employee and the location of employment have come to be defined in ways such as to broaden coverage.

Second, as noted previously, the federal Act excludes various categories of employees on the basis of the type of employment. Except for the District of Columbia—primarily an urban community —which does not exclude agricultural labor, the other states tend to follow the federal law. Only New York covers domestic servants in private homes; only Wisconsin covers family employment; only

[9] The authors have found two techniques useful in approaching this problem. The first technique is to include, as part of the textual materials for the course, copies of the *Social Security Bulletin* for September (of the year in question), containing the Annual Statistical Supplement or separate statistical compilations, and copies of the latest issue of the U. S. Department of Labor's *Comparison of State Unemployment Insurance Laws*, which of late has been issued annually. It is obvious that a text cannot help being dated almost immediately as to the factual data; even the government reports are always somewhat behind the times. Yet the publications listed above do provide a set of comprehensive source materials. (The larger institution also is likely to have in its library a labor reporting service of some type through which one can keep completely up to date if this is felt desirable.) The second technique is to take the unemployment insurance law of the state in which the college or university is located, use it as a prototype, and subject it to detailed inquiry, spending a week or more upon presentation and analysis. Copies of the state law usually can be secured without difficulty. The specific sources used in the following section are: U. S. Department of Labor, Bureau of Employment Security, *Comparison of State Unemployment Insurance Laws as of December, 1955*, 1956; and *Social Security Bulletin*, XIX, No. 9 (September, 1956); and the Annual Statistical Supplement for 1955. We have also found valuable as sources the following: *Employment Security Review* and *Labor Market and Employment Security*, both government publications; *American Economic Security* for a business point of view, and *Economic Outlook* for a labor organization viewpoint.

Alaska and Hawaii cover employees in nonprofit organizations.[10] Thus the tendency here is to hew close to federal specifications.

Given these coverage qualifications, the average number of employees blanketed under the state acts was thirty-six million as of December, 1955, with over one and one-half million eligible employing units. This compares with approximately twenty million employees covered in 1938. The rate of growth of covered employees has been larger than the rate of growth of the labor force. Coverage varies rather widely in different industries: manufacturing and wholesale and retail trade account for the bulk of total coverage, while mining and finance run low.

But more employees than the "average" tend to have some wage credits at one time or another during the year. The numbers with some wage credits approximate one-half to one-third again as many as the average number of employees covered, tending toward the latter figure of late. Of these, somewhat over 80 per cent have enough wage credits (to be defined shortly) to qualify for at least minimum benefits. Protection is thus broader than "average" coverage figures would indicate.

QUALIFICATIONS FOR BENEFITS

It is here that state laws have developed most of their complexities. Qualification requirements are of several different basic types; we shall discuss each of them in turn.

Qualifying wages or employment. To be eligible for unemployment benefits, an individual must be more than merely in a covered employment. He must meet a number of other requirements, the first of which is that he must have earned a specified amount of wages or have worked for a certain period of time within his base period, or both. (The "base period" or "base year" is a period of time, commonly one year, which precedes the period in which benefits start, usually with a lag of one quarter.) The purpose of these qualifying requirements is to admit to participation in the benefits of the system only such employees as have a *bona fide* attachment to the labor force of covered workers.

Earnings requirements are usually stated in terms of a multiple of the weekly benefit or as a flat qualifying amount. In the nineteen states that used the benefit multiple in 1955, the multiple ranged from twenty to sixty, with thirty the most common. Thus, if we assume for illustrative purposes the benefit rate to be 50 per cent

---

[10] Alaska, Hawaii, and the District of Columbia are construed as states in the following presentation.

and the eligibility requirement (benefit multiple) 30 per cent, the individual must have fifteen weeks of full-time employment in his base period. Sixteen states using the flat qualifying amount require earnings of $200 to $800, with $300 the median figure. Other combinations are also found. Frequently there may be additional requirements, such as that these earnings be in more than one quarter. A few states (four in 1955) require that an individual must have worked a specified number of weeks, with at least a specified weekly wage.

The net effect of these requirements is to reduce the number of otherwise eligible individuals. Some estimates indicate that 20 per cent, plus or minus, of the otherwise eligible may be so disqualified. While there is a reasonable basis for this type of requirement, one may raise a question as to the inherent logic of these particular methods. (The student might ask himself two questions here: (1) should only employees "genuinely attached" to the labor force be eligible for benefits, and (2) if so, how "genuinely attached" should be defined.)

The method of job separation. Next, the individual must *not* have been separated from his job for a series of reasons if he is to qualify for benefits. That is, certain types of job separations disqualify an individual (either temporarily or permanently) from receiving benefits. The purpose of such qualifications is to restrict benefits to those who become unemployed through no fault of their own; that is, it is generally held that an employee who "voluntarily" leaves his job should take the consequences.

The series of disqualifying reasons includes: voluntary separation from work, discharge for misconduct, refusal of suitable work, and unemployment due to a labor dispute. In some cases and in some states the disqualification results in a denial of benefits for a temporary period; in New York, for example, in 1955, voluntary leaving disqualified an individual for six weeks. In other cases the disqualification may be "permanent" (for the duration of unemployment); in New Jersey in 1955, voluntary leaving resulted in disqualification for the duration of unemployment. In some cases the disqualification is mandatory, in others it may be optional and at the discretion of the administrative agency.

In general, the above listed reasons for disqualification admit of exceptions, depending upon the circumstances involved. Thus, as of January 1, 1956, all states disqualified an individual for voluntarily leaving his employment without "good cause." But if the quit was for "good cause," benefits were not denied. (What constitutes "good cause" becomes, of course, a complicated matter and one with which administrative agencies have to concern themselves regularly.) The penalty for discharge for misconduct may result in disqualification for the duration of unemployment, or it may be scaled down according to the type of misconduct. Thus, "aggravated misconduct" disqualifies for a longer period than "lesser misconduct."

Refusal to accept suitable work also disqualifies an individual. In addition to the federal specifications on suitable work, other criteria have been developed to evaluate the suitability of an offer of work. These include: (1) the degree of risk to a claimant's health, safety, and morals; (2) the claimant's physical fitness, prior training, experience, and earnings; (3) the length of his unemployment and local job market prospects, and (4) the distance of the job from his home. It should be noted that the suitable work criteria are imposed not only as an initial test, but throughout the period of unemployment, whereas the job separation cause is a "once and forever" action. Labor dispute disqualifications, in general, last as long as the labor dispute, though there is a pattern of exceptions and qualifications for lockouts, location of the dispute, and indirect actions. Finally, certain special groups of individuals are disqualified: students not available for work while attending school and women who quit their jobs to assume marital obligations or to bear children.

Able to, and available for, work. Next, an individual must be able to work and be available for work. These are continuing requirements, extending through the period for which benefits are claimed. Here the states set their own eligibility requirements, since there are no federal specifications except the labor standard provisions. "Able to work" implies physical and mental ability. The unemployment insurance system as presently structured is an economically oriented system; it is not set up for the purpose of providing accident or sickness benefits (which may be covered in part by workmen's compensation or by private accident and health plans). One evidence of ability to work is the filing of a claim and registration for work at a public employment office, which is required under all state laws, ordinarily on a weekly basis.

Availability for work is a more complex issue.[11] The customary interpretations of availability include the following: (a) indication of availability as evidenced by registration at the appropriate public employment office, (b) actively seeking work or making a reason-

[11] For a useful analysis and discussion, see Ralph Altman, *Availability for Work: A Study in Unemployment Compensation* (Cambridge: Harvard University Press, 1950).

able effort to obtain work, and (c) willingness to accept suitable work (as previously defined).

Subsequent disqualifying factors. Even though an individual meets all the above requirements, there are still certain factors that may preclude him from starting to collect benefits or from continuing to receive benefits once he has started. Fraudulent misrepresentation not only disqualifies an individual, but all state laws contain some provision for recovery of benefits paid. Other income received may disqualify an individual, usually through a reduction in benefits. Thus workmen's compensation, old age benefits, private pensions, wages in lieu of notice, or dismissal payments commonly restrict unemployment benefits. Partial employment does not disqualify an individual, but it may reduce his benefits. Thus in 1956, all states allowed an individual to earn some sum each week without reducing his benefits; the size of the sum varied from $2 to one-half the weekly benefit amount, with $3 a median figure.

All the above restrictions are designed to carry out the intent of the unemployment insurance system, given the basic premises of that system. One may quarrel with these basic premises, but if one accepts them, the subsequent regulatory framework is logical, though one might also be disposed to dispute the application of the regulations in specific cases.

BENEFIT LEVELS

If an individual meets all the above qualifications, what benefits can he collect? The following seeks to provide an answer to this question.

First, it should be noted that the federal Act sets no standards for unemployment insurance benefits. The result, unlike coverage and financing, has been the development of differentiated and complex formulae for determining employee benefit rights. The following are the principal factors involved in benefit calculation.

Benefit year. The period in which an employee may receive his benefits is called a "benefit year." This is usually a one-year period; in forty-three states it is an "individual benefit year" related to the date of his unemployment. In seven other states the potential benefit year begins for all claimants on a date specified in the law, usually April 1.

Waiting period. All but three states require a waiting period before benefits are payable. This is an "uncompensable period" in which the employee must have been otherwise eligible for benefits. One week (with modifications) is the most common initial period in forty-seven states. The purposes of such a period are two in number. First, it excludes from coverage those unemployed who secure re-employment within this period; that is, it permits unemployment compensation to be applied to those who more fully need it. The belief here is that an individual should be expected to, and be able to, finance a week of unemployment. Second, like a "deductible insurance," it reduces the cost or, conversely, for a given premium it permits a higher benefit.

The weekly benefit amount. Numerous formulae are used to compute the weekly benefit amount, but they all depend upon certain basic factors. First, benefits vary with the employee's past wages (customarily during the base period or some portion thereof) within minimum and maximum limits. Second, the formulae are generally weighted so that the lower paid employee receives a proportionately larger benefit than does the higher paid. The minimum effective weekly benefit in 1954 was $5; the maximum, without dependents' allowances, was $45.

Dependents' allowances. Eleven states provide dependents' allowances. A rather rigorous set of restrictions is set up to define dependency. The allowance formulae vary, from a fixed sum per dependent ($1 to $7) with a maximum allowed amount (such as $20), to systems whereby the supplementary payment depends upon the "primary" weekly benefit.

Duration of benefits. In 1956 thirty weeks was the maximum effective period during which a claimant could collect benefits. Twenty-six weeks was the median figure. The exact maximum for a given individual depended upon the specific formula used, the formula in the majority of the states being related to the weekly benefit amount.

The net effect of the weekly benefit calculation is to weight benefits in favor of the lower bracket wage earner. A question here: Does this discriminate against the high-wage earner? The low? At present, although benefit weeks have lengthened, average benefits do not come up to the 50 to 65 per cent of wages envisaged in the 1935 Act.[12] As we shall see in the next chapter, this has been one of the bases upon which labor organizations have built their supplementary unemployment benefit approach.

[12] Analysts differ on the 50 and 65 per cent figures. This is the effective range, however, within which most opinions fell.

COSTS—FINANCING

The federal Act specified a 3 per cent tax on employers against which could be offset up to 90 per cent of any state contributions. Additionally, the employer could be credited with any reductions under an approved experience rating plan. No tax on employees was provided for in the Act. We shall cover the principal cost-finance topics under a number of subheads.

Employee contributions. Although nine states at one time or another utilized employee contributions, only Alaska, Alabama, and New Jersey did so in 1956. (California, Rhode Island, and New Jersey utilize employee contributions for a related system of disability insurance.) The tax in both states is on the first $3,000 of wages, and in Alaska on the first $3,600. The rates vary: in Alabama, from 0.1 per cent to 1.0 per cent as the employer's rate varies under experience rating; in New Jersey the rate is 0.25 per cent; in Alaska, 0.5 per cent.

Experience rating. Unemployment insurance is essentially an alleviative system. But it also contains a "preventive" component whereby an employer who reduces his unemployment (or who is so placed that his employment is "normally" stabilized) can have his tax reduced. The procedure used is called experience rating. In Chapter 14 we shall discuss more fully the economic ramifications of this procedure; here we will present some of the details of application.

Experience rating formulae of the different states vary greatly, but they all contain a number of common elements. First, all formulae measure the employer's experience with unemployment: how much unemployment he has had in his establishment in some specified period. This factor is customarily measured in terms of benefit payments to employees severed from jobs in his company. Second, this measure is compared with a measure of "exposure," usually the payroll for the period in question. In a sample formula, the benefits paid are put in the numerator and the "exposure" (payroll) in the denominator. A fraction results from the division; this is the "experience ratio." What tax the employer then pays may depend not only upon this ratio (a higher ratio would require a higher tax) but also upon the size of the state unemployment reserve fund (a smaller size fund moves the tax structure up and vice versa) and upon the employer's individual reserve (unless a specified reserve is reached and maintained, a tax reduction is not allowed).[13] All states now have in effect some experience-rating system. The reason is clear; no state feels it can put its industry at a competitive disadvantage by not having such a plan. While social insurance costs are but one of many factors involved in plant location (attraction of new industry or retention of present), they are one over which state legislatures can exercise directly some degree of control.

The result of experience rating has been to change the effective tax paid from 3.0 per cent (or 2.7 per cent to the state) to a lower figure. Calculations for 1955 indicate that the average contribution (tax) rate for fifty-one states and territories was 1.2 per cent. Alaska, Massachusetts, and Rhode Island were at the 2.7 per cent maximum; Colorado was low with 0.2 per cent.[14] A second result probably has been to keep the benefit structure lower than it would otherwise have been. This has happened for two reasons. First, given a lower tax rate, employer pressures have tended to resist any increase in benefits which would require an increase in tax rates. Second, state legislatures have been reluctant to raise rates unless such a raise were general among the states; to do so unilaterally would be to add a factor of competitive disadvantage. This should not be taken to imply that there have been no benefit increases. Benefits (levels and duration of) have climbed since the passage of the federal Act. But they have not kept pace with wage changes, and it is probable that experience rating has had a braking effect upon benefit liberalization.

Other cost-financing details. State laws include a number of other features designed to make the unemployment insurance system work more rationally. For example, the three-year experience rule for experience rating has a special proviso in all states whereby one company taking over another may acquire the latter's experience record under certain conditions. Or again, special methods are set up to identify the employer to be charged with benefits when an employee becomes unemployed. In eight states, as of January, 1956, the most recent employer is charged with all benefits on the basis that he has primary responsibility for the unemployment. Thirteen states charge base period employers in inverse chronological order, while twenty-three charge benefits against all base

13 The student should secure a copy of the plan used in his state and work out arithmetic examples using different figures. The best over-all exposition of different plans is found in D. Gagliardo, *American Social Insurance* (rev. ed., New York: Harper and Brothers, 1955), pp. 261–71.

14 *The Labor Market and Economic Security*, June, 1956, p. 25.

period employers in proportion to the wages earned by the beneficiary with each employer.

Nearly all states have developed "noncharging" provisions, wherein certain classes of benefits are not counted as benefit wages. Benefit charges may be omitted for benefits based upon short periods of employment (such as less than four weeks), upon minimum wage payments (such as less than $175 paid in wages), or for benefits paid following a period of disqualification. The logic behind the noncharging approach is that certain types of benefits inherently are not allocable to a given employer (or should not be).

Twenty-two states permit the employer to make voluntary contributions. The purpose of such provisions is to increase the balance in the employer's reserve so that he is assigned a lower rate, one which will save him more than the amount of the voluntary contribution.

ADMINISTRATION

Since there are no specific requirements in the federal Act as to the form of the state administration or its place in the state government, a number of differing agency types have developed. The most common type in 1956 was the independent board or commission found in nineteen states. A second common type found in fourteen states was an independent department of the state government. Finally, seventeen states have the administrative agency located in the state department of labor. To some extent the form of the administrative agency is an accident of political pressure, of existing state government units, and of historical growth. But, irrespective of the form, the purpose is clear: to administer the state act in conformity with its intent as well as content.

The administrative procedure set up for the processing of claims is similar in all states. The unemployed individual files a claim for benefits following specified steps and using specified forms. This is usually done at his local public employment office, although in unpopulated areas another public official may substitute for an employment office. The claim is then centrally reviewed (in some states locally) and benefit amount and duration determined. Benefit claimants customarily receive their checks by mail, but must report regularly (usually weekly) at the local public employment office. All states provide an appeals procedure for the individual whose claim is denied. The appeals agency is an impartial tribunal, variously composed in different states. In all but four states in 1956 an additional second appeals stage was provided. Appeal agency decisions can be reviewed by the courts, but only as to matters of law and not of fact. All but three states provide for an advisory council —usually with equal employer and union representation—whose purpose it is to help in policy formulation and administrative problem solving.

The administration of the state acts is financed by the federal government, through grants from the general federal treasury. After July 1, 1953, the 0.3 per cent federal tax was reserved for employment security purposes. The annual excess (if any) of such taxes over the cost of administration is to be placed in a federal Unemployment Account (an emergency reserve) until a total of $200 million is reached. Subsequent excess collections are to be allocated to the various state accounts in the proportion their covered payrolls bear to the aggregate.

Administrative provision is also made for the handling of interstate claims. At present the principal procedure is for the "liable" state to make the original determination of eligibility and benefits, and the "agent" state to receive and initially transmit the claim and subsequently pay the benefits (reimbursed by the "liable" state) and make subsequent determinations. The advantage of this procedure in permitting desirable labor mobility is obvious.

Operational Data and Trends in Unemployment Insurance

The above material was designed to present an over-all view of the nature of state unemployment insurance programs. Without burdening the reader with excessive details, it may prove desirable to highlight a few operational statistics[15] and indicate trends in the program.

COVERAGE AND CLAIMS

Table 7.1 presents data on coverage and claims for selected years of operation under the state unemployment insurance system.

While coverage has increased 50 per cent since the beginning of operations and has resulted in the inclusion of a greater proportion of the civilian labor force (54 per cent in 1954 in contrast to 43 per cent in 1940), this has been accomplished by the growth of employment in already covered industries rather than by blanketing in new occupations. The change in the federal law as of Janu-

[15] Unless otherwise indicated, these data have been abstracted from relevant *Social Security Yearbooks,* and *Annual Statistical Supplements* to the *Social Security Bulletin.*

TABLE 7.1

COVERAGE AND CLAIMS UNDER UNEMPLOYMENT INSURANCE

Year	Coverage* (in thousands)	Payrolls Covered by†		Initial Claims** (in thousands)	Continued Claims‡ (in thousands)
		Amount (in millions)	Per Cent of Civilian Wages-Salaries		
1940	23,096	$32,352	65.7	11,140	66,676
1941	26,814	41,985	69.7	8,526	42,341
1942	29,349	54,548	71.8	6,323	33,761
1943	30,821	65,871	72.0	1,884	7,664
1944	30,026	68,886	71.0	1,502	5,480
1945	28,203	66,411	69.4	6,048	30,633
1946	30,213	73,145	70.3	9,844	67,333
1947	32,276	86,234	72.6	9,702	51,859
1948	30,127 (July)	95,731	73.0	10,919	50,981
1949	31,697	93,520	71.9	17,660	102,612
1950	32,887	102,835	72.7	12,251	78,654
1951	34,858	118,243	72.9	10,836	50,393
1952	35,557	127,320	72.9	11,174	54,311
1953	36,667	138,657	73.7	11,349	51,468
1954	35,372	136,594	73.1	15,781	97,236
1955	36,590	148,144	74.1	11,874	66,940

Sources:

* Social Security Yearbook, 1945, p. 76; Social Security Bulletins (Coverage in average monthly number of workers.)

† Social Security Bulletin, XVIII, No. 9 (September, 1955), p. 16; Annual Statistical Supplement, 1955, p. 7.

** Social Security Yearbook, 1945, pp. 79–80; Social Security Bulletins.

‡ Social Security Yearbook, 1948, p. 26; Social Security Bulletins. Data for 1949 on show continued claims in terms of weeks of unemployment covered.

ary 1, 1956, lowering the minimum coverage figure from eight to four employees will increase the number covered, although not as significantly as one might expect, since employers in this group are but a small fraction of the total employer group.

The number of initial claims follows closely the level of economic activity. Thus, in the full-employment economy of 1943–1944, one found few claims; conversely in 1949 and 1954 the opposite was true. (The student should ask himself why there were so many more claims in 1946–1947 than in 1943–1944, since 1946–1947 was a full-employment period also.)

While it is difficult to prove from the data, disqualifications and appeals have probably increased more than proportionately because of an increasing tightening of state administrative standards and the application of more rigorous disqualification standards.

Beneficiaries and Benefits

Table 7.2 presents data on beneficiaries and benefits.

TABLE 7.2

Beneficiaries and Benefits Under Unemployment Insurance

Year	Number of Beneficiaries (Average Weekly Number)	Amount of Benefits (in thousands)
1940	982,392	$518,700
1941	621,065	344,321
1942	541,495	344,084
1943	115,454	79,643
1944	79,306	62,385
1945	464,996	445,866
1946	1,152,203	1,094,850
1947	852,404	776,165
1948	821,057	793,265
1949	1,666,100	1,737,279
1950	1,305,000	1,373,426
1951	796,900	840,411
1952	873,600	998,237
1953	812,100	962,221
1954	1,614,900	2,026,866
1955	1,099,500	1,350,268

Source: *Social Security Bulletins* and *Social Security Yearbooks.*

The year 1954 represented an all-time high in numbers of beneficiaries and benefits. The major causal factor was the reduction in the level of economic activity. But before a true comparison could be made, it would be necessary to correct for changes in the number of people covered and changes in the benefit structure. If these corrections were made, the increase would not be as significant.

The Unemployment Trust Fund

The following table presents a picture of the unemployment trust fund from its inception through 1955.

In terms of total figures, the nineteen-year record is impressive. In only three calendar years—1945, 1950, and 1954—did out-payments exceed in-payments plus interest earned. Moreover, at the end of 1954 the trust fund balance stood at eight billion dollars, higher than for any years except 1952 and 1953. At the rate of 1954 withdrawals, the highest year in history, benefits could be paid for four years without any additional in-payments (assuming away here any individual state differences in fund size or benefit payments).

TABLE 7.3

THE UNEMPLOYMENT TRUST FUND

Year	State Deposits (in millions)	State Withdrawals (in millions)	Interest (in millions)	Balance (in millions)	Ratio of Withdrawals to Deposits and Interest (per cent)
1936	$ 65	(less than $500,000)	$ 1	$ 65	—
1937	567	$ 2	8	638	(less than 1)
1938	829	404	9	1,072	48
1939	830	429	27	1,500	51
1940	861	517	60	1,805	56
1941	1,008	342	58	2,516	32
1942	1,139	344	74	3,379	28
1943	1,328	78	89	4,711	06
1944	1,317	63	55	6,016	05
1945	1,161	461	129	6,833	36
1946	916	1,104	144	6,775	104
1947	1,097	787	147	7,217	63
1948	989	852	246	7,572	69
1949	998	1,762	176	6,954	150
1950	1,191	1,342	163	6,948	99
1951	1,495	845	175	7,757	51
1952	1,372	996	194	8,310	64
1953	1,350	970	217	8,892	62
1954	1,135	2,032	212	8,193	151
1955	1,215	1,352	199	8,242	96

Source: *Social Security Bulletin, Annual Statistical Supplement,* 1955, p. 12.

But, what size fund should have been expected in 1955? Since unemployment still does not seem to contain the niceties of actuarial calculation, it is not likely that the magnitude of the fund can be ascribed to previous (and precise) actuarial prediction. Therefore, two other approaches can be used in looking at the fund. At one extreme, if one assumes that fiscal and monetary policy can be used to prevent unemployment from rising over some critical point, then only a "minimum contingency fund" need be provided. The fund appears to be well over such a minimum, and hence this approach does not appear to have been chosen consciously. Conversely, if one assumes one does not know fully the unemployment future and, therefore, maximum emergency reserves should be provided, then the fund can be allowed to grow continually at a greater or lesser rate, depending upon varying economic and political pressures.

This latter course appears to have been the one followed, with actual growth an "accidental" as much as a "planned" matter. A basic reason for the growth rate is found in the continuous and unprecedentedly high levels of economic activity and employment since 1940. Thus the pattern of experience has been different (and more favorable) than was envisaged in the calculations made for the Social Security Act of 1935. The fund has grown, even though experience rating about halved the effective tax rate. Economic and political pressures have been effective in reducing the tax rate; probably they also have been responsible for a failure of the benefit rate to increase as rapidly or as fully as upward changes in the price level. Thus, even a reduced in-payment structure may permit fund growth if employment experience is favorable and if a relatively reduced benefit structure lessens withdrawal rates. Interestingly enough, the fund increase has not resulted in any basic change in our thinking about its size or use. We are apparently still apprehensive enough about unemployment to be willing to commit ourselves to accumulating the largest fund compatible with other interests.

One might get the impression from the above that the fund is a federal fund. This, of course, is not the case. The totals presented in Table 7.3 merely represent the summation of individual state funds (technically "reserve accounts"). In this fact resides a problem that is not self-evident from the above discussion. This problem arises out of the fact that not all states have the same unemployment experience.[16] Some are hit much harder than others in periods of economic recession: Massachusetts and Rhode Island in 1949–1950 illustrate the case. Hence at different times, individual state funds have approached dangerously low figures. The affected state has several alternatives open to it in such a situation. While it is difficult to cut benefits, possible increases can be forestalled. Since there is customarily a relationship set up between individual state fund size and tax rates under experience rating, a lowering of the fund may call forth increased tax rates. This is a second alternative, and one most commonly followed. Thus in 1951 (following the

[16] Many states have recently conducted studies to analyze in detail their employment-unemployment experience, the operation of their state funds, and thence to make projections as to future patterns. This provides a base for policy action. The interested student can check to see if such a report has been made in his state. Several examples of such studies include William Haber, *How Much Does It Cost, a Report to the Michigan Employment Security Commission* . . . (Ann Arbor, September, 1951), and State of Minnesota, *A Report of the Financial Experience and Actuarial Requirements of the Minnesota Unemployment Compensation Program* . . . (St. Paul: Minnesota Division of Employment and Security, 1952). Federal studies also have been undertaken; see, for example, *Unemployment Insurance*, Senate Document No. 206, 80th Congress, 2nd Session (Washington, D. C.: U. S. Government Printing Office, 1948), pp. 30–42.

1949–1950 recession) the effective rate in Massachusetts and Rhode Island was 2.7 per cent, while the average for the country was 1.6 per cent. A third alternative is to secure an interest-free loan from the federal Unemployment Account.[17] A state can secure such a loan by request if at the end of any calendar quarter the balance in its fund is less than the amount of benefits paid by it during the preceding twelve months. At present there is no re-insurance system in the rigorous sense of the term, but individual states do have recourse to federal loans.

An Evaluation of the Unemployment Insurance System

What can be said by way of evaluating the unemployment insurance system? In Chapter 1, three general criteria were laid down. They included the questions: (1) Did the program accomplish the purpose(s) for which it was designed? (2) Was the program rationally structured and soundly administered? (3) Did the program produce undesirable economic consequences? We shall generally reserve for Chapter 14 the discussion of the third criterion, and shall concentrate here upon the first two.

Purposes and Accomplishment of Unemployment Insurance

In a general sense the purpose of the unemployment insurance program was to alleviate the undesirable economic consequences arising out of short-term unemployment which regularly employed individuals would experience even though the aggregate demand for labor was not insufficient. This general purpose was carried into effect by the law in two specific ways. First, by providing a high benefit level, designed to approximate 50 to 65 per cent of the unemployed individual's previous income; and second, by extending the benefit level over a relatively short period of time (sixteen weeks was the maximum in the first state laws passed after 1935).

Appraising performance in terms of the general purpose, one might conclude that unemployment insurance has accomplished the objective for which it was designed.[18] The specifics, however, have not been met in the form in which they were set up. First, in place of 50 per cent of previous wages, the average has dropped to 30 to

---

[17] This was originally set up in 1944 as a federal Emergency Reserve, designed to handle what was expected to be the vast immediate post-war unemployment problem. It was abolished in 1952 and re-established in 1954.

[18] For a useful analysis see the *Vanderbilt Law Review*, VIII, No. 2 (February, 1955). This issue is devoted to economic security matters.

40 per cent (though some individual states have maintained the higher ratio). Second, and conversely, the benefit period was lengthened to a median figure of twenty-six weeks in 1954. Thus the trend has been to provide a lower benefit for a longer period of time.

With a given in-payment structure, one or the other of benefit levels or benefit duration must be the limiting or balancing factor; both cannot be indefinitely extended. Hence, it is not fully justifiable to criticize the failure of benefits to keep pace with wage and price-level increases, for the duration of benefits has increased at the same time. Thus, if one took the net amount receivable (by multiplying benefit by duration) by an unemployed person, this would not exhibit quite the same lag characteristics as would benefit levels alone. One has to make a choice between what one wants (or what combination one wants) in benefit levels and benefit duration. This is fundamentally a problem in economic choice: scarce resources against unlimited wants.

If one took the evaluatory sentiments of employers and unions and arrayed them against each other, one would find generally opposing views, though with different emphases. Labor views would be critical of general accomplishment; not only has the system not "improved," but it has not kept pace. Labor would also be critical of some specialized aspects: administration, experience rating, and disqualifications.[19] Management, while not generally unsympathetic toward the system, would criticize administration (on opposite grounds from labor) and financial procedures.[20]

Before trying to present our evaluation on general accomplishment, let us take a look at the structure and administration of the system.

Structure and Administration of Unemployment Insurance

In assessing the structure and administration of an economic security program, one can do so using an ideal frame of reference: one can start with a clean slate upon which one can draw what one conceives to be a desirable program. Or one can take a "realistic" frame of reference and operate within it, granting that such a method should not necessarily imply a fatalistic approach.

[19] See, for example, *Labor Looks at Unemployment Insurance* (Chicago: University of Chicago Press, 1945).

[20] See, for example, various issues of *American Economic Security*, the publication of the Chamber of Commerce of the United States.

Let us take the ideal framework first. Under these circumstances we would feel that societal purposes would best be served by an unemployment insurance program with the following characteristics. First, the program should be federal rather than state. This would permit economy of administration, uniformity of interpretation, and, most important of all, equalization of the unemployment burden. Since unemployment is now distributed unevenly among the states, a federal program would eliminate these differential impacts. Second, coverage should be extended to the same degree as under OASI. Third, the salary limit should be raised to $4,200 as under OASI. Fourth, experience rating should be eliminated (for reasons we will discuss in Chapter 14). Fifth, an examination should be made of the unemployment trust fund, the benefit structure, and the tax structure, to reconcile different needs and demands. Sixth, benefit levels should be increased to approximate the 50 per cent level, though our suggestion here is tempered by the fact that the duration of benefits has increased through the years.[21] (The closer the benefit level approaches the wage level, the more rigorous the administration must be to prevent abuses.) Seventh, examination should be made of the desirability of developing a system of disability insurance such as now found in four states. (Whether such a plan should be tied into unemployment compensation or workmen's compensation and whether more attention should be paid to long-term disability are matters discussed in Chapter 11.) The one-week waiting period does not appear to work a great hardship; hence, its abolition is not recommended. Nor is sentiment strong about changing generally current administrative practices, definitions, and interpretations; grave injustices do not appear in present applications of availability for work, ability to work, and suitable work criteria. Some would feel present interpretations far too harsh; others, that they were too lax. But economic security programs (as do most social programs) inevitably involve compromises between those who would go too fast and those who would drag their feet.

But what if one does not have a clean slate upon which to write? In such a case the following recommendations might be in order. First, it is unlikely that we shall have (or can have) a federal system. Hence, if we wish to preserve state rights in this area, we shall have to accept diseconomies of administration and lack of uniformity of interpretation as a price. But we could have a federal re-insurance system which would accomplish the purpose of equal-

---

[21] A model workmen's compensation bill suggested by the U. S. Department of Labor would set weekly benefits at the 66⅔ per cent of the average weekly wage of all workers covered by the system.

izing the unemployment burden. Likewise, we would find it difficult to abolish experience rating or to introduce nationwide disability insurance. All the other items listed under the ideal system above would be feasible, and their incorporation into the present system is recommended. (Such recommendations are by no means novel; both Democratic and Republican administrations in recent years have made proposals of one type or another along these lines.)

Given these criteria, our summary evaluation would be that the present system has acomplished in *major* part the purposes for which it was set up, but that it could be made a much more effective system without a marginal increase in costs of the same magnitude.[22]

Administration of the program has been uniformly honest and efficient, improving through the years. Criticism has, of course, been raised by employers and unions (usually on opposite sides) that administration has been pro-labor or pro-employer and hence has lessened the possibilities of accomplishing the purposes for which the program was set up. While the validity of some of this criticism cannot be denied, maladministration has not been of a magnitude such as to impair at all seriously the unemployment insurance system.[23]

Summary

In the United States the major public program for the alleviation of the economic consequences of unemployment is the unemployment compensation (or insurance) system. This is a combined federal-state program, with the federal government setting down a framework of minimal specifications within which the several states are free to write their own acts, which all have done.

[22] The Bureau of Employment Security published in 1955 the results of a series of studies undertaken on the effectiveness of the unemployment insurance system. Our interpretation of the data would lead to a single conclusion: if one assumes either that individuals have no savings (and hence when unemployed cannot make ends meet on unemployment compensation) or that even if they have savings the system should underwrite them until they get a new job, then the present program is not doing what it should. But if one assumes the converse, then the present program gets a better grade. For a brief summary of the findings of the Bureau, see *A Digest of the Survey of Unemployment Compensation Beneficiaries in Pittsburgh, Pennsylvania* (U. S. Department of Labor, Bureau of Employment Security, 1955).

[23] Thus, while we agree that a disservice has not been done by the publication of the following articles, we do not feel that the contentions made in these articles were borne out. The articles include, among others, H. Whitman, "Chiseler's Holiday," *Collier's*, CXXI (June, 1948), 13 ff; K. Coolbaugh, "Job Insurance Needs Investigation," *Saturday Evening Post*, CCXXI (July 26, 1947), 116; C. Stevenson, "Is Rainy-Day Money a Give-Away Show?" *Nation's Business*, XXXVII (November, 1949), 29–30+.

An unemployment insurance program requires answers to a number of basic questions: who is to be covered, what shall be the eligibility requirements for benefit collection, how much benefits shall be and for how long they shall be paid, who shall pay the costs and how much they shall be, and how the program is to be administered. While the federal government imposes certain minimal requirements upon the states in the answering of these questions, the states are given considerable latitude in the programs they enact. Hence, one finds an extremely complicated as well as diverse set of laws in this country. The state programs have been amended continually, but because of interstate competitive relations, such changes have tended to be less marked than for wholly federal laws such as the OASI program.

In concluding this chapter it may be noted first, that the unemployment insurance system *has* been an effective instrument in alleviating the undesirable economic consequences of short-term unemployment. But, second, it may be suggested that the program falls short of the goals it could achieve, and hence there is need for a continuing examination so as to create a more fully effective unemployment insurance system in the United States.

Suggestions for Additional Reading

ADAMS, JOHN F. (director). *A Review of the Financial Experience and Actuarial Requirements of the Minnesota Unemployment Compensation Program, Including an Economic Survey of Minnesota.* St. Paul: Division of Employment and Security, State of Minnesota, 1952.
An interesting and detailed examination of a state economy and its implications for the unemployment insurance program. The student might wish to compare this report with those published by a number of other states.

ALTMAN, RALPH. *Availability For Work: A Study in Unemployment Compensation.* Cambridge: Harvard University Press, 1950.
An interesting study of one phase of the administration of an economic security program, and how such administration has important economic as well as operational implications.

BECKER, JOSEPH M. *The Problem of Abuse in Unemployment Benefits.* New York: Columbia University Press, 1953.
Like the Ralph Altman study noted above, this is an analysis of the administration of an economic security program, dealing with the various ways in which abuses develop and exist.

FORSBERG, ALLEN B. (ed.). *Selected Articles on Unemployment Insurance.* New York: The H. W. Wilson Co., 1926.
Mainly of historical interest, this collection is a very handy summary of positive and negative viewpoints on unemployment insurance. It would be hard to find between two covers another such composite presentation.

RIESENFELD, STEFAN A., and RICHARD C. MAXWELL. *Modern Social Legislation*. Brooklyn: The Foundation Press, 1950. Pp. 461–580.
A legal presentation of problems in coverage, benefits, and administration, including case materials.
—— "Unemployment Insurance—A New Look," *Employment Security Review*, XXI, No. 8 (August, 1954), entire issue.
A series of articles dealing with the philosophy, the operation, and the economics of unemployment insurance.

8

Private Approaches:
Unemployment

Introduction

This chapter is more appropriately titled private "approaches" than "supplements," since the approaches taken by employers and unions against unemployment are not only preventive as well as alleviative, but also broader than supplements to the public system of compensation as discussed in Chapter 7. The major approaches include private unemployment insurance programs; dismissal compensation or the severance wage as it is sometimes called; employment stabilization; and work and wage guarantees, including the conventional guaranteed annual wage (GAW) and the newer supplementary unemployment payment (SUP) or supplementary unemployment benefit (SUB). We shall discuss each of these methods in turn and attempt to relate them to the over-all American economic security system.

General Comments

The methods used in private approaches to unemployment are clear: the employer, either by himself or through collective bargaining, seeks to reduce the incidence of unemployment in his establishment and, for such cases as do arise, may additionally seek to supplement public alleviative measures. Why should the employer do this? There are several very good reasons, based on humanitarian as well as economic grounds. On the preventive side, stabilizing employment affords operational advantages to the employer: manpower savings through reduction in the costs of labor turnover and machine savings in the more intensive utilization of equip- ment. Stabilization also permits a reduction in unemployment insurance taxes through the experience rating system, and, if accompanied by an approved guarantee, provides exemption from the overtime provisions of the Wage and Hour Act. On a humanitarian basis, stabilization reduces the incidence of unemployment and, hence, employee fears about the threat of economic insecurity.[1] On the alleviative side—that of the private unemployment supplement— one finds the same reasons as are found for pensions and accident and illness insurance: namely, to supplement what is considered an otherwise inadequate level of benefits.

How far should an employer go in seeking to stabilize employment? The answer here is the same as for any pecuniary business decision: to the point where the marginal cost of stabilizing is equal to (or at least does not exceed) the marginal benefit, this assuming that the employer has some degree of control in the situation (which realistically is the usual case). There is a point below which stabilization is socially undesirable (in that labor mobility is unduly restricted) and also beyond which the costs of further reduction exceed the gains.

Private supplements to unemployment compensation are a new development. The first collective agreement embodying this approach was signed in 1955. Under present practice, protection via the private supplement is provided by the employer on the basis of a contribution of so many cents per hour into a fund which then can be used to pay the supplements. Customarily, the cents-per- hour fund payment is part of the total wage package or settlement. Hence, employer decision-making on this problem involves determining jointly with the union (or unilaterally in the nonunionized case) what portion of the over-all wage bargain will be allotted to the supplement. We shall discuss these matters more fully later in this chapter, after discussing other types of programs first.

Private Unemployment Insurance Systems

Private unemployment insurance systems (other than the newer unemployment compensation supplements) are primarily of his-

---

[1] For a fuller discussion, see J. L. Snider, *The Guarantee of Work and Wages* (Boston: Harvard University, Graduate School of Business Administration, 1947), pp. 109–10; and H. Feldman, *Stabilizing Jobs and Wages* (New York: Harper & Brothers, 1940), pp. 10–11.

torical interest, but they are worth a brief comment, since they highlight employer and union attempts to deal with this form of insecurity.[2]

Private unemployment insurance programs can be classified into three groups, depending upon the originating parties involved: those developed by unions, those developed by employers, and those collectively bargained. (So far as the authors know, a fourth alternative, unemployment insurance written on an actuarial basis by a commercial insurance company, never came into being, although some carriers were working upon such policies in the 1920's.)

Trade-union plans, dating back to at least 1831, never developed more fully than to provide protection for between approximately 35,000–60,000 or so union members under some thirteen international and twenty additional local union programs in the 1920's. Yet some protection was afforded in specific cases (though the benefits were very low), and the experimentation was useful. Company plans, of which some thirteen were paying benefits in the early 1930's, varied from the employment guarantee approach to the out-and-out unemployment benefit, as found in the Dennison Manufacturing Company. In this company plan, benefits were liberal; up to the middle of 1930, employees with dependents received 80 per cent of their weekly earnings, with a waiting period of but one day. Collectively bargained plans covered more employees— some 63,500 in 1928—than either union or company plans. Again, the approach varied from guarantees to benefits. The most outstanding benefit plans were found in the clothing industry, with some attempt being made to approach actuarial soundness through the use of risk pooling and the setting up of reserve funds.

The passage of the Social Security Act in 1935 led to predictions that private plans would either terminate or function under public regulation. As a matter of course, the former generally happened. All these private plans are interesting for two reasons: (1) they illustrate company and union concern with a burdensome type of economic insecurity and (2) they also illustrate the incredible difficulties involved in trying to combat this form of insecurity on a piecemeal basis, where actuarial data do not exist and where many forces are beyond the control of the employer and the union. (It is granted that it might not have been too difficult to undertake a modest program on a "limited liability" basis, as was the case in the clothing industry. But a piecemeal appoach such as this was not

[2] For a useful reference, see B. M. Stewart, *Unemployment Benefits in the United States* (New York: Industrial Relations Counselors, 1930).

likely to lead to comprehensive and systematic coverage for the economy as a whole.)

Dismissal Compensation

Private unemployment insurance, insofar as the benefit payments technique was used, made no *formal* distinction as to whether a man was laid off and was expected to return, whether he was laid off and his return was uncertain, or whether he was permanently severed, say, for economic reasons. The evidence, however, leads one to presume that the benefit approach was oriented more toward job separations due to layoffs, where the man was expected to return, than it was to cases where he was permanently separated. For this latter case, a different technique developed—that of dismissal compensation or severance wages.

Dismissal compensation may be defined as "the payment of a specific sum, in addition to any back wages or salary, made by an employer to an employee for *permanently terminating* the employment relationship for reasons beyond the control of the employee."[3] In general, dismissal compensation is paid for a severing of the employment relationship, rather than for a period of unemployment; thus, payments are not contingent upon the former employee remaining unemployed. Such compensation is not customarily paid if discharge is for cause, including fault, incapacity, or incompetence.[4]

While exact figures are not available on the extent of dismissal compensation plans in industry, rough estimates would indicate a coverage of about one million employees in 1955.[5] Some 10 per cent of union agreements appear to contain a separation allowance provision.

Why should an employer be interested in providing this form of protection against economic insecurity? One can visualize employer interest in protective plans where the employee is expected to remain with the company—pension, and accident and sickness plans, for example. But in the other case the employment relation-

[3] E. D. Hawkins, *Dismissal Compensation* (Princeton: Princeton University Press, 1940), pp. 5-6 (italics supplied). This is a very useful source book on dismissal compensation, along with the National Industrial Conference Board analysis, "Severance Pay Plans," *Studies in Personal Policy No. 141*, New York, 1954.

[4] Some recent cases indicate that severance pay is now being given for "temporary layoffs," though not for discharge for cause. See "Severance Pay Clauses in Recent Union Agreements," *Management Record*, XIII, No. 10 (October, 1951), 359 ff.

[5] Based upon an extrapolation of figures contained in *Collective Bargaining Negotiations and Contracts* (Washington, D. C.: Bureau of National Affairs, Inc. 1950), pp. 15–3 and 15–52.

ship is permanently severed. Two reasons appear for employer interest in situations where his employee leaves "permanently." One is the increasing belief that the cost of doing business—the cost of production—should include a charge for those employees "scrapped" because of the changes wrought by a dynamic economy. The other is that labor organizations have evinced increasing interest in this type of protection; and, since collective bargaining is a two-way process, union interest is likely to evoke employer response.

DETAILS OF DISMISSAL COMPENSATION PLANS

The following summarizes the basic operational details of severance pay plans.

Coverage. While earlier plans tended to be restrictive in coverage—including, for example, only white-collar employees of the company, or, if blue-collar, only a select group—the present tendency is to widen the umbrella of protection to, say, all employees who have passed their probationary period.

Qualification for benefits. The fact that coverage has tended to increase recently does not mean that a "covered" employee thereby is automatically eligible to receive benefits. Two additional qualifications are found. The first is that the employee must be a certain age (a much less common requirement today) or have had some degree of attachment to the company, ranging all the way from three months to ten years, with one year the most common. (There is an increasing tendency to get away also from the "attachment" qualification by requiring that the individual be merely a "regular" employee of the company—"regular" being defined as having passed the probationary period.) The second qualification relates to the manner of job separation. Usually the job separation must be for reasons beyond the control of the employee; hence, voluntary quits and discharges for cause commonly disqualify the individual. Some companies have escape clauses in which dismissal pay is not required where acts of God, national emergencies, or other forces are the "cause" of the separation. Conversely, some companies make such payments for separations due to total incapacity, military service, retirement, or death.

Benefit levels. The following variables are most commonly taken into account in calculating dismissal pay: (1) the wage or salary at the time of separation (or for some average period prior to that), (2) length of service, and (3) age and need. The latter—age and need—are less commonly applied today than previously and are tending to disappear. The common forms of benefit calculation provide either a "uniform payment" system, such as that all severed employees shall receive two weeks' pay or a "service rule" where pay is graded on the basis of length of service. Thus, an individual might get one week's pay for each year of service. Or, there might be a system of classes set up, such as one week's pay for one to two years of service, two weeks' pay for two to three years of service, three weeks' pay for three to ten years service, and so on. More complex formulae are sometimes found, taking into account age, need, or possible moving expenses.

Here again in these benefit structures is an illustration of the "cultural" belief that loyalty to the company (evinced by a long employment attachment) should be rewarded. The rewards do not, however, go up proportionately in most plans: a twenty-year man does not get twenty times as much as a one-year man.

Benefit payments are commonly made on a lump-sum basis, although some periodic and combination payment plans exist. Not all states permit unemployment insurance payments to be made if the individual receives severance wages, the belief being that this constitutes "double payment." As a result of recent decisions made in conjunction with supplementary unemployment insurance payments, this "double payment" objection is likely to decrease in the future.

Costs, financing, and administration. In the majority of present cases, the employer finances the plan, most frequently on a pay-as-you-go basis. With an increasing use of such plans, it would appear logical that some type of funding be adopted. If the dismissal pay plan is negotiated, then both its content and administration may be subject to joint determination. Commonly, however, the employer is given administrative initiative in operating the plan, with the union having the right to protest management actions where it feels it has been aggrieved.

EVALUATION

Since dismissal compensation has many characteristics in common with wage guarantee plans, particularly the new supplementary unemployment benefit plans, we will defer evaluation until later in this chapter.

Employment Stabilization

Employment stabilization may be defined as the process whereby an employer seeks to regularize his business operations so as to provide as nearly continuous employment as possible for his work force. At one extreme, such stabilization may be very informal; at the other, it may become formalized and may be accompanied by explicit work and/or wage guarantees to the employees. We shall discuss these guarantees in the next section of this chapter, concentrating at this point upon stabilization itself and upon the procedures used.

The rationale of employment stabilization has already been commented upon: it afford both pecuniary and nonpecuniary advantages to the employer, and in so doing also benefits the employee and the community. Employment stabilization is not a cost-free process, however; employing economic logic only, the rational approach would be to push stabilization to the point where the marginal benefits were equal to (or were not exceeded by) the marginal costs of the program. Nonpecuniary factors—such as the social standing of the plant in the community—frequently may influence economic standards, and hence the employer may make stabilization decisions which take these other factors into account.

Formal data on the extent of employment stabilization as such do not exist. Certainly, its use must be very widespread, however, for the very logic of business operations would seem to call for it. If one took a spectrum and labeled one extreme "no stabilization" (a fiction as far as actual operations are concerned) and the other "perfect stabilization" (also a fiction), there is little doubt that most companies have purposefully moved, or tried to move, *further* away from the "no stabilization" extreme. It is probably true also that most companies have a long way to go before getting close to the other extreme (the reaching of which, incidentally, would be both impossible and undesirable, economically and socially).

Granting the logical compulsion of stabilization, can business enterprises achieve it in some degree? That is, can they move toward the "stabilization" end of the spectrum? The answer seems to be that, while certain unstabilizing forces are outside the control of any company, and while certain other forces affect different companies differently, there are various stabilization procedures that all companies can utilize, and there are certain others that specifically situated companies can employ. Hence, it *is* possible to move toward the "perfect stabilization" end of the spectrum, even if different companies move at different rates and come to rest at different points. And, while "perfect stabilization" would make for undesirable rigidities (if, indeed, along with "no-stabilization," it were conceivably possible), there is little doubt of the logic of movement toward stabilization.

Approaches to Employment Stabilization

Employment stabilization is a two-step process: (1) uncovering unstabilizing forces and evaluating their quantitative significance where possible and (2) introducing appropriate measures to counter these unstabilizing pressures.

Unstabilizing forces are of two general types: those "internal" to and those "external" to the company, though in some cases this distinction is blurred. Internal forces are those arising out of inefficient internal business procedures: erratic selling, poor materials scheduling which de-activates part of the work force part of the time, and poor over-all production planning. Internal pressures are less serious insofar as their impacts tend to be very short-lived (unless they cause company bankruptcy). Likewise, their remedy is essentially found in educating the entrepreneur to use "better business methods." External pressures can be classified on the basis of the unemployment categories developed in Chapter 6. Thus, these unstabilizing forces may be secular, cyclical, seasonal, and technological.

Given the unstabilizing force (or forces), the approach is to overcome it (or them) to whatever degree possible through the use of counteracting measures. As noted previously, there is little doubt that employers have some degree of freedom in the application of these counteracting measures. Thus, while there are some unstabilizing forces about which he can do little, the employer normally has some "elbow room." But he must *want* to act, and he must have or acquire the knowledge with which to act. If these conditions are met, three basic categories of counteracting measures are found: those associated with markets and products, with production methods and general operations, and with personnel practices. We shall discuss each of these in greater detail.[6]

Markets and products. By stabilizing the markets for its products, the company can stabilize production, and thus employment. The market-product approach can take various turns. Thus, a cyclically affected company may seek to add product lines whose sales tend to be more fully maintained in a depression. A seasonally affected company does the same: the classic illustration is the han-

---

[6] There are many source materials on stabilization techniques. See, for example, American Legion, Employment Stabilization Service, *To Make Jobs More Steady and to Make More Steady Jobs* (St. Paul: Webb Publishing Co., 1942); Ernest Dale. "Annual Wages and Employment Stabilization Techniques," *Research Report 8* (New York: American Management Association, 1945); Industrial Relations Counselors, *Steadier Jobs*, New York, 1954.

dling of both ice and fuel oil. A company engages in research so as to have new products continually emerging, thus preventing the possibility of secular decay.

The approach need not necessarily be in terms of adding or changing products as such. It may rather involve the timing of the introduction of given (as well as new) products. Thus, a company changes the time of new model introduction so that the slack season comes in the summer months, when the entire plant can shut down for vacation. Or, new product (or new model) introduction can be coordinated in various ways so as to minimize unstabilizing impacts.

Market techniques of various types, for given product lines, can be applied as regularizing devices. Thus at one extreme, the company may seek, through advertising or other means, to regularize a seasonally unstable consumer demand. In its relations with wholesalers, jobbers, and others, the company may seek to regularize their purchases by offering off-season discounts, by guaranteeing delivery at specified prices and times, and by providing warehousing services.

Production methods. The integration of sales forecasting with production planning provides a concrete basis for stabilization. Such integration involves a forecast of sales, setting up of production levels, and control of stock levels. Production for "stock" is another frequently used procedure. Shifting to maintenance work in slack seasons also has been widely used, although this may be difficult if the company is unionized and craft lines are involved.

Personnel methods. Centralizing personnel functions and records is a useful device in that it permits the company to operate with an eye on its over-all operations; thus, one department is not hiring from the outside at the same time that another is laying off. Training for versatility, using interdepartmental transfers, and scheduling vacations during slack periods are other personnel procedures that have been used successfully in the past.

In all the above cases, the business logic is simple: it may be good business (depending upon cost-benefit relationships) to apply operating procedures that seek to stabilize sales, production, and employment ("stabilize" here as elsewhere making allowances for growth potentials). It is probably the case that most employers could do something more than they are doing in the way of stabilizing. And while the greatest successes of stabilization are in overcoming seasonal fluctuations, other causal forces can be attacked successfully to some degree.

Work and Wage Guarantees

An employer who regularizes his business operations may wish to go further and offer the fruits of stabilization to his employees in the form of various types of work or wage guarantees. Such guarantees not only serve useful industrial relations functions, but also may exempt the employer from the overtime provisions of the Fair Labor Standards Act, and reduce his state unemployment tax. For conventional guarantee plans, to be defined shortly, stabilization is a necessary prerequisite condition. This is true because the very nature of such guarantees "demands" a prior stabilization condition if the employer is not going to be forced to default in the critical case. Stabilization is not as vital an issue in the new supplemental unemployment benefit programs, since such plans commonly call for the employer to build up a reserve benefit fund and also limit his obligations to the assets in the fund, plus any agreed-upon and continuing cents-per-hour out-of-pocket payments.

NATURE OF CONVENTIONAL GUARANTEE PLANS

Conventional guarantee plans "guarantee" to the eligible employee a given amount of work per year with no specification as to income, a given income per year (in the strictest sense the "Guaranteed Annual Wage") or provide a similar arrangement for some shorter period. The term "guarantee" was put in quotation marks in the above sentence because the conventional plans customarily contain escape clauses of one type or another. *The important point to note in conventional guarantee plans is that the emphasis is upon fulfilling the guarantee through keeping the employee at work*; or, phrased another way, *the focus is upon the employee who is kept on the job.* Technically, such conventional plans need not inevitably work out in this manner; but historically, it is the way that a majority of them have evolved. *In contrast, and as will be noted in greater detail later in this chapter, the newer supplemental benefit plans focus upon the employee who is displaced from his job.*[7] The immediate connection in conventional guarantees is

---

[7] The literature on guarantee plans is voluminous. For useful source materials on these plans, see J. W. Garbarino, *Guaranteed Wages* (Berkeley: University of California, Institute of Industrial Relations, 1954); Jack Chernick and G. C. Hellickson, *Guaranteed Annual Wage Plans* (Minneapolis: University of Minnesota Press, 1945); A. D. H. Kaplan, *The Guarantee of Annual Wages* (Washington, D. C.: The Brookings Institution, 1947); and M. W. Latimer, *Guaranteed Wages* (O. W. M. R. Report [Washington, D. C.: U. S. Government Printing Office, 1947]). The first item is an accurate and popular style pamphlet; the last, the "Bible" on the subject. The second and third items present factual details on many types of plans.

through the whole complex array of techniques designed to stabilize employment; in the new plans the direct relation is through an
addition to labor cost of so many cents per hour.

EXTENT AND HISTORY OF CONVENTIONAL GUARANTEE PLANS

The most recent detailed analysis of conventional guarantee
plans was made by the Bureau of Labor Statistics in 1945. The
results of this survey were incorporated in the Latimer Report,
published in 1947.[8] While there have been some changes since this
date in conventional guarantee plans (primarily in the form of
additions), the 1945 data present an accurate picture of the nature
and development of such plans. The Bureau of Labor Statistics
canvassed some 90,000 employers in March, 1945, as to the use of
guarantee plans. The criterion of acceptability for such plans was
that they guarantee in advance a period of employment equal to at
least three months a year, or an equivalent amount of wages.

The results of the survey were as follows. A total of 347 plans
were tabulated. Of these, 196 plans were still in operation, and 151
had been discontinued, the latter including 96 cases which operated
under the Wisconsin unemployment compensation law in 1934–
1935. As of January, 1946, the 196 plans covered approximately
61,000 employees. A 1952 Bureau of Labor Statistics examination
of some 2,000 collective agreements revealed 184 with guarantees of
some sort—many limited in nature—covering 246,000 employees.
Thus the later picture was not markedly different in aggregate
terms, since the 1952 criteria were less rigorous than the 1946.[9]

The first of such plans (or among the first) was started in 1894
as a result of negotiations between the National Association of
Machine Printers and Color Mixers and the National Wall Paper
Company. The guarantee was for eleven months, and in 1896 was
extended to twelve months. The greatest period of growth was in
the 1930's and 1940's, with some 102 plans started in 1934, 96 of
which were passed under the tax exemption provisions of the Wisconsin unemployment insurance law. As of January, 1946, the
median number of years current plans had been in existence was
eight. The majority of plans (111 plans) were in companies with
less than 100 employees, and in turn the majority of plans (100

---

[8] See the M. W. Latimer *Report*, Appendix C.

[9] See "Guaranteed Employment and Wages under Collective Agreements,"
Monthly Labor Review, LXXIV, No. 5 (May, 1952), 555–59. Also see Industrial
Relations Counselors, "The Guaranteed Wage: An Active Issue," *Industrial Relations
Memos, No. 131*, 1953.

plans) were in wholesale or retail trade, or food and kindred manufactured products. These two sets of statistics point up the types
of environmental factors conducive to stabilization. The student
should ask himself: Would plans of this type be easily introduced
in "prince and pauper" industries? In the large corporation? Why,
or why not?

Of the 347 tabbed plans, 151 had been discontinued, and among
these were the 96 abortive Wisconsin cases. But why the mortality
among the other 55 plans? Opinions differ. The Latimer Report
indicates that discontinuance was largely the result of special individual circumstances, in a number of cases related to the general
state of business conditions at the time, but more specifically the
result of problems facing the individual employer. Other analysts
are more biting in their comments. Thus W. A. Berridge and C.
Wolfe are more critical, suggesting that inherent instability may
also have been important.[10]

EXAMPLES OF PRESENT CONVENTIONAL PLANS

The "Big Three" among conventional plans, and the best known,
are the Procter & Gamble Company, George A. Hormel & Company,
and Nunn-Bush Shoe Company plans. The first two are work or
income guarantee plans; the latter a flexible wage plan. Other
newer conventional plans—such as the Rice-Stix Dry Goods Company (St. Louis)—International Brotherhood of Teamsters plan,
dated 1953—are similar in nature and scope to the earlier plans. We
shall examine here briefly the details of a number of such plans.

Coverage. There is some tendency to restrict work or wage
guarantees to certain classes of employees in the same way that
restrictions are imposed in unemployment insurance or dismissal
compensation. Two reasons appear for such restrictions. The first
is the conventional belief that the employee should have some
"permanence" about his attachment to the company before it is
obligated to him; this is essentially the type of ethical belief we
have noted in conjunction with other programs. The second reason
is cost and safety: limiting the guarantee to some portion of the
work force makes it less likely that default will be necessary if heavy
economic weather is encountered. The Hormel plan covers "all
employees," as do certain other contemporary programs. The
Quaker Oats plan covers (as of 1954) all full-time employees with
at least six months' service (about 90 per cent of all production

---

[10] See W. A. Berridge and C. Wolfe, *Guaranteed Employment and Wage Plans*
(New York: American Enterprise Association, Inc., 1948), particularly pp. 21–27.

workers). The Procter & Gamble plan, as of 1946, extended its guarantee to all hourly-rated employees with 24 consecutive months of employment, ranging from some 75 to 95 per cent of total hourly-rated employees for a 1936–1941 period. But, as of 1953, the Rice-Stix plan covered only the first 420 employees on the seniority roster (some 60 per cent of total employees).[11] Thus, conventional guarantees tend to have some limitations in coverage, and while this coverage is tending to expand rather than contract, there is less than complete protection for all employees in the companies in question.

Qualification for benefits. In general, in work and wage guarantee plans, coverage and eligibility are more nearly synonymous than is true in other security programs. There are, however, additional qualifications found in some plans. Voluntary quits, discharge for cause, absence beyond regularly provided sick leave or vacation, failure to report for work or to accept suitable work are among the more important disqualifying factors. Except for these restrictions, the eligible employee is blanketed under the guarantee.

Benefits. Benefits under guarantee plans are, of course, the guarantees themselves: so many hours of employment in the given period, so much income, or some other arrangement. Thus, the Procter & Gamble plan guarantees 48 weeks of work per year to eligible employees. The Hormel plan guarantees 52 paychecks per year. The Nunn-Bush flexible wage plan does not guarantee any definite amount of hourly pay. The Company allocates to a fund X per cent of the value added by manufacture. From this "wage fund" a specified number of eligible employees are guaranteed wages during a 52-week period. The amount paid out in wages is directly dependent upon company revenues.

Costs and financing. Conventional plans appear to have been financed, where necessary, by the employer essentially on a pay-as-you-go basis via charges against payroll. There appears to have been little tendency to fund against future contingencies. The fundamental approach to guarantees has, however, been of a different nature: an approach that would minimize the necessity for any explicit outlays to meet the guarantees. This approach involves the precedent step of "stabilization" and hence of meeting the obligation simply through the process of doing business in such a way that the people to whom the guarantee is extended are kept at work. While this description may have been less valid for those

---

[11] See "Experience under Three Guaranteed Wage Plans," *Monthly Labor Review*, LXXVII, No. 7 (July, 1954), 769–70.

companies which abandoned their plans than for those who retained them, it probably characterizes the majority.

Administration. Since the majority of guarantee plans have been employer initiated, it would be expected that the employer would exercise administrative control over them. This has tended to be true also in several of the earlier plans where the company—or some part of it—was unionized. In several of the newer plans in unionized companies, the certified labor organization has tended to play a more important role in administration.

Administration has presented two major issues: first, those matters concerned with stabilization as such, and, second, the problems that arise if the guarantee is not "automatically" met by stabilization. In this latter case, conscious "remedial" steps must then be taken so as not to default on the guarantee.

Evaluation of the conventional stabilization approach may be deferred until after we present, in the next section, some highlights on the "new look" in guarantee plans.

The New Approach to Guarantee Plans

The new types of guarantee plans, oriented toward supplementing unemployment insurance payments for employees separated from their jobs, had their genesis in the years of World War II. During this period and earlier, a number of CIO unions, particularly the United Steelworkers of America, had interested themselves in wage and employment guarantees as part of their long-range wage policy. In 1943, the steelworkers included, as part of the negotiating pattern with the "Big Steel" companies, a demand for a guarantee for forty hours' straight-time pay for each week of a proposed two-year contract. The disputed case was brought before the National War Labor Board, which, while rejecting the demand, urged that an official study be made of the problem. This led to the Office of War Mobilization and Reconversion inquiry, headed by Murray W. Latimer and subsequently to the publication of the so-called "Latimer Report."[12]

The Latimer Report noted that conventional guarantees would be difficult to achieve in a cyclical industry such as steel, but suggested that an "unemployment compensation supplement" would be feasible.[13] Action was not seriously pressed during subsequent full-employment years by the unions, which concentrated instead upon securing health, welfare, and pension plans. Both the steel-

[12] See the reference in footnote 7, p. 223.
[13] See the Latimer *Report*, pp. 97–124, for details.

workers and the United Automobile Workers (CIO) did, however, continue to work upon the details involved in such plans, and to make them part of token demands upon the employers. In 1951–1952 the issue was argued again by the steelworkers, this time before the Wage Stabilization Board as that agency was constituted during the Korean conflict. Again the union request was denied. Still later, after further action, the issue was joined in the 1955 negotiations between the UAW and Ford and General Motors, with an historic contract, embodying a modified new-type guarantee, being signed with Ford on June 6, and with General Motors shortly thereafter.[14] We shall examine these plans in greater detail after a brief look at their composition before modification.

Early Versions of New-Look Plans

The new-look plans are best typified in their "tentative versions" by those of the autoworkers and the steelworkers.[15] While the plans differ in details, particularly as to financing, they have certain common elements which we shall discuss.

"One-Week" guarantee to "all employees." The *one-week* guarantee to *all employees* characterized the UAW plan. This short-term guarantee would require the employer to pay the employee for a full week unless the latter were properly notified previously that his services would not be needed for the ensuing week. This is actually equivalent to "40-hour call-in-pay," and was designed to put pressure upon the employer to regularize his week's work-schedule. This part of the plan did not appear in the final contractual version.

"One-Year" guarantee to "eligible employees." A *one-year* guarantee to *eligible employees* characterized both plans. In the case of the steelworkers' plan, eligible employees would be those with three years of service; in the autoworkers', all those employees with seniority status. In the steelworkers' version, the amount of the guarantee would be 30 times the employee's basic hourly wage rate, running for 52 weeks from the date of unemployment, with all benefits

---

[14] A good résumé up through 1953 is to be found in Industrial Relations Counselors, "The Guaranteed Wage: An Active Issue," pp. 2–5. An excellent analysis and summary is found in Jack Chernick, "A Guide to the Guaranteed Wage," *Bulletin No. 4* (New Brunswick: Rutgers University, Institute of Management and Labor Relations, 1955).

[15] For full details see USW–CIO, *A Guaranteed Wage Plan for the Workers in the Steel Industry* (Union exhibit before the Wage Stabilization Board, Case No. D–18–C), and UAW–CIO, *Preparing a Guaranteed Employment Plan* and *Questions and Answers about the UAW–CIO Guaranteed Employment Plan* (Detroit: UAW–CIO Education Department Publications 321 and 330, respectively).

paid by the state unemployment insurance system deducted from company payments. The plan envisaged a guarantee of about 75 per cent of straight-time wages. The UAW plan provided for a 52-week guarantee. Payments would supplement unemployment compensation and would be such as to permit employees to "maintain the same standard of living as when fully employed." This could be viewed as 100 per cent of take-home pay. Both plans contained elaborate "incentive" guarantees to prevent their abuse: guarantees that would preclude the separated employee from merely sitting back and drawing benefits if work were available.

Financing and administration. In the steelworkers' plan, a trust fund would be set up, with the employer paying, for example, 10 cents per hour per man into the fund. Employer liability would be limited to this obligation. As hours worked decreased (as in a cyclical downturn), the in-payment obligation would be reduced. The UAW plan involved a combination of trust fund, pay-as-you-go, and reinsurance. The added pay-as-you-go obligation presumably would offer an extra incentive to the employer to stabilize; if he did not stabilize, he would have the equivalent of a partial payroll to meet without having employees performing productive operations. Thus, pay-as-you-go would make this week's layoffs raise this week's costs immediately. Both plans envisaged an employer–union administrative agency of some type not only for purposes of over-all supervision, but more importantly to adjudicate cases of individual eligibility (initial and continuing) as they arose. This unit would be over and above any applicable state unemployment insurance administrative agency.

The "One-Year" guarantee plan discussed above brings out sharply the differences between conventional and new-type guarantees. While an implicit "stabilization" approach is found in both UAW and USW plans, and is formalized to some extent in the UAW pay-as-you-go proposal, the major emphasis is upon the displaced worker and upon supplementing his unemployment compensation.

How intensely the unions were wedded to these particular plans is not readily apparent. At one extreme, they could be viewed as bargaining points, to be modified in the face of the realities of collective negotiation. At the other, one could envisage them as plans in which the unions had an unyielding belief. The 1955 negotiations, which resulted in the introduction of these new-style guarantees, did modify rather markedly the proposals outlined above. But we do not know if the unions will be content with the modified versions of 1955, or if they will eventually seek to obtain the original versions. There is some evidence, as of late 1956, that the unions will push ahead toward trying to secure something like the original versions.

THREE PLANS: 1955–1956 MODELS

Developments in new-style guarantees are occurring so fast that anything written today is likely to be somewhat out of date tomorrow. Yet it may prove instructive to examine three of the major types of plans negotiated in 1955. These are the historic Ford–UAW plan (to which the GM plan is similar); the Can Companies (American and Continental)–USW plan, and the CIO Glass Workers–Libby-Owens-Ford and Pittsburgh Plate Glass Company plan.[16] We will examine each of the plans under the customary headings, using the terms "auto plan," "steel plan," and "glass plan," respectively, as shorthand designations.

Coverage. The glass plan is the most liberal, extending to all except "temporary" employees. The auto plan is next, covering hourly rated employees with one year's seniority. The steel plan is most restrictive, encompassing only qualified employees with three years' seniority.

Qualification for benefits. The auto and steel plans extend to employees laid off for lack of work or apply in case of a reduction in force. The glass plan covers employees laid off for a full pay period or sick for two consecutive pay periods. Since all except the glass plan are unemployment insurance supplements, the separated employee would be presumed to meet the relevant state insurance requirements. There is a waiting period of one week (two weeks in sickness cases in the glass plan). The plans provide for specific ways for the employee to build up "wage credits" used to determine the exact duration for which an employee can collect benefits; that is, all employees need not necessarily be entitled to collect for the maximum benefit period. The plans were not to go into effect until June 1–October, 1956, depending upon the plan.

Benefit levels. The steel plan is the most liberal. It provides a maximum of fifty-two weeks of benefits for any one layoff, at a level of 65 per cent of take-home pay. This plan permits the separated employee to draw up to $2 per week for each dependent up to four. It also has a special proviso as follows: if it proves legally impossible

---

[16] The details of these plans were obtained from a miscellany of current newspaper accounts, labor reporting services, and economic periodicals.

to pay benefits concurrent with unemployment compensation, the companies will pay the employee a lump-sum benefit at the end of his period of unemployment or at expiration of state benefit.

The auto plan provides benefits for a maximum of twenty-six weeks, and with a $25 maximum an employee would receive—when combined with unemployment insurance—65 per cent of his take-home pay for the first four weeks, and 60 per cent for the next twenty-two weeks.

The glass plan is really not an unemployment insurance supplement as are the above. It is rather a deferred savings plan with vested rights. The individual who is laid off for a full pay period or sick for two consecutive pay periods may apply for anywhere from $15 to $30 from his security account(defined below) as long as the withdrawal does not exceed 10 per cent of the funds in his account. The companies are to set up an individual fund (the "security account") for each employee. Up to $600 of the individual fund may be used to pay for idleness due to layoff or prolonged illness. If more than $600 accumulates in the fund, the excess is to be distributed as vacation pay. Each employee retains a vested right to his security fund, which he will receive in a lump sum if he quits, is dismissed, or retires.

Costs and financing. The costs in all plans are to be borne by the employer through 5-cent-per-hour payment per employee. In the auto plan (omitting the special "defense" fund), a $55 million trust fund is set up, with elaborate provisions made for changing its size. The glass plan provides for a minimum security account of $600 per employee, but once this is reached, in-payments do not stop; rather they are earmarked for distribution as vacation-pay extras. The steel plan is more flexible than either of the above.

Administration. The three plans call for joint company–union administration. The major areas of joint concern include such matters as the size of the supplemental benefit due an employee; the period for which he is eligible to collect such benefits, which involves, as in the Ford plan, an evaluation of "wage credits"; and adjudication of differences in disputed cases. The steel and glass plans are independent of the question of the legality of paying unemployment supplements at the same time unemployment insurance payments are being made. The auto plan is, however, contingent upon such legality. Legal developments in mid-1956 make it appear that "dual payments" will be approved generally, although there may be court tests of administrative rulings.[17]

[17] See *Labor Relations Reporter*, XXXVIII, No. 9 (June 4, 1956) 38 Analysis 17.

Approximately two million employees have now been brought under the coverage of the new plans. Thus, in approximately one year, coverage was extended to well over twenty times as many employees as had been included under conventional plans in a sixty-five-year period. Obviously, it takes but a few companies the size of Ford and General Motors to effectuate this. By mid-1956, the SUB program was paying benefits to displaced employees in the three major automobile companies, and comment was to the effect that the plan was "meeting its first test well."[18] (Some later reports, however, indicated administrative complexities and difficulties.)

Private Unemployment Approaches: Some Evaluatory Comments

Private approaches to unemployment are of various types. In turn, each of these types is many-dimensioned and capable of being discussed on various levels and in innumerable detail. We shall select a number of major headings upon which to concentrate our discussion.[19]

SOME GENERAL CONCLUSIONS OF THE CRITICS: CONVENTIONAL PLANS

The following typify some of the more general conclusions that various analysts have reached concerning conventional private unemployment approaches:

First, employer stabilization programs are both desirable and useful, though some critics doubt how effective such programs can really become and other critics feel that such approaches should be purely voluntary—that if labor organizations can use these ap-

[18] See *Business Week*, July 21, 1956, pp. 46–54.

[19] While much of the literature available on this subject sheds more heat than light, it is nonetheless instructive. Most of the source material focuses upon employment stabilization and wage guarantees, both old and new styles. The following are suggested to the student as comprising a reasonably balanced list. For stabilization programs, see the volumes by J. L. Snider and H. Feldman, cited in footnote 1, p. 215. For a discussion of conventional guarantee plans see A. D. H. Kaplan, cited in footnote 7, p. 223. For union positions on the new plans see particularly the two UAW publications cited in footnote 15, p. 228. For employer positions on the new plans, see Chamber of Commerce of the United States, *The Economics of the Guaranteed Wage*, and *Jobs? or Jobless Pay?*, Washington, D. C., 1954, 1955, respectively, and National Association of Manufacturers, *Guaranteed Annual Wage and Its Implications to a Free Economy*, New York, 1954. For the views of outside analysts, see especially S. H. Slichter, "Labor's New Victory," *The Atlantic Monthly*, September, 1955, pp. 63–66, and "One View of the Effects of the Ford-GM Contracts," *Monthly Labor Review*, LXXVIII, No. 10 (October, 1955), 1115–1118. As a final suggestion, see H. J. Ruttenberg, "Pay By The Year," *Harpers*, CCXI, No. 6 (December, 1955) 24, 29–33.

proaches as collective bargaining pressure levers, much of the "desirability" is lost. There is a general sentiment that such programs may accomplish their purposes in a very limited way. Further, in terms of the types of programs thus far developed, they are not likely to be accompanied by undesirable direct or indirect effects, except for some possibly undesirable "rigidities."

Second, probably because of its limited use thus far, dismissal compensation has not been publicized and discussed to the degree that other programs have. There is, however, some feeling that the cost of production ought to include a readjustment allowance for the worker who is permanently separated from his job for technological or other reasons. On this basis, there is likewise some sentiment that dismissal compensation would be a feasible mechanism for providing such a readjustment allowance. There are, however, numerous specific problems associated with this approach that are also common to guarantees. We shall examine these shortly.

And third, conventional guarantee plans have also tended to receive general approbation, provided they were "voluntarily" introduced. (There has been considerable doubt expressed, however, as to how extensive such plans could ever become in the economy and there has been inter-industry criticism.) This matter of "voluntarism" is interesting. As long as the employer was free to experiment with such plans on his own, employer associations and others had not been particularly critical, although, conversely, unions had not been very enthusiastic or optimistic. When various unions began to suggest bargaining collectively over these plans, employer groups marshaled weighty evidence to show why, from their point of view, the approach was not feasible, at least not for the economy at large. Many of the reasons developed have also been identified with the new types of plans.

THE UNEMPLOYMENT SUPPLEMENT PLANS

If employers and unions were not particularly vocal about the conventional plans noted above, the dam broke when the new plans crystallized; torrents of argumentation and discussion appeared on both sides as well as from "neutrals."[20]

[20] See the references cited in footnote 19, p. 232. See also the papers and comments by Arthur Larson, S. E. Harris, Nat Weinberg, E. P. Schmidt, and S. Brandwein in "The Impact of Employment Security Problems," *Proceedings* of the Seventh Annual Meeting of the Industrial Relations Research Association, 1954; and W. Papier, "Guaranteed Annual Wage Proposals: Their Implications for Unemployment Compensation," *Industrial and Labor Relations Review*, VIII, No. 2 (January, 1955), 265–74. For an over-all analysis of many broader issues, see S. E. Harris, *The Economics of Social Security* (New York: McGraw-Hill Book Co., Inc., 1941).

We shall select a number of "problem areas" associated with new-type guarantee plans, discuss certain relevant issues therein, and try to integrate a number of points into a concluding statement.

"Duplicate" unemployment systems. One of the major criticisms leveled against the new plans is that they duplicate programs existent in an already complex security system, proliferating administrative agencies in a wasteful way, and uneconomically utilizing resources. There is little doubt that these charges are in many respects true. But this is one of the prices paid for free collective bargaining. Moreover, it takes two to make a bargain, and a number of employers agreed to such union demands in 1955. One alternative approach would be to deny to employers and unions the right to bargain over certain matters. A moment's reflection indicates, however, the incredible difficulties involved in trying to stake out allowable areas of collective bargaining, though this ought not to stop us from trying to make decisions about the "good" and the "bad."

It has been said sometimes that if unemployment compensation benefit levels had kept pace with changes in the price level, these new plans would not have developed. If benefits had averaged around 50 to 65 per cent—which appears to have been the original intention of the unemployment insurance system—instead of slipping well below that, it is claimed that the existing system would have been acceptable. Further, it is held that if the states had been willing to adjust their plans even as late as 1955, the new plans would not have appeared on the bargaining agenda.

One cannot prove what would or would not have happened had circumstances been different. But we feel that by 1955 the die had been cast, the unions' stake in these plans was high, and, irrespective of what changes took place in unemployment insurance, it was likely that the unions would press their claims. And, irrespective of what the states do in the near future to increase benefit levels, union pressure for the new plans is not likely to abate. Hence, it is wishful thinking to say that these plans are uneconomical duplication and thereby to wish them away. If they are uneconomical, this is the price of employer and legislative shortsightedness in refusing to adjust benefits to price-level changes. It is also the price of free collective bargaining and the right of unions to act as "idea men." These are not fatalistic views, but they are, perhaps, realistic.

"Unethical" systems. It is also charged that the new plans are unethical: Why should an employee who, as an accident of fate, works for an employer with a supplement plan be entitled to collect

more for being unemployed than another employee not so fortunately placed? Again, there is more than a grain of merit in this contention. But life is full of such differentials: Is it not equally unethical for an employee to have a higher wage merely because he is lucky enough to work for a prosperous company? By parity of reasoning, one could extend the argument to many other facets of the job and the wage. If the unemployment supplement is financed by an employer payment of X cents per hour into a fund, isn't this merely a foregone direct wage increase? Would the same objection be raised if the X cents were paid directly to the employee as wages? If these new plans are unethical on this basis, then any differential advantage that was obtained by individual A over individual B might be so construed. Improving the unemployment insurance system so as to provide parity of treatment for the unemployed would be a much more equitable approach. But, if employers and unions are free to bargain, these differentials are likely to result, at least in the short run. And, since unionism is presumed to "pay off," this is one of the gains it may try to secure for those who are its members.

The incentive effect. Critics claim that the new plans will destroy incentive: Why should a man seek work if he can collect a 100 per cent benefit when idle? At the moment the question is partially academic, since the plans negotiated in 1955 settled approximately at a 65 per cent compromise level rather than the 100 per cent original proposals. But there is some evidence that the unions intend to push eventually for the 100 per cent figure. As was noted in Chapter 1, there is a paucity of proof as to the disincentive level for an individual, let alone for a group. It is our belief, however, that a 100 per cent benefit level would have extremely undesirable disincentive consequences (quite apart from the cost considerations involved); this would be true even if an elaborate system were set up to protect the 100 per cent plan from abuse. Here is an instance in which the contemplated plan has not yet been adopted. And it might be desirable to take a long, hard look before figuratively or actually accepting a feature of the plan about which there is such an absence of favorable evidence.

Economic issues. Numerous economic issues have arisen in conjunction with the new supplement plans. We shall look at two in particular.[21]

---

[21] See Chapter 14 for additional discussion. See also Campbell McConnell, "Pros and Cons of the Guaranteed Annual Wage," *Labor Law Journal*, VII, No. 7 (July, 1956), 414–24.

One criticism is that such plans put another block in the pathway of labor mobility. Insofar as the plans are on a company-by-company basis, with no interchange, this charge is true. The impediment is less serious than in the case of, say, pensions where an employee must attach himself in most cases to a given employer for a much longer period of time in order to be eligible. But there may be short-term immoblity, immobility which would not be created if the unemployment insurance system were expanded. Mobility is, however, a vexing problem. One of the purposes of an employment program in any company is to reduce labor turnover to whatever minimum is economically feasible. To do this, the employer utilizes a variety of personnel practices of which the unemployment supplement may be one. Yet, the very accomplishment of reducing turnover may reduce desirable mobility. We need to know more about desirable mobility levels before we can say much about the effect of the new-type plans. In general, however, it is safe to conclude that such plans do reduce mobility. Whether they reduce it to an undesirable level is a matter of conjecture.

A second economic issue involves the impacts of the plan upon the ability of businesses to survive. It is claimed that such plans are likely to cause serious financial difficulties for business enterprises and, if imposed upon the small enterprise, to drive it out of business. If the supplemental plan is financed by a fixed cents-per-hour contribution to a fund, if there is no additional out-of-pocket cost, and if the liability of the firm is limited to the fund, then it is hard to see why such a plan should cause a company any more difficulties than would any other wage charge. Moreover, if fund in-payments vary directly with work force size, then burden decreases as layoffs (and presumably an unfavorable economic climate) increase. The fear for the small employer rests upon the assumption that his employment instability is greater. This is not necessarily true, and hence the small company may be in no more of a disadvantageous position than the large one. The plan may have serious consequences, however, for the unstable firm, possibly adding to its problems if the union is able to bargain through a supplement.

Operational issues. Another set of criticisms relate to the operating practices of companies and unions. For example, it is held that a company which formerly subcontracted certain operations will now no longer do so, since by doing them at home employment can be maintained at a time when layoffs might otherwise have occurred. Thus, it is claimed that this new system will operate so as to shift the layoff burden to a whole host of suppliers. There is little doubt that this is a possibility. But with the guarantees extending generally at present only to the one-year or more service employee, the need for such changes in company operations is likely to be small.

A more pressing operational problem exists for the union, particularly the union with an increasing proportion of high seniority workers. Suppose the supplemental benefits are paid substantially to the short service worker, with seniority protecting the long service worker. Yet, payments made into the fund are on the basis of total payroll. Why should not the long service employee prefer the X cents per hour added directly to his wage, since there is little likelihood of his ever getting it through an unemployment supplement? (This type of pressure, incidentally, was sufficient to prevent the introduction of the plan in several companies in 1955.) The glass plan, in which an individual has a fully vested personal security account, is not as subject to this pressure. If employees view the other plans as quasi-insurance types—as, say, fire insurance—where one collects only if the undesirable event happens, then it is not likely that serious pressures will build up. But if the plans are viewed as individual forced saving-deferred payment plans, then difficulties are likely to arise. One suspects that employees accept the latter more than they do the former view. Therefore, it is likely that some difficulties will be encountered in this direction.

Political issues. It has been suggested that the piecemeal introduction of guarantee plans will lead to political problems within and among states.[22] Thus, it is held that employers who have such plans will push for increases in unemployment compensation benefits in their states, thus reducing demands on their own funds and in effect transferring part of the burden elsewhere. This may lead to conflicts of various types among employers on the state level. The same problem may be repeated between states. An additional result may be the transference of deliberations over unemployment insurance from the legislature to the bargaining table. There is little doubt that all these problems are real and that they may be heightened by the further partial introduction of supplement plans. It is hard to envisage a way out of these conflicts except to note in an almost trivial fashion that differences of various types have existed and persisted in these areas for long periods.

[22] For an excellent analysis of this, see W. Papier, *op. cit.*, pp. 265–74.

A CONCLUDING COMMENT

In evaluating private approaches to unemployment the following conclusions appear.

First, such approaches permit useful experimentation. There are some dangers, but the benefits are likely to outweigh the dangers—benefits that would include among others augmenting our built-in stabilizers, stimulating technical progress, and increasing industrial expansion.

Second, we have seen the limited coverage of severance wage plans and conventional guarantee programs. And supplemental plans at best are likely to reach only about 25 per cent of the employees now covered under unemployment insurance.[23] Where the supplements may be needed most is where they are least likely to develop. There are significant gaps in the protection afforded by private plans. Hence, as was concluded in the last chapter, *there is a real need to press for a more adequate system of unemployment compensation.* This is a goal toward which real effort should be extended.

Summary

Private approaches to the economic insecurity created by unemployment have had a long history in the United States, antedating unemployment compensation by a half-century.

Approaches of employers and unions to the unemployment problem have taken various forms. Private insurance systems of various types were experimented with on a limited basis. Although such systems were restricted in their usefulness, and although they were superseded after 1935, they afford an interesting example of one approach to an economic and social problem. A current variant of such an approach is found in the increasingly important system of the dismissal wage, which seeks to compensate an individual severed from a job through no fault of his own.

The most important contemporary private approach is that of employment stabilization, wherein the employer seeks to regularize his operations so as to maximize the work opportunities of his employees. Employment stabilization may be accompanied by a formal work or wage guarantee. In conventional guarantee plans the emphasis is upon keeping the employee at work. Newer guarantee plan types focus upon the employee who is displaced and seek to

---

[23] See S. H. Slichter, *op. cit.*, p. 66. Professor Slichter, as of the end of 1955, did not believe such plans would become widespread. See *Labor Relations Reporter,* XXXVII, No. 7 (November 28, 1955) 37 Analysis 13.

provide a supplement to his unemployment benefits.

Nothwithstanding the realized or potential usefulness of such private plans, federal and state unemployment insurance approach does have a fundamentally important place in our society, and efforts should be extended to make it as effective as possible.

Suggestions for Additional Reading

CHAMBER OF COMMERCE OF THE UNITED STATES. *Jobs? or Jobless Pay? The "Real" Issue Behind the "New" Guaranteed Wage Proposals.* Washington, D. C.: Chamber of Commerce of the United States, 1954.

The reader should consult this pamphlet for its presentation of one point of view on wage guarantees, new style.

CHERNICK, JACK. *A Guide to the Guaranteed Wage. Bulletin No. 4.* New Brunswick: Rutgers University, Institute of Management and Labor Relations, 1955.

The most recent and one of the best accounts of old and new style guarantees. Particularly helpful at the level of the individual firm.

HAWKINS, EVERETT D. *Dismissal Compensation.* Princeton: Princeton University Press, 1940.

One of the best available descriptions and analyses of "voluntary and compulsory plans used in the United States and abroad." The book is particularly useful in its treatment of historical analysis and administrative operations.

LATIMER, MURRAY W. (research director). *Guaranteed Wages* (Report to the President by the Advisory Board). Washington, D. C.: U. S. Government Printing Office, 1947.

Notwithstanding criticism from various sources this is the standard authority on the subject and well worth careful study. See particularly the appendixes, particularly Appendix F on the economics of wage guarantees.

UAW-CIO (Education Department). *UAW-CIO Guaranteed Employment Plan.* (Publication No. 330.) Detroit: UAW-CIO Education Department, Undated.

The reader should consult this pamphlet in conjunction with the one put out by the Chamber of Commerce. A rather different point of view is to be found.

YODER, DALE. *Personnel Management and Industrial Relations,* 4th ed. Englewood Cliffs, N. J.: Prentice-Hall, Inc., 1956.

A detailed analysis of personnel administration and labor relations practices and procedures and how they tie into the types of problems discussed in the last three chapters. Chapters 18 and 19 are particularly relevant.

9

Problems of Occupational
Disability

Introduction

When a worker is forced to leave his job because of injury or sickness, he may often incur a greater risk to his economic security than if he left because of changing economic circumstances. For serious disability (the consequence of the injury or sickness) may cause prolonged unemployment, and may have severe personal and economic consequences in addition to the cost of the unemployment.

Job-connected disability, however, presents a less important aggregate problem in economic security than does unemployment. This is because fewer people are affected, either directly or indirectly, by industrial disability; and because over periods of time economic losses due to unemployment are far greater than those caused by disabilities.

Occupational disability became a serious threat to economic security when, in the late nineteenth century, the place of our nation's work shifted from agrarian to industrial grounds. It was the first hazard to economic security, the costs of which were redistributed (nearly a half-century ago) by public policy in the form of social insurance. Only very recently have injuries and sickness from nonwork causes begun to come under private and public insurance systems. In this chapter we will discuss the problem of occupational disability, its origins, and the development of the present-day workmen's compensation legislation which seeks to deal with it. The following chapter discusses these laws in greater and evaluative detail. Chapters 11 and 12 will consider nonoccupational disability.

The Problem of Occupational Disability

SCOPE OF THE PROBLEM

According to the U. S. Bureau of Labor Statistics,[1] an occupationally disabled worker is one who, because of a job-connected accident or sickness, is unable to perform his usual work one or more days after his injury. Disabilities fully repaired by healing are classified as "temporary." Those involving more serious injuries and permanent impairment or loss of a member or of its function are termed "permanent disabilities." Both temporary and permanent disabilities may be totally or partially disabling depending upon the degree of physical impairment caused by the injury.

Hence, industrial disability figures may include, on the one hand, a worker who is forced to miss a day's work because of a sprained ankle and, on the other, a worker who has permanently lost his sight. Included, too, are occupational diseases, which, because many evolve over long periods of time, tend to be understated by reported occupational injury data. The list of illnesses that come as a natural consequence of employment is nearly inexhaustible: "The fisherman's rheumatism, the waiter's fallen arches, the surgeon's hypertension, the miner's silicosis, the boilermaker's deafness, the bus driver's peptic ulcer, and the housemaid's bursitic knee are all, like a thousand other complaints, more or less directly attributable to the environmental conditions under which their victims work."[2]

Job-connected injuries, sickness, and deaths are a frequent occurrence in an industrial economy, which is perhaps one reason they are not often the subject of public discussion. The occupationally disabled far outnumber war casualties, and they are more numerous than motor vehicle accident victims. In fact, job-connected disabilities account for nearly one-fifth of all accidental injuries each year.

Judging by the experience shown in Table 9.1 (p. 242), we can expect some two million disabling injuries annually (including dis-

---

[1] The complete definition of disabling work injury, as approved by the American Standards Association, may be found in "Techniques of Preparing Major BLS Statistical Series," *Bulletin 1168* (U. S. Department of Labor, Bureau of Labor Statistics, 1954), p. 34. Students interested in the concepts, background, and scope of the Bureau's work-injury studies are advised to consult Chapter 5 of this bulletin: "Work-Injuries and Accident-Cause Statistics."

[2] Berton Roueché, "Annals of Medicine," *The New Yorker*, XXXI, No. 2 (February 26, 1955), 35–36.

TABLE 9.1

Estimated Number of Disabling Work Injuries, All Industries,
1939–1955

Year	All Disabling Injuries	Deaths	Permanent Disabilities	Temporary Total Disabilities
1939	1,603,500	16,400	109,400*	1,477,700
1940	1,889,700	18,100	89,600*	1,782,000
1941	2,180,200	19,200	100,600*	2,060,400
1942	2,267,700	18,100	102,600	2,147,000
1943	2,414,000	18,400	109,700	2,285,900
1944	2,230,400	15,900	96,100	2,118,400
1945	2,020,300	16,500	89,900	1,913,900
1946	2,056,000	16,500	94,200	1,945,300
1947	2,059,000	17,000	91,800	1,950,200
1948	2,019,900	16,000	88,500	1,915,400
1949	1,870,000	15,000	81,000	1,774,000
1950	1,925,000	15,500	84,900	1,851,600
1951	2,100,000	16,000	91,000	2,000,000
1952	2,040,000	15,000	84,000	1,941,000
1953	2,034,000	15,000	84,000	1,935,000
1954	1,860,000	14,000	76,000	1,770,000
1955†	1,930,000	14,200	76,800	1,839,000

* Death cases include cases of permanent total disabilities.
† Data are preliminary.

Sources: U. S. Department of Labor, Bureau of Labor Statistics, "Handbook of Labor Statistics, 1950," *Bulletin 1016*, p. 178; 1951 *Supplement*, p. 57; *Monthly Labor Review*, LXXVII, No. 4 (April, 1954), 423–24; LXXIX, No. 4 (April, 1956), 439.

ease). About 14,000 of these workers will die as a result of their injuries, and another 76,000 will be permanently maimed or crippled. These figures do not include an estimated forty to fifty million non-lost-time accidents requiring minor medical treatment.

But these injuries do not occur evenly throughout all types of work. Table 9.2 indicates on an absolute basis which industries account for the greatest numbers of disabilities and includes some rather surprising figures.

According to these data, more deaths occur in agricultural employments than in manufacturing, a fact reflecting the improved accident prevention programs of manufacturing industries and the effect of mechanization of farms. Except for manufacturing, work in finance, service, and government is responsible for more injuries than any other single industrial classification. Before judgments can be made about the magnitude of the occupational disability

TABLE 9.2

ESTIMATED NUMBER OF DISABLING WORK INJURIES BY INDUSTRY,
1954–1955

(1955 Data Preliminary)

Industry	All Disabling Injuries		Deaths	
	1954	1955	1954	1955
All industries	1,860,000	1,930,000	14,000	14,200
Agriculture	310,000	310,000	3,800	3,700
Mining	52,000	52,000	800	800
Contract Construction	205,000	210,000	2,400	2,400
Manufacturing	390,000	410,000	2,000	2,100
Transportation	167,000	170,000	1,200	1,300
Public Utilities	18,000	18,000	200	200
Trade	340,000	360,000	1,300	1,400
Finance, Service, Government, and Miscellaneous	378,000	400,000	2,300	2,300

Source: *Monthly Labor Review*, LXXIX, No. 4 (April, 1956), 431.

problem in any given employment, however, these aggregate data, of course, must be standardized. This is done by calculating accident "frequency" and "severity" rates.

The accident frequency rate. The accident frequency rate is calculated to show the number of accidents that are occurring and is stated in number of man-hours of exposure to make it comparable from time to time and place to place within and between industries. It is defined as the number of disabling accidents per one million man-hours worked.[3]

While the frequency rate indicates the trend of accidents and enables comparisons between industries, plants, and even between departments within a firm, it does not distinguish serious accidents from less serious ones. All disabling work injuries (the consequence of the accident), regardless of severity, enter the numerator of the frequency rate calculation. Hence, accident data include a second calculation—the severity rate—which states on a standard basis the relative seriousness of occupational injuries.

[3] Frequency rate $= \dfrac{\text{Number of Disabling Accidents}}{\text{Man-hours} \div 1,000,000}$. Thus, if a small manufacturing firm that employed, say, 250 workers for a regular work year of 2,000 hours each, had six disabling accidents, its accident frequency rate would be $\dfrac{6}{500,000 \div 1,000,000}$ or 12, which would place the firm close to its industry's average.

The accident severity rate. The accident severity rate is an average-time-lost-per-accident measure. It is defined as the average days lost per one thousand man-hours worked.[4]

For injuries resulting in temporary disability, the "days lost" figure is the actual number of days the injured worker is forced to be away from his job. Permanent disability and death cases require that days lost be stated in terms of standard time charges varying with the degree of disability. Actual days lost could not otherwise be calculated meaningfully in these two categories. A standard table of time charges is prepared for this purpose by the American Standards Association[5] and is used in severity rate calculations.

Frequency and severity rates for selected industries (and industry groups) are presented in Table 9.3 (p. 245). 1954 frequency rates showed a distinct improvement over 1953, with an all-time low of 10.5 recorded for manufacturing in December, 1954. 1955 rates were slightly higher than 1954's.

These data show that there may be vast differences in frequency and severity rates from industry to industry. They suggest, too, a fact borne out by fuller study of a larger sampling of rates, that there is no close correlation between accident frequency and severity rates for all employments.[6] Although manufacturing, for example, always shows a fairly high frequency rate, it tends to have a low severity rate. Construction, on the other hand, always shows both high frequency rates and high severity rates. Average frequency and severity rates change considerably from year to year, however, and rarely show any clearly established patterns.

The 1954 average accident-frequency rates both for manufacturing and nonmanufacturing industries, for example, showed encouraging improvement over 1953. The manufacturing rate dropped to 11.9 disabling injuries per million employee-hours worked, a rate of 11 per cent below the 13.4 cited in Table 9.3, and a new low for the third straight year. Yet despite this general downward trend,

---

[4] $\text{Severity Rate} = \dfrac{\text{Days Lost}}{\text{Man-hours Worked} \div 1,000}$.

[5] See "Manual on Industrial-Injury Statistics," *Bulletin 667* (U. S. Department of Labor, Bureau of Labor Statistics, 1940), pp. 181–84.

[6] Industrial injury data are available from several sources. Nationally, the U. S. Bureau of Labor Statistics, through the *Monthly Labor Review*, is the most important single source. Data covering specific areas are also compiled by the National Safety Council and various federal agencies, such as the Department of Agriculture and the Bureau of Mines. State agencies, typically Industrial Accident Boards and Commissions, are usually responsible for publication of these data on the state level. For detailed bibliographic notes on sources of accident data, see Herman M. Somers and Anne R. Somers, *Workmen's Compensation* (New York: John Wiley and Sons, Inc., 1954), p. 328.

TABLE 9.3

INJURY RATES FOR SELECTED INDUSTRIES, 1953

Industry or Group	Injury Rates*			All Cases	Average Days Lost or Charged Per Case			Per cent of Disabling Injuries Causing		
	Frequency		Severity†		Permanent Partial Disability	Temporary Total Disability	Death & Perm. Total Disability	Perm. Partial Disability	Temp. Total Disability	
	1953	1952								
All Manufacturing	13.4	14.3	1.2	86	871	18	0.4	5.4	94.2	
Lumber & Wood Products**.	43.6	49.6	4.1	92	944	17	.5	4.6	94.9	
Elec. Machinery	6.5	7.0	.6	76	685	19	.1	7.8	92.1	
Contract Construction . . .	32.9	35.3	3.2	107	1,256	17	1.0	2.4	96.9	
Trucking & Warehousing . .	33.2	(‡)	2.2	66	1,306	14	.5	1.8	97.7	
Wholesale & Retail Trade .	12.1	12.4	.6	55	1,104	14	.3	1.9	97.8	
Hotels	13.2	14.4	.7	50	1,492	16	.3	1.2	98.5	
Laundries & Dry Cleaning .	8.6	9.1	.6	72	1,692	17	.2	2.6	97.2	
Local Transit Systems . . .	15.2	(‡)	1.5	102	1,402	54	.6	1.1	98.3	
Elementary & Secondary Schools . . .	10.0	(‡)	.2	24	(5)	10	.1	.4	99.5	

* Injury frequency rate = disabling work injuries per million hours worked. Included are work injuries causing: (a) death or permanent physical impairment; (b) inability to perform regular job duties on one or more days after injury date. Occupational diseases are included in "injuries."

† Injury severity rate = average number of days lost for each 1,000 employee-hours worked. Computations include standard time charges for deaths and permanent disabilities.

** Except furniture.

‡ Not available.

Source: Adapted from *Monthly Labor Review*, LXXVII, No. 11 (November, 1954), 1227.

ten manufacturing classifications had increased rates of 5 per cent or more over the previous year's record. Jewelry, silverware, and plated ware industry experienced a 25 per cent increase, and veneer mills rose 18 per cent. At the same time, the seriousness of injuries during 1954 was about the same as it was in 1953.

Analysis of the circumstances surrounding accidents can provide some insight into this picture. Accident frequency—that is, the number of accidents—is subject to control by safety and prevention measures. Accident severity, however, tends to be primarily a matter of chance. Thus, although a downward trend in accident frequency can be credited to improved safety performance, it does not follow that these safety activities will have the same effect on severity rates. Other factors enter in too. For instance, the poor accident records of the World War II period are not generally ascribed to poor safety and prevention measures but rather to the influx of many new and inexperienced workers into the labor force.

NATURE AND COST

Disability is the most costly and tends to be the most severe of all noneconomic barriers to employment. In addition to the opportunity and maintenance cost of unemployed workers and their families, disability brings about considerable costs of its own—both of a monetary and of a personal nature.

Compare disability, for example, with the noneconomic employment barrier of advanced age. Loss of work for either of these reasons will shut off wage earnings. However, age barriers to employment are more or less fixed institutionally over fairly long periods of time. To the worker this means that possible economic insecurity because of old age is a cost that must be met at a future date, and within ranges, it is capable of prediction. Furthermore, it will be incurred at a time when family obligations of the wage-earner tend to be smallest. His children will no longer be financially dependent upon him; he will have paid for his housing, furnishings, and insurance; his fixed financial commitments, if any, will be at their lowest level. So that while workers may or may not be able to prepare for this cost successfully, its incidence can be estimated safely.

Occupational disability, on the other hand, can never be predicted for an individual worker. It seems to occur most frequently among younger workers whose financial and family obligations are greatest and among the lowest paid workers who are least able to meet these financial obligations.[7] Over and above the cost of a shut-off income supply (which for the severely disabled may be permanent) are medical and hospital costs as well as inestimable personal costs that in cases of severe disability arise from family sacrifices. The pain and suffering of the injured worker are, of course, incalculable.

As a hazard to individual income security, therefore, disability must be viewed more as a risk than a cost the incidence of which can be predicted. This is not to say that direct and hidden dollar costs of industrial disability are not gigantic. Estimates of the total of income losses, medical expenses, workmen's compensation payments, damage awards, damaged property, and production losses have ranged from 1 up to 10 per cent of national income.[8] While

---

[7] Somers and Somers, op. cit., p. 10.

[8] Domenico Gagliardo, American Social Insurance (New York: Harper and Brothers, 1949), pp. 448–52; Somers and Somers, op. cit., pp. 9–15.

this ratio will change from time to time, the latter estimate is undoubtedly too high. Somers' recent estimate of from three to five billion dollars a year, or slightly over 1 per cent of national income, is probably a close approximation. These estimates do not include the great amounts of money spent in avoiding occupational disability through safety programs and health measures. For example, nontraumatic loss of hearing due to industrial noise, just recently held compensable in a few states, is now under strong attack by safety- and cost-minded employers. It was estimated that in 1955 employers would spend about $100 million in efforts to reduce this disability hazard alone.[9]

The impact of the dollar costs on individual workers is best illustrated in the light of their financial circumstances. Before workmen's compensation, when damage awards were few, charity was the primary alternate source of income to seriously disabled workers. Workmen's compensation has done much to relieve this situation, but serious gaps remain. For example, a Minnesota study in 1952[10] revealed that permanently and totally disabled workers whose workmen's compensation benefits had expired were living on an annual real income of $661—much of it from charity.

To the worker whose arm is amputated traumatically in a revolving cutter, the costs, the pain and suffering, and the problems of physical and occupational rehabilitation are no different from those of another worker suffering loss of a leg as a result of a fall in a friend's home. Both encounter the same problems: obtaining and paying for medical and hospital care, continuing to meet nondeferrable expenses of a family, and, finally, returning to productive employment after healing.

For a long time, American public policy made no basic distinction between these two kinds of injuries. In order to recover money damages for his injury, either worker had recourse only in the common law of liability. If he could prove his injury stemmed directly from the negligence or fault of the factory or home owner, he could recover money damages. With the greater risks of occupational disability that accompanied the industrial development of the late nineteenth century, however, and in response to this growing hazard to the economic security of the nation's workers, social policy began to distinguish between accidents and sickness caused by the work

[9] *Wall Street Journal*, November 16, 1955, p. 1.

[10] Before Minnesota joined the seventeen other jurisdictions which put no time or dollar limits on benefits for permanent disability. Earl F. Cheit, "The Effects of Selected Workmen's Compensation Benefits in Minnesota," *A Report to the Legislative Interim Commission on Workmen's Compensation* (Mimeographed, 1952), pp. 86–94.

environment and those that were not. This recognition took three forms: (1) employer-initiated safety programs, which, though unimportant at first, have today become significant factors in holding down the toll of industrial injuries;[11] (2) the industrial hygiene movement aimed at industrial sickness; and (3) workmen's compensation legislation (which seeks through insurance to redistribute part of the costs of occupational disability) in which fault or negligence is not an issue.

Emergence of the Problem of Occupational Disability

American history from the Civil War through the close of the nineteenth century is a story of rapidly expanding industrial capitalism. In a single generation the United States changed from an agrarian country which had to import most of its manufactures from abroad into an industrialized nation exporting products all over the world.

Rail transport expanded rapidly; coal, iron, and petroleum resources were exploited vigorously, and the manufacture of cotton, iron, steel, and other products increased phenomenally. In 1890, for the first time in this country's history, the wealth created by manufacturing surpassed that created by farming. By external measures, too, industrial growth was phenomenal. In 1860, America ranked fourth among nations in the volume and value of factory goods; in 1894, it ranked first, with factory production worth more than that of Germany and Great Britain combined.[12]

To operate the factories turning out this record production, employers recruited to the cities more and more workers—many of them women and children—from farms and from abroad. And with the growth of industrial cities came new problems in the mode and character of American life, particularly in the economic and social life of the worker. During the first fifteen years of the twentieth century, much of the country's energies, particularly at local levels, was directed toward adjusting public policy to the needs of the new economic environment. A concentrated attack was launched on the political, social, and economic problems created by an industrial society—child labor, slums, growing health and accident hazards, to

[11] Today, in addition to safety programs aimed at existing employment hazards, new safety regulations are adopted as work processes and materials change. The increased industrial use of atomic energy, for example, has required new regulations to protect against the hazards of radiation. See *The New York Times*, October 31, 1955, p. 52.

[12] For a statistical summary of this economic revolution, see Arthur M. Schlesinger, *Political and Social Growth of the American People, 1865–1940* (New York: The Macmillan Co., 1941), p. 43.

name a few—and with remarkable results. More social legislation (including workmen's compensation) was enacted during this period than during any previous time in American history.

Professional concern for occupational health and safety can be traced back to 1837, when the first United States report on occupational health was issued, which was long before the movement to legislative reform got under way. Between that time and 1900, over fifty discussions and state reports on occupational health and accident hazards appeared, and by 1910 the industrial health movement had gained support from magazines, state agencies, and professional associations.[13]

In 1867, Massachusetts enacted legislation providing factory inspection services; two years later the first Bureau of Labor Statistics was created in that state to study the accident problem; and in 1877 the Massachusetts legislature acted to insure that employers safeguard hazardous machinery. In 1892 a safety department was established in the Joliet Works of the Illinois Steel Company where the American industrial accident prevention movement subsequently was born.[14]

The exact magnitude of the occupational health and accident hazards of the period cannot be determined accurately. The few data available are not comprehensive and are largely estimates. Farm work was by no means "safe." Hours were long, and the work was strenuous and subject to natural physical hazards. Yet its hazards were relatively few compared with those introduced by mechanized work (including mechanized work on farms). Power-driven machines, and machine tools in particular,[15] created new and serious accident hazards. But it would be inaccurate to attribute the rising accident rate to mechanization alone. Each industry, because of its environment or operations, had its own peculiar hazards —cave-ins and explosions in the coal mines, moving locomotives, lead poisons, overhead cranes, and the pace of the new industrial tempo all contributed to the employment hazards. So, too, did the interdependence of employees in the factory system.[16] In addition,

[13] John R. Commons and associates, *History of Labor in the United States, 1896–1932.* (New York: The Macmillan Co., 1935), III, 359–70.

[14] Ronald P. Blake (ed.), *Industrial Safety* (Englewood Cliffs, N. J.: Prentice-Hall, Inc., 1943), pp. 12–22.

[15] For an informative enumeration of these hazards, see "Machine Tools and Their Hazards," *Bulletin 129* (U. S. Department of Labor, Bureau of Labor Standards, 1951). (One of a series.)

[16] See Crystal Eastman, *Work Accidents and the Law* (Russell Sage Foundation, 1916 ed.; [Reprinted in Paul H. Douglas, Curtice N. Hitchcock, and Willard E. Atkins (eds.), *The Worker in Modern Economic Society,* Chicago: University of Chicago Press, 1923, pp. 401–12]).

there were the problems of the fatigue of long hours, child labor, the use of "cheap" immigrant labor, and the failure of the large factories, which today produce the most enviable safety records, to assume much responsibility for the injured.[17]

Somers estimates that the "peak in industrial accident rates was reached during the first decade of the century, probably about 1907–1908. In the year ending June 30, 1907, 4,534 workers were killed in railroading alone; 1907 was also the blackest year in mining: 2,534 men were killed in bituminous mines alone."[18] Frederick L. Hoffman of Prudential Life Insurance Company, whose estimates for early accident experience are as good as any available, guessed the total occupational 1908 death toll at between 30,000 and 35,000.[19] A more conservative estimate by Dr. E. H. Downey,[20] put occupationally caused deaths at 25,000, permanent disabilities at 25,000, and temporary disabilities lasting over three days at 2,000,000. Frederick Lewis Allen writes[21] that ". . . in the single year 1901, one out of every 399 railroad employees was killed; and one out of every 26 was injured. Among engineers, conductors, brakemen, trainmen, etc., the figures were even worse than this: in that single year, one out of every 137 was killed."

THE COMMON LAW OF INDUSTRIAL ACCIDENTS

With the sharp rise in the number of occupational injuries, the costs of disability became an acute problem. The physical losses, of course, were borne by the injured worker in all cases. But what of the financial burden of job-connected disability? Was this also to be the private responsibility of the worker?

Before 1841, there were no rules of law or court decisions to answer this question, although recourse to the law was available to the occupationally injured and the nonoccupationally injured alike. As job injuries became increasingly frequent and severe, the courts were called upon to decide how the financial burden of this disability should be distributed. In these decisions the courts de-

[17] Arthur H. Reede, *Adequacy of Workmen's Compensation* (Cambridge: Harvard University Press, 1947), p. 345.

[18] Reprinted by permission from Herman M. Somers and Anne R. Somers, *Workmen's Compensation* (New York: John Wiley & Sons, Inc., 1954), p. 9.

[19] Frederick L. Hoffman, "Industrial Accidents," *Bulletin* of the Bureau of Labor Statistics (Washington, D. C.: September, 1908), p. 418. Quoted in Philip Taft, *Economics and Problems of Labor* (3d ed.; Harrisburg: The Stackpole Co., 1955), p. 123.

[20] Taft, *op. cit.*, p. 123.

[21] Reprinted with permission from Frederick Lewis Allen, *The Big Change* (New York: Harper and Brothers, 1952), p. 56.

veloped the nation's first public policy toward occupational disability as a source of economic insecurity.

In retrospect the body of common law of employers' liability that emerged from these cases seems unduly harsh. For the small-scale industrial organization, frictionless labor market, and close employment relationship between master and servant—on which it was based—were all casualties of the economic revolution.

At common law, an employee injured in an accident in the course of his work could recover damages only through a personal injury suit against his employer. The success of such a suit depended upon showing that the job-connected injury arose from the employer's negligence. Although a master owed his servants due care (the violation of which was negligence), formidable difficulties faced an employee seeking to discharge his burden of proof against his employer. He frequently encountered reluctance on the part of his fellow employees to testify, probable loss of employment, and a serious (often insurmountable) financial burden.

Second, and even more onerous, was the array of common-law rules of master and servant that blocked easy recovery for industrial injuries. The oldest of these was the defense of contributory negligence which was always available in suits based upon a claim of negligence. This tenet had been introduced into the common law of England in 1809.[22] In operation it defeated an employee's claim to damages if he had in any way contributed to the negligence of his employer.

Two further defenses grew out of later cases. In 1842, the leading American case involving master-servant relations was decided. In *Farwell v. Boston and Worcester R.R. Co.* a Massachusetts court denied an engineer's claim for damages based upon the negligence of a switchman and established "fellow-servant" and "assumption of risk" defenses in America. The court held that "since the engineer was not in the relation of a stranger to the railroad, the employer's liability, if any, was governed by the implied contract of employment entered into with the engineer at the time of hiring and that such a contract does not extend to indemnify the servant against the negligence of anyone but the master himself."

Two important concepts were implied in this holding. First, servants were now denied recovery for injuries arising from a fellow-servant's negligence. This was an exception to the well-established tort doctrine of *respondeat superior* which held a master responsible

---

22 In the case of *Butterfield v. Forrester,* 11 East. 60 (K.B. 1809) cited in Walter F. Dodd, *Administration of Workmen's Compensation* (New York: The Commonwealth Fund, 1936), chaps. i and ii.

to third persons for injuries inflicted by his agents. The second principle—the "assumption of risk" doctrine—made the hazards of an occupation noncompensable. For many years hence, cases consistently holding to the "assumption of risk" defense partially justified this position on the theory that the wage rate of an occupation reflected its hazards. This quite painful application of Adam Smith's principle of equal net advantages[23] together with the contributory negligence and fellow-servant defenses were the cornerstones on which was built the laissez-faire approach of the common law to occupational disability.

Dissatisfaction with the Common Law and the Enactment of Employer's Liability Laws

With occupational injury and death rates reaching alarming proportions, the continued application of these common-law rules was producing tragic results. The vast majority of the occupationally injured or their survivors realized either inadequate damages awards or, all too frequently, no awards at all. In the face of the wastes, uncertainties, delays, and high costs of law suits, widespread dissatisfaction arose with this approach to industrial disability. In the late part of the nineteenth century, many legislative attempts were made to find a new remedy. These took the form of employers' liability legislation which was patterned, in part, after earlier attempts made in England to mitigate the effects of common-law defenses to injury claims. Between 1885 and 1910 most of the states enacted such employer liability legislation.

The first of the three common-law defenses to come under legislative attack was the fellow-servant rule. Next, by stating that an employee's knowledge of safety violations is no bar to a suit for recovery, the assumption-of-risk doctrine was weakened. The defense of contributory negligence, however, yielded most reluctantly under the more liberal legislative (and judicial) attitudes.

In addition to modifying the three common-law defenses, employers' liability laws sought to bring relief to injured workers in

---

[23] Smith observed that where there was liberty, wages would make the advantages and disadvantages of occupations equal. See Adam Smith, *The Wealth of Nations* (Modern Library ed.; New York: Random House, Inc. 1937), p. 99: "The whole of the advantages and disadvantages of different employment of labour and stock must, in the same neighbourhood, be either perfectly equal, or continually tending to equality. If in the same neighborhood there was any employment evidently either more or less advantageous than the rest, so many people would crowd into it in the one case, and so many would desert it in the other, that its advantages would soon return to the level of other employments."

two ways.[24] The first of these was a legal denial of the right to "contract out" of liability. No longer would contracts be binding in which workers agreed not to hold their employers liable for injuries sustained at work. And, secondly, the right to suit was extended to death cases.

Employers' liability laws, following one or more of these three forms, were enacted in almost all the states by the time that accident tolls were reaching their peak (1907–1908). But they did not provide an adequate solution to the problem of occupational disability. Damage awards were still scarce (usually inadequate) and bore no rational relation to the injury. The costs, wastes, and delays, as well as the employer-employee antagonisms of litigation, were still present under employers' liability, just as under common law. And, as with the common law, the emphasis still tended to be to conceal accidents rather than to study them frankly and to attempt to reduce them.

RISE OF WORKMEN'S COMPENSATION LEGISLATION

While America was experimenting with legislation designed to modify the results of the common-law rules of employers' liability, a far-reaching experiment was taking place in some European countries. Germany took the lead in the early 1880's, and by 1910 virtually all the countries of Europe had adopted some system of workmen's compensation.

These events did not go unnoticed in the United States. The United States Department of Labor took official notice in its 1893 publication of a report on compulsory insurance in Germany. Shortly thereafter, bills following the European models were introduced in several states (but failed to gain passage). It became apparent through the unsuccessful attempts of several states to enact workmen's compensation legislation that a thorough study was necessary to determine the needs of compensation systems, their requirements, how they might relate to our legal system and, important to employers, what their costs might be. Intensive commission investigation of the problem of occupational disability was the next step.

Some thirty-one investigatory commissions were established between 1909 and 1913. Nine others were in operation in the next six years. These investigating bodies, through joint conferences, hearings, and intense study, recommended unanimously that employers' liability be abolished. From these investigating committees emerged: (1) a severe indictment of the record of employers' liability legis-

24 Commons, *op. cit.*, p. 567.

lation, and (2) the foundation for recommendations that later evolved into workmen's compensation laws. Their recommendations were supported by the American Association for Labor Legislation, the National Civic Federation, the American Bar Association, the American Federation of Labor, and by a poll of the National Association of Manufacturers.

FAILURE OF THE EMPLOYERS' LIABILITY STATUTES

Committee data documenting the failure of the employers' liability systems aroused considerable public concern. They showed that: (1) contrary to their purpose, employers' liability laws were not enabling workers to recover damages for injuries. Damage awards were sparse and uncertain, and where they were granted, they came long after the disability and were usually inadequate; and (2) since employers' liability was a system based on lawsuits, it was costly and produced ill will between employers and employees, thus failing to produce any stimulus to safety programs. In short, it was no better than the inadequate, uncertain, and costly remedy at common law. A new approach was needed to the problem of occupational injury and disease. It was found in workmen's compensation.

Workmen's compensation laws were enacted in four states in 1911, in eleven states in 1912 and 1913. After 1920, only six states (each of which later enacted systems) did not have workmen's compensation legislation; today such laws are in effect in all states and federal jurisdictions. Much credit for this reform must go to the investigatory commissions.

Workmen's Compensation Laws

LIABILITY WITHOUT FAULT

New York was one of the first states to take the lead in the movement toward workmen's compensation. In 1910 it enacted a compulsory law covering twelve specified occupations wherein employers were made liable for specified compensation payments to their injured workers, whether or not the injury stemmed from employer fault. The extent of this departure from the traditional common law of employers' liability is nowhere better dramatized than in the language of the New York Court of Appeals[25] which declared

[25] *Ives v. South Buffalo Railway Co.*, 201 NY. 271 (1911). Quoted and discussed in Harry A. Millis and Royal E. Montgomery, *Labor's Risks and Social Insurance* (New York: McGraw-Hill Book Co., Inc., 1938), pp. 194–96.

the law unconstitutional the following year. Said the New York court in this case:

". . . This is a liability unknown to the common law and we think it plainly constitutes a deprivation of liberty and property under the Federal and State Constitutions . . . if the legislature can say to an employer, 'you must compensate your employee for an injury not caused by you or by your fault,' why can it not go further and say to the man of wealth, 'you have more property than you need and your neighbor is so poor that he can barely subsist; in the interest of natural justice you must divide with your neighbor so that he and his dependents shall not become a charge upon the state'?"

A popular referendum and, later, state and United States Supreme Court decisions and legislative devices[26] overcame constitutional objections, however, and today all states have workmen's compensation laws based upon the principle of "liability without fault." Yet, while the constitutional barrier in the Ives case did not deter the movement toward workmen's compensation, it indirectly weakened the laws of a majority of jurisdictions. Over two-thirds of the states gave employers an "election" of being covered by the Act or remaining exempt—but without full protection of common law defenses. Today the laws of nearly one-half the states have some form of elective provision.[27] The extent to which they operate to restrict effective coverage of workmen's compensation acts cannot be estimated.

The principle of liability without fault is quite simple. The employer is assessed the compensable costs of job-connected injuries to his employees not because he is responsible for them, not because he caused them, not because he was negligent, but simply because of social policy. The premise has been discarded that behind every disability there is a negligent party. Under modern industrial conditions the employment relationship itself is reason enough for assessing the employer to compensate his injured employees. Since the employment of labor involves the risk of disability, by social policy the employer must defray its costs.

But while the interpretation of liability without fault is clear enough, its theoretical justification has raised some questions. For one thing, if considered apart from its consequences, the common-law principle that an employer should be responsible only for accidents stemming from his fault has an appeal of justice and fair play. Some early acts applied only to hazardous occupations, holding the

---

[26] Stefan A. Riesenfeld and Richard C. Maxwell, *Modern Social Legislation* (Brooklyn: The Foundation Press, 1950), pp. 153–62.

[27] See Table 9.4.

employer responsible for operating a hazardous business. But as workmen's compensation laws were extended to most kinds of work, liability without fault could be justified only by reference to broader norms.

Many norms have been formulated.[28] An important early theory was that of the "trade risk." This theory held that the employer must bear the costs of the risks of his trade and, implicitly, that these costs would be shifted forward in the product price. (A slogan attributed to Lloyd George proclaimed that "the cost of the product should bear the blood of the workingman.") The implications of this justification (among them that workers are relieved of all accident costs) have been sharply criticized, and a more thorough formulation has been that of the "least social costs" principle, contending that economic losses were reduced to a minimum by workmen's compensation legislation.[29] These theories, and particularly some of the legal justifications, were important to the acceptance and subsequent broadening of workmen's compensation laws.

The policy of protecting the economic security of the worker by making employers liable for job-connected disability is not a radical policy from the viewpoint of the economics of the labor market. In fact, it can be interpreted simply as a more efficient result economically than would be the case in a perfectly competitive labor market. Let us examine this point.

THE COMPENSATION PRINCIPLE

If all that is implied in the principle of equal net advantages were empirically descriptive of labor supply and demand conditions, employers' common-law defense of assumption of risk would be economically persuasive. For under this condition, wage rates for individual occupations would reflect fully their relative advantages and disadvantages, including the risk of disability. It would follow that, other things being equal, employments where accident rates are relatively high (say agriculture where the death rate is three times that of manufacturing) would pay correspondingly higher wage rates than less hazardous jobs requiring similar skill and training. Large numbers of workers would be attracted to the better jobs (tending to keep the wage rate down) and employers would have

[28] Discussions of these can be found in E. H. Downey, *Workmen's Compensation* (New York: The Macmillan Co., 1924), pp. 19–20; and in Clarence W. Hobbs, *Workmen's Compensation Insurance* (New York: McGraw-Hill Book Co., Inc., 1939), pp. 61–62. See also Riesenfeld and Maxwell, *op. cit.*, pp. 138–40.

[29] Edwin E. Witte, "The Theory of Workmen's Compensation," *American Labor Legislation Review*, XX, No. 4 (December, 1930), 411–18.

to bid up wages to attract workers to the less attractive (and more hazardous) jobs.

But do wage rates in fact reflect differences in job hazards? To some extent, yes. Structural steel workers, for example, may be paid a higher wage when working on high construction where the danger from falls is great; test pilots receive a high wage reflecting their hazardous work; seamen receive additional pay for duty in war zones. In fact, in any business organization, wage structures based upon standard methods of job evaluation will, in some measure, be influenced by the relative hazard factor of working conditions.

But wage differentials generally bear very little relation to the relative attractiveness of work. The worker in actual labor markets is not informed completely about attractive alternative job opportunities nor would he always be willing or able to accept them if he did know about them.[30] And no one today would contend seriously that wage rates do include a "risk" portion reflecting the value of an occupation's injury risk. "Assumption of risk" at common law denied damages for injured employees because it was assumed that they had knowledge of the risks of their employment, and hence were left to their own resources if they took the work.

But even the most stringent application of this principle assumed only in part that the wage rate had an adequate risk portion. In a famous and frequently cited case in New York in 1924[31] a girl who had contracted tuberculosis while working in a candy factory was denied recovery. The court concluded it was from the plaintiff's own testimony that:

". . . We learn that the walls of the cellar were wet to the touch; that a cesspool backed up liquids which wet the floor; that the cellar was devoid of windows to light or air it; that dead rats were left about; that the odors were vile; that no fires were kept in the upstairs room; that the plaintiff worked in a drafty place; that the upstairs was damp. It is common knowledge that such conditions are deleterious to health. The plaintiff was chargeable with such knowledge. We think that the plaintiff, as a matter of law, assumed the risk attendant upon her remaining in the employment. . . ."

What if the many conditions needed to make the labor market perfectly competitive were realized? Then to attract labor, employers would have to pay a "risk" premium in the wage rates for hazardous occupations. It would follow, therefore, that other things being equal, the average wage rate would be higher under these competitive conditions than in their absence.

---

[30] Gordon F. Bloom and Herbert R. Northrup, *Economics of Labor Relations* (rev. ed.; Homewood: Richard D. Irwin Co., 1954), pp. 231–38.

[31] *Wager v. White Star Candy Co.* 217 N.Y. Supp. 173.

But in the actual labor market, employers have an incentive not to pay the full risk rate because (1) their competitors cannot be expected to follow suit, and (2) the incentive to spend money on safety measures is reduced, since the greater portion of the cost of disability is borne by the disabled worker. The employer's private cost of the full "risk" wage exceeds the benefits he would receive from paying this wage.

Under these circumstances, if injuries are to be compensated, it is necessary for government action to assess a social cost that will pay for the full needed social benefits. This could take two forms. Wage rates could be adjusted by legislation in hazardous occupations, or employers could be made liable for the cost of injuries to employees. Of these two approaches, the latter (workmen's compensation) can be shown to be economically more efficient in principle.

Forcing employers by legislation to pay a risk wage rate for hazardous jobs would result in a small increment in the wage rate. But this would provide less protection for the worker in the event of disability than does an insurance-like payment, withheld and paid at the time of the injury. For in accordance with the principle of diminishing utility,[32] the disutility of one great loss would more than offset the added utility of small increments of income spread over time. Or, conversely, the utility of payment at the time of disability is greater than that of the increments in the wage rate. Hence, liability without fault is not an expensive social reform, but rather a more efficient method, in principle, of achieving what the labor market would achieve if it were perfectly competitive.

COMMON LAW AND EMPLOYER'S LIABILITY STATUTES ARE STILL IMPORTANT

The emergence of the workmen's compensation principle, however, has not eliminated case law from the field of industrial disability. Wholly aside from the vast numbers of cases interpreting the compensation laws, there are wide areas where liability is determined through litigation.[33] These include employees who are not covered by the compensation acts, either because they are not working in a covered employment or because they are exempt or excluded by law. Elective laws, discussed earlier, remove consider-

---

[32] A good brief discussion of the law of diminishing utility applied to insurance is presented by Paul A. Samuelson in *Economics* (3d ed.; New York: McGraw-Hill Book Co., Inc. 1955), pp. 419–21.

[33] Railroad employment is the most important example. See Chapter 13 for a discussion of the Railroad Employees Liability Act.

able numbers of workers from coverage, as do some cases of third-party (nonemployer) liability and the area covered by employers' liability laws.

Workmen's compensation laws were not enacted in a vacuum. They grew in response to the pressing needs of the occupationally disabled—needs that were not being met by existing institutions. Let us turn now to the question of the extent to which the compensation principle was enacted to answer these needs.

Objective of Workmen's Compensation

In comparison with the complex workmen's compensation laws of today, the original acts of the states were very simple. They were all based upon the liability-without-fault principle, and each was enacted to provide prompt and adequate relief to victims of industrial accidents and to improve accident prevention. Most state laws were in large measure based upon the experience of Germany and England in workmen's compensation and upon some of the findings of the American legislative commissions.

But despite their original simplicity and the common origins and problems which led to their enactment, workmen's compensation laws have never been nor are they today uniform from state to state. Local problems and constitutional, statutory, and political barriers account for this diversity. Early legislatures were forced to enact provisions which would circumvent some of these problems and make concessions to others. And over the years the modifying forces of local considerations and political opposition have continued to grow rather than to diminish. It is a situation, one scholar laments, in which

". . . about half of the State laws are compulsory, the others are elective. Under some laws in the latter group, an employer and all his workers are presumed to be covered by the law unless the employer—and in some States, the worker himself—individually rejects it, and under others, an employer must positively elect to be covered by the workmen's compensation act so as not to come under the employers' liability laws with the common-law defenses abrogated. Some laws are in part compulsory and in part elective. Insurance is handled in three ways: in some States, through an exclusive State fund; in others, by private carriers; and in another group, by State funds competing actively with private carriers and operating under the same regulations."[34]

Table 9.4 illustrates the lack of uniformity of the workmen's compensation laws of the fifty-four state, federal, and territorial

[34] Max D. Kossoris, "Workmen's Compensation in the United States," *Bulletin 1149* (U. S. Department of Labor, Bureau of Labor Statistics, 1954), p. 2.

TABLE 9.4

COMPARISON OF COVERAGE, INSURANCE AND EXEMPTION PROVISIONS OF
WORKMEN'S COMPENSATION ACTS OF ALL AMERICAN JURISDICTIONS

(November, 1955)

Juris-diction	Coverage Compul-sory	Coverage Elec-tive	Insured through State Fund	Insured through Private Carriers	Insured through Self-Insurance	Employers Exempted If Fewer Employees Than
Alabama		x	—	x	x	8
Alaska	x		—	x	x	No exemptions
Arizona	x*		Compet.	x	x	3a
Arkansas	x		—	x	x	5b
California	x		Compet.	x	x	No exemptions
Colorado		x	Compet.	x	x	4
Connecticut		x	—	x	x	3
Delaware	x		—	x	x	3
D. C.	x		—	x	x	No exemptions
Florida		x	—	x	x	3
Georgia		x	—	x	x	10
Hawaii	x		—	x	x	No exemptions
Idaho	x		Compet.	x	x	No exemptions
Illinois	x†		—	x	x	No exemptions
Indiana		x**	—	x	x	No exemptions
Iowa		x**	—	x	x	No exemptions
Kansas	x		—	x	x	5b
Kentucky	x		—	x	x	3
Louisiana	x		—	x	x	No exemptions
Maine		x	—	x	x	6
Maryland	x		Compet.	x	x	No exemptions
Massachusetts	x		—	x	x	4a
Michigan	x		Compet.	x	x	4a
Minnesota	x		—	x	x	No exemptions
Mississippi	x		—	x	x	8
Missouri		x	—	x	x	11c
Montana		x**	Compet.	x	x	No exemptions
Nebraska		x	—	x	x	No exemptions
Nevada	x		Exclusive	—	—	2a
New Hampshire	x*		—	x	x	5
New Jersey		x	—	x	x	No exemptions
New Mexico		x	—	x	x	4b
New York	x		Compet.	x	x	4c
North Carolina		x	—	x	x	5b
North Dakota	x		Exclusive	—	—	No exemptions
Ohio	x		Exclusive	—	—	3
Oklahoma	x		Compet.	x	x	2
Oregon		x	Exclusive	—	—	No exemptions
Pennsylvania		x	Compet.	x	x	No exemptions
Puerto Rico	x		Exclusive	—	—	3b
Rhode Island	x		—	x	x	4a
South Carolina		x	—	x	x	15
South Dakota		x	—	x	x	No exemptions
Tennessee		x	—	x	x	5

TABLE 9.4 (*Continued*)

| Juris-diction | Coverage | | Insured through | | | Employers Exempted If Fewer Employees Than |
	Compul-sory	Elec-tive	State Fund	Private Carriers	Self-Insurance	
Texas		x**	—	x	—	3
Utah	x		Compet.	x	x	No exemptions
Vermont		x	—	x	x	8
Virginia	x		—	x	x	7
Washington	x		Exclusive	—	—	No exemptions
West Virginia		x	Exclusive	—	—	No exemptions
Wisconsin	x		—	x	x	3
Wyoming	x		Exclusive	x	—	No exemptions
Federal Employees	x		Congressional Appropriation —		—	No exemptions
U. S. Long-shoremen	x		—	x	x	No exemptions

* Employees may reject Act.
† Elective as to occupational diseases.
** Compulsory for specified employments.
ᵃ Applies only to compulsory coverage.
ᵇ Does not apply to specified employments.
ᶜ Applies only to nonhazardous employments.

Source: U. S. Department of Labor, Bureau of Labor Standards, *Bulletin 161*, Supplement to "State Workmen's Compensation Laws as of September, 1954," November, 1955.

jurisdictions for three important aspects of the laws: (1) compulsory vs. elective coverage; (2) permitted manner of insuring liability; and (3) exemptions to coverage for small employers. Other important aspects of the laws, such as medical and indemnity benefits, also vary from state to state.[35]

Students of workmen's compensation, dismayed at the diversity of standards, see little likelihood that this situation will soon be remedied,[36] either by state action alone or by federally enacted standards. In the next chapter we will consider the question of how

[35] State industrial accident boards and commissions will furnish interested students with copies of the workmen's compensation laws they administer. Also available is a brief pamphlet published by the U. S. Department of Labor, Bureau of Labor Standards, "How Good Is Your Workmen's Compensation Law?" *Bulletin 70*, 1944. The student will find it valuable to obtain his state's law and study its provisions in the context of Chapters 9 and 10, and to use the Bureau's pamphlet as a guide in its evaluation.

[36] Kossoris, *op. cit.*, p. 2. The U. S. Department of Labor, through its Bureau of Labor Standards, has published a tentative copy of a "model workmen's compensation bill" which, it hopes, will be followed by the states in the continual process of revising their compensation laws.

effective and adequate the workmen's compensation remedy can be, both in specific jurisdictions and in general, in the light of differences in standards and administrative practice.

Summary

Unemployment caused by occupational disability is a less serious aggregate problem in economic security than is unemployment due to labor-market causes. But work-connected injuries and sickness are costly noneconomic barriers to employment and tend to present a serious threat to individual economic security. Disability (sometimes permanent) shuts off earnings and brings with it extensive hospital, medical, and maintenance costs.

Although work has always produced disabling injuries and sick-ness, the rate of these disabilities began to rise in this country as it began to be industrialized in the late nineteenth century. Early interest in combatting the problem resulted in scattered safety legislation, a few individual employer safety programs and eventually an industrial hygiene movement aimed at preventing industrial ill-ness. But during the period of the peak rates of occupational disability, injured workers had as their chief recourse a law suit at common law in which recovery required demonstrating employers' negligence as a cause of disability.

This system, which permitted employers to defend on the grounds of contributory negligence the negligence of fellow employees or the assumption of the risks of employment by the claimant, produced serious hardships. Lawsuits were costly, time-consuming, produced serious antagonisms, and only infrequently resulted in adequate recoveries. Dissatisfaction with this approach to the problem led to the widespread enactment of employers' liability laws which weakened employers' common law defenses. But, since lawsuits were still required for recovery, and since these laws gave no incentive for safety programs, they were little improvement over the common law. Against this background, American legislatures turned with interest to a German legislative experiment: workmen's compensation laws, which provided benefits to injured workers on an insurance basis without the need of a law suit or proof of fault. The liability without fault principle of workmen's compensation was first enacted early in the twentieth century, and today all states have these laws.

Suggestions for Additional Reading

BOWERS, EDISON L. *Is It Safe to Work?* Boston: Houghton Mifflin Co., 1930. The impact of industrial accidents and the failures of workmen's compensation and rehabilitation to deal adequately with them are the central themes of this very readable essay.

Downey, E. H. *Workmen's Compensation.* New York: The Macmillan Co., 1924.
Long considered a classic, this volume is a basic work in the field of early workmen's compensation development.

Reede, Arthur H. *Adequacy of Workmen's Compensation.* Cambridge: Harvard University Press, 1947.
A detailed examination of the development of the coverage and benefit provisions in workmen's compensation.

Riesenfeld, Stefan A., and Richard C. Maxwell. *Modern Social Legislation.* Brooklyn: The Foundation Press, 1950. Pp. 127–62.
A legal treatment of the history, nature, and types of workmen's compensation laws.

Weiss, Harry. "Development of Workmen's Compensation in the United States." Unpublished Ph.D. thesis, University of Wisconsin, 1933.
A comprehensive study of the forces which led to the enactment of workmen's compensation laws by the states.

10

Workmen's Compensation

Introduction

Today in each of the forty-eight states and all territorial jurisdictions, workmen's compensation is the major economic security program for occupational disability. The laws of all the states are based upon the principle of liability without fault, but because they are individual state laws, their benefit and coverage provisions vary widely from jurisdiction to jurisdiction. Before discussing the provisions of workmen's compensation laws and their effectiveness, it may be useful to state briefly how they operate.

Workmen's compensation laws usually begin by stating which employments they cover—most public and private employments with stated exclusions and exemptions (see Table 9.4). The laws entitle covered employees who are disabled as a result of injury or disease causally related to their employment to indemnity medical and hospital benefits.[1] The employee must file a notice of injury with his state industrial accident board to receive these benefits. When the injury or disease results in death, stated indemnity benefits are paid to survivors.

The benefits paid under workmen's compensation laws are, by law, secured through insurance. As Table 9.4 indicates, in most jurisdictions this insurance is available only from private carriers. Seven states sell insurance to the exclusion of all private carriers, and eleven states offer insurance in competition with private carriers. How much employers pay for this compulsory workmen's compensation insurance coverage varies with the type of work in

[1] We use the more limited term "disease" here since, technically, occupational disease is the only compensable type of sickness.

which their employees are engaged. Premiums are stated per $100 of covered payroll. For clerical employees whose work is relatively safe, the insurance premiums may be as little as 10 cents for $100 of payroll. For hazardous work, such as construction or mining, the rate may be as high as $15 or $20 per $100 of payroll.[2]

Let us now examine the benefit and coverage provisions of the laws in greater detail.

Qualification for Benefits

Although the benefits that an occupationally disabled worker receives under workmen's compensation vary widely from state to state, the right of a worker to these benefits is determined in all jurisdictions by three basic elements:[3]

First, a worker must be an "employee" working in a "covered employment"—as these terms are defined by the state law. Table 9.4 indicates that in some jurisdictions, employees working for firms with less than a given number of persons on the payroll—usually between three and five, although ranging as high as fifteen in South Carolina—will not be covered. The table also indicates that about one-half the jurisdictions make no such eligibility requirement. Typically, therefore, covered employments would include most public employments and all private employments except domestic servants, farm laborers, merchant seamen, railroad employees, and the so-called casual employees whose work is not in the usual course of the trade of the employer. The table also shows that in about one-half the states—those with elective laws—election is needed for coverage; and, in addition, that some states exclude "nonhazardous" employments, as well as a few specified employments such as professional athletics. The question of who is an "employee" raises a considerable volume of litigation, particularly in the case of casual employees and those working for independent contractors. Both of these elements of coverage, however, are fairly well established.

Second, "employees" working in "covered employments" can receive benefits only for disabling injuries and sickness the nature and origin of which are compensable by statute. In adopting from English law the phrase "personal injury by accident," a majority of American jurisdictions embraced the concept of injury as associated

[2] Possible economic effects of these costs, and their differences, are discussed later in this chapter in the section entitled "Does Workmen's Compensation Produce Undesirable Economic Effects?"

[3] Stefan A. Riesenfeld and Richard C. Maxwell, *Modern Social Legislation* (Brooklyn: The Foundation Press, 1950), pp. 162–291.

with a traumatic occurrence. The rigor of this definition became troublesome, however, in cases where disabilities emerged from gradual deterioration of a bodily member due to work causes or from repeated accidents. American courts have developed a liberal definition of the concept of an "accident" so as to compensate cases such as these. In revising the laws, legislatures are increasingly discarding the word "accident." More emphasis is now being placed upon the third requirement (discussed below) that the injury be traceable to the employment.

Legislative coverage of occupational diseases developed much more slowly than did other injury coverage. Massachusetts pioneered in this area when in 1910 it followed the Federal Employees Act and provided "blanket" coverage for all occupational diseases. Other states developed the "schedule" system, providing coverage only for diseases specified by law. Today blanket or full coverage is provided by thirty-one jurisdictions; schedule coverage is provided by twenty-one. Mississippi and Wyoming are the only jurisdictions which provide no coverage of occupational diseases.

Third, the covered employee's disability (caused by either injury or disease), to be compensable, must have resulted from the employment—again as specified by statute. The requirement that there be a proper relationship between the employment and the disability has become a thorny legal question and policy issue. Almost every American law, again borrowing from England, extended coverage to accidents "arising out of and in the course of employment." This phrasing was intended to reduce to a minimum questions about the origin of the injury, but litigation concerning the interpretation of these words is almost endless.

Two types of issues arise. First, should an admittedly compensable disability be compensated when it occurs under "unusual" circumstances? Typically, should workers be covered while traveling for their employer? After or before working hours? Off duty, going to and from work? Or, at work when a worker takes a devious route? And so on. For the most part, court interpretations of these issues have tended to take a liberal view of what is "in the course of employment."[4]

Secondly, and perhaps more important as far as policy is concerned, are those disabilities where the causal link with the em-

---

[4] For conflicting views on effects of the trend toward liberal interpretation of the phrase, "arising out of and in the course of employment," see Samuel B. Horovitz, "The Litigious Phrase: 'Arising Out of' Employment," NACCA Law Journal, III and IV (May and November, 1949), 15–67 and 19–90; and Bruce S. Black, "The Anomalies of Workmen's Compensation," Industrial and Labor Relations Review, VII, No. 1 (October, 1953), 43–50.

ployment is not clear. That is, did the injury "arise out of" the employment? Disabilities such as nontraumatic loss of hearing and coronary and pulmonary afflictions may be caused by employment, but, of course, they are also associated with nonwork hazards of life. Allocating liability for these types of disability presents serious policy issues,[5] perhaps the major ones facing workmen's compensation today. Let us now turn to the question of what benefits are paid to an eligible disabled employee.

Types and Amounts of Benefits

Two basic types of benefits are provided by workmen's compensation laws: (1) cash or indemnity payments and (2) payments for medical services. Although rehabilitation services, which are an important recent development, consist partly in medical services, they should ideally extend well beyond them. Hence, they are considered separately here.

CASH OR INDEMNITY PAYMENTS

Cash benefits are immediately payable to disabled workers in only one American jurisdiction, Oregon. All other jurisdictions require that the disability extend beyond a "waiting period" which ranges typically from three to seven days and is designed to reduce compensation costs and to discourage possible malingering. Although the overwhelming majority of job-caused disabilities are of very short duration and hence do not involve benefit payments (because of the waiting periods), they do account for substantial aggregate medical benefits.

Disability extending beyond the waiting period is classified for benefit purposes into "total" and "partial." A temporary total disability is one which is repaired by healing, thus enabling the injured worker to return to his job. Permanent total disability involves injuries such as loss of sight, both arms, or legs, which except for cases of successful rehabilitation, make further employment impossible. Cash benefits for total disability are usually weekly payments calculated as two-thirds of the average weekly wage at the

[5] Studies by the American Heart Association have led one of its members, Dr. Richard J. Clark, to the conclusion that ideal criteria for compensability of these injuries are virtually impossible, and, therefore, that ". . . all heart and degenerative diseases, barring those cases clearly and specifically caused by well defined accidents on the job, should be excluded from Industrial Accident provisions and should be covered by a Sickness Insurance System. . . ." "The Challenge of Occupational Disability," *Proceedings* of the Committee on Workmen's Compensation, Council on Industrial Health, American Medical Association, January 25–26, 1955, p. 34.

time of the injury, subject to weekly maximums and limits on duration of payments and total amount.[6] Table 10.1 shows these limits and indicates the benefits payable in all American jurisdictions at the time of this writing.

Disabilities where at least partial employment is possible are also divided into temporary and permanent cases. Most serious partial disabilities involve total disability in their early stages until healing (say, from an amputation) is complete. Temporary partial disabilities are not as significant, numerically, as are serious permanent partial injuries and are most often compensated by a formula paying two-thirds of the difference between the disabled worker's earnings (during disability) and his prior average earnings.

Since it is extremely difficult to determine the exact degree of permanent partial disability, most acts set forth "schedule disabilities" which list the maximum amount and duration of compensation payments for specific injuries. The weekly benefits are calculated by the same formula used in cases of total disability.

Thus, *in addition to* the portion of wages made up during the period of disability, a permanent partial disability payment "schedule" would provide the following payments (using but several examples, ranging from one extreme to the other): (1) for the loss of a little finger, 66⅔ per cent of the daily wage at the time of injury for 15 weeks; (2) for the loss of one arm and one leg, 66⅔ per cent of the daily wage at the time of injury for 400 weeks.

Death benefit payments to survivors are also an important benefit provision, and, like indemnity payments, they vary greatly from jurisdiction to jurisdiction. In many, these payments to dependents are limited both in time and amount. Limits range from a high of $20,000 (Wisconsin) to a low of $3,500 (Puerto Rico). A majority of the jurisdictions pay less than $10,000 in cases of death.

In summary, cash or indemnity payments serve two purposes: first, they make up a portion of the wage loss suffered by workers with "nonscheduled" disabilities and by dependents of fatal cases; and, second, in the case of permanent partial disabilities, these benefits additionally seek to make up a portion of anticipated future reductions in earnings which the disability is presumed to bring about. Of necessity, the second of these indemnities must be subject to loose estimation; it is not possible to calculate with any degree of precision what reductions in earning power, if any, such

___

[6] The operation of benefit formulas and the effect of statutory benefit limits are best understood in the context of specific examples. Students will find it helpful, using the laws of their home states, to compute benefits that are payable to injured workers with different incomes and suffering different degrees of disability.

TABLE 10.1

Comparison of Cash and Medical Benefit Provisions for All American Jurisdictions

Jurisdiction	Cash Benefits						Medical Benefits	
	Permanent Total Disability			Temporary Total Disability				
	Weekly Max.	Maximum Period	Stated Max.	Weekly Max.	Maximum Period	Total Max.	Full Benefits	Dollar or Period Limits*
Alabama	28.00	400 wks^d	$11,200	28.00	300 wks	$8,400		$1,000
Alaska			12,000 to 15,000^b		24 mos			4 yrs
Arizona	150.00	life		100.00	433 wks			
Arkansas	25.00	450 wks	8,000	150.00	450 wks	8,000	x†	
California	35.00	life^c		25.00	240 wks	9,600	x†	1,000
Colorado	31.50	life		40.00	p.d.**		x	
Connecticut	40.00	p.d.**		31.50	p.d.**		x	
Delaware	35.00	p.d.**		40.00	p.d.**		x	
District of Columbia	35.00^d	p.d.**		35.00^d	p.d.**	11,000	x†	
Florida	35.00	p.d.**		35.00	350 wks			1,125^a
Georgia	30.00	400 wks	10,000	30.00	400 wks	10,000		
Hawaii	50.00^d	p.d.**	20,000^e	50.00	p.d.**	20,000	x	
Idaho	23.00^b / 40.00	400 wks^b, e		23.00^b	400 wks^b, e		x	
Illinois	34.00^b / 40.00	life	8,000^b, e / 10,750	34.00^b / 40.00	p.d.**	9,250^b / 12,000	x	
Indiana	33.00	500 wks	12,500	33.00	500 wks	12,000	x†	
Iowa	32.00	500 wks		32.00	300 wks		x†	1,500^a
Kansas	32.00	416 wks		32.00	416 wks			2,500
Kentucky	27.00	520 wks	11,500	27.00	520 wks	11,500		2,500
Louisiana	30.00	400 wks		30.00	300 wks			1,000
Maine	30.00	500 wks	12,000	30.00	500 wks	12,000	x†	
Maryland	35.00	p.d.**	15,000	35.00	312 wks	5,000	x†	

TABLE 10.1 (Continued)

Jurisdiction	Cash Benefits						Medical Benefits	
	Permanent Total Disability			Temporary Total Disability				
	Weekly Max.	Maximum Period	Stated Max.	Weekly Max.	Maximum Period	Total Max.	Full Benefits	Dollar or Period Limits*
Massachusetts	35.00[b] up	p.d.**		35.00[b]	p.d.**	10,000	x	
Michigan	32.00[b] 42.00	p.d.**		32.00[b] 42.00	500 wks	†	x†	
Minnesota	40.00	p.d.**		40.00	310 wks	†	x	
Mississippi	25.00	450 wks	8,600	25.00	450 wks	8,600	x	
Missouri	35.00	300 wks[e]		35.00	400 wks		x†	
Montana	26.50[b] 32.50	500 wks		26.50[b] 32.50	300 wks			2,500
Nebraska	30.00	300 wks[e]		30.00	300 wks[e]		x	
Nevada	34.50[d] 47.76	life		30.00[b] 41.54	433 wks			6 mos[a]
New Hampshire	33.00	341 wks	11,250	33.00	341 wks	10,500	x†	
New Jersey	30.00	450 wks[d]		30.00	300 wks		x†	
New Mexico	30.00	550 wks		30.00	550 wks		x†	
New York	36.00[d]	life		36.00	p.d.**	6,500	x	
North Carolina	32.50	400 wks[d]	10,000	32.50	400 wks	10,000	x†	
North Dakota	31.50[b] 45.50	life		31.50[b] 45.50	p.d.**		x	
Ohio	40.25	life		40.25	520 wks	8,000	x†	
Oklahoma	28.00	500 wks		28.00	500 wks		x†	
Oregon	23.08[b] 61.15	p.d.**		26.54[b] 61.15	p.d.**		x†	
Pennsylvania	32.50	700 wks	20,000	32.50	700 wks	20,000		450[a]
Puerto Rico	20.00	340 wks	3,500	20.00	104 wks		x	
Rhode Island	32.00	p.d.**	16,000	32.00	p.d.**	16,000	x†	
South Carolina	35.00	500 wks	8,000	35.00	500 wks	8,000	x†	

TABLE 10.1 (Continued)

Jurisdiction	Cash Benefits						Medical Benefits	
	Permanent Total Disability			Temporary Total Disability				
	Weekly Max.	Maximum Period	Stated Max.	Weekly Max.	Maximum Period	Total Max.	Full Benefits	Dollar or Period Limits*
South Dakota	28.00	300 wks^e	9,000	28.00	312 wks			300^a
Tennessee	30.00	400 wks^e	10,000	30.00	300 wks	10,000		1,500
Texas	25.00	401 wks		25.00	401 wks			4 wks^a
Utah	30.00^b 40.50	260 wks^e		30.00^b 40.50	313 wks	8,580 10,725	x†	
Vermont	28.00^b up	330 wks	6,500	28.00^b up	330 wks			2,500^a
Virginia	27.00	500 wks	10,800	27.00	500 wks	10,800		
Washington	23.08^b 46.15	life^d		23.08^b, d 42.69	p.d.**		x	60 days^a
West Virginia	30.00	life		30.00	208 wks			
Wisconsin	45.50^d	life		45.50^d	p.d.**		x	1,600^a
Wyoming	21.23 27.69^b		7,500 13,850^b	23.85^b	p.d.**		x†	
Federal Employees	121.15^b	life		121.15	p.d.**		x	
Longshoremen	35.00^b	p.d.**		35.00	p.d.**	11,000	x	

* All but five limited benefit jurisdictions provide both dollar and period limits. For the remainder, dollar limits only are shown in the table. Time limits are listed for these five.

† Benefits limited by law but may be extended without limit by administrative agency.

** Period of disability.

^a Limited dollar (in some cases time) extensions may be authorized.   ^b Varies with number of dependents.

^c Benefits reduced to 40 per cent after 400 weeks.

^d Added benefits for specific cases, such as those requiring constant attendance or those involving loss of mental faculties.

^e Added benefit payments at reduced rates.   ^f Not to exceed 500 times the weekly amount.

Source: U. S. Department of Labor, Bureau of Labor Standards, *Bulletin 161*, Supplement to "State Workmen's Compensation Laws as of September, 1954," November, 1955.

disabilities will cause. Hence, the figures arrived at are compro-
mises of various types.

PAYMENTS FOR MEDICAL SERVICES

During the early development of workmen's compensation laws,
little or no provision was made for medical benefits.[7] Today, however, as Table 10.1 indicates, some thirty-seven jurisdictions put no
limit on medical benefits provided to the occupationally disabled.
The benefits are provided as they are indicated medically. They
include physician and hospital service, surgical and medical care,
and, in all states but five, any necessary artificial appliances that
may be required by the disability.

This liberalization in medical benefits has been characterized as
the greatest single improvement or development in workmen's compensation legislation. While the trend is clearly in the direction of
only medically indicated limits on benefits, seventeen jurisdictions
still have limits of time or amount. Referring again to Table 10.1,
time and dollar limits on medical benefits go as low as four weeks
(Texas) and $300 (South Dakota.)

Medical benefits account for about one-third of total benefit payments under workmen's compensation, and it is estimated that at
least seven million disabilities a year are treated under workmen's
compensation medical care programs.

REHABILITATION SERVICES

Most promising of the recent benefit developments is the growth
of provisions for vocational rehabilitation.[8] Under early workmen's
compensation laws, after the limited medical care called for by law
had been provided, the disability was "fixed" as it stood. And when
treatment ran out or no further benefit from it was apparent, permanent total disability was often presumed. With the advances medicine has made in overcoming many of the physical handicaps of
disability and with the growth of facilities and knowledge for
vocational training, the area of permanent total disability has been
reduced and can no longer be presumed.

Vocational rehabilitation has been slow in developing in workmen's compensation laws. A few states—notably Massachusetts,
Oregon, California, and North Dakota—established rehabilitation

---

[7] See Bruce A. Greene, "Workmen's Compensation in the United States," *Bulletin
1140.* (U. S. Department of Labor, Bureau of Labor Statistics, 1954), pp. 25–28.

[8] Jerome Pollack, "Workmen's Compensation in the United States," *ibid.*, pp. 40–
45.

training and instruction provisions in their workmen's compensation acts before 1920. The federal Vocational Rehabilitation Act of 1920 gave some technical and financial assistance to the states under a cooperative program for all cases of disability regardless of origin.

Today the workmen's compensation laws of only five jurisdictions provide rehabilitation facilities. About twenty more provide added indemnity or retraining allowances and utilize federal, state, or private facilities available to them to provide rehabilitation services.

These brief observations about rehabilitation provide a logical point at which to begin an evaluation of workmen's compensation.

Appraising Workmen's Compensation

Protection against the hazards of occupational disability through workmen's compensation laws was the objective of the first social insurance programs both here and abroad. Its rapid development, due to both the need for such protection and the soundness of the liability without fault principle, ended abruptly within a decade of its introduction in the United States. Today, nearly a half-century after the first American law, critical concern with the role and success of this pioneering social insurance is greater than it has ever been. The remainder of this chapter, therefore, will be devoted to a discussion of the problems which have caused this concern.

As we have already seen, the provisions of state workmen's compensation laws are not uniform. However, all jurisdictions initially sought the same objective—economic rehabilitation of the occupationally injured. Marshall Dawson, an eminent workmen's compensation scholar, outlines this objective as follows:[9] (1) to pay certain, prompt, and reasonable compensation to victims of work accidents; (2) to eliminate delays, costs, and wastes of personal injury litigation; (3) to study and attempt to reduce the number of accident cases rather than to conceal them. As a result of some twenty-five years of compensation experience, (4) prompt and adequate medical treatment and (5) rehabilitation for workers unable to return to their former jobs have become added objectives.

How fully have these objectives been realized? This question cannot be answered without making value judgments about which there may be some legitimate disagreement. Nor can it be answered

[9] Marshall Dawson, "Problems of Workmen's Compensation Administration in the United States and Canada," *Bulletin 672* (U. S. Department of Labor, Bureau of Labor Statistics, 1940), pp. 5–6.

completely, for unlike all other forms of social insurance, neither are basic data collected in one place, nor are they available from jurisdiction to jurisdiction in complete or comparable form. Thus, some of the most elementary questions about the performance of the laws or the fate of injured workers cannot be answered in some jurisdictions. For example, only a few states know how promptly benefit payments are made to injured workers and whether the full payment required by law has indeed been made. Most of the available data show little more than the number of injured workers and the total compensation paid. This paucity of information has been deplored many times at the annual meetings[10] of the administrators of the state laws. Yet most jurisdictions have failed to follow the lead of states like Wisconsin, whose excellent statistical reports draw wide praise.

Does Workmen's Compensation Pay Certain, Prompt, and Reasonable Compensation to Victims of Work Accidents?

Few jurisdictions gather and report data on promptness of payment, and for those who do, comparisons are not easy to make because of varying provisions in the systems: different waiting periods, different methods of computing time of accidents, and different methods of administering the law. A Bureau of Labor Statistics survey showed a six weeks' lag between time of accident and first payment for the period from 1919–1920 to the middle thirties (where data were available). Some states, notably Wisconsin and New York, currently report pay lags of about three weeks. The national average probably is about one month. The continued use of the "agreement" method of claims administration (discussed below) leaves open the possibility of defeating intended statutory benefit amounts. These factors make it difficult to judge whether or not benefits are paid promptly and with certainty, and they indicate that there is much room for improvement on this performance standard.

Cash benefits are frequently referred to as the "heart" of a workmen's compensation system, and with good reason, for they provide income which enables a worker and his family to live during the period of disability. Yet, despite its importance to the compensation

---

[10] Proceedings of the annual meetings of the International Association of Industrial Accident Boards and Commissions are an important source of data and evaluations of current workmen's compensation experience. They are published by the U. S. Department of Labor as bulletins of the Bureau of Labor Standards under the title "Workmen's Compensation Problems."

principle, in most jurisdictions this part of the compensation law has not accomplished its purpose.

Most of the early workmen's compensation laws stated that weekly cash benefits should be one-half to two-thirds of the worker's weekly wages at the time of his injury. Minnesota, for example, provided in its April 25, 1913, enactment that the weekly maximum benefit be 50 per cent of wages with a maximum payment of $10, not to fall below a weekly minimum of $6. This maximum weekly figure was in fact close to the average weekly wage prevailing at that time, and, with very limited exception, injured workers received the full 50 per cent of their average weekly wage provided by the law.

However, in the years since the widespread enactment of workmen's compensation laws, both the average weekly wage (real and money terms) and the weekly benefits of compensation have increased. Unfortunately, the former have tended to outstrip the latter. Thus, although today most jurisdictions seek to restore about 60 per cent to two-thirds of the average weekly wage and post higher dollar and duration limits than did their earlier laws, benefits have not kept pace with rising wages. As a result, the maximum dollar limits provided by most laws become in effect upper limits on benefits, and today very few injured workers receive benefits amounting to from 60 per cent to two-thirds of their lost weekly earnings.

The most recent comprehensive study of the weekly wages restored by indemnity benefits[11] reveals that in only six of fifty United States jurisdictions do the cash benefits of the June, 1953, laws restore 60 per cent of the 1952 average weekly wage. Allowing for dependents' allowances (and the assumption of four dependents) only two of the fifty jurisdictions reach the 60 per cent figure. Some are restoring less than 40 per cent. These data make it fairly clear that, in general, injured workers today are heavier coinsurers than they were under the original workmen's compensation laws.

Since the benefits in some jurisdictions fall below what many consider to be a minimum budget, or even an adequate one by relief standards, it is obvious that over-all benefit performance cannot be judged reasonable by almost any standard.

What is a reasonable or (as it is more frequently stated) an adequate benefit? How high should cash benefits be? The model bill of the U. S. Department of Labor proposes that the maximum be

[11] Dorothy McCamman and A. M. Skolnik, "Workmen's Compensation: Measures of Accomplishment," *Social Security Bulletin*, XVII, No. 3 (March, 1954), 7.

set, without weekly dollar limits, at two-thirds of the average gross weekly wages of all covered employees in the state.[12]

Practical considerations guided benefit decisions in the earliest compensation laws. Benefits could not be so high as to be too costly to employers or to give workers an incentive to feign injury or to malinger. On the other hand, they could not be so low as to be inadequate for the support of the injured worker and his family. Admittedly, these outside limits cannot be translated readily into dollars and cents statements.[13] Yet it seems clear that today's benefit levels are in the aggregate closer to the lower limits than they are to the upper limits. Of course, both sides of the benefit issue must always be considered in shaping policy, but today's benefit levels focus primary attention on the dangers to the living standards of injured workers rather than on the possibility of malingering or of excessive costs.

A discussion of the "reasonableness" or adequacy of indemnity benefits should take into account three additional factors, the first of which has already been mentioned briefly.

There are wide variations between states. As we have emphasized several times earlier, differences are considerable from jurisdiction to jurisdiction. Thus, workers injured in Wisconsin or Arizona and those covered by the Federal Employees Compensation Act will receive benefits which restore a considerably greater portion of their wage loss than workers suffering identical injuries in most other states.

There are differences within jurisdictions. Even within a given jurisdiction, the percentage of the wage loss restored differs greatly among degrees of disability. Studies have demonstrated repeatedly[14] that benefits restore a larger portion of lost wages to workers suffering temporary disability than they do in cases involving

---

[12] See "Discussion Draft of Proposed Model Workmen's Compensation Law," U. S. Department of Labor, November, 1955, Sec. 16, p. 21. In addition to this benefit proposal, the law, which is in large part based upon the Wisconsin and New York laws, would: (1) broaden coverage of employments; (2) provide full coverage of occupational diseases; (3) extend benefit duration to life for permanent total disability; (4) provide unlimited medical benefits; (5) provide for rehabilitation centers; (6) broaden second-injury funds; and (7) penalize illegal employment of minors. Through the drafting and publication of this model bill, the Department of Labor hopes to arouse interest in revising the state laws. Interested students may obtain copies of the proposed law from the Department.

[13] For a discussion of this issue, see Earl F. Cheit, "Adequacy of Workmen's Compensation," *Insurance Law Journal*, No. 387, April, 1955, p. 247.

[14] Herman M. Somers and Anne R. Somers, *Workmen's Compensation* (New York: John Wiley & Sons, Inc., 1954), pp. 80–81.

death, permanent total, or severe permanent partial disability. The Social Security Administration study referred to above reported that temporary disability cases lose, on an average, about two-thirds of their weekly wage, with the most seriously disabled suffering even greater proportionate wage losses.

The system cannot be judged by indemnity benefits alone. No attempt should be made to conceal the inadequacy of workmen's compensation indemnity benefits, but because the whole performance of workmen's compensation is so frequently judged by reference to this criterion alone, it is important to recognize that the systems have tended to become more liberal in other respects. Broader coverage, more lifetime benefits for permanent total cases, improved benefit duration and rehabilitation progress—these improvements should also be considered in judging the adequacy of the system.

If we accept E. H. Downey's premise that the "compensation system should comprise all injuries, all persons employed therein and all personal injuries which arise in the course of industrial pursuits,"[15] then all state systems must be judged deficient in compensation coverage of work accident victims. For, as we have noted before, exclusions, exemptions, and other eligibility requirements restrict the scope of workmen's compensation. Actually, the scope of compensation protection has been widened considerably over the years; all jurisdictions today have laws; their numerical exemptions have been reduced and in some cases eliminated; the hazardous employment requirement has been dropped from some laws. Nevertheless, substantial numbers of employees remain outside the protection of workmen's compensation.

Six requirements limit workmen's compensation coverage. Benefits can be paid only to (1) "employees" (2) working in covered employments (3) who suffer injuries covered by statute (4) and are incapacitated for a period longer than the waiting period (5) by an injury caused by and sustained in the course of the employment, and (6) who elect coverage in jurisdictions offering the option. How many victims of work accidents are denied benefits by the combination of these limiting factors is not known accurately, since adequate data are not available. Carl Hookstadt's pioneering studies of workmen's compensation coverage have provided some measure, however. Hookstadt concluded that for the states that had laws in

15 E. H. Downey, *Workmen's Compensation* (New York: The Macmillan Co., 1924), p. 21.

1920, some 30 per cent of otherwise eligible employees were not covered as a result of exclusions and exemptions.[16]

In bringing these figures up to date, Harry Weiss concluded that in 1933, only 24 million of an eligible 33 million "employees" were covered. A study by Arthur H. Reede reveals that, exclusive of the unemployed, unpaid family workers, the self-employed, and other groups for whom coverage is not normally contemplated by workmen's compensation (such as railroad workers and federal employees), 67.4 per cent of the remaining "eligible" employees were covered in 1920, 75.2 per cent in 1930, and 81.5 per cent in 1940.

The most recent estimate, made by the Social Security Administration, places 1952 coverage at about the 80 per cent figure estimated by Reede in 1940.[17] There are wide differences, however, within these broad national estimates. Urban areas and industrial states, for example, have much higher coverage than the rural and nonindustrial states.

Furthermore, covered workers receive compensation only for injuries specified by statute. This further reduces coverage in some states, especially in the case of occupational diseases. Also, the link between injury and employment must be established legally, and, except for Oregon, the waiting period requirement must be fulfilled. This latter provision alone takes perhaps two-fifths of all temporary injuries out of coverage. In some states, poor enforcement, as well as elective provisions, tends to reduce coverage.

In sum, therefore, remarkable strides have been made in providing compensation to victims of industrial accidents. All state and territorial jurisdictions and the federal government provide coverage against the hazard of occupational disability. Some early restrictions, such as those applying to "nonhazardous" occupations, have been legislated away; other restricting forces such as a rigorous definition of accident have been liberalized by court and legislative action. Yet coverage is still denied to many victims of work accidents. It may be that Downey's criterion is too inclusive. Short waiting periods, though costly to individual workers, do permit allocation of benefit resources to the more seriously disabled. But there are no compelling reasons to exclude employers on the basis of numbers employed or, for that matter, to exempt casual or domestic employees, if these groups are defined carefully. There-

[16] This study and those by Harry Weiss and Arthur H. Reede are discussed in Arthur H. Reede, *Adequacy of Workmen's Compensation* (Cambridge: Harvard University Press, 1947), pp. 8–30.

[17] McCamman and Skolnik, *op. cit.,* p. 4.

fore, although we seem to be moving slowly in the direction of improved coverage, much work remains.

HAS WORKMEN'S COMPENSATION ELIMINATED DELAYS, COSTS, AND WASTE?

By introducing the concept of liability without fault, workmen's compensation laws eliminated many of the delays and costs made necessary by the common law. In fact, the administrative approaches of workmen's compensation are sometimes suggested as possible solutions to the many automobile accident claims which today cause court delays, costs, and wastes not unlike those associated with occupational injuries at common law. Despite the transfer from court to commission determination of injury claims, however, prompt and efficient benefit payment is not yet ideal because of problems in administration and because of legal contests, which still tend to play a significant role in the administration of workmen's compensation. These problems are discussed later in this chapter together with the administration of workmen's compensation laws.

HAS WORKMEN'S COMPENSATION HELPED TO REDUCE ACCIDENTS?

Accident Facts, published annually by the National Safety Council, indicates that since shortly after the widespread enactment of workmen's compensation in America, the long-run general trend in accident frequency and severity rates has been downward. There is some disagreement, however, about whether or not workmen's compensation laws have contributed substantially to this trend.[18] There are several reasons why we might assume that it has.

First, it is obviously to an employer's self-interest to install safety measures for prevention of accidents when he is liable for the payment of compensation benefits. His insurance premiums, if he is not a small employer, will be "merit rated"—that is, if he produces a good accident record, he will be rewarded with lower insurance costs.

Secondly, it is to the self-interest of the insurance carrier to prevent accidents, and compensation carriers allocate a portion of their

---

[18] W. F. Dodd says: "It is perhaps safe to say that workmen's compensation has had little effect" [on the industrial accident rate]. See W. F. Dodd, *Administration of Workmen's Compensation* (New York: The Commonwealth Fund, 1936) p. 698. The Director of the Bureau of Labor Standards, however, writes that "the greatest contribution which workmen's compensation has made to the economic and physical well-being of workers is the stimulus it has given to accident prevention efforts." See "Workmen's Compensation in the United States," *op. cit.,* p. 29.

premium collections to safety services for their assureds. Some states have sought to stimulate preventive measures by enacting provisions which assess penalties against employers for accidents stemming from safety code violations.

Finally, workmen's compensation systems in themselves make accident control more possible, since the assembling of accident data is a part of their operation. Over half the states have established independent safety and inspection programs and placed them under the responsibility of their workmen's compensation administrations.

At the same time, however, it must be noted that the employer's self-interest in reducing accidents is strong whether or not he is covered by workmen's compensation. Benefit costs are but a fraction of total accident costs to employers; furthermore, smaller employers are not eligible for merit rating, and many of those who are can, on small premiums, realize only small incentive savings from a good safety record. The value of penalty provisions is not clear, and the poor reporting of accident data in many states leaves this promising avenue of control unexploited in many areas. Even the self-interest of insurance carriers has been known to give way when it becomes a matter of rejecting possible assureds because of questionable safety records.

On balance, therefore, we can do little more than hazard some guesses about the effects of workmen's compensation on accident prevention. First, whether or not they provided great incentives, workmen's compensation laws did, in fact, stimulate initial employer interest in accident prevention. And, to a lesser degree, the workmen's compensation movement has provided a measure of continued drive and direction to the safety movement, now supplemented by the work of many other safety agencies, voluntary and governmental.

Second, it seems safe to assume that compensation incentives, with all their weaknesses, have provided some impetus to prevention. An excellent illustration is the estimated $100 million per year employers are currently spending to make jobs more quiet—partly as a result of the recent decisions holding that nontraumatic occupational "loss-of-hearing" is compensable.

However, there is still elective coverage in many jurisdictions; there are exemptions; and small employers have little, if any, insurance incentives. Some industries, like manufacturing, have produced good over-all results. Others, like coal mining, still tend to be very hazardous. Moreover, the largest companies are producing excellent safety records, but the smaller firms are producing poorer ones. While workmen's compensation may have contributed to the goal of accident prevention, the goal itself has not yet been fully achieved.

DOES WORKMEN'S COMPENSATION PROVIDE PROMPT AND ADEQUATE MEDICAL TREATMENT?

We have already seen in Table 10.1 that, either by law or in practical operation, thirty-seven American jurisdictions provide full medical treatment—that is, the degree of care medically indicated, without legal limitation to a specified time or amount. Even in those jurisdictions where limitations apply, employers and insurance carriers frequently report that they provide unlimited medical treatment to seriously injured workers.

When one considers that the original workmen's compensation acts provided little or no medical benefits, the progress that has been made in this area is probably the greatest single achievement of workmen's compensation since its inception in this country. Furthermore, since there is now a well-established trend toward acceptance of medically indicated medical treatment as the only "adequate" treatment, it appears quite certain that all jurisdictions will employ this benefit policy in the near future.

This optimism is based not on humanitarian considerations, but rather on the principle of the economy of full medical treatment. It has often been demonstrated that the maximum medical treatment is also the optimal one; that prompt adequate medical care reduces compensation costs in at least three ways. First, it reduces the number of cases of "avoidable disability"—cases of a minor nature which might otherwise become more serious. Secondly, it reduces the degree of disability. And, finally, it reduces the period of care, thereby avoiding prolonged indemnity and other costs.

In the states where benefits are limited, the results are far from satisfactory. A recent study by the Council on Industrial Health of the American Medical Association reveals that in fourteen American jurisdictions more money is presently being allocated to acquisition of workmen's compensation insurance than is being spent for medical treatment.[19]

Not all the problems of medical care have been solved, although those that remain are mainly problems of quality and administration. For example, fee schedules of charges permitted by some states may be too low to attract the best medical practitioners to

[19] *Some Monetary Aspects of Workmen's Compensation* (Chicago: American Medical Association, 1955), p. 4.

compensation cases. The quality of medical care may be poor because of the injured worker's ignorance in his choice of a physician in jurisdictions where such free choice is permitted or because of the pressure of an insurance carrier on a physician where it is not. Since, there is little statutory supervision over medical care, problems of inadequate services arise, particularly in the case of workers who could have been rehabilitated if more competent initial treatment had been provided.

In addition, partisan medical testimony may have the effect of defeating the ends of efficient claims administration.[20] Yet, on balance, this phase of workmen's compensation, more than any other, must again be cited as having most nearly achieved its purposes.

DOES WORKMEN'S COMPENSATION PROVIDE REHABILITATION SERVICES FOR WORKERS UNABLE TO RETURN TO THEIR FORMER JOBS?

Probably no phase of workmen's compensation offers more promise of achievement and, at the same time, shows greater gaps in over-all performance than does the relatively new field of rehabilitation. Unfortunately, this must also be said of the restoration to useful employment of the nonoccupationally handicapped, who account for over 90 per cent of all such cases.

Rehabilitation is, in part, an outgrowth of the workmen's compensation movement, but only a very few state laws have brought rehabilitation activities within their scope. The important federal Vocational Rehabilitation Act of 1920 gave technical and financial assistance to state programs for all disabled persons regardless of the origin of disability. Today most state rehabilitation work depends on this federal-state system which meets but a fraction of the need.[21]

The following data, issued by the Director of the Federal Office of Vocational Rehabilitation, illustrate the problem:[22] In 1954, federal-state rehabilitation programs restored an estimated 58,000 disabled persons to gainful employment. Nonpublic programs performed this important service for some 40,000 more. Yet, during this period an estimated 250,000 persons were disabled and required rehabilitation services to become employable. Furthermore, although rehabilitation services are usually most effective if given immediately after

---

[20] *Medical Relations Under Workmen's Compensation in Illinois* (Chicago: American Medical Association, 1953).

[21] Jerome Pollack, "Medical Care and Rehabilitation Under Workmen's Compensation," *American Journal of Public Health*, XLV, No. 5 (May, 1955), 648–50.

[22] *The New York Times*, November 29, 1955, p. 31.

the disability, the present backlog of unattended cases is estimated at two million persons.

This rather dismal record tends to overshadow the remarkable achievements and renewed efforts in rehabilitation of the disabled.[23] In 1955, for example, the Office of Vocational Rehabilitation expanded its grants to training centers, established traineeships for training in workshops and gave more funds to rehabilitation groups in forty-one states. Private centers, too, most notably those of the United Mine Workers of America and the Liberty Mutual Insurance Company, have made great contributions towards rehabilitating the disabled and restoring them to useful economic activity. Yet, the fact remains that rehabilitation resources and personnel are woefully inadequate to their task.[24]

Other deterrents to rehabilitation success exist:[25] poor cooperation between federal and state agencies, poor administration of the laws, and some disincentives to rehabilitation in the laws themselves. Furthermore, as medical progress has made rehabilitation feasible for greater numbers of persons, the scope of the task has become greater. For as it becomes possible to restore more and more types of disability to useful service, persons with these handicaps outnumber the services available to them.

Ample evidence now exists that rehabilitation services can be justified, not only on humanitarian grounds—which often carry little weight in legislative debate—but purely on economic grounds as well.[26] The Liberty Mutual Insurance Company reports, for example, that by putting thirty-five paraplegics back to work through rehabilitation, it has saved over 1.5 million dollars in compensation costs.

Is the System Structured Rationally?

Since workmen's compensation laws do not operate independently of the industrial disability problem which they seek to alleviate, it follows that if the system is structured rationally it should exert a positive influence on industrial injury experience. The merit

[23] An enlightening dramatization of what rehabilitation can accomplish under workmen's compensation laws is the film "Team Play in Action" designed to demonstrate the Ontario workmen's compensation system. This film is available on loan for classroom use through the Ontario Commission.

[24] See the "Proceedings of the National Conference on Workmen's Compensation and Rehabilitation," *Bulletin 122* (U. S. Department of Labor, Bureau of Labor Standards, 1950).

[25] Dawson, *op. cit.*, p. 169.

[26] Willis C. Gorthy, "Rehabilitation: Its Effects in Reducing Compensation Costs," in "Workmen's Compensation Problems," *Bulletin 180* (U. S. Department of Labor, Bureau of Labor Standards, 1953), pp. 35–43.

rating and penalty provisions discussed earlier were adopted with this goal in mind. Although the effects of these provisions are in dispute, other provisions have achieved their purpose—for example, the "nurse credit" in insurance rates to companies which make nursing service available to their employees. To this extent the system is structured rationally.

Under some compensation laws, instances arise of resisting claims through litigation, of paying lump-sum benefits in place of regular payments, of shoddy medical practices and benefit abuse; but, for the most part, these are due to inadequate supervision and administration, rather than to structural failures of the laws. They are more faults of omission than commission.

One serious structural shortcoming of workmen's compensation laws is that they may unwittingly offer disincentives to speedy rehabilitation of injured workers. Two situations arise.

First, *workmen's compensation laws may tend to deter seriously injured workers from seeking rehabilitation aid.* Under present laws, injured workers often see in rehabilitation the possible forfeiture of their maximum cash benefit claims.[27] Compensation benefits are based in part on the degree of disability or disablement, and since these cases are serious and hence costly to insurers, many of them result in litigation where the degree of disability is the issue in dispute. When an injured worker is disputing an insurance carrier's contention that he is not as disabled as he claims, he will not readily seek rehabilitation services or do anything else to show that he may not be disabled.[28]

In order to be resolved, this apparent conflict between maximum cash benefits and rehabilitation will require not only more enlightened claims administration, but perhaps benefits which, for serious "nonscheduled" injuries, are paid as a matter of right and are not forfeited by rehabilitation or temporary employment success.

Second, *workmen's compensation laws have tended to deter employers from hiring handicapped workers.* Employers avoid hiring handicapped workers for fear that further injury could result in a total disability claim. In a well-known case in Oklahoma in 1925,[29] it was held that an employee who had previously lost sight in one eye could bring a claim against his employer for permanent total

[27] Ashley St. Clair, "Medicolegal and Social Problems in Disability Cases," *Industrial Medicine and Surgery*, XX, (March, 1951), 109–12.

[28] Rehabilitation authority Dr. Howard A. Rusk reports that he succeeded in rehabilitating only 3 per cent of 300 cases in litigation, whereas his usual success with rehabilitation cases is 90 per cent. *Medical Aspects of Compensation* (New York: Commerce and Industry Association of New York, 1953), pp. 68–69.

[29] *Nease v. Hughes Stone Co.,* 244 PAC. 778.

compensation for loss of the other eye in the course of his employment. It is reported that "Seven thousand one-eyed, one-armed and one-legged workmen were fired over night in that state. Oklahoma employers were unwilling to take on handicapped workers for fear that additional injury would cost them permanent total disability awards."[30]

Second-injury funds have been adopted to meet this situation in all but five states. Money for these funds is collected by a moderate assessment on employers (in most states for death cases where there are no dependents eligible for benefits; in a few states, in each case of serious disability). The second injury fund operates to protect employers from total disability claims in cases involving second injuries. Employers are made liable only for the disability of the second injury, and the fund pays the rest of the benefits for total disability.

This remarkable device, if broad enough in its coverage, provides an important incentive to employment of handicapped workers. Moreover, it has proved to be relatively inexpensive, since experience shows that not a great many charges are made against the second-injury funds.

Is the System Administered Soundly?

Sound administration is as important to an adequate workmen's compensation program as are substantive provisions of the law. Adequate benefits lose their value if they are not promptly paid or are not paid in full.

Fewer evaluative data are available to review this aspect of workmen's compensation than any other. We do know that some jurisdictions, most notably Wisconsin, win repeated acclaim as models of good administration. We know, too, that studies of administration do not present a very satisfactory over-all picture. The problems that arise are summarized below.

First, in five jurisdictions the legislation has never been given over to administrative determination. And where workmen's compensation laws are court-administered, the results have not been good. They have provided poor and inadequate records, and, as Dawson has written, except in contested cases they have provided no administration at all. The administrative machinery is lacking for the detailed work required of an injury compensation program.

[30] "Workmen's Compensation," *CIO Guidebook Series*, No. 1 (Washington, D. C.: Congress of Industrial Organizations, 1952), p. 56.

Second, administrative procedures in the remaining jurisdictions follow three basic approaches. Claims are paid by direct settlement; by agreement; or, after a hearing. The direct-settlement method enables cheap and speedy claims payments since claims in noncontested cases are paid directly upon notice of disability. But quick and economical claims administration alone does not insure that claims are paid justly. The "hearing" system, used only in New York, seeks to insure just payment by providing a hearing for every claim. The "agreement" method, most widely used of the claims techniques today, seeks to gain equity on the assumption that workers can agree with a settlement proposed by employers or carriers. Serious problems of cost and waste arise under the hearings approach, and the greatest weakness of the agreement system is its possibilities for abuse. Students of administration seem agreed that a closely supervised direct-settlement method is probably the best approach. But this raises another problem in administration.

Third, workmen's compensation administrative offices in a majority of jurisdictions are frequently without adequate personnel and budgets, nor do they enjoy the status and tenure protection needed for completely independent judgment. It is impossible to operate a closely supervised direct-settlement system under these circumstances.

Fourth, partly because of the lack of professional administrative direction and partly because of the incentives to do so, far too many compensation claims (about 10 per cent) are contested and result in the kind of lengthy and costly litigation which the system was designed to circumvent in the first place.

And lastly, not all the litigation and administrative indecision can be laid to these causes, however, for some of the basic concepts in workmen's compensation pose some theoretical issues of great importance, such as the proper standards for determining the measure of benefits and disability rating.[31]

Does Workmen's Compensation Produce Undesirable Economic Effects?

According to Social Security Administration estimates, the cost to employers of workmen's compensation insurance (and self-insurance) is about 1.5 billion dollars a year, or about 1 per cent of their total payrolls. Since insurance can be provided more efficiently to larger companies, and since it will reflect safety records, premiums

---

[31] Stefan A. Riesenfeld, "Basic Problems in the Administration of Workmen's Compensation," *Minnesota Law Review*, XXXVI, No. 2 (January, 1952), 119–142.

may vary widely among individual employers. Moreover, in any given state, insurance costs will differ from employer to employer depending upon the degree of work hazards. In Wisconsin, for example, employers presently pay insurance premiums of 8 cents per $100 of payroll to insure clerical workers. They pay $18 per $100 of payroll to insure ice harvesters. Insurance costs vary from state to state, too, depending upon the benefit provisions of the law and the distribution of employments in a given area.

At the time workmen's compensation laws were first being enacted, a major opposing argument was that they would put home industry at a competitive disadvantage, deter location of industry within the state, and possibly even drive business firms away. Although all states have workmen's compensation laws today, the argument is still an important one in legislative debate over liberalization of the laws.

Do interstate cost differentials in fact produce such undesirable economic effects? It seems fairly well agreed that workmen's compensation costs at an average of 1 per cent of payrolls are not sufficiently significant to play an important role in location decisions or in competitive advantage—in the short run. Long-run effects, too, are probably exaggerated. Yet it must be recognized that along with other factors such as taxes, power resources, and labor, employers take workmen's compensation costs into account when deciding where to locate their firms.

A more serious economic effect on individual firms or industries as well as on their insurance carriers arises when workmen's compensation coverage is extended to heretofore noncompensable injuries. It is possible that the full cost impact of new claims would be assessed against the firm or industry in which the majority of claims arise. This possibility has been averted by rating procedures which spread these new costs in part throughout all employers in the state.

Another phase of workmen's compensation insurance costs—one which is not so wholly related to the benefit level and the distribution of industry—has raised questions about economic impact. That is, these costs seem to move countercyclically. With rising employment and prosperity, costs tend to go down; with declining levels of employment, they tend to rise. This movement is sometimes attributed to abuse of the system. It is argued that workers have an incentive to malinger when benefits may restore much of their lost earnings and when re-employment opportunities are few; and they may be helped in this process by dishonest physicians, who, during periods of economic decline, are willing to prolong treatment of compensation cases where payment is assured by the compensation system. Also, workers who are laid off may seek to gain compensation for injuries (real or feigned) incurred while they were employed.

There is some evidence that the system is sometimes abused.[32] But there are no data to show that this problem is a serious cost burden or that it is outside of administrative control.

Insurance costs are sometimes criticized as being excessive for the amount of benefits paid by workmen's compensation. The exact proportion of insurance premiums that reaches disabled workers is the subject of some disagreement. According to the National Council on Compensation Insurance,[33] 62.5 cents of every net premium dollar collected is paid out to workers in the form of indemnity and medical benefits. The CIO contends[34] that only 47 cents reaches the disabled worker.

More important than the fact of this difference, which is in part due to definition of losses and premium income, are the questions that it raises: Is workmen's compensation liability being insured efficiently? Or, more directly, do the acquisition and administrative costs of workmen's compensation put an unreasonable cost burden on this social insurance program? The choice of a stock or a mutual carrier may make some cost differences, but insurance authorities are inclined to minimize "legal-organizational structure" per se and to put more emphasis on an individual company's performance for such factors as service, financial strength, and record of cost allocation.[35]

The issue is made far more complex when the alternatives are private carriers on the one hand and state insurance on the other. For in addition to the difficulties of measuring the many variables involved (such as service to policyholders and claimants, safety engineering, and other components of insurance costs), ideological preferences tend to make the issue more a political one than an economic one. Private insurance, as we have seen earlier, is the dominant method by which workmen's compensation liabilities are insured today, although eleven jurisdictions offer the state fund

[32] See, in this connection, Joseph S. Keiper, *Forces That Spiral Workmen's Compensation Costs* (New York: Commerce and Industry Association of New York, 1953); and Henry H. Kessler, *Low Back Pain in Industry* (New York: Commerce and Industry Association of New York, 1955).

[33] *Annual Report*, National Council of Compensation Insurance, March 4, 1954, p. 6.

[34] *CIO Council Guidebook Series*, No. 1, p. 11.

[35] C. A. Kulp, *Casualty Insurance* (3d ed.; New York: The Ronald Press Co., 1956), chap. xv.

alternative, and eight have state insurance exclusively. If insurance premiums one day become a more significant precentage of payrolls, the issue will probably assume more significance, although it seems unlikely that it will ever be resolved with certainty on economic grounds alone.

Summary

The principle of liability without fault has more than proved its *utility* in the field of occupational disability. But problems have arisen out of the *application* of this principle. In some jurisdictions, the benefits and administration of workmen's compensation laws are adequate to the needs of an occupational disability program, but in others they are not. As a result, there are many workers today who would prefer to have their injury claims processed through the courts—who are convinced that the tort remedy available in the railroad field is superior to workmen's compensation. Compensation claimants' attorneys oppose extension of the compensation principle into the railroad, tort, or admiralty fields; indeed, despite all its drawbacks, court administration in some states is defended by trade union groups because of the higher awards being gained.

Lagging workmen's compensation benefits have made court awards in damage suits very attractive. Therefore, if all the objectives sought in workmen's compensation are to be gained more fully, widespread reform in the laws is indicated. Although trade unions have succeeded in negotiating supplemental benefits,[36] (discussed in Chapter 12), the tort alternative to providing adequate compensation to the occupationally disabled will remain attractive[37] until widespread reform is accomplished. Such reform is the objective of the "model bill" of the United States Department of Labor. It remains to be seen whether or not it will succeed in bringing those jurisdictions which have neglected their workmen's compensation programs up to "model" standards.

Suggestions for Additional Reading

DAWSON, MARSHALL. "Problems of Workmen's Compensation Administration in the United States and Canada," *Bulletin 672.* U. S. Department of Labor, Bureau of Labor Statistics, 1940.

[36] Duncan M. MacIntyre, "Workmen's Compensation and Private Benefit Programs," *Industrial and Labor Relations Review,* VII, No. 1 (October, 1953), 63–72.

[37] See Arthur J. Altmeyer, "The Future of Social Security in America," *Social Service Review,* XXVII, No. 3 (September, 1953), 251–68. Altmeyer makes the argument that a partial re-introduction of the tort remedy is necessary to overcome inadequacies in benefits.

Based on a field survey of Canadian and American jurisdictions, this study provides expert insight into the operating problems of workmen's compensation.

DODD, WALTER F. *Administration of Workmen's Compensation.* New York: The Commonwealth Fund, 1936.
Many of the generalizations and insights of this valuable book are important today to an understanding of workmen's compensation administration.

KULP, C. A. *Casualty Insurance,* 3d ed. New York: The Ronald Press Co., 1956. Chapters 5, 6, 7, 17, 18.
Chapter 6 is a good, brief discussion of workmen's compensation. The other chapters present the various aspects of workmen's compensation insurance and rate-making.

RIESENFELD, STEFAN A., and RICHARD C. MAXWELL. *Modern Social Legislation.* Brooklyn: The Foundation Press, 1950. Pp. 162–440.
A legal presentation of problems in benefits, coverage, and administration, including case materials.

SOMERS, HERMAN M., and ANNE RAMSAY SOMERS. *Workmen's Compensation.* New York: John Wiley and Sons, Inc., 1954. Chapters 3–8.
Comprehensive and up-to-date analysis of workmen's compensation. Excellent treatment of benefit adequacy, insurance, and rehabilitation.

11

Nonoccupational Illness
Problems

Introduction

The nature and importance of occupational injuries and disease and the legal responsibility of employers for them were discussed in the last two chapters. This chapter deals primarily with the economic problems created by nonoccupational accidental injuries and sickness (for which we here use the collective term "illness") and public approaches to their solution. Most of the public programs to be discussed will also pay benefits for job-connected illness, but these benefits will usually be offset by any workmen's compensation payments received.

We shall treat first the types of losses caused by nonoccupational accidental injuries and sickness, the probability of incurring such losses as revealed by three independent surveys, and the total costs of nonoccupational illnesses.

A general discussion of the various private and public methods of attacking the economic problems created by nonoccupational illnesses will be followed by a discussion of the arguments advanced for and against a more extensive social accidental injury and sickness insurance program.

Next we shall discuss in detail current public alleviative programs including special public assistance programs, limited disability provisions under OASI, and temporary disability insurance legislation.

Finally we shall consider the historical developments and present status of social medical expense insurance.

Losses Caused by Nonoccupational Accidental Injury and Sickness

As in the case of occupational illness discussed in Chapter 9, an accidental injury or sickness may cause a financial loss through loss of income and through medical expenses. The potential loss of income may be estimated in the manner outlined in Chapter 3 for computing the income loss caused by death, but the cost of maintenance should not be subtracted and the income loss may be partial or temporary. The income loss caused by total and permanent disability will exceed the income loss caused by death because the maintenance cost continues.

Medical expenses themselves take the form of hospital bills, physicians' and surgeons' charges, nurses' fees, medicines, and appliances. The possible variation in the amount of these expenses is great.

Probability of Loss

The probability of an accidental injury or sickness loss is much more difficult to state than the probability of death for at least three reasons.

First, it is relatively easy to tell whether a person has suffered an accidental injury, but it is almost impossible to determine whether certain individuals are sick. Some persons will claim that they are sick for various reasons, while apparently they are not. Others are sick, but they will not admit it.

Even if this problem did not exist, what is illness? Is a slight cold a sickness? Is a minor cut on a finger an accidental injury? Someone has stated that we are all ill; it is just a matter of degree. For statistical purposes it is necessary to draw a definitional line somewhere. Hence most statistical reports on accidental injury and sickness are concerned only with *disabling* illnesses. An illness is usually considered to be disabling if it prevents the individual from performing his regular activities for at least one day. Consequently, these studies exclude many illnesses. Most of the excluded cases are minor, but some are serious. Moreover, because of differences in character or occupation, the same illness may disable one person but not another, thus complicating the definitional problem.

Second, a person may be ill more than once during a year, and each illness may last for a different period. The probability structure would be a complex one to describe even if the exact probabilities were known. Furthermore, the economic loss depends not only upon the frequency and duration of the illness, but also upon its seriousness in terms of income loss and medical expenses.

Third, births, deaths, and certain illnesses are reported on a regular basis to public authorities, but most illnesses are not so reported. The imperfect data that are available are based upon special studies, and most of these studies are limited to certain groups of people, such as those residing within specified areas.

THREE STUDIES OF THE PROBABILITY OF LOSS

Three extensive studies have been made of these problems, however. The results are applicable to the general population or a large part of it. These studies include the report of the Committee on the Costs of Medical Care, the National Health Survey, and a recent study by the United States Public Health Service. The major findings of each study are presented below. The object of the presentation is not to show changes over time because the studies are not comparable. Our purpose is rather to emphasize the economic importance of illness, to present different types of relevant information, and to point out the dependence of the survey results upon the survey techniques. Both occupational and nonoccupational illnesses are included in these three surveys.

Committee on the Costs of Medical Care. The Committee on the Costs of Medical Care was established in 1929 to study the financial problems created by accidental injury and sickness. The results of its five years of research are still quoted widely, and it is considered by many to be the most accurate extensive report on the health of the nation.

The committee studied each of 8,758 families in seventeen states and the District of Columbia for twelve consecutive months. The survey covered the period 1928–1931, since not all the families were surveyed for the same twelve months. Parts of the survey were based upon the experience of 11,500 families. Certain sections of the country were not included in the analysis, but the data are considered to be fairly representative of the health situation of white families in the United States.[1]

In this survey a person was considered to be ill if he was totally or partially disabled for at least one day or if he received medical attention of any kind. If his only medical expense was medicine and

[1] For a more complete discussion of the committee's study, see I. S. Falk, M. C. Klem and N. Sinai, *The Incidence of Illness and the Receipts and Costs of Medical Care among Representative Family Groups* (Chicago: University of Chicago Press, 1933).

he was not disabled, he was considered to be ill if he spent at least 50 cents on the medicine. This is a fairly liberal definition of illness. According to the committee's data, during any year

47 per cent of the population will not be ill,
32 per cent will be ill once,
14 per cent will be ill twice,
5 per cent will be ill three times, and
2 per cent will be ill four or more times.

The average number of illnesses per person per year is approximately .84.

Among those who become ill, 52 per cent will be disabled. Among those who are disabled,

42 per cent will be disabled from one to five days,
46 per cent will be disabled from six to 25 days,
9 per cent will be disabled from 26 to 75 days,
2 per cent will be disabled from 76 to 349 days, and
1 per cent will be disabled 350 days or longer.

The average number of days lost per disability is approximately sixteen.

We may conclude from this survey that most of the population will either suffer no loss or a small loss in a given year, but a large number of families will suffer substantial losses.

National Health Survey. The most extensive survey in terms of the number of families interviewed is the National Health Survey. During the winter of 1935–1936, interviewers visited 703,092 urban households in eighteen states.[2] Certain limitations in the survey procedure and the period of the year in which the survey was conducted may make it dangerous to generalize on the basis of the information collected, but the study did provide us with much detailed information on the health status of the large group studied. It is the most frequently quoted study today.[3]

This survey attempted to find out how many persons were disabled, not how many were ill. A person was considered to be dis-

---

[2] Interviewers also visited 36,801 households in rural areas in three states, but the results of these interviews are less meaningful.

[3] For more details on the study, see U. S. Public Health Service, *Illness and Medical Care Among 2,500,000 Persons in 83 Cities, with Special Reference to Socio-Economic Factors* (Washington, D. C.: U. S. Government Printing Office, 1945).

For an excellent critical analysis of this survey and that conducted by the Committee on the Costs of Medical Care, see George W. Bachman and Lewis Meriam, *The Issue of Compulsory Health Insurance* (Washington, D. C.: The Brookings Institution, 1948), chap. vi.

abled if he was suffering from a sickness, accidental injury, or impairment that kept him from his work, school, domestic duties, or other activities.

The National Health Survey showed that 4.4 per cent of the urban population was disabled on the day of the visit. About 1.2 per cent had been disabled for the whole twelve months preceding the visit.

During the preceding year, 17.1 per cent had suffered a disabling illness of one week or more. About three-tenths of these illness had been chronic; that is, the disease symptoms had been observed for at least three months preceding the visit of the interviewer. Seventenths of the illnesses were acute.

The average duration of the disabling illnesses lasting for at least seven days was 58 days. The acute cases had an average duration of only 21 days, but the chronic cases lasted, on the average, 154 days.

The importance of the distinction between disability and illness is made clear by the fact that although only 4.4 per cent of the population was disabled, on the day of the visit, 17.7 per cent reported a chronic disease or impairment.

The National Health Survey leads to the same major conclusion as the report of the Committee on the Costs of Medical Care. Accidental injury and sickness are extremely important economic insecurities.

Population survey of 1949–50. The most recent estimates of the prevalence of disabling illness in the United States are based upon two surveys conducted by the Public Health Service, the Social Security Administration, and the Office of Vocational Rehabilitation.[4] Twenty-five thousand households were interviewed in February, 1949, and another 25,000 in September, 1950. The surveys covered the civilian noninstitutional population, fourteen to sixty-four years of age.

In this survey, a person was assumed to be disabled if he was prevented from doing his regular work or performing other duties on the day of the interview or if he had been able to work only occasionally.

The survey revealed that 4.19 per cent of the civilian noninstitutional population, aged fourteen to sixty-four, were disabled; 4.72

[4] Theodore D. Woolsey, "Estimates of Disabling Illness Prevalence in the United States," *Public Health Monograph 4, U. S. Public Health Service Publication 181* (Washington, D. C.: U. S. Government Printing Office, August, 1952).

per cent were disabled in the February survey and 3.67 per cent in the September survey.

In the February survey

25 per cent were disabled for one week or less,

24 per cent were disabled for over one week, but not over three months,

14 per cent were disabled for over three months, but not over one year, and

37 per cent were disabled for over one year.

The corresponding figures in the September survey were 18 per cent, 21 per cent, 15 per cent, and 46 per cent. The differences are due primarily to the high frequency of minor respiratory aliments during the winter months.

The Social Security Administration in a recent report[5] based largely upon the 1949–50 surveys estimated that on an average day in 1954 approximately 2.9 million persons, aged fourteen to sixty-four, had been disabled for six months or more. Including children under fourteen and persons aged sixty-five and over increased the estimate to 5.3 million or about 3.3 per cent of the total civilian population in the United States. About 4.1 million of these disabled persons were in the civilian noninstitutional population, and 1.2 million were in institutions.

These more recent estimates reinforce the findings of the earlier surveys.

FACTORS CAUSING VARIATION IN THE PREVALENCE OF ILLNESS

The prevalence of illness depends upon age, sex, race, income, employment status, residence, marital status, and the season of the year. The findings of these three studies and others of the same general nature are not always in agreement on the effects of these factors, but the more common findings are enumerated below.

1. The very young and the aged are ill more often than the average person and the illnesses of the aged are of much longer duration, but age is a relatively unimportant factor for persons aged twenty to fifty. The probability of a *long-term* illness, however, increases markedly as a person ages.

2. Females are more likely to be ill than males, but they are less likely to be disabled for long periods of time.

3. Disabling illnesses of all durations are more common among nonwhites than whites.

[5] See "Estimated Prevalence of Long-Term Disability, 1954," *Social Security Bulletin*, XVIII, No. 6 (June, 1955), 20–21.

4. Low-income groups suffer more frequent and more serious illnesses than the middle- and upper-income groups, but otherwise income does not appear to be an important factor.
5. Employed persons are, on the average, a much healthier group than the unemployed. Certain occupations are more hazardous than others, while some are associated with undesirable moral and economic characteristics.
6. The effect of a rural or urban residence upon the probability of illness is not clear, but the urban group appears to be more healthy.
7. Unmarried persons are more likely to be ill than married persons, especially at the older ages.
8. Illness is much more common in the winter than in the summer, primarily on account of the numerous short-term illnesses in the winter caused by mild respiratory diseases.

Causes of Illness

According to the National Health Survey, the six leading causes of illnesses disabling for a week or more and the per cent of disabling illness caused by them are as follows:[6]

Respiratory diseases	30 per cent
Communicable diseases	17 per cent
Accidental injuries	9 per cent
Confinements	9 per cent
Degenerative diseases	9 per cent
Digestive diseases	8 per cent

Fortunately the causes of long-term disability are among the less frequent causes of illness. The National Health Survey indicated that the following caused the longest average periods of disability.[7]

Orthopedic impairments	344 days
Tuberculosis	246 days
Nervous and mental diseases	189 days
Cardiovascular-renal diseases	122 days
Rheumatism and allied diseases	120 days
Cancer and other tumors	100 days

Note that sickness is about ten times more likely than an accidental injury to be the cause of illness. Among the accidental injuries, only about one-quarter are occupational injuries. Nonoccupational illness is clearly a much more important problem than occupational illness.

[6] Bachman and Meriam, *op. cit.*, p. 259.
[7] *Ibid.*, p. 156.

Total Costs of Nonoccupational Illness

The Social Security Administration makes periodic estimates of (1) the aggregate loss of earning power due to temporary non-occupational disability and (2) private expenditures for medical care.[8]

Temporary nonoccupational disability includes all disabilities lasting six months or less and the initial six months of disabilities which last longer. It is estimated that this form of disability causes the average worker to lose seven working days a year. On this basis, the estimated income loss due to nonoccupational short-term illness in 1954 was $6.2 billion.

It has also been estimated that temporary nonoccupational disability is responsible for about one-fifth of the nonoccupational disability income losses, partial disability accounting for about one-half and long-term total disability losses for the remainder.[9] If this estimate is correct, the total nonoccupational disability income loss in 1954 was about $31 billion.

Personal expenditures for medical care in 1954 totaled about $10 billion.[10] Of this, about 31 per cent was incurred for hospital services, another 31 per cent for physicians' services, 10 per cent for dentists' services, 6 per cent for other professional services, and 23 per cent for medicines and appliances.

Thus the total personal cost of nonoccupational illnesses in 1954 was estimated at about $41 billion, or $670 per employed person. The aggregate loss to the economy is much greater because of the many indirect effects, such as decreased efficiency and the private nonpersonal and public expenditures for medical care. The uneven incidence of illness among families intensifies the problem.

Methods of Attacking the Problems of Illness

The methods used to attack the problems created by nonoccupational accidental injuries and sicknesses are preventive and alleviative, both private and public.

[8] Social Security Bulletins, January and February, 1950; December of 1951, 1952, 1953, 1954, and 1955; and January, 1956.

[9] Commission on Health Needs of the Nation, Building America's Health, IV, (Washington, D. C.: U. S. Government Printing Office, 1952), 303. The complete report of five volumes summarizes the statistical findings of many studies.

[10] For a discussion of the limitations of this estimate, see Oscar N. Serbein, Paying for Medical Care in the United States (New York: Columbia University Press, 1953), pp. 47–52.

PREVENTIVE EFFORTS

The methods used to prevent premature death also help to reduce the number and duration of accidental injuries and sicknesses. Since these methods were discussed in Chapter 3, they need not be reconsidered here. One preventive method which was not discussed in Chapter 3, but which reduces the wage loss due to permanent disability, is vocational rehabilitation. Individuals, private nonprofit agencies, insurers, employers, unions, and government have all been active in this area, as has been indicated in Chapter 10. Further expansion of these activities is needed and can be expected.

ALLEVIATIVE METHODS

The increasing industrialization of our society and the loosening of family ties have had an even greater effect upon the role of the sick and injured than they have had upon the dependents of deceased persons and the aged. The sick and injured can seldom be absorbed easily into some relative's household. They must either assume the loss themselves, collect insurance payments, or accept aid from outside sources.

Self-assumption is the most economical and most satisfactory way to meet losses which are small relative to the person's income, but insurance or outside aid is essential when the economic impact of the illness is a serious one. Thus, for the lower income groups, such aid is generally needed.

Voluntary private insurance is, by far, the most important private method of alleviating the financial burden of nonoccupational illness. This method will be considered in detail in the next chapter.

Public alleviative methods have been limited until recently to public assistance programs based upon need, the provision of medical facilities to deal with certain illnesses such as tuberculosis and mental disease, and programs benefiting special groups such as the armed services, veterans, Indians, and prison inmates.[11] Until the 1954 authorization of the OASI disability "freeze" and the 1956 addition of limited OASI disability income payments, the only general social accidental injury and sickness insurance program was the temporary disability insurance legislation in four states.

Few people disagree with the principle of subsidizing certain groups of the population on the basis of need, but there has been

[11] For an excellent discussion of federal, state, and local government activities in providing medical care, see *Ibid.*, chaps. xix–xxv.

considerable opposition to the inclusion of accidental injury and sickness in our social insurance system. That this opposition has been successful for the most part is evidenced by the statements of the preceding paragraph. However, the proponents of social accidental injury and sickness insurance have scored important victories with the recent OASI changes.

ARGUMENTS FOR SOCIAL ILLNESS INSURANCE

The major arguments presented by various groups in favor of an extensive social accidental injury and sickness insurance program providing disability income *and* medical expense benefits are the following:[12]

1. The need is great. Many families cannot afford the average cost of illness; most families cannot afford a serious loss.

2. Benefits should be granted as a matter of right instead of on the basis of need. The acceptance of charity is degrading.

3. Our social insurance system provides a floor of protection against the economic problems caused by premature death and old age. Why is the financial protection against accidental injury and sickness losses so limited?

4. Private insurance is inadequate. Not all persons are eligible; the cost is too high because of the high costs of administration; and the benefits are limited.

5. Adequate medical expense insurance could encourage insureds to take advantage of preventive medicine, thus reducing the total costs of illness through early diagnosis and care.

6. The total cost of illness would not be increased; the cost would simply be redistributed in such a way that those better able to bear the cost would pay a larger share of the total cost.

7. Freedom of choice of doctors would not be affected by the introduction of social medical expense insurance. Medical care would be improved because financial barriers would not prevent the physician from giving each person the best possible care. Adequate service would be available in all sections of the country.

8. The medical profession would gain in many ways. It would have the inner satisfaction associated with doing a better job; its skill would increase because cases would be studied more intensely; and financial considerations would be less important in determining where doctors practice.

---

[12] For a detailed discussion of the arguments for and against the adoption of a social insurance program providing medical expense benefits, see Domenico Gagliardo, *American Social Insurance* (rev. ed.; New York: Harper and Bros., 1955), chap. xix. Also see the reports on the many hearings before Congress on this subject.

Arguments Against Social Illness Insurance

The major arguments presented in opposition to social accidental injury and sickness insurance are the following:

1. Most families can bear the average cost of illness if they are willing to budget as much for this item as for items such as alcohol and tobacco. The remainder should be frankly subsidized. The public assistance programs and increased emphasis on rehabilitation are the best ways to handle this problem.

2. When benefits are granted as a matter of right, it is difficult to deny them. Old age, premature death, and unemployment losses are definite in time and place, but it is difficult to determine whether a person qualifies for illness benefits. In periods of unemployment, illness benefits, especially loss-of-income benefits, are subject to great abuse. The private insurance companies discovered this in the thirties. Since administrative discretion is involved, political factors may enter into the decision. Even if the insurance is initially written under very strict terms, there will be constant pressure to liberalize the qualifications and benefits.

3. Private insurance protection is becoming more widespread each year. At the close of 1941, less than twenty-million persons had hospital expense protection and less than ten million had surgical or physicians' care expense insurance. At the close of 1955, more than 100 million had hospital expense protection; about ninety million had surgical expense protection; and over fifty million had protection against the expenses of a physician's care. New forms of insurance providing protection against long-term illness have been developed, and more of the substandard lives are becoming eligible for coverage. Admittedly, private insurance will never cover everyone, but the ineligibles will be a small number and they can be cared for through a public assistance program.

4. Preventive medicine is useful, but prevention is largely a matter of education, and its effectiveness should not be overestimated.

5. The cost of illness would increase. Medical facilities would be overutilized and claimed disability would increase.

6. Freedom of choice of doctors would be restricted. Unless there was a limit to the number of patients that a doctor would serve, the time he would be able to spend on each patient would be very short. Medical care would deteriorate because doctors would lose incentive and personal interest in their patients. The doctors would become cogs in a bureaucratic machine.

7. The medical profession would lose the dignity and respect associated with individual freedom. Their work would become less enjoyable and less rewarding.

An Opinion

Certainly, accidental injury and sickness protection deserves a more important position in our public economic security system.

There is merit to an extensive social accidental injury and sickness *insurance* program, but there are underwriting problems, possible adverse effects on the medical profession, and possible loss of freedom of choice of medical facilities.

As an initial step, a more adequate public assistance program should be created to help those persons who are indigent or medically indigent. This program should pay medical expenses and provide an income for the disabled.[13]

Eventually, disability income protection under OASI should be extended to the point where it will provide a floor of protection against all serious disability income losses. However, because of the underwriting problems involved, the present limited protection should be extended gradually, and each extension should be carefully planned.[14]

The authors are, bluntly, uncertain about the desirability of social medical expense insurance. Because of the impressive improvement in private insurance protection including employer, union, and collectively bargained plans, and the possible adverse effects of a social insurance program, they favor a "wait and see" attitude in this area.

Current Public Alleviative Approaches

The most important public assistance and social insurance programs include the public assistance plans providing aid to the blind and the totally and permanently disabled, the disability freeze and disability income protection provided under OASI, and temporary disability insurance legislation in four states.

PUBLIC ASSISTANCE PROGRAMS

The public assistance programs providing old-age assistance and aid to dependent children were discussed in Chapter 4. The aid-to-dependent-children programs provide some protection against accidental injury and sickness, since physical or mental incapacity of the parent may be the reason for the dependency. Furthermore, under both programs, medical care allowances may be included in the cash payments, or there may be direct payments to vendors of medical services such as doctors and nursing homes. In fact, in 1955 about 7 per cent of the total payments under the old-age assistance

13 For further comments, see page 307. Also see Chapter 18 for additional discussion of public assistance programs.
14 For further comments, see page 310.

plans and 3 per cent of the payments under the aid-to-dependent-children plans were vendor payments for medical care.

In 1956, Congress authorized the separate matching of assistance expenditures for medical care under the special public assistance programs. Consequently, vendor payments may be expected to increase in the future. Effective July 1, 1957, the federal government will pay one-half of the first $6 of the average monthly expenditure per old-age assistance recipient in the form of medical or other remedial care, including expenditures for insurance premiums for such care or the cost thereof. The *total* grant-in-aid under the aid-to-dependent-children plans will be one-half the monthly expenditures not counting the amount by which these expenditures exceed 3 times the number of child recipients plus 6 times the number of adult recipients.

Two additional special public assistance programs—Aid to the Blind and Aid to the Totally and Permanently Disabled—are devoted solely to the problems of accidental injury and sickness. Aid-to-the-blind plans became effective at about the same time as those providing old-age assistance and aid to dependent children, but plans providing aid to the totally and permanently disabled were not enacted until 1950 when federal grants-in-aid were authorized for the first time.

Plans providing aid to the blind. All states have plans providing aid to the blind which have been approved under the Social Security Act. The requirements for federal approval are essentially the same as those established for old-age assistance plans.

Over half the plans have no age requirement, the minimum ages under the other plans being sixteen, eighteen, or twenty-one. Almost nine-tenths of the plans have no citizenship requirement. About one fourth of the plans use the residence requirement established by the federal government for approval, but almost one-half simply require that the person be a resident of the state for one year preceding his application for benefits. Approximately one-sixth of the states have no residence requirement. Four-fifths of the plans have specific property requirements of various types; the other one-fifth simply consider property in determining eligibility. A need for assistance is generally presumed to exist if the income or other resources are insufficient to provide a reasonable subsistence compatible with decency and health. About one-third of the plans have legal maximum benefits, and one-third have no maximum benefits. Almost all the maximum payments equal or exceed the federal matching maximum. Usually there is no provision for recovery of the amounts paid, but under many plans the state has a claim against the estate.

The federal government computes its share of the expenditures under the aid-to-the-blind programs in the same way that it determines the amount that it will contribute to approved state programs providing assistance to the aged. In 1957, separate matching of assistance expenditures for medical care will begin on the same basis as under the old-age assistance programs.

Like the old-age programs, the aid-to-the-blind plans have been liberalized from time to time. It is easier to qualify for a benefit now than it was in the thirties, and the benefits are more adequate.

Plans providing aid to the totally and permanently disabled. Forty-five states have federally approved plans providing aid to the totally and permanently disabled. In order to be approved, these programs must satisfy essentially the same requirements as the aid-to-the-blind programs. The disability assistance programs are of special interest because of their recent addition to the group of special public assistance plans.

All plans have a minimum age requirement of eighteen years; about half also have a maximum age requirement of sixty-five. A person under eighteen is assumed not to have suffered an income loss, while a person over sixty-five may be eligible for old-age assistance. More than nine-tenths of the plans have no citizenship requirement. About six-tenths of the plans have a durational residence requirement of one year preceding the date of application, while over one-tenth have no requirement. All plans take income and property into account in determining the need for assistance, with about four-fifths of the plans having specific property limitations. Administrative maximum benefits, legal maximum benefits, and no maximum benefits are each found in about one-third of the plans. Only about one-fifth of these maximum payments are less than the federal matching maximum. Most plans do not provide for recovery of the amounts paid, but often the total assistance constitutes a claim against the estate of the recipient.

The federal government's contribution to these programs is computed in the same way as under the aid-to-the-blind programs. Separate matching of expenditures for medical care will begin in July, 1957.

The federal grants have been increased and the disability programs considerably liberalized in the short time the plans have been in existence.

Operations. The operations of these two programs are summarized in Table 11.1. The number of recipients of aid to the blind has increased slowly but steadily except during World War II when blind persons re-entered active employment in large numbers. Recipients of aid to the totally and permanently disabled have more than quadrupled in the six years that such aid has been available. The average monthly benefits under both programs have increased as the cost of living rose and the plans became more liberal.

TABLE 11.1

ASSISTANCE PROGRAMS PROVIDING AID TO THE BLIND AND THE
TOTALLY AND PERMANENTLY DISABLED: RECIPIENTS, TOTAL
PAYMENTS, AND AVERAGE MONTHLY PAYMENTS, BY PROGRAM,
1936–1955

(Includes Payments for Medical Care)

Year	Recipients (in thousands)		Total Payments (in thousands)		Average Monthly Payment	
	Aid to the blind	Aid to the totally and permanently disabled	Aid to the blind	Aid to the totally and permanently disabled	Aid to the blind	Aid to the totally and permanently disabled
1936	45	—	$12,813	——	$26.11	——
1937	56	—	16,171	——	27.20	——
1938	67	—	18,958	——	25.22	——
1939	70	—	20,752	——	25.44	——
1940	73	—	21,826	——	25.38	——
1941	77	—	22,901	——	25.82	——
1942	79	—	24,660	——	26.54	——
1943	76	—	25,143	——	27.95	——
1944	72	—	25,342	——	29.31	——
1945	71	—	26,557	——	33.52	——
1946	77	—	30,748	——	36.67	——
1947	81	—	36,353	——	39.58	——
1948	86	—	41,382	——	43.54	——
1949	93	—	48,532	——	46.11	——
1950	98	69	52,866	$ 8,129	46.56	$45.41
1951	97	127	55,507	57,937	49.05	49.46
1952	99	164	61,324	90,945	54.91	53.50
1953	100	195	65,748	115,441	55.67	53.44
1954	102	224	67,830	137,100	56.37	54.93
1955	105	244	71,127	156,456	58.09	56.18

Source: *Social Security Bulletin, Annual Statistical Supplement,* 1955, p. 49.

About 4 per cent of the total payments under the aid-to-the-blind plans in 1955 were vendor payments for medical care, while about 14 per cent of the total payments under the plans providing aid to the totally and permanently disabled were used for this purpose. Vendor payments will increase after the new separate matching program begins.

The number of recipients and, to a lesser extent, the total cash payments under both programs should increase less rapidly in the future and may eventually decrease because (1) disability benefits have been added to OASI and (2) part of the past increase in the number of totally and permanently disabled recipients has been caused by the adoption of new state programs and a backlog of eligible cases.

In June, 1956, the number of recipients of aid to the totally and permanently disabled was 3.4 per 1,000 population aged eighteen to sixty-four. This proportion ranged from .6 per 1,000 in Michigan and Wisconsin to 9.0 per 1,000 in Louisiana (20.7 in Puerto Rico and 9.8 in the Virgin Islands). Differences in economic status, the date the plan became effective, and the provisions in the plan are the primary reasons for the variations among the states.

The June, 1956, average monthly payments under the aid-to-the-blind programs ranged from $32.44 in West Virginia ($7.85 in Puerto Rico) to $103.27 in Massachusetts. Under the programs providing aid to the totally and permanently disabled, the average monthly payments varied between $24.59 in Mississippi ($8.62 in Puerto Rico and $19.47 in the Virgin Islands) and $118.42 in Connecticut.

In 1955 the federal government paid about half the costs of these two programs. The federal government's share of the expenditures for the aid-to-the-blind plans ranged from 33.2 per cent in Pennsylvania to 72.2 per cent in West Virginia. Its share of the cost of the aid-to-the-totally-and-permanently-disabled plans ranged from 33.0 per cent in Connecticut to 75.5 per cent in Mississippi.

Evaluation. The public assistance programs providing aid to the aged and dependent children were evaluated in Chapter 4, which should be reread because the remarks apply to all public assistance programs. Two additional observations apply to the two programs discussed in this chapter.

The blind have been singled out for separate and more liberal treatment than the totally and permanently disabled persons who are not blind. In part this is due to the more objective tests that are possible; in part it is due to the prevailing attitude in our country toward the blind. In fairness to the other groups, we should explore the possibility of absorbing the aid-to-the-blind programs into those for the totally and permanently disabled.

Many needy persons who suffer an income loss due to disability, medical expenses, or both, are not eligible for benefits under these programs. A more equitable approach would be (1) the extension of the eligibility requirements under these special public assistance programs to include more bona fide cases of disability and (2) the provision of medical expense benefits for the indigent and the medically indigent. However, this extended program would have to be strictly administered, so as to prevent abuses and accomplish its purpose.

OASI DISABILITY BENEFITS

Disability benefits were included under the Old-Age and Survivors Insurance System for the first time in 1954 and extended in 1956, although many persons had advocated their inclusion as early as the thirties. The disability benefits are the disability freeze, disability income payments beginning at age fifty, and income payments for disabled children.

Disability freeze. In order to qualify for the disability freeze benefit, a person must (1) be currently insured and (2) have at least twenty quarters of coverage out of the last forty quarters, including the quarter in which he becomes disabled. The second requirement makes its more difficult to qualify for disability benefits than survivorship benefits and thus reduces the cost of the program. A person is considered to be totally and permanently disabled if (1) he has been unable to engage in any substantially gainful activity because of a physical or mental impairment for at least six full consecutive months and (2) this impairment is expected to result in death or continue for a long indefinite period. Blindness is assumed to cause total and permanent disability.

The disability freeze benefit protects a fully or currently insured worker against losing this status or having his benefit reduced as a result of total and permanent disability. If any part of a calendar quarter falls in a period of disability, that quarter is not counted in determining whether a person is fully or currently insured. However, for years after 1950, the first and last quarter of the period of disability may be counted if they improve the worker's status. For years prior to 1951, only the first quarter may be counted. In computing the average monthly wage, earnings and months in any calendar *year*, any part of which was included in a period of disability, are not counted. However, the earnings and months in the year in which the disability began may be counted if the primary insurance amount is increased as a result. (Prior to the 1956 amendments, calendar *quarters* falling in a period of disability were excluded except that the quarters which were quarters of coverage were included.) The period of disability ends on the last day of the month in which the worker reaches age sixty-five or recovers from his disability.

For example, assume that a person reaches age sixty-five in February, 1966. In order to be fully insured on that date, he must have thirty quarters of coverage or one-half the number of quarters between December 31, 1950, and January 1, 1966. If this person had worked in covered employment from 1952 on and had earned four quarters of coverage each year, but became totally and permanently disabled on January 1, 1958, he would have earned only twenty-four quarters of coverage. If it were not for the disability freeze, he would not be entitled to any retirement benefits. Because of the freeze, he is entitled to these benefits, since the quarters between December 31, 1957, and January 1, 1966, do not count as elapsed time. He has twenty-four quarters of coverage out of the twenty-eight quarters which have elapsed. Moreover, because of the freeze, the average monthly wage will be computed on the basis of the earnings and the number of months between December 31, 1950, and January 1, 1958.

The disability freeze affects benefits payable on or after July 1, 1955. If the application for benefits is filed before July 1, 1957, the period of disability is assumed to have begun on the first day of disability. This rule made it possible for many disabled persons who had lost their fully insured status to become eligible for retirement benefits on July 1, 1955, while others received larger checks because their average monthly wage was increased. The benefits available to those filing applications on July 1, 1957, or later will be much less liberal, since the period of disability will never be assumed to have begun more than one year prior to the date of application for benefits. It is assumed that by that time there should be no excuse for failure to file an application within a year. It is difficult to determine whether the claim is a proper one if more than a year has elapsed.[15]

Disability income payments beginning at age fifty. In order to qualify for disability income payments beginning at age fifty or six months after the beginning of the disability, whichever comes later, the person must satisfy the eligibility requirements for the disability

---

[15] If a person is disabled but is unable to qualify for the disability freeze, the drop-out provisions discussed in Chapter 4 may help him to reduce the loss of benefits caused by his disability.

freeze and, in addition to this, must be fully insured. Blindness is not, however, *assumed* to cause total and permanent disability. The monthly payments are equal in amount to the primary insurance amount to which the person would be entitled if he were sixty-five years of age. The payments stop at age sixty-five when the person qualifies for retirement benefits.

The first month for which disability income payments will be made is July, 1957. After December, 1957, no payments will be made for any month before the person applies for benefits.

Income payments to disabled children. If a child has been totally and permanently disabled since before he reached eighteen, is unmarried, and either (1) is dependent upon a parent, step-parent, or adopting parent who is entitled to OASI retirement benefits or (2) was dependent upon a parent who died after 1939 and was entitled to OASI survivorship benefits, he may receive the appropriate OASI child's insurance benefit even though he may be now eighteen years of age or more.

For example, a fully insured worker, aged thirty-two, has a son, aged six, who is totally and permanently disabled. If the worker should die during the next year, the mother and son would receive survivorship benefits until the son reached eighteen. Because of the disability provisions, the son's benefit would then be continued for life and the mother's benefit would be continued as long as he remained in her care. On the other hand, if the father should live to age sixty-five, the son would receive a child's benefit at that time, although he would then be thirty-nine years of age. There would also be a mother's benefit if the child was in her care.

The first month in which disabled children's benefits were payable was January, 1957.

The amount of all OASI disability income payments is reduced by the amount of any other federal disability benefit or workmen's compensation benefit.

The costs of these disability benefits are paid out of the OASI payroll tax on employers, employees, and the self-employed. To meet the costs, the tax rates for employers and employees were increased, effective 1957, by ¼ per cent. The tax increase for self-employed persons was ⅜ per cent. A federal Disability Insurance Trust Fund was created into which these tax increases are appropriated and from which the disability income benefits for workers, aged 50 and over, are paid. The federal Disability Insurance Trust Fund operates in essentially the same fashion as the federal OASI Trust Fund discussed in Chapter 4. Note, however, that the tax rate is not scheduled to increase.

The most important problem in the administration of the disability benefits is determining when a person is totally and permanently disabled. The Department of Health, Education, and Welfare either makes the disability determination itself or, more commonly, makes an agreement with a state agency to do the work for it. In either case, the standards are set by the Department of Health, Education, and Welfare to promote uniformity among the states. State agencies administering vocational rehabilitation programs are specifically mentioned in the law because Congress and the President wanted to encourage greater efforts in the field of rehabilitation.[16] However, other agencies such as those administering workmen's compensation and nonoccupational disability insurance programs may also be used. It is assumed that these agencies have had more experience in this area than the federal agency. If a state agency is used, the case may be appealed to the Secretary. Decisions by the Secretary may be appealed to the federal courts.

EVALUATION

Objections are few to the inclusion of the disability freeze benefits under OASI, but many persons were and are still strongly opposed to the addition of disability income benefits. Others feel that the benefits are too limited.

Because these benefits have been made available so recently, it is too early to discuss trends in the operations of the benefits. Moreover, it is difficult to evaluate the benefits fairly. There is no doubt that these benefits represent an important addition to the OASI System, but it is also clear that the system still does not provide a floor of protection against all serious disability income losses. The age at which the benefits begin is too high and the definition of disability is too severe. However, as an initial step, the benefits appear to be adequate.

Temporary Disability Insurance Legislation

HISTORICAL DEVELOPMENT

Only four states—Rhode Island, California, New Jersey, and New York—have laws providing cash payments for employees who are *temporarily* disabled because of an accidental injury or sickness. This legislation is aimed *primarily* at the economic problems associated with *nonoccupational* illnesses; but three of the laws pay benefits in certain cases *when the illness is job-connected*; here the

---

[16] In fact, benefits are withheld if an applicant refuses without good cause to accept rehabilitation services offered by a state rehabilitation agency.

subject matter might have been discussed in the last two chapters were it not for complexities of presentation.

The basic emphasis is different, however, from both unemployment and workmen's compensation. The latter is an economic security program providing protection against *job-connected* illness. The former, through its "able to work" and "available for work" requirements provides indemnification for the *healthy* person who is unemployed.

Rhode Island adopted the first law of this type in 1942. California passed its act in 1946, New Jersey in 1948, and New York in 1949. Interest in this type of legislation dates back, however, to the 1915–1920 era when workmen's compensation was being introduced.[17] Bills advocating the passage of temporary disability income legislation were debated in many states, but none passed. During the twenties, interest in the subject waned.

The depression years saw a renewal of interest in this type of coverage, and many persons felt that temporary disability insurance should be provided under the Social Security Act. The problems of unemployment and old-age seemed much more important at the time, however, and the opposition to the inclusion of any form of accidental injury and sickness insurance was strong. As a result, the Act as passed contained no reference to disability insurance.

However, the Committee on Economic Security in its deliberations considered the matter of accidental injury and sickness insurance and suggested further study of this problem. It pointed out that it might be desirable to coordinate unemployment insurance and temporary disability insurance. A similar recommendation was made in 1939 by the President's Interdepartmental Committee to Coordinate Health and Welfare Activities.

In 1939 the late Senator Robert Wagner introduced a bill which provided, among other things, for federal grants-in-aid to states having approved temporary disability insurance legislation. The bill was not reported out of the Senate Committee on Education and Labor, but it received much publicity, and many states began to study the problem seriously.

Most of those who favored the passage of temporary disability insurance legislation felt that this insurance should be combined with unemployment insurance for several reasons. First, unemployment insurance provides protection against loss of income due to lack of work but not due to disability. Therefore, temporary dis-

17 Alfred M. Skolnick, "Temporary Disability Insurance Laws in the United States," *Social Security Bulletin*, XV, No. 10 (October, 1952), 11–24. Much of the material which follows is based upon this article.

ability insurance is a natural extension of unemployment insurance. Furthermore, the two systems should be related because it is logical to continue the checks of an unemployed person on the same basis if he becomes disabled after the date of unemployment. Second, some states had required employees to contribute to the cost of unemployment insurance and had discovered that these taxes were not necessary. In these states the cost of temporary disability income insurance could be met through the diversion of part or all of an existing tax instead of through the imposition of a new tax. And third, administrative expenses would be reduced if the two programs were integrated.

For these reasons, Rhode Island, California, and New Jersey patterned their temporary disability insurance plans along the lines of their unemployment insurance plans. Six other states—Idaho, Maryland, Montana, Nevada, Tennessee, and Vermont—did not pass temporary disability income legislation, but they amended their unemployment insurance laws as a partial solution to the problem. The amended laws provided that unemployment insurance benefits would not be terminated simply because an unemployed worker was disabled after he had filed his claim and registered for work.

Washington passed a temporary disability insurance law in 1949, which was similar to those in New Jersey and California, but it was defeated in a public referendum in 1950.

New York, on the other hand, passed a law patterned after its workmen's compensation act. Those who favored this approach argued that temporary disability is more closely related to occupational disability than to unemployment. Furthermore, since New York employees did not contribute to the cost of unemployment insurance, a new tax would be required in any event. Consequently, there were no financial advantages to be gained by relating temporary disability insurance to unemployment insurance. Finally, unemployment insurance is strictly a government operation, while workmen's compensation insurance may be underwritten by commercial insurers and the New York legislators preferred to have these insurers participate.

The opposition to temporary disability insurance legislation maintains that such legislation reduces the responsibility and freedom of choice of the individual; creates additional tax needs through extra administrative expenses; and is unnecessary because of the important advances in private insurance protection.

Since 1939, over half the state legislatures have debated the merits of temporary disability insurance legislation, but only four states have laws. No state has passed an act of this type since 1949, but the debates continue. In 1955 temporary disability insurance legislation was introduced in thirteen state legislatures.

We shall now summarize the coverage, the qualifications for benefits, the benefits, the financing, and the administration of the four existing state plans.

CONTENT OF THE LAWS[18]

Coverage. The employments covered under the Rhode Island, California, and New Jersey acts are the same as those covered under their unemployment insurance acts except that individual workers can elect not to be covered on religious grounds. The employments covered under the New York act are not the same as those covered under the Unemployment Insurance Act or the Workmen's Compensation Act.

The types of employees excluded under all four laws are agricultural laborers, railroad workers, government employees, and employees of nonprofit institutions. Domestic employees are excluded under all acts other than that of New York.

The New Jersey and New York laws also exclude service for persons who do not employ four or more workers for more than twenty weeks in New Jersey and thirty days in New York. The California law also excludes service for persons whose quarterly payroll is less than $100.

Qualifications for benefits. In addition to working in covered employment, a person must satisfy the following types of requirements:

1. *Qualifying wages.* In Rhode Island a worker must have earned at least thirty times his weekly benefit amount in the base period, which is the four calendar quarters preceding his application for disability benefits.

A California worker must earn during the base period, which is approximately the first four of the last five calendar quarters preceding his application for unemployment or disability benefits, thirty times his weekly benefit amount or one and one-third times his high-quarter wages, but in no case less than $300.

A New Jersey worker must have earned $15 or more from one employer in each of seventeen weeks during, roughly, the fifty-two week period preceding his application for either disability or unemployment benefits.

---

[18] Many of the important detailed provisions of these laws have been omitted for the sake of brevity and clarity of exposition. For a detailed summary of the laws, the student is referred to U. S. Department of Labor, Bureau of Employment Security, *Comparison of Temporary Disability Insurance Laws,* January, 1954.

A New York worker must have completed four or more consecutive weeks of employment prior to the commencement of disability. If he terminates his employment, in most cases he will retain his eligibility for four weeks. After four weeks, he may qualify if he is eligible for unemployment compensation or if he has earned at least $13 in covered employment in twenty of the thirty weeks preceding his last day in covered employment.

2. *Labor force status.* The purpose of the temporary disability insurance legislation is to make income payments to those persons who cannot work or cannot seek work because of disability. The wage qualification does not always accomplish this objective because a person may qualify on the basis of a past employment record. Therefore, all states other than Rhode Island require that claimants who have been unemployed for more than a few weeks prove their continued attachment to the labor force.

3. *Definition of disability.* In general, a person is assumed to be disabled if he is unable to perform his regular or customary work because of a mental or physical condition. New Jersey and New York require that unemployed workers be unable to perform the duties of *any* occupation.

New York is the only state which specifically limits the coverage to nonoccupational illnesses, but workmen's compensation benefits usually reduce the disability benefits in the other states. Rhode Island is the only state that covers routine pregnancies, but California and New York pay benefits for certain disabilities following the termination of normal pregnancy.

4. *Disqualifying income.* The purpose of temporary disability insurance legislation is to replace income that has been lost. The worker should not be placed in a position where he is almost as well off disabled as not, for this leads to false claims and malingering. For this reason the states may disqualify a claimant with other sources of income.

Until 1946, workmen's compensation benefits were ignored in Rhode Island, but at present the workmen's compensation benefit plus the disability benefit is not permitted to exceed 85 per cent of the worker's average wage or $58, whichever is less. In California only the difference between the disability benefit and the workmen's compensation benefit is paid. No disability benefits are payable in New York or New Jersey if the claimant is receiving workmen's compensation benefits.

In California and New Jersey, continuing wages plus the disability benefit may not exceed the worker's wage prior to the disability. In New York, no benefit is payable if the worker is *entitled* to receive from his employer (or from a fund to which the employer has contributed) an amount equal to or greater than the disability benefit.

Benefits in New Jersey and New York are also reduced by private and public pension benefits.

5. *Other disqualifications.* All states disqualify a person who is receiving unemployment insurance benefits.

Except in Rhode Island, if a person is ineligible for unemployment compensation for such reasons as involvement in a labor dispute or discharge for misconduct, he is ineligible for disability benefits.

Benefits. The benefits are determined by three factors: the benefit amount, the duration of the benefits, and the waiting period.

1. *Benefit amount.* Both Rhode Island and California provide a weekly benefit which is a function of the total earnings during the base-period quarter of highest earnings. In both states the minimum benefit is $10. The Rhode Island maximum benefit is $30, while the California maximum is $40. The California act also provides hospital benefits of $10 a day.

In New Jersey the disability benefit for employed workers is two-thirds of the first $45 and two-fifths of the remainder of the average weekly wage during the eight weeks preceding the disability. Weeks in which the employee earned less than $15 from one employer are excluded. For unemployed workers, the same formula, but a longer and more distant base period, is used. The minimum benefit is $10; the maximum, $35.

The New York benefit is one-half the average weekly wage during the last eight weeks in covered employment. The minimum benefit is $10, but if the average weekly wage is less than $10, the benefit is the average weekly wage. The maximum benefit is $40.

2. *Duration of benefits.* The duration of the disability income benefits in all states, except New York, varies directly with the earnings during the base period. The maximum duration is twenty-six weeks, but Rhode Island limits pregnancy benefits to twelve weeks. California limits hospital benefits to twelve days in a one-year period.

In New York the benefits are payable for twenty weeks in any fifty-two consecutive week period.

In all four states the duration of disability benefits for employed workers is separate from the duration of unemployment benefits. This separation also holds for unemployed workers in Rhode Island and California.

3. *Waiting period.* A waiting period reduces the cost of the program by eliminating the frequent small losses which add up to a large total. Claims adjustment expense and the temptation to feign claims are also reduced.

Rhode Island has established a waiting period of one calendar week in a benefit year. California, New Jersey, and New York require a waiting period of seven consecutive days at the beginning of each uninterrupted period of disability. California, however, requires no waiting period for hospitalized patients.

Type of insurer. Three different methods have been used to insure these benefits. All eligible employers in Rhode Island are insured under a monopolistic state fund. In California and New Jersey all eligible employers are insured under a competitive state fund *until* the appropriate agency approves a self-insured plan or a privately insured plan. New York requires that the employer actively purchase approved benefits from a competitive state fund or a private insurer unless he can satisfy the appropriate agency that he can safely self-insure this obligation. Disability benefits for unemployed workers formerly covered under a private plan and for persons working for an employer who failed to purchase the required insurance are paid by a special state fund in New York and by the state disability fund in California and New Jersey.

California will not approve a private plan unless it is more liberal than the state plan in at least one respect and at least equal in all other respects. Furthermore, a majority of the employees must consent to the private plan. Even if the plan is approved, those employees who prefer to retain their membership in the state plan may do so.

The private plans in California usually pay two-thirds of the worker's weekly compensation at the time of disability, subject to a minimum payment of $10 and a maximum of $40. There is a flat hospital benefit of $10 a day for twelve days. The benefits continue until recovery or the end of twenty-six weeks, whichever occurs first. If maternity benefits are included, they are paid for six weeks at most. There is a waiting period of seven days for sickness except when the individual is confined in a hospital. The protection under the private plan continues for fourteen days after a person terminates his employment or takes a leave of absence without pay unless he enters uncovered employment, in which case the protection ceases immediately.

New Jersey requires that approved private plans be as liberal as the state plan in all respects. A majority of the employees must agree to the plan if the plan is contributory. If the majority agree, all employes are automatically covered. The typical New Jersey private plan benefits are essentially the same as the typical California private plan benefits. Workers leaving covered employment have their private plan protection continued for two weeks.

New York approves a private plan if it provides benefits which are at least as favorable from an over-all point of view as the state plan. The temporary disability income benefits must be at least 60 per cent of the statutory benefits. If these benefits are less than 100 per cent of the statutory benefits, there must be other benefits such as medical expense benefits to make up the difference. Private plans existing on the date the disability benefit was enacted were permitted to continue throughout the term of the contract and could be extended by collective bargaining agreements even if they did not provide the equivalent of the statutory benefits. As a result of these two requirements, the plans in New York are more heterogeneous than those in the other states.

The New York employer decides how he will insure his obligation. No majority vote of employees is necessary. Workers who terminate their employment are insured under the private plan for four weeks after they leave covered employment.

Financing. Rhode Island requires that employees pay a tax of 1 per cent on the first $3,000 of wages to finance the disability benefits. Employers pay nothing. Prior to the enactment of temporary disability income legislation, Rhode Island had required its employees to contribute to the cost of unemployment insurance. The disability tax was at first a diversion of part of this unemployment tax. At the present time, there is no unemployment tax on employees.

In 1946 the federal Unemployment Tax Act was amended to permit states which had required employee contributions for unemployment insurance to recover these contributions for the purpose of financing disability income plans. Rhode Island, California, and New Jersey benefited from this amendment.

California also levies a 1 per cent tax on the first $3,000 of earnings of employees covered under the state plan. Employers pay nothing.

A California worker insured under a private plan is not permitted to pay more than 1 per cent of the first $3,000 of his wages toward the cost of the plan. Most employees pay this 1 per cent tax, but sometimes employers pay part of or all the cost under the privately insured plans. The total cost may be more or less than 1 per cent because the private insurers, unlike the state insurer, take into account the underwriting characteristics and loss experience of the group in determining the premium. Also, the benefits under the private plan must be more liberal and this affects the total cost.

The state fund pays all the benefits to qualified workers who have been out of covered employment for more than fourteen days. These benefits are financed out of the interest earnings on an invested principal consisting of the employee contributions for unemployment insurance in 1944, 1945, and part of 1946. If these interest earnings are not sufficient, an assessment is levied on the state fund, private insurers, and self-insurers.

The New Jersey plan is financed in essentially the same way as the California plan except for the following important differences. (1) An employee covered under the state plan pays a tax of ½ per cent on the first $3,000 of wages, while his employer pays a tax of ¼ per cent. (2) The employer's contribution to the state plan is subject to modification through a form of experience rating.

In New York, employees may not pay more than ½ per cent on the first $60 of weekly earnings toward the cost of the plan, unless there is a special agreement to the contrary. The employer pays the additional cost, if any. Both the state fund and the private insurers use premiums which reflect in approximately the same way the underwriting characteristics and loss experience of each insured group. Consequently, adverse selection against the state fund is much less likely.

Benefits for unemployed workers were initially financed out of a separate fund created through a special employer-employee tax, collected from January 1 to June 30, 1950. This fund has been exhausted, and the state fund, self-insurers, and private insurers are currently assessed for whatever amount is needed.

Administration. In Rhode Island, California, and New Jersey, the unemployment insurance agency administers the law, while in New York the Workmen's Compensation Board is the administrator.

Workers covered under the state plans in Rhode Island, California, and New Jersey mail their claims to the appropriate state office. Medical certification is required on all claims, and claims must be submitted within a stated period after the beginning of disability. On the basis of information provided in the claims report and unemployment insurance records, the benefit rate and probable duration of benefits are determined. Unscheduled visits by claims examiners are used to check on the disability status of the claimant, especially when the claim is doubtful, and another medical certification may be requested if the claim is continued. However, most of the claims administration is handled by mail.

Employees covered under private plans deal with their employer or an insurer, but each claim must be reported to the appropriate state agency.

In New York, all claimants must send a written notice of disability to the employer who turns it over to his insurer, if any. Unemployed workers, on the other hand, must send written notice of disability to the chairman of the Workmen's Compensation Board.

In all four states, under both private and public plans, provision is made for appeal to several administrative boards and eventually to the courts if a claimant is dissatisfied with the award he receives.

The state funds are operated essentially on a pay-as-you-go basis. However, some reserves have been accumulated because the employee contributions, interest earnings, and recoveries from the Federal Unemployment Trust Fund have exceeded the benefits and administrative expenses. These reserve amounts are invested in interest-bearing government securities, and the interest and principal can be used to reduce the current tax, improve the benefits, or serve as a contingency fund.

OPERATIONS

Table 11.2 summarizes the current operations under the four state temporary disability insurance laws.

About one-quarter of the employees covered under unemployment insurance in the United States are covered under these state laws. The New York law covers almost half this number.

In California slightly less than half the covered employees with slightly less than half the taxable payroll are insured under private plans. In New Jersey about two-thirds of the covered employees with about two-thirds of the taxable payroll are insured under private plans. In New York it is estimated that over 90 per cent of the covered workers are insured under private plans.

New York pays the highest average weekly benefit, but the lowest average weekly number of beneficiaries relative to the total covered employment. The opposite is true of Rhode Island.

The private plans are apparently more liberal than the public plans in terms of the average weekly benefit. This result is not unexpected because of the criteria established for the approval of private plans. Data are not available to support a further conclusion that because of greater administrative costs private plan benefits are

TABLE 11.2

OPERATIONS UNDER THE FOUR STATE TEMPORARY DISABILITY INSURANCE LAWS, 1955

State	Covered employment (in thousands)	Taxable payroll (in millions)	Average weekly number of beneficiaries (in thousands)	Average weekly benefit amount	Contributions collected (in millions)	Net benefits paid (in millions)	Administrative expenses (in millions)
Rhode Island	221	$ 594	4.8	$22.85	$ 5.9	$ 5.6	$ .35
California	3,144	9,464	*	–	*	80.6	3.41[3]
State	1,680	4,919	25.3	30.38	48.7	45.8	–
Private	1,464	4,545	*	36.00	*	34.8	–
New Jersey	1,469	4,170	*	–	*	35.5	1.32[3]
State	558	1,385	6.8	26.74	9.5	9.5	–
Private	911	2,785	*	*	*	26.0	–
New York	4,653	12,400	44.0	–	*	92.4	1.45[3]
State	–	–	.6[2]	25.59[2]	*	.8[2]	–
Private	4,653[1]	12,400[1]	43.4	36.43	*	91.6	–

* Not available.

[1] Apparently includes the State Fund.

[2] State program refers to the separate fund for unemployed workers.

[3] Represents state costs of administering state program and of supervising private plans.

Source: *Social Security Bulletin, Annual Statistical Supplement,* 1955, p. 13.

more expensive on the average than those provided under state plans.

Under at least two of the state plans, the 1955 benefits and administrative expenses of the state fund exceeded the 1955 taxes, but the reserves increased because of interest earnings, assessment income, or both.

EVALUATION

Temporary disability insurance legislation was designed to provide a minimum income during periods of temporary disability (primarily nonoccupational) to persons who were attached to the labor force: that is, employed or temporarily unemployed at the time they were disabled. The general objective of this legislation has been achieved without any apparent serious adverse economic effects. The original Rhode Island legislation had many obvious defects, but all these have been corrected, at least in part.

The most important differences of opinion about temporary disability legislation have centered on its following aspects: (1) eligibility requirements and benefit determinations, (2) the attachment of disability income insurance to an existing insurance plan, (3) the role of private and public insurers, (4) the relative importance of temporary disability insurance, and (5) the need for compulsion.

Eligibility requirements and benefit formulas have been designed for administrative convenience. Some of the flat coverage rules result therefore in cases where new employees are not eligible for benefits until some time after they enter covered employment. In other cases, it is doubtful whether the eligible person is still attached to the labor force. Some employments are excluded from coverage merely for administrative reasons. Benefits, for the same reasons, are sometimes determined upon the basis of wages which are no longer representative.

The arguments favoring the attachment of temporary disability income insurance to unemployment insurance or workmen's compensation insurance have already been noted on pages 311-12. Some persons believe that temporary disability insurance is sufficiently different to merit separate treatment. For example, at one time the Social Security Administration favored the inclusion of both short-term and long-term disability insurance under OASI.[19]

One of the most debated issues is the role of private and public insurers. Those in favor of a monopolistic public fund argue that

[19] See "Issues in Temporary Disability Insurance," *Social Security Bulletin*, XII, No. 6 (June, 1949), 3–8, 14. Many of the arguments concerning the role of public and private insurers are also summarized in this article.

(1) the benefits provided by private insurers are necessarily more costly because of increased administrative expenses and taxes; (2) the state incurs extra costs of supervision if private plans are permitted; (3) a state fund must always exist to take care of the groups that the private insurers will not underwrite, and this state fund is subject to adverse selection; (4) the employee has no say in the choice of the private insurer even though he contributes to the cost; (5) a compulsory state plan is simpler to explain to employees; and (6) the tax rate should be uniform for all groups.

Opponents argue that private insurers would administer claims more efficiently than a monopolistic state fund and that legitimate decreased benefit costs will offset increased administrative costs. Furthermore, the expense comparison is unfair, for part of the increased administrative costs of private plans consists of state taxes from which a state monopolistic fund is exempt. The opponents also believe that monopolistic fund benefits are not likely to be supplemented by private plans. They point to the almost nonexistent role of private group insurers in Rhode Island and the more adequate benefits under private plans in states where they are permitted. A similar argument holds that the further development of private accidental injury and sickness insurance would be retarded as a result. The opponents also feel that private plan benefits are much easier to explain to employees than state plan benefits. Finally, they argue that the chance of a short-term accidental injury or sickness is to some extent within the control of an individual and, for this reason, the premium rate should vary among groups. The equal tax rate should be a last resort.

Most of these opponents favor a competitive state fund because they feel that a yardstick is essential and there should be some method of providing benefits to temporarily unemployed workers. However, a large number in this group feel that the competitive state fund should be a "fair" competitor, paying the same taxes and subject to the same regulations as other insurers. This is the situation in New York.

The other opponents, whose views have not been accepted by any state legislature as yet, feel that the state should go no further than making the insurance compulsory, as it has in the case of workmen's compensation in most states. However, under this arrangement the original stimulus for this legislation—payments to disabled temporarily unemployed persons—would not be taken care of.

Temporary disability can cause important losses, but these losses are not as severe as long-term disability losses. Thus, it is argued by some that concentration upon the problems of short-term disability results in an unfortunate use of scarce resources. Others feel that this legislation represents a further attempt on the part of the government to dictate how a person should spend his income. They feel that the problem is not sufficiently great to warrant this restriction of freedom. Some moderates in this group do not oppose compulsory short-term disability insurance, but they believe that the benefits should be set at a minimum level.

The most important issue in most states which have considered the legislation in recent years is whether the coverage is necessary. The number of persons covered and the percentage of short-term income loss paid under voluntary private plans have grown tremendously since Rhode Island enacted its legislation in 1942.[20] Those favoring the bill feel that a large segment of the population is still not covered and probably never will be covered.

To a certain extent, temporary disability insurance legislation has been responsible for the growth in private plans. Employers who were forced to provide this protection to employees in the four temporary disability insurance states extended this insurance in many cases to cover employees in other states. Labor unions often pressed for extension of this sort if the employer did not act voluntarily. Insurers experimented with smaller groups than they had written before and opened up new markets for themselves. Finally, the threat of compulsion usually leads directly to more voluntary action.

The New York plan appears to be the most satisfactory compromise between varying objectives. Eligibility requirements and benefit levels are a reasonable compromise between equity and administrative ease. Joint financing recognizes that the employer and the employee both benefit from the program. Private insurers are given the maximum opportunity to develop their own coverages, but the state plan is an ever-present fair yardstick. Costs are distributed partly on the basis of pooling and partly on the basis of the experience of the individual group.

One may question, however, whether temporary disability insurance legislation of the current type does make the optimum use of our resources. A waiting period of approximately one week does not exclude many nonserious illnesses while a maximum duration of twenty-six weeks or less reduces the effectiveness of the program in dealing with long-term illnesses. More attention should be directed, on the private and public levels, toward more adequate long-term disability insurance.

[20] See Chapter 12 for more detailed information.

Social Medical Expense Insurance

HISTORICAL TRENDS

No general social insurance scheme in the United States includes nonoccupational *medical expense* insurance except the plans established under the California temporary disability insurance legislation and some of the plans established under the New York law. The other general social insurance programs, other than workmen's compensation, freeze the eligibility status of the insured for death and retirement benefits or pay a disability *income*. They do not pay medical expenses or provide medical services.

Opposition to social medical expense insurance has been much stronger than opposition to disability income insurance, because more segments of the population, especially the medical profession, feel that they would be adversely affected. However, there has always been intense interest in the subject during this century, particularly in the thirties and forties.

It has already been stated that nonoccupational temporary disability insurance legislation dates back to the introduction of workmen's compensation in the United States. Compulsory medical expense insurance first attracted widespread public attention in 1912. Bills establishing compulsory medical expense insurance were introduced in several state legislatures, but none passed and during the twenties the issue was almost dropped.

In 1929 the Committee on the Costs of Medical Care was formed in response to increasing dissatisfaction with medical costs and medical resources. The committee report emphasized the uneven incidence of medical expense, but the majority of the committee felt that, although compulsory medical expense insurance "may ultimately be necessary and desirable in some states, . . . for most states and probably for almost all of them at the present time, it is much more desirable . . . to develop voluntary insurance for medical care."[21] The committee approved the group-practice principle and suggested grants-in-aid to increase the medical resources in certain areas.

The Depression intensified public interest in the problem because the average family was hard-pressed if there were *any* medical expenses. The Committee on Economic Security considered seriously the advisability of including compulsory medical expense

[21] Committee on the Costs of Medical Care, *Medical Care for the American People* (Chicago: University of Chicago Press, 1932), p. 130.

insurance under OASI, but the Social Security Act contained no reference to this insurance.

The year 1935 marked the beginning of the National Health Survey and the appointment by the President of an Interdepartmental Committee to Coordinate Health and Welfare. The National Health Survey produced some extensive information on the frequency and severity of illness. The Interdepartmental Committee submitted a report which was largely responsible for the 1939 Wagner Bill already referred to in connection with temporary disability insurance.

The Wagner Bill provided for federal grants-in-aid to states having approved medical expense plans.[22] The bill emphasized the provision of medical care for the needy, but it also provided that temporary disability insurance plans would not be approved unless all those covered under temporary disability insurance were also covered under an approved compulsory medical expense insurance plan. The bill died in committee, but was widely discussed.

The appearance of the Beveridge Report in England in 1942 was the next stimulus, and in 1943 Senators Robert Wagner and James Murray introduced a bill which would have created a Unified National Social Insurance Scheme. The same bill was introduced in the House. A second Wagner-Murray-Dingell bill was introduced in 1945. Both bills called for a federal system of medical expense benefits and compensation for temporary disability. President Truman recommended the passage of a National Health Act in November, 1945, and the third Wagner-Murray-Dingell Act was introduced to carry out his recommendations. This third bill was the high-spot in the movement for compulsory medical expense insurance.

Under this bill, the eligibility requirements were similar to the requirements for currently insured status under OASI. The benefits were hospitalization; care by physicians, including surgeons and specialists, in the patient's home, the doctor's office, or a hospital; care by a dentist; nurses' services; laboratory and related services; eye examinations; and appliances, including eye glasses. Hospital benefits were limited to a certain amount per day for a stated number of days, but other limitations were to be applied only if they appeared necessary to prevent abuses, to limit the use of scarce resources such as dental and home nursing services, or to reduce the cost of the program. No benefits were available for confinement in an institution for mental or nervous diseases or for tuberculosis.

22 The Wagner Bill and others are discussed in detail in Gagliardo, *op cit.*, chap. xviii.

All legally qualified hospitals, physicians, dentists, and nurses were eligible to participate, but they did not have to serve under the plan. The participants were to be reimbursed on a fee-for-service, per capita, or salary basis which it was presumed would be determined by the participants of each class in a local area. The number of patients per participant would be limited, but otherwise there would be freedom of choice. Patients preferring nonparticipants would receive no benefits under the system.

The Surgeon General was to be the Chief Administrator of the plan, but he was to decentralize the operation as much as possible. It was estimated that the benefits could be provided for insureds and their dependents if covered employees and their employers each paid a tax of 1.75 per cent on the first $3,600 of the employee's ·earnings. The bill did not pass, but was given wide publicity and had many supporters.

Senators Taft, Ball, Donnell, and Smith were opposed to the Wagner-Murray-Dingell bill, but they felt that some action was necessary. They sponsored proposals which, in effect, would have provided federal grants-in-aid to the states with approved plans providing medical care for the indigent and the medically indigent. These bills and the successors to the Wagner-Murray-Dingell bill all failed.

Since the late forties, interest in social medical expense insurance has declined. Compulsory medical expense insurance measures still appear on the Congressional calendar, but they do not appear to have widespread support. Neither major political party advocated compulsory medical expense insurance in its 1956 platform. For these reasons, the future of this legislation is uncertain, but no immediate action is likely.

One of the most important factors in the decline in interest is the significant growth of voluntary accidental injury and sickness insurance, reflecting in part high levels of personal income and trade union activity. The 1929 remark of the Committee on the Costs of Medical Care, which is quoted on page 324, is still relevant in this respect.

Federal Reinsurance Plan

In 1954 the Eisenhower Administration introduced a bill which would have created a federal reinsurance pool. The purpose of the bill was to encourage the extension of private insurance plans.

A private insurer was permitted to reinsure benefits under approved contracts in the federal reinsurance pool. The pool would promise to pay three-fourths of the excess losses suffered under these contracts during the reinsurance policy period. The standards and the reinsurance premium to be paid to the pool were to be determined by the Secretary of Health, Education, and Welfare. The reinsured contract had to represent an extension of existing coverage with respect to the benefits offered or persons eligible for the insurance. The Administration expressed a definite desire to extend coverage to aged persons, substandard lives, and catastrophe losses.

The pool was to consist of a $25 million capital fund provided by the Treasury. Administrative expenses during the first five years were to be paid out of general revenues. However, the pool was intended to be self-sustaining and the capital fund was to be repaid as soon as possible. The pool was to operate only in areas where private reinsurance pools were not able to provide the coverage under similar terms and conditions.

The prospects for passage of the bill seemed excellent, but it was defeated in the House and never voted on in the Senate. The defeat was due to the combined efforts of those who felt that the bill was weak and those who believed that it provided an opening wedge for "socialized medicine." Many private insurers maintained that the pool could not be self-sustaining, and they were opposed to a federal subsidy since they associated it with possible federal control. The vagueness of the bill also disturbed many.

The bill was modified and reintroduced in 1955, but it died in committee that year. In 1956 the bill was not introduced until the closing days of the session and it again died in committee. However, present indications are that the idea is still very much alive.

The objectives of the reinsurance scheme are commendable, but it is to be doubted that the program can operate effectively unless it is subsidized by the federal government. A subsidized operation deserves closer scrutiny than the present vague legislation will permit. For example, it is important to know who will be subsidized and what federal controls will be imposed. Finally, a reinsurance program will not solve the needs of the indigent nor the medically indigent.

A Concluding Note

This chapter has discussed a variety of approaches to the economic problems created by nonoccupational accidental injury and sickness. Evaluations of these various approaches have been presented at several points throughout the chapter. The student is encouraged to form his own opinions on this highly controversial subject.

Summary

In a given year, about half the population will be ill and about one-quarter of the population will be disabled. Over 3 per cent has been disabled for six weeks or more.

Nonoccupational accidental injuries and sicknesses cause about forty times as many illnesses disabling for a week or more as job-connected accidental injuries and sicknesses. In 1954 the average personal cost of nonoccupational illness due to loss of income and medical expenses was around $700, and this cost was distributed very unevenly among American families.

Preventive and alleviative methods, both private and public, have been used to attack the financial problems caused by non-occupational illnesses. This chapter is primarily concerned with public alleviative approaches.

The important public programs are the special federally supported state public assistance programs which provide aid for the blind and the totally and permanently disabled, the disability freeze and disability income programs under OASI, and temporary disability insurance legislation in four states.

The recent addition of the disability freeze and disability income benefits to OASI and their limited nature reflect the intense opposition to an extensive social accidental injury and sickness program.

The OASI disability freeze enables a totally and permanently disabled person to retain the insurance status and average monthly wage he had earned at the date of disability. The OASI disability income benefits enable a totally and permanently disabled person to receive a monthly income beginning at age fifty. Children who are disabled prior to age eighteen also receive a monthly income under certain conditions after they reach age eighteen.

Temporary disability insurance legislation in four states protects workers against short-term disability income losses. Three of the states coordinate temporary disability insurance with unemployment insurance; the fourth regards it as a supplement to workmen's compensation. One state requires insurance in a monopolistic state fund; the other three states permit commercial insurers to compete with a state fund. Two states tax the employee only, while the other two tax both the employer and the employee. No two plans have the same eligibility requirements or benefit formulas. The maximum benefit in any state is $40 for twenty-six weeks.

Opposition to social medical expense insurance has been most intense, especially from the medical profession. Compulsory medical expense insurance bills received widespread support in the thirties and forties, but neither major political party has indicated any current strong interest in the subject. A federal reinsurance scheme is the most recent suggestion.

Suggestions for Additional Reading

COMMISSION ON THE HEALTH NEEDS OF THE NATION. *Building America's Health.* Washington, D. C.: U. S. Government Printing Office, 1952. Five volumes.
This extensive report summarizes and interprets the findings of many statistical surveys on the health needs of the nation.

GAGLIARDO, DOMENICO. *American Social Insurance,* rev. ed. New York: Harper and Bros., 1955. Chapter 19.
An extensive discussion of the arguments for and against social medical expense insurance and the legislation that was introduced during the thirties and forties.

NEW YORK STATE, DEPARTMENT OF LABOR, DIVISION OF RESEARCH AND STATISTICS. *Studies in Disability Insurance.* New York, 1949.
This study describes the issues which must be resolved before a compulsory temporary disability insurance program can be established.

SCOTT, J. A., D. J. B. COOPER, and S. SEUFFERT. *The National Health Service Acts, 1946 and 1949.* London: Eyre and Spottiswoode, Ltd., 1950. Parts I and II.
A description of the social insurance system of England, particularly the medical care program.

U. S. CONGRESS, 83D, SECOND SESSION, HOUSE, HEARING BEFORE THE INTERSTATE AND FOREIGN COMMERCE COMMITTEE. *Health Reinsurance Legislation.* Washington, D. C.: U. S. Government Printing Office, 1954.
Hearings on the federal reinsurance proposal which died in committee.

U. S. CONGRESS, 84TH, SECOND SESSION, SENATE, HEARINGS BEFORE THE FINANCE COMMITTEE. *Social Security Amendment of 1955.* Washington, D. C.: U. S. Government Printing Office, 1956.
Hearings on the OASI disability income provisions which were enacted in 1956.

U. S. DEPARTMENT OF HEALTH, EDUCATION, AND WELFARE. *Annual Report.* Washington, D. C.: U. S. Government Printing Office, 1955.
The annual reports of the Department comment on the current operations of the federal public assistance and social insurance programs.

12

Voluntary Private Accidental
Injury and Sickness Insurance

Introduction

The social insurance programs providing benefits for accidental injury or sickness have been discussed in Chapters 9, 10, and 11. These programs include workmen's compensation laws which provide disability income and medical expense benefits for job-connected injury and disease; OASI which freezes the eligibility status of totally and permanently disabled persons and provides them with a monthly income beginning at age fifty; and, in four states, temporary disability insurance legislation, dealing essentially with the non-job connected economic insecurities of accidents and sickness.

Important gaps in this social insurance protection against accidental injury and sickness remain. For example, the OASI disability income payments do not begin until age fifty, and only one state program requires medical expense benefits for nonoccupational illness. Voluntary private accidental injury and sickness insurance, therefore, is extremely important in covering non-job connected illnesses and in many cases also job-connected illnesses.

In this chapter we shall consider the voluntary protection provided by private insurers. We shall classify the private insurance plans according to the type of insurer, for each type of insurer has a different underwriting philosophy and we are interested in the important characteristics of each approach.

The three major types of insurers are commercial insurers, Blue Cross and Blue Shield associations, and independent insurers. The last class includes all types of insurers not included under the first two classes.

Under each category we shall discuss the benefits currently available, their role in the economic security system, and important trends in their development.

Commercial Insurance Contracts

The commercial insurer is the most important type of insurer in the private accidental injury and sickness field. Commercial insurers underwrite almost all the protection against loss of income caused by disability and they share with Blue Cross and Blue Shield associations the leadership in underwriting medical expense coverages.

Commercial insurers write both individual and group coverages. The major characteristics of each of these major classifications of coverages are discussed below.

INDIVIDUAL INSURANCE

Individual insurance contracts may be divided into three classes: income contracts which protect insureds against loss of income only, income-medical expense contracts which protect insureds against both loss of income and medical expenses, and medical expense contracts which protect insureds against medical expenses only. Included in the first two groups are commercial policies, semi-commercial policies, noncancellable policies, industrial policies, and limited policies. Included in the third group are basic medical expense policies and major medical expense policies. We shall discuss the major provisions of the most typical contracts under each classification, but the reader should remember that there are a very large number of different forms available. Our discussion is primarily intended to indicate the major types of protection available.

Individual income and income-medical expense contracts. Commercial policies are the most frequently sold income and income-medical expense contracts. They are issued only to persons engaged in nonhazardous occupations. The policy may protect the insured against losses due to accidental injury and sickness or the coverage may be restricted to accidental injuries.

In the past, accidental injury benefits were usually payable only if the insured suffered a bodily injury effected solely through accidental means. The cause must have been accidental. Today, however, most of the leading insurers simply require that the claimant have suffered an accidental bodily injury. The distinction is clearly important if the insured does not also have a sickness policy; it is also important if the insured has a sickness policy because the accidental injury benefits are much more liberal, as indicated in the following paragraphs.

The most important accidental injury benefits include the disability income benefits, benefits for dismemberment and loss of sight, and medical expense benefits.

There are two types of disability income benefits—total disability benefits and partial disability benefits. A person who is totally and continuously disabled within a specified period, such as twenty days, following the date of an accident will receive a specified weekly indemnity. He is considered to be totally disabled if he is unable to perform any and every duty pertaining to his occupation. The test is not whether his income stops. The requirement that the disability commence within a stated period after the accident is included because, as the interval between the accident and the date of disability increases, it becomes more difficult to determine whether the disability was caused by the accident. Payments are usually continued for fifty-two weeks or until recovery, if earlier. Payments will be continued for life if the insured is unable to engage in *any* occupation. This requirement is interpreted by most insurers and courts to mean any occupation for which the insured is suited by education, training, or experience.

A person who is partially and continuously disabled within some period, such as twenty days, following an accident or immediately following a period of total disability will receive a specified weekly indemnity which is usually two-fifths of the total disability weekly indemnity. Partial disability is defined as the inability to perform at least one important daily duty pertaining to his occupation. The payments are generally continued up to twenty-six or fifty-two weeks, never for life.

Insureds who lose one or more members or the sight of one or both eyes within a certain period following the accident may commonly elect to receive a lump-sum payment equal to the weekly indemnity for a number of weeks; for example, one hundred weeks for the loss of a hand or foot.

Medical expense benefits, which are often not included, may be written on a blanket or on a specific basis. Under the blanket coverage there is one aggregate limit for all types of expenses covered. For example, one policy pays hospital bills, nurses' fees, and charges for treatment by a physician or surgeon incurred within twenty-six weeks following the accident up to the limit specified in the policy. Under the specific coverages, there are separate limits for each type of expense covered. For example, under one policy the insureds may purchase one or more of the following specific benefits: (1) actual hospital room and board charges up to $10 per day for not more than one hundred days plus miscellaneous hospital expenses up to $100; (2) surgical fees according to a schedule of allowances; (3) nurses' fees up to $5 per day for not more than one hundred days; and (4) charges for a physician's care in the hospital up to $3 per day for not more than one hundred days. Blanket coverage is more liberal than the specific coverages because the types of covered medical expenses included in the insured's claim do not affect his recovery from the insurer.

Accidental injuries caused directly or indirectly by suicide or war are excluded. Moreover, no benefits are paid for injuries sustained while the insured is in the armed services in time of war or while the insured is riding in an airplane other than a fare-paying passenger on a scheduled airplane. There are usually other minor exclusions.

Sickness benefits, which are written only in conjunction with accidental injury benefits, include only a total disability income benefit and medical expense benefits. Sickness losses are much more difficult to underwrite than accidental injury losses because of the possibility of feigning sickness. Therefore, insurers are more cautious when they underwrite this type of insurance.

A person who is totally and continuously disabled by sickness will generally receive a specified weekly indemnity for 52 or 104 weeks beginning with the fifteenth day of total disability. The fourteen-day waiting period (or some other waiting period) reduces the cost of the insurance considerably because it eliminates the frequent short-term illnesses. Total disability is defined as the inability to perform any and every duty of his occupation.

Partial disability benefits are seldom included, but some contracts distinguish between total confining disability and total nonconfining disability benefits. A disability is confining if the insured must stay indoors. These contracts are usually less liberal than the more common contract because the total confining disability benefit is the same as the usual total disability benefit, while the total nonconfining disability benefit is less liberal in duration and sometimes in amount. Some contracts will continue the payments for life if the insured is house confined.

The medical expenses in the sickness policy are almost always written on the less liberal specific basis.

No sickness benefits are usually payable if the sickness was contracted prior to the fifteenth day of the policy period. Moreover, no benefits are payable if the insured is not under the care of a physician or if the loss is incurred while the insured is a member of the armed services. Sometimes the latter exclusion applies only in time of war.

Commercial accidental injury and sickness contracts are issued on a yearly basis and are renewable at the option of the insurer. The insurer usually also has the right to cancel the contract during the policy period if he wishes to do so. This cancellation right in itself is undesirable from the insured's point of view, but it enables the insurer to offer more liberal benefits than would otherwise be possible.

Premiums for the accidental injury benefits are dependent primarily upon occupation and sex. Age is not important. Premiums for sickness insurance depend primarily upon sex. There may also be broad age groupings such as eighteen to forty-nine and fifty to fifty-four. The premiums are quoted on an annual basis, but they may be paid semi-annually, quarterly, or monthly.

Each applicant must pass the underwriting standards established by the insurer. Factors considered by the underwriter are the applicant's age, his physical condition, his occupation, and his moral and financial reputation.

Semi-commercial contracts provide essentially the same types of benefits as commercial contracts. However, because persons in more hazardous occupational groups may purchase these contracts, the benefits are written for smaller amounts and there are usually more restrictions on the benefits. The borderline between semi-commercial and commercial contracts is a hazy one, but the contracts with the fewest restrictions and the largest benefit amounts are designed for persons in relatively safe occupations.

Noncancellable (and guaranteed renewable) contracts are extremely important. The insurer may not cancel the contract within the policy period, and the insurer must renew the contract at the insured's request up to some advanced age specified in the contract. This right to renew adds greatly to the economic security of the individual.

Noncancellable contracts provide a specified weekly indemnity if the insured is totally and continuously disabled by disease or by an accidental injury within some specified period, such as twenty days, following the accident. The sickness benefits are not payable until after a waiting period, and the average noncancellable waiting period exceeds the average commercial sickness contract waiting period.

Total disability may be defined as the inability to perform the duties of any occupation, or a "this occupation" standard may be used for some initial period, such as fifty-two weeks. Some policies require house confinement.

Most long-term noncancellable contracts limit both accidental injury and sickness benefits to ten years per disability, and no payments are made beyond age sixty-five, but many provide lifetime benefits in case of accidental injury. Only one contract provides a life indemnity for sickness and that benefit is reduced fifty per cent if the disability is not house-confining.[1]

Medium-term noncancellable contracts providing sickness benefits lasting forty-eight to sixty months and short-term contracts providing sickness benefits lasting twelve to thirty-six months are also available. Accidental injury benefits are limited to the same period or are payable for life. Some of these contracts are written on a less liberal aggregate basis: they limit the indemnity for all disabilities to a stated number of dollars or a stated number of payments. Some require house confinement before any total disability benefits are paid.

Long-term noncancellable contracts are issued only to relatively safe occupational groups. Medium-term contracts are issued to most insurable occupational groups and short-term contract to all insurable occupational groups.

Other benefits in noncancellable contracts include waiver of premium benefits, partial disability benefits, and medical expense benefits. Almost all noncancellable contracts provide for the waiver of future premiums in case of total and permanent disability. Most contracts provide short-term benefits in case of partial disability, but long-term contracts restrict the payments to periods of partial disability following a period of total disability. Medical expense benefits are the least common benefit.

The exclusions in noncancellable contracts are approximately the same as those found in commercial contracts.

Noncancellable premiums are level premiums similar to those paid for life insurance contracts. Sex and occupation are important rating factors, but the most important factor is age, because of the

[1] For a description of current noncancellable contracts, see David G. Scott, "Noncancellable Coverages," *Best's Insurance News, Fire and Casualty Edition,* LIV, No. 3 (July, 1953), 25–27, 66–67. For a discussion of long-term noncancellable disability income insurance, see O. D. Dickerson, *Long-Term Guaranteed Renewable Disability Insurance* (Chicago: Health and Accident Underwriters Conference, 1955).

level premium and long term. Underwriting practices are very strict, and a physical examination by a doctor is required of about half the applicants.

Industrial contracts are designed primarily for low-income groups. Premiums are payable weekly or monthly and are usually collected at the home of the insured. The benefits are essentially the same as those provided under the commercial and semi-commercial contracts, but they are much lower in amount and somewhat more restricted.

Limited policies are policies which protect the insured for a very short period of time or against special types of illnesses. Examples are the railway travel policy and polio insurance contracts.

Commercial policies and noncancellable policies play major roles in the search for economic security because they provide valuable protection for many persons against both loss of income and incurred medical expenses. Industrial policies provide less protection, but this protection is important to the low-income groups. The limited policies play a relatively minor role in our economic security system, but they may be very helpful in individual cases.

Individual medical expense contracts. Basic medical expense contracts are the most frequently sold individual accidental injury and sickness contracts. They may protect an individual or a family. The probability of incurring medical expenses looms greater than the probability of a loss of income, and the average person insures against unexpected medical expenses first. His principal concern is hospital expenses.

A typical hospital expense policy pays daily hospital room and board charges up to a specified amount, commonly $5 to $10, for a specified period, commonly thirty to ninety days. Hospital expenses other than room and board charges incurred during the same specified period are covered up to a specified dollar amount or five to ten times the daily room and board allowance. Maternity benefits are limited to ten times the daily room and board allowance.

Typical exclusions are treatments for venereal disease, injuries covered under a workmen's compensation law, and injuries caused by war or attempted suicide. No benefits are payable for injuries sustained while the insured is engaged in air travel other than as a fare-paying passenger on a scheduled airline. Maternity confinements are not covered unless the policy has been in force ten months, and sometimes treatments for appendicitis, tonsillitis, and similar illnesses are also excluded during the first ten months.

A separate policy or an addition to the hospital policy may provide surgical benefits, physicians' care benefits, or both. The surgical benefit is a schedule of allowances toward the actual cost of several specified surgical operations. An in-hospital physicians' care benefit provides $3 to $5 per visit beginning with the first or fourth visit for a specified number of days or until a maximum amount, such as $150, has been paid. Sometimes benefits are payable on essentially the same basis even if the physician treats the patient in his office or at the patient's home. The exclusions under all of these coverages are about the same as those under the hospital expense coverages.

Basic medical expense coverages are usually cancellable by the insurer, and the insured faces the possibility of losing the coverage if his health deteriorates, but cancellation does not affect the benefits payable on account of illness commencing while the policy is in force.

Basic medical expense insurance enables the insured to budget systematically the medical expenses associated with less costly illnesses. It provides valuable protection if the insured becomes ill shortly after the policy is issued. Like the medical expense coverages in the income-medical expense contracts, it has a limitation in filling the economic security gap in that it provides little protection against the sizable medical expenses associated with long-term serious illnesses unless the insured is willing to pay the premiums necessary to purchase extremely high limits. If he has that much money to spend, it would probably be more economical for him to self-insure the less costly, more frequent illnesses himself because these losses are relatively expensive for an insurer to adjust.

Major medical expense insurance contracts are designed for the person who wants to insure against sizable medical expenses at a reasonable cost. Individual and family contracts are issued. The main features of this important form of protection may be summarized as follows: (1) Almost every type of medical expense such as hospital bills, nurses' fees, medicine costs, surgical fees, and physicians' charges is covered. There are few, if any, limits on specific types of medical expenses. (2) The insurer agrees to contribute to the medical expenses only when they exceed a specified amount called the "deductible." The insured may select the deductible in accordance with his financial resources and desires. (3) Usually the insurer promises to pay only part, commonly 75 or 80 per cent, of the excess expenses in order to give the insured some incentive to keep the costs down. (4) The maximum contribution of the insurer is limited to $5,000, $7,500, or $10,000.

Treatments for mental or nervous disorders, except when treated in a general hospital, and for injuries covered by workmen's compensation are excluded. Other exclusions tend to be of minor importance.

Most major medical expense policies are cancellable, but a few quasi-noncancellable contracts are available. The contracts are not truly noncancellable, since the insurer reserves the right to change its schedule of rates for all insureds in a given class if that is necessary.[2] A rate increase might force the insured to discontinue his protection.

Age is the most important factor affecting premiums even if the contract is cancellable. Other factors include income, sex, and occupation.

Medical expense policies cover only one of the two types of losses caused by accidental injury and sickness, but they are the most important coverages which commercial insurers write against that type of loss. Major medical expense insurance is a recent innovation (1948), but it has already established itself as an important part of our economic security system.

Disability provisions in individual life insurance contracts. Individual life insurance contracts also provide some accidental injury and sickness benefits. Most life insurance contracts provide in the policy itself or through a rider for the waiver of future premiums if the insured is totally and permanently disabled prior to age sixty. A relatively small but increasing number of contracts also promise to pay $5 or $10 per month per $1,000 of insurance usually beginning with the sixth month of disability. This coverage is always attached as a rider on the life insurance policy and an additional premium is charged. The benefit is extremely important, for it is the only noncancellable lifetime indemnity coverage available today against disability due to either accidental injury or sickness.

GROUP INSURANCE

The advantages, nature, and history of group insurance have already been discussed in Chapter 5. Several additional factors are relevant for group accidental injury and sickness insurance. First, the fact that an individual's protection cannot be cancelled unless

---

[2] Similar provisions are found in some basic medical expense contracts, but very rarely in income or income-medical expense contracts.

the group contract is cancelled is especially valuable in accidental injury and sickness insurance. Second, because age is a much less important factor in accidental injury and sickness insurance than in life insurance, group accidental injury and sickness insurance is written on groups that would not be eligible for group life insurance. Third, group accidental injury and sickness insurance grew less rapidly than group life and pension plans until the forties. Now it is the most rapidly growing field of group insurance because of an increasing awareness by the public of the need for accidental injury and sickness protection, the more frequent inclusion of this protection in collective bargaining agreements, and the increased interest of private insurers.

Group accidental injury and sickness insurance includes temporary disability income insurance (called group accident and health insurance), dismemberment insurance, and medical expense insurance, both basic and major. Usually the plans cover only nonoccupational illnesses, but occupational illnesses are sometimes included. The only exclusion may be self-inflicted injuries.

Unlike group life contracts, most group accidental injury and sickness contracts do not permit a terminating group member to convert his group coverage to an individual contract. However, the medical expense benefits are usually continued for a three-month period if the insured terminates his membership because of total disability and remains totally disabled for that period.

Premiums depend upon the percentage of females in the group and, in the case of the disability income and dismemberment coverages, upon the industry. The age and income composition of the group are important in group major medical expense insurance. Premiums are adjusted partly according to the experience of the particular group and partly according to the total group experience of the insurer.

Group temporary disability income insurance contracts. These contracts provide an income for the person who is temporarily disabled. The insurer promises to pay a specified weekly income for a maximum period of thirteen, twenty-six, or fifty-two weeks. Payments usually begin with the first day of disability due to an accidental injury and with the fourth or eighth day of disability due to sickness. The weekly income is usually two-thirds of the employee's wage, but typically does not exceed $35 or $40. If the plan covers occupational illnesses, workmen's compensation payments are deducted from the group insurance benefits. Maternity benefits, if included, are usually limited to six weeks.

Group accidental death and dismemberment contracts. These contracts provide for the payment of a lump sum if there is a loss of life, limb, or sight through solely external, violent, and accidental means within ninety days after an accident.

Group basic medical expense contracts. Included here are group hospitalization contracts, group surgical contracts, different forms of group physicians' care contracts, and minor coverages.

Typical group hospitalization insurance contracts promise to pay daily room and board charges up to $3–$15 for a period of hospital confinement up to 30–180 days. Sometimes the daily benefit is paid even if the actual charge is less. Reimbursement for other hospital expenses incurred within the covered period is limited to five to thirty times the daily room and board allowance. Maternity benefits are usually included, but the benefit is limited. For example, the maximum covered confinement is commonly fourteen days.

Group surgical insurance contracts promise to pay the cost of surgical operations up to the limit specified in a schedule. The maximum allowance is usually $200. In a few states, participating doctors have agreed to charge low-income groups a scheduled fee established by a local medical society, and the group surgical contract may provide these scheduled amounts.

There are three group insurance plans covering the charges for a physician's care. The group in-hospital plan pays $3 or $4 per day of confinement to cover the costs of physician's visits (nonsurgical) in the hospital. The group total disability insurance plan pays $2 for an office call and $3 for a home call if the insured is totally disabled. Charges for hospital calls are reimbursed up to $3 per call or $3 per day of confinement. The group comprehensive insurance contracts pay essentially the same benefits as the group total disability contracts, but total disability is not required and periodic health examinations and immunizations may be included in the protection. Under all three plans, the maximum payment is about $150 or $200 per illness.

Dependents, including a wife or husband and children from fourteen days to nineteen years of age, may be insured for the same or slightly less liberal benefits under each of the medical expense plans except the total disability plan because it would be difficult to tell if a dependent was totally disabled. If dependents are covered, all insureds with dependents may pay the same rate; insureds with two or more dependents may pay more than those with one dependent; or there may be three dependent rates—a wife-only rate, a children-only rate, and a wife-and-children rate.

Group major medical expense insurance. This is the most rapidly growing form of group medical expense insurance because of the important need it fills and because of its recent introduction. Its principal characteristics have already been noted in connection with individual contracts. It is sufficient to note here that group major medical expense contracts are more liberal than the individual equivalents. For example, most individual contracts limit the period within which the expenses associated with an illness must be incurred to a stated period such as two or three years; there are usually no time limits in the group contracts.

Group life insurance contracts. These contracts commonly provide that life insurance will be continued in force without charge for twelve months if a person under age sixty-five terminates his membership because of total disability and remains totally disabled. Most new contracts, however, provide for the waiver of premiums for life in case of total and permanent disability. A few provide for the payment of the face amount in case of death or total and permanent disability.

Group pension plans. Such plans may provide some assistance for a disabled person through their early retirement provisions. Under some plans, only totally disabled persons can retire early. Under others the amount of the early retirement pension is greater for a totally disabled person. A relatively few plans include total and permanent disability income insurance as a separate feature. Usually they provide a specified income beginning within a few months after the occurrence of the disability and continuing to the date of normal retirement. A relatively few plans also waive future premium payments in case of total and permanent disability. Some of these waiver-of-premium benefits enable the insured to retire at the normal retirement age with the same income that he would have received had he continued to participate in the plan at the same salary up to that time.

The most frequently issued forms of group accidental injury and sickness insurance are temporary disability income insurance, the medical expense coverages, and dismemberment insurance. The last form is too limited to be considered a vital part of the economic security system. Long-term disability income losses are seldom covered under group insurance plans.

TRENDS IN COMMERCIAL INSURANCE CONTRACTS

The first commercial accidental injury and sickness insurance contracts were issued about the middle of the nineteenth century, but it was not until the latter part of that century that the coverages were broadened and the industry became established. About the same time, life insurers introduced waiver-of-premium riders in their contracts.

The next important development was the writing of the first non-cancellable policy in 1915 in response to criticisms of the cancellation provisions in commercial contracts. In 1917, some life insurers added total and permanent disability income riders to their contracts. As competition became intense in the twenties, the contracts were further liberalized and lifetime income payments for total and permanent disability became common.

Group disability income insurance was first written in 1912 as a result of the Montgomery Ward group life insurance negotiations discussed in Chapter 5, but this form of insurance did not make much progress until the late twenties because both insurers and employers were directing most of their efforts toward the problems caused by premature death and old age. Meanwhile some group life and group pension plans included total and permanent disability income protection.

The thirties witnessed disastrous experience with lifetime indemnity coverages because of a combination of inadequate premiums, inadequate reserves, inadequate underwriting, and many improper claims. Almost all insurers withdrew from that field or seriously restricted their coverages. On the other hand, medical expense insurance began to grow because the Depression emphasized the need for this form of protection and a new competitor—the Blue Cross movement[3]—was born. Group hospitalization policies were issued for the first time in 1934; group surgical policies in 1938.

As economic conditions improved during the forties, commercial life insurers cautiously re-entered the lifetime indemnity field, and accidental injury and sickness insurers began to liberalize their coverages. These liberalizations were made on a much sounder basis than they had been made in the twenties. The interest in medical expense coverages continued to grow rapidly, and group policies covering charges for physicians' care appeared in 1943. The most significant development was the first writing of a major medical expense policy in 1948. This policy was written on a group basis at the request of a society of employees of the General Electric Company which was seeking this form of protection for its members.

[3] See pages 346–47 for the history of the Blue Cross movement.

During the fifties, further improvements occurred, reflecting increased competition, experience, and consumer interest. Policies are becoming more standardized and easier to read; more noncancellable policies are being issued; policy provisions are being liberalized with respect to definitions of disability, duration of benefits, and exclusions; more substandard lives are being insured; major medical expense insurance is being developed and improved; and small deductibles are being included in basic medical expense coverages. This is an important period of experimentation, and many new approaches will be tried in the quest for economic security.

Blue Cross and Blue Shield Plans

The most important competitors of the commercial insurers are the Blue Cross associations and the Blue Shield associations.[4] Their underwriting philosophy and their contracts differ significantly from those of commercial insurers. We shall now consider the contributions of these associations to our economic security system.

BLUE CROSS PLANS

Blue Cross associations and commercial insurers are about equally important in the field of hospitalization insurance. A Blue Cross association is a voluntary nonprofit hospital expense prepayment plan which has applied for and received the approval of the Blue Cross Commission of the American Hospital Association. There are about eighty locally autonomous Blue Cross associations in the United States. Almost all the associations cover a state or part of a state, and, except in North Carolina, the plans are not competing. The promoters of most associations are hospitals in the plan area. Member hospitals usually elect the board of directors whose members represent the hospitals, the medical profession, and the public. Generally the member hospitals guarantee the plan benefits.

Initially, Blue Cross contracts were sold only to members of eligible groups, and the majority of current contracts are still being issued on that basis. Each association has its own standards, but groups as small as five persons have been covered. The percentage

---

[4] For an excellent discussion of the advantages which Blue Cross and Blue Shield enjoyed in their competition with commercial insurers and how they are losing those advantages, see C. A. Kulp, *Casualty Insurance* (3d ed.; New York: The Ronald Press Co., 1956), pp. 359–60.

For a discussion of some recent problems, see Donald L. MacDonald, "Blue Cross Troubles: a Price of Delusion," *The Weekly Underwriter* CLXXV, No. 20 (November 17, 1956), 1134–37.

of the group which is required to participate decreases as the size of the group increases. If an individual leaves the group, he may purchase an individual contract without proving insurability.

Each association makes contracts with its subscribers and its member hospitals. All associations do not use the same contracts, and over half of them offer more than one form of contract to their subscribers.[5]

Subscriber contracts. A typical Blue Cross contract with a subscriber promises to provide certain hospital services in a member hospital for a stated period of time, regardless of the cost of the services. If a subscriber wants better accommodations than those provided under the plan, he receives a limited cash allowance to help cover his expenses. In either case the subscriber receives no cash directly; his hospital bill is reduced.

For example, the contract may provide subscribers with room and board, general nursing service, use of the operating room and other hospital services in ward or semi-private accommodations of member hospitals for seventy days in each period of separate and unrelated disability in each membership year. Thus if the subscriber is hospitalized for seventy days or less, he may have no hospital bill to pay.

Partial benefits such as a 50 per cent allowance on all specified benefits are sometimes provided for an additional specified period, such as ninety days. Maternity benefits are usually limited to ten days. If the subscriber wants private accommodations, some specified amount, such as $8 per day, is allowed on the charges for room and general nursing services. All other benefits are provided on a full service basis.

The most common variation of the typical contract provides essentially the same benefits, but there is always a dollar limitation, usually $6 per day, on the charge for room and board and general nursing service. Other variations have dollar limitations on some of or all the hospital extras or small deductibles, such as $10 and $25, applicable to these charges. Under these contract variations, the subscriber is much more likely to have some hospital bill to pay.

Special benefits are provided for Blue Cross subscribers who may be hospitalized in a nonmember hospital or in an institution which belongs to a different Blue Cross plan. Not many Blue Cross subscribers are hospitalized in nonmember hospitals, since less

---

[5] For an excellent analysis of 195 group contracts offered by eighty Blue Cross plans, see Oscar N. Serbein, Jr., *Paying for Medical Care in the United States* (New York: Columbia University Press, 1953), pp. 120–27.

than one-third of the general nongovernmental hospitals with less than 10 per cent of the hospital beds fall in that category. Benefits in these nonmember hospitals are limited to some specified amount, and the money is often paid to the insured after he has paid the hospital bill.

Because of the local autonomy of Blue Cross associations and territorial variation in hospital costs, a subscriber hospitalized in a member institution in a different area used to receive the same benefits that he would have received in any nonmember hospital. However, more than three-fourths of the plans now belong to the Inter-Plan Service Benefit Bank. The bank is a financial arrangement which makes it possible for a participating plan to provide the service benefits of other participating plans under which the subscriber may be hospitalized for the number of days to which he is entitled under his own plan.

Firms which wish to provide uniform coverage for employees in two or more plan areas may purchase a contract from the stock insurer, Health Service, Incorporated, which is owned by the Blue Cross Commission. Part or all of the benefits are reinsured by local plans.

All contracts exclude workmen's compensation cases, cases where hospitalization is furnished by law, hospitalization primarily for physiotherapy or diagnostic studies, and rest cures. Other common exclusions are care for tuberculosis, nervous and mental diseases, venereal disease, alcoholism and drug addiction. Pre-existing conditions may be excluded entirely or for the first six to twelve months. A waiting period may also apply to treatment for tonsillitis or adenoids.

Dependents may be insured for the same or slightly less liberal benefits. Dependents include the husband or wife and children, usually from birth to age nineteen.

The premium structure is usually very simple. There is one rate for single persons and another for a person with dependents. There are no variations among groups and no dividends. However, a few plans divide each group into more classes on the basis of the number and type of dependents in the same way as the commercial insurer. Also, a few plans have experience rated some very large insureds.

Contracts with member hospitals. The contracts with the member hospitals prescribe the schedule of payments which these hospitals will receive for the services rendered Blue Cross subscribers. Three principal methods have been used: (1) A straight *per diem* is paid for each day of care, the *per diem* being based on the hospital's average charges. Some plans vary the *per diem* by the type of treatment or length of stay. Others pay separate amounts for room and board and hospital extras. (2) All or part of the billed charges are paid. (3) The payments are based upon service cost statements provided by the hospitals, but in no case may the payments exceed the charges to nonmembers. Costs are interpreted liberally to include depreciation and obsolescence, interest, and an increase in a contingency fund. The third method is the most common.[6]

TRENDS IN BLUE CROSS CONTRACTS

Hospital expense prepayment plans have been traced back to 1880 in Minnesota and Oregon, but the modern movement is considered to have started with the Baylor University Hospital Plan in 1929. A group of teachers in the Dallas city schools who were impressed by the need for protection against hospital expenses approached the hospital administrators with the original idea. As a result of their talks, all Dallas teachers who belonged to a Sick Benefit Fund were promised twenty-one days of hospitalization in a semi-private room for a premium of 50 cents a month. Other groups joined the plan as its popularity grew.

Hospital administrators throughout the country studied the plan and many of them adapted the underlying principles to their own situation. They discovered that through such plans they could provide a valuable form of protection and cut down the amount of free service that they were providing. The Depression and increasing hospital services had intensified their financial problems.

The fear of excessive competition among two or more plans in a given area and the disadvantages of limiting coverage to one hospital suggested the joint participation of several hospitals in a single plan. The first joint plan was established in 1932 in Sacramento, California, and was followed in 1933 by plans in six other cities.

In 1933 the American Hospital Association approved the principle of prepaid hospital expense and appointed a special committee to study the growing movement. The committee reported a few months later on the essentials of an acceptable plan. In 1936 the AHA established a Commission on Hospital Service (now the Blue Cross Commission) as a clearing house and center for information and advice. In 1937 the Commission began to approve plans meeting their standards and Blue Cross was born.

[6] Some hospital administrators are strongly opposed to this approach.

Contracts have been improved from time to time. As in the case of the commercial insurers, increased competition, experience, and consumer interest are responsible for these improvements. The number of days of coverage has been increased; the list of hospital extras has been lengthened; and full service benefits have become more common. The independent plans are learning to work together, and today the Blue Cross subscriber can receive service benefits in a different plan area. Individual contracts are becoming more common.

BLUE SHIELD PLANS

Blue Shield associations are voluntary nonprofit prepayment plans covering surgical fees and charges for physicians' care which have applied for and received the approval of the Blue Shield Commission of the American Medical Association.[7] There are about eighty locally autonomous plans, most of them being organized on a statewide basis. A local medical society usually initiates and controls the plan, the daily operations of the plan generally being handled by the staff of the local Blue Cross plan. Most of the plans are underwritten by the participating physicians.

Most Blue Shield contracts are sold to members of eligible groups, but individual contracts are available. Conversion rights are included under the group contracts.

Subscriber contracts. The variations among the subscriber contracts offered by a given plan are minor, but there are significant variations among the different plans.[8] All plans provide surgical benefits; most cover charges for physicians' care in the hospital; and about one-seventh will cover charges for physicians' care at the doctor's office or at the patient's home. The benefits are approximately the same as those provided under commercial group contracts, but there are usually more exclusions and no coverage during a specified period for pre-existing illnesses, tonsillitis, and adenoids. Dependents are eligible for the same or slightly less liberal benefits and children are usually considered dependents from birth to age nineteen.

Most contracts are partial service contracts. The patient is responsible for the difference between the benefit and the doctor's regular charge, but if the subscriber's family income from all

[7] A few Blue Cross plans include surgical and physicians' care benefits in their hospital contracts, while several Blue Shield plans include hospital benefits in their contracts. In a few areas Blue Cross and Blue Shield plans compete.

[8] Serbein, *op. cit.*, p. 319.

sources is less than a specified amount, commonly $2,000 for single subscribers and $3,000 for family subscribers, participating physicians agree to accept the benefit as full payment. An increasing number of plans now permit persons in an intermediate income group—higher than the income level eligible for service benefits in the basic plan but lower than some specified amount—to receive service benefits if they are willing to pay an additional premium.

About one-fourth of the plans are written on a cash indemnity basis, while a few provide full service benefits. No Blue Shield plan has ever changed from a service program to a straight indemnity program.[9]

About 90 per cent of the physicians in the United States are participating physicians, but in certain plan areas the percentage is much less than the average. About five-sixths of the plans promise to pay 50 or 75 per cent of the cash indemnity if the subscriber is treated by a nonparticipating physician. Most of the other plans pay the same cash indemnity, while a few pay no benefits.

If a subscriber covered under a full service or partial service plan is treated by a participating physician in another plan area, there is no guarantee that the physician will accept the benefit as full payment, but in practice this is what usually happens.

The premium structure for Blue Shield contracts is approximately the same as for Blue Cross contracts.

TRENDS IN BLUE SHIELD CONTRACTS

Medical society sponsored prepayment plans covering surgical fees and charges for physician's care date back to 1929 in Washington and Oregon. They were an outgrowth of earlier prepayment plans controlled by lay persons which started in the 1880's when employers entered into contracts for the provision of service to workers injured on the job. The physicians found that the lay associations were forcing the doctors to compete for their subscribers on a price basis.

The movement did not grow rapidly until 1939 when the California Physicians Service was established on a statewide basis by the California Medical Association. The governor of California had proposed a social medical expense insurance bill and the doctors resolved to prove that a voluntary plan would work. Soon plans were being formed in other areas.

Blue Cross plans encouraged the movement, for their subscribers were requesting coverage against doctors' bills, and commercial

[9] Frank E. Smith, "Blue Shield Develops," *A Look at Modern Health Insurance* (Washington, D. C.: Chamber of Commerce of the United States, 1954), p. 122.

insurers were providing this protection. In 1942 the American Medical Association approved the principal of prepayment plans sponsored by medical societies. During the next three years the Council on Medical Service and Public Relations coordinated the existing plans and gave guidance to local medical societies which were interested in establishing new plans. Some plans began to display the Blue Shield symbol. In 1946 a definite set of standards was made public and the formal approval program started.

The coverages are gradually being liberalized. Physicians' care in the hospital, in the doctor's office, or at home is being provided in more contracts; benefit amounts are being increased; exclusions and waiting periods are becoming less numerous; and service benefits are becoming more common. Several Blue Shield plans are issuing major medical expense insurance contracts similar to those being sold by commercial insurers.

Independent Plans

The independent plans include all accidental injury and sickness plans other than those underwritten by commercial insurers and Blue Cross and Blue Shield associations. The plans may be divided into three major categories: (1) paid sick leave plans, (2) supplementary workmen's compensation benefit plans, and (3) medical expense plans.

PAID SICK LEAVE PLANS

Paid sick leave plans are the only important nonoccupational disability income plans in addition to those underwritten by commercial insurers. These sick leave plans may be formal or informal: the benefits may be paid according to a predetermined formula or they may be awarded on some discretionary basis at the time of need. The plans are self-insured by the employer.

The plans usually continue the employee's salary in full, beginning with the first day of absence from work. There is usually a maximum number of days of sick leave per year and this maximum may be a function of the length of service.

SUPPLEMENTARY WORKMEN'S COMPENSATION BENEFIT PLANS

Plans under which a firm seeks to supplement workmen's compensation payments have become more common in recent years. A variety of practices are used in these supplementary payment plans.[10] The most common single method for both salaried and hourly employees is to pay the employee his full compensation, from which workmen's compensation is deducted. Most commonly also, companies tend to maintain a distinct, separate, self-insured program for such supplemental payments.[11]

While this approach does not appear quantitatively significant at present for hourly rated employees, it does loom importantly for salaried employees, and will probably increase in the future. (Interestingly enough, this type of supplement does not appear to have given rise to any of the legal, ethical, and economic issues that have arisen in conjunction with unemployment supplements. Nor, so far as we know, has anyone studied the incentive-disincentive effects of the 100 per cent benefit, which was the most common practice, as noted in the paragraph above. These plans would appear to merit further investigation.)

MEDICAL EXPENSE PLANS

In 1954 there were 304 independent medical expense plans in the United States.[12] About half of these plans had enrollments of less than 5,000. Because the plans are a very heterogeneous group, their operations and benefits will be discussed only in general terms.

Two-thirds of the independent plans are industrial plans whose membership is restricted to the employees of a single establishment or union and to their dependents. Most of these plans are controlled and operated directly by a union or group of unions, the funds usually being provided at least in part by employers. The second most common group is jointly financed and controlled by the employer and the employee or union. Employee-sponsored plans are the third most common, and employer-sponsored the least common.

An example of a liberal industrial plan is the medical program of the United Mine Workers of America Welfare and Retirement Fund. This program provides medical care and rehabilitation services for miners and their dependents and survivors of deceased miners. Services provided by approved physicians and hospitals (located primarily in coal mining areas) are covered in full, but the

[10] Harland Fox, "Company Supplements to Workmen's Compensation." *Management Record*, XVII, No. 1 (January, 1955), 19–22.

[11] Sometimes a paid sick leave plan or group temporary disability income insurance is used.

[12] Agnes W. Brewster, "Independent Plans Providing Medical Care and Hospital Insurance," *Social Security Bulletin*, XVIII, No. 4 (April, 1955), 8–17.

hospital treatment of adult dependents has sometimes been limited to a specified number of days.[13] The welfare and pension programs of the fund are financed by employer payments equal to a specified royalty rate per ton of coal mined.

The nonindustrial plans include plans sponsored by a community, a cooperative, a fraternal, a medical society (plan not approved by Blue Shield), or a private group clinic. Community plans are sponsored by the public and are open to groups or to individuals in the community. Cooperative plans resemble community plans, but each member has a say in the nonmedical administrative aspects of the plan. Fraternal societies sometimes sell commercial-type accidental injury and sickness contracts to their members; a few offer limited direct medical services such as hospital treatment for tuberculosis. The medical society plans resemble the Blue Shield plans, but their sponsors either have not applied for or have not gained Blue Shield approval. Private group clinic plans are prepayment plans operated under the direction, control, and ownership of a group of doctors.

An example of a liberal nonindustrial community plan is the Health Insurance Plan of Greater New York, a nonprofit corporation which contracts with various medical groups to provide the service. The plan provides medical care by a doctor and home nursing service. Service provided within one of the plan group practice areas by approved physicians is covered in full[14] with limited cash payments being made if for any reason the subscriber cannot be served by his medical group. Each subscriber is entitled to one physical examination per year. Only groups of employees are insured.

The independent plans are classified by type of sponsorship and type of benefit, including dental benefits, in Table 12.1. Each type of benefit is offered by a larger percentage of the industrial plans than of the nonindustrial plans.

All but one of the employer-sponsored industrial plans offer hospitalization, surgical, and physicians' care benefits. The position of the union-sponsored plans is understated because many of them exist to supplement benefits provided under insured plans subject to collective bargaining. Although the table does not list disability income benefits, some industrial plans do pay an income to disabled workers.

[13] Serbein, op. cit., pp. 212–15.
[14] A $2 charge may be made for each visit by a doctor between 10 P.M. and 7 A.M.

TABLE 12.1

INDEPENDENT MEDICAL EXPENSE PLANS, BY TYPE OF SPONSORSHIP
AND BY TYPE OF BENEFIT, 1954 SURVEY

Type of Sponsorship	Type of Benefit					
	Any Benefit	Hospitali- zation	Surgical	Physi- cians' Care	Out-patient Diagnostic Services	Dental
Total	304	252	250	208	164	47
Industrial	204	177	181	144	119	39
Union	73	56	58	40	41	14
Employer-employee .	63	58	59	46	37	17
Employee	42	38	39	32	18	6
Employer	26	25	25	26	23	2
Nonindustrial . . .	100	75	69	64	45	8
Community . . .	37	33	14	13	8	2
Cooperative . . .	24	15	21	21	13	2
Fraternal	18	13	15	9	6	4
Private group clinic .	15	11	13	15	15	—
Medical society . .	6	3	6	6	3	—

Source: Based on Agnes W. Brewster, "Independent Plans Providing Medical Care and Hospital Insurance," *Social Security Bulletin*, XVIII, No. 4 (April, 1955), Table 9, p. 14.

Community plans emphasize hospitalization, while group clinic and medical society plans emphasize surgical and physicians' care benefits.

About one-half of the plans provide service benefits only, while one-third provide cash indemnity benefits only. The others provide some service benefits and some cash indemnity benefits. Among the plans providing at least some service benefits, two-thirds of them provide the doctor's care and diagnostic service benefits through the plan's own group practice clinic. Hospitalization benefits were provided by the plan's own hospital or obtained through arrangements with community hospitals. A few plans did not limit the amount of service to be provided in a given year.

Ninety per cent of the nonindustrial plans cover the dependents of members. All the community, cooperative, and medical society plans provide this protection. On the other hand, less than half the industrial plans cover dependents. Employer-sponsored plans had the lowest percentage (31 per cent) of plans protecting dependents.

Premiums do not generally vary among subscribers, but an additional premium is charged for each dependent, up to three or four dependents.

Trends in Independent Plans

Four significant trends have been noted since 1950.[15] First, union-sponsored plans are becoming more common and they are offering more comprehensive benefits. Second, benefits are being extended to dependents. Third, more plans are providing benefits through their own group-practice clinics and hospitals. And finally, more plans provide benefits for retired workers.

The independent plans include many novel approaches to the medical expense problem, and the more popular plans will continue to adopt some of their ideas. However, in some states, legislative barriers have been erected which hinder this type of useful experimentation.

Operations of Private Accidental Injury and Sickness Insurers

The recent past has witnessed a remarkably rapid increase in voluntary private accidental injury and sickness insurance. As evidence of this progress two types of data will be presented—the number of persons insured and the percentage of illness losses covered by private illness insurance benefits.

The Health Insurance Council, an organization of various commercial insurance trade associations, reports annually on the number of persons covered under private insurance contracts. The figures do not include persons covered under workmen's compensation insurance, total and permanent disability riders on life insurance contracts, or commercial contracts covering accidental injuries only. The figures do include workers covered under private plans in the four states with temporary disability insurance legislation.

The first annual report indicated the number covered as of December 31, 1947, while the latest report available as of this writing depicted the situation as of December 31, 1955. Table 12.2 summarizes and compares the 1950 and 1956 reports on the annual survey.

Coverage under major medical expense policies was not included in the surveys until the end of 1952 when 533 thousand persons were covered under group policies and 156 thousand persons under individual policies. The corresponding figures at the end of 1955 were 4,759 thousand and 482 thousand.

The data indicate (1) a tremendous growth in all forms of coverage, especially the physicians' care and major medical expense

[15] Brewster, op. cit., p. 11.

TABLE 12.2

NUMBER OF PEOPLE PROTECTED UNDER PRIVATE ACCIDENTAL INJURY
AND SICKNESS CONTRACTS, END OF 1949 AND END OF 1955

(in thousands)

Plan	End of 1949	End of 1955	Per Cent Increase
Loss of income:			
Commercial insurance			
Group insurance . . .	10,260	19,238	87.5
Individual insurance . .	13,687	14,238	4.0
Paid sick leave*			
Private industry . . .	4,560	3,100	−32.0
Civilian government service	4,750	4,800	1.1
Union administered plans* .	1,700	600	−64.7
Employee mutual benefit			
associations* . . .	1,460	600	−58.9
GRAND TOTAL . . .	36,417	42,576	16.9
Deduct for duplication . .	2,281	3,132	
NET TOTAL	34,136	39,444	15.5

	Hospital	Surgical	Physicians' Care	Hospital	Surgical	Physicians' Care	Hospital	Surgical	Physicians' Care
Medical expense:									
Commercial insurance									
Group insurance	17,697	15,590	2,736	39,029	39,725	20,678	120.5	154.8	759.1
Individual insurance	14,729	9,315	2,350	26,706	22,445	6,264	81.3	141.0	166.6
Blue Cross plans and plans sponsored by medical societies	34,315	14,628	8,508	50,726	39,165	29,451	47.8	167.7	246.2
Independent plans:									
Industrial	1,785	1,835	1,830	2,916	2,926	2,599	63.4	59.5	42.0
Community-consumer	1,600	1,600	1,600	738	627	614	−53.9	−61.8	−61.6
Private group clinics	275	285	305	476	487	526	73.1	70.9	72.5
University health plans	100	100	100	400	300	900	300.0	200.0	800.0
GRAND TOTAL	70,501	43,353	17,429	120,991	105,675	61,032	71.6	143.8	250.2
Deduct for duplication	4,457	2,210	567	13,329	13,748	5,526			
NET TOTAL	66,044	41,143	16,862	107,662	91,927	55,506	63.0	123.4	229.2

* Net figures after adjustment for duplication of other coverage.

Source: The Health Insurance Council, A Survey of Accident and Health Coverage in the United States (New York: 1950), and The Extent of Voluntary Health Insurance Coverage in the United States (New York: 1956).

coverages; (2) the greater popularity and more rapid growth of medical expense coverages as compared with loss of income coverages; (3) the dominant role of the commercial insurers and the Blue Cross-Blue Shield movements; and (4) the increasing importance of group insurance.

The Social Security Administration uses a different yardstick to determine the growth of private accidental injury and sickness insurance. It reports annually the total nonoccupational short-term disability income losses and medical expenses and the percentage of the losses covered by private insurance benefits. Table 12.3 summarizes the record of private insurance according to this measure in 1948 and 1954. The data are presented in such a way that it is possible to compare the benefits with the losses including or excluding the expenses of the insurers.

The growth of all forms of private accidental injury and sickness insurance is impressive. The percentage of medical expenses covered is now greater than that of disability income losses covered, but the opposite was true in 1948. Hospital bills are the most completely covered type of expense, but the most rapidly growing type of insurance covers doctors' charges.

Of the insurance benefits covering income losses, 55 per cent were paid by sick leave plans, 41 per cent by commercial insurers, and 4 per cent by other insurers. These data emphasize the liberal individual payments under the sick leave plans because relatively few people are covered under these plans. Of the medical expense benefits, 45 per cent were paid by Blue Cross-Blue Shield associations, 45 per cent by commercial insurers, and 10 per cent by the independent insurers.

In interpreting these data it should be remembered that complete coverage is impossible for underwriting reasons. In fact if the expenses of the insurer are included in the losses, the per cent would be less than unity even if all losses were paid. Furthermore, complete coverage may not be desirable if it is more economical to assume some of the losses as operating expenses.

Unfortunately, the data do not tell us to what extent some families benefited more than others from private insurance benefits. The benefits may be widespread in their impact or a small percentage of the families may have a large percentage of their losses covered. Furthermore, there is no information on the types of benefits paid. It makes a difference both to the family and to society whether the benefits were used to pay for a few serious losses or for many nonserious losses.

TABLE 12.3

Private Insurance Benefits in Relation to Disability Income Losses and Private Expenditures for Medical Care, 1948 and 1954

(in millions)

Type of Loss	1948			1954		
	Loss	Insurance Benefits	Per Cent of Loss Covered by Insurance	Loss	Insurance Benefits	Per Cent of Loss Covered by Insurance
Income loss:*						
Disability income loss	$4,629	$729	15.8	$6,157	$1,361	22.2
Net cost of medical expense insurance†	271	—	—	456	—	—
Total	$4,900	$729	14.9	$6,613	$1,361	20.5
Medical expenses:						
Hospital services	$1,663	$455	27.4	$2,970	$1,442	48.5
Doctors' services	2,233	151	6.8	2,963	737	24.8
Dentists' services	833	—	—	975	—	—
Other professional services	423	—	—	583	—	—
Medicines and appliances	1,785	—	—	2,197	—	—
Total	$6,937	$606	8.7	$9,688	$2,179	22.4
Net cost of medical expense insurance†	256	—	—	577	—	—
Total	$7,193	$606	8.4	$10,265	$2,179	21.2

* Short-term nonwork-connected disability (lasting not more than six months) and the first six months of long-term disability.
† Premiums earned less benefits incurred.

Source: U. S. Department of Health, Education, and Welfare, Social Security Administration, "The Growth of Voluntary Health Insurance, 1948–54," *Social Security Bulletin*, XVIII, No. 12 (December, 1955), 11–14, 29. U. S. Department of Health, Education, and Welfare, Social Security Administration, "The Growth in Protection Against Income Loss from Short-Term Sickness: 1948–54," *Social Security Bulletin*, XIX, No. 1 (January, 1956), 3–8.

Evaluation[16]

Private accidental injury and sickness insurance has expanded significantly but few people would claim that the present coverage is completely adequate. In this section we shall consider separately the protection afforded, the underwriting practices, the premium structures, and the type of control.

PROTECTION AFFORDED

Private insurance contracts are available which protect insureds against long-term disability income losses, short-term disability income losses, and medical expenses.

Commercial insurers issue both cancellable and noncancellable individual policies under which the insurer promises to pay a monthly income for the duration of a long-term total disability caused by accidental injury. On the other hand, relatively few policies (and almost all of them are cancellable) pay a monthly income for more than ten years if the disability is caused by sickness. Partial permanent disability payments are always limited to a relatively short period. Disability income riders on life insurance policies protect the insured against long-term total disability income losses, regardless of the cause, but it is necessary to purchase a sizable amount of life insurance before the disability income amount is reasonably adequate. Group plans seldom provide any long-term disability income protection. Long-term disability is the weakest area in private accidental injury and sickness insurance, but commercial insurers appear to be gradually solving some of their important underwriting problems and long-term disability income protection should be continually improved. The 1956 amendments to OASI will probably hasten these improvements.

Temporary disability income benefits are readily available from commercial insurers on an individual or group basis and under paid sick leave plans. The cause of the disability may be an accidental injury or sickness. Waiver of premium benefits are also readily available in individual life insurance and noncancellable contracts.

Under almost all disability income contracts, disability is not defined in terms of a loss of income. Administrative reasons have been cited to justify the definitions used, but, in the opinion of the authors, a more logical definition based upon the loss of income is needed. The need for a change in the present definitions is being

---

[16] For an extensive objective critique of commercial accidental injury and sickness insurance, see Kulp, *op. cit.*, pp. 391–98.

discussed more frequently both within and outside the insurance industry.

Individual sickness contracts almost always require that the sickness commence during the policy period. Therefore, a claim may be denied on the grounds that the illness was pre-existing even though the insured was unaware of its existence at the time he purchased the contract. However, most states do not permit commercial insurers to deny claims on this basis after the policy has been in effect for two or three years. Many insurers follow this practice voluntarily in the other states. The other exclusions under most disability income contracts are not too important for the average person.

Many types of medical expense coverages are available. The prospective insured may choose among commercial individual and group insurance contracts, Blue Cross and Blue Shield plans, and independent plans.

Some medical expense plans usually provide complete protection for nonserious illnesses, but most contracts always require the insured to pay part of the bill himself. When the medical facilities are costless, the insured is more likely to seek early treatment, which should reduce the severity of the illness. On the other hand, complete protection may encourage overutilization of the medical resources.

Many plans provide full or partial service benefits. The loss of freedom of choice of medical facilities is slight under most of these contracts, but some are very restrictive in this respect. In fact, a few plans require treatment in one hospital by a limited group of doctors. To some persons, however, even this severe restriction is not important.

Until recently, medical expense insurance was primarily a device for budgeting the cost of nonserious illnesses over a number of years. Protection against financial catastrophes at a reasonable cost is a recent innovation, but it is growing rapidly. In the opinion of the authors, major medical expense insurance is the most promising addition to private accidental injury and sickness insurance in many decades.

Few medical expense plans include diagnostic and preventive services among their benefits. It is debatable whether they should. In most cases it is probably cheaper for an insured to pay for such services as periodic health examinations and immunizations at the time he incurs the expense because the expense is certain and the insured saves the expense loading of the insurer. On the other hand, (1) insureds are more likely to appear for these preventive services when they have already been paid for, thus reducing the other services which are necessary, and (2) the cost per examination is reduced by distributing the overhead expense among more persons.

The exclusions under the medical expense contracts are more numerous and more important than those under the disability income contracts, but they are being reduced.

Age limitations are common in both the disability income and medical expense contracts, especially those of commercial insurers. These limitations are not too important in the case of disability income insurance because the insured's earning power would normally stop at some advanced age, but the need for medical expense insurance increases at the advanced ages. However, medical expense coverages are available which will protect the insured for life, and the age limits under other contracts are being increased.

Opinions as to the adequacy of the present plans vary depending upon the standard desired. Those who believe that the plans should provide complete protection against all types of medical expenses would consider the present plans very inadequate. The authors believe that private accidental injury and sickness insurance should be available which would pay all the losses which the insured family cannot, without more than temporary inconvenience, handle out of its current income and small savings accounts. On this score, private insurance rates fairly high and its record is improving, but there are still some important gaps and weaknesses to be overcome.

UNDERWRITING

A larger percentage of applicants is ineligible for private accidental injury and sickness insurance than for private life insurance. Advanced age and poor health are the principal reasons for the rejections. Moreover, individual contracts can usually be cancelled if the insurer finds it necessary to take this step.

Within the past few years, much more attention has been paid to substandard lives and more advanced age groups are now eligible for coverage. Moreover, noncancellable policies are becoming more common.[17]

Group insurance is another solution to the problem of individual uninsurability because all members of an eligible group are insurable. Moreover, under most noncommercial group insurance plans terminating members are usually permitted to purchase individual

---

[17] At least one author questions whether enough underwriting safeguards are being included in these noncancellable policies. See Kulp, *op. cit.*, p. 407.

insurance contracts without proving insurability. An increasing number of commercial insurers are extending the same privilege to their group insureds. However, not all members of the population are members of eligible groups, although very small groups of various types are currently being insured.

There will always be some persons who will be ineligible for private insurance. Others will not choose or be able to afford the protection, and the protection purchased will probably always be incomplete for many others. Therefore, there is a need, in the opinion of the authors, for at least a public assistance program dealing with these problems which is broader than Aid to the Totally and Permanently Disabled and Aid to the Blind. This opinion was developed in detail in Chapter 11.

PREMIUM STRUCTURES

As stated in Chapter 5, private insurance premiums should not, on the average, be excessive and they should distribute the cost equitably. One indication as to whether the premiums are excessive, on the average, is the benefit ratio or ratio of benefits incurred to earned income. Other things being equal, a high ratio is favorable, for it indicates that most of the premiums are being returned to policyholders in the form of benefits.

Table 12.4 lists the 1954 benefit ratios of each type of insurer. Paid sick leave plans are not included. The ratio exceeds 70 per cent in each case except commercial individual insurance where the insured receives more individual attention and, consequently, the cost of selling and servicing the protection is greater.[18] Since these ratios vary from year to year, slight differences among the ratios should be ignored. On the whole, the picture is favorable to private insurance, but it can be improved.

There are two schools of thought concerning the equitable distribution of the insurance costs. The arguments of both schools have some merit. One school maintains that it is socially and economically desirable to use an average premium for all insureds, regardless of their age, sex, and group experience. The objective of this school is the widest possible pooling of risks. The other school argues that a uniform distribution of the costs is not a fair distribution according to private insurance standards. The mem-

[18] Kulp points out that the quality of the agent and the service he provides must be considered in deciding whether acquisition costs are too high. See Kulp, op cit., p. 396. Unfortunately many accidental injury and sickness insurers do not train their agents adequately, and some individual agents are much more interested in commissions than in service to policyholders.

TABLE 12.4

EXPENDITURES FOR INCOME AND MEDICAL EXPENSE BENEFITS AS A
PER CENT OF EARNED INCOME, BY TYPE OF INSURER, 1954

Benefit and Type of Insurer	Benefits as Per Cent of Income
Loss of income:	
Commercial insurers	
Group insurance	72.6
Individual insurance	42.0
Others	74.4
Medical expenses:	
Commercial insurers	
Group insurance	82.6
Individual insurance	51.0
Blue Cross associations	89.3
Blue Shield associations	80.8
Independent plans	
Employee benefit associations	96.1
Union-administered	91.2
Community	83.7
Consumer	82.9
Medical society	88.1
Private group clinics	97.3

Source: *Social Security Bulletin*, December, 1955, p. 13, and January, 1956, p. 4.

bers of this school also believe that a uniform premium will work
only if all insurers charge the same uniform premium, for otherwise
the insureds will seek out the insurer charging the lowest premium.
Even if the premium were uniform, it might be higher than some
of the healthier insureds would be willing to pay. Hence compulsion might be necessary if these people are to be insured.[19]

TYPE OF CONTROL

The insured usually has little or no direct control over the types
of contracts offered. Stockholders, the present management, physicians, and hospitals control most of the plans. However, this lack of
control by the insureds is not too important as long as the plans
continue to experiment and to liberalize their coverages. Competition has forced the plans to listen to the demands of insureds.

However, there have been abuses in some employee welfare
plans as noted in Chapters 5 and 18. Most of the abuses have arisen
out of the accidental injury and sickness features of the plans. It

[19] John H. Miller, "Rates and Reserves—Personal Commercial and Non-cancellable
Contracts," *Accident and Sickness Insurance* (Philadelphia: University of Pennsylvania Press, 1954), pp. 190–91.

has also been claimed that some doctors and hospitals have abused accidental injury and sickness insurance and that doctor- and hospital-controlled plans do not police their colleagues adequately. On the whole, however, the administration of private accidental injury and sickness insurance appears to be satisfactory.

A Concluding Note

The most obvious characteristic of private accidental injury and sickness insurance is at the same time a strong point and a weakness. The multitude of contracts available with their heterogeneous benefits and costs gives the insured considerable freedom of choice. Moreover, the competition among insurers has produced many important improvements. On the other hand, the field is so complicated that relatively few insureds understand it well enough to make intelligent choices.

Summary

Private accidental injury and sickness insurance is underwritten by three major classes of insurers: (1) commercial insurers, (2) Blue Cross associations and Blue Shield associations, and (3) independent insurers.

Commercial insurers underwrite both disability income and medical expense benefits. The two most important forms of individual insurance providing both types of benefits are commercial insurance, which is cancellable by the insurer, and noncancellable insurance. The income benefits vary depending upon whether the disability is partial or total and whether the disability is caused by an accidental injury or sickness. The medical expense benefits may be written on a general or on a specific basis and are often not included in the contract.

Most of the individual insurance contracts issued by commercial insurers are basic medical expense insurance contracts. These contracts protect the insured against small and moderate medical expenses, usually on a specific basis. The most important recent development is major medical expense insurance which pays, on a blanket basis, all or most of the medical expenses in excess of a specified deductible.

Group insurance underwritten by commercial insurers protects more persons than individual insurance. The most common benefits protect the insured against a temporary disability income loss, specific types of basic medical expenses, such as hospital expenses, and major medical expenses.

Blue Cross associations and Blue Shield associations are the most important competitors of the commercial insurers. A Blue Cross association is a nonprofit hospital expense prepayment plan approved by the American Hospital Association. There are many types of Blue Cross contracts, but the typical contract provides a specified number of days of service in ward or semi-private accommodations of member hospitals. The subscriber receives limited cash allowances if he wants better accommodations or if he is hospitalized in a nonmember hospital.

A Blue Shield association is a nonprofit prepayment plan covering surgical fees and charges for physicians' care which has been approved by the American Medical Association. There are many Blue Shield contracts, but the typical contract provides specified dollar amounts for surgical operations. Participating physicians agree to accept the benefit as full payment if the subscriber's income is below a certain amount.

The independent insurers underwrite medical expense plans primarily, but paid sick leave plans self-insured by employers are important disability income plans. The independent insurers include the nonindustrial insurers—community plans, cooperatives, fraternals, medical societies, and private group clinics—and the industrial insurers—unions, employers, and groups of employees. Most of these plans provide some service benefits, and in some plans the protection is very comprehensive.

Suggestions for Additional Reading

DICKERSON, O. D. *Long-Term Guaranteed Renewable Disability Insurance.* Chicago: Health and Accident Underwriters Conference, 1955.
This monograph deals with the problem of long-term disability and the history and current status of long-term guaranteed renewable disability insurance.

FAULKNER, EDWIN J. *Accident and Health Insurance.* New York: McGraw-Hill Book Co., Inc., 1939.
A dated but useful text on private accidental injury and sickness insurance.

HERRICK, KENNETH. *Total Disability Provisions in Life Insurance Contracts.* Homewood: Richard D. Irwin, Inc., 1956.
This book traces the history of total disability provisions in life insurance contracts and discusses the present status of this coverage.

ILSE, LOUISE WOLTERS. *Group Insurance and Employee Retirement Plans.* Englewood Cliffs, N. J.: Prentice-Hall, Inc., 1953. Chapters 1, 2, and 7 through 10.
This text describes group accidental injury and sickness protection underwritten by commercial insurers and Blue Cross—Blue Shield associations.

KULP, C. A. *Casualty Insurance,* 3d ed. New York: The Ronald Press Co., 1956. Chapter 14.

An objective description, analysis, and evaluation of private accidental injury and sickness insurance.

McCahan, David, (ed.). *Accident and Sickness Insurance.* Philadelphia: University of Pennsylvania Press, 1954.
A collection of lectures on accidental injury and sickness insurance, primarily underwritten by commercial insurers.

Serbein, Oscar N., Jr. *Paying for Medical Care in the United States.* New York: Columbia University Press, 1953.
This authoritative volume analyzes in detail all types of medical expense insurance.

Strong, Jay V. *Employee Benefit Plans in Operation.* Washington, D. C.: The Bureau of National Affairs, Inc., 1951. Chapters 6 through 8.
An analysis of the group insurance plans of 923 firms. The last chapter discusses collective bargaining on welfare programs.

13

Economic Security Programs
for Special Groups

Introduction

In addition to the programs created under the Social Security Act and the related economic security measures discussed in earlier chapters, at least five major systems, underwritten by governmental units, deal with the old age, illness, and unemployment risks to economic security. These relate to veterans, railroad workers, federal civil servants, state and local government employees, and individuals receiving aid under the general assistance programs.

These programs differ in two respects from those considered earlier. First, their coverage is limited to special groups of workers; and, second, the objective of the benefits paid under these programs is in some cases somewhat different from that of the Social Security Act. We have omitted from this discussion still other special programs, such as the Merchant Marine Act, which extends to seamen the same rights as railroad workers enjoy under their federal Employers' Liability Act and the Longshoremen's and Harbor Workers' Act, which provides workmen's compensation benefits similar to those of the Federal Employees' Compensation Act. Each of these, and others, while they are important to their industries, were omitted to enable discussion of the programs which, by the standard of numbers of workers protected, are the most important ones applying to special groups.

In Table 13.1 these economic security measures for special groups are compared with the systems we have been discussing in terms of the risks with which they deal and the size of their coverage and benefits.

TABLE 13.1

PERSONS RECEIVING PAYMENTS AND AMOUNT OF
SUCH PAYMENTS UNDER SOCIAL INSURANCE AND
RELATED PROGRAMS, 1954
(Corrected to July 19, 1955)

	Average Monthly Number of Persons Receiving Payments (Thousands)	Annual Amount of Payments (Millions)
Old-age benefits		
Old-Age and Survivors' Insurance	4,589.6	$2,698
Railroad retirement	307.7	325
Federal Civil Service and other federal . . .	249.2	459
State and local government retirement	292.0	385
Veterans' programs	65.7	79
Old-age assistance	2,565.0	1,685
Survivorship benefits and aid to dependent persons		
Monthly survivorship benefits:		
Old-Age and Survivors' Insurance	1,891.9	880
Railroad retirement	167.2	93
Federal Civil Service	60.2	33
State and local government retirement	48.0	35
Veterans' programs	1,112.2	629
Workmen's compensation	——ᵃ	75
Lump-sum survivorship payments:		
Old-Age and Survivors' Insurance	——ᵃ	93
Railroad retirement	——ᵃ	16
Federal Civil Service and other federal . . .	——ᵃ	9
State and local government retirement	——ᵃ	40
Veterans' programs	——ᵃ	16
Aid to dependent children	2,174	650
Disability		
Workmen's compensation	——ᵃ	525
Veterans' programs	2,735.9	1,842
Railroad retirement	84.9	104
Federal Civil Service and other federal . . .	138.0	256
State and local government retirement	45.0	40
State programs for temporary disability . . .	81.6	190
Railroad temporary disability insurance . . .	31.5	49
Aid to the permanently and totally disabled . .	224.0	153
Aid to the blind	102.0	73
Unemployment		
State unemployment insurance	1,614.9	2,026
Railroad unemployment insurance	110.4	157
Veterans' unemployment allowances and self-employment	89.3	107
General assistance (cases)	351.0	298

ᵃ Not available.

Source: *Social Security Bulletin*, XVIII, No. 9 (September, 1955), 30, 65, 76.

It is apparent from this table that the programs for special groups are indeed important in relation to our better known economic security measures. This is particularly true of some of the veterans' programs which, in terms of the scope and degree of coverage they provide, are the largest of all programs applying to special groups.

Veterans' Economic Security Programs

A system of veterans' benefits has been maintained by this country since the Revolutionary War. In fact, pension precedents established at that time are still used today in appeals for veterans' pensions. In times of war, veterans' benefit programs have always been re-examined and usually have been extended.

Although the veterans' benefit program includes economic security measures protecting against the hazards of death, old age, dependency, illness, and unemployment (which are in some respects comparable to our regular social insurance programs covering these hazards), the whole program, both in scope and nature, goes far beyond the system of job-oriented economic security dealt with in this book. It is instructive, however, to enumerate some of the veterans' benefit programs which have been provided by our government over the years: *disability compensation to veterans and dependents; pensions; aids in land acquisition; cash bounties; domiciliary care; Civil Service preference; insurance; medical and hospital care; vocational rehabilitation; guardianship service; retirement of disabled emergency officers; readjustment benefits (G. I. Bill) providing re-employment rights, education benefits, readjustment allowances, and loans.*[1] This list does not include veterans' benefits provided under state laws.

CHANGING PHILOSOPHY OF VETERANS' BENEFITS

From the period of the American Revolution, the government has always in some measure accepted the view that it is responsible for the economic security of those who served it in time of war. There has never been any question about compensating the survivors of war casualties or veterans who were disabled in the service of their country. But how to discharge this responsibility to other veterans in their best interest has been the subject of strong polit-

[1] For the most complete and up-to-date study of veterans' benefit programs, see U. S. Congress, 84th, House, 2nd Session, House Committee on Veterans' Affairs, *A Report on Veterans' Benefits in the United States* (Washington, D. C.: U. S. Government Printing Office, 1956), Committee Prints 243, 244, 246, 247, 259–262, 270, 275.

ical and economic forces since the Revolutionary War, and changing concepts of this responsibility have led to a new approach in veterans' benefits.

A long-prevailing philosophy, particularly as evidenced by the various pension acts, was that the government ought to help the veteran when he is down—because he is a veteran. In part, there has always been the desire to protect veterans from indigency, to pay them a debt of gratitude, or simply to reward them for faithful service. Basically, this philosophy governed veterans' benefits until World War II. The veteran was largely left to make his own economic adjustment on return from duty to civilian life, and if he failed, the government sought to come to his aid. Under this approach, the emphasis was on picking up the pieces of economic wreckage, rather than on avoiding them if possible.

An attempt to improve the program after World War I failed because of the deeply imbedded concept that something was owed to the veteran. Veterans were a minority group, had no general social security system, and could point to much precedent for pension benefits. But World War II, and the legislative programs for economic security that preceded it, changed this picture. Veterans were no longer a small minority group. In 1955, they represented 13.5 per cent of the total population, or 20.5 per cent of the population over eighteen. Including wives and children of veterans, nearly one-half of the population is now eligible for veterans' benefits. Furthermore, after World War II, veterans had gained protected status under the Social Security Act, and in some instances under the Federal Employees' Compensation Act.

By this time, it was thus possible successfully to introduce a new approach to veterans' benefits—one which most observers feel has worked well. A program of benefits was designed to launch the veteran in his civilian role and to help him compete on equal terms with nonveterans. Readjustment benefits, including education benefits, unemployment allowances, job counseling and re-employment rights have replaced the pension approach as the attempt has been to bring the veteran into the mainstream of competitive economic activity on a forward-looking basis.

READJUSTMENT BENEFITS

The Servicemen's Readjustment Act of 1944—best known as the G. I. Bill of Rights—was the central piece of legislation in this new philosophy of veterans' benefits programs. As amended and later applied to Korean War veterans, it provided a variety of benefits to aid the veteran in readjusting to civilian life.

Education benefits under the first G. I. Bill of Rights expired on July 26, 1956, after providing education opportunities to nearly eight million veterans at a total cost of about $14.5 billion. An estimated two million veterans attended colleges and universities, and some 600,000 disabled veterans became self-supporting through the program.

A major innovation of the 1944 Act was the loan guaranty program which was devised as an alternative to the bonus. It was less expensive for the government and was designed to serve better the ends of the veteran by providing credit to enable him to get started in farming, in a business, or in buying a home. The system also provided an investment outlet for large amounts of savings accumulated at the end of World War II.

Readjustment allowances—payments to unemployed or partially employed veterans—were also provided under the Act with the purpose of providing minimum income during readjustment. Nearly ten million veterans filed claims, and total expenditures of around $4 billion were made.

DISABILITY COMPENSATION

As Table 13.1 indicates, disability compensation is one of the most important veterans' programs. This type of payment has existed in some form since before the American Revolution. Today, a compensation system provides benefits for service-connected disabilities as follows: total disability, $181 per month, with rates for partial disability ranging down to $17 per month for a 10 per cent disability. Totally disabled veterans receive additional compensation for dependents. Also, there are statutory awards for specific losses of bodily members and for disease.

PENSIONS AND SURVIVORS' BENEFITS

Although they are not now available to World War II or Korean War veterans, pensions are still being paid by the Veterans' Administration to veterans of wars prior to World War I and to some veterans of that war. Survivorship benefits are still available for survivors of veterans killed in wartime service and, if specified requirements are met,[2] for survivors of veterans whose deaths were not service-connected.

[2] For service-connected death, the following schedule of monthly benefits will be paid to dependents: Widow, no children, $87; widow, one child, $121; each additional child, $29; no widow, one child, $67; no widow, two children, $94; no widow,

TABLE 13.2

BENEFICIARIES AND BENEFITS UNDER
VETERANS' PROGRAMS, 1940–1954

(in thousands)

Year	Retirement Beneficiaries	Benefits	Survivorship Beneficiaries	Benefits Monthly	Lump Sum
1940	29.2	$19,770	323.2	$105,696	$ 3,960
1941	36.6	24,423	318.5	111,799	4,352
1942	42.0	28,956	315.9	111,193	4,120
1943	46.8	32,632	322.7	116,133	4,350
1944	59.1	49,250	372.7	144,302	4,784
1945	59.1	54,730	542.1	254,238	5,049
1946	62.5	57,370	790.5	333,640	7,491
1947	61.6	54,285	901.5	382,515	13,270
1948	59.8	64,221	950.0	413,912	12,358
1949	57.4	61,731	971.2	477,406	12,427
1950	53.5	57,586	991.7	491,579	12,709
1951	57.3	62,350	1,011.2	519,398	12,885
1952	78.4	87,220	1,044.2	572,983	15,142
1953	71.8	86,284	1,086.0	613,475	16,118
1954	65.7	79,096	1,122.2	628,801	16,193

Source: *Social Security Bulletin*, XVIII, No. 9 (September, 1955), 30; Federal Security Agency, *Social Security Yearbook*, 1945, p. 18; and 1948, p. 4.

Table 13.2 lists retirement and survivorship benefits under the veterans' program from 1940 to 1954. Retirement benefits and beneficiaries are on the decline, since veterans of the most recent wars are no longer entitled to such benefits.[3] Survivorship benefits and the number of beneficiaries have increased considerably, especially in the post-World War II period. Since benefits are paid from Congressional appropriations, there is no trust fund nor actuarial reports.

three children, $122; each additional child, $23; dependent father or mother, $75; dependent father and mother, $80.

Where death is not service-connected, monthly survivors' benefits will be paid if (a) a veteran of World War II or the Korean conflict had a service-connected disability—a requirement which no longer applies to veterans of World War I; and (b) the "other income" of a surviving widow or children is not above a given limit. Benefits are smaller in either case than for service-connected death.

Honorably discharged veterans with wartime service are entitled to lump-sum funeral expense benefits of $150.

[3] The sudden increase in 1952 is misleading, since in 1951 the Veterans' Administration began to classify under old age pensions both disability pensions and old-age pensions awarded to veterans prior to World War I.

INSURANCE

The Veterans' Administration issued United States Government Life Insurance policies to servicemen from World War I until 1940 when National Service Life Insurance policies were introduced. If they wanted the coverage, the servicemen paid for this insurance. The contract was very similar to that issued by commercial insurers, and there was no exclusion of war deaths. The original policy was a term policy which paid only in case of death, but servicemen had the right to renew the policy at the expiration of the term without proving insurability. They could also convert the term policy to a level-premium contract with a cash value at any time.

Because the expenses of the operation were to be paid by the government out of tax revenues, the initial premiums were low. The actual cost was much less than the initial premium because the actual death claims were far fewer than the estimated death claims. In part, this was due to the fact that the mortality table used was too conservative, but also the fact that insurance funds were not used to pay claims if the death occurred in service or was service-connected.[4]

Because it was expensive for the government, because commercial insurers argued that coverage after service was not justifiable, and because of numerous administrative and personnel problems, National Service Life Insurance was replaced by the Servicemen's Indemnity Act of 1950. This Act provided $10,000 of protection free to every serviceman. For all but disabled servicemen, the only policy to which they could convert was five-year renewable term. The premiums are lower than those of commercial insurers because there is no loading for expenses, but the insurance funds are used to pay all death claims. As a result of Congressional action in August, 1956, no *new* insurance protection will be issued by the government after 1956.

These insurance programs were justified on the social grounds that these servicemen have devoted part of their lives to serving their country. However, the bonus feature of the programs should be acknowledged and appreciated.

Table 13.3 presents some data on veterans' life insurance. In 1944, the amount of veterans' life insurance in force was almost

4 For more information on government life insurance, see Dan M. McGill, *An Analysis of Government Life Insurance* (Philadelphia: University of Pennsylvania Press, 1949); Charles K. Reid, *Fundamentals of Government Life Insurance and Related Benefits* (Philadelphia: American College of Life Underwriters, 1953).

equal to the total amount of commercial life insurance in force during that year. Apparently, many veterans did not recognize the bonus feature of the insurance, for two years later the amount of insurance in force was only about 30 per cent of the 1944 figure. Veterans of the Korean conflict are reacting in the same way, but with a somewhat better reason. The death benefits are sizable and increasing; other benefits such as cash values and disability payments are increasing but are much less important. Note the increase in other benefits in 1946 reflecting the surrender of policies by many veterans.

TABLE 13.3

VETERANS' LIFE INSURANCE

(in thousands)

	Insurance in Force		Benefits Other Than Dividends	
Year	No. of Policies	Amount	Death	Other
1941	1,312	$ 5,034,000	$ 15,189	$35,853
1942	5,125	28,950,000	19,270	28,692
1943	13,663	97,656,000	34,344	25,377
1944	16,473	123,754,000	86,078	23,149
1945	13,488	98,426,000	243,601	28,784
1946	6,140	36,599,000	283,888	70,675
1947	6,619	38,469,000	296,624	70,343
1948	5,964	37,665,000	320,352	40,238
1949	6,112	38,234,000	346,664	45,401
1950	6,978	45,286,000	361,577	50,915
1951	7,557	50,984,000	431,598	65,553
1952	7,364	49,479,000	440,245	68,195
1953	6,689	44,097,000	396,696	62,807
1954	6,469	42,741,000	422,066	63,110
1955	6,439	42,728,000	252,956	60,251

Source: *Life Insurance Fact Book* (New York: Institute of Life Insurance, 1956), p. 88.

The Veterans' Administration establishes a full legal reserve on these contracts similar to those maintained by commercial insurers. Their assets are invested in special 3 per cent government bonds.

ARMED SERVICES PROGRAM

The armed services provide a liberal retirement plan for their career members. Not all branches have exactly the same plan, but, in general, a serviceman who has completed twenty years of service may retire (with the consent of his branch) on a monthly income for life equal to 2½ per cent of his highest base pay, plus the allowance for length of service times the number of years of service. The maximum annuity is 75 per cent of his present pay.

The annuity continues during the lifetime of the annuitant but not after his death. If the serviceman dies while on active duty, his family is entitled to a lump sum equal to six months' pay and the burial benefits and service-connected death compensation available to the families of veterans. If the serviceman dies after he has left the service, his status is that of a veteran.

All these benefits are provided without cost to the members of the armed services. They are paid out of annual Congressional appropriations.

A Concluding Comment

Although veterans' benefit programs have been reshaped to follow a more forward-looking approach to the problems of economic security, they are still beset by many difficulties. Attempts to revise and modernize measures such as disability compensation and medical benefits still meet with strong (and often successful) resistance. Thus, while an improved system of veteran's benefit programs has slowly evolved over the years, it remains a program shaped as much by power and politics as by sound economic and public policy.

Economic Security Programs for Railroad Employees

Old Age, Death, and Permanent Disability

In 1875 the American Railway Express Company established the first formal private pension plan for railroad workers; by 1934, almost ninety such plans had been instituted, and the railroad industry was considered a leader in the private pension field. These plans typically provided a pension of 1 per cent of the worker's average salary over the ten-year period preceding his retirement for each year of service. Most of these plans were self-insured, and few, if any, were fully funded. Consequently, they encountered financial difficulties during the depression. In 1934, because the orderly operation of these pension plans was essential at a time when employment opportunities for younger men were scarce, Congress enacted legislation which created a liberal compulsory retirement system underwritten by the federal government and financed by taxes levied on the railroads and their employees.

In enacting this law, the Congress argued that the safety of passengers and freight was endangered by the continued employment of older workers. But the United States Supreme Court declared the law unconstitutional on the grounds that certain provisions took property without due process of law, and the power to regulate interstate commerce did not include the power to establish a compulsory retirement system for workers in interstate commerce. A 1935 Act creating essentially the same system was declared unconstitutional by the Supreme Court of the District of Columbia, but the decision was ambiguous and the system actually started to operate in a small way in 1936. Operations under this system and litigations concerning its operations ceased in December, 1936, following a joint conference of railroads and railroad unions. At this conference the details of a mutually satisfactory compulsory retirement system were worked out, and in 1937, Congress enacted these details into law. The 1937 Act has since been amended seven times.

BENEFITS

The railroad retirement system provides three basic types of benefits: retirement annuities; death and survivorship annuities; and annuities for total disability. There is a close relationship between the system and the OASI program, and all railroad workers with less than ten years of railroad service have their earnings treated as covered wages under OASI for benefit purposes. Also, the railroad retirement system has a "Social Security Minimum" applicable to all benefits so that benefits payable under this system will always be at least as large as the OASI benefits that would have been payable if the railroad wages had been covered by OASI. As a result, most railroad survivors' benefits are payable under this "Social Security Minimum."

Retirement annuity. To be eligible at age sixty-five for a retirement annuity, a railroad worker must have had at least ten years of creditable service in covered railroad and related work. At age sixty he is eligible with thirty years of service. Credit is provided for military service. The program includes benefits for wives of retired workers.

Survivorship benefits. Under a survivors' benefit program, payments are made to specified survivors of workers who were "completely" or "partially" insured. At least ten years of service with the industry and current connection with the industry for a stated number of work quarters are required.

Disability benefits. Disability annuities are payable to workers who are permanently disabled for any regular gainful employment if the disabled worker has had ten years of covered railroad service. Workers who are permanently disabled for their regular occupations (but not necessarily for other work) are eligible for a disability annuity at age sixty, if they are currently connected with the industry at the time of disability and have had ten years of service, or under age sixty with twenty years of service covered by law.

The retirement annuity for a worker retiring at age sixty-five is determined by applying the following formula to his average monthly compensation: 2.76 per cent of the first $50 of average monthly compensation, plus 2.07 per cent of the next $100, plus 1.38 per cent of the next $200, the sum to be multiplied by the years of service.[5] Disability annuities are computed in the same way. A scale is provided for computing survivorship benefits.

Above the "Social Security Minimum," the minimum annuity is the smallest of the following amounts: $4.14 times the years of service, $69, or the average monthly compensation. For the fiscal year 1954-1955 the average retirement annuities were $109.57 a month, and the average monthly disability annuity was $97.08.

UNEMPLOYMENT AND TEMPORARY DISABILITY

As early as January, 1933, the Railway Labor Executives' Association proposed a federal law designed to stabilize employment and pay unemployment compensation through payroll reserves. Their desire for a national law was based on the whole historical pattern of railroad labor relations. Wages, hours, and conditions of work in the railroads were not governed by state boundaries, but were set for the whole industry. Experience under the state unemployment compensation acts convinced the Association that a federal approach was needed, and the efforts of this Association (and others) were rewarded when, in June, 1938, the Railroad Unemployment Insurance Act was put into effect. The law has been amended several times since. Its most important amendment (in 1946) extended the system to provide cash sickness benefits, similar to those paid for unemployment, for workers temporarily unable to work because of sickness (which included maternity sickness) or injury.

Benefits paid under the Act or designed to protect workers against income losses from unemployment caused by labor market fluctuations or temporary disability—occupational or nonoccupational. Benefits are administered much like the unemployment benefit programs of the states. The system provides for disqualifications for several causes (such as failure to apply for work, leav-

[5] For example, if the average monthly compensation is $210 and the worker has thirty years of service, the retirement annuity is:

$$[2.76\% \ (\$50) + 2.07\% \ (\$100) + 1.38\% \ (\$60)] \ 30 =$$
$$[\$1.38 + \$2.07 + \$.83] \ 30 =$$
$$[\$4.28] \ 30 = \$128.40$$

ing suitable work without cause, fraud, or participation in a strike) and stipulates a waiting period both for unemployment and disability benefits. Benefits for disability or unemployment are payable after a seven-day waiting period—the first seven days of unemployment for the first "registration period" covered by the claim. After a claimant's first registration period in any benefit year, benefits are payable after the fourth day of unemployment. Special maternity benefits may be paid for 57 days before confinement and for a maximum of 116 days. These are in addition to general disability benefits.

ELIGIBILITY AND BENEFIT LEVEL

To qualify for benefits, a covered worker (note that coverage is the same as under the Railroad Retirement Act) must have received at least $400 in pay from an employer covered by the Act in the calendar year preceding his benefit year. Benefits are based on calendar year earnings, or on an annual figure computed by expanding ½ the basic wage earned on the last date of employment in the base year, whichever is greater.

Calendar (or Computed Base Year) Year Earnings	Daily Benefit
$ 400– 499	$3.50
500– 749	4.00
750– 999	4.50
1,000–1,299	5.00
1,300–1,599	5.50
1,600–1,999	6.00
2,000–2,499	6.50
2,500–2,999	7.00
3,000–3,499	7.50
3,500–3,999	8.00
4,000 and over	8.50

During the fiscal year 1954–1955, the average daily unemployment benefit payment under this program was $7.02. Sickness benefits (excluding maternity) averaged $6.95 a day, and maternity benefits averaged $7.24 a day. An average weekly unemployment and sickness benefit (excluding maternity) of $36 was paid for each week of total unemployment and sickness.

COVERAGE AND OPERATIONS OF THE RAILROAD RETIREMENT SYSTEM AND UNEMPLOYMENT INSURANCE ACT

Although the Railroad Retirement and Unemployment systems do not affect nearly as many workers as the Social Security Act, they do cover all employees in an important industry. Both programs are administered through the Railroad Retirement Board, membership to which is gained by Presidential appointment with Senate confirmation. The retirement system is financed by joint contributions of employers and employees. Currently, each contributes 6¼ per cent of the employee's compensation, up to $350 a month. Employee representatives working for unions pay 12.5 per cent. Taxes collected from workers and employers are placed in a special account in the treasury's general fund, and that part of the account which is not needed to pay current benefits and administrative expenses is invested in interest-bearing United States government obligations. At least once every three years the Railroad Retirement Board is required to make an actuarial report and to estimate the tax rate required to make the system self-supporting. The present contribution rate of 12½ per cent has been shown to be insufficient by about 3 per cent of payroll.

The unemployment and temporary disability programs are financed wholly by a payroll tax on employers. The rate of contribution varies from .5 per cent to 3.0 per cent depending upon the size of the balance in the Railroad Unemployment Insurance account.

In 1954, an average of 1,249,000 workers per month worked in employments covered by the Railroad Retirement and Unemployment Insurance Acts. A total of 1,682,000 employees worked in covered employment. Coverage figures for the Act for the past decade are presented below in Table 13.4.

TABLE 13.4

EMPLOYEES COVERED BY RAILROAD RETIREMENT AND
RAILROAD UNEMPLOYMENT INSURANCE ACTS

(in thousands)

Year	Number of Employees	
	Average*	Total
1945	1,680	3,016
1946	1,622	2,660
1947	1,598	2,476
1948	1,558	2,313
1949	1,403	2,102
1950	1,421	2,053
1951	1,476	2,053
1952	1,429	2,032
1953	1,405	1,968
1954	1,249	1,682

* Average of twelve mid-monthly employment figures.

Source: Railroad Retirement Board, *Annual Report* (Washington, D. C.: U. S. Government Printing Office, 1955), p. 218.

Table 13.4 reveals that the average monthly coverage of the Act (1,249,000 employees) is 11 per cent below the 1953 figure and 26 per cent below that of the war-time high reached in 1945. It is the lowest figure of any year since 1940. Although these figures indicate the secular decline in employment in the railroad industry, the system is nevertheless important in terms of its coverage.

OCCUPATIONAL DISABILITY

As we indicated in Chapter 9, work on the railroads has always been among the most hazardous occupations and once had the worst accident record. Hence, it is not surprising that accident compensation should long have been a concern among railway workers. They were active in the fight for compensation legislation, and in 1908 won enactment of the Federal Employers' Liability Act which, although it has been amended many times, is the basis for occupational injury compensation on the railroads today.

It is important at the outset to stress that the Federal Employers' Liability Act is not a workmen's compensation law. It does not include the principle of liability without fault. Compensation for occupational injury on the railroads must still go through the regular court channels, and the injured employee (with some exception) has the burden of proof of negligence. But that burden has been considerably lightened because the common law defenses of assumption of risk and fellow servant have been denied the employer by law. Furthermore, even contributory negligence will not wholly deny a claim, but will merely reduce it.

Injured railway workers take their claims to the courts, and usually depend upon jury awards for their compensation. This situation is condemned as archaic, in view of the compensation principle; yet the failure of compensation laws to keep pace with rapid changes in wages and other costs, together with the liberal jury awards of recent years, have caused the railway worker to defend the system of employers' liability. If it were to be changed to a compensation system, it would be over the strenuous objection of railway unions and compensation claimants attorneys who are convinced that workmen's compensation is not sufficiently liberal to compete with the success of jury awards.[6]

It should be noted that the occupationally injured have two other sources of income: (1) the temporary disability benefits under the

[6] For a good summary of the arguments on both sides, see Herman M. Somers and Anne R. Somers, *Workmen's Compensation* (New York: John Wiley and Sons, Inc., 1954), pp. 322–25.

Railroad Unemployment Insurance Act, and (2) the disability benefits under the Railroad Retirement Act.

Economic Security Programs for Federal Employees

The federal government, in its role of employer, has done much to insure the economic security of its many thousands of civilian employees. Programs protecting against the risks of death, old age, and occupational illness have long been part of the terms of federal employment, and in 1955, for the first time, unemployment compensation was made available to federal employees.

OCCUPATIONAL ILLNESS

The oldest of the federal programs is the Federal Employees' Compensation Act—the workmen's compensation system for federal government workers. In fact, it is the oldest of the American workmen's compensation systems, dating back to 1908 in its original form. Since the law covers employees of all branches of the federal government, its total coverage is in excess of 2.5 million workers.

Like the state workmen's compensation systems considered earlier, the federal system provides indemnity and medical benefits for disability that is causally linked to employment—due either to disease or accidental injury. The federal system differs from the state laws in several respects, particularly in benefit administration, but its most significant difference is that the federal system is generally more liberal. Its full medical benefits and liberal death and indemnity allowances (with no limit on total disability length or amounts) are considered by many to be a "model" of achievement in the workmen's compensation field.

The Act is financed by Congressional appropriations and administered by the Bureau of Employees' Compensation in the Department of Labor. All administrative functions of claims adjustment and administrative supervision are conducted by the Bureau. Administrative costs of the federal Act are often the subject of discussion, for, while they cannot be considered comparable to private insurance expense ratios, they are nevertheless sufficiently lower (running about 4 per cent of total benefits) so that they are sometimes cited as evidence of the advantage of a state-financed program.

UNEMPLOYMENT

Until 1955, federal employees were not eligible for unemployment compensation benefits under the state unemployment compensation laws. As of January 1, 1955, however, they gained coverage under the state laws and are eligible for benefits with the same status—for purposes of the system—as employees of private industry.

OLD AGE AND DEATH

Actually, there are several different retirement plans covering civilian employees of the federal government and quasi-governmental agencies. Special plans cover groups such as foreign service officers. The most important of these plans is the Civil Service Retirement System which was established in 1920. This system covers most federal employees including all nonelective officers and employees in the three branches of the federal government except those excluded by an executive order (part-time workers, dollar-a-year men, temporary employees) and those included under some other retirement plan. Special eligibility requirements and benefits apply to Congressmen and persons dealing with criminals. There is a tendency to bring these special groups under OASI coverage.

The federal Civil Service Retirement System provides four types of benefits.

Retirement annuities. Retirement is compulsory at age seventy, but annuities are payable to persons sixty years of age with thirty years of service or sixty-two years of age with fifteen years of service. Optional retirements now constitute about four-fifths of all retirements under the plan. The annuity is calculated at 1½ per cent of the average annual pay during the highest five consecutive years for the first five years of service (or, alternatively, 1 per cent of such average pay plus $25 for each year of such service), plus 1¾ per cent of such pay for the next five years of service (or, alternatively, 1 per cent of such pay plus $25 for each year of such service), plus 2 per cent of such pay times the remaining years of service (or, alternatively, 1 per cent of such pay plus $25 multiplied by such years of service). The alternative basis can be applied only for workers whose average annual salary is below $5,000. In all cases the maximum annuity is 80 per cent of the average annual basic pay.

Disability annuities. Disability annuities are payable to workers with over five years of service who are disabled (and unable to follow their usual occupations). The annuity is calculated in the same way as the retirement annuity, with a minimum benefit of 40 per cent of the highest five years' average annual pay.

Survivorship benefits. The most important survivorship benefits were made available in 1948. These are payable if an employee has completed five years of service and is either an active employee or an annuitant.

Financing the Civil Service Retirement System

The Federal Civil Service Retirement System is jointly financed. Employees today contribute 6½ per cent of their regular compensation.[7] A matching contribution is made by governmental departments, and, when necessary, Congress appropriates additional funds. The amounts of the Congressional appropriations are not fixed by law.

The system is administered by the United States Civil Service Commission through a retirement division. At present, the system is a smaller operation than either the Railroad Retirement System or the Social Security Act. But it has increased in importance since its inception, and will probably equal the railroad system within a decade or two. It is already the largest single-employer retirement system in the United States. When the system began in 1920, it had a membership of approximately 330,000 with an annual covered payroll of about $400 million, and only employees in classified Civil Service and certain special groups were eligible for membership. With growing federal payrolls and more liberal eligibility provisions, the system today covers 1,700,000 employees with a payroll of nearly $7.5 billion.

A Special Note on Financing of the System. As is the case with the OASI and Railroad Retirement funds, the annual receipts to the Civil Service Retirement and Disability Fund exceed the annual expenditures. Each year the Board of Actuaries makes its estimates of the annual appropriation necessary to make the system self-supporting, but the Congressional appropriation is often less than the recommended amount.

The 1955 report of the Civil Service Commission Retirement Board stresses that despite a sizable fund ($5,635,772,000) the deficiency under the fund is increasing. In fact, it is estimated that about one-half of the funds on hand at the end of fiscal 1955 would be needed merely to pay benefits to persons already on the benefit rolls if the system were to be terminated today. The system's Board of Actuaries has recommended that the fund be placed on a full reserve basis: not only should the deficiency be prevented from increasing, but it should eventually be liquidated. It is feared that

---

[7] This rate of contribution has risen over the years as follows: 2.5 per cent in 1920; 3.5 per cent in 1926; 5 per cent in 1942; 6 per cent in 1948. Workers who have left their jobs after five years of government service, but with less than twenty years, may request a refund of their contributions, plus interest. Or they may be eligible for benefits at age sixty-two. The refund option is not available to workers after twenty years of service.

the present system makes younger employees too dependent upon future Congressional appropriations; that benefits may be reduced when the true costs of the program are realized; and that if the system is not fully funded, the benefits for present beneficiaries may be unjustifiably increased, thus increasing the cost even further. The following observation of the Board of Actuaries should be of interest to students not only because of its importance to this program, but also because it is partially applicable to the Railroad Retirement Act as well:

> The argument has been made that reserves should not be built up to meet the Government's obligations, that since any moneys set aside are to be invested in the Government's own securities, the Government is in effect borrowing from itself and in the end the outlay will be the same whether the Government set aside a lesser amount now and paid its interest or appropriated a great amount later. In support of this argument the hypothetical case of government without a debt was cited and it was stated that in order to have a reserve fund such a government would need to go into debt in order to issue the bonds in which to invest. This argument is novel and it would seem to mean one of two things.
>
> It might mean that a government, without a debt, would have the privilege of incurring any deferred pension liabilities for the public to meet that it wishes to incur, because if it does not take such deferred liabilities into account in its bookkeeping, it is in a good financial position.
>
> We would assume that in such case any system would have to be non-contributory because there would be no way of investing reserves from employees' contributions. This theory has operated to the disadvantage of taxpayers in many cases where it has been used, and to a loss to employees in others. The other alternative would seem to be that such a government should set aside funds to meet its obligations, when it incurs them, but not invest them but hold them in case.
>
> Perhaps there is a third possibility, namely, that if no provision to meet pension costs is made as the costs accrue, future benefits may be cut if future costs are too high. This argument may be sound in a system like the Social Security System, where almost the entire public is involved, but it hardly applies to a staff pension system where employees are rendering definite service to the employer in return for a definite promise of a stated pension. In the latter case, the pension is not like social insurance, but it is in the nature of deferred compensation.[8]

While these views are perhaps not generally accepted, they merit attention and thought. Many would probably argue that it is sufficient to prevent the deficiency from increasing, since the system will almost certainly operate indefinitely.

[8] Board of Actuaries of the Civil Service Retirement and Disability Fund, *Thirty-Second Annual Report* (Washington, D. C.: U. S. Government Printing Office, 1952), p. 31.

Economic Security Programs of
State and Local Governments

State and local government employees are protected by widespread economic security programs today. It is estimated that over three million persons—75 per cent of all persons employed by these governments—are currently insured under one of several retirement programs. Retirement systems are the most important benefit programs unique to state and local government employees. These employees are covered by their respective state workmen's compensation laws, and although many such governmental units elect to act as self-insurers of their workmen's compensation liabilities, their employees receive the same protection as they would in private covered employment.

STATE AND LOCAL GOVERNMENT RETIREMENT SYSTEMS

Although state and local government retirement systems vary widely from one locality to another, a few generalizations can be made about their coverage, benefits, and operations. Most of the governmental units establish three types of retirement plans—in the order of liberality of their benefits. These plans cover policemen and firemen, teachers, and all other employees. In general, all three of these plans are contributory, but they differ in type and amount of benefits. Typically, only the plans applying to policemen and firemen provide survivors' benefits. Eligibility requirements tend to be high for all the plans, and the benefits are less liberal than those received by federal civil servants. Finally, although eligibility requirements are high, most of the plans offer both disability and old-age annuities.

OPERATION OF STATE AND LOCAL RETIREMENT SYSTEMS

The estimated three million workers covered by these programs are more than the number covered under the Railroad Retirement and Civil Service Retirement plans combined. Table 13.5 indicates the number of beneficiaries and the amount of benefits paid under state and local retirement systems from 1940 to 1954.

The steady increases over time reflect gradual increases in the number of plans, the number of employees, their salary and benefit levels, and the maturing of existing plans. Total lump-sum benefits have increased substantially. Average retirement and survivorship benefits have increased as well, but only gradually and less markedly than in the case of other plans.

TABLE 13.5

BENEFICIARIES AND BENEFITS UNDER STATE AND LOCAL RETIREMENT SYSTEMS

Fiscal Year Ending June 30	Retirement		Survivorship		
			Family Beneficiaries	Benefits	
	Beneficiaries	Benefits		Monthly	Lump Sum
1940	113.0	$103,000	25.0	$16,000	$12,500
1941	117.2	106,750	26.0	16,500	13,000
1942	126.7	115,400	28.0	17,700	12,600
1943	136.0	124,900	29.0	18,400	13,400
1944	146.0	134,500	30.0	19,000	15,000
1945	155.0	143,000	32.0	20,000	15,500
1946	167.0	158,000	34.0	21,000	16,000
1947	180.0	175,000	35.0	22,000	16,000
1948	190.0	190,000	36.0	23,000	17,000
1949	200.0	203,000	38.0	25,000	18,000
1950	213.0	230,000	40.0	26,000	20,000
1951	230.0	273,000	42.0	29,000	25,000
1952	250.0	310,000	44.0	30,000	30,000
1953	270.0	343,000	46.0	32,000	35,000
1954	292.0	385,000	48.0	35,000	40,000

Source: *Social Security Bulletin*, XVIII, No. 9 (September, 1955), 30; Federal Security Agency, *Social Security Yearbook*, 1945, p. 18; and 1948, p. 4.

Because these plans are operated at the state and local levels, national figures would not indicate any sudden over-all changes in coverage or benefit levels. No national figures are available on the actuarial status of these plans, but it is generally agreed that many of them are being operated essentially on a pay-as-you-go basis, while others are fully funded.

Today the Social Security Act permits states to enter voluntary agreements with the federal government to accept federal OASI coverage for employees of the state or of its political subdivisions. Thus, protection is being extended beyond the scope of the state and local systems.

General Assistance

Under the provisions of the Social Security Act discussed in Chapter 4, special public assistance programs provide aid to four specified groups: the aged, dependent children, the blind, and the permanently and totally disabled. Many persons who are in need of money to meet their basic needs, however, are not eligible for assistance under these provisions because of their inability to meet age, disability, residence, or other requirements. For these persons, the state and local aid program—commonly referred to as general assistance—is the only source of aid.

Although the general public assistance program is the most basic and the oldest of assistance programs in this country, today it is essentially a "residual" program. That is, it comes to the aid of those persons who are not included in federally-aided programs or who are not getting sufficient aid from these programs to meet their needs. For this reason, the types of persons on general assistance rolls tend to change with the times and with the adequacy and scope of coverage of other programs.

For example, during periods of depression, one can expect to find on these rolls persons who are able-bodied and fully capable of full-time gainful employment, but who are unable to find work due to labor market conditions. During periods of economic prosperity, the persons on general assistance rolls tend more to be those who are disabled or sick or who are survivors or dependents of such persons. Federal programs, such as the 1950 Social Security Act amendment providing aid to the permanently and totally disabled, should aid in lightening the load, as did unemployment compensation before it and the other programs of the Social Security Act. Nevertheless, while these programs have tended to take the major burden from the general assistance program and have made it essentially a residual one, experience reveals that there will still be many persons who will be unable to meet the criteria of these other programs and must rely for their basic needs on general assistance.

Table 13.6 indicates the number of general assistance cases and amount of benefits paid them for the years 1936 to 1954.

Just as special assistance programs should become less important as the OASI first line of economic security defense becomes more extensive in its coverage and more liberal in its provisions, so, too, should general assistance programs carry a smaller and smaller load of the burden as all these programs expand. Table 13.6 indicates that this has been the case. It must be remembered that only two decades ago, general assistance was, in fact, the *major* economic security program. The gradual reduction in case loads from 1936 through the present period is due to the fact that other programs have taken over the burden. (The system still increases and decreases its load with changing economic circumstances.)

ADMINISTRATION OF GENERAL ASSISTANCE

General assistance programs are truly local in nature. They receive no federal aid, and their cost is distributed between the states and localities, with the localities bearing slightly under one-half of it. Since administration is wholly local, the system is administered in many thousands of localities—counties, town, and villages.

TABLE 13.6

GENERAL ASSISTANCE CASES AND BENEFIT PAYMENTS

1936–1954

Year	General Assistance Cases (in thousands)	Average Monthly Pay. Per Case	Total Payments (in thousands)
1936	1,510	$24.13	$439,004
1937	1,626	25.36	406,881
1938	1,631	25.06	476,203
1939	1,558	24.89	482,653
1940	1,239	24.28	404,963
1941	798	24.40	272,649
1942	460	25.23	180,571
1943	292	27.76	110,978
1944	258	28.77	88,762
1945	257	32.72	86,912
1946	315	39.47	120,928
1947	356	42.79	164,830
1948	398	47.39	198,838
1949	562	50.47	282,252
1950	413	46.65	295,383
1951	323	47.09	195,254
1952	280	49.82	171,779
1953	270	50.53	151,436
1954	351	57.27	198,106

Source: *Social Security Bulletin*, XVIII, No. 9 (September, 1955), 65.

General assistance evolved from the local poor relief systems which existed in the colonial period, and has not completely shaken some of its features of those days. One of these is the principle of local responsibility based on the doctrine that towns and settlements would be responsible for their own paupers, but not for those of other communities. Some states maintain residence requirements today, which have the effect of denying payments to new residents.[8]

Another feature of the early relief systems—the imposition of primary responsibility on the family—is today an important part of general assistance in many states, with the right of suit for enforcement available in some of them.

ADEQUACY OF GENERAL ASSISTANCE PAYMENTS

General assistance payments are made on the basis of needs and are intended to fill the gap between the recipient's resources and his needs. But the limited funds of the local agencies often put a lower

[8] Discussed by Stefan A. Riesenfeld and Richard C. Maxwell, *Modern Social Legislation* (Brooklyn: The Foundation Press, 1950), p. 685.

limit on benefit levels than this theoretical level. Table 13.6 indicates that the long-term tendency for average monthly payments per case is upward and has more than doubled (in money terms) from 1936 through 1954. In general, however, payments under this program tend both to be smaller than comparable special assistance programs and to show greater diversity from state to state, as is shown in Table 13.7.

TABLE 13.7

RANGE OF AVERAGE BENEFIT PAYMENTS UNDER UNEMPLOYMENT INSURANCE,
SPECIAL ASSISTANCE AND GENERAL ASSISTANCE

(June, 1955)

	Average Payment	
Program	Highest State*	Lowest State*
Unemployment Ins. (weekly) . . .	$ 29.73 (Mich.)	$17.85 (Florida)
Old-Age Assis. (monthly)	85.10 (Col.)	27.69 (W. Va.)
Aid to the Blind (monthly)	128.12 (Minn.)	32.13 (W. Va.)
Aid to Perm. and Tot. Dis. (monthly) .	107.13 (Conn.)	24.16 (Miss.)
General Assis. (monthly)	78.06 (N. Y.)	12.69 (Miss.)

* Omitting territories outside continental United States.

Source: U. S. Congress, 84th, 1st Session, Senate and House, Hearings before the Joint Committee on the Economic Report, Subcommittee on Low-Income Families, *Low Income Families* (Washington, D. C.: U. S. Government Printing Office, 1955), p. 46.

SUGGESTED REFORMS IN GENERAL ASSISTANCE

Plagued by ancient traditions, a wide diversity of administrative regulations and standards, and inadequate funds, the general assistance program operates under a heavy handicap in its important role as our residual economic security program. As noted above, the program has improved its benefit levels and has been relieved of some of its obligations by the Social Security Act. Also, there is a distinct trend among states to reduce residence requirements. Aside from the benefit levels, there is still need for vast improvement.

The American Public Welfare Association has gone on record in favor of several specific reforms. These include: (1) further reduction in the residence requirements; (2) establishment of reciprocity between the states; (3) the inclusion of all needy persons under the program, regardless of the cause of their need; (4) broadening of the aid to the permanently and totally disabled to take further burden off the general public assistance programs; and (5) a unified public assistance program. The idea of several categorical relief programs sponsored or aided by the federal government, and a general relief program without that aid has been under critical attack for some time. The American Public Welfare Association has recommended that a single federal general assistance program be adopted to replace all categorical programs.[9]

A concluding comment. In some respects, the general assistance program raises the basic issue in economic security: To what extent does an individual who lacks basic resources have an enforceable right to receive from society a minimum standard of living?[10] Historically, no such common law right existed. And although, after 1900, states began to single out certain categories of needy individuals and to give them assurances of basic income, the assistance program has always maintained its relief aspects. It has been indigency relief rather than enforcement of rights. Perhaps it is inevitable that the residual program should maintain this character, but it is not necessary that it remain so wholly inadequate. It could be modernized and made to reflect an ". . . affirmation of worth, not a testimony of inadequacy."[11]

Summary

Despite many differences between the economic security programs for special groups, all of them (with the exception of the veterans' and general assistance programs) have one striking similarity. Each seeks to provide essentially the type of protection that most workers engaged in private industry would receive from a combination of the Old-Age and Survivors' Insurance program and group insurance and pension plans. This raises the question of whether it might not be more logical for purposes of equitable treatment and cost of administration to include groups such as railroad workers under the Old-Age and Survivors' programs. It would then be possible to use the special programs for providing the additional coverage that would be deemed desirable. This would clearly demark Social Security Act coverage as social insurance; the additional coverage would clearly *not* be, and would be funded along the same lines as private pension and insurance schemes.

Clearly, of the special groups, the veterans' programs are the most liberal. In view of the combined roles that their benefits seek

---

[9] See U. S. Congress, 84th, 1st Session, Senate and House, Hearings before the Joint Committee on the Economic Report, Subcommittee on Low-Income Families, *Low-Income Families* (Washington, D. C.: U. S. Government Printing Office, 1955), pp. 86–88, 90, 131, 167–68.

[10] See A. Delafield Smith. "Public Assistance as a Social Obligation," *Harvard Law Review*, LXIII, No. 2 (December, 1949), 266–88.

[11] *Ibid.*

to play, however, they cannot be compared to the programs of the social insurance type, although the programs of the Veterans' Administration and the armed forces resemble the social assistance programs in some respects.

For all the programs, both those of the assistance and of the social insurance nature, the economic effects seem clearly desirable and comparable to those of the social insurance and assistance programs.

Suggestions for Additional Reading

GAGLIARDO, DOMENICO. *American Social Insurance,* rev. ed. New York: Harper & Bros., 1955.
Chapters 6, 7, 8 present a detailed discussion of provisions and operations of various economic security programs for special groups.

GRIGSBY, MARJORIE W. "Workmen's Compensation Under the Federal Laws," *Archives of Industrial Hygiene and Occupational Medicine,* American Medical Association, IX (June, 1954), 451–75.
A careful analysis of the operation of the Federal Employees' Compensation Act.

HOGAN, JOHN D., and FRANCIS A. J. IANNI. *American Social Legislation.* New York: Harper & Bros., 1956. Chap. 5.
Chapter 5 on social assistance is useful.

REID, CHARLES K. *Fundamentals of Government Life Insurance and Related Benefits.* Philadelphia: American College of Life Underwriters, 1953.
This pamphlet provides an analysis of life insurance for veterans.
Note: Operating statistics for the Railroad Retirement and Unemployment programs can be found in the *Annual Reports* of the Railroad Retirement Board; those for the Civil Service program in the *Annual Report* of the Civil Service Retirement Board. The *Social Security Bulletin,* especially the September statistical supplement for each year, contains operating data on all programs and detailed statistics on public and general assistance.

RIESENFELD, STEFAN A., and RICHARD C. MAXWELL. *Modern Social Legislation.* Brooklyn: The Foundation Press, 1950. pp. 685–747.
Legal background and foundations for the present-day Public Assistance programs are presented here. Also case materials on legal issues in administration of the program.

U. S. CONGRESS, 84TH, HOUSE, 2ND SESSION, HOUSE COMMITTEE ON VETERANS' AFFAIRS. *A Report on Veterans' Benefits in the United States.* Washington, D. C.: U. S. Government Printing Office, 1956. Committee Prints 243, 244, 246, 247, 259-262, 270, 275.
Detailed report on the operation and historical background of present-day veterans' benefit programs.

14

Economics of Security Programs

Introduction

In previous chapters we have discussed the problems of economic insecurity arising out of old age, death, unemployment, accidents and sickness. And, we have likewise looked at the ways in which society has adjusted itself to these problems through both public and private economic security programs. This process of social adjustment involves various administrative, economic, legal, political, and other issues. In this chapter we shall single out a number of the more basic economic issues and analyze them in greater detail.[1] In this analysis we shall treat, first, a number of general issues more or less common to all economic security programs. Following this we shall focus upon a number of specialized issues as they relate to particular economic security programs.[2]

General Economic Issues

HOW MUCH ECONOMIC SECURITY CAN OUR SOCIETY AFFORD?

The word "afford," as it is used in the heading above, can be defined in two ways. First, it can be interpreted essentially as a budgetary phenomenon: How much of an individual's (and of the nation's) income can be "devoted" to economic security? Second,

---

[1] The student specializing in law, political science, sociology, or social work may wish to append materials from his own discipline to this analysis.

[2] These lines were written before the appearance of Eveline M. Burns' detailed and provocative book, *Social Security and Public Policy* (New York: McGraw-Hill Book Co., Inc., 1956) which is a most useful volume for any student wishing to become conversant with this field.

it can be viewed as a normative issue: How much economic security can society "tolerate" before wholly undesirable disincentive effects appear?

For the second of these problems we can offer only conjectures. As was noted in Chapter 1, there is a dearth of evidence—theoretical or empirical—as to the impact of security upon incentive and hence upon the motivating forces of a dynamic economy. In that chapter several conclusions were suggested. First, economic security programs apparently have not had any markedly detrimental aggregative effects upon incentive, though, certainly, individual examples of abuse can be found. (But conversely, neither can it be demonstrated that such programs have had any markedly beneficial effects upon incentives.)[3] Second, merely because such economic security programs have been "neutral" up to now in their incentive effects, it should not be taken to imply that they will continue to be neutral regardless of the scope or form of the program. For example, benefits that restore all or nearly all of wage losses would have potentially dangerous (and detrimental) effects upon incentive.[4]

But what of the first problem, the budgetary aspects of economic security? How much economic security can society afford? The answer is twofold: (1) as much as its resources will allow, and (2) given this limiting factor, as much as it is willing to spend for such programs. Both monetary and physical productivity factors are involved.

Any economic security program presupposes a given "standard" or "level" of protection or care for those persons covered. And the level of standard that can be adopted is restricted, in the limiting case, to the productive capabilities of the society. For example, it is difficult to visualize the aged being provided for in the backwoods-frontier regions of the early United States under the equivalent of our present-day Old-Age and Survivors Insurance system (even if the frontier philosophy had been willing to accept such an approach). The aged were taken care of, but "retirement at sixty-five" could not be tolerated, and when a person finally had to stop work, he was cared for in the same cabin as was occupied by the rest of the family. Productive capacity simply was not such as to permit separate facilities to be built or for the retired person to "live in

---

[3] But see Arthur Larson, *Know Your Social Security* (New York: Harper & Brothers, 1955), p. 23, where he argues that while it cannot be proved statistically, it is generally agreed that the "secure worker is the better worker."

[4] For an analysis in an allied area, see Earl R. Rolph, *The Theory of Fiscal Economics* (Berkeley: University of California Press, 1954), chap. x, "Taxes and the Incentive to Work."

style," supported by the family.[5] In a real sense we could not have had an OASI program of today's dimensions one hundred years ago; the productive capacity of the country could not have supported it. To be sure, the aged had to be taken care of (they were an overhead cost to society); but instead of "retiring in their own homes," as is increasingly true today, they were frequently provided for by more intensively utilizing the capacity of the family homestead.[6] Or, if provided for in public institutions, the care was minimal in most cases.

Given the fact that the productive capacity of the economy ultimately limits the level at which economic security can be provided, it is nevertheless true that society has considerable choice within this limit as to the level or standard it wishes to select. Thus, a second answer to the question of how much it can afford is how much it is willing to pay, and this a cultural as much as an economic answer. Where there is a correspondence (even if only rough) between an individual's in-payments and his benefits in an economic security program, willingness to pay additionally involves two specific questions.[7]

How much present income (in the real sense) is the individual willing to forego for protection in the future against the risks of economic insecurity?[8] In the individual case this becomes a matter of individual choice, and one finds a range of such choices from persons with no protection to those who are "insurance poor." In the case where the economic security program is of a negotiated type, as in an employer-union relationship, the individual may have a choice (or vote) in the initial deliberations on whether or not to attempt to negotiate such a program. Once the program has been accepted, the individual is restricted in the freedom he has in choos-

[5] Just as fiction is frequently more revealing than fact in many instances, it is also the case here. For an account, less rigorous than the backwoods illustration given above, of the way a somewhat later generation cared for the aged, see Mildred Walker, *The Southwest Corner* (New York: Harcourt, Brace and Co., 1951). (Thus, succinctly, on page 11, Miss Walker notes: "The southwest corner was the way New England handled social security in the very early days.") For a still later account, see the short story by Edna Ferber, "Old Man Minnick," in *Your Town* (World Reprint ed.; Cleveland: World Publishing Co., 1948).

[6] For a humorous and nostalgic account of this, see James Thurber's tales of his grandfather's life in the family homestead in *My Life and Hard Times* (New York: Harper & Brothers, 1933).

[7] See the interesting discussion in John J. Corson and John W. McConnell, *Economic Needs of Older People* (New York: The Twentieth Century Fund, 1956), chap. xiii.

[8] This type of problem can be handled readily through the use of indifference curve analysis.

ing present as against future goods. The same restraints apply in the case of any compulsory program.

The second specific question relates to the level of security society is willing to provide (and is economically capable of providing). Private and public retirement programs give an individual the right to claim goods and services at a later date in exchange for goods and services foregone now. (Thus, under OASI an individual gives up—pays—up to $94.50 a year in exchange for the right to collect benefits at age sixty-five.) The individual, therefore, has a "legal" claim which he has the right to exercise in the future. But, in the future, those in society who have not retired are the people who will have to produce the goods and services which the retired person can claim. And, for a variety of reasons the nonretired group may not be able to do this. One could visualize, for example, a society in which the majority of persons were in the older age group.[9] In such a case the productive segment of the population, even if provided with considerable capital equipment, may not be able to produce the needed goods. A more realistic case of the same nature arises out of a state of war and a war economy. Here it may not be possible to permit the aged to exercise their claims; the productive segment of the economy simply may not be able to turn out military and civilian goods in sufficient quantity. Hence we come around the full circle again to the earlier noted idea that the productive capacity of a society looms importantly in the question of how much economic security can be afforded. And while one notes an increasing amount of our economy's resources being devoted to economic security, the process is not unidirectional. It could well be that the pressure of future events might require a reversal of the trend.

ISSUES IN THE FINANCING OF ECONOMIC SECURITY PROGRAMS

Financing economic security programs involves a number of problems, some of which are related to the individual, others to the economy. We shall analyze briefly a number of these problems.

Who bears the costs of economic security programs? "Bear" is defined here in terms of the individual or group upon whom the burden ultimately falls; we are not concerned with the legal or financial mechanics of who initially pays or how the payment is made. Three different situations may be recognized.

---

[9] The student should check on changes in age distributions in the United States for an indication (though less severe than indicated above) of this type of problem. See Chapter 3 of this volume for age distribution data.

First, economic security programs like the Employment Act of 1946 are financed out of general revenues, and hence the burden is diffused through the economy, dependent upon the ways in which revenues are produced. The same or parallel analyses can be used with respect to public works programs, to the costs of administering governmental intervention in substandard conditions, and to other cases where there is no direct relation of payments to benefits or where there are no compulsory, ear-marked taxes involved.

Second, where the individual provides for his own economic security, such as through the purchase of accident and sickness insurance or of a retirement annuity, he in turn bears the cost. This is done by the individual giving up present goods and services (or by reducing savings) in exchange for "future protection."

Third, there are cases where the program is compulsory and where the employee and/or employer pays a premium or a tax. This is the incidence problem. In the case of private programs—health, welfare, pension—the employer may initially pay the entire "premium" or only some part of it. Does this imply that he likewise bears the burden? The answer to this question depends upon whether one believes that the employees would have received the equivalent of the premium or tax in higher wages had there been no economic security program.[10] It may be conjectured that the employees would have received, via wage increases, some portion—perhaps a major portion, though not necessarily all—of the premium or tax.[11] Hence a portion—and perhaps a major one—of the costs of employer-employee security programs is borne by the employees themselves.[12] In the case of public programs, the analysis appears to indicate that the burden is more fully diffused, with some belief that employees again bear the major share of the burden.[13]

[10] See the argumentation in *Potlatch Forests v. International Woodworkers*, 22 Labor Cases 67, 355.

[11] This would perhaps vary from time to time. Thus, in a period when a direct wage increase would not or could not have been forthcoming, "fringes," as in an economic security program, might have been. Hence in some cases (wage stabilization periods or "depressed" periods such as 1949–1950) the burden is not shifted (at least not immediately) to employees. In such cases the employees have the choice of accepting the economic security program or "nothing," since a direct wage increase would be unlikely. *But*, economic security programs may be a method through which some gains can be negotiated by labor organizations. Hence there is the problem not only of cost but also of ingenuity in presenting and securing demands.

[12] Since the employer pays an income tax on income *after* his security program tax (or premium) has been deducted (as a "wage cost") while the employee pays an income tax on an amount *including* his security program contribution, there is a certain logic in the belief that the employer contributions are deferred pay, and hence paid for by employees.

[13] The most recent study on this is by R. A. Musgrave, J. J. Carroll, L. D. Cook, and L. Frane, "Distribution of Tax Payments by Income Groups: A Case Study for

Is the financing of economic security programs deflationary? Inflationary? In the case of compulsory public programs, any in-payment made to the government is a tax, and as such its collection is deflationary.[14] If the tax receipts were in some way sterilized, the net result would also be deflationary. But the collected tax is not sterilized; it passes into the flow of economic activity. If the tax is used to effect a transfer payment (that is, if it is paid out to a recipient of an economic security program) then the situation that develops is equivalent to that which existed prior to the collection of the tax, providing the propensities to consume and save are equal for taxpayer and recipient. There is a lag problem involved inasmuch as collection and disbursement are not coincidental in time. Since public economic security program taxes are collected regularly through the year, this lag is likely to be regularized and minimized. If the collected tax is paid out to government employees, there results a production of goods and services, and under specified conditions there may actually be an expansion of production.[15] Thus the net impact of the collection of economic security program premiums or taxes need not be deflationary.

In the case of private programs where the premium payment is compulsory and where the service received is not necessarily or continuously equal to the in-payment, the type of analysis used above can be applied. If the program is voluntary and/or if there is a close correspondence of benefit and payment, a different approach must be used. In this case the analytical treatment is the same as is used for any personal expenditure on consumer goods.

What are the implications of alternative methods of financing economic security programs? Certain types of economic security programs inherently call for financing on a pay-as-you-go basis. Thus, except for accumulating contingency reserves, this would be

---

1948," *National Tax Journal*, IV, No. 1 (March, 1951), 1–53. See particularly pp. 23–25, where the authors present their summaries. Musgrave and his associates conclude that in a competitive system, the entire burden is borne by wage earners, but that in the realistic case complete backward shifting is unlikely for various reasons, among them being the fact that unions may cite the intent of the law and restrain employers from such shifting. For analysis, as well as a useful summary of the literature, see S. E. Harris, *Economics of Social Security* (New York: McGraw-Hill Book Co., Inc., 1941), Part III, particularly chap. xiii. Harris concludes (pp. 440–41) that a substantial part of the burden falls elsewhere than on the wage earner. Older analyses tended to emphasize more fully the fact that the employee bore the full burden; the modern tendency is less so.

14 For an extended discussion of this question, see S. E. Harris, *op. cit.*, Part I.

15 For a useful discussion, see T. Haavelmo, "Multiplier Effects of a Balanced Budget," *Econometrica*, XIII, No. 4 (October, 1945), 311–18; and the further discussion by G. Haberler, R. M. Goodwin, E. E. Hagen, and T. Haavelmo in *Econometrica*, XIV, No. 1 (January, 1946), 148–58.

true (with minor exceptions) of insurance programs such as accidental injury and sickness, and workmen's compensation, whether private or public. Conversely, the very nature of private pension programs calls for the accumulation of reserves (although in some cases in the past, companies operated on an out-of-pocket basis.) In the case of public old-age and unemployment programs, either approach could be used.[16]

The choice made on these latter two programs has been dictated in part by other than economic considerations and is moreover in part a result of the sheer accidents of historical development. If unemployment insurance is to be financed from sources other than general revenues, then it is logical to build up reserves in years of great plenty to carry over in years of famine.[17] But partly because employment experience since 1940 has been much different (and more favorable) than was anticipated and partly because of various pressures upon state legislatures, the size of the reserve and its growth bear little relation to any particular set of logical economic criteria.[18]

In the case of the old-age program, there have been various shifts between pay-as-you-go and full-reserve approaches, and the present system stands somewhere between either extreme, probably closer to the former.[19] Proponents of pay-as-you-go have taken their positions either out of a belief in the economy of such an approach (or related approaches) or out of a conviction that the states rather than the federal government should administer such a program.[20]

If it is the factual case that both public old-age and unemployment programs have resulted in the accumulation of combined re-

[16] Students interested in the public finance aspects of economic security programs should consult the *National Tax Journal* which publishes relevant items. Thus, in the December, 1954, issue there is an interesting article by L. H. Kimmel, "Is the Old-Age and Survivors Insurance Trust Fund Valid?"

[17] *Genesis*, 41: 25–36.

[18] Various states have, however, undertaken detailed studies in an attempt to bring some actuarial rationality into cost calculations. See the references in Chapter 7.

[19] This does not mean that the Social Security Administration has been capricious in its approach to the problems involved. Far from it! Under the direction of Chief Actuary Robert J. Myers and others, numerous actuarial studies have been undertaken for a series of differing situations. See Chapter 5 of this text for additional discussion.

[20] The student should check such sources as L. Meriam, K. T. Schlotterbeck, and M. Maroney, *The Cost and Financing of Social Security* (Washington, D. C.: The Brookings Institution, 1950); Chamber of Commerce of the United States, *Improving Social Security* (Washington, D. C.: 1953); and the papers presented in the symposium on "Social Security—A New Look" in *Proceedings* of the Sixth Annual Meeting, Industrial Relations Research Association, 1953, pp. 163–99, for illuminating discussion on these issues.

serves at the end of 1955 of $30 billion, what are the economic implications of such accumulations? What of the private pension counterparts? We shall not consider here such issues as investment outlets, effects on the interest rate, liquidation problems, and the like.[21] We are rather concerned with the general economic implications of fund accumulation and reduction.

If public program in-payments exceed out-payments, the excesses are required under law to be invested in United States obligations. Given this fact, a number of possible alternatives can be discerned. If the funds now provided the government via economic security program in-payments were raised alternatively by other types of personal taxes, the net impact on the level of economic activity would be likely the same, lags excepted, if propensities to consume and save of the two taxable groups were similar. If the funds were raised by government borrowing, then the results would depend upon the source from which the loans were obtained. If the banking system were the source, then the results would be inflationary; hence, in this case, an economic security program would contribute to stability. If the public were the source, then the results would depend upon the propensities to save and consume, and any of a number of alternatives would be possible.[22] Conversely, if the fund were reduced (if out-payments exceed in-payments) the above analysis would be applicable, except that results in the opposite direction might be expected in given cases. Thus, fund reduction (and hence debt repayment) may be deflationary in the same sense as is general public debt reduction.

In the case of private economic security programs where funds are accumulated, a major determinant is the savings-investment relation. In-payments to such a program arbitrarily increase the level of savings. Investment (in the real sense, not merely in the purchase of securities) is, however, likely to be undertaken by other groups in the economy. And, unless these groups are willing to make use of the larger accumulation of savings, the impact of fund increases is deflationary. Thus, such economic security programs can be a valuable source of savings for the investment required by

21 See for example, I. Friend, "New Influences in the Stock Market," *Fortune*, XLVII, No. 3 (March, 1953), 108–09; 173ff; and James E. Walter, "Some Implications of Private Pension Funds," *Southern Economic Journal*, XXII, No. 2 (October, 1955). See also Chapter 18 of this text for comments on investment problems.

22 The student should construct cases where borrowing from the public is inflationary in the above case and where it is not. Hint: Vary the propensities to save and consume of the different groups in question, and assume in one case that the savings are automatically invested; in the other, that they are not.

economic progress; on the other hand, in the early thirties, they would have added fuel to the deflationary spiral.

One final comment: Pay-as-you-go programs are less subject to the vicissitudes of economic change than are funded programs. While pay-as-you-go may be impractical (or impossible) in some types of private programs, the alternative is always available for public programs. And even if hyper-inflation should wipe out the assets of private program funds, public programs would be un-affected and could continue operating (or start operating again). This factor is not necessarily decisive in choosing the program type (there are advantages to funded systems, in leveling out the premium or in providing for contingencies), but it is worth calling attention to in light of economic activity and price level movements over the last generation.

General Impacts of Economic Security Programs

What are the impacts of economic security programs upon the functioning of the economy? We shall look at a number of problems.

The impacts of economic security programs upon entrepreneurship. Do economic security programs of the formalized type, whether public or private, discourage entrepreneurship? Formal economic analysis of the firm would indicate that the costs of such a program would change the position of the cost curve of the firm. But, while formal analysis is capable of indicating the consequences of the change in the cost curve, it does not itself tell us about the effect upon entrepreneurial activity, partly because this is a problem of a different order.

Several different impacts on entrepreneurial activity may be found. First, in the short run, there may be a sort of negative "shock" impact arising out of the instituting of an economic security program. And this may have "slightly" unfavorable consequences for the entrepreneur, a "discouraging" influence on his "outlook." Observations would lead one to believe, however, that these "unfavorable" or "discouraging" consequences are not necessarily translated into specific business activity. There are no recorded instances in which a businessman deliberately closed his doors or another decided not to enter business because of the imposition of, say, the Old-Age and Survivors Insurance program. Nor would such programs appear markedly to influence the fields of economic activity which an entrepreneur chooses to enter; we would not feel that the absence of an unemployment insurance tax would be critical in influencing an entrepreneurial decision to enter the field of agriculture, for example. All this should not be taken to imply that the government can act with impunity; there may be levels at which the programs might be self-defeating. And "differentiated" programs, discussed below, may have important impacts.

Second, in the long run, it is probable that the influence is even minimized as far as the psychological aspects are concerned. Thus, economic security programs become an ingrained part of the environment within which business is done; and they are accepted as an integral element of the business framework. This should not be taken to imply that entrepreneurs are thereby oblivious to the costs involved or to *changes* in these costs. Far from it; all the proof one needs can be obtained from business responses in hearings on proposed changes in workmen's compensation rates, for example. But the fundamental program tends to grow into the framework within which economic activity takes place, and it becomes a customary factor in doing business.

Third, "differential" economic security programs do, however, have an influence upon entrepreneurial decision-making and hence upon the location of industry and pricing. These programs are only one of many factors considered, for example, in plant location. But, as one factor, they do contribute to decisions made with respect to location and pricing, and in some cases they may be the critical factor. And while, as noted above, such programs may not have a marked influence upon fields of economic endeavor entered or not entered, they do influence the choice of geographic area in which to locate. "Differential" programs are "differentiated" essentially on a state-by-state basis. This is one reason why we find states generally unwilling to be very far in the forefront in economic security programs, for these programs customarily involve a premium or a tax of some type, and a state is usually not desirous of increasing these costs for fear of driving out established businesses or failing to attract new businesses.[23]

The influence of the structure and content of economic security programs. The structure, content, and the administrative operation of a security program may have an important effect upon economic activity. A given program, even if it is designed wholly and only as a security measure, may have discernible economic impacts of vari-

---

[23] See various issues of the magazine *Industrial Location* for a discussion of concrete location factors. For a regional analysis of the problem see The Commonwealth of Massachusetts, *Report* of the Special Commission Relative to the Textile Industry . . . (Boston: May 12, 1950), pp. 43–49, 51; and *Report* on the New England Textile Industry by the Committee Appointed by the Conference of New England Governors (Cambridge: 1953), pp. 245–55.

ous types. Moreover, some programs have had incorporated into them, deliberately or otherwise, features designed to accomplish other purposes than economic security itself. Here the impact may be even more pronounced.

Several examples may be cited to illustrate these possibilities. Take private pension programs, for example. Such programs generally have not incorporated vesting rights for the employee. That is, the employer's contribution generally has not belonged to the employee; the latter could not take the contribution with him when he left the employ of a given employer.[24] Hence, nonvested pension programs probably have the effect of restricting labor mobility, or conversely, of tying the employee to the employer. As was noted in Chapter 8, employment guarantees as well as pension plans may restrict mobility. While we need to know more about "desirable" *versus* "undesirable" levels of labor mobility, and while it is one of the industrial relations functions of management to reduce labor turnover, it is nevertheless true that the artificial erection of walls retarding the free flow of economic activity is undesirable.[25] This holds true not only for labor mobility, but for resource allocation, pricing, distribution, and for all the other phases of economic activity. Good cases can be made for regulating certain types of economic activity, but an economic security program hardly seems the appropriate vehicle for such control.

A second example is found in the Old-Age and Survivors Insurance program provision which limits benefits if earnings by a retired person exceed a given amount. At present, the law provides that between the ages of sixty-five and seventy-two a benefit recipient can earn up to $1,200 a year without loss of benefits. After $1,200 has been earned, one month's benefit is deducted for each $80 of

24 This would appear to be a denial of the belief that it is the employee who bears an important share of the burden of economic security programs. In the nonvesting case, the employer retains his (the employer's) contribution; if the payment were merely a foregone wage increase, one would assume it belonged to the employee and he should be able to take it with him. The fact that vested rights are slowly but surely on the increase makes it appear, however, that there is some logic to the assertion that certainly a part of the burden of economic security programs rests upon the employee.

25 Professor George P. Shultz has pertinently noted to us that, while employee services are generally available on a "here and now basis" to all employees, this is not true of certain classes of financial services. In the latter case, there is a "time-lock" wherein the employee must remain with the company to benefit from the service. In the extreme case (a nonvested pension) he "loses all" if he leaves the company. There are modified "time-locks" in many employee services: vacations graduated on the basis of length of service, or employee discounts similarly graduated. But here the employee does not lose all if he leaves the company, since he has "collected" in the interim.

earnings or fraction thereof. Such "retirement earnings" have been liberalized greatly through the years, and the age limit has come down from seventy-five to seventy-two.

The original purpose of this provision is not difficult to discern, resting upon the "lump of labor" theory. This theory, in one version, assumes that there is only so much work available, and hence only so many employees needed. One way, therefore, in which new entrants into the labor force can get jobs is through the relinquishing of jobs by the retirement of older workers. But, at present, the view appears to be that earnings below $1,200 annually are not sufficient to pose a threat to the younger worker; that is, it is only after $1,200 that the potential displacement threat becomes actual. Likewise, after age seventy-two, an individual apparently is not presumed to threaten the jobs of others.[26]

One may ask the question, however, whether an economic security program should have as an integral purpose the regulation of the supply of labor. J. Douglas Brown contends that it should not, noting that "the essential purpose of social insurance is to afford security and not to regulate the supply of labor."[27] Dean Brown notes, however, that the contingency of dependency is likely to be reduced by earnings, and hence that the amount of benefit above a modest sum should be reduced by an amount equivalent to the earnings received. Thus the result tends to be a compromise, with present trends indicating a liberalization of earnings and a lowering of the age. Both these factors in turn tend to lessen the influence of an economic security program in regulating the supply of labor. These are moves in the right direction. An economic security program need not necessarily be "economically neutral (nor is it possible for it to be "neutral" in many situations). But a program is perhaps most rationally structured when it does not implicitly or explicitly seek to accomplish, or in fact does not accomplish, the regulation of other phases of economic activity.

A FINAL COMMENT ON ALTERNATIVE ECONOMIC SECURITY APPROACHES

The previous discussion has centered upon problems related primarily to the *present* United States economic security system and

---

[26] Arthur Larson holds that cost is an important factor in these provisions, and that if benefits were payable to people if they continued to work, the cost would skyrocket, increasing an estimated two billion dollars a year. Larson, *op. cit.*, p. 31.

[27] J. Douglas Brown, "Concepts in Old-Age and Survivors' Insurance," *Proceedings* of the First Annual Meeting, Industrial Relations Research Association, 1948, p. 102.

to alternative ways of structuring security programs within that system. In closing this section it may be well to comment briefly upon more basic alternatives—those of differing systems.

One basic alternative is whether economic security should be a matter of complete private action and initiative or should involve the government. But, government *is* an active participant in present programs and during our lifetime is not likely to remove itself. Moreover, it has been clearly demonstrated that there is a useful role to be played by the government in providing the *basic* layer of protection against economic insecurities.

If it be assumed that the government, broadly defined, has a legitimate place in formal economic security programs, a second alternative is whether the federal government, state governments, or some combination should exercise jurisdiction. Here one can also take a somewhat deterministic view, but there is perhaps more freedom of choice. What criteria would one apply in making such a decision? On the one hand would be the yardsticks of economy and uniformity; here an all-federal program would probably best fit the specifications. On the other hand, if one applies the criterion of states' rights, then a combined program fits better. Which of these criteria one does apply is a matter for one's own value judgments. Our own preference would be for a combined program, even if it sacrificed some economy and uniformity. But this does not mean that lack of economy and uniformity should be at a premium. Far from it. We have commented at various places in this text on ways of undertaking voluntary action toward efficiency and standardization.

If federal and state governments undertake programs of economic security, what form should such programs take? The range of possibilities is great, from a Townsend Plan at one extreme through a rigid insurance program to the setting of individual wage rates at levels which compensate for the risks of economic insecurity involved. For reasons developed in Chapters 7 and 9, a "tax" system is preferable economically to a wage adjustment program. Administratively, the tax system is much to be preferred; the difficulties in wage adjustment appear incredibly difficult, in addition to which there are the ethical problems inherent in this type of control.

If a tax system is preferable, should it be the type which uses general revenues, the type which applies special taxes such as transaction taxes, or the type in which all groups are blanketed on some sort of complete pay-as-you-go basis? Or should it be of some "social insurance form," such as we now have? Considering costs only, good cases can be made for the first three types, although there are some hidden dangers. But the latter approach, utilizing the social insurance basis, appears more compatible with our cultural mores, and hence is much more acceptable to the populace at large. For the present at least, tempering economics with social reality, the existing system is the most operable.[28]

Specialized Economic Issues

In the above section, attention has been given to a variety of economic issues relevant to economic security programs in the general sense. In this section the focus will be upon issues that are essentially germane to particular programs. We will select three issues, one of which is analytically "new," the other two being older, standardized problems. This selection is by no means exhaustive, but it illustrates the range of subject matter.

COMPENSATORY INFLUENCES OF ECONOMIC SECURITY PROGRAMS

How effective are economic security programs in providing income or other types of payments when economic insecurity appears? The following data cast some light upon this question.

First, in the case of accidents, sickness, death, and old age, it is difficult to speak of the "compensatory" or "counterbalancing" influences of economic security programs. This is true because, unlike unemployment, it is not customary to view accidents, sickness, death, or old age as accompanying (or causing or resulting from) changes in the level of economic activity. Hence, it is likewise not customary to view accident and other types of indemnification as a compensatory influence in the way that unemployment insurance payments are.

But, the injured, the dependent, and the aged are an overhead cost to society. And payments made under private and public economic security programs for accidents, death, and old age are one means through which these overhead costs can be met. Hence, while such payments are not compensatory in, say, a counter-cyclical manner, they do provide an income flow which permits a more socially desirable way of caring for those dependent, and, which in turn helps maintain the level of economic activity.

Table 14.1 summarizes benefits paid under a number of economic security programs for selected years. While the figures are for disparate years and hence not fully comparable, they do reveal clearly the trends in economic security payments. The magnitude of

[28] See J. Douglas Brown, "The American Philosophy of Social Insurance," *The Social Service Review*, XXX, No. 1 (March, 1956), 3–8.

TABLE 14.1

Economic Security Program Payments for Selected Years*

Date	OASI and Other Public Retirement Programs (Federal and State)†	Unemployment Insurance, Employment Service and RR Unemployment Insurance†	Workmen's Compensation, RR and State Disability Insurance†	Date	Life Insurance Death Benefits**	Private Pensions**	Private Accident and Health Programs; Paid Sick Leave‡	Public Aid†	Other Public Programs (Health, Medical, Other Welfare; Federal and State)†	Total (Millions)	Gross National Product† (Billions)
1939–1940	398.3	570.6	246.0	1940	994.9	176.5	No Data	3,657.1	1,466.3	7,509.7	95.7
1944–1945	793.3	166.1	356.9	1945	1,279.7	216.4	No Data	1,037.8	2,123.8	5,974.0	218.3
1949–1950	1,821.7	2,201.4	700.4	1950	1,589.7	319.3	1,538	2,488.8	9,101.2	19,760.5	263.0
1953–1954	5,134.1	1,898.3	1,179.0	1954	2,072.2	456.8	2,954	2,774.7	7,721.3	24,190.4	360.6

* All figures in millions except gross national product in billions.

† Adapted from Ida C. Merriam, "Social Welfare in the United States," *Social Security Bulletin*, XVIII, No. 10 (October, 1955), Table 1, pp. 6–7.

** *Life Insurance Fact Book, 1955*, p. 34. Includes individual annuities as well as insurance pension plan payments under private pensions. The figures understate total payments, since a significant number of plans exist outside insurance companies.

‡ *Social Security Bulletin*, XVIII, No. 12 (December, 1955), Table 2, p. 13; XIX, No. 1 (January, 1956), Table 6, p. 7. Includes income loss payments and medical care expenditures. Excludes payments under public programs and government sick leave.

such payments is apparent when set against national income for the relevant years.

Unemployment insurance is, however, more relevantly viewed against the backdrop of changing levels of economic activity. How much of a countercyclical influence is it? The most thorough investigation of this subject has been made by Daniel Creamer, whose studies are summarized here.[29]

Unemployment insurance benefits were not payable by all states until 1939. There have been three recessions in labor income since then: 1945–1946, 1948–1949, and 1953–1954. Creamer's data cover the first two of these three periods. (A cursory examination of the period 1953–1954 leads us to believe that the conclusions reached by Creamer for the earlier periods would be applicable here also.)

For the recession period February, 1945–March, 1946, Creamer calculates (using seasonally adjusted monthly data) a loss in private payrolls of $5.7 billion. During this period the total compensation to the unemployed was $698 million, or 12.1 per cent of the payroll loss. For the period September, 1948–April, 1950, the payroll loss was $7.4 billion; the unemployment payments $1.5 billion, or 20.2 per cent of the loss. Using quarterly rather than monthly data, the unemployment payments compensate for 18.7 and 24.3 per cent, respectively.[30] Creamer has also calculated these ratios for a given group of states, and with several exceptions there is evidence of an *inverse* relation between payroll loss and the relative offset from unemployment compensation.

Three conclusions appear warranted from the investigations of Creamer and from other data. The first is that in the relatively mild recessions of 1945–1946 and 1948–1949, compensating payments to the unemployed were significant in maintaining purchasing power. Such payments ranged from 12 to 25 per cent of payroll losses, contingent upon the method of calculation used. But second, following Creamer, it can be noted that the evidence suggests "that

[29] See Daniel Creamer, *Personal Income during Business Cycles*, A Study of the National Bureau of Economic Research (Princeton: Princeton University Press, 1956), particularly pp. 96–103. For the period analyzed by Creamer (1939–1952), the new supplementary unemployment payments were nonexistent. Hence, unemployment insurance and public assistance are the payment categories scrutinized. See also the work by Ida Merriam, "Social Security Programs and Economic Stability," *Policies to Combat Depression*, also a National Bureau of Economic Research publication, 1956. For an earlier study, see Sam Arnold, *Effectiveness of Unemployment Benefits in Maintaining Purchasing Power* (Columbus: Ohio State University, Bureau of Business Research, 1943). For a later study see Ida C. Merriam, "Social Welfare Expenditures in the United States, 1954–55," *Social Security Bulletin*, XIX, No. 10 (September, 1956), pp. 3–10.

[30] See Creamer, *op. cit.*, pp. 99–100, for an explanation of why the quarterly figures differ from the monthly.

in more severe business recessions the relative offset under present laws would be decidedly less than it was in the 1948–1949 recession."[31] Finally, economic security program payments of all types are "built-in stabilizers," which not only have a counter-cyclical usefulness (for specific programs such as unemployment compensation) but which also provide a steady stream of income payments to various classes of recipients. This stability factor has a usefulness all its own.

EXPERIENCE OR MERIT RATING IN UNEMPLOYMENT COMPENSATION

"The primary and announced purpose of experience rating . . . is to provide a financial incentive, in the form of a reduced contribution rate, for the individual employer to make a real effort to stabilize his employment."[32] While Great Britain experimented with this approach prior to 1920 and then abandoned it, the "merit rating" idea was incorporated into the Wisconsin Act in 1932. Today all state laws make provision for some form of merit or experience rating. (While the two terms are technically interchangeable, the latter has become the more customary.) The necessity for such adoption was discussed in Chapter 7, along with experience rating formulae and the employer contribution rate changes resulting from the utilization of this system.

But, the mere fact that all states have experience rating plans does not mean that the approach is economically logical (though this has led to the oft-repeated statement that "experience rating is indefensible in theory but thoroughly acceptable in practice"). What are the presumed advantages of experience rating? The disadvantages? The following discussion seeks to get at the more relevant issues.[33]

The major contentions for experience rating are two in number, as follows:

1. On an economywide level, such a system is viewed as a way of allocating or distributing the social costs of unemployment among indus-

[31] *Ibid.*, p. 103.

[32] Charles A. Myers, "Experience Rating in Unemployment Compensation," *American Economic Review*, XXXV, No. 3 (June, 1945), 339. This article, along with the following by Professor Myers, provides an excellent analysis of the subject: *Employment Stabilization and the Wisconsin Act* (Washington, D. C.: Social Security Board, September, 1940).

[33] Perhaps still the two best sources on this topic are Herman Feldman and Donald M. Smith, *The Case For Experience Rating in Unemployment Compensation and a Proposed Method;* and Richard A. Lester and Charles V. Kidd, *The Case against Experience Rating in Unemployment Compensation,* both published by Industrial Relations Counselors, New York, 1939. The analysis herein leans heavily upon these studies.

tries in the order in which they are "responsible" for unemployment. This is held to be analogous to the way in which, for example, the costs of industrial accidents are distributed among companies in order of their safety "experience."

2. On the individual-enterprise level, the purpose of experience rating is, as was noted in the opening paragraph of this section, to stabilize employment in the individual firm by providing a monentary incentive in the form of a reduced contribution rate. (If employment stabilization were a cost-free process, one would presume that the entrepreneur would carry it to the point where his unemployment compensation tax was minimized. If it were not cost free, then economic logic would dictate that it be carried to the point where its marginal costs would not be greater than the marginal tax savings.)

The arguments arrayed against experience rating are more numerous. Whether they are also more persuasive is a matter we shall analyze further.

1. It is held to be economically and ethically undesirable, as well as operationally impossible, to allocate the social costs of unemployment via experience rating. Assume a highly unstable industry, and assume that the employer is thus able to do little in the way of stabilizing his employment. Further assume his contribution rate is therefore high. If the employee bears the burden of the high rate he is really paying the cost of unemployment inherent in his own job. If the tax is shifted to consumers and the employer bears none of the burden, there is no incentive for him even to attempt to stabilize. If the employer bears the burden, he is a victim of economic happenstance. And even if the burden is shared, there is little justice; it merely means that three parties carry the yoke, and injustice is compounded. Moreover, say the critics, the analogy with workmen's compensation is not valid, since unemployment is largely a *market* phenomenon, unlike industrial accidents which occur because of conditions within the plant.

2. Rather than being countercyclical in nature (and hence acting as a stabilizing force), experience rating "adds fuel to the flames." In boom periods, when employment is high (for reasons inherent in the functioning of the economic system), tax rates are low (when they should be high). Conversely, in depressed periods, the contribution rate is high (when it should be low). Thus the entire system operates out of phase.

On the individual firm level the principal counter-arguments are three in number.

1. The major criticism rests upon the contention that the employment experience of a business is largely beyond its control; that market forces and not employer activities are the critical causal factors. Hence, experience rating is a misdirected form of social policy, since it rewards

one employer for a record not of his doing and penalizes another on the same basis.

2. Experience rating may in part tend to be self-defeating. Employers, in attempting to secure more favorable tax rates, are likely to engage in a variety of practices (some ethically defensible, others not so) that *may* increase employment stability for a small core of employees, but which *will* greatly increase instability for another group. For example, an employer can increase his use of part-time employees, can discharge individuals before they become eligible for unemployment insurance, or can utilize other practices that at one and the same time decrease employment stability for given employees and yet that do not in any way officially blemish the employer's records. Hence it is held that experience rating may actually increase unemployment for that marginal group of employees who can stand it least.

3. Finally it is contended that such a system will prove administratively cumbersome if not unworkable. Experience rating implies the keeping of detailed and perhaps voluminous reports on each employer's accessions and separations. Moreover, it is now to the economic interest of an employer to challenge unemployment insurance payments to individuals in specified cases; a successful challenge means a better employment record and hence a lower contribution rate. Therefore, unemployment insurance may become a legalistic battleground, defeating in part its operation. This legalism may, additionally, be carried over into struggles to prevent benefits from rising so as to keep the contribution rate low.

Let us take a more critical look at various of these contentions, recognizing that we do not have a clean slate upon which we can trace an ideal system, but rather that the system of experience rating is a reality in all forty-eight states.

Can an employer stabilize his employment? What degree of control does he have? What forces, operating through the market, are beyond his ability to regulate? This is perhaps the most important of all the questions involved, since answers to the others depend in no small measure upon the answers to it.

The customary answer is that the employer has little control over his total employment experience, particularly that arising from cyclical and secular causes where market forces are the more crucial, although he does have more control over other unemployment types. While there has been little recent empirical research in this field, earlier studies tend to support this position. Thus Charles A. Myers concludes by noting that employers can do something in the way of ironing out day-to-day or intermittent irregularities in employment or reducing seasonal unemployment. And Myers also indicates that a reduced contribution rate is a tangible financial incentive *initially*, though he wonders if it need be continued once a firm has seen the inherent desirability of stabilized operations.[34]

Thus, the general conclusions to which one comes are as follows: First, the stabilization of employment is a multi-layered matter. Second, over the basic and quantitatively more important employment layer (secular, cyclical) the employer has relatively little control. Third, over the layer of daily and seasonally changing levels of employment, he has a higher degree of control. Fourth, a financial incentive may help to reduce unemployment of the latter type, though there is some doubt as to whether a continuing incentive is necessary.

If these arguments have merit, then one can in turn reach certain conclusions on experience rating as a social policy. Such a system should not be used to allocate the social costs of that unemployment included in the basic layer, since such unemployment is largely outside the employer's control. But, such a system might well be used in conjunction with the secondary layer of unemployment. The relationship of this approach to commerial insurance premium structures is readily apparent. Given this approach, there would be a minimum rate *all* employers would pay. Above that, reductions of a supplementary rate would be possible, contingent upon the employer's experience.

The organizational and administrative difficulties of such a system should not be minimized, however. Critical decisions would have to be made on the choice of the basic rate and the supplementary rate, and this would involve a variety of interindustry and interfirm comparisons. Day-by-day administration of such a system would be far from routine. Moreover, such an approach would not of itself equalize the burden among the various states, and federal minimum-maximum specifications would be desirable. Whether such a system would be self-defeating (a criticism noted above) is difficult to answer without experience as a guide; one may conjecture that it would not. Nor would such an approach have the desirable counter-cyclical characteristics; to achieve this would involve, at the very least, a complicated lag-formula system.

But, if the present system does not operate as envisaged above, and if, in fact, we have a miscellany of experience rating plans, what practical suggestions can be given? One would be that the federal government enact a set of minimum standards for experience rating. Such standards would require uniformity among the

---

[34] See the previously cited works by C. A. Myers, particularly "Experience Rating in Unemployment Compensation," p. 347.

states and would meet in part the multi-layered nature of the unemployment problem.[35]

ECONOMIC SECURITY TRUST FUNDS AND THE TAXATION QUESTION

An interesting sort of attack on (and defense of) economic security trust funds has appeared now and again in the past decade or two.[36]

The trust fund "fraud" thesis is usually spelled out in the following steps. (We will use the OASI fund as the example.)

1. The government taxes employers and employees covered under the OASI program. But it taxes (at present, at least) more than is needed to meet current out-payments. Therefore a reserve (a trust fund) is built up and by law is invested in United States government securities. This is the first taxation stage—single taxation.

2. The securities held in the reserve (trust fund) are interest-bearing. In order to pay the interest on these obligations, the government taxes the general public. This is the second taxation stage—"double" taxation, and the stage which is viewed as "fraudulent" by certain critics.

A variety of minor rebuttals have been made to this argument: that if the excess of taxes over out-payments were invested in private rather than in government securities we would have government ownership of private industry (and hence "socialism"); or that the contention might have some merit only if the excess receipts caused the government to spend more than it otherwise would have.

But these rebuttals do not get at the core of the false reasoning involved in this type of argumentation. That there are two stages of taxation is obviously the case. But this is not double taxation. Nor is it fraudulent. Assume that present taxes were lower—that they were just sufficient to meet present benefit requirements, and hence that no trust fund could be built up. Assume that the system remains on such an annual "pay-as-you-go" basis. Now "pay-as-

---

[35] See Feldman and Smith, op. cit., p. 59. See also *Unemployment Insurance,* Senate Document No. 206, 80th Congress, 2nd Session (Washington, D. C.: U. S. Government Printing Office, 1948), pp. 30–42. One improvement was made in federal specifications as of January 1, 1955, in that an employer could qualify for reduced benefits with only one rather than three year's experience. Hence the "new" firm is not discriminated against.

[36] See, for example, John T. Flynn, "Our Present Dishonest Old Age Pension Plan," *Reader's Digest,* L, No. 5 (May, 1947), 4–8; "The Old Age and Survivor's Insurance Fund," in Recommendations for Social Security Legislation, The Reports of the Advisory Committee on Social Security to the Senate Committee on Finance, Senate Document No. 208, 80th Congress, 2nd Session (Washington, D. C.: U. S. Government Printing Office, 1948), p. 48; George B. Robinson, "The Old Age Reserve Fund is Not 'Illusory'," *Quarterly Journal of Economics,* LX, No. 1 (November, 1945), 136–53.

you-go" has a particular connotation here. What it means is that each year those who are actively covered under the system pay the benefits of those who have become eligible to retire. As the percentage of the retired aged increases (which is the developing case in this country) those actively covered under the system will have to pay increased taxes to meet the obligations imposed by the given benefit structure. Disregarding discount complexities, one can show that the interest paid on the trust fund and raised by taxation is equal to the increase in taxes that would be required to meet obligations in the absence of such a fund. Thus there is no "double taxation." There might be some legitimacy to the criticism that the taxes are paid by different groups; that in the case of a trust fund, the "general public" helps support the OASI beneficiary, whereas on a pay-as-you-go approach the OASI group finances itself. But this is not the same as double taxation or fraud.

A simple arithmetic example will bring out the above. Assume $1,000,000 is needed this year to pay benefits, and $1,002,000 next year. Using the trust fund approach, $1,100,000 is raised via OASI taxes this year, and the excess $100,000 invested in United States securities at 2 per cent. Next year $1,000,000 will be raised from OASI coverage and $2,000 via general taxation as interest on trust fund securities. Thus, $2,000 comes from general taxation. In the absence of this fund, the $2,000 would have to be raised via OASI taxes. Hence $2,000 = $2,000 and there is no double taxation. It may be argued that an extra $100,000 was levied in the first year to build up the trust fund. But, ultimately if the trust fund is reduced to zero, the process of its reduction means that additional funds will be available, thus permitting taxes to be reduced in that year. Hence, again the two alternatives systems balance each other out.

The Social Security Advisory Council's rebuttal to the "double taxation" thesis was a "half-taxation" argument, which while interesting also is not wholly valid. This rebuttal ran as follows:

Assume that in a future year, OASI benefit payments exceeded taxes collected by $2,000. If there were a $100,000 trust fund invested in 2 per cent United States securities, $2,000 would be earned, and total receipts from taxation and interest would equal benefit payments. But assume there was no reserve fund. Then it would be necessary to raise the $2,000 via, say additional OASI taxes. *And* (and this is the core of the argument) another $2,000 would have to be raised to pay interest on $100,000 of public debt that would now be held by someone other than the OASI trust fund. Therefore, the trust fund results in half, rather than double taxation.

One does not, however, get something for nothing in this case; if one did it would be profitable to pursue this policy and thus achieve one-fourth, one-eighth, and subsequent geometric reductions in the tax load. Counterbalancing factors negate this "something for nothing" possibility. If no reserve had been created, the excess taxes (or tax base) that would have been used in building it up could have been used for other purposes. Hence there would have been no need to have public debt in the hands of others (there would have been no public debt) and in turn no need to levy taxes to make interest payments. But assume that a public debt did exist and it was in the hands of others. If this were the case, then taxes would have been less in an earlier period (or periods) since public borrowing was used instead. Thus the additional tax burden now (to meet public debt interest payments) would have been balanced by the lower earlier tax load. There is, of course, a difference in who pays the taxes. But this is not a "half-taxation" argument. Again arithmetic examples could be used to illustrate the problems involved.[37]

Whether a trust-fund approach should or should not be used for the various social insurances has been endlessly debated.[38] There are valid arguments for and against such an approach. But we are not convinced that the double-taxation (or half-taxation) argument is one of them.

Summary

In this chapter we have presented a number of the more important and interesting economic issues involved in programs of economic security. It is difficult to treat these issues within a formal analytical framework, such as might be done when examining, say, business price policy in light of the theory of the firm. A welfare economics approach might be used, but this requires a degree of sophistication in presentation and utilization that is hard to achieve. Yet the relative absence of a formal framework does not mean that an economic approach cannot be used. Far from it; we have tried in the above to indicate ways in which such an approach can be employed.

Thus, in trying to answer the question of how much security a society can afford, we noted that this involves first the question of

[37] As an exercise the student might wish to work out several such examples.

[38] See Harris, *op. cit.*, chap. ix, and "Financing Old-Age and Survivor's Insurance," Report on Issues in Social Security to the Committee on Ways and Means of the House of Representatives, 79th Congress, 1st Session (Washington, D. C.: U. S. Government Printing Office, 1946), particularly pp. 103 ff. See also Chapter 4, this volume.

the productive capacity of that society, and given more than minimal capacity, it involves secondly a choice by society as to what proportion of its resources it wishes to devote to economic security programs. The choice might well vary under different conditions; thus in a war economy, economic security programs might have to be restricted.

A variety of financial problems are created through the operation of economic security programs. Who pays the costs of such programs? There is some reason to believe that employees finance their own security in large measure although not completely. The specific method of financing such programs creates its own problems, particularly where reserves are utilized, and deflationary or inflationary pressures may be built up depending upon the method chosen.

Economic security programs may have impacts other than those of a financial nature as noted above. What of the impact upon entrepreneurship? It is our feeling that "differentiated" programs may have marked consequences (or at least may be a factor of importance) upon businessmen's behavior, but that programs comprehensive in nature tend to become part of the setting within which economic activity takes place and hence their effect is minimized. Similarly, such programs may have various "side-effects" as, for example, in influencing labor supply. We would feel that such side effects should be minimized, and if it is desirable to control these other economic activities it should be done by direct means rather than through an economic security program.

Economic security programs are important built-in stabilizers in the economy; the benefit payment record under unemployment compensation illustrates this. Yet, some programs work contrary to economic balance, as in the case of the tax structure under experience rating. Conversely, it is not valid to conclude that the accumulation of trust funds under various security programs has the contrary result of "double taxation."

But, in all these matters, the economist's verdict is not final. It should be taken into account, but only along with relevant legal, political, psychological, and social considerations.

Suggestions for Additional Reading

BURNS, EVELINE M. *Social Security and Public Policy.* New York: McGraw-Hill Book Co., Inc., 1956.
A social, political, economic, and operational analysis of many of the facets of economic security. Very useful as a constant reference when studying the American economic security system.

CREAMER, DANIEL. *Personal Income During Business Cycles.* Princeton: Princeton University Press, 1956.
An analysis of the role of unemployment insurance benefits (among other factors) in maintaining personal income in business cycles. Pages 96–103 are particularly useful to the student interested in economic security programs.

HARRIS, SEYMOUR E. *Economics of Social Security.* New York: McGraw-Hill Book Co., Inc., 1941.
While this book is factually dated, it provides one of the best comprehensive treatments existent on the economic phases of security problems.

MERRIAM, IDA C. *Social Security Programs and Economic Stability.* Paper presented at the Universities-National Bureau Committee for Economic Research Conference on Policies to Combat Depression, (held at Princeton, New Jersey, May, 1954). New York: National Bureau of Economic Research, 1954.
An interesting examination of the stabilizing influences of social security systems upon the economy. Includes both qualitative and quantitative analysis.

RAINWATER, P. L., "The Fallacy of Experience Rating"; Stanley Rector, "The Frailty of the 'Fallacy' of Experience Rating"; P. L. Rainwater, Rebuttal to article by Stanley Rector. All in *Labor Law Journal,* II (February, 1951), 94–104; II (May, 1951), 338–49; II (October, 1951), 753–62; respectively. Additional argumentation on the experience rating issue.

15

Problems of Substandard Conditions

Introduction

The working and living conditions of American workers for the first time became a matter of widespread concern around the turn of the twentieth century. There were being generated employment and living conditions which a changing public opinion would not long tolerate. We discussed earlier the deplorable accident record of this period. Conditions of work were equally poor (although not all of them were as harsh as in the case of the candy girl whose fate was described in Chapter 9). Frederick Lewis Allen writes of this period that to read "reports of qualified observers of poverty at its worst in the big city slums and grim industrial towns at the beginning of the century is to hear variation after variation upon the theme of human misery, in which the same words occur monotonously again and again: wretchedness, overcrowding, filth, hunger, malnutrition, insecurity, want."[1]

What were employment conditions at the time? First, there was widespread employment of children which increased steadily until 1910. Census records reveal that 16 per cent of all children ten to fifteen years old were gainfully employed in 1880, and 18.4 per cent in 1910. These estimates are probably conservative, since child labor in home work and street trades could not easily be recorded. Much of this child labor was most heavily concentrated in agri-

[1] Reprinted with permission from Frederick Lewis Allen, *The Big Change* (New York: Harper and Brothers, 1952), p. 57.

culture and manufacturing, where accident rates among children were high. The average earnings of employed children, except for the war years, was reported at from three to five dollars a week.[2]

Second, adult American workers of the period labored under similarly adverse conditions. Allen writes[3] that the average wage of the period for American workers was between $400 and $500, with unskilled workers averaging under $460 in the North and $300 in the South. A report[4] of male earnings in the "principal trades and industries" for the decade preceding World War I reveals that one-fourth of the heads of families earned less than $400 a year; and one-half of them earned less than $600. One-fourth of regularly employed women in the "principal manufacturing industries" earned less than $200 a year and two-thirds earned less than $400. Women and children were employed in greatest proportions in the low-paid industries, such as textiles and glass. For women, a work week in excess of fifty-five to sixty hours was not uncommon.

Nature of the Problem

Oppressive working conditions, such as those briefly sketched above, pose a problem in economic security which cannot be resolved by approaches like the social assistance and insurance measures considered in earlier chapters. Rather, they must be dealt with through direct control and intervention. This is true because the problem is associated with employment rather than with unemployment.

In the preceding chapters, the problems in economic security which were discussed were problems of unemployment. That they should be of great importance is not surprising, for in an industrial society the only means by which a worker can earn a livelihood is through the sale of his personal services in a free labor market. Whether unemployment arises directly out of labor market operation or is caused indirectly by other factors such as accidents, illness, or old age, social insurance measures seek primarily to alleviate its undesirable consequences. Protection against substandard working conditions cannot be provided by these methods, however, for it is not the inability of workers to get a wage contract that is at

[2] S. Howard Patterson, *Social Aspects of Industry* (New York: McGraw-Hill Book Co., Inc., 1929), p. 200.

[3] Allen, *op. cit.*, p. 55.

[4] These data are taken from an interesting compilation of studies on working conditions for the period from 1900 to World War I by W. Jett Lauck and Edgar Sydenstricker, *Conditions of Labor In American Industries* (New York: Funk and Wagnalls, 1917), chap. ii.

issue here, but rather their inability to get a wage contract that meets the minimum standards under which a society will permit its members to be employed. Hence a different type of labor market functioning is involved.

This distinction has significance beyond its use as a definition. For unlike unemployment-caused insecurity, control of substandard conditions requires, and has indeed involved, intervention into the wage contract and intervention directly into the labor market. And, so, two questions arise: Should the government intervene in the freedom of individuals to enter contracts for employment? Can it intervene? The courts permitted qualifications of this freedom in the name of economic security only after extended resistance.

CHANGING ATTITUDES TOWARD SUBSTANDARD CONDITIONS

Because of the vast improvement in the conditions of work over the past one-hundred years, most working conditions during this period would probably be termed "substandard" by today's standards. The terms of employment which free societies accept as reasonable have changed enormously over the years, as have educational, health, and living standards—and they will probably continue to do so.

The changing attitudes toward child labor are illustrative. Of eighteenth-century England, Professor Herbert Heaton writes that ". . . a child of four or five years could, if well brought up, 'earn its own bread.' In the straw-plaiting regions they began work at four years, and by their sixth birthday were (in 1801) earning 2/- to 3/- a week, climbing to a wage of 10/- to 12/- by the time they were eight or nine."[5]

In the American colonies, one of the chief benefits derived from manufactures was considered to be the job opportunities created for children. As recently as 1910, it was estimated that about one-fifth of all boys between ten and fifteen years of age were employed. Today the Fair Labor Standards Act prohibits the employment in interstate commerce of children under sixteen in all employments and under eighteen in hazardous work.

Similarly, the acceptable minimum standards for working conditions, working hours, and pay have changed with a changing social and economic environment. These changes have been achieved through legislation, the efforts of trade unions, the actions of

[5] Reprinted with permission from Herbert Heaton, *Economic History of Europe* (New York: Harper and Brothers, 1936), p. 350.

employers and, in the case of improved hours and wages, were made possible by advances in productivity.

Development of Protective Legislation

Before considering the provisions of the protective labor laws which are in effect in all American jurisdictions today, it is useful to note several generalizations about their development.

Historically, movements for improving working standards have been directed more at a specific situation which had aroused public interest than at goals based on abstract principles. Definitions of minimum acceptable working conditions have been determined by contemporary economic, social, and political circumstances. Clyde Dankert notes that arguments for reduced hours at any particular time ". . . usually bear a close relationship to the objective conditions prevailing at that time."[6] The appearance early in the twentieth century of a child labor movement in the South, for instance, was due less to a belief that children should be educated as well as protected from working conditions interfering with their adult development, than it was to the realization of the inhumane effects of the widespread employment of children by the new southern mills.

For these reasons, arguments in support of government intervention into substandard conditions have changed with the times and the conditions. Thus we may note that shorter hours were first advocated as necessary for leisure and for better citizenship. But later, with the coming of the factory system, this approach was abandoned for the argument that shorter hours were necessary to protect the worker's health.

Experience under the Fair Labor Standards Act has been similar. The original 1938 Act, as well as its 1949 and 1955 amendments, was justified by arguments which are traditionally offered in support of minimum wage legislation—the need to provide minimum living standards, to reduce poverty, to increase purchasing power, and to lessen employer exploitation of the worker. Important to the 1938 law, however, was the argument that the overtime penalty provisions would aid in spreading employment in that immediate post-depression period. The 1955 amendment, which increased minimum wages during a period of high, full employment, found important justification in the arguments that since the low wages paid in southern states were acting as an inducement to northern industry to migrate south, they were an

---

[6] Clyde E. Dankert, *An Introduction to Labor* (Englewood Cliffs, N. J.: Prentice-Hall, 1954), pp. 519–20.

unfair competitive advantage against northern employers and a threat to trade union wage standards.[7]

In short, demands that certain working conditions be declared substandard have varied at different times and have been based on many grounds, including those of civic improvement, safety, health, morals, and more recently, economic effects.[8] Although these demands at all times had the specific objective of improving the conditions of work, they did not necessarily focus on an abstract goal or on a single set of principles.

Behind this combination of objective and value judgment criteria for improved working conditions, there occasionally lurked the selfish motive of setting job standards for women which would reduce their competitive threat to men.

Support for protection has come from many and varying sources. Sometimes an aroused public opinion was the initiating factor, as in the case of the child labor movement in the South. Trade union support, which today is frequently at the head of campaigns to improve legislative standards, dates back to the interest of the Knights of Labor in child labor legislation and the eight-hour day, which this union gained for its members for a short time. Yet trade union support has by no means been uniform. In fact, for a time, trade unions actively opposed the enactment of minimum wage legislation and never gave much support to men's hours movements.

Employers have improved working conditions on their own initiative, partially in response to the pressures of trade unions and of competition, and in part when the economies of such action were apparent. Finally, reform movements frequently had as their nucleus of support organizations like the Consumers' League and Women's Trade Union League (in the case of women's hours) and various public spirited middle class individuals and groups who carried the brunt of the fight for minimum wage legislation.

Cultural, economic, and social philosophy, in the broad sense, appear to have played a more minor role in the movements for legislative protection. Humanitarian considerations, it is true, were responsible for the recognition that, particularly with respect to

[7] See statements of employers' groups endorsing a higher federal minimum wage as protection against low-wage competition in U. S. Congress, 84th, 1st Session, Senate, Hearings Before the Committee on Labor and Public Welfare, Subcommittee on Labor, *Amending the Fair Labor Standards Act of 1938.* (Washington, D. C.: U. S. Government Printing Office, 1955), pp. 1320–54, Part 3.

[8] H. A. Millis and R. E. Montgomery, *Labor's Risks and Social Insurance* (New York: McGraw-Hill Book Co., Inc., 1938), p. 249; Frank T. de Vyver, "Regulation of Wages and Hours Prior to 1938," *Law and Contemporary Problems,* VI, No. 3 (1939), 323–24.

children and women, conditions of work were cruel and inhuman by virtually any standard. From these premises came the regulation of child labor. Other arguments came to be more significant, and the movement eventually extended to hours regulation for women and men, and finally to wage regulation.

Origins of the Problem of Substandard Conditions

Also, prior to analyzing the standards set by protective labor laws, several questions should be asked. Why do working conditions fall to "low" levels? Who or what is responsible? The answers to these questions have, of course, changed from the time of the master-slave relationship to the present-day wage system.[9] Since slaves were owned by a master who could buy and sell them, they were wholly at their master's disposal. The status of the serf in the period of feudalism was only slightly better. While a lord did not own his serfs, their freedom was narrowly limited by their legal obligations in a lord's service, and government action was used to insure that economic force did not give the serf power to change these conditions.[10]

None of these legal ties bind today's workers, since the essence of the contemporary wage system is the workers' freedom of choice. Workers are legally free to choose their occupations and to change them; to accept or reject working conditions that please or fail to please them; to change employers, to work in any part of the country that they choose, or indeed, to refuse to work altogether.

Given these legal labor market freedoms and concomitantly those of the employer to hire and fire, it should follow that under competitive labor market conditions employers would be the custodians or administrators of working conditions determined by the basic market forces of competition. It was one of Adam Smith's premises in his theory of equalizing differences (referred to in Chapter 9) that under a free wage system, competing bids for labor would regulate working conditions effectively in different occupations. The regulating force of competition lies in the threat to an employer posed by his employees' alternative opportunities.[11] Em-

[9] Discussed by Maurice Dobb, *Wages* (London: Pitman Publishing Co., 1948), pp. 1–17.

[10] Thus the first real government regulation of working conditions was the oppressive fourteenth-century Statutes of Laborers which set maximum wages—a policy followed in the later Elizabethan Statutes of Apprentices.

[11] The effect of competition on restricting the scope of bargained terms is presented concisely by Tibor Scitovsky in *Welfare and Competition* (Chicago: Richard D. Irwin, Inc., 1951), chap. ii.

ployees who are informed of job alternatives and who are willing and able to accept them, will force employers to offer wage contracts at least equal to these alternatives.

If it is assumed that labor market competition will regulate working conditions in a free economy, and the government intervenes in a free labor market to prohibit certain pay or employment practices that would prevail in the absence of such intervention, one is saying in effect that competition as a regulating force of working conditions has failed. Yet, this statement seems to conflict with common sense.

Competition appears to play a paradoxical role in its effects on working conditions. On the one hand, our competitive system leads all nations of the world in its ability to amass capital and to become increasingly productive. Furthermore, the gigantic increases in real national income due primarily to productiveness have, over the years, been distributed generously to American workers in the form of reduced hours of work and higher (real) wages. Working hours during the past century have been shortened from an approximate sixty-nine-hour week to the present forty-hour week. Average non-agricultural wages have increased from about 9 to 10 cents an hour to current levels of about $1.90. Our competitive economy has produced a situation which led the manager of Buick Division of General Motors to comment that "the man on the assembly line can buy what he makes."[12] Buick's 90,000 employees enjoyed average earnings of $5,460 in 1955 compared with an average of $4,200 for a smaller work force in 1950.

On the other hand, various social, political, and economic criteria have been used over the years to demonstrate that an unregulated wage system produces substandard conditions, and that at the beginning of the twentieth century, deplorable working conditions existed in this country.

These two apparently contradictory situations can be reconciled, however, when the distinction is made between labor market competition on the one hand and product market competition on the other. In part, the reasons that labor market competition does not always bring about acceptable working conditions[13] are similar to the reasons that it fails to bring about wage rates that fully reflect the accident hazard of occupations. The reasons are not wholly the same, however, and since they involve the effects of the product

[12] First National City Bank *Monthly Letter*, March, 1956, p. 35.

[13] For a discussion of labor market competition as a regulator of working conditions, see Francis M. Boddy, (ed.), *Applied Economic Analysis* (New York: Pitman Publishing Co., 1948), chap. v.

market, let us examine them more fully. There are three general reasons why competition may not adequately regulate working conditions, to which a fourth may be added. These are as follows.

BARRIERS TO LABOR MARKET COMPETITION

Although workers enjoy full legal rights to choose among labor market alternatives, they are neither willing nor able to exercise these rights fully. Hence, the competitive regulating force of working conditions is seriously weakened by the labor market imperfections referred to earlier: poor knowledge of alternatives, institutional (noneconomic) barriers to accepting alternatives, economic barriers to geographic mobility, and economic and social barriers to upward occupational mobility. To expect of free *legal* labor market choice the full exercise of *economic* labor market choice which will fully regulate working conditions is, in Dobb's words, to depend upon so "one-sided a picture as to contrast in some respects grotesquely with reality."[14]

SUPERIOR BARGAINING POWER OF EMPLOYERS

Partly because of these barriers to labor market competition and partly because of the very nature of the employment relationship, employers enjoy bargaining advantages over their employees in setting conditions of work.[15] In general, competition among workers for jobs tends to be greater than competition among employers for workers (though experiences of the past fifteen years are a short-run modification). Employers have better information about alternatives; moreover, they control revenues and payments.

Labor is much more difficult to move than is capital, and it is much more perishable. Since most workers with little savings cannot store their services, they have poor waiting power. These and other reasons explain in large part why our present-day public policy toward collective bargaining encourages the development of trade unions as a means of gaining equality in bargaining power between employer and employee.

It must be stressed in considering the above two points that they are by no means applicable without exception. For instance, the employment of women was once opposed as a social evil on the

---

[14] Dobb, *op. cit.*, p. 6; for an interesting picture of the relation of the worker to his labor market in 1923, see Douglas, Hitchcock, and Atkins, *op. cit.*, pp. 226–228. For a more recent analysis see Herbert S. Parnes, "Research on Labor Mobility," *Bulletin* 65 (New York: Social Science Research Council, 1954).

[15] Discussed by K. W. Rothschild, *The Theory of Wages* (New York: The Macmillan Co., 1954), chap. ix.

grounds that women were being underpaid and exploited. Yet to-day women represent nearly 30 per cent of the labor force. And in the secretarial and other office jobs in which demands for their skills are highest, women's working conditions tend to be excellent by almost any standard. Another illustration is that, despite possible labor market imperfections, the current keen competition for the services of engineers has forced employers to bid up their working conditions. This happens wherever demands for labor are strong. During periods of rising prosperity, the overwhelming majority of workers enjoy working conditions far better than the statutory minimums. Yet, even in these times there are some who do not.

While our competitive system has produced the highest standard of living in the world, certain aspects of the system, in the absence of regulation, do produce substandard working conditions. In 1954, for example, a total of 3.7 million American families of two or more persons received incomes of less than $1,000.[16]

KEEN PRODUCT MARKET COMPETITION[17]

Despite the obvious virtues of competition among sellers of goods and services, it is nevertheless true that where such competition is keen and is combined with the labor market imperfections referred to above, substandard conditions of employment tend to result. Employers have a strong incentive to maximize their employees' output during the immediate period of their employment. The Webbs observed that, as a result of the introduction of the factory system, "competition is always forcing him [the employer] to cut down the cost of production to the lowest point. Under this pressure, other considerations disappear in the passion to obtain the greatest possible 'output per machine.' "[18]

The desire to increase productivity and reduce costs by greater employment of the fixed costs of the factory led to long hours of work and to the employment of children. Children were worked without consideration for the subsequent effects on their adult health or lack of education; adults were worked long hours and under serious hazards, with low pay. Over a period of years, workers became less productive and had to be replaced. The result was not only inhumane; it was socially inefficient.

[16] See U. S. Congress, 84th, 1st Session, Senate and House Hearings Before the Joint Committee on The Economic Report, Subcommittee on Low-Income Families, *Low-Income Families* (Washington, D. C.: U. S. Government Printing Office, 1955), pp. 24–30.

[17] Rothschild, *op. cit.*, pp. 51–52.

[18] Sidney and Beatrice Webb, *Industrial Democracy* (London: Longmans, Roberts and Green, 1897), p. 327.

Although maximum short-run productivity may not produce maximum long-run productivity, price competition forces employers to maximize short-run output. And as long as there is an adequate labor supply, employers have incentives to follow this policy. The private cost to an employer of doing so is less than the full social cost of depreciating workers. Where labor market competition cannot be counted upon to remedy this situation, government intervention is necessary. By intervening here to achieve optimal working conditions, the government performs one of its most important economic functions,[19] and as a result everyone benefits—employers gain greater long-run productivity, and workers enjoy better health and living standards.

LABOR IS A HUMAN COMMODITY

Unequal bargaining power and the lack of competitive regulation, despite their effects on the terms of sale, might be tolerable except for one additional factor—the commodity involved is an unusual one. Like most other commodities in the economy, labor has a price and is bought and sold in a marketing process. But unlike any other commodity, labor is distinctive in that the service can never be isolated from the person who performs the service. In short, it is a human commodity. The attention currently commanded by the "human relations" aspects of employment is ample evidence of how widely this fact is appreciated today. The terms of the sale of labor involve human conditions which are not a part of any other market considerations.

Approaches to the Problem of Substandard Conditions

Recognition of the need for regulating working conditions developed along similar lines in America and in England, although at different times. In both countries the government intervened to protect those least able to protect themselves—those whose lack of bargaining strength prevented them from a full exercise of their legal labor market freedoms.

Dissatisfaction with substandard working conditions in England came in the late eighteenth century shortly after formalized adoption of laissez-faire policies and was soon followed by legislative efforts to correct them. The first such enactment was the (1802)

---

[19] An excellent discussion of this function, an issue basic to much of the material in this book, appears in William J. Baumol and Lester V. Chandler, *Economic Processes and Policies* (New York: Harper and Brothers, 1954), pp. 119–34.

Factory Act designed to protect pauper children who had been made apprentices. Only a few such laws were enacted for some time, but after 1850 the area of regulative control expanded, until by World War I all the leading industrial countries of Europe exercised extensive controls over working conditions, hours, and wages.

Working Conditions

Almost all states, and many municipalities and other jurisdictions, have sought to regulate conditions of work to insure certain minimum standards—particularly in the case of working women and children. Since there is very little uniformity in this type of legislation, it is difficult to estimate the degree or quality of protection that it affords,[20] but certain generalizations about the laws can be made.

Most of the laws apply primarily to women and children. For these two groups, most states prohibit work in specified industries or occupations—those declared hazardous or a health menace; and require that seating, rest, and toilet facilities be available. Some jurisdictions require lunchroom facilities, stated meal periods, and that sanitary drinking water be provided by the employer. A few states have enacted "equal pay" legislation seeking to attain for women the pay status of men.

Some of this legislation reflects the needs of particular geographic areas. Alaska's law, for instance, requires that employers provide physical examinations for all employees recruited outside of Alaska and return transportation for those rejected on physical grounds. Mining states—Arizona, for example—prohibit payment of wages in script and forced purchases at the "company store."

Where this protective legislation has been extended to include men, it sometimes requires "safe employment devices and safeguards" and, in a few states, provides for minimum pay for call-ins and split-shift work. Other regulations require approved ventilation standards (particularly in laundries), payment of wages at least twice monthly, time off for voting, and adequate lighting.

Because of enlightened personnel administration, trade union pressures, and the cost savings to an employer of a satisfied working force, many of the standards of these laws are not as high as the "going practice." Yet, for some employees, particularly those in unorganized areas, these laws can be a genuine source of protection.

---

[20] A state-by-state summary of legislation affecting working conditions appears in *Labor Policy and Practice Manual*, III (Washington, D. C.: Bureau of National Affairs, Inc., 1956), Sec. 100.

CHILD LABOR[21]

In America the first protective measures–also child labor laws–were enacted during the nineteenth century. Although a few states adopted such laws during this period, major protective labor legislation in America did not appear until after 1900.

Of all labor legislation, the need for laws regulating the employment of children was most generally accepted and received the most early widespread support. Nevertheless, the development of child labor legislation was piecemeal and slow. It was hampered by problems of law and enforcement as well as by powerful, though limited, opposition. In addition, the problem of child labor was extremely complex. Elizabeth Sands Johnson writes that from the time of the earliest nineteenth-century laws, it became apparent that adequate protection of children required: "(1) a minimum age below which they should not be allowed to work; (2) a minimum of education which they should acquire before entering employment; (3) a maximum number of hours for their employment; and (4) some rules to protect them against especially hazardous or unhealthful occupations."[22]

Let us examine state and federal legislative efforts to achieve protection for children in these areas.

Action by the states before 1900. During the nineteenth century there was some support for the protection of children (some of which came from the Knights of Labor) and, in fact, a substantial number of laws were enacted. Following the early leads of the New England states, most notably Massachusetts and Connecticut, other states also adopted child labor measures, and by the turn of the century, twenty-eight state laws had been enacted. These early laws were recognized as a justifiable exercise of a state's police power, since the welfare of children (minors) as wards of the state was bound up with the welfare of the state.

Early child labor laws embodied a variety of standards, but were, for the most part, limited to work in manufacturing. They set the minimum age limit at twelve years and the work day at ten hours. Only a few of the laws made some provisions for required education.

[21] For an excellent review of child labor legislation from its beginnings through the middle 1930's, see John R. Commons, *History of Labor in the United States* (New York: The Macmillan Co., 1935), III, 403–56. A more recent treatment of the legal problems of regulating child labor may be found in Glenn W. Miller, *American Labor and the Government* (Englewood Cliffs, N. J.: Prentice-Hall, 1949), pp. 146–48 and 245–65. Both sources were drawn upon in preparing this section.

[22] Reprinted by permission of The Macmillan Co. from John R. Commons, *op. cit.*, pp. 403–04.

Despite this apparent progress in regulating the employment of children, census data for the period indicated that the percentage of employed children ten to fifteen years old was increasing. This was partly due to poor enforcement and limited coverage of the laws and, in part, to the new industrial expansion of the South, an area in which labor laws were yet to be enacted (and in which they were to encounter their stiffest opposition).

Action by the states after 1900. A great deal of state child labor legislation was enacted after the turn of the century and until the period of the first federal action in 1916. A Child Labor Committee was formed in the South in reaction to the widespread employment of children in that area. Later another committee was formed in New York, and eventually a national group began operation. By 1909, all but six states had minimum age requirements for factories. And during the period of greatest growth of labor and protective legislation (from 1911 to 1913), thirty-one states took action to improve child labor legislation.

These laws sought to: (1) create administrative devices which would enable conclusive evidence of age that could not be circumvented by parents; (2) set up hours provisions that bore a rational relation to the amount of work that a child could (reasonably) do; and (3) make some educational provisions.

All states now have child labor laws. Like workmen's compensation laws, they are constantly being revised, and (again like workmen's compensation) certain elements are common to all of them, although their standards differ considerably.[23] State child labor laws seek to:

1. Set a minimum age at which a child may legally accept work, qualified occasionally by school hours requirements
2. Limit the maximum hours per day that a youth may be employed
3. Limit employment during night hours
4. Set age limits on certain dangerous occupations
5. Require employment certificates
6. Require school attendance

The International Association of Governmental Labor Officials (IAGLO), an organization of the state administrators of laws relating to labor, has prepared standards which it considers to be minimum required regulations, and from time to time the Bureau

[23] Summaries of state child labor laws are published from time to time by the U. S. Department of Labor, Bureau of Labor Standards. The most recent is "State Child-Labor Standards," *Bulletin 158,* 1952.

of Labor Standards issues a tabulation indicating the number of jurisdictions which meet these minimum standards. The latest comparison for state child-labor laws (November, 1954) is reprinted in Table 15.1.

TABLE 15.1

MAJOR STANDARDS RECOMMENDED BY THE
INTERNATIONAL ASSOCIATION OF GOVERNMENTAL LABOR OFFICIALS FOR
STATE CHILD LABOR LEGISLATION AND THE EXTENT TO WHICH EXISTING
STATE CHILD LABOR LAWS MEET THESE STANDARDS

	Recommended Standards	Extent to which State Child-Labor Laws Meet Recommended Standards
Minimum age	16 years, in any employment in a factory; 16 in any employment during school hours; 14 in non-factory employment outside school hours.	23 States, Alaska, and Puerto Rico approximate this standard in whole or in part (Ala., Conn., Fla., Ga., Ill., Ky., La., Maine, Md., Mass., Mont., N. J., N. Y., N. C., Ohio, Pa., R. I., S. C., Tenn., Utah, Va., W. Va., Wisc.)
Hazardous occupations	Minimum age 18 for employment in a considerable number of hazardous occupations.	Few, if any, States extend full protection in this respect to minors up to 18 years of age, though many State laws prohibit employment under 18 in a varying number of specified hazardous occupations.
	State administrative agency authorized to determine occupations hazardous for minors under 18.	21 States, D. C., Alaska, Hawaii, and Puerto Rico have a State administrative agency with such authority (Ariz., Colo., Conn., Fla., Kans., La., Maine, Md., Mass., Mich., N. J., N. Y., N. C., N. Dak., Ohio, Oreg., Pa., Utah, Wash., W. Va., Wisc.)
Maximum daily hours	8-hour day for minors under 18 in any gainful occupation.	15 States, Alaska, D. C., and Puerto Rico have an 8-hour day for minors of both sexes under 18 in most occupations (Calif., Ky., La., Mont., N. J., N. Y., N. Dak., Ohio, Oreg., Pa., Tenn., Utah, Va., Wash., Wisc.)
		7 other States have this standard for girls up to 18 (Ariz., Colo., Ill., Ind., Nev., N. Mex., Wyo.)
Maximum weekly hours	40-hour week for minors under 18 in any gainful occupation.	5 States (Ky., N. J., Tenn., Va., Wisc.) Alaska and Puerto Rico have a 40-hour week for minors under 18 in most occupations; 4 States (La., Oreg., Pa., Utah) a 44-hour week for such minors.

TABLE 15.1 (*Continued*)

Maximum weekly hours	40-hour week for minors *under 18* in any gainful occupation.	7 other States (Ala., Fla., Ga., Md., N. C., R. I., W. Va.) and Hawaii have a 40-hour week for minors *under 16* in most occupations, and 3 States (Miss., N. Mex., N. Y.) a 44-hour week for such minors. Wash. has a 40-hour week when school is not in session.
Work during specified night hours prohibited	13 hours of night work prohibited for minors of both sexes *under 16* in any gainful occupation.	10 States, Hawaii, and Puerto Rico meet or exceed this standard, at least for most occupations (Iowa, Kans., N. J., N. Y., N. C., Ohio, Okla., Oreg., Utah, Va.)
		13 States and D. C. prohibit 12 or 12½ hours of night work for minors under 16 (Ala., Ariz., Ill., Md., Mass.—12½ hours; Minn., Mo., N. Mex., N. Dak., Pa., R. I., Tenn., Wyo. The Alabama law prohibits such work for 12 night hours during the regular school term.)
	8 hours of night work prohibited for minors of both sexes *between 16 and 18* in any gainful occupation.	11 States, D. C., and Puerto Rico meet or exceed this standard, at least for most occupations (Ark., Conn., Fla., Kans., Ky., La., Mass., Mich., N. J., Ohio, Tenn.)
Employment Certificates	Required for minors *under 18* in any gainful occupation.	24 States, D. C., Hawaii, and Puerto Rico require employment or age certificates for minors *under 18* in most occupations (Calif., Conn., Del., Fla., Ga., Ind., Ky., La., Md., Mass., Mich., Mont., Nev., N. J., N. Y., N. C., Ohio, Oreg., Pa., Utah, Va., Wash., Wisc., and where continuation schools are established, Okla.). One other State (Ala.) requires such certificates for minors *under 17*.

Source: U. S. Department of Labor, Bureau of Labor Standards (Washington, D. C.: November, 1954).

This table reveals both the gains that have been made in the regulation of child labor and the gaps that remain. Factory employment, which was the focal point of the initial drives against the evils of child labor, is now regulated approximately up to recommended minimum age standards in twenty-five jurisdictions. But hazardous occupations, including agriculture where child labor violations are most frequent and accident rates highest, are not at all well regulated.

The table indicates further that less than one-third of the states meet IAGLO recommended standards for maximum weekly hours (a forty-hour week for minors under eighteen in any gainful occupation), and for the prohibition of work during specified night hours. Ironically, the best regulation (in twenty-four states and Hawaii and Puerto Rico) is achieved in connection with required employment certificates.

Federal approaches to regulation of child labor. Because of the diversity in state child labor standards and the failure of some states to enforce their laws adequately, it became apparent that genuinely effective control could be achieved only by federal legislation. Even before 1900 pressure was building, and despite the fact that the states had enacted considerable legislation, by 1914 demands for federal action could no longer be ignored.

By 1916, support was so widespread that Congress, by a great majority, enacted the first federal child labor law. It was the first in a series of federal attempts at regulation. Of these, the first four failed to survive legal hurdles, and the fifth provided little protection.

The first federal attempt to regulate child labor was based upon the constitutional power of the Congress to regulate interstate commerce. It declared unlawful and punishable by fine and/or imprisonment the interstate shipment of mined products on which children under sixteen had been employed and cannery or manufactured products on which children under fourteen had been employed. It also prohibited a work day longer than eight hours, a work week longer than forty hours, and night work.

To base this federal regulation on the commerce clause of the Constitution was a rather novel use of this power, but it was not an unreasonable approach, since there was convincing precedent that federal regulation of this type could meet court approval. Earlier laws had successfully regulated the shipment of lottery tickets and the transportation of women across state lines for purposes of prostitution.

Since major opposition to the passage of the law came from the South, it was not unusual that the new law received its first test in North Carolina. In 1918 the United States Supreme Court held[24] the law unconstitutional on the grounds that Congress had exceeded its authority under the commerce clause; that however desirable the purpose of the law and undesirable the situation it

24 *Hammer v. Dagenhart*, 247 U.S. 251 (1918).

was meant to correct, this was a matter for the local police power of the states.

Congress responded promptly to the challenge of this decision by enacting a new child labor law in the same year. Its standards were the same as the first law, as were the arguments raised for and against it. But its enforcement provisions were quite different. The new law was based on another (and the only other regulative) constitutional authority of the Congress to regulate labor—the power to tax. Its connection with the child labor problem was even less direct, but there was a somewhat analagous precedent for control based on this power. It had been used to prohibit the manufacture of white phosphorous matches. The new law provided a penalty of a 10 per cent tax on the net profits of violators.

The bill was passed as an amendment to a revenue act, and became a law in 1919. It was challenged immediately and successfully—again in North Carolina. Upon appeal, the United States Supreme Court ruled[25] the child labor law unconstitutional on the grounds that it was not a tax that imposed incidental restraints, but that it was in fact a regulation using the power to tax as a penalty. The court concluded that its provisions went far beyond the taxing authority in supervising a course of conduct in business.

The poor standards of state child labor legislation in the year of the Bailey case (1922), impelled supporters of federal regulation to seek a new approach. In only thirteen states were child labor standards comparable to those of the unsuccessful federal laws, and the employment of children was still widespread. Since the only two apparent avenues of congressional authority had been blocked by the Supreme Court's interpretation of the Constitution, the only possibility that remained was to change the Constitution specifically to authorize federal child labor regulation. A child labor amendment giving Congress "power to limit, regulate and prohibit the labor of persons under 18 years of age" was presented to the states for ratification in 1924.

Despite its apparent strong support, it failed because of local opposition based on the fear that it would give Congress too much authority. Only twenty-one of the required thirty-six states ratified it by 1933, and only six more had done so by 1939 when the issue arose whether or not its long delay still left it open to further ratifications. Although the Supreme Court ruled favorably, it was of no importance, since the federal control of child labor had finally been achieved by that time with the passage of the Fair Labor Standards Act in 1938.

25 *Bailey v. Drexel Furniture Company,* 259 U.S. 20 (1922).

An early federal control which did succeed, although briefly, set minimum age standards for the employment of children in the Codes for Fair Competition of the National Industrial Recovery Act. The standards of the Codes varied, but typically they provided for a minimum age of sixteen, although some went as low as fourteen. Eighteen was set as the minimum age in hazardous employment. The Codes succeeded in curtailing the employment of children,[26] but the regulations fell in 1935 along with the rest of the NIRA when the United States Supreme Court held[27] that in enacting the Codes, the Congress had exceeded its powers to regulate interstate commerce.

Following the Schechter decision, Congress acted to control child labor in an area which seemed safely within its powers, namely, contractors supplying the federal government. In 1936 the Walsh-Healy Public Contracts Act was passed prohibiting contractors who supply the federal government (with manufactures or products or finished materials) in values over $10,000 from employing children under sixteen and women under eighteen. It does not apply to agriculture, retail trade, or the service occupations. This was the only successful enactment of federal child labor regulation before the passage of the Fair Labor Standards Act, which marked the end of a twenty-two year period of unsuccessful federal action in this field.

Hours

Attempts to regulate working hours of adults, particularly women's hours, were in many cases linked to the child labor regulations discussed above. In fact, in some states the same law controls working hours of both women and children, and in a few states, general hours laws cover all workers.

Although movements to control working hours for women and men are related both in time and in motivating forces, because of some differences in timing, theory, scope and coverage, hours regulation for these two groups will be discussed separately here. Although hours regulation prior to the Fair Labor Standards Act was primarily a matter of state legislation, the federal government in its role as employer was actually the first to limit hours and undoubtedly influenced the actions of some employers and legislative groups. But federal regulation comparable to that of child labor has never been attempted in this field. The discussion below,

26 Miller, op. cit., p. 255.
27 Schechter Poultry Corporation v. U. S., 295 U.S. 495 (1935).

therefore, concerns state regulation, with a brief added comment on federal action.

WOMEN'S HOURS

Successful regulation of women's working hours dates back almost as far as the first child labor laws. New Hampshire enacted a ten-hour law in 1847, and a few other New England states followed. By 1896, thirteen such regulatory laws had been passed. These laws were, for the most part, limited to manufacturing, and by and large were not very effective, either because they were unenforceable or because they lacked realistic hours limits. Moreover, a court decision in 1895 declared an Illinois eight-hour law for women unconstitutional.[28] The court ruled that such laws interfered with the right of freedom of contract and liberty and that there was not present the necessary protection to health, safety, or morals which might make such interference justifiable.

In the view of this Illinois court, at least, the theory that hours protection should be extended to children by the state as their guardian did not apply to women. The court did not agree that special protection for women was needed on the grounds that women were unable fully to gain their rights in the labor market. But it was the recognition of these differences in women's bargaining ability that played a prominent part in the thinking of the United States Supreme Court when, in 1908, the first women's hour law reached the court.[29] In declaring an Oregon ten-hour law for women constitutional, the court brushed aside the arguments of the Ritchie case (as did an Illinois court in a later decision) and upheld the law which applied to mechanical establishments, factories, or laundries.

As a result, there was from 1909 to 1917 a great flood of state legislative activity in this field. The principle had been firmly established, had won legal acceptance, and most states enacted women's hours laws. After World War I, however, the movement never regained its pre-war momentum, and the legislative revisions were limited to newer rules such as prohibitions against night work and required rest periods.

The current status of hours regulation is summarized from time to time by the United States Department of Labor publications. The most recent summary[30] indicates that, while almost every juris-

[28] *Ritchie v. People*, 155 Illinois 98 (1895).
[29] *Muller v. Oregon*, 208 U.S. 412 (1908).
[30] U. S. Department of Labor, Bureau of Labor Standards, *Bulletin 116.* "State and Federal Hours Limitations," 1950. (This bulletin includes all hours regulations.)

diction has in some way regulated the hours of women, the extent and quality of coverage (as in the case of working conditions legislation) tends to vary widely among jurisdictions. However, the following generalizations about them appear to be warranted: (1) for reasons of health and safety, most women's hours laws limit work in specified industries or occupations; (2) almost all the women's hours laws provide for maximum hours—only a few do not. Frequently there is a stated maximum of an eight-hour day and a forty-eight-hour week, but there are many exceptions, particularly in the South; (3) the effect of the maximum hours requirement is considerably weakened by the exemptions (most frequently domestics, agricultural workers, and waitresses) which appear in virtually all the laws. Coverage in some of the laws is limited to certain industries or establishments.

MEN'S HOURS

Regulation has never been as comprehensive in its scope or coverage of men's working hours as it has of the hours of women and children. Until fairly recently, laws were enacted almost exclusively in those employments where protection was very badly needed because of hazardous conditions or where they were fairly easy to enact because of advantageous political or administrative situations.

In 1840 a presidential order stipulated a ten-hour maximum work day in government Navy yards.[31] As early as 1868, Congress, with some success, limited the work day on contracts for government buildings and roads to ten hours. An early case[32] upheld state and municipal employees' hours laws and those covering state workers under contract.

Regulation of hours in hazardous work was first approved by the Supreme Court in 1898,[33] when the court upheld a Utah law which regulated the hours of men working in mines. Later cases upheld the right to regulate hours of special groups such as railroad employees, mining workers, bus drivers, and others on the grounds of safety.

In *Holden v. Hardy,* the court stated that ". . . the fact that both parties are of full age and competent to contract does not necessarily deprive the State of power to interfere where the parties do not stand upon an equality or where public health demands that

---

[31] Discussed by Matthew A. Kelly, "Early Federal Regulation of Hours of Labor in the United States," *Industrial and Labor Relations Review,* III, No. 3 (April, 1950), 362–74.

[32] *Atkin v. Kansas,* 191 U.S. 207 (1903).

[33] *Holden v. Hardy,* 169 U. S. 366.

one party to a contract shall be protected against himself."[34] This doctrine, as we have seen, found general application in the case of women's hours laws. Men's hours laws, however, except for those applying to state and federal government employees, tended to remain limited to those situations in which the additional grounds of health or safety were present. And with but one important exception,[35] courts recognized these bases as proper for the regulation of men's working hours.

Although men's hours laws gained recognition and approval between 1911 and World War I, they did not play a part in that period of vigorous legislative activity. Public interest in men's hours laws was never great, and no particular movement to enact this legislation ever developed.

Attempts to achieve shorter hours have been an important part of trade union programs since the 1890's. Since unions have been successful in gaining this objective and because of the general feeling that men are better able than women to protect themselves in the labor market, this area of regulation has not been one of major legislative or public interest in the over-all movement to improve substandard conditions. Little has been done by the states since the passage of the Fair Labor Standards Act. Only a few states today have general maximum hours laws for men.

FEDERAL REGULATION OF WOMEN'S AND MEN'S HOURS

With the exception of work on railroads, Congress has never sought to enact legislation which would state maximum hours of work for men or for women. Its approach in the few areas in which it has attempted regulation has always been not to prohibit excessive hours of work, but rather to make excessive hours expensive through penalty "overtime" payments. The Codes of Fair Competition of the National Industrial Recovery Act provided for overtime payments, as did the 1916 Adamson Act and the Walsh-Healey Act. Each of these set the work day and provided for overtime payments. Apart from the instances in which the federal government was acting as employer, these were the only federal regulations in this field prior to the Fair Labor Standards Act.

Wages

Wages were the last of the conditions of employment to be regulated by government intervention. In working to the wage core

[34] *Ibid.*, p. 397.
[35] *Lochner v. New York*, 198 U.S. 45 (1905). The Supreme Court refused to uphold a New York ten-hour law applying to bakery workers.

of the employment relationship, state governments had regulated the length of the work day, its conditions, and the time and method of wage payments. Child-labor and hours movements were well under way by the time Massachusetts enacted the pioneer minimum wage law in this country in 1912—one which set nonmandatory minimum wages for women and children. In many respects the minimum wage laws were to be an extension of these movements. With but limited exception, they applied exclusively to women and children and were justified as protecting these two groups from low wages resulting from competitive labor market conditions.

STATE ATTEMPTS AT REGULATION

Although eight states quickly followed the lead of Massachusetts in enacting minimum wage laws (most of which called for enforcement), and despite apparent Supreme Court approval,[36] the movement never gathered much momentum. Only fifteen states had enacted such laws when the movement encountered a serious legal setback. In 1923, the minimum wage law of Washington, D. C. was held[37] unconstitutional as an interference with the freedom of contract.

The effect of this decision was nearly ruinous. Laws in six other jurisdictions were declared unconstitutional; other states avoided court tests at the cost of full compliance; and by 1933, wage laws existed in only nine jurisdictions, and some of these were not in effective operation.

Most early minimum wage laws were based upon a concept of the minimum wage needed for living. In the Adkins case the court implied that a criterion more directly related to the value of the services performed by the employee might be a more appropriate basis for such legislation. Laws which embodied this concept and set minimum wages for "reasonable value of services" were enacted in some states. The New York law, however, was challenged and held[38] unconstitutional despite its new basis. It was not until 1937 that the United States Supreme Court gave full approval to state minimum wage laws by holding[39] the Washington law a valid exercise of state police power.

[36] In *Settler v. O'Hara*, 243 U.S. 629 (1917), the U. S. Supreme Court split evenly, J. Brandeis abstaining, on the constitutionality of Oregon's minimum wage law, leaving intact its approval by the lower court.
[37] *Adkins v. Children's Hospital*, 261 U.S. 525 (1923).
[38] On the grounds of a violation of the due process clause of the Fourteenth Amendment. *Morehead v. New York ex rel. Tipaldo*, 298 U.S. 587 (1936).
[39] *West Coast Hotel Co. v. Parrish*, 300 U.S. 379 (1937).

Some favorable legislative response followed this decision, and state legislatures enacted laws or broadened existing ones, in some cases even extending coverage to men. Yet only four of the twenty-nine state minimum wage laws presently in effect were enacted after the Fair Labor Standards Act.

CURRENT STATUS OF STATE MINIMUM WAGE REGULATION[40]

State minimum wage laws are in effect today in twenty-nine states—twenty-one of these apply to women and children and eight[41] apply to all workers. The nineteen states which do not have minimum wage laws are, by and large, southern and border states.[42]

Standards required by these state minimum wage laws vary greatly. Wage orders in industrial areas vary from 50 cents to $1.00 an hour, in nonindustrial areas from 20 to 60 cents. The highs are $1.00 for women workers in New Jersey and $1.00 for men and women in Massachusetts. These standards are somewhat deceiving, however, since some of the laws restrict coverage to certain industries, and in some states (such as Kansas), although there is a minimum wage law, no wage orders are currently in effect.

Situations such as these have focused attention on a problem of long-standing—namely, how shall state minimum wages be set? There are three alternative methods, all of which are in use today. Minimum wages may: (1) be set by the legislature which, as a matter of law, declares the minimum figure—Alaska follows this procedure; (2) be fixed or revised by the agency responsible for administration of the law—this practice is followed in Arkansas; or (3) be set by a wage board which hears recommendations of an appointed tripartite commission, and then sets the minimum—Minnesota now employs this method.

Although it is sometimes argued that the use of legislative procedures results in a less flexible and somewhat more haphazardly set

[40] For the current status of state minimum wage laws and other provisions affecting working conditions, see "State Minimum-Wage Laws and Orders," *Bulletin 247* (U. S. Department of Labor, Women's Bureau, 1953). This bulletin together with its July 1, 1954, supplement, presents the laws, an analysis of the occupation covered by each wage order, class of employee covered, and wage rates and hours of work. A companion study shows for each wage order the supplementary provisions that affect wages and working conditions. See "State Minimum-Wage Order Provisions Affecting Working Conditions," *Bulletin 259* (U. S. Department of Labor, Women's Bureau, 1955).

[41] Connecticut, Idaho, Massachusetts, New Hampshire, New Mexico, New York, Rhode Island, and Wyoming (which excludes minors).

[42] Alabama, Delaware, Florida, Georgia, Indiana, Iowa, Maryland, Michigan, Mississippi, Missouri, Montana, Nebraska, North Carolina, South Carolina, Tennessee, Texas, Vermont, Virginia, and West Virginia.

minimum, which agency sets the wage is less important than how a criterion of wage adequacy can be translated into dollars and cents. All the standards to which agencies refer (such as the "necessary cost of living") produce results about which there may be legitimate value judgment differences when they are converted to an actual wage.

For an estimated twenty million workers who are outside the coverage of federal minimum wage regulation, therefore, state laws offer a wide variety of standards—in some cases better protection than under the federal law, and in others no protection at all. For the most part, however, state minimum wage protection falls far below federal standards.

FEDERAL APPROACHES

Prior to the enactment of the Fair Labor Standards Act, attempts to intervene in the wage area were made almost wholly by the states, although from time to time there had been pressure for federal action—some as early as World War I.

Proponents of federal wage regulation argue that a uniform standard overcomes interstate cost differentials which are always cited in opposition to increasing a state minimum wage level. A novel state approach to this problem[43] was initiated in 1931 by Franklin D. Roosevelt. As Governor of New York, he succeeded in persuading seven states (Connecticut, Maine, Massachusetts, New Hampshire, New York, Pennsylvania, and Rhode Island) to sign an interstate wage compact. It provided for uniform wages and hours and was ratified by three of the states when passage of the Fair Labor Standards Act made its operation seem unnecessary. It later became ineffective.

Federal minimum wage action prior to 1938 was limited to the Davis-Bacon Act (1931), which provided for the payment of prevailing wages on federal construction contracts over $2,000; to the Walsh-Healey Act (1936), which required overtime and "prevailing wage" payments for industries holding government contracts in excess of $10,000; and to the NIRA Codes.

Summary

Government intervention into conditions of employment began as a movement to protect women and children. Although some state protective legislation applies to men today, the state laws, generally

[43] de Vyver, *op. cit.*, p. 330.

speaking, have neither, gone far beyond this scope, nor have they fully achieved the original objective. Wage and hour laws are still the continuing business of state legislatures, but interest in them has subsided substantially since the enactment of the Fair Labor Standards Act. In the past fifteen years, rising levels of income and a public policy favorable to collective bargaining have brought working conditions for many workers in intrastate commerce well above the minimum levels which existing state regulation could properly achieve. But for significant numbers of workers, particularly in some areas of the South, improved legislative standards could achieve better conditions of work. Let us now consider the development of present-day federal standards in the Fair Labor Standards Act.

Suggestions for Additional Reading

BUREAU OF NATIONAL AFFAIRS, INC. "Wages and Hours," *Personnel Policy and Practices,* II (Washington, D. C.).
Presents an up-to-date summary of legislation, both state and federal, covering working conditions, wages and hours.

CIVIC, MIRIAM. "State Minimum Wage Laws in Action," *The Conference Board Business Record,* VII, No. 11 (November, 1950), 440–44.
One of the few studies of the effects of state minimum wage laws.

COMMONS, JOHN R. *History of Labor in the United States.* Vol. III. New York: The Macmillan Co., 1935.
The entire third volume of this classic series is devoted to working conditions. It presents a detailed and comprehensive analysis of the development of legislation in this field.

COMMONS, JOHN R., and JOHN B. ANDREWS. *Principles of Labor Legislation,* 4th ed. New York: Harper and Brothers, 1936. Chapters 2, 3, 4, and 6.
This book is still valuable for its expert insights into principles and administrative problems of labor legislation.

MILLER, GLENN W. *American Labor and the Government.* Englewood Cliffs, N. J.: Prentice-Hall, 1949. Chapters 10–14.
A good textual treatment of state and federal government intervention into labor standards.

16

Fair Labor Standards Act

Introduction

In 1938 government regulation of child labor, working hours and wages was brought together under the Fair Labor Standards Act.[1] The inclusive provisions of the Act were unique in comparison with the scope and operation of the state protective labor laws which preceded it.[2] It is true that as early as 1913 in a few states (Oregon, California, and Washington) minimum wage laws for minors and women provided wide administrative discretion in establishing " 'standard conditions of labor' demanded by their well being."[3] None of these laws, however, prohibited child labor or established a fixed minimum wage applicable to women and men alike. Since its enactment, the Fair Labor Standards Act has become the accepted conceptual term for comprehensive protective labor legislation in contrast to the more limited laws which were discussed in the preceding chapter.

Not only was the Fair Labor Standards Act comprehensive, but each of its several standards tended to be more rigorous and more inclusive than previous state protective labor legislation. Its child

[1] 52 U.S. Stat. c. 1060 (1938). The law is most widely referred to as the "Wage and Hour Law."

[2] Strictly speaking, this cannot be said when comparing the Act with earlier federal laws, since . . . "The Fair Labor Standards Act is a reenactment of subsection (3) of Section 7(a) of Title I of the National Industrial Recovery Act." Orme W. Phelps, *The Legislative Background of the Fair Labor Standards Act* (Chicago: University of Chicago Press, 1939), p. 5.

[3] Louise Stitt, "State Fair Labor Standards Legislation," *Law and Contemporary Problems,* VI, No. 3 (Summer, 1939), 454. Copyright 1939 by Duke University.

labor requirements were higher than those of the provisions of many of the 1938 state laws; it fixed an absolute wage minimum, departing from the administrative arrangements of flexible minimum wage-setting to which all state minimum wage laws had adhered; and while its hours provisions did not set absolute maximums, it was the opinion of students at the time that the law would probably give more impetus to a movement toward a shorter workweek than had been generated by the state hours laws. Furthermore, the new law extended wage and hour protection to men, discarding the widely held theory that, except for special cases where health or safety were involved, only women and children required government protection against the economic pressures of the labor market.

Finally, it extended regulation of working conditions far beyond the narrow limits of earlier federal control which, it will be recalled, was limited to situations in which the government was the employer, or was being furnished goods by contractors, or was interested in safety. Based on the constitutional authority of Congress to regulate interstate commerce, the Fair Labor Standards Act covered employees who were engaged in (1) "commerce," and (2) "the production of goods for commerce." In short, it covered all employees in interstate commerce activities except those who were specifically exempted.

Despite its comprehensive and far-reaching provisions and its new extension of federal authority into working conditions, however, the Fair Labor Standards Act was but an extension of a movement for improved labor standards legislation which, as noted in the last chapter, had begun over 100 years earlier in this country and over one and one-half centuries earlier in England. Federal intervention, though narrowly circumscribed, originated in the ten-hour order of President Van Buren in 1840 and involved a long history of federal attempts at control of child labor as well as the action of governmental agencies in helping the states obtain sound and workable protective labor legislation.[4] Of these influencing forces, the primary antecedents of the Fair Labor Standards Act were the National Industrial Recovery Act, the President's Re-Employment Agreement and the Codes of Fair Competition.[5]

[4] See, for example, "Criteria for Minimum-Wage Determination," *Monthly Labor Review*, XLVI, No. 1 (January, 1938), 201–04. This is the report of a study designed to aid state agencies in formulating criteria that go into the cost-of-living bases for many state minimum wage laws.

[5] A comparison of the provisions of the NIRA, the Agreement, and the Codes with the Fair Labor Standards Act reveals how closely they correspond. See Phelps, *op. cit.*, pp. 5–8.

The Fair Labor Standards Act[6]
Legislative History

The National Industrial Recovery Act was held[7] unconstitutional in 1935, and in the following year the United States Supreme Court refused to uphold New York state's minimum wage law.[8] As a result, an important plank in the platform of the Democratic party in the 1936 presidential election was the enactment of federal wage and hour controls, by constitutional amendment if necessary. The party's victory brought immediate attention to the question of how this pledge would be fulfilled.

Eighteen months elapsed between the time the seventy-fifth Congress convened and June 25, 1938, when President Roosevelt signed the Fair Labor Standards Act. The first six months of this period were marked by intensive administrative maneuvering and momentous decision-making for each of the branches of government. The Administration and the Congress were faced with the problem of fulfilling the campaign pledge for federal wage and hour standards. President Roosevelt, deeply concerned about possible opposition from the judiciary and the probable refusal by the Court to uphold a federal protective labor law, sought to obtain enactment from the Congress of his Court reorganization measure as well as the labor standards legislation. Forsythe observes that the President considered the wage and hour bill to be "one of his strongest weapons available to force passage of the Court bill. For this reason it was indicated that the legislation would not be submitted until after there had been action on the Court plan."[9]

Meanwhile, the United States Supreme Court upheld the constitutionality of the Railway Labor Act of 1926 as revised in 1934, the newly enacted National Labor Relations Act, and a minimum wage law of the state of Washington.[10] Since these decisions reduced much of the pressure for the Court reorganization bill, the Administration decided to introduce a wage and hour bill. Some thirteen

[6] For a detailed and thorough presentation of the general legislative history of the Act and an analysis of the legislative fate of the many proposals that were considered before its final passage, see John S. Forsythe, "Legislative History of the Fair Labor Standards Act," *Law and Contemporary Problems, op. cit.,* pp. 464–90. This material was drawn upon in the preparation of this section.

[7] *Schechter Poultry Corporation v. U.S.,* 295 U.S. 495 (1935).

[8] *Morehead v. New York ex rel Tipaldo,* 298 U.S. 587 (1936).

[9] Forsythe, *op. cit.,* p. 465.

[10] *Virginia Railway Company v. System Federation #40,* 300 U.S. 515 (1937); *National Labor Relations Board v. Jones and Laughlin Steel Co.,* 301 U.S. 1 (1937); *West Coast Hotel Co. v. Parrish,* 300 U.S. 379 (1937).

months later the President signed a bill which had been buffeted through three sessions of Congress and had "undergone amendment after amendment until practically the only point in common with the original bill was the legislative number."[11] The Fair Labor Standards Act became law on June 25, 1938, and began effective operation on October 24th of that year.

BASIC PROVISIONS

In its statement of findings and policy, Congress declared that it was the purpose of the Fair Labor Standards Act:

. . . to correct and as rapidly as practicable to eliminate . . . labor conditions detrimental to the maintenance of the minimum standard of living necessary for health, efficiency, and general well being of workers . . . without substantially curtailing employment or earning power.

To achieve this purpose, the law established labor standards for (1) minimum wages, (2) maximum hours, and (3) control of child labor. The original provisions have been amended twice—a major revision was effected in 1949, and a more limited one in 1955.

General coverage. The original law extended protection to "employees" who were "engaged in commerce" or in the "production of goods for commerce" and who were not specifically exempted from coverage. A multitude of legal issues and uncertainties are involved in these standards.[12] In 1939, reflecting early uncertainties with the law, a lawyer wrote with respect to coverage that at least one question ". . . can be answered with certainty. When an employer inquires whether the wage and hour requirements of the law apply to his business, an attorney can with comparative safety always answer in the negative."[13]

Despite legal vagaries, however, some elements of the test of coverage became well-established. In each case, coverage was made to depend upon the activities of the individual employee—not upon his employer's over-all business, nor on the work of fellow employees, nor on the industry involved. Thus, one of two employees working side by side might be engaged in commerce while the other might not. The definition of "employee" was broadly interpreted, so that the designation of a worker as an "independent contractor,"

[11] Forsythe, *op. cit.*, p. 466

[12] For an analysis of the legal problems involved in coverage, see Stefan A. Riesenfeld and Richard C. Maxwell, *Modern Social Legislation* (Brooklyn: The Foundation Press, 1950), pp. 606–37.

[13] Frank E. Cooper, "The Coverage of the Fair Labor Standards Act and Other Problems in Its Interpretation," in *Law and Contemporary Problems, op. cit.*, p. 333.

for example, would not deny him protection of the Act if he worked in the usual employer-employee relationship. Whether or not work involves commerce or the production of goods for commerce was also made dependent upon the duties of individual employees. Although there evolved no definitive tests of what is commerce, employees have been held covered even when they have worked only part-time on work going into interstate commerce for an employer whose interstate commerce activities constitute less than 1 per cent of his total business.

Exemptions are more important numerically than the fringe cases of coverage and will be considered in detail later in this chapter.

Minimum wages. Section 6 (a) of the Fair Labor Standards Act provided that:

Every employer shall pay to each of his employees who is engaged in commerce or in the production of goods for commerce wages at the following rates—(1) during the first year from the effective date of this section, not less than 25 cents an hour, (2) during the next six years from such date, not less than 30 cents an hour, (3) after the expiration of seven years from such date, not less than 40 cents an hour, or the rate (not less than 30 cents an hour) prescribed in the applicable order of the Administrator . . . whichever is lower, and (4) at any time after the effective date of this section, not less than the rate (not in excess of 40 cents an hour) prescribed in the applicable order of the Administrator . . .

The Fair Labor Standards Act set a goal of a 40-cent-an-hour minimum wage rate, to be attained over a seven-year period in order to reduce any possible adverse employment effects of the legislated minimum wage. It should be recalled that in 1938, 10,390,000 workers—19 per cent of the civilian labor force of 54,610,000—were unemployed.[14]

Not all, nor even a major portion of the 1938 wage rates were subject to immediate revision as a result of the new minimum. In manufacturing, for example, average gross hourly earnings were 63 cents; in bituminous coal mining, 88 cents; and in wholesale trade, 70 cents.[15] Yet, for the estimated eleven million workers covered by the Act in September, 1938, at least 300,000 were earning less than 25 cents an hour; 550,000 were earning below 30 cents an hour; and 1,418,000 below 40 cents.[16]

[14] *Economic Report of the President* (Washington, D. C.: U. S. Government Printing Office, January, 1955), p. 153.

[15] *Ibid.*, p. 162.

[16] *Monthly Labor Review,* XLIX, No. 6 (December, 1939), 1439–46.

In order to attain the minimum wage rate for each covered industry as rapidly as possible, at the same time retaining flexibility through the period of transition, the Act instructed the Administrator to appoint a committee for each industry. These committees were to investigate and recommend to the Administrator the highest wage that the industry could afford to pay without curtailing employment. Industry committees began to function shortly after the Act was passed.[17] Their valuable work was abetted by the effects of World War II on wages and prices, and the committees reached the 40-cent objective well before the October, 1945, deadline.

Maximum hours. Section 7 (a) provided that:

No employer shall, except as otherwise provided in this section, employ any of his employees who is engaged in commerce or in the production of goods for commerce—

(1) for a workweek longer than forty-four hours during the first year from the effective date of this section,

(2) for a workweek longer than forty-two hours during the second year from such date, or

(3) for a workweek longer than forty hours after the expiration of the second year from such date

unless such employee receives compensation for his employment in excess of the hours above specified at a rate not less than one and one-half times the regular rate at which he is employed.

This section of the Act followed the same gradual approach as the wages section, although the goal was to be attained in this case the second year after the Act went into effect. It is estimated that of the eleven million workers covered by the Act as of September, 1938, 1,384,000 were working more than forty-four hours per week; 1,751,000 were working more than forty-two hours per week; and 2,184,000 were working more than forty hours per week.[18]

This provision (with one exception discussed below) sets no maximum daily or weekly hours beyond which work is prohibited. Rather, it assesses an overtime penalty on long working hours. Also, it is noteworthy that the overtime penalty of one and one-half times is based upon the regular rate of pay, and not upon the statutory minimum rate.

The United States Supreme Court has emphasized several times that the hours section of the Fair Labor Standards Act has a dual purpose.[19] On the one hand, it is designed to compensate workers

[17] Z. Clark Dickinson, "The Organization and Functioning of Industry Committees Under the Fair Labor Standards Act," *Law and Contemporary Problems, op. cit.,* pp. 353–67.

[18] *Monthly Labor Review,* XLIX, No. 6 (December, 1939), 1439–46.

[19] See Riesenfeld and Maxwell, *op. cit.,* pp. 604–05.

for the duress of long hours worked in excess of the statutory minimum; and on the other, it is designed to spread employment through its overtime penalties.

Control of child labor. Section 12 (a) provided that:

. . . no producer, manufacturer or dealer shall ship or deliver for shipment in commerce any goods produced in an establishment situated in the United States in or about which within thirty days prior to the removal of such goods therefrom any oppressive child labor has been employed.

"Oppressive child labor" is defined by Section 3 (1) as the employment of children under sixteen, unless employed by parent or guardian. Employment in mining and manufacturing is prohibited in all cases for employees under sixteen. For children fourteen to sixteen, employment is not oppressive if it does not interfere with schooling, health and well being—as determined by the Chief of the Children's Bureau. Work in occupations designated as "hazardous" by the Children's Bureau is oppressive for children below eighteen. Appropriate agencies in the states issue certificates of age for children seeking employment.

Exemptions from coverage. A series of four specific provisions exempts otherwise covered employees from each of the three basic labor standards insured by the Act.

1. *Exemptions from minimum wage requirements.* To avoid curtailing employment for groups whose positions might be placed in jeopardy by too high a minimum wage, the Act authorized the Administrator to issue special certificates to handicapped workers, messengers, apprentices, and learners. Certified workers in these groups may be employed at a rate below the statutory minimum. Since this exemption is intended only to avoid possible restriction in employment opportunities, it does not extend to the hours (or overtime) provision of the law. Thus messengers, learners, apprentices, and handicapped workers must be paid one and one-half times their regular rate of pay for hours in excess of those specified by statute—after 1940, forty hours per week.

2. *Exemptions from hours (overtime) requirements.* Three exemptions were provided. First, industries found by the Administrator to be "seasonal" were given an exemption for fourteen weeks in any calendar year. Employees in these industries could work up to twelve hours a day, fifty-six hours a week, without overtime payment. Beyond these limits, overtime applied. Secondly, a fourteen-weeks exemption per calendar year was provided employees working in "agricultural processing—such as processing milk, processing cream into dairy products, ginning and compressing cotton. Third, employees who come under the Interstate Commerce Commission's jurisdiction with respect to hours (such as motor carriers) were exempt from overtime provisions.

The final hours exemption related to collective agreements. In order to encourage regular employment, exemption from overtime penalties was provided if an employer and a certified union entered into a collective agreement which provided either a maximum of fifty-two weeks of employment for 2,000 hours (changed to 2,080 hours in 1941); or twenty-six weeks of work for 1,000 hours. Where such contracts were bargained, employers were permitted to average out overtime, and to work employees up to twelve hours a day, or fifty-six hours a week without incurring the overtime penalty. If the 2,080 or 1,040 hour maxima were exceeded, the overtime exemption was lost.

3. *Exemptions from child labor provisions.* We have already noted that children working for a parent or guardian were exempt in part. Children working in agriculture, while not legally required to attend school, and children employed as actors in motion pictures or theatrical productions were also exempt.

4. *Exemption for wage and hour provisions.* Complete exemption from the coverage of the Fair Labor Standards Act was provided for some dozen groups of employees. Most important of these are the several classes which fall into the agricultural and white collar group.

First, employees classified as executives, administrative, professional, outside salesmen, or working in local retailing or retailing primarily intrastate commerce in nature, were exempt. By law the Administrator is empowered to set up regulations which define the scope of these exemptions.

Second, seamen, fishermen (including canning), workers employed in agriculture, and those working in agriculture or horticulture in the "area of production" were exempt.

Finally, employees such as air carriers, switchboard operators, and employees of small local newspapers were given exemptions.

Enforcement provisions. Three means of enforcement were established. First, willful violation of the Act could be punishable criminally by fine and imprisonment. Secondly, the right of civil suit was given employees whose employers violated wage and hour provisions. Suits for unpaid amounts as well as for damages, fees, and costs were authorized. Finally, violations of the Act could be restrained by injunctions.

CONSTITUTIONALITY[20]

The first challenge of the Fair Labor Standards Act reached the Supreme Court in 1940, and in 1941, the Court reversed a lower

[20] In view of past decisions of the U. S. Supreme Court on state laws regulating conditions of work, there was a great deal of speculation about whether or not the Court would uphold the Fair Labor Standards Act. Two opinions, one holding the new Act constitutional, the other holding it unconstitutional, were prepared in 1939 by legal scholars as suggestive of what the Court might do. See Robert L. Stern and R. S. Smethurst, "How the Supreme Court May View the Fair Labor Standards Act," *Law and Contemporary Problems, op. cit.,* pp. 431–53.

District Court decision and held[21] the new Act constitutional. Darby Lumber, which had been charged with a violation of the wage and hour provisions, claimed that the Fair Labor Standards Act, in violation of the rule in *Hammer v. Dagenhart*, used the power to regulate commerce to regulate essential interstate business. The Court repudiated this narrow view of what was a permissible regulation of commerce and overruled *Hammer v. Dagenhart*. The Court's earlier decision in *West Coast Hotel v. Parrish* had already determined that wage regulation did not violate the Fourteenth Amendment. In the Darby case the Court held that the Act did not violate the due process clause of the Fifth Amendment. Another decision[22] upheld the operation of the industry committees as a permissible delegation of powers, and they operated until they completed their work in 1944.

REVISIONS OF THE ACT

Two important amendments have been made to the original Fair Labor Standards Act. Before turning to the details of the coverage and administration of the Act, its rationale, and an appraisal, let us discuss these amendments.

1949 revisions. In 1944, when the last industry committee had reached the minimum wage goal set forth in the Fair Labor Standards Act, that wage level (40 cents an hour) was already considered by many persons to be obsolete. The inflationary pressures of World War II had pushed gross hourly earnings in manufacturing from a 1938 level of 63 cents to $1.02—some 61 per cent; in construction, hourly earnings had risen from 91 cents to $1.32; in wholesale trade from 70 cents to 99 cents; and in laundries, from 42 cents to 61 cents. During this same period, prices, as measured by the Consumers' Price Index, rose from a 1938 index level of 60.3 to 75.2[23]

It was with these facts in mind that President Truman in his "State of the Union Message" on January 5, 1949, stated that the minimum wage should be fixed at 75 cents an hour. This major aim was more fully spelled out by William R. McComb, Wage and Hour Administrator, in his testimony in the hearings on proposed legislation. Said Mr. McComb:

The most vitally required change in the Fair Labor Standards Act is to increase the minimum wage. This proposal should no longer be in the realm

[21] *United States v. F. W. Darby Lumber Company,* 312 U. S. 100 (1941).
[22] *Opp Cotton Mills, Inc. v. Administrator,* 312 U.S. 126 (1941).
[23] Wage and price data from the *Economic Report of the President,* January, 1955, pp. 162–76.

of controversy. The 40-cent minimum wage has shrunk to 23 cents in 1938 dollars. It is a modest proposal . . . Most industries could afford to pay a minimum wage well above 75 cents . . . While I estimate that only 7 per cent of the 22,600,000 workers covered by the minimum wage provisions of the Act are earning less than 75 cents an hour, this 7 per cent represents 1½ million human beings. These 1½ million workers desperately need the benefits of a modest 75-cent minimum wage.[24]

In the nine months which elapsed between the time the administration bill was introduced and the time the measure reached the President's desk, the proposed amendments went through many changes. The President received his recommended 75-cent minimum, but he also received amendments he had not sought.

The 1949 amendments may be summarized as follows:

1. *Wage and hour provisions.* (a) The minimum wage was increased from 40 to 75 cents an hour. (b) Rules governing overtime exemptions for annual wage plans were made more flexible. The maximum of 2,080 hours for fifty-two-week plans was raised to 2,240 hours. Overtime rates are required over the lower figure, but exemption is not lost unless the upper figure is exceeded. Similarly, the ceiling of 1,000 hours on twenty-six-week plans was raised to 1,040 hours. (c) Contracts permitting fixed weekly wages for employees with irregular hours were authorized if they were limited to sixty hours a week, guaranteed the minimum statutory rate and provided overtime for more than forty hours. (d) The concept "hours worked" was defined to exclude wash-up time and clothes-hanging time unless these are covered by contract or custom. (e) "Regular rate of pay" was defined to exclude certain gratuities. The effects of these latter changes are discussed later in this chapter.

2. *Child labor provisions.* (a) Whereas the earlier law simply prohibited shipment of goods on which oppressive child labor had been employed, the new law *specifically prohibited the employment of child labor.* (b) It set the minimum age for hazardous work at eighteen and eliminated the exemption for children working for parents. (c) It added exemptions for minors in radio and television, but limited the agriculture exemption to hours outside required school hours for the district where the child or parents reside.

3. *Coverage.* The 1938 law covered employees engaged in commerce, or in the production of goods for commerce or in any occupation necessary to such production. The amendments reduced coverage to apply to employees engaged in commerce or in the production of goods for commerce or in any *closely related* process or occupation *directly essential* to such production.

4. *Exemptions.* Only two of the original exemptions—fishing and air carriers—were somewhat curtailed. Exemptions to agricultural process-

[24] U. S. Congress, 81st, 1st Session, House, Hearings Before the Committee on Education and Labor, *Amendments to the Fair Labor Standards Act of 1938,* I (Washington, D. C.: U. S. Government Printing Office, 1949), 51–52.

ing, local newspapers, and telephone exchanges were enlarged, and new exemptions—for agricultural irrigation, taxicab operators, forestry and lumbering, and telegraphic agencies—were added.

5. *Enforcement.* The new law gave the Administrator the authority to sue for an employee's back wages with the consent of the employee. Such suits had not previously been authorized.

1955 revisions. In his *Economic Report* to the Congress in January, 1955, President Eisenhower proposed that the minimum wage be increased to 90 cents an hour and that ". . . both Congress and the States . . . consider the question of bringing substantial numbers of workers, now excluded from the protection of a minimum wage, under its coverage."[25]

After lengthy hearings, Congress rejected the Administration bill and approved one which increased the minimum wage to $1 an hour, but did not extend coverage of the Act.[26] Changes became effective March 1, 1956.

An important issue in the hearings on the 1955 amendments was whether or not workers in the retailing industries should be brought under the Act. Although they were not included in the bill, the United States Department of Labor announced plans for an extensive fifteen-month study to determine the feasibility of such coverage for the national retail industry.[27]

COVERAGE OF THE ACT

According to the most recent United States Department of Labor estimates (September, 1953), the Fair Labor Standards Act sets minimum standards for about twenty-four million, or 55 per cent of the forty-four million[28] American wage and salary workers for whom this protection might be contemplated. Table 16.1 indicates the degrees to which coverage extends to employees of major industries.

Table 16.1 reveals that virtually all workers in mining and manufacturing are covered by the Fair Labor Standards Act, whereas in retail trade, agriculture, forestry, fisheries, and domestic service, coverage is virtually nonexistent. Two factors deny Fair Labor

[25] *Economic Report of the President,* January, 1955, pp. 58–59.

[26] Other 1955 amendments provided that the Wage and Hour Administrator's annual report must make an evaluation and appraisal of the minimum wage set by the Act; that it must also make recommendations for future revisions of the law; and that the reports of industry committees for minimum wages in Puerto Rico and the Virgin Islands must be published in the *Federal Register* to take effect fifteen days after such publication.

[27] *Wall Street Journal,* March 15, 1956, p. 2.

[28] Excludes executive, administrative, professional, government, and self-employed persons as well as armed forces personnel.

TABLE 16.1

PERCENTAGE DISTRIBUTION OF
WAGE AND SALARY EARNERS PROTECTED BY
THE FAIR LABOR STANDARDS ACT, SEPTEMBER, 1953

	% of wage and salary workers protected by FLSA
Mining	97.3
Manufacturing	95.8
Transportation, Communications, and Utilities	87.0
Wholesale Trade	66.7
Finance, Insurance, Real Estate	58.5
Construction	23.9
Services and Related Industries	17.7
Retail Trade	3.3
Agriculture, Forestry and Fisheries	.5
Domestic Service	.0
Total, All Industries	54.5

Source: U. S. Congress, 84th, 1st Session, Senate, Hearings Before the Committee on Labor and Public Welfare, Subcommittee on Labor, *Amending the Fair Labor Standards Act of 1938* (Washington, D. C.: U. S. Government Printing Office, 1955), p. 1587, Part 3. (Data prepared by U. S. Department of Labor.)

Standards Act protection to these groups: (1) the requirement, discussed earlier, that coverage extend only to employees "engaged in commerce or in the production of goods for commerce"; and (2) exemptions which exclude many workers who meet coverage requirements.

The effects of these two limitations on Fair Labor Standards Act protection are demonstrated below in Table 16.2.

This table reveals that of the twenty million workers not protected by the Act, some 13.6 million do not meet (interstate) coverage requirements; and about 6.4 million wage and salary earners who do meet these requirements are specially exempt by one or more of the provisions we have already discussed briefly. Retail trade accounts for about one-third of the exempt group. Agriculture, forestry and fisheries, and service industries represent another one-third of the workers exempt from the Act. A more detailed breakdown of the 6.4 million exempt workers, by exemption, is presented below in Table 16.3.

The full effect of this spotty coverage cannot easily be gauged. Undoubtedly some of the workers who fall outside the protection of the Act are not in need of it. This would apply to employments in

TABLE 16.2

DISTRIBUTION OF EMPLOYEES NOT PROTECTED
BY THE FLSA, BY INDUSTRY DIVISION,
September, 1953
(thousands)

Industry		Workers Not Protected by FLSA	
	Total	Not Covered	Covered, but Exempt
Manufacturing	683	86	597
Mining	21	19	2
Construction	1,951	1,867	84
Wholesale trade	846	262	584
Retail trade	6,698	5,558	1,140
Finance, Insurance, Real Estate . .	744	414	330
Transp., Communications, Utilities .	515	286	229
Services and Related Industries . .	3,447	2,995	452
Agr., Forestry, and Fisheries . . .	3,052	101	2,951
Domestic Service	2,021	2,021	—
Total, All Industries	19,978	13,609	6,369

Source: *Amending the Fair Labor Standards Act of 1938*, p. 1780. (Data prepared by U. S. Department of Labor.) Table excludes proprietors, self-employed persons, unpaid family workers, executive, administrative, and professional employees and armed forces personnel.

TABLE 16.3

EXEMPTIONS UNDER
THE FAIR LABOR STANDARDS ACT

Exemptions	Number Exempt
Farm workers	3,032,000
Employed by exempt retail trade or retail service establishments	1,360,000
Outside salesmen	1,203,000
Engaged in handling or processing agricultural commodities in the area of production	233,000
Employed in laundries or cleaning and dyeing plants	132,000
Seamen	117,000
Employed in small logging operations having 12 or fewer logging employees	110,000
Engaged in fishing or in canning, processing or distributing fishery products	61,000
Switchboard operators of small telephone exchanges	43,000
Employed by small newspaper concerns	32,000
Employed by local transit companies	32,000
Employed in local retailing capacity by manufacturers or wholesalers . .	10,000
Taxicab operators	4,000

Source: *Amending the Fair Labor Standards Act of 1938*, p. 1780. (Data prepared by U. S. Department of Labor.)

which trade union wage and hour standards are in effect. Most organized workers enjoy working standards well above the minimum requirements of the Act. But those who do not and who cannot look forward to favorable market forces must depend upon state minimum wage laws. As we have already seen, not all states have adopted such laws. State laws that do exist rarely apply to men, and their standards, by and large, are low. Table 16.4 illustrates the legislative gap between the twenty million workers not protected by the law and those protected by state minimum wage legislation.

Before turning to this table, it may be well to note how it was prepared and to advise caution in its interpretation. The distribution of *unprotected* workers by states is an estimate based upon the distribution of *covered* workers by state, and hence may tend to understate the number of unprotected workers in the agricultural and fishing states and to overstate these numbers in industrial areas.

Allowing for the possible errors of estimate, the table nevertheless reveals very clearly the great gaps between the numbers of workers who are unprotected by federal standards and those covered by state standards—16.5 million workers. Although not all these workers are in need of state protection, the over-all coverage record (qualified as it is) is still in great need of improved legislation.

Let us now turn to the qualitative issues in coverage to determine the rationale behind the exemption and limiting provisions.

RATIONALE OF COVERAGE AND EXEMPTIONS

At the present time the civilian labor force is comprised of about sixty-seven million persons. Of these, twenty-two million work in occupations for which Fair Labor Standards Act coverage was not intended.[29] For the forty-five million who remain, however, we have seen that protection is not available to the 13.6 million workers who are not covered nor to the 6.4 million who are exempt. What are the reasons for these limits on coverage and exemptions? It may be instructive to look at this matter in some detail so as to get a flavor of political processes.

Limitations on coverage. In the 1955 Senate hearings, the United States Department of Labor listed three factors which limit coverage:

1. Congress cannot legislate beyond its constitutional authority which, in the case of the commerce clause, is "to regulate commerce

---

[29] Proprietors, self-employed, and unpaid family workers—twelve million; government employees—six million; executive, administrative, and professional employees—four million.

TABLE 16.4

Estimated Number of Workers Not Subject to Fair Labor Standards Act Coverage, and Workers Covered by State Minimum Wage Laws and Orders, by States

	Number of Workers			Number of Workers	
	Not Subject to FLSA[1]	Covered by State Min. Wage Laws[2]		Not Subject to FLSA[1]	Covered by State Min. Wage Laws[2]
Alabama . . .	280,000		New Hampshire	80,000	62,000
Arizona . . .	60,000	17,000	New Jersey . .	820,000	82,000
Arkansas . . .	100,000		New Mexico . .	40,000	
California . .	1,200,000	615,000	New York . .	2,560,000	1,065,000
Colorado . . .	120,000	50,000	North Carolina .	440,000	
Connecticut . .	400,000	245,000	North Dakota .	20,000	13,000
Delaware . . .	60,000		Ohio	1,380,000	92,000
Florida . . .	180,000		Oklahoma . .	160,000	
Georgia . . .	340,000		Oregon . . .	200,000	65,000
Idaho	40,000		Pennsylvania .	1,860,000	50,000
Illinois . . .	1,560,000		Rhode Island .	160,000	36,000
Indiana . . .	660,000		South Carolina .	220,000	
Iowa	220,000		South Dakota .	20,000	
Kansas . . .	180,000		Tennessee . .	300,000	
Kentucky . . .	260,000	87,000	Texas	720,000	
Louisiana . .	260,000		Utah	60,000	20,000
Maine	120,000		Vermont . . .	40,000	
Maryland . .	320,000		Virginia . . .	320,000	
Massachusetts .	800,000	601,000	Washington . .	260,000	100,000
Michigan . . .	1,160,000		West Virginia .	300,000	
Minnesota . .	320,000	81,000	Wisconsin . .	480,000	205,000
Mississippi . .	120,000		Wyoming . .	40,000	
Missouri . . .	520,000				
Montana . . .	60,000		Washington, D.C.	60,000	57,000
Nebraska . . .	100,000				
Nevada . . .	20,000	13,000	Total . .	20,000,000	3,556,000

Sources:

[1] Estimate of distribution by States of twenty million uncovered workers derived from coverage estimates in U. S. Department of Labor, Wage and Hour and Public Contracts Division, *Annual Report* (Washington, D. C.: U. S. Government Printing Office, 1950), p. 318.

[2] *Amending the Fair Labor Standards Act of 1938, Ibid.*, p. 1781 (U. S. Department of Labor data).

. . . among the several States . . ." The Fair Labor Standards Act is limited in application to employees "engaged in commerce or in the production of goods for commerce." Court interpretation has given broad scope to the coverage phrases of the Act to "extend it far beyond interstate commerce . . . to a whole complex of activities which precede commerce, broadly defined as production for commerce."[30] Yet coverage of the Act is restricted by the fact that "It does not . . . extend at all beyond commerce to the other complex of activities which follow commerce . . . The effect on commerce of labor conditions in production of the article which subsequently moves, is recognized, though the effect on the same commerce of labor conditions in the distribution of the article which has moved, is not."[31]

2. A second factor limiting coverage is the required relationship between the individual's work and commerce. Since this is made the basic test for coverage, it "tends to obscure what may be essentially national, as opposed to local, nature of the business organization to which his employment contributes."[32]

3. And finally, in delineating covered employments, the Act sacrifices ". . . application of other employments which may have an equal effect on interstate commerce and the business of the nation as a whole."[33]

Exemptions. Fair Labor Standards Act protection is neither intended nor appropriate for workers who are professionals or for those who are identified with management (executives, administrators, and white collar workers). But why does the law fail to protect certain nonmanagerial and executive groups? Reasons for these exemptions, as they appear in the legislative history of the exemption, are briefly outlined below together with a notation of the number of workers exempt in each case.[34]

1. *Farm workers.* It was argued, first, that most farm workers probably cannot be reached by Congress; and, second, that it is too hard to regulate wages and hours in an industry that is subject to natural and seasonal forces. (Number exempt: 3,032,000.)

2. *Employees in local retailing, exempt retail trade, retail service, and outside salesmen.* These groups were exempt under the original Act to insure that employees of small local retailers—such as butchers and grocers for whom the Act might prove too burdensome financially—would be exempt. Outside salesmen were considered comparable to the executive, administrative, and professional group and exempt for the same reasons. (Number exempt: 2,573,000.)

3. *Handlers and processors of agricultural commodities.* In adopting this exemption it was argued that the costs of processing cannot be

---

[30] U. S. Congress, 84th, 1st Session, Senate, Hearings Before the Committee on Labor and Public Welfare, Subcommittee on Labor, *Amending the Fair Labor Standards Act of 1938* (Washington, D. C.: U. S. Government Printing Office, 1955), p. 1779.

[31] *Ibid.*   [32] *Ibid.*   [33] *Ibid.*

[34] *Ibid.*, pp. 1782–87, where brief summaries of legislative history for each exemption to the Act may be found.

passed on to consumers but must be borne by the farmer. Also, these workers do not work under industrial conditions. (Number exempt: 233,000.)

4. *Laundry, cleaning, and dyeing plant employees.* A 1949 amendment covering this group of workers was adopted despite the fact that some launderies were exempt as "retail establishments" to insure that none would lose his exemption by performing service for non-home customers. (Number exempt: 132,000.)

5. *Seamen.* These men, it was argued, were already subject to the jurisdiction of the Maritime Commission which had authority to fix wages on some vessels. Also, overtime pay was not in accord with the practices of the industry. If men worked only forty hours, ship operators would have to hire much larger crews, which would not be feasible. Furthermore, the Courts might construe seamen's work as a twenty-four-hour-a-day job. (Number exempt: 117,000.)

6. *Workers in forestry and lumbering.* In order to compete with large operators, it was contended that these employees should be made exempt. Also, it would be difficult to enforce the law for the woods employees of small operators. (Number exempt: 111,000.)

7. *Fishing and fisheries.* This exemption was justified on the grounds that the industry is greatly affected by natural forces which make wage and hour regulation impracticable. (Number exempt: 61,000.)

8. *Small telephone switchboards.* The reason for this exemption was the possible threat to rural telephone service if small companies who pleaded that they could not afford to do so were forced to comply with the Act. (Number exempt: 43,000.)

9. *Small newspapers.* Since these are essentially small local businesses, it was felt that they should enjoy the exemption for that group. (Number exempt: 32,000.)

10. *Local interurban trains, streetcars, and buses.* Since most of these do not cross state lines, they would not be covered. In addition, it was contended that there was great difficulty involved in regulating late hours due to peak morning and evening loads. (Number exempt: 32,000.)

11. *Taxicab company employees.* Few of these cross state lines, and it was felt that those who were covered would have to compete with those who were not. (Number exempt: 4,000.)

A comment. If an important aim of the Fair Labor Standards Act is to protect workers, because they are unorganized and/or in employments in which working conditions are substandard, then the interests of these workers must be brought before the Congress. Today, trade unions strongly back expanded coverage.[35] But no one spoke authoritatively for this point of view in 1949 when revisions of the minimum wage involved changes which curtailed coverage

[35] See, for example, *Labor's Economic Review,* I, No. 3 (March, 1956), 25–32.

of the law. Four exemptions were enlarged, six new ones added, and only one curtailed.

In looking at the aims of the Act and its present pattern of coverage, the United States Department of Labor concludes that these gaps in protection ". . . because of their size and importance to our economy, merit thorough consideration as to why the present act does not apply to them," and suggests that it should be ascertained ". . . whether any valid reason exists today for continuing limitation on the accomplishment of the economically sound and humane purposes of the act.[36]

ECONOMIC EFFECTS OF THE ACT

Earliest United States Department of Labor estimates (referred to earlier in this chapter) of the wage and hour status of workers covered by the 1938 Act revealed that 300,000 covered workers were earning less than 25 cents an hour; 550,000, less than 30 cents an hour; and 1,418,000, less than 40 cents an hour. It was estimated that 1,384,000 workers were working in excess of forty-four hours a week; 1,751,000, more than forty-two hours a week; and 2,184,000, over forty hours a week. A later study[37] concluded that on October 24, 1939, the date the Act became effective, 650,000 workers in manufacturing, wholesale trade and motor carriers—some 5½ per cent of all covered employees—would be subject to wage increases to 30 cents an hour; that the wage increases would average 1.9 per cent in all manufacturing, 13.5 per cent for cottonseed oil, 8.2 per cent in saw mills, and 4.9 per cent in the canning industry; and that only 30 per cent of some 2,400,000 workers then working more than forty-two hours a week were receiving overtime.

What effects would the required adjustments have on wages, employment opportunities, prices, and profits? These questions were of great concern to the Congress which, it will be recalled, prefaced the new law with the policy statement that it was the purpose of the law to eliminate substandard conditions ". . . without substantially curtailing employment or earning power." As Chapter 17 will indicate, economists have long been concerned about these issues of public policy, but have never been agreed as to the probable effects of minimum wage laws. Their differences of opinion are apparently due partly to different points of view regarding the desirability of minimum wage legislation and partly to the notable lack of empirical information on these questions.

[36] *Amending the Fair Labor Standards Act of 1938, op. cit.,* p. 1781.
[37] *Monthly Labor Review,* L, No. 3 (March, 1940), 546.

The new law raised wage rates and reduced hours (or penalized overtime)—this is agreed. But did it have other (possibly undesirable) economic consequences? Since reliable and comprehensive data are not available, there has been little more than speculation about this question. Nowhere is the lack of empirical information about the effects of the Fair Labor Standards Act more clearly indicated than in the Congressional hearings on the 1949 revision.[38]

When the law was amended in 1949 with the 75-cent minimum to become effective January 25, 1950, the Department of Labor undertook a major study[39] to determine its effects. Three avenues of inquiry were followed.

First, field surveys were made in five low-wage manufacturing industries (southern sawmilling, fertilizer, men's dress shirts and nightwear, women's seamless hosiery, and wood furniture except upholstered) to determine the impact of the new law on wage structures.

Second, every complaint of a plant slowdown, shutdown, or job curtailment due to the law was investigated thoroughly. A wide range of firms and industries was covered.

Third, a comparison was made of wage movements for seventeen industries, some high-wage, others low-wage, for several periods to determine the effects of the law.

Results of this study, briefly summarized below, were perhaps partly influenced by the fact that the period after 1950, because of the Korean War, was one of rising prices and employment. The data reveal that, except for the payment of the required increase, the over-all effects of the new minimum were minor for the firms studied.

Wage changes. Upward wage adjustments in the five low-wage industries were extensive. In southern sawmilling, for example, the direct wage bill rose by 14 per cent. With but few exceptions, the increases in the wage bill were greater than any effected by the industry committees under the original Act. As might have been predicted, percentage wage differentials were reduced, both between high- and low-wage industries and regions. Wage rates of employees working at or above the new 75-cent minimum wage were not significantly affected. For employees outside of coverage, wage rates that were below the new minimum increased—in some cases as much as those of covered employees. The study of wage move-

---

[38] *Amendments to the Fair Labor Standards Act of 1949.*
[39] See Chapter 17, this text, for further discussion of this study.

ments in the seventeen industries indicated that low wages increased more in covered industries than in noncovered industries.

Non-wage effects. Despite the fact that the new higher minimum required significant wage increases, its effect on employment, plant shutdowns, hiring policies, technological change, and overtime work was minor. In the relatively few instances where minor employment declines did occur, the decisions to reduce employment were influenced by other factors as well as the minimum wage. No plant closings were attributed by their managers solely to the 75-cent minimum wage requirement.

Some firms indicated that the new minimum had the effect on their hiring policies of placing more emphasis on younger, more experienced workers. Although a few cases of curtailed overtime were reported, over-all effects on prices and overtime work were similarly small and insignificant. Finally, no direct evidence could be found that the new minimum accelerated the rate of technological change.

Effects in firms reporting adjustment problems. These firms, it will be recalled, were those which reported difficulties in adjusting to the new minimum wage. Not only were they untypical of all firms, but were, in fact, those least able to meet the wage and hour requirements of the new law. Even in these firms, however, the new minimum wage law did not have any serious over-all effects.

The hand cigar and oyster canning industries were especially hard hit. Together with a few other industries, they experienced unemployment and even a few closings, although most of the unemployment resulted from job elimination or elimination of slower workers. Even in these extreme cases, however, the causal picture was not clear, since other unfavorable market forces were influential in the employment decisions.

It will be useful for the student to consider the meaning of these findings in the context of the next chapter. Do they indicate, for example, that the new higher minimum wage was returning to workers more than the value of their marginal product? And a more immediate consideration: Can the pattern of these findings be extended to the latest Congressional action of increasing the minimum wage to $1 an hour?

Tables 16.5 and 16.6 below, which are excerpts from two tables presented in the extensive statistical exhibits prepared by the United States Department of Labor for the Senate committee hearings, reveal some significant facts about the impact of the new $1 minimum wage level.

TABLE 16.5

ESTIMATED NUMBER OF WORKERS EARNING LESS THAN $1.00 AND $1.25 AN HOUR, AND THE DIRECT WAGE EFFECTS OF THESE MINIMUM WAGE RATES

Hourly Minimum Wage Rate	Workers Earning Less Than Specified Amounts		Direct Increase in Annual Wage Bill	
	Number[1]	% of Total Employment	$ Amount (Millions)	% of Total Wage Bill
	(000's omitted)			
All workers subject to the Act:				
Total	24,000	100.0	82,000	100.0
Under $1.00 . . .	2,100	8.7	560	.7
Under $1.25 . . .	5,000	20.9	2,300	2.8
$1.25 and over . . .	19,000	79.1	79,700	97.2

[1] Estimates based on employment level of September, 1953.

Source: *Amending the Fair Labor Standards Act of 1938*, p. 1628. (Data prepared by the U. S. Department of Labor.)

Table 16.5 shows that the new $1 wage minimum involves direct pay increases to 2.1 million workers (representing 8.7 per cent of covered employees) and a direct wage hike of $560 million, or a .7 per cent raise, in the total covered wage bill. The indirect effects which occur when old differentials are adjusted are unpredictable.[40]

Table 16.6 indicates that the geographic distribution of this cost impact is largely in the South, where some 850,000, or 28 per cent, of production workers were earning less than $1 an hour, compared with 10 per cent in the country as a whole, 8 per cent in the Northeast, 4 per cent in the Middle West, and 1.8 per cent in the Far West.

It is clear that the 1955 amendments produced one of the greatest simultaneous wage boosts in our history. And the full impact of the amendments throughout wage structures cannot be assessed for many months. Can we infer from the earlier study that the effects of this wage adjustment on employment and prices will again be negligible? Some small businesses, such as junk yards, waste processors, candy markets, and upholstery producers, particularly in the South, found that the higher minimum wage was an immediate and

[40] Findings from the study cited above seem to indicate, at least in the short run, that these differentials are not maintained. Thus, an issue in the 1955 strike of the shoe workers at the International Shoe Company was the union's demand for ". . . correction of wage inequities resulting from an increase [on March 1, 1956] in the minimum wage from 75¢ to $1 . . ." *Wall Street Journal*, November 15, 1955, p. 2.

TABLE 16.6

ESTIMATED PERCENTAGE OF PRODUCTION WORKERS IN MANUFACTURING
EARNING LESS THAN $1.00 AND $1.25 AN HOUR, BY U. S. AND REGIONS
(April, 1954)

Straight-time Average Hourly Earnings	Percentage of Production Workers				
	U.S.	South	N.E.	Mid-West	Far West
Under $1.00	10.2	28.2	8.0	4.1	1.8
Under $1.25	22.4	50.0	21.4	11.5	6.3
$1.25 and over . . .	77.6	50.0	78.6	88.5	93.7

Source: *Amending the Fair Labor Standards Act of 1938*, p. 1628.

heavy burden. Among larger businesses—southern saw mills and work clothing manufacturers—considerable wage rate adjustments were needed, for not only a majority of workers earned less than $1 an hour, but few of the highest paid received much more than that.

The United States Department of Agriculture predicted specific increases in prices for food, cigarettes, and clothing as a result of the new minimum wage.[41] And there are indications of slight price increases in clothing and textiles made in the South.[42] Lumber mill operators expressed doubt that they would raise prices, but suggested, however, that their overtime would probably be cut back. Shoe and costume jewelry manufacturers made specific announcements of price increases that could be attributed, at least in part, to the higher wage minimum. From an over-all point of view, most observers seemed to agree with Labor Secretary Mitchell that the new 1955 $1 minimum wage was being ". . . absorbed with a great deal of ease," and that generally there could be foreseen no ". . . impact of the minimum wage increase of a nature that would cause unemployment. . . ."[43]

ADMINISTRATION OF THE ACT

The myriad problems that arise in the administration of the Fair Labor Standards Act can be grouped into problems of how to fix standards and how to enforce them.

Fixing standards. Although the Fair Labor Standards Act defines basic wage and hour standards, it leaves to the Administrator considerable areas of discretion in defining and delimiting the law's

[41] *Wall Street Journal*, January 9, 1956, p. 9.
[42] *Ibid.*, March 1, 1956, p. 1.
[43] *Ibid*, March 16, 1952, p. 2.

applicability. The Administrator is also called upon to interpret the law for employees who are uncertain of their status. A great many questions must be decided. Who is an executive, an administrator, or an outside salesman within the meaning of the Act? What employments are "closely related" or "directly essential" to the production of goods for commerce? For that matter, who are "employees"? How is overtime to be computed? Who qualifies for retail exemption? For seasonal industry exemption? What is the "Area of Production"?

The Act gives the Administrator power to issue binding and authoritative regulations in connection with specific provisions of the Act. It also makes provision for employers or others affected by these regulations to appeal to the Administrator for their revision. These important regulations, which now number nineteen, cover the many phases of the law which the Administrator must supervise.[44]

The Administrator must set standards for employment of learners and must revise these standards in the light of current economic conditions. He must issue certificates for the employment of apprentices, messengers, and handicapped workers. In addition, he must maintain wage standards in Puerto Rico and the Virgin Islands, where they are still determined by industry committees.

Shortly after passage of the Act in 1938, the Administrator was beseiged by employers and unions seeking authoritative rulings as to the applicability of the Act in specific situations. In lieu of such rule-making power (which was not given to the Administrator in the Act) the Wage and Hour Division began, in November, 1938, to issue interpretative bulletins—a practice which it has followed ever since.

The first interpretative bulletin (October 12, 1938) made clear its nonofficial status by noting:

. . . interpretations announced by the Administrator, except in certain specific instances where the statute directs the Administrator to make various regulations and definitions, serve only to indicate the construction of the law which will guide the Administrator in the performance of his administrative

---

[44] A list of the current regulations provides some indication of the scope of this area of administration. They cover: certificates of age, employment of minors, child labor, utilization of state agencies for investigation and inspections, record keeping, vocational training, apprentices, learners, messengers, handicapped workers, sheltered workshops, seasonal industries, student workers, cost of facilities, area of production, white-collar workers, thrift and savings plans, profit-sharing plan or trust, agreed basic rates on overtime, and "talent" fees. For the complete text of these regulations and the interpretive bulletins, see Bureau of National Affairs, Inc., *Labor Policies and Practices*, III (Washington, D. C.: 1956).

duties, unless he is directed otherwise by the authoritative rulings of the courts, or unless he shall subsequently decide that a prior interpretation is incorrect.[45]

Today, fifteen interpretative bulletins cover such areas as general enforcement policy, coverage, methods of wage payment, overtime compensation, retail and service trades, and agricultural processing. While these bulletins do not have the status of substantive regulations, they do carry weight with the Courts, which are faced with the question of interpreting the Fair Labor Standards Act.[46]

Enforcing standards. Despite the many problems involved in fixing standards, the most difficult task of the Administrator is to enforce them. Although the law has always made private suits for back pay available to workers, experience indicates that enforcement cannot be left to the worker's own initiative. Rather, business establishments are inspected to insure compliance with required standards—through law suit if necessary. Enforcement is an especially vexing problem since the number of inspections is relatively small because of limited personnel, and the percentage of violations, although many are good-faith errors, is very large.

Inspections. In the first annual report of the Wage and Hour Division (1939), Administrator Harold J. Jacobs stated:

> The Administrator has proceeded on the assumption that the Division should work toward a sustained program of inspecting on a systematic basis the establishments of all employers subject to the provisions of the act. Experience in the enforcement of other labor laws has demonstrated the necessity for such procedure. The goal of the Division is to make annual routine inspection of each covered employer. This goal probably will not be achieved for several years, but it is one which, in fairness to both employers and employees, should not be put in the too distant future.[47]

In 1946, Wage and Hour Administrator L. Metcalfe Walling reported:

> It has been conservatively estimated that there are currently about 550,000 establishments with employees subject to the Fair Labor Standards Act, with a total of nearly 20,000,000 covered employees . . . most of the establishments which are inspected are found to be in violation of the major provisions of the Fair Labor Standards Act and Public Contracts Act. Nevertheless, because of budgetary limitations, the Divisions must attempt to obtain compliance in all of these 550,000 covered establishments through inspections of only 45,000, or 8 per cent, of them each year.[48]

[45] Cited by Samuel Herman in "The Administration and Enforcement of the Fair Labor Standards Act," *Law and Contemporary Problems, op. cit.,* p. 379.

[46] Riesenfeld and Maxwell, *op. cit.,* p. 607.

[47] U. S. Department of Labor, Wage and Hour and Public Contracts Division, *Annual Report* (Washington, D.C.: U. S. Government Printing Office, 1939), p. 45.

[48] *Ibid.* (1946), p. 24.

In 1955, when an estimated 800,000 establishments were covered by the law, Administrator Newell Brown disclosed that inspections reached 39,300 establishments, or just under 5 per cent of those covered. The Division hopes to increase inspections to 67,000 establishments in 1956.[49]

Violations. A great many firms which are covered by the Fair Labor Standards Act operate in violation of its provisions. Table 16.7 (which presents data for the Fair Labor Standards Act and the Public Contracts Act) indicates just how extensive this problem is. The proportion of investigated establishments found to be in violation of the minimum wage and overtime provisions is about the same today as it was in 1939—an astonishing figure of 50 per cent. Child labor violations, which are not reported in the table, presently run at about 9 per cent of nonagricultural establishments investigated.

Wage and Hour officials have always stressed the fact that a large majority of these violations are not intentional. Whether or not they are intentional, however, violations of the standards of the Act deny full protection of the law to employees and indicate how strongly additional inspection and enforcement are needed to bring working standards up to the requirements of the law. In the last fiscal year, violations of minimum wage provisions were found in some 12 per cent of investigated cases, and, as in past years, over one-half of the establishments investigated were found "in violation of the basic provisions of the Fair Labor Standards Act. . . ."[50]

SOME SPECIAL PROBLEMS

Experience under the Act reveals that some of its standards, though clear in definition, present important policy problems when interpreted in specific situations. For example, the requirement that employees covered by the law must be paid overtime pay for all hours worked in excess of forty, at the rate of one and one-half times their regular rate of pay, has produced a series of complicated issues which revolve about the questions: What are "hours worked," and what is "the regular rate of pay"?

Hours worked. According to the Act, to "employ" means, in part, "to suffer or permit to work." Thus, "hours worked" include not only time an employee is *required* to be on duty, but also time he is *permitted* to be on duty, whether required or not. Two types of questions have arisen: Should "hours worked" include (1) idle time

[49] *The New York Times,* February 27, 1956, p. 9.
[50] *Ibid.*

TABLE 16.7

RESULTS OF INVESTIGATIONS IN NONAGRICULTURAL ESTABLISHMENTS UNDER FAIR LABOR STANDARDS ACT (1938–1953) AND PUBLIC CONTRACTS ACT (1942–1953)

Fiscal Year	Total Establishments Investigated	Per Cent Investigated	In Violation of Min. Wage and/or O.T. Reg.		Amount	Restitution Agreed to or Ordered	
			Back Wages Owed	Per Cent in Violation		Per Cent of Back Wages Owed	Avg. Per Case
1939	402	42%	—a	96%	$ 51,828	—a	$322
1940	3,851	62	—a	96	1,714,494	—a	746
1941	53,248	44	—a	86	11,540,889	—a	573
1942	74,914	53	—a	72	20,920,956	—a	724
1943	61,170	43	—a	75	16,824,021	—a	854
1944	54,431	46	—a	83	18,620,369	—a	903
1945	44,271	50		86	15,824,377		830
1946	43,832	48	$21,623,739	81	13,360,826	62%	782
1947	40,350	49	18,575,149	76	8,864,186	48	593
1948	30,053	51	10,757,914	63	4,256,761	40	444
1949	31,916	54	12,186,957	62	4,279,085	35	399
1950	25,881	48	9,559,628	72	4,081,193	43	457
1951	31,889	53	11,202,561	84	6,666,995	60	469
1952	39,109	52	15,663,912	84	8,467,668	54	496
1953	38,649	54b	16,652,697	79	8,282,043	50	511
Total	573,976	49%	—a	78%	$143,755,691	—a	$654

a Not available.
b Based on 38,026 covered establishments.

Source: U. S. Department of Labor, Wage and Hour and Public Contracts Division, *Annual Report* (Washington, D. C.: U. S. Government Printing Office, 1953), p. 53.

when, say, men are awaiting orders, and (2) time spent by employees getting ready for work, such as underground miners walking between the portals of the mine and the working face at the beginning and the end of each day? The United States Supreme Court held[51] that "hours worked" should include both these instances, and the latter decision gave rise to the important "portal-to-portal" pay problem.

It appears that portal-to-portal pay began during the period of wage stabilization as a "fringe" item won by the United Mine Workers. It was soon adopted in slaughter houses, bakeries, and powder plants, and employees were being paid for time spent changing uniforms, obtaining tools and materials, and traveling to work areas, in addition to regular working time. When the United States Supreme Court held[52] in 1946 that such activities were "hours worked" and refused later to rehear the case, the legal basis for portal-to-portal pay could no longer be questioned.

Employee law suits for back pay at overtime rates were instituted against employers in several areas, and management became genuinely alarmed when the United Automobile Workers, CIO, talked of suits against all automobile companies. The United Steel Workers also threatened suit for several hundred million dollars against steel companies.[53]

In 1947, Congress enacted the Portal-to-Portal Act designed to curtail the basis for portal-to-portal pay claims. The law, which was amended slightly in the 1949 Fair Labor Standards Act changes, was passed on the grounds that the Court holdings in this issue went beyond the intentions of the Act. The Portal-to-Portal Act stated that time spent in preliminary or postliminary activities or in travel to the work site cannot be considered as "hours worked" unless payment for these activities is the custom of the industry or is expressly agreed to in a collective agreement.

Regular rate of pay. If a covered employee regularly works a forty-hour week at a wage rate of $2 an hour, and one week works, say, five additional hours on Saturday, his weekly pay is easily established at $95.[54] But what if this worker is employed under a union agreement which specifies that work from 8:00 A.M. to 5:00 P.M. Monday through Friday and from 8:00 A.M. to noon on Saturday is to be paid at the "regular rate" of $2 an hour, but that work outside

[51] *Skidmore v. Swift and Company,* 323 U.S. 134 (1944); and *Tennessee Coal, Iron and R.R. Co. v. Muscoda Local,* 321 U.S. 590 (1944).
[52] *Anderson v. Mt. Clemens Pottery Co.,* 328 U.S. 680 (1946).
[53] *Business Week,* November 23, 1946, pp. 102–06.
[54] $[(40 \times \$2.00) + (5 \times \$3.00)]$

of these hours shall be paid at the "overtime" rate of one and one-half times the "regular rate," and he works thirty hours at the "regular rate," and fifteen hours at the "overtime rate"? Should his weekly pay be $105 or $110.70?[55]

OVERTIME ON OVERTIME. This was essentially the issue that arose between New York longshoremen and stevadoring companies, and which culminated in the famous Overtime-on-Overtime case.[56] In 1938 the Wage and Hour Administrator had ruled that premium payments under contracts could be credited towards the overtime required by the Act. But in the Bay Ridge case, the United States Supreme Court upset this position, holding that such premium pay for work outside of "regular hours" was not genuine overtime as required by law and, therefore, that such premium rates would have to be included in calculating the "regular rate" on which the overtime was based. It held that in order to compute overtime, the total weekly compensation must be divided by the number of hours worked. Therefore, in the above example the employee was owed $5.70.

Interestingly, the International Longshoremen's Association joined employer and government lawyers to oppose the workers' claims in this case, fearing that the Union would lose an advantageous contract clause. And immediately after the decision, a House subcommittee began work on a measure that would exempt employers from its effects. With the backing of employers (who, with good reason, were fearful of an avalanche of suits for back pay), trade unions, and the Wage and Hour Division, Congress enacted on July 20, 1949, the "overtime-on-overtime" law which permitted premium pay of 150 per cent to be excluded from the computation of regular rates. The 1949 amendments to the Fair Labor Standards Act expanded the overtime-on-overtime law—actually they repealed it and reenacted it in a broader form. The amendments forbade claims for overtime-on-overtime and permitted employers to include as overtime, premium pay for work outside the regular work day or week, if the premium is fixed by employment contract and is 150 per cent of the "regular rate" on other days.

BELO PLANS. When the Fair Labor Standards Act was passed in 1938, some employers—particularly those whose employees worked irregular hours—sought to make pay arrangements which would permit them to pay the same weekly wage as before the Act, despite

---

[55] [(30 × $2.00) + (15 × $3.00)] or [(40 × $2.33) + (5 × $3.50)]
[56] *Bay Ridge Operating Company v. Aaron*, 334 U.S. 446 (1948).

its overtime requirements. The arrangement of the A. H. Belo Corporation, Texas newspaper publishers, for a fixed hourly rate, time and one-half for hours over forty-four, and a weekly guarantee of $40 was challenged by the Wage and Hour Administrator. The Administrator contended that the $40 weekly minimum and the 67 cents an hour in the pay arrangement were inconsistent; that the weekly $40 guarantee was the only real weekly rate and that the "regular rate" of pay should be $40 divided by the number of hours worked each week. The United States Supreme Court disagreed with this interpretation and held[57] that since the plan specified a basic hourly rate and time and one-half for overtime and was mutually satisfactory to the contracting parties, it carried out the intention of Congress. Thus, "Belo plans" gained official status.

While Belo plans were especially attractive to employers whose employees had to work irregular hours, they provided an opportunity for abuse, and the United States Supreme Court struck down several purported Belo-type plans on the grounds that they were defeating the purposes of the Act.[58]

It became uncertain whether or not Belo-type plans were lawful. In the 1949 amendments, Belo plans were specifically authorized, but were limited to prevent possible abuse. Today an employee whose work requires irregular or fluctuating hours may be paid a regular weekly amount. But these contracts for a regular weekly wage must offer: (1) a wage equal to or better than the minimum wage; (2) time and one-half for all hours over forty; and (3) the guarantee must be limited to sixty hours.

GUARANTEED PAY PLANS. It will be recalled that in the original Act, union-negotiated annual pay plans had to provide an annual guarantee, but not in excess of 2,080 hours of work in fifty-two weeks to gain the overtime exemption. This rigid requirement was relaxed somewhat in the new 1949 law in the hope that it would make such plans more attractive to employers. Under the amended law, employers may now work employees up to an absolute limit of 2,240 hours without losing the exemption. Time worked during the hours of added flexibility (between 2,080 hours and 2,240 hours) simply requires overtime for hours worked beyond 2,080. Similarly, the twenty-six-week guarantee has a more flexible ceiling—1,040 hours rather than 1,000 hours. However, an annual guarantee plan must provide at least 1,840 hours of employment in order to qualify for eligibility; this is the minimum figure allowed.

[57] *Walling v. A. H. Belo Corporation*, 316 U.S. 624 (1942).
[58] See Riesenfeld and Maxwell, *op. cit.*, pp. 646–56.

Other Federal Standards Laws

Two additional federal measures regulate labor standards, and although their coverage is much smaller than that of the Fair Labor Standards Act, they are nonetheless important in their particular fields. The Davis-Bacon Act of 1931 (amended in 1936) and the Walsh-Healey Act of 1936 regulate firms doing business with the government; and both laws provide the means by which the government's purchasing policies can be used as leverage to protect labor standards.

THE DAVIS-BACON ACT

This law applies to public works contracts—government construction projects (construction and repair) which exceed $2,000. The law declares that it is government policy to pay to "mechanics and laborers employed directly upon the site of the work" the prevailing minimum wage rates for such work. Since construction work is performed at specific sites, the relevant prevailing wage rates are typically those of the local building trades in individual towns, sites, or civil subdivisions that are affected. By setting a wage floor, the law seeks to achieve two purposes: (1) to protect labor standards, and (2) to prevent unfair competition for government business by contractors who obtain such business by paying low wages.

The prevailing wage for a locality is determined by the Secretary of Labor in accordance with procedures outlined in the Act. Interested persons may obtain the prevailing wage rates for given localities at given times from the United States Department of Labor. A prevailing wage determination, however, does not necessarily mean that labor will be available at that rate. Thus in a recent case[59] when a contractor had to pay above the "prevailing wage" set by the Secretary of Labor, he was not entitled to recover the difference from the government.

The law is enforceable by termination of contract, by blacklisting the violators from government business, or by withholding amounts due.

THE WALSH-HEALEY ACT

Labor standards protection of the Walsh-Healey Act covers employees of firms ("regular dealers" or "manufacturers") supplying the federal government with new or used materials. It applies to manufacturing, assembling, and handling.

[59] See *Monthly Labor Review*, LXXVII, No. 5 (May, 1954), 558–59.

Executives, administrators, professional workers, office, custodial, and maintenance workers, as well as agricultural workers and farm producers are exempt from coverage. For covered firms, the law stipulates standards in five areas: it prohibits child labor (males under sixteen and females under eighteen cannot be employed); it prohibits prison labor; it specifies certain safety and health standards; it sets minimum wages as specified by the Secretary of Labor; and it requires overtime at the rate of one and one-half times the basic rate for more than eight hours a day or forty hours per week.

Administration of the law is assigned to the Wage and Hour and Public Contracts Division. Among the tasks of administration are the granting of exemptions, making final decisions on violations, rulings and interpretations, determining questions of who is a "manufacturer" or "regular dealer." The task of determining minimum wages is the most important of the provisions of the law.

The law provides that ". . . all persons . . . will be paid . . . not less than the minimum wages determined by the Secretary of Labor to be the prevailing minimum wages for persons employed in similar work or in the particular or similar industries or groups of industries currently operating in the locality in which the materials are to be manufactured."

These minimum wages are set after investigation of the industry, consultation with industry and labor officials, and public hearings. In many cases such hearings produce substantial agreement and the rate is agreed upon. The minimum wage determinations of the Secretary of Labor are published in the annual reports of the Director of the Wage and Hour and Public Contracts Administration. They show the industry covered, the date of the ruling, the rate, and the employees covered.[60]

In setting the minimum wage, the Secretary has taken the position that in industries like cement and steel where long-distance shipment is too expensive, the government may permit different minimum wage rates for different localities without doing damage to one of the major goals of the Act—namely, the prevention of unfair competition for government business by business firms who get the contracts because they pay lower wages than do competitors.

In industries where distribution costs are smaller and where slight labor cost differentials may make considerable differences in the ability to win contracts, the Secretary has sought to prevent wage differences between localities. This has meant the protection

[60] U. S. Department of Labor, Wage and Hour and Public Contracts Division. *Annual Report* (Washington, D. C.: U. S. Government Printing Office, 1953), pp. 66–69.

of unionized and high-wage bidders in some cases. It was impossible to appeal the Secretary's ruling until 1952, when the law was amended to permit such appeals to the Courts. The Walsh-Healey Act promptly received its most important challenge since its enactment on the question of what, precisely, is a "locality."

In 1953 the Secretary of Labor fixed a $1-an-hour minimum wage for the cotton, silk, and synthetic branches of the textile industry for government contract work. Some 158 textile companies in the South and in the New England areas joined in suit, challenging this action on the grounds that the Walsh-Healey Act gave power to fix wages only for a geographic locality, and therefore could not on an industrywide basis.

On December 1, 1955, the U. S. Court of Appeals ruled in *Mitchell v. Covington Mills*[61] that the federal government has the authority to set minimum wages on a nationwide basis in industries working on government contracts. To do otherwise, said the Court, would "freeze the competitive advantage of concerns that operate in low-wage communities and would in effect offer a reward for moving into such communities."[62] On March 26, 1956, the United States Supreme Court refused to review this decision. Today the power of the Secretary of Labor to set industrywide minimum wages is established.[63] The economic problems in such wage determination are discussed in Chapter 17. This ruling will undoubtedly affect the outcome of similar cases which have been filed against the Secretary of Labor by wool manufacturers and soft coal mine operators on the same grounds.

The law is enforceable by government suit for violations and by blacklisting.

Summary

At the time the Fair Labor Standards Act was passed, its comprehensive and far-reaching extension of government authority into working conditions was viewed with some apprehension. For although it was an extension of a century-old state movement for improved labor standards legislation, its child labor and wage and hour provisions set standards well above existing state standards. And subsequent amendments have tended to increase this gap.

Yet all available data seem to indicate that the Fair Labor Standards Act and its companion legislation—the Davis-Bacon and

---

[61] Discussed in *Monthly Labor Review, LXXIX,* No. 3 (March, 1956), 325.

[62] *The New York Times,* December 2, 1955, p. 6.

[63] *Wall Street Journal,* March 27, 1956, p. 3.

Walsh-Healey Acts—have had but negligible impacts on employment, prices, and profits.

Today there is widespread support for extension of the Fair Labor Standards Act's coverage to groups which are still not protected. In all likelihood, this extension will be the next amendment to this important piece of legislation.

Suggestions for Additional Reading

Law and Contemporary Problems, VI, No. 3 (Summer, 1939).
    The entire Number of this Duke University law publication is devoted to articles interpreting the original Fair Labor Standards Act.

RIESENFELD, STEFAN A., and RICHARD C. MAXWELL. *Modern Social Legislation.* Brooklyn: The Foundation Press, 1950. Pp. 585–655.
    A concise discussion of the history of wage and hour regulation, together with a legal presentation of questions of coverage, benefits, and administration of the Fair Labor Standards Act. (Includes 1949 amendments.)

U. S. CONGRESS, 84TH, 1ST, SESSION, SENATE, HEARINGS BEFORE THE COMMITTEE ON LABOR AND PUBLIC WELFARE, SUBCOMMITTEE ON LABOR. *Amending the Fair Labor Standards Act of 1938.* Washington, D. C.: U. S. Government Printing Office, 1955. 3 parts.
    These hearings on the 1955 amendments to the Fair Labor Standards Act contain several original studies of the Act prepared by the Bureau of Labor Statistics for use of the Committee.

U. S. DEPARTMENT OF LABOR, WAGE AND HOUR AND PUBLIC CONTRACTS DIVISION. *Results of the Minimum Wage Increase of 1950: Economic Effects in Selected Low-Wage Industries and Establishments.* Washington, D. C.: U. S. Government Printing Office, 1954.
    Report of an extensive study of the economic impact of increasing the mimimum wage from 40 to 75 cents an hour.

U. S. DEPARTMENT OF LABOR, WAGE AND HOUR AND PUBLIC CONTRACTS DIVISION. *Annual Report.* Washington, D. C.: U. S. Government Printing Office, 1955.
    The annual reports of the Division are the original sources of operating data for the Fair Labor Standards Act, the Davis-Bacon and Walsh-Healey Acts. They also present background discussion of the laws and comment on their amendments and Court interpretation.

17

Economic Issues in
Substandard Conditions

Introduction

As has been noted in the previous two chapters, the problems of substandard conditions do not exist apart from the realities of labor market operation. Nor do the remedies, realized or proposed. Rather, problems and remedies are both embedded in a changing economic and social framework. A summary of the issues involved follows:

First, society expects a certain minimum performance from its economic institutions. Failure to achieve this level of performance may create economic insecurity.

Second, in western capitalistic countries, the marketing mechanism—the labor market—has been the chief economic institution by means of which wages, hours, and working conditions have been "determined."

Third, since at least the early part of the nineteenth century in England, and later in this country, society has felt that the marketing mechanism has malfunctioned in part or at times, and has not met minimal performance levels. In some cases, society also has held that the marketing mechanism was not designed (or expected) to perform in certain ways.

Fourth, two schools of thought exist on the subject of remedies for these problems. The first generally maintains that interferences with the marketing mechanism are undesirable and likely to be self-defeating (that there are, in effect, "economic laws" with which society should not tamper). Those groups opposing minimum wages fall in this category. The second school holds that society can beneficially intervene and can improve substandard conditions, and that such intervention can take the form of various economic security programs.

Fifth, society has (using the United States now as the example) tended to follow the second school of thought, increasingly so in the twentieth century.

And, lastly, our task in this chapter is to look at the way in which society has intervened in substandard conditions and, using the materials developed in the last two chapters, ask the questions: What are the economic issues in, and the implications of, intervention as a type of economic security program? We shall analyze three topics, treating them in the following order: working conditions, hours, wages. While common threads run through all three, there are enough differences to warrant separate discussion.

Working Conditions

Defined rigorously, working conditions involve the work an employee performs and the environment in which it is done. But the term has come to be applied also to *who* may do the work. In turn, government intervention has been of two types. First is the positive regulation of the work environment: requiring that minimal specifications be met. Second is the negative regulation of the work force: deciding what groups will be excluded from labor force participation and under what circumstances.

REGULATION OF LABOR SUPPLY

The latter topic, "regulation of the labor force," is easier to handle analytically, and we will discuss it first. The basis for this type of regulation is more a matter of social welfare than it is of economics. If society concludes that it is to its best interest to prohibit, say, children under twelve from working at all or children under sixteen from working in mines, the grounds for such a conclusion rest upon concern for the mental, moral, and physical well-being of the young.

Such regulation, however, is not directly imposed upon one or more of the "resultants" (wages, hours, working conditions) of the operation of the marketing mechanism. Rather, it is imposed upon one of the causal forces involved in producing these resultants, in this case labor supply. It is doubtful that economists, when speaking about the self-adjusting characteristics of marketing mechanisms, specified any minimum qualifications for labor force participation and hence for labor supply. The market would adjust to whatever supply existed, but the existing supply was looked upon as a cultural-social, rather than as an economic factor. If this were the case, then society might be interested, for reasons noted above, in specifying those individuals and groups who might not be part of the labor supply. As society applied such regulation, it invariably involved curtailing the supply: society was more rigorous than was the market.

The economic effect of this type of intervention expresses itself through a reduction of labor supply which therefore shifts the short-run supply-curve to the left, and in so doing increases the price of labor. But in a dynamic economy, such government regulation tends to become intertwined with other economic and social changes. Hence it is doubtful if succeeding generations in the economy are aware of what dimensions the supply curve of labor would have had, had the old system persisted and had society not curtailed labor force participation for certain groups.

The long-run economic effects may, however, be quite different. By such intervention with respect to, say, child labor, the future physical condition of the youth of the nation may be improved and hence the future supply curve of labor may be to the right of what it otherwise might have been.

An analogy from athletics may be appropriate to this whole train of discussion. Disregarding obvious differences, both athletic games and economic pursuits are played under a framework of rules. In the interest of the participants in the game (players, schools, clubs) rules may be imposed and may be changed. However, institution of, and changes in, rules may occur in both the areas discussed in the opening paragraph on working conditions. Thus the athletic "labor supply" may be regulated, as in cases where freshmen are prohibited from engaging in varsity competition. Or the "working environment" itself may be subject to rules and rules changes. In football, for example, the flying-wedge was abolished—this is in the interest of reducing the number of deaths the game produced, and with long-run advantages thereto. So in economic games, the rules may be changed in what society deems is its best interest.

Interestingly enough, opposition to government intervention of this type has not been entirely a matter of the economics of short-run increases in costs. Legal and social considerations also have been important. Although these latter arguments may have been mere rationalizations of a real concern over increased costs, employers and others have contended strongly that denial of freedom of contract was at the root of their opposition. Likewise there were oft-repeated moralistic beliefs that "idleness breeds mischief" and that to prevent children and women from working was to put them into the hands of the devil.[1]

Regulation of this type represents the earliest governmental intervention in substandard conditions. In the United States it can be traced back to the first half of the nineteenth century. By now it has become an accepted part of government control of economic activity. And, it is difficult to say that such intervention has detrimental long-run economic implications. There is essentially nothing that can be self-defeating in such regulation. Society has, in the larger interest, simply set up a different framework of rules. Moreover such intervention may actually be beneficial, in that future labor supplies are more productive than they otherwise would have been.

But, as was noted in Chapter 15, in conjunction with the discussion on protective labor legislation for women, one qualification needs to be made. All protective labor legislation need not necessarily arise for altruistic social reasons: it may also result from the efforts of various pressure groups to restrict labor-supply competition. Here social rules-making becomes tinged with monopolistic practices. The student should be aware of this in his study of such labor legislation.

REGULATION OF THE WORKING ENVIRONMENT

Government regulation of the work environment imposes a minimal performance requirement upon the employer. Instead of "negative" behavior, of refraining from hiring child labor, he is obligated to positive action, that of maintaining his workplace in accordance with legal specifications. The immediate consequences of increased costs may be the same under both types of regulation, but the routes through which they are reached are different.

The basis for government intervention of this type is the same as that involved in regulating labor supply. The psychological and physical well-being of employees requires certain standards of ventilation, lighting, sanitation, and materials handling. There is no guarantee that the market will provide such standards. Hence government action may be necessary.

There are several important differences, however, between this case and that previously discussed. Thus, while labor supply is a

---

[1] For an interesting contemporary statement, see William G. Long, "Let's Allow Our Teen-Agers to Work," *Reader's Digest*, LXVIII, No. 405 (January, 1956), 71–74.

determinant in market action, the work environment is much more a resultant. As was noted in the last section, it is not necessarily a function of the market to regulate participation in the labor force. But, conversely, the market may both compensate for inherent job differences and regulate the work environment. This the market may do in two ways.

First, it may *regulate*, by "forcing" continuous employer readjustments in the working environment so that it becomes equalized among establishments. For example, if the working conditions of employer "A" are substantially below a competitor's, he may have difficulty in retaining his present work force or in attracting new employees. This will "force" a change in the resultant, in employer "A's," and hence, the total working environment.

Second, the market may *compensate* for differences in the inherent characteristics of jobs (including a work environment component) by means of wage differences. If the market does not necessarily *regulate* job content, some economists have held that it *reflects* innate differences in the agreeableness of jobs through differences in wages.[2] Thus the marketing mechanism is at least presumed to be "aware" of job differences.

There are, however, two realistic limitations to the above notions of readjustment. First, wage differentials may not, in fact, compensate for the innate differences in jobs. Certainly penalty rates exist for extra dirty or hazardous tasks. But economists from Senior's day on have stressed that the market does not always evaluate job differences as one might expect it would.[3] We have commented upon this matter in earlier sections of this book. Second, there is no necessary guarantee that "continuous employer working condition readjustments" will be upward (that they will be improvements). Moreover, even if the adjustment is upward, there is no certainty that the final equilibrium will be at a minimally acceptable level, however this be defined by society.

Social attitudes, and hence actions in this area, have been of two types. First, society has not sought to correct the malfunctioning of the market (where it has malfunctioned) by adjusting wage rates and job content. Wage administration of this type involves incredibly difficult ethical, economic, and administrative problems. It is our judgment that this is not a proper function for the state;

---

[2] See, for example, Nassau William Senior and his discussion of Adam Smith in *An Outline of the Science of Political Economy* (New York: Farrar and Rinehart, 1939), pp. 200–04.

[3] See, for example, E. H. Phelps Brown's review of "The Social Foundations of Wage Policy" (by Barbara Wooton) in *Economica*, New Series, XXII (November, 1955), 349–54. See also the discussion in Chapters 7 and 9 of this volume.

we feel that the government should not administratively attempt to set wages so as to reflect innate differences in the agreeability or disagreeability of jobs. Our feeling is that market malfunctioning in this respect would be far and away the lesser of two undesirable states of affairs.

But, second and conversely, the government has in many cases specified minimal work conditions: safety, sanitation, space, ventilation, and comfort requirements such as seating arrangements for female employees. The government, in fact, has acted thus, since the market did not guarantee what society felt were minimally acceptable conditions. The preventive rather than the curative route was followed; society did not accept the view that any type of working environment was satisfactory, provided wage rates (whether set by the market or the government) reflected working condition differences.

In requiring that the employer conform to minimum specifications, the government imposes a "continuous" performance requirement upon him. Such performance customarily involves an increase in expenses, which in turn increases the cost of employing labor. (This is why, for example, an employer may be reluctant to hire women, since the overhead cost of providing minimal working conditions for them may be higher than for men.) Depending upon the ease of substituting other factors of production for labor, there may be a short-run reduction in employment. The long-run impact may be the opposite; the increased well-being of the work force may result in increased productivity more than enough to offset the cost increases. There is a limit, however, to this process; for no matter how greatly working conditions are improved, the employee's output can only approach a physical maximum.

Even if the employer's long-run costs are increased (assuming not all the burden is passed back to the employee or forward to the consumer), a good case still can be made for this social approach. Substandard working conditions are likely to have undesirable mental and physical impacts upon groups in the work force. At a later date it may be necessary for the state to care for these groups: they become an overhead cost to society. Hence it may be not only economical but also more socially desirable to use the preventive rather than the curative approach. The analogy with unemployment and workmen's compensation is clear.

In summary, society demands a certain minimal performance from its economic institutions. If the marketing mechanism, as such an institution, does not meet this performance level (or if it was not designed for such a purpose), intervention by the state may be required. It is hard to see how intervention can be self-defeating in the case of working conditions, for in the long run no one is made worse off, while many may be better off. And even if it could be shown in some way that the output of goods and services was reduced by intervention, it would be a healthy rather than an ailing society that would have the opportunity of consuming them.[4]

Hours of Work

Hours of work, like working conditions, are neither necessarily nor uniquely determined by or with a given wage rate.[5] Hours cannot be changed readily by the unilateral action (or individual bargaining) of individual employees demanding certain hours or working conditions with a given wage rate. Rather, changes are likely to occur as a result of collective action at various levels: the firm, the area, the industry, the economy.

Government intervention on hours has been both preventive and punitive. In the first case, certain classes of employees are prevented (through absolute limits) from working over a given number of hours per given time unit. In the second case, the employee may work more than the specified maximum, but only if he is paid penalty rates. Here the first case is the easier to analyze, and we shall examine it first.

PREVENTIVE REGULATION

The case for preventive regulation is based upon two factors which vary in different situations: (1) the well-being of the employee and/or (2) the well-being and safety of the clientele using the services of the employee. The case involving the well-being of the employee himself is analogous to that discussed in the previous section on working conditions, and it need not be reanalyzed here.

The second situation requires, however, a slightly different type of treatment. Here it is the well-being of the consuming public which is the basis for government intervention. In the rendering of certain services, of which public transportation is the best example, the safety (and the life) of the consumer is entrusted to an employee or an employee group. In rendering the service, the em-

---

[4] For a brief but interesting account of the rise of such social regulation in England, see A. P. Usher, *An Introduction to the Industrial History of England* (Boston: Houghton Mifflin Co., 1920), particularly chap. xvi, "The Protection of Health and Welfare by the State."

[5] K. W. Rothschild, *The Theory of Wages* (New York: The Macmillan Co., 1954), chap. iv.

ployee must maintain a basic performance level so that the customer is not endangered. Such performance entails a minimum physical well-being which, in turn, requires that "proper" rest be obtained. Conversely, such rest is presumed to be obtainable only if the employee does not work more than a given maximum number of hours in one stretch, or if he has "proper" rest pauses.

Under the pressure of product market competition for business, there is no necessary guarantee that the market will limit maximum hours to this "safe" number, as has been noted in Chapter 15. Hence, society has imposed arbitrary hour restrictions for such groups as locomotive engineers, airline pilots, and bus drivers. While these limits are frequently higher than the actual work day, they may become effective in critical cases. Further, while there are obvious individual differences between employees as to their fatigue "thresholds," society has set down blanket restrictions, in the interest of administrative simplicity.

It is impossible to argue against such regulations. One might be disposed to question the specific maxima in a given case, but the over-all sensibility of this approach has been proved by time and experience. In one respect there is no economic basis upon which one can argue pro or con. One cannot say that such regulations are self-defeating; there is nothing about which to be self-defeating. One can merely note that society has changed certain phases of market operation, in the interest of the health and safety of the consumer.

PUNITIVE REGULATION

Punitive pay regulations had their inception in a lump-of-labor-spread-the-work philosophy. If there was only so much work available at a given time, it was viewed as ethically undesirable to permit some employees to get more than their "share" of it. In the past three decades, an "ethical" share has been most commonly viewed as that done in an eight-hour day or a forty-hour week. If more work than this is available, it should be given to those not receiving their share. To put pressure on the employer to ration out available work, various government regulations require that he pay premium rates (as time-and-one-half) for hours worked over the maximum. This, in turn, would presumably lead him to hire additional help at regular rates and thus to increase employment (and reduce unemployment in the case at hand).

A second basis for punitive wages has become increasingly important, primarily in rates negotiated by employers and unions. This is the "normal life" concept. The employees is presumed to wish to lead a life which, in terms of his work schedule, conforms to the general pattern. Hence, if the employer wishes him to work overtime, or more particularly in this case, Saturdays, Sundays, holidays, or odd hours, the employee should receive premium pay.[6] Here the emphasis is not upon work-sharing; it is rather on pressuring the employer to schedule his work in accord with current work-leisure patterns.

It is difficult to find a basis for judging such punitive wage payments as self-defeating, although there may be certain negative impacts. A number of interesting implications are, however, developed.

First, such requirements reduce employer flexibility in work scheduling. If the business enterprise is on "cost-plus" contracts from a government agency, overtime payments may not be significant. But in competitive situations the opposite may be true, although overtime may indicate a "good" state of business and may more than pay for itself. In the competive case the employer may try to "cut down" on work done rather than provide overtime, let alone hire extra help.[7] Moreover, there are many situations in which it is more logical to pay overtime than to hire extra help. Hiring and separating additional help is not a cost-free process. Therefore, until the employer is convinced that additional business is permanent, it may be preferable to pay overtime. (Two incidental problems are frequently presented to the employer through the use of overtime. Thus, employees working overtime may find their total take-home cut when overtime is curtailed. They may then press for "maintenance of take-home in the face of a reduction in hours." Again, administering overtime in the plant and "distributing it equitably" is frequently a complicated problem for the employer.)

Second, overtime pay presents problems to the economy-at-large. Thus, in times of full employment when additional output is necessary, it may be forthcoming only at a premium. Such a situation adds fuel to the flames of inflation, or at least makes administrative problems in checking inflation much more difficult.

Third, overtime pay provisions pose interesting questions for wage theory. While overtime pay does not necessarily weaken the logic of marginal productivity theory, it makes for difficulties in its application.[8]

---

[6] The steel negotiations of mid-1956 strikingly illustrate this development.

[7] One of the authors was a participant in such a case. In a work experience in which he was involved and in which Saturday work was sometimes done, the "word went out" after the passage of the Fair Labor Standards Act: "No more Saturday work." Not only was no extra help added, but hours for existing employees were cut.

[8] For an analysis see Richard A. Lester, *Economics of Labor* (New York: The Macmillan Co., 1941), pp. 199–202.

A Note on the Shorter Work Week

What if the statutory punitive maximum work week were lowered from forty to, say, thirty hours per week? Under employment conditions of the last fifteen years, it is not likely that such a move would be undertaken for work-sharing purposes (though it is a method through which adjustments could be made to the possible impacts of automation).

If such a decision were made, given recent employment experience, it is likely to be a reflection of public sentiment that gains in productivity should, in part, be realized through a reduction in working hours. It is our belief that such a decision is best made by employees themselves (or employers and unions) rather than by state edict. Hence, we would not be disposed to suggest further governmental intervention in this respect. The various problems involving the cultural, economic, and social consequences of such a reduction in hours have been analyzed extensively elsewhere and need not be treated here.[9]

Wages

Government intervention in substandard wages has been more recent and has provoked more controversy than has either regulation of working conditions or hours. In part, businessmen have joined the controversy because wages have a money dimension easily recognizable, because the impacts of an increase in wages are readily perceived in cost terms, and because wage changes have important economic implications. In part, economists have been much more vocal about the wage question because ethically and logically it is more readily grappled with. Labor leaders, politicians, administrators, and others have contributed to the debate.

Economic analysis on minimum wages falls into three categories: first, arguments against wage-setting; second, arguments for wage-setting; and third empirical studies of the impacts of minimum wages. After an introductory comment, we shall examine each of these categories and then conclude with a number of evaluatory comments.

[9] For a general discussion, see Harry A. Millis and Royal E. Montgomery, *Labor's Progress and Some Basic Problems* (Vol. I of *Economics of Labor;* [New York: McGraw-Hill Book Co., Inc., 1938]), chap. ix. For a useful summary on hours and productivity, see Max D. Kossoris, "The Facts about Hours of Work *vs.* Output," *Factory Management and Maintenance,* CIX, No. 2 (February, 1951), 68–73. For a discussion of the "coming shorter work week" see Daniel Seligman, "The Four-Day Week: How Soon?" *Fortune,* L, No. 1 (July, 1954), 81–83; 114–18.

The Basis for Minimum Wage Setting

In the broadest sense, the basis for setting minimum wages rests upon a belief that the marketing mechanism has malfunctioned. Malfunctioning may occur in two ways which may, but need not necessarily, be connected.

First, the market may not operate in such a way as to provide a "living wage" for those who supply labor services. This failure has important economic and ethical implications: economic in that an institution does not perform optimally; ethical in that the wage earner may be forced into degrading situations of various types. The latter argument is found particularly in the case of minimum wages for women. "Elimination of poverty" is the phrase sometimes used in conjunction with this type of wage-raising legislation.

Second, the employer, deliberately or otherwise, may exploit the worker in the sense of paying him less than "his due." Minimum wage regulation may, therefore, be applied to reduce the degree of employer control in the labor market, and hence to reduce exploitation. In summary, poverty and exploitation are the two major themes most commonly encountered in minimum wage arguments.

The Contemporary Case Against Minimum Wage Regulation

While well-developed positions against minimum wages can be found in the writings of such earlier twentieth-century American economists as John Bates Clark and F. W. Taussig, the most illuminating recent argumentation has been developed by George J. Stigler.[10]

While aggregative effects of minimum wage setting are considered (particularly by Stigler), the general emphasis of this group of economists is upon the economics of the individual firm. Both competitive and noncompetitive cases are analyzed. Two basic assumptions, whether explicitly stated or implicitly introduced, are important for the argumentation. The first is that the firm follows marginal principles in its profit maximizing efforts. The second is that restrictions are placed upon discontinuities in both demand and cost functions.

Given these assumptions, the argument can be presented simply. We shall use a graphic rather than arithmetic method, but the logic is the same in either case.

---

[10] George J. Stigler, "The Economics of Minimum Wage Legislation," *American Economic Review*, XXXVI, No. 3 (June, 1946), 358–65. See also R. G. Hawtrey, *Cross Purposes in Wage Policy* (New York: Longmans, Green and Co., 1955), pp. 87–88, 91–95, 124–25.

Let us take the competitive case first.

Using Figure 17.1, assume the employer purchases his labor in a competitive labor market. In such a case the supply of labor to him will be perfectly elastic, and average outlay, AO, and marginal outlay, MO, will be the same. D is the demand curve for labor (value of the marginal product or marginal value product, whichever is lower). In the case at hand, given at wage of W_1, the employer will hire Q_1 units of labor.[11]

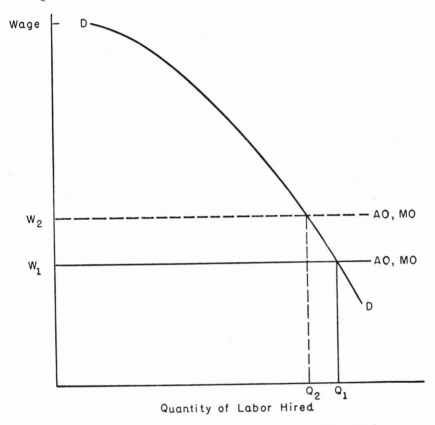

Fig. 17.1. *Quantity of Labor Hired in a Competitive Labor Market.*

Assume now the state sets a minimum wage of W_2. Under such conditions, employment will decrease from Q_1 to Q_2; this consequence is inevitable in the nature of the situation. Who becomes unemployed? Those who are the less efficient, whose services are

[11] For an excellent analysis of the application of marginalism in such cases, see R. L. Bishop, "Cost Discontinuities, Declining Costs, and Marginal Analysis," *American Economic Review,* XXXVIII, No. 4 (September, 1948), 607–17.

less than the minimum wage. Hence, unless one does not view a decrease in employment as undesirable, the imposition of a minimum wage is self-defeating.

Is there any way out of this dilemma? A number of alternatives present themselves, all of which are based upon increases in labor productivity to offset the higher wage. First, the workers themselves may become more efficient or work harder. Second, employers may introduce previously unprofitable techniques or they may be "shocked out of lethargy" to become more efficient. (If one assumes a given demand for goods and services, such adjustments may also be self-defeating in that *fewer* workers are needed if they become more efficient.)

It is Stigler's contention, however, that neither of these means is likely to provide much of a counter-force to the unemployment impacts of the minimum wage. He notes in particular that the shock theory seems inapplicable to low-wage paying industries, where the impact of the regulation is the greatest.

In the case of employer control (monopsony) in the labor market, a skillfully set minimum wage may increase both wages and employment. Figure 17.2 illustrates this.

Under monopsony, the supply curve of labor to the employer is not a horizontal line, but positively sloped. Marginal and average outlays diverge. Using the logic of marginalism, the employer will hire labor to the point where the demand and marginal outlay curves are equated (point one). The wage paid will be W_1 (point two); the employer moves down from the marginal to the average curve.[12]

Assume again that the state sets a minimum wage. The supply curve now becomes a horizontal line for its effective length, and average and marginal outlays again coincide. A minimum, W_2, set just above the going wage would maximize the possible increase in employment. At W_3 the maximum has been reached; up to that point an increase in wages will also result in an increase in employment. At a wage higher than W_3, employment would fall to less than what it was under the nonregulated market.

Stigler is not very optimistic, however, about the possibilities of administratively setting wages so as to achieve the results desired. Because of diversities of conditions among occupations and firms, and because of variations through time, he feels a uniform

---

[12] This involves one species of "exploitation." The student might wish to (1) think about the logic of this variant and (2) ask himself what other types of exploitation might be found.

national minimum is unsuitable. Conversely, there is no reasonably accurate method to derive such demand and supply schedules, and hence administratively setting different rates for different conditions would be an incredibly difficult if not impossible job.[13]

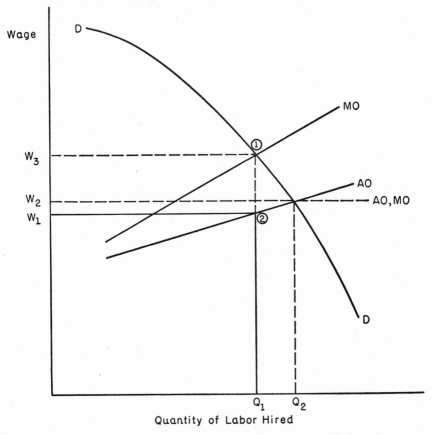

Fig. 17.2. *Quantity of Labor Hired in an Employer-Controlled Market.*

On the question of the aggregate employment effects of a minimum wage, Stigler feels that "the net effects of the minimum wage . . . are adverse." The higher the minimum wage, the greater will be the number of covered workers who will be discharged.

[13] A "Kinky" demand curve creates a discontinuity within which wages may move appreciably with no change in the level of employment. Again, however, there are incredibly difficult problems involved in setting minimum wages in such cases. See Paul M. Sweezy, "Demand Under Conditions of Oligopoly," *Journal of Political Economy*, XLVII, No. 4 (August, 1939), 568–73; and Raymond F. Mikesell, "Oligopoly and the Short-Run Demand For Labor," *Quarterly Journal of Economics*, LV, No. 1 (November, 1940), 166.

Thus, considering both the economy and the firm, the minimum wage is held to be an undesirable type of state intervention. To reduce poverty, Stigler feels that there are other, more desirable means, such as granting assistance to the poor with regard to their need. To reduce employer exploitation, Stigler would remove the condition of labor immobility which gives rise to it. This can be done, he suggests, by increasing employment information, by vocational training, and by loans to cover moving costs. These, he feels, are more rational procedures to achieve the purposes that the minimum wage is not capable of accomplishing.

The Contemporary Case for Minimum Wage Regulation

The leading spokesman against the previously noted position has been Richard A. Lester, whose criticisms have been directed not only against conventional minimum wage doctrines but also against the whole body of marginalism.[14]

Lester's minimum-wage criticisms can be summed up under three major headings: that the economists typified by Stigler have an inadequate understanding of first, labor market operation, including wage determination therein; second, policies and functioning of management in manufacturing concerns; and third, the economic effects of minimum-wage fixing as observed in practice.

Labor markets, contends Lester, are not like commodity markets, in large measure because of a complex of job factors, and because psychological, social, and institutional (union) pressures are absent in the latter type of market. Hence, demand, supply, and price considerations are considerably tempered in labor markets. Unlike a reduction in commodity purchases, a reduction in the work force of an employer frequently involves significant costs: separation costs, adverse effects upon morale, transfers, increases in unemployment tax rates. Conversely, a firm may increase its wage level for various nonmarket reasons. Moreover, in the labor market itself, Lester contends that it is simply not the case that each worker receives the value of his marginal product under competition. Hence, there is frequently a range within which wages can move without any damaging effects. Finally, institutional rules in the labor market (such as seniority) may make it impossible for the employer to separate the least efficient employees if a minimum wage is introduced.

[14] See particularly R. A. Lester, "Shortcomings of Marginal Analysis for Wage-Employment Problems," *American Economic Review*, XXXVI, No. 1 (March, 1946), 63–82; and "Marginalism and Labor Markets" (including rejoinders by Fritz Machlup and G. J. Stigler), *American Economic Review*, XXXVII, No. 1 (March, 1947), 135–57.

The view on managerial policies and actions is also criticized by Lester. It is his contention that employers do not react to an increase in wages in the way Stigler says they would—namely, through a reduction in labor employed. Lester asks first how a minimum wage is supposed to lead to a curtailed output and the "discharge of a large number of workers." Through increased prices? On the basis of marginalist reasoning, Lester holds this unlikely. Through the substitution of machinery for labor? In the short-run there may be fixed coefficients and the possibility of substitution is small. Through cut-backs in production? But costs increase in the general case under such conditions, and if a firm is wedded to a given sales volume, this is unlikely. Conversely, Lester holds that "better management" is an adjustment technique that has been widely used to counteract increased wage scales due to unionism or government intervention.

Finally, Lester contends that the empirical evidence simply does not substitute the position of these economists. As we shall discuss this in detail in the next section, it will not be necessary to enlarge upon the matter here.

In summary, Lester contends that "marginalism has become suspect" for both pecuniary and nonpecuniary reasons. Therefore, its applicability to minimum wage issues is also suspect, and on this basis Lester contends that it should not be used as a tool to assess the impact of government intervention in substandard wage conditions.

EMPIRICAL STUDIES ON THE IMPACTS OF MINIMUM WAGES

A number of empirical studies have sought to assess the impacts of minimum wages. These studies all have been on the national level; we have had relatively few recent inquiries into the impacts of state laws.[15] (It is our conjecture that state minimum-wage laws affecting women have "caused" little if any unemployment. Such laws tend to "lag" wage changes and hence one would assume their impacts to be limited.) While several of these broader empirical studies have involved theoretical considerations, the majority have focused upon reporting "what has happened." Hence we include them in this section.[16]

[15] See Miriam Civic, "State Minimum Wage Laws in Action," *The Conference Board Business Record,* VII, No. 11 (November, 1950), 440–44.

[16] For a useful critique of minimum wage studies as well as suggestions to make them more meaningful, see Jean A. Wells, "An Appraisal of Studies of Minimum Wage Legislation," *I L Research,* II, No. 1 (December, 1955), 9–12.

The studies can be divided into three classes, contingent upon the statutory minimum wage in force.

The period 1938–1950. This is the period in which the 40-cent minimum was reached early and then maintained until 1950. Some four principal empirical inquiries have been reported upon for this period, none of them dating later than 1941–1942.[17]

Harry M. Douty, reporting on the seamless hosiery industry, notes that the establishment of a wage minimum of 32.5 cents an hour had an appreciable effect upon the industry's wage structure. Almost half the workers in the industry were directly affected by the wage order. Yet, Douty concludes that there is no evidence to show that the minimum wage resulted in the dislocation of employment through plant failures. There was some transfer of employment from low-wage to high-wage firms. But available data do not indicate that the total volume of employment was materially affected. Douty is of the opinion that managerial performance was stimulated and improved.[18]

Robert J. Myers and Odis C. Clark reach somewhat similar conclusions for the cotton garment industry.[19] Few displacements resulted from the introduction of the 30-cent and the 32.5-cent minimum rates in the cotton garment industry in 1939 and 1940, and most of the separated workers experienced little hardship in occupational readjustment. (The Myers-Clark analysis focuses upon workers in those firms existent at both the beginning and terminal dates of the study. Hence, the analysis does not reveal anything about possible unemployment arising from firms which went out of business. But within this limitation the inquiry does not indicate any serious unemployment impacts of the minimum wage.)

John F. Moloney holds that the minimum wage has tended toward some reduction in employment in southern industries, but this has been more than offset by a rising volume of production.[20] Moloney further notes that the Act has encouraged better management practices and the installation of labor-saving equipment. He

[17] The student should ask himself why no studies were made on the impact of the minimum wage during the period, say, 1942–1950.

[18] See Harry M. Douty, "Minimum Wage Regulation in the Seamless Hosiery Industry," *Southern Economic Journal*, VIII, No. 11 (October, 1941), 176–90. See also A. F. Hinrichs, "Effects of the 25-Cent Minimum Wage on Employment in the Seamless Hosiery Industry," *Journal of the American Statistical Association*, XXXV, No. 209, Part 1 (March, 1940).

[19] Robert J. Myers and Odis C. Clark, "Effects of a Minimum Wage in the Cotton Garment Industry, 1939–1941," *Monthly Labor Review*, LIV, No. 2 (February, 1942), 318–37.

[20] John F. Moloney, "Some Effects of the Federal Fair Labor Standards Act upon Southern Industry," *Southern Economic Journal*, IX, No. 1 (July, 1942), 15–23.

feels, however, that the full impact of the law will not be realized until the volume of production again declines.

Other commentary runs in the same vein as the above. Herbert R. Northrup, in a useful survey article, summarizes the experiences of a number of industries and concludes that minimum wages did not produce the dire results expected, in no small part because of the impact of other employment-increasing forces.[21] Lloyd Reynolds notes that the only large group of workers displaced were several thousand pecan shellers who had been receiving as little as 8 cents per hour, and who were replaced by machinery.[22]

Do these studies indicate that the unemployment impact of a minimum wage is greatly exaggerated and hence not to be feared? The studies hardly indicate that. The basic reason, of course, is that the Act never had a chance to be tested under static conditions. The wage minima were hardly introduced when a rearmament and then a war economy gave a tremendous impetus to production and employment. Inflationary pressures subsequently wiped out any meaning that could be attached to a 40-cent minimum. Hence from 1941–1942 on, the minima had no real meaning, and this was true even in the periods of unemployment following World War II.

The period 1950–1956. With the 40-cent minimum all but meaningless after World War II, pressures arose to have it increased. The change was finally made and became effective January 29, 1950, with the minimum increased to 75 cents an hour. A number of studies have been made for this period; again, however, their usefulness is limited by the post-June, 1950, course of history, and by subsequent "full-employment" and inflationary movements. The period is a small-scale replica of 1938–1950.[23] A Department of Labor study summarizes the impacts of the 75-cent minimum thus:

Though causing significant payroll increases, the 75-cent rate had only very minor determinable effects on employment and other non-wage variables in the five low-wage manufacturing industries surveyed. [These included: southern sawmilling, fertilizer, men's dress shirt and nightwear, men's seamless hosiery, wood furniture.] Even within as selected a group of establishments as those

[21] See Herbert R. Northrup, "Minimum Wages and Employment," *The Conference Board Business Record*, VII, No. 4 (April, 1950), 141–47. Northrup's article contains a useful theoretical summary also.

[22] Lloyd Reynolds, *Labor Economics and Labor Relations* (2d ed.; Englewood Cliffs, N. J.: Prentice-Hall, Inc., 1954), p. 663.

[23] A useful summary of various Department of Labor Studies is found in U. S. Department of Labor, Wage and Hour and Public Contract Divisions, *Results of the Minimum-Wage Increase of 1950: Economic Effects in Selected Low-Wage Industries and Establishments* (Washington, D. C.: U. S. Government Printing Office, 1954).

with reported adjustment problems, the non-wage consequences of the 75-cent requirement were on the whole not very substantial. *The Korean development undoubtedly helped the affected firms meet their higher wage bills.*[24]

The post–1956 experience. Wage increases after 1950 made the 75-cent minimum less effective than would have been true in the absence of such upward changes. The 75-cent minimum was not so far removed from the realities of the wage structure as was 40 cents after World War II. Nevertheless, various groups pressed for an increase. After considerable debate, a $1 minimum was enacted in 1955, effective March 1, 1956, the date at which these lines were written.[25]

While it is too early to ascertain the effects of the new minimum, the Department of Labor made a series of studies as to the probable number of employees affected for different minima.[26]

It was estimated that the increase from 75 cents to 90 cents would mean pay raises for 1.3 million factory workers, or about 5 per cent of the 24 million workers subject to the Act. The average increase would total 9 cents per hour. The industries mainly affected would be lumber products, apparel, tobacco, textiles, leather, and food. As a percentage of the relevant labor force affected, the regional figures would be: Far West, 1.1 per cent; Middle West, 2.3 per cent; North East, 4.1 per cent; South, 20.2 per cent. The 90-cent minimum would have had about as great an impact on low-wage industries as did the 75-cent rate in 1950. An increase to $1 an hour, the figure finally chosen, would affect over two million employees.[27]

It is interesting to note the Administration's philosophy on minimum wages:

Minimum wage laws do not deal with fundamental causes of low incomes. Accordingly, this condition can be corrected only to a limited extent by such laws. However, as pointed out in the last *Economic Report*, minimum wage

[24] *Ibid.*, p. 19, italics added.

[25] For a fascinating account of the thinking which goes into such legislation see U. S. Congress, 84th, First Session, House, Committee on Education and Labor, *Proposed Legislation to Increase the Minimum Wage* (Washington, D. C.: U. S. Government Printing Office, 1955).

[26] Convenient summaries are to be found in *Business Week*, February 19, 1955, pp. 168–69, and U. S. Department of Labor, Press Release (Statement of James P. Mitchell, April 14, 1955, on amendment of the Fair Labor Standards Act).

[27] In a sense, the $1 figure represented a compromise between the Administration's original 90-cent proposal and the $1.25 figure suggested by others. Dean Arthur Upgren of the Amos Tuck School of Business Administration, Dartmouth College, recommended the 90-cent figure because he felt that unemployment effects would appear if a higher rate were chosen. See 36 *Labor Relations Reporter* 139, May 23, 1955.

laws can assist the comparatively small number of workers who are at the fringes of competitive labor markets.[28]

An Evaluation

We can pull together the minimum-wage discussion with the following comments.

First, wages are a cost of production. Other things being equal, an increase in wages increases production costs. Under static conditions, where competition exists, unemployment will result. In the static-imperfect competition case, a skillfully set minimum wage may increase employment.

Second, minimum wages are imposed in a dynamic rather than in a static economy, and one in which imperfect competition is the rule rather than the exception. Three possibilities follow from such conditions. First, unemployment need not result if the entrepreneur increases his selling efforts or in other ways tries to market the same amount of goods at higher prices. Second, and conversely, he may try to become more efficient so as to keep costs the same for a given level of production. How much of this is done or can be done is an empirical problem about which we have relatively little information. It is our hunch, however, that the possibilities are greater than sometimes visualized. Third, however, the possibility of substituting capital for labor is greater over the long run, and this may be a negative offset to the two positive forces noted above.

Third, if society is willing to accept an alteration in the level of returns to the factors of production, minimum wages need not result in unemployment. Thus, if entrepreneurs will accept a reduced rate of profit, the impact of a minimum wage can be absorbed. Here is a case where realistic pressures shift the forces operating in economic markets. Such alterations, if they do occur, are likely to take place only over a longer period of time.

Fourth, the relatively optimistic statements of the last two paragraphs should not be taken to imply that society can act without restraint in setting wage minima. Far from it. Any attempt to, say, take the economy's "average" wage and make it the minimum would result in economic chaos. Structural dislocations of many types and price rises would occur that would cancel much of the wage increase. And such minimum wages tend to increase the unemployables by imposing higher standards of employability. One cannot lift oneself economically by this type of bootstrap;

[28] *Economic Report of the President,* January, 1956 (Washington, D. C.: U. S. Government Printing Office), p. 67.

minimum wages are neither a substitute for productivity nor a panacea that will produce a utopian wage structure.[29]

Fifth, if the minimum wage approach appears to be restricted in its usefulness in raising the basic wage, it also appears to us to possess limitations as a technique to prevent exploitation in imperfect labor markets or to raise wages where discontinuities make a wage-range possible. To be done efficiently and justly, such wage-setting requires industry-by-industry and firm-by-firm treatment. We would agree with Stigler that there is no "tolerably accurate method" of deriving the demand and supply schedules necessary to fix such a wage. Moreover, even if there were, we would be concerned about the administrative bureaucracy that might become necessary to implement the program. We would feel that trade unionism is a more suitable institution for correcting such malfunctioning along with mechanisms to increase the degree of competition in labor markets.

Finally, if these minimum-wage limitations appear, does the mechanism possess any justification as a device of economic policy? Our answer would be, yes, that minimum-wage law can "help tidy up the ragged lower edge of the wage structure."[30] Such a ragged lower fringe may exist in a number of circumstances: sweated industries in general, inefficient marginal firms, and the employment of women. What society in effect does is to set up minimum specifications and then tell employers that they must either meet these or go out of business. Is this inhumane treatment? We suspect no more so than the rigors of normal business competition.

Can a minimum wage law be self-defeating if it merely seeks to regulate wages at the fringes? In practice, regulation has lagged behind general wage movements. This in itself has minimized the impact. Moreover, in the case of national minima, increased economic activity and rising prices have cancelled the effects of the 1938 and 1950 wage settings (and, we suspect, will minimize the

[29] Some contemporary economic thinking does focus, however, upon the problems and possibilities of changing *basic* wage structures through minimum wage legislation. Thus R. G. Hawtrey notes that minimum wage legislation of the general type aims not only at "correcting lapses of wages below the basic wage but at maintaining or raising the basic wage itself." If such legislation is to be successful, monetary policy must provide the mechanism through which adjustments are made. For a provocative discussion, see Hawtrey, *op. cit.*, pp. 91–96. We are less optimistic about the desirability and possibility of monetary policy accomplishing the required adjustments. We do not feel, however, that this contradicts our position in Chapter 6 of this text, where we held that monetary and fiscal policy *can* be used to maintain high levels of employment.

[30] See Reynolds, *op. cit.*, p. 665, This is the same line of reasoning as that found in the 1956 *Economic Report of the President, op. cit.*, p. 67.

1956 increase). As long as care is exercised in rate setting (so that structural distortion is minimized) and insofar as high levels of economic activity are maintained (not necessarily with rising prices) we would feel that the self-defeating possibilities can be minimized.

Hence, we would feel that the minimum-wage mechanism is a useful tool of social policy. But we would not agree with its most enthusiastic adherents in holding that it is one of the (if not the) means for achieving an ideal basic wage. Nor would we agree with its critics who can see naught but disaster flowing from its application.

Minimum Labor Standards and Competitive Conditions

Does government intervention in substandard conditions jeopardize the competitive position of the firms, industries, regions, and countries affected? Or, conversely, has it no effect? Or is the answer, "It depends"? Let us return to this problem, to which passing attention has been given in many of the chapters of this volume.

It is a well-established principle, if not a truism, in economic theory and business practice that labor is a factor of production and that whatever affects the costs of hiring that factor affects the allocation of resources and the pricing of produced goods and services.[31] Certainly, government intervention in substandard conditions is a force affecting the cost of labor, just as was noted in Chapter 14 that other economic security programs have a similar impact.

As a specific example, do high wages and optimal working conditions impose a competitive disadvantage upon the firm, industry, region, or country that provides them? The answer is *no*, if (1) all participants compete under the same set of rules, and (2) the high wages and optimum conditions *flow out of* high productivity. Here productivity precedes and permits the improvements. Thus an American automobile company, with much higher wages and fringes than its English counterpart, need have little fear of foreign competition, for the higher productivity which made the wages possible sustains the American competitive position.[32]

But the answer may be *yes*, if the higher wages and optimal working conditions are imposed by government edict upon a sys-

---

[31] The literature here is voluminous. For a good summary, see Edgar M. Hoover, Jr., *The Location of Economic Activity* (New York: McGraw-Hill Book Co., Inc., 1948).

[32] We omit here, and subsequently, all the details involved in similarities and differences between interregional and international trade.

tem that may not necessarily be able to "afford" them and if they are imposed unequally among firms, industries, regions, and counties. A system may be able to "afford" such intervention by the government if the other factors entering into the cost of production —abundant natural resources, cheap power and fuel, nearness to market, economical transportation, low taxes—are sufficient to counterbalance the degree of intervention. It is further true that, even if the government does intervene with undesirable immediate consequences, there will be a long-run return to "equilibrium." But such a balancing movement takes time, and may involve painful readjustments.[33]

Is government intervention likely to be the critical element, or only one of several, in determining competitive positions and in affecting the allocation of resources and the pricing of goods and services? The answer depends upon both the degree of intervention and the area in which is occurs. As we have emphasized throughout this book, social insurance programs are likely to be but one of many elements involved. Likewise, the regulation of hours and working conditions is but one of many possibilities, though here intervention may have a more critical impact at times.[34] In the case of wages, the impact may be most pronounced of all. It is "differential" intervention, however, which is important. Interestingly enough, differentiation can arise in two opposing ways. Thus, if state A imposes regulations and B does not, such intervention may work to the detriment of the former. But suppose the federal government imposes a uniform minimum national wage. Though it is "uniform," such a wage minimum yet is differentiating in its impacts; it places a heavier burden upon the low-wage areas, such as the South, and removes one element of competitive advantage from such regions.

All this poses a series of interesting questions, particularly as regards wage regulation. Should nationally set minimum wages, as under the Fair Labor Standards Act, be uniform throughout the country? Or should "regional" minima be imposed, making exceptions for "low" wage areas? Under the Walsh-Healey Act, which specifies prevailing minimum wages for certain classes of govern-

---

[33] We are less optimistic here than is R. A. Lester. See his *Economics of Labor* (New York: The Macmillan Co., 1947), chap. xix, "The Economics of Labor Standards." See also his *Labor and Industrial Relations* (New York: The Macmillan Co., 1951), Part III.

[34] Thus it was frequently contended that prohibiting women from working on the third shift in textile mills in Massachusetts placed industry in that state at a competitive disadvantage.

ment contracts, should "prevailing" be interpreted on an industry or on a regional basis?[35]

The legislative or judicial answers that have been given to the above questions have had as many political overtones as they have had economic ones. Yet it is possible to look at the questions from an economic viewpoint.

The decision one comes to on these questions is conditioned chiefly by which of two basic sets of assumptions one chooses to accept. Regional differentials may arise from differing natural resources, labor supplies, proximity to markets, and other "inherent" characteristics. *But* they may also arise from all kinds of artificially induced means: plant subsidies, tax concessions, restrictive labor legislation, and the undercutting of other labor standards. Here is a case where the participants do not compete under the same set of rules.[36]

If one views differentials as arising essentially from the first set of causes, then regional variations in minimum wages would be logical. If one views them as developing essentially out of the second set of causes, then a national minimum is the more appropriate.[37] Such a national minimum would tend to counterbalance the artificial inducements.[38] Whether it would also overbalance

[35] For a discussion of the nature and (from one point of view) the impact of the Walsh-Healey Act, see John V. Van Sickle, *The Walsh-Healey Public Contracts Act* (No. 445 in the Series, National Economic Problems; [New York: American Enterprise Association, Inc., 1952]).

[36] In the above discussion we have extensively utilized the following sources: Seymour E. Harris, *New England Textiles and the New England Economy, Report to the Conference of New England Governors* (Cambridge: February, 1956); *Report on the New England Textile Industry by Committee Appointed by the Conference of New England Governors, 1952* (Cambridge: May, 1953); *Subsidized Industrial Migration: the Luring of Plants to New Locations* (Washington, D. C.: American Federation of Labor, 1955); the previous work cited for John V. Van Sickle; and Gerard D. Reilly, Reuben S. Haslam, and Rudolph Modley, "Threat of the Walsh-Healey Act," *Harvard Business Review*, XXIX, No. 1 (January, 1951), 86–98. See also the *Annual Reports* of the Wage and Hour and Public Contracts Divisions, U. S. Department of Labor.

[37] Ideally, the most "logical" method would be to set the minima on a regional basis just compensating for the artificially induced means. This is a "sophisticated" sort of neutrality equivalent to the political form which would have us arm nations differentially so as to preserve the balance of strength among them. The incredible administrative difficulties in trying to do this in the wage field are apparent. A case might be made, however, for using industry committees such as was done in the early days of the Fair Labor Standards Act.

[38] In fairness it ought to be said that such a minimum may also subsidize a variety of restrictive union practices. There is little doubt that many such practices promote desirable labor standards. But some may be socially or economically undesirable. The case also highlights the problems involved when a union has organized only a part of an industry; this is true of textiles.

natural regional advantages would depend in large measure upon where the minimum was set.[39]

In the case of the Fair Labor Standards Act, the minimum wage is national in scope. As such, and even though it is a marginal rather than an average minimum, it impinges more heavily upon the lower-wage South than upon the North. This in turn alters the competitive position of the two areas, presumably offering something of a deterrent to industrial growth in the South, and making it less desirable to shift plants from the North. Can such a minimum be justified? We think yes, if for no other reason than that it eases the transitional problems faced by a regional economy such as New England, losing 43 per cent of its textile employment from 1947 to 1955, in part because of artificial inducements of other areas.

It is true that such a uniform minimum is a type of internal tariff protecting northern industry. On this basis it might be better not to impose a national minimum, but to let industry migrate and then to assist, say, New England by means of subsidies and other measures. Administratively, however, a national minimum is probably a more reasonable way of achieving the desired result. Therefore, we would conclude that a case can be made for a national minimum.

In the case of the Walsh-Healey Act, should the "prevailing minimum wage" be set in terms of industries or localities? The trend has been increasingly to focus upon the industry rather than upon a series of localities. The Fulbright Amendment of 1952, however, granted judicial review of prevailing minimum wage determinations and other administrative actions. As a result, a number of determinations made upon an industry basis have been challenged by affected companies and, as of the present, are being litigated, although by denial of review, the Supreme Court in March, 1956, upheld an industry-wide minimum in cotton, silk, and synthetics.[40]

The Walsh-Healey question is less easily answered. This is true because the impact of an industry determination is more pronounced than a national minimum; the former reaches more completely into many localities than does the latter. As such, there is a greater possibility of local distortions, if the affected firms choose to

[39] For other argumentation see Gordon F. Bloom and Herbert R. Northrup, *Economics of Labor and Industrial Relations* (Philadelphia: The Blakiston Co., 1950), pp. 340–47.

[40] See 37 *Labor Relations Reporter* 433–34, and earlier issues for information on company challenges of wage setting in cotton, synthetic, and silk textiles and for court interpretation.

bid on government contracts. Again, the results are like the national minimum: northern firms may get a share of government business which they might find it otherwise hard to secure; southern firms may refrain from contract bidding.

There are many forces making for wage equalization: the re-direction and relocation of economic activity; industrywide and pattern collective bargaining; union policies. Should government action hasten the process? We would be somewhat less insistent upon industry determinations under the Walsh-Healey Act because of the possibilities of local distortions. Yet if various regions under-cut what are considered desirable (not "excessive") labor standards, such determinations may serve a useful corrective purpose. Some of the innocent may get burned along with the noninnocent; this is probably an unavoidable consequence if various artificial induce-ments cannot be reached in other ways.

Summary

We may pull together the threads of thought in this chapter with several concluding observations.

First, the market mechanism does not necessarily or always func-tion so as to provide a minimally acceptable set of rules of the game. Therefore, society may deem it desirable to intervene in what it considers substandard conditions, in an effort to eliminate a source of economic insecurity.

Second, such intervention may serve a variety of useful purposes. But it may have certain self-defeating tendencies, and certainly it is not a process by means of which one can artificially raise oneself by the bootstraps. Improvement at the margin and gradualism are two desirable, if obvious, approaches of economic security programs of this type.

Third, intervention, if imposed on a differential basis by varying regions or states, may change the competitive position of the affected areas, since labor conditions are a factor taken into account in plant location and in the pricing of output. Hence, a "liberal" region may find itself in a dilemma: it would like to raise its labor standards, but it is fearful of doing so if its competing neighbor does not. Complete national regulation is politically unfeasible; hence, the various states must of necessity move modestly in attempting improvements. We have records of states that moved too rapidly, with subsequent local economic difficulties. Persistent education and effort can help materially, however, in gradually improving the level of labor standards. The record is clear on this account.

Suggestions for Additional Reading

CHAMBER OF COMMERCE OF THE UNITED STATES. *Economics of Minimum Wage Legislation.* Washington: Chamber of Commerce of the United States, 1955.
A presentation of one point of view on the minimum-wage question. Includes comments on economic issues, as well as on matters of coverage under minimum wage acts.

CIVIC, MIRIAM. "Minimum Wages on the March." *The Conference Board Business Record*, XIII, No. 3 (March, 1956), 114–19.
An up-to-date, factual summary of federal and state minimum wage legislation, including an analysis of administrative procedures. Useful in conjunction with theoretical speculation about the impacts of such wages.

HAWTREY, R. G. *Cross Purposes in Wage Policy.* New York: Longmans, Green and Co., 1955. See particularly pp. 91–96.
This volume should be examined not only for its comments on conventional minimum-wage setting, but also for its ideas on changing *basic* wage structures through legislative means.

THOMAS, MAURICE WALTON. *The Early Factory Leglislation, A Study in Legislation and Administrative Evolution.* Leigh-on-Sea, Essex: The Thames Bank Publishing Co., Ltd., 1948.
An account of the early development of factory legislation in Great Britain. Particularly helpful in showing how ethics, politics, and other pressures combine with, or temper, economic forces in molding social legislation.

U. S. CONGRESS, 84TH, FIRST SESSION, HOUSE, COMMITTEE ON EDUCATION AND LABOR. Hearings on *Proposed Legislation to Increase the Minimum Wage.* Washington, D. C.: U. S. Government Printing Office, 1955.
A fascinating study of the way in which the legislative process operates. Useful narrative and statistics.

18

Some Concluding Observations

Public Policy Toward Economic Security

In 1956, the United States Department of Health, Education, and Welfare announced that it had prepared for nationwide distribution a comic book explaining to young people and encouraging them to take advantage of the benefits of the Social Security Act. Newspapers reported the project with routine interest. If there were no other evidence of the degree to which we have committed ourselves to legislative programs providing economic security, this venture alone, undertaken by an administration whose party was in large measure opposed to the principle of social insurance only a generation ago, would be dramatic proof of that commitment.

We have already observed that at least seven federal and state social insurance or public assistance programs pay benefits for old age; that at least eight provide survivors' benefits for dependent persons; that three alleviate the effects of unemployment due to labor market causes; and that at least a dozen systems pay disability benefits. Related programs which we have not discussed include the housing and school-lunch programs, and the accommodation and encouragement being given to private programs. In short, it is clear that problems of poverty and economic insecurity have been of continuing concern in this country.

It is common to think of our public economic security programs primarily as depression-born measures designed to meet immediate needs of the time and to think of them only secondarily (as they became consolidated programs) as designed to insure against risks to income security. This is partially true, however, only with respect to the participation of the federal government in such programs. For, as we know, social welfare measures actually began in the colonial period, and although they have been undertaken at all levels of government, they were mainly local programs in their earliest forms. State programs became important in the middle nineteenth century, and federal measures gained importance after the depression.[1]

ECONOMIC ORIGINS OF PUBLIC PROGRAMS

Although the depression shifted emphasis and accelerated federal activity in the field of economic security, it was not *the* causal force behind the rise of public programs. As we have seen, they arose as an answer to the problems caused by an industrial society in which an increasing number of persons had to depend for a livelihood upon a wage system.

Complexity of economic life. At the home-work stage of economic development, when the consumer was his own producer and production was the only limit on consumption, the only economic problem was production. However, with the development of the handicraft period and the need for specialization, exchange, and money, the worker's well-being came to depend not only upon what he produced, but also upon the ratio at which his goods exchanged for other commodities. And as the economy grew more complex and interdependent, this ratio of exchange was influenced more and more by forces completely beyond the worker's control. He could become unemployed for reasons wholly beyond his influence and quite aside from his willingness to work. At the same time the newer factory methods of production were creating greater accident and sickness hazards and presenting employers with incentives to operate long hours at fast production tempos, and often to employ child labor.

Limitations of labor market competition. The inherent hazards of an industrial society—unemployment, illness, and long strenuous hours—though socially undesirable, would be compensated (or reduced) in perfectly competitive labor markets. But it was apparent very early that buyers and sellers in the labor market were not meeting on equal terms—that their bargaining power was unequal and that labor supplies in the market behaved differently than did

[1] This point is developed by Ida C. Merriam in "Social Welfare in the United States, 1934-1954," *Social Security Bulletin*, XVIII, No. 10 (October, 1955), 3-14 (with cited references to earlier articles on the same subject).

other commodity supplies. When the price of labor decreased, its supply was not curtailed (nor did it return to the old equilibrium rate under a market adjustment). Rather, reductions in the price of labor tended to increase labor supplies, often accelerating sub-standard conditions. Not only was the labor market failing to compensate for these income interruptions, but unemployment became more costly by virtue of the fact that with increasing industrialization, wages tend to be the primary source of income. And the alternative of going back to live off the land and await better times was rapidly disappearing.

Problems of older workers. Rarely did the farm worker outlive his usefulness, but in urban economic life employment opportunities diminish as the worker grows older. Moreover, as Professor Eveline M. Burns has pointed out, "the spread of large scale enterprise and chain stores in retail trade has further limited the opportunities of old people to engage in marginal economic ventures, and the increasing standardization of wages through collective bargaining and minimum wage legislation has made it more difficult for the less than 100 per cent efficient worker to secure employment by accepting a lower wage rate reflecting his lessened earning power."[2]

Breakdown of "family security." The city wage-earner's life is not conducive to the development of the family as an economic resource in times of need. In the first place, city dwellings tend to be small; and, secondly, family units are broken up because of geographic and occupational mobility.

Changing concepts of responsibility. Finally, as the cumulative effects of these economic and social factors became more widely understood, popular concepts about economic responsibility changed. For example, the proposition (once rather widely heard) that "only the lazy are unemployed" dropped from use in the depression when it became abundantly clear that an individual's economic well-being was not dependent solely upon his initiative.

EVOLUTION OF PUBLIC PROGRAMS

All industrial societies have been confronted with the need for programs of economic security and labor protection, and all have contributed solutions to the problems herein discussed. Professor

[2] Eveline M. Burns, *The American Social Security System* (Boston: Houghton Mifflin Co., 1949), p. 26.

Herbert Heaton enumerates six questions which must be considered in formulating public policy on economic security:

1. "Which workers are to be protected?
2. "At what age should persons be allowed to begin work?
3. "For what hours should work be permitted?
4. "What should be done to protect the health, strength and safety of workers?
5. "Could or should the state regulate wages?"
6. Should those unemployed as a result of sickness, old age, accidents, or labor market conditions ". . . be cast aside to depend on savings, family, friends, or union or to fall back on poor relief?"[3]

Professor Burns sees the development of social insurance answers to certain of these questions as having taken place in two stages in this country. Stage I, from 1911 to 1935, ". . . is characterized by the application of the social insurance principle to relatively few risks and only to selected groups. There is either no government contribution or, at most, a nominal or token contribution."[4]

Stage II, since 1935, ". . . is marked by a growing but uneven extension of social insurance to cover not only new risks but more importantly, new population groups . . . the system begins to include a more substantial contribution from general tax revenues."[5]

In the evolution from Stage I to Stage II, the benefit provisions and coverages of our economic security programs have undergone great changes. The Social Security Act, for example, dealt first with the pressing needs of the depression period; its longer range provisions assured the aged a retirement income. Insurance coverage and benefits have outstripped the public aid provisions of the Act in importance. In the same way, workmen's compensation evolved from a simple indemnity system to one which placed more and more emphasis on medical and rehabilitation benefits. As time has gone on, all economic security measures have tended to include more risks, to broaden coverage, and to liberalize benefits. It is ironic, however, that while the trend towards more liberal systems has been made possible by growing economic prosperity, the speed of economic growth has often left the programs lagging; this is true in the regulation of substandard conditions as well as in social insurance.

[3] Reprinted by permission from Herbert Heaton, *Economic History of Europe* (New York: Harper & Brothers, 1936), pp. 693–94.

[4] Eveline M. Burns, "Social Insurance in Evolution," *American Economic Review*, XXXIV, No. 1, Part 2 Supplement (March, 1944), 200.

[5] *Ibid.*, p. 201.

Philosophy of social insurance. To the extent that they have succeeded in securing income against risks, our economic security measures owe their success to two closely related factors in addition to prosperity—our philosophy of social insurance and our acceptance of it. Professor J. Douglas Brown (in the 1955 Hillman Memorial lecture) stated[6] that American social insurance has succeeded because it: (1) protects against hazards to economic security, not as a matter of benevolence of government or employer, but as a matter of right; (2) extends coverage to all and is limited only for constitutional or administrative reasons; (3) seeks to keep emphasis upon the individual—the size of his benefits are (in part) determined by his earnings; (4) emphasizes protection of the family unit, particularly through protection against the various hazards that it might face; and finally, (5) makes contributions (particularly in the case of Old-Age and Survivors' Insurance) to many of the systems joint. Persons who are beneficiaries are also contributors.

Acceptance of the principle of economic security. Certainly this philosophy explains, at least in part, why social insurance programs are accepted almost universally today. Both major political parties clearly endorse them. In fact, it is difficult to detect any difference in the degree of their endorsement. In July, 1955, the United States House of Representatives (which was then nearly evenly divided politically) passed by a 372 to 31 vote a bill proposing sweeping changes in the Social Security Act with virtually no debate and no hearings.[7]

President Eisenhower recently paid warm public tribute to a university professor who, in interpreting the United States abroad, stressed among other things that as a result of legislative measures which originated with the New Deal but are now endorsed by both parties, social insurance programs have become part of the accepted framework of our governmental structure and have made individual Americans economically secure.[8]

Economic Security and the "Welfare State"

The focus of all preceding chapters has been upon the basic categories of individual economic insecurities in our economy, their

[6] J. Douglas Brown, "The American Philosophy of Social Insurance," *The Social Service Review*, XXX, No. 1 (March, 1956), 3–8.

[7] Providing in part benefits to women retired at age sixty-two, to all workers permanently disabled at age fifty, and to children totally disabled before age eighteen when present children's benefits expire.

[8] *The New York Times*, March 22, 1956, p. 19.

causes, and the methods used in combating them. This emphasis may tend to obscure the full perspective of government activities in private economic affairs; it may also create an exaggerated picture of the rate of growth of these programs and the impression that problems of economic security have been "solved." Each of these possible impressions is worth examining briefly.

GOVERNMENT AID TO BUSINESS

State intervention in economic affairs goes far beyond measures to protect individual economic security. In an instructive survey entitled "The Spreading of State Welfare," *Fortune* magazine recently sought to trace the extent of "government welfare." It reported that "the endlessly staggering fact about the United States government . . . is the number of things it has a policy about . . ."[9] Admittedly, definitions of welfare or welfare state are in large measure a function of political disposition, but no matter what views one holds, the vast array of state services to business organizations cannot be ignored when questions of state interference in economic affairs are raised. *Fortune* lists twenty-eight federal departments and agencies which (in 1952) ". . . render services of distinct benefit to business, exclusive of contracts (for example, munitions) or business generated by foreign aid."[10] These services range from ". . . stocking inshore ocean beds with young lobsters . . . [to] . . . furnishing isotopes."

GROWTH OF ECONOMIC SECURITY PROGRAMS

Since the thirties, state participation in social welfare programs has been strengthened by federal programs administered through states and localities. Today 60 per cent of social welfare funds are contributed by the states and about 40 per cent by the federal government, and when federal grants-in-aid are considered, state and local programs administer some 69 per cent of social welfare funds.[11]

Although economic security programs have grown in number in the past fifty years and have gained greater acceptance and more liberal benefits and coverage, their over-all size in relation to the rest of the economy is not growing today. Federal "Labor and Welfare" expenditures, as a percentage of total national income,

---

[9] *Fortune*, February, 1952, pp. 100–17.
[10] *Ibid*, p. 102.
[11] Includes social insurance, health, education, and veterans' programs.

have remained virtually constant since the end of World War II. And when the abnormal needs of the depression and immediate post-depression era are considered, "Labor and Welfare" expenditures have dropped markedly, relative to national income since 1938.[12]

"Social Welfare Expenditures," measured in relation to gross national product, show a similar pattern. Table 18.1 presents these figures for the period 1934 to 1954.

TABLE 18.1

CIVILIAN PUBLIC SOCIAL WELFARE PROGRAMS IN RELATION TO
GROSS NATIONAL PRODUCT (FISCAL 1934–1954)

Fiscal Year	Gross National Product (billions)	Social Welfare Expenditures as a Per Cent of GNP						
		Total	Soc. Ins.	Public Aid	Health and Medical Services	Educ.	Other Welfare Services	Veterans' Programs
1934–35	$ 68.7	11.5	0.6	5.9	0.9	3.2	0.2	0.7
1935–36	77.6	9.6	.5	4.4	.9	3.1	.1	.6
1936–37	86.8	8.9	.5	4.0	.8	2.9	.1	.6
1937–38	88.0	9.2	.9	3.7	.9	3.1	.1	.6
1938–39	88.2	10.8	1.3	4.8	.9	3.1	.1	.6
1939–40	95.7	9.5	1.3	3.8	.8	2.9	.1	.6
1940–41	110.5	8.2	1.1	3.2	.7	2.6	.1	.5
1941–42	140.5	6.1	.9	1.9	.6	2.1	.1	.4
1942–43	178.4	4.1	.7	.8	.5	1.7	.1	.3
1943–44	202.8	3.5	.6	.5	.4	1.5	.1	.3
1944–45	218.3	3.6	.6	.5	.5	1.6	.1	.4
1945–46	202.1	5.8	1.3	.6	.5	1.8	.1	1.5
1946–47	221.5	7.5	1.2	.7	.5	1.9	.1	3.0
1947–48	245.0	7.7	1.2	.7	.6	2.2	.1	2.8
1948–49	260.5	8.2	1.4	.8	.7	2.4	.1	2.7
1949–50	263.0	9.0	1.8	.9	.8	2.8	.2	2.5
1950–51	311.8	7.6	1.5	.8	.8	2.5	.2	1.8
1951–52	336.8	7.4	1.7	.8	.8	2.5	.2	1.4
1952–53	358.4	7.3	1.8	.8	.8	2.5	.2	1.2
1953–54	360.6	7.9	2.3	.8	.8	2.7	.2	1.1

Source: *Social Security Bulletin*, XVIII, No. 10 (October, 1955), 9.

THE PROBLEM REMAINS

Despite the recognized need for economic security programs, their widespread adoption, and the fact that Americans currently enjoy a high level of full employment, poverty continues to be an

[12] This argument is more fully developed in "The Welfare State," *Economic Trends and Outlook*, I, No. 1 (April, 1956), 1–3.

acute problem. In 1955, public assistance—involving a means test—
from federal-state programs[13] amounted to:

NUMBERS OF PERSONS RECEIVING PUBLIC ASSISTANCE
(USING A MEANS TEST)
(September, 1955)

	(thousands)
Old-age assistance	2,553
Aid to blind	104
Aid to dependent children	2,191
Aid to the permanently and totally disabled	241
General assistance (cases)	290

Moreover, the latest available Department of Health, Education,
and Welfare data, summarized below in Table 18.2, reveal that the
income distribution in the United States, while gradually improving
upward, still leaves wide gaps. It should be noted that of the
families with incomes under $1,000, slightly under one-third are
farmers.

TABLE 18.2

PERCENTAGE DISTRIBUTION OF FAMILIES
BY TOTAL MONEY INCOME, 1948 AND 1954

Total Money Income Class	Families of Two or More Persons		
	1954		1948
	Current Dollars	1948 Dollars	
Total	100%	100%	100%
Under $1,000	9	10	10
$1,000 to $2,000	11	12	15
$2,000 to $3,000	12	15	20
$3,000 to $5,000	31	33	34
$5,000 and over	37	30	21

Source: U. S. Congress, 84th, 1st Session, Senate and House, Hearings Before the
Joint Committee on the Economic Report, Subcommittee on Low-Income Families,
Low-Income Families (Washington, D. C.: U. S. Government Printing Office, 1955),
p. 29.

THE ROLE OF ECONOMIC SECURITY MEASURES TODAY

Social insurance measures and protective labor legislation are
designed to assure minimum income to persons affected by the

[13] U. S. Congress, 84th, 1st Session, Senate and House, Hearings Before the Joint
Committee on the Economic Report, Subcommittee on Low-Income Families, *Low
Income Families* (Washington, D. C.: U. S. Government Printing Office, 1955), p. 37.

major risks to economic security which we have been discussing. They are not designed to replace savings, but rather to supplement them; not to discourage incentive to return to productive work, but to hasten a speedier return. These economic security measures involve government activity which is not unique, but rather is a part of a broader pattern of state intervention into economic affairs. And, finally, while the record of achievement is noteworthy, much work must be done before these measures fulfill their accepted goals.

The Future of Economic Security Programs I: A Unified Social Insurance System?

What path will our public economic security measures follow in the future? With each passing year these plans become a more fully accepted part of our economic structure. Today, proposed changes in benefits raise fewer and fewer debates on whether the principles are sound and more and more questions as to whether or not the added costs and benefits are in balance and are desirable in view of the rest of the economy.[14]

This fact and its results as seen in the evolution toward more liberal systems prompt the question of whether or not our system of economic security will evolve into a final unified phase—Stage III, in Professor Burns' terms, where "coverage is no longer limited to wage earners, or to the basic threats to income security, but is extended, through a unified social insurance system, to all, or virtually all citizens for most of the 'hazards of life.' "[15]

Under a system like that of New Zealand, for example, minimum income is assured to all members of the country. Similarly, a universal American system would provide benefits for health services, children's allowances, pregnancy—in short, it would provide minimum income protection to all American citizens.[16] Although wide acceptance of social insurance principles and programs indicates possible support for such an eventual development, the factors in opposition to it in this country make such a development appear unlikely in the near future.

SOCIAL PHILOSOPHY

What is acceptable to the American people as a matter of social policy is, of course, subject to considerable change and is a function

[14] See, for example, First National City Bank, *Monthly Letter*, April, 1956, pp. 44–47.

[15] Burns, "Social Insurance in Evolution," *op. cit.*, pp. 202–03.

[16] *Ibid.*

not only of the time, but also of changing economic conditions. But for the immediate future, it seems unlikely that such a program would be acceptable to many Americans. Certain groups obviously have a stake in preventing such a program which goes somewhat beyond their political philosophy. Many private insurance carriers, for example, would resist moves to make the government an insurer of risks they now insure. Our present system, as we have seen, is administered through all levels of government and, in fact, state and local governments account for about two-thirds of all social welfare expenditures today. That these governments would yield their pivotal position in this picture without a struggle is not probable.

In fact, not only would such a measure be resisted, but it would be hard to point to a single group of any significance at the present time which would propose such a unified program of social insurance. Trade unions, the economic groups which might be expected to lead such a move, would not now think of doing so. A majority of trade union sentiment has never even favored a national job-accident insurance program. Furthermore, a national program of income maintenance would be resisted because of the threat it would pose to the role of trade unions in collective bargaining. Nor would trade unions be inclined to accept such a move as a matter of personal philosophy.

Finally, leaders of liberal thought might well find such proposals repugnant. There is increasing evidence that liberal thinking does not view further extension of government into the affairs of men as an unmixed blessing. And the argument of security versus liberty, once considered "outdated" and fashionable only in "conservative" circles, is now being heard in more liberal quarters.[17]

ECONOMIC POLICY

There are several immediate reasons of economic policy which would tend to hold back development of a unified social insurance program. First, there is the fear, already felt in connection with the possible social security changes, that increasing the tax burden to provide greater benefits might make it so heavy as to leave in question its benefits to those of lower incomes. For example, if the tax on self-employment income were increased to the presently proposed 6¾ per cent by 1975, a self-employed person with a wife and two children and an annual income of $4,200 would pay $276 in

17 Max Ascoli, "The Future of Liberalism," The Reporter, XIV, No. 9 (May 3, 1956), 12–16.

income taxes under the present rates, and his social security tax burden would be $283.50—a total tax load of $559.50. It is conceivable that further extension of benefits which would require heavy taxes would put a burden on low-income families and tend to lose rather than gain support for the program.

Alternative means of financing could, of course, be devised. But this would weaken the contributory features of the system. Benefits would no longer be partly determined by wages, and this is a feature of the system that is generally regarded to have been one of the most effective contributing factors in its success. Moreover, it might be questioned whether income security financed by fiscal policy to create full employment would not achieve the end more efficiently, more cheaply, and with greater productive results.

Finally, although they are not now dominant issues, work disincentives and the inflationary impact of an income maintenance program would become much more important.

LACK OF INTEREST

Although social insurance programs have gained general and nearly unqualified acceptance, interest in them has, with some exceptions discussed below, tended to dwindle. Trade unions have become the chief spokesmen for benefit changes against the opposition of employers' groups. Often, the result, particularly in state legislatures, is a stalemate or adoption of compromise legislation with little attention to the over-all objectives of the program. In effect, liberal leaders have taken the position that since we now have social legislation, we should turn to other issues.[18] But, as we have pointed out earlier, many serious problems remain. How these problems are to be solved is of far greater current importance to the future of our economic security programs than are theoretical discussions about a unified national program.

SOME PROBLEMS OF PUBLIC PROGRAMS

Inadequacy. Economic security legislation, like any other, tends to become rigid through time. The processes for amending legislation are laborious. As a result, a great deal of attention, re-evaluation and revision is necessary to keep the laws up to date. The normal tendency for such legislation to become obsolete is aggravated by the rapid pace at which our whole economic environment has been changing. In the twenty-year period beginning with 1929

[18] Arthur Schlesinger, Jr., "The Future of Liberalism, *The Reporter*, XIV, No. 9 (May 3, 1956), 8–11.

average hourly earnings rose in this country some 113 per cent, prices about 55 per cent, and real earnings about 52 per cent.

This dynamic growth, together with the rapid development of medical technology, rehabilitation, and living standards, has put our economic security programs in relatively poor perspective. This has been particularly true of workmen's compensation, which has suffered for two reasons. Because it is a state program with no strong political group to further its cause, it has lagged in many jurisdictions, and as its rehabilitation promise has become greater, its relative fulfillment has been more dismal. Second, whereas other programs have tended more to become instruments of economic policy (such as the use of minimum wage legislation to offset geographic competition advantages), such policy uses have given little aid to workmen's compensation. Minimum benefit payments and the use of dependents' allowances have liberalized job-accident laws in some jurisdictions. In fact, there is a general tendency to drop the strict insurance approach whereby benefits are paid solely on the basis of what is paid in, and to provide minimum benefits and dependents' allowances. But inadequacy tends to be the greatest single problem of public measures.

Gaps in coverage. The many gaps in coverage of public economic security programs generally are due to those risks, which though covered by one or more programs, are not fully covered; and those risks for which widespread coverage is not yet part of any program. Most of our social insurance programs could be cited as examples of the first type. They do not provide protection for risks such as extraordinary catastrophes or series of misfortunes. Even for those risks falling within a program, persons may be denied coverage because incapacity or other limiting circumstances deny them the needed labor force attachment. Workmen's compensation and unemployment compensation programs would be examples of this latter situation.

Since benefits for nonoccupational disability are limited, it might be cited as the leading risk for which public programs do not provide widespread coverage. Coverage gaps of this type also characterize most protective labor legislation. Workers in retail industry and in agriculture, for example, are denied protection of the Fair Labor Standards Act, and the state acts by and large have even poorer records for coverage of risks and persons.

These gaps have made the residual program of public assistance all the more necessary. Until recently, in fact, that program was the first line of defense in paying greater sums in benefits than the federal social security program. Although this balance is now reversed, the assistance programs carry a far heavier burden than they would if the gaps in coverage were closed.

Overlapping. These omissions are compounded by the overlapping benefits which may occur along with them. For example, it is possible for a worker injured on the job to have no recourse but common law or, in many states, only a very small benefit payment. At the same time, it is possible for benefit payments under combined programs to exceed a worker's lost earnings: dependents of workers killed at their employment who are covered by workmen's compensation and OASI survivors' benefits are a case in point. Another example is a worker suffering permanent total disability and receiving OASI retirement benefits.[19]

Other programs, too, involve possible dual payments. Sometimes overlapping benefits can weaken the benefit structure of one law. Thus the practice in Rhode Island of supplementing workmen's compensation with payments from its temporary disability insurance program is sometimes cited as a factor holding down the workmen's compensation benefit level.[20]

That this problem should arise is not surprising when one considers the vast number of economic security programs which, although they cover different populations, deal with the same risks. Disability insurance programs, veterans' programs, or care for seamen may overlap with workmen's compensation; railroad retirement may overlap with veterans' benefits; and railroad and general unemployment benefits may overlap with other benefits. Many of the programs have sought to avoid the inequities that can arise from dual payments. The Minnesota legislature recently provided an offset to its workmen's compensation permanent total disability benefits for social security payments. And the unemployment compensation laws of most jurisdictions, the temporary disability insurance laws, and the OASI disability provisions, or disqualification, have "offset," provisions. Overlapping is presently not a serious over-all problem, but it underscores the need for a more rational relationship among our various economic security programs.

Administration and finance. At the 1955 ceremony in recognition of the twentieth anniversary of the Social Security Act, Professor Edwin E. Witte, distinguished social insurance scholar, paid de-

---

[19] For a discussion of such cases in New York, see U. S. Department of Labor, Bureau of Labor Standards, "Adequacy of Workmen's Compensation," *Bulletin 180* (Washington, D. C.: U. S. Government Printing Office, October, 1954), pp. 102–06.

[20] State of Minnesota, Department of Employment Security, *Report on a Study of Sickness and Disability Insurance* (St. Paul, 1954), p. 59.

served tribute[21] to the highly successful record of the administration of the Social Security Act. Problems which seemed almost insurmountable to the framers of the Act have been overcome.

This record has been duplicated in the administration of many economic security programs. Still, the total administrative picture is far from satisfactory. The great proliferation of programs and agencies, the many sources of benefits, the complex and sometimes strained intergovernmental relations—such as that between state workmen's compensation agencies and state divisions of vocational rehabilitation—do little to effectuate the purposes of the laws. Not only is this confusing to the possible beneficiary, but it requires much more information and communication, and imposes extra costs.

Furthermore, as earlier chapters have indicated, administrative standards are not uniformly high and in some instances are, indeed, poor. Lack of conformity and varying interpretation among state and local programs are still troublesome issues. These problems are best illustrated by the varying disqualification provisions and workmen's compensation coverage from state to state, the failure of some states to issue orders under minimum wage laws, and of others to enforce orders that have been issued. Not only can serious doubt be raised about the efficiency with which monies are being allocated to given programs, such as workmen's compensation where nearly one-half of premiums do not go into benefit payments, but also about the issue of the luxury of so many programs covering the same risks. But it is not realistic as we have tried to indicate, to expect solutions to these problems to come from unification.

The Future of Economic Security Programs II: Rise of Private Programs

The preceding discussion has sought to make clear two points. First, that despite the development of American public economic security measures and their general acceptance in our economy, there are important economic and social reasons why at this time it appears unlikely that the trend towards more comprehensive social insurance will soon result in a single minimum income program. And, second, that the development of these systems has produced a series of problems involving inadequacy, coverage, gaps, overlapping, and administrative problems that cannot be ignored if the laws are to serve their purposes adequately. As a result of the

[21] Edwin E. Witte, "Twenty Years of Social Security," *Social Security Bulletin,* XVIII, No. 10 (October, 1955), 15–21.

Model Bill venture of the United States Department of Labor, together with trade union demands for guaranteed annual wages and increasing congressional interest in social security in the past few years, economic security measures have been brought back into the mainstream of economic affairs. Movements for reform have gained some new impetus, and while these movements may bring about relief from these problems, another important development is at hand—namely, the private economic security programs which in part supplement public measures. These private programs, particularly the bargained ones, have risen in importance, in large part as a result of the very problems which have occurred in public programs. And they have become so linked with our public programs that it is no longer realistic to talk about economic security in America in terms of public programs alone. The future of social insurance cannot be considered without reference to the private programs.

Private Programs for Economic Security

Private insurance has always played an important role in the American philosophy of social insurance. As we indicated earlier, social insurance, with an eye to maintaining incentives and to keeping costs manageable, has never sought to do more than provide basic protection. In the past decade, Americans have been buying private insurance at a rapid rate, as individuals and groups have sought added protection suited to their needs, abilities, and desires.

Today, however, privately bargained supplements to social insurance have produced a situation in which, Professor J. Douglas Brown says, "Instead of a two-layer system of protection, social and private, we have a three-layer system with a juicy slice of supplementary protection inserted into the sandwich as a result of vigorous collective bargaining."[22]

When we add to this the employment stabilization programs of some employers, private economic security measures fall into three categories: private individual insurance; private group insurance, including among other plans those designed to supplement social insurance; and noninsurance measures, such as employment stabilization programs. Let us look at them in turn.

Private individual insurance. In a country where great stress is placed upon the individual's responsibility for his own economic salvation, private insurance will always and rightly play an important role in economic security. American insurance experience

[22] Brown, *op. cit.*, p. 8.

clearly bears this out. Individual insurance protection, sold by private carriers, has had tremendous growth in the past two decades. Most American families today look to private insurance to supplement their Old-Age and Survivors' Insurance benefits, and all indications are that this trend will continue and grow. A recent University of Michigan survey revealed that 86 per cent of the surveyed families owned some form of life insurance.[23] Thus the role of this private economic security measure as it relates to social insurance is clearly defined and, as indicated in Chapter 5, despite its problems seems to be serving its function well.

Private group insurance. Private group insurance programs are clearly becoming the most important of the private economic security measures, but the role of these programs is yet to be defined. Even in the life insurance field, as Chapter 5 indicated, group annuities have grown at a faster rate than have private individual insurance. And in the other areas—such as workmen's compensation, disability insurance, unemployment and Old-Age and Survivors' Insurance—group supplementary payments are in force; in fact, they are currently a part of the bargaining demands of nearly every union.

Noninsurance measures. Perhaps least well-known of the economic security measures are those important programs and techniques designed to stabilize production, sales, and, hence, employment. Private approaches to economic security problems are confined largely to the field of unemployment, where, as Chapter 8 indicated, they perform a valuable service.

Although different events have triggered supplementary programs, they all have the common objective of providing additional benefits to those provided by law. Historically, a large number of plans were employer–initiated; World War II and the Inland Steel decision played a prominent role in pension bargaining; supplements to workmen's compensation grew gradually, whereas supplementary unemployment benefits became an important bargaining issue in the 1955 automobile negotiations and gained recognized status in a very short period. No doubt organized labor's demand for group supplementary benefits has been a means of applying pressure to gain legislative action on the laws. Trade unions have sought supplements for another reason, too: because ceilings on benefit differentials have been held low and, in general, have failed to reflect the increased earnings of the highly organized.

[23] *Life Insurance Fact Book, 1956,* p. 16.

Supplementary benefits are to a large extent a practical outgrowth of successful collective bargaining and are not integrated into our social insurance scheme. Professor Brown has observed that "Since even the trade-union leaders who have won supplementary benefits remain uncertain of their proper relation to social insurance systems, it is understandable if such supplementation is not yet made an amendment to our philosophy of social insurance."[24]

SOME PROBLEMS OF PRIVATE INSURANCE

Like the social insurance systems they supplement, private insurance programs involve similar problems in administration and coverage as well as new problems unique to nonstate systems. And some of these—such as the need for regulation—are made ever more pressing by the rapid rate at which supplemental programs are growing.

Administration. Although supplemental benefit programs involve a distinct administrative structure, this need not always be expensive. Thus supplementing workmen's compensation benefits need not require costly administrative determination—if benefit decisions are based upon those of the Industrial Commission. But in cases where the private plan must determine whether or not an employee is entitled to benefits and must administer the law's provisions and provide for possible review, rehabilitation, and re-employment, administrative costs may be great. This might be particularly true where standards differ from those of the social insurance program. For example, early administrative experience in the recently negotiated supplementary unemployment benefits proved somewhat costly.[25]

Benefits and incentives. Since (at least in theory) the disincentive factor acts as an upper limit on social insurance benefits, it follows that private supplements to public benefits make the benefit incentive question a pertinent one. Although it does not follow that work incentives are destroyed by private measures, the issue takes on more importance with them. Some perverse incentives have arisen in firms where private disability programs pay more than workmen's compensation and workers have an incentive to conceal injuries and claim them under the private program as a home injury. Indeed, this situation provided one of the incentives behind the move to gain supplementary workmen's compensation benefits. It is also possible for benefits to exceed wages, as we have seen,

24 Brown, *op. cit.*, p. 8.
25 *Wall Street Journal*, May 24, 1956, p. 1.

because of overlapping public and private programs. All this points up the need for a more rational integration of the two systems.

Gaps. It is easy to overemphasize the extent of the coverage of private programs. Actually, there are great gaps. A recent study[26] of disability retirement in industrial pension plans, for example, concludes that the disability insurance must be supplemental in nature and cannot get complete coverage, which is why the AFL-CIO emphasizes a public disability insurance provision in the Social Security Act.[27]

The United States Department of Health, Education, and Welfare has sought to expand private health insurance to cover the hazards of catastrophic illness, and by pooling costs and setting up federal government reinsurance. In May, 1956, the major American insurance companies rejected this pooling proposal.[28]

The need for regulation. A serious problem involved in private welfare and pension plans is that they present easy opportunities for abuse. Concern over this possibility led to the enactment in 1947 of Section 302 of the Taft-Hartley Act which required joint administration of such plans. Experience since then, however, has quite clearly indicated that more stringent regulation is necessary if serious abuses are to be avoided.

A careful inquiry—the first of its kind—was recently conducted by the United States Senate into the administration of welfare and pension plans. The printed record of these hearings[29] is a sad commentary on what can happen to private plans that fall into corrupt hands.

The report[30] makes clear that corruption and abuses are an exception. An overwhelming majority of plans are administered honestly. Where corruption and questionable practices were uncovered, all parties involved in private welfare and pension plans shared in the blame. Union officials were found to be receiving kickbacks, mixing monies from the funds with their own accounts, and receiving salaries and bonuses for nonexistent duties. Management officials

---

[26] Michael W. Blumenthal, *Disability Retirement in Industrial Pension Plans* (Princeton: Industrial Relations Section, Princeton University, 1956).

[27] See, for example, *Labor's Economic Review,* I, No. 5 (May, 1956). Also see Chapter 12, this text.

[28] *The New York Times,* May 11, 1956, p. 14.

[29] U. S. Congress, 84th, 1st Session, Senate, hearings before a Subcommittee of the Committee on Labor and Public Welfare, *Welfare and Pension Plans Investigation* (Washington, D. C.: U. S. Government Printing Office, 1954), 3 parts.

[30] U. S. Congress, 84th, 1st Session, Subcommittee of the Committee on Labor and Public Welfare, *Welfare and Pension Plans Investigation* (Committee Print, January 10, 1954), 50 pp.; (Committee Print, July 20, 1955), 50 pp.

shared in the blame, although in their case information was more difficult to obtain. Where plans were nonunion and thus unilaterally administered by management, operations were secret, and information was hard to secure. Some practices which the committee uncovered, however, included investment of fund money in securities of the employer for not altogether appropriate motives. Placement of such unilaterally administered insurance contracts involves some questionable practices. A tendency to place such contracts with insurance firms whose directors are also directors of the assured firm was noted. Open bids were not always taken.

Insurance agents were found by the subcommittee to be guilty of corrupt practices, as well as of receiving high commissions, charging high administrative costs, and in some instances, embezzling premiums outright, sometimes in collusion with unions or management. These serious abuses clearly indicate the need for regulation.

The Senate subcommittee recommended a federal disclosure law to be administered by a federal agency such as the Securities Exchange Commission. The law would require: (1) that all funds covering over twenty-five employees be registered with the regulating agency, and (2) that such registration include detailed reports and disclosures of its operations. The act would be enforced by criminal penalties.

It is noteworthy that this report and its recommendations were soundly praised by the AFL-CIO which endorsed the conclusions and urged the Congress to enact the disclosure law.[31] At this writing the proposal is in congressional committee.

EFFECT OF PRIVATE PLANS ON PUBLIC MEASURES

Private insurance plans to aid the economic security of employees may be either negotiated by collective agreement or unilaterally installed by employers, typically in nonorganized firms. In terms of number of workers covered, the latter type is less important than the former and does not appear to influence greatly the course of public economic security programs. The negotiated supplements, however, do not operate independently of the public measures.

As a wage, they pose no issue. If we assume that bargained supplementary benefits are traded for wages, it follows that they are not different from what wage rate differentials might be between union and nonunion workers. If they are not traded for wages, but de-

---

[31] The National Association of Insurance Commissioners voted in opposition to federal regulation and in favor of state control. *St. Louis Post-Dispatch,* May 31, 1956, p. 6D.

manded as something past due, union and covered workers would
have greater wage increases than they would have in the absence of
these "fringes."

Is it simply a case of union versus nonunion working conditions,
or is it a case of high value productivity employees getting higher
wages than less productive ones? What does this mean for the
economic security of nonorganized workers? Actually, bargained
supplements tend to influence public economic security programs
in two directions. On the one hand, by drawing attention to the
inadequacy of public programs relative to the private plans and by
giving employers an incentive to support public programs, they
operate to liberalize economic security systems. Thus when it is
understood, for example, that workers are concealing plant injuries to claim that they were injured at home because private disability plan benefits are superior to workmen's compensation, favorable pressures may come to bear upon the state system. Also, union
demands for annual wage guarantees and the resulting SUB plans
clearly give employers an incentive to strengthen unemployment
compensation laws, as well as drawing attention to them. An equally
direct incentive to employers was presented by union demands for
noncontributory pensions linked to social security retirement benefits. In 1949, employers responded by backing higher social security
benefits.

Widespread adoption of private pension plans could also be an
argument for the "ease" of inaugurating a new state program—disability insurance, for example. For if many employers presently
support a noncontributory plan, a state plan probably would not be
more costly. On the other hand, the opposite result can occur—as it
has in at least one state. The widespread adoption of private plans
was offered by a majority of a legislative advisory council in Minnesota as an argument against the adoption of a state disability insurance program, largely on the grounds that so many private plans
were in existence that there was no need for a state program.[32] Thus
those who are most in need of such protection—those not covered by
group plans—were denied it.

This effect, however, has not been the dominant one. Private
plans have focused attention on the gaps and inadequacies that
remain in public programs. And by giving employers an incentive
to expand social security, all workers have received higher benefits.

[32] See State of Minnesota, Department of Employment Security, *Report on a Study
of Sickness and Disability Insurance* (St. Paul: 1954).

ECONOMIC SECURITY FROM GOVERNMENT OR BUSINESS?

Although the use of union bargaining power to obtain improved public economic security legislation has been sharply criticized by some groups, its pattern seems clearly established. And it has raised an important question of business philosophy. Congressional hearings on the 1950 Social Security Act amendments revealed that businessmen could be counted upon actively to support increased benefits. Some of this support came from persons and groups who had earlier opposed the enactment of social security legislation. Why?

This change in the attitude of business toward improved social security resulted from the so-called fourth round of post-World War II collective bargaining—the pension round. Backed by the authority of the Inland Steel decision,[33] trade union demands for pensions produced results. Many large companies, such as Kaiser and Ford Motor Companies and the Aluminum Company of America, bargained pension plans with their unions. These plans provided flat pensions for eligible retired workers. The pension, however, included social security payments. Therefore, as social security benefits rose, the employers' contribution to the flat sum pension would decrease. Since these bargained pensions were noncontributory, the incentive to back higher social security benefits was obvious and strong. Thus the 1950 Social Security Act amendments were backed by the United States Chamber of Commerce and many business organizations and business leaders, including Mr. Charles E. Wilson of General Motors.

Businessmen's stake in an improved Social Security Act, generated by the leverage of union pension bargaining, posed an uneasy question for many of them who, if they did not oppose the legislation, at least would not support its liberalization. Should business rally to the support of the proposed amendments to increase social security benefits? The question provoked an interesting divergency in point of view from two leading business publications, *Business Week* and *Fortune*.

Business Week[34] said, yes, there were reasons enough for such action in addition to the financial incentive, including the fact that the Social Security Act was inadequate to its task. Not only could companies with private plans reduce their cost load, but private plans could not do the whole and necessary job of providing retirement income for workers. Therefore, the magazine concluded edi-

33 See Chapter 5, p. 133.
34 April 8, 1950, p. 120

torially, private plans must supplement an adequate public program. This produces incentives that aid in keeping trained people in the firm, although it cannot be the first line of protection against the hazards of old age for all workers.

The editors cited other advantages of social security over private plans. First, social security can cover all workers in the country and thus avoid the problems of pensions that apply only to a given employer; second, such a plan could be financed on a pay-as-you-go basis; and, finally, increased social security benefits can cut down on the load of old-age assistance as well as on the abuse of relief programs. From the record of business support, it is quite apparent that this line of reasoning was more or less adopted by much of the business community.

Fortune, although not necessarily in disagreement with *Business Week,* took a different approach to this general question. In a lucid and persuasive series of articles,[35] the late *Fortune* editor, Russell W. Davenport, developed what he felt should be the philosophy of American businessmen toward economic security measures. His argument was based on the answers to two questions: first, is the demand of American workers for more welfare (economic security) measures a justified demand? Davenport concludes that it is—that we must recognize and agree that it is a basic economic right as fundamental as the other rights of American citizenship. Second, since the demand for economic security is a justified one, can it be met in any way without recourse to an authoritarian state? He feels that it can, but that American business has failed by backing additional government measures. He advocates instead a new capitalistic venture.

He would have businessmen take the responsibility for the economic rights of American workers and seek methods of providing stable employment and health and welfare plans. Business has erred in permitting government to be the protector of the economic rights of employees. Government will probably have to continue to provide some floor of protection, but it should not be considered as the primary source of responsibility for man's economic rights.

All states, he argues, have given recognition to man's basic economic rights. Socialist states have done so, but they can give effective exercise to these rights only by government monopoly. To avoid this occurrence in the United States, he concludes, our gov-

[35] Russell W. Davenport, "The Greatest Opportunity on Earth," *Fortune,* XL, No. 4 (October, 1949), 65–69, and 200–08; "Pensions: Not If but How," *Fortune,* XL, No. 5 (November, 1949), 81–83, and 218–25; "Health Insurance is Next," *Fortune,* XLI, No. 3 (March, 1950), 63–67, and 142–52.

ernment should yield that responsibility to private business and make its private exercise possible through tax and other incentives.

Economic Issues in Private Programs

In addition to those discussed earlier, two economic issues raised by various public and private economic security programs deserve consideration. First, the issues raised by the funds being accumulated under private insurance programs; and second, the possible impact of the whole economic security system—private and public.

One significant result of private health and welfare plans is the accumulation of great sums of money in the financing and funding of the programs. It is estimated that pension funds *alone* each year receive about one-third of the annual amount Americans can save for new investment. It is well known, for example, that the Sears-Roebuck pension fund owns over one-fourth of the company's stock; and that General Motors' pension fund every year amasses for new investment about $100 million of new money.[36] Insurance companies are by law required to invest almost exclusively in fixed dollar obligations. Where such legislation does not apply, these great accumulations of capital have created new situations, the full results of which cannot be gauged.

Institutional trustees, both of pension and welfare plans, have become the most important new source of equity capital, in fact nearly the only one. According to Peter F. Drucker, "The New York Stock Exchange estimates that for every dollar of new money they spend on buying common stock, only 5 cents are invested directly by private investors—and this in a period of rapidly rising stock-market prices."[37]

Fiduciary investors place but a small fraction of their capital (perhaps about one-sixth) into common stock. Of course, this is due partly to requirements of their trusteeship, and, in part, it simply reflects the conservatism of their fiduciary relationship. Where they do purchase equities, they choose the so-called "blue chips" to the exclusion of others. Thus, not only is there the possibility of a shortage of venture capital in general, but for the less well-known businesses the problem of attracting equity capital becomes ever more serious. There is every indication that this is the case today.

[36] See Peter F. Drucker, "The New Tycoons," *Harper's Magazine*, CCX, No. 1260 (May, 1955), 39–44.
[37] *Ibid*, p. 40.

When fiduciary trustees do purchase equities, the question arises: How actively should they participate in the management of the company? This is a particularly thorny problem. On the one hand, they can take the position, as many have, that they are investors and not entrepreneurs and so should refrain from any active control. On the other hand, they can take active part in the company's control—as a duty of common stock ownership. The former view may permit a minority group to control the company, and the latter makes the possibility of abuse too easy. Thus when President Dave Beck of the International Brotherhood of Teamsters Union, during a bitter stock fight to unseat Montgomery Ward's management, announced that his union was voting its sizable block of shares for the incumbent management and at the same time that his union had just arrived at a satisfactory collective agreement with that management, many wondered if active ownership was the solution.

Funds accumulated through pension and welfare plans can be a source of badly needed capital for nonindustrial projects. The work of the International Ladies' Garment Workers Union is a case in point. In October, 1955, the union completed a cooperative housing development on New York's lower east side with the aid of a $15 million union loan from pension and welfare fund reserves. At its May, 1956, convention, union president David Dubinsky announced that the union intends to put $15 million of its pension and welfare reserves into government-insured mortgages for small home construction. Thus, the union is following a policy of using part of its $167 million health and retirement reserves to ease the housing shortage for low and middle income groups—and at the same time receives a better rate of return than is now received from government bonds.[38]

The Future of Economic Security: A Concluding Comment

Two general conclusions about the future problems of economic security seem to emerge from the above discussion. First, although there are differences among specific public programs, it is apparent that they are accepted today, and there is little likelihood that they will change form in the very near future. Second, the role of private benefits in relation to our public systems must be re-examined and redefined. For while the private programs seem to be fulfilling the role in economic security which has been traditionally assigned to them—that of adding a layer of protection to the basic protection

[38] *St. Louis Post-Dispatch,* May 17, 1956, p. 10.

offered by social insurance—their rapid growth has created new problems of equity, administration, regulation, and cost that cannot long be ignored.

Economic Security and Economic Behavior

The economic behavior of Americans has been the subject of much recent discussion and attention, for to the extent that great consumer spending, that a willingness to incur record-level personal debt, and that apparent decline in the need felt for savings are valid indicators, Americans have all-time record confidence in their economic future.

One hypothesis which is offered in explanation is that this behavior is at least in part attributable to the very economic security measures which we have been considering. The argument runs as follows: Why do individuals save? Or, more accurately, why do they take a portion of their income and not spend it for consumption? Two motivations are the need for money for transactions and liquidity. But the motives for these demands are diminishing. Charge accounts and paying by check, which have become nearly universal, have reduced the demand for money for transactions. And, the argument continues, economic security measures have cut down the desire for money for liquidity purposes, for they protect against the risks to income that made great liquidity necessary—thus the conclusion that a sense of security is making people spend more and save less.

Students will recognize a hypothesis which has long had circulation in connection with the Guaranteed Annual Wage—namely, that this device does not operate independently of the problem it is seeking to curtail. Whether or not the whole system of economic security measures is having this effect on consumption patterns seems now to be the critical question and one which more observers seem to be answering positively.

A Rational System of Economic Security

A decade ago Professor Burns wrote of the need for a "rational system" of social security. That need is no less today, although the picture has been altered. First, several new entrants, such as collectively bargained group plans, have made an appearance; second, private insurances have moved into newer risks, such as major medical expense insurance; there is greater interest and acceptance of the fact that alleviative methods are insufficient; and there is a recognized need for improved preventive measures. This can be seen in workmen's compensation where the new emphasis is being directed toward rehabilitation and also in the broader area of public dependency. The United States Department of Health, Education, and Welfare, in fact, recently announced plans for a nationwide study of the causes of dependency, with a view towards developing rehabilitation methods in this area.[39]

In addition, interest in liberalizing the field has grown. During the last decade not only have private supplements become important in every field of social insurance, but all public economic security measures have been considerably liberalized—this includes two amendments to the Fair Labor Standards Act, OASI, workmen's compensation, unemployment compensation, and all programs applying to specific groups.

Despite these developments, the need for a rational system of economic security is as pressing today as it was ten years ago. The relationship between public and private programs is still uncertain and needs to be clarified; and, as we have indicated, the administrative, adequacy, and coverage problems of all the programs are serious. In some instances these seem to be working out. Thus the Fair Labor Standards Act today, although it still needs better enforcement and more widespread coverage, is a first-rate piece of protective legislation. But at the other extreme, programs such as workmen's compensation are badly in need of a change.

Actually, it is hard to generalize about the future of all systems. Professor Somers sees the future of workmen's compensation largely in the future of disability legislation in general.[40] Because of our deep-rooted acceptance of economic security measures, their need and legitimacy today, we have an excellent opportunity to fill in the gaps and to strengthen standards. We are agreed that risks are to be covered; we are defining them; and we are improving benefit standards. Although the outlook need not be pessimistic, we must remember that today, at the peak of our prosperity, nearly five million persons are dependent wholly or in part on federally aided public assistance programs.

Suggestions for Additional Reading

BURNS, EVELINE M. "Social Insurance in Evolution," *American Economic Review*, XXXIV, No. 1, Part 2, Supplement (March, 1944), 199–211.

[39] *St. Louis Post-Dispatch*, May 31, 1956, p. 3.

[40] Herman M. Somers and Anne R. Somers, *Workmen's Compensation* (New York: John Wiley and Sons, Inc., 1954), p. 289.

An examination of the progress of social insurance and the problems it will face in further evolution of the program.

———. *Social Security and Public Policy.* New York: McGraw-Hill Book Co., Inc., 1956.

This book deals basically with the policy questions of social security, and is a valuable analytical work for students desiring familiarity with social security institutions.

BROWN, J. DOUGLAS. "The American Philosophy of Social Insurance," *The Social Service Review,* XXX, No. 1 (March, 1956), 3–8.

This short article is a concise statement of the philosophy of social insurance and some of the issues surrounding the new private economic security programs.

Economic Security for Americans: Final Edition. Third American Assembly. New York: Columbia University Press, 1954.

Conclusions of the American Assembly on questions of economic security.

STRONG, JAY V. *Employee Benefit Plans in Operation.* Washington, D. C.: The Bureau of National Affairs, Inc., 1951.

A study of the operating problems in all types of employee private benefit programs.

Index of Authors and Sources Cited

(Italicized entries refer to first citation of sources quoted by title only. Annual reports, proceedings, periodical items are not included in this listing.)

Index of Subjects

533

Date Due

FEB 1 0 1996			